This invaluable textbook captures the profound dynamism in the international political economy. Like Lairson and Skidmore's earlier work, the new book provides a sophisticated synthesis of the intersection of politics and economics, and treats the student with respect, even as it explains complicated issues or concepts. The new volume incorporates the 2008 global fiscal crisis, the full emergence of China as a global power, and the ever-changing politics of global inequality, sustainable development, and environmental diplomacy. This book will be a welcome addition to the international political economy classroom!

Gregory White, *Smith College*

This book is by far the most comprehensive, insightful, and accessible introduction to the rapidly expanding field of international political economy. The authors expertly draw upon both theoretical perspectives and real-world experience to offer an analysis of global political economy that is unsurpassed by any other textbook.

Francis Adams, *Old Dominion University*

This is probably the best comprehensive textbook treatment of the international political economy field, and ideal for an advanced course on international political economy or globalization. It provides students with needed background in political science theory and the history of globalization, and includes an excellent discussion of economic concepts necessary to study the politics of trade, finance, and development. Lairson and Skidmore then apply these concepts to the central questions of modern globalization, such as the global economic crisis of 2008, the rise of China, and environmental sustainability.

Sean D. Ehrlich, *Florida State University*

This is a classic in the undergraduate curriculum. Lairson and Skidmore offer a first-rate introduction to the study of international political economy that provides students with a wealth of perspective and information about the causes and consequences of globalization. Today's students will be well served to begin their analysis of the past, present, and future of global economic relations with Lairson and Skidmore's excellent new edition.

Orfeo Fioretos, *Temple University*

International Political Economy

This text offers a rethinking of the field of international political economy in an era of growing but uneven globalization. Even as global integration advances, states play central roles as partners with the largest of global firms, as the catalysts of competitiveness and economic growth, as the creators of global institutions, and in promoting and responding to global interdependence. Indeed, the struggle for power and wealth within and among states underscores the primacy of politics in understanding current realities. At the same time, new issues and actors complicate the global agenda as it expands to address the environment, global health, and food security. By offering a clear explanation of basic concepts, contextualizing the presentation of theoretical debates, and placing current events in historical context, *International Political Economy* ensures students a deep understanding of how the global economy works and the ways in which globalization affects their lives and those of people around the world.

Key Content and Features

- Engages debates over the reach and significance of globalization.
- Examines the sources and consequences of global financial instability.
- Explores the origins and consequences of global inequality.
- Compares various strategies of development and state roles in competitiveness.
- Discusses the role of key international economic institutions.
- Considers the impact of the rise of China on the global economy and the potential for war and peace.
- Illustrates collective efforts to fight hunger, disease, and environmental threats.
- Includes numerous graphs and illustrations throughout and end of chapter discussion questions.
- Links key concepts for each chapter to a glossary at the end of the book.
- Provides a list of acronyms at the outset and annotated further readings at the end of each chapter.
- Offers additional resources on a website related to the text, including a list of links to IPE-related web pages.

Thomas D. Lairson is Visiting Professor of Political Science at Jindal Global University and Emeritus Professor of Political Science at Rollins College.

David Skidmore is Professor of Political Science at Drake University.

International Political Economy

The Struggle for Power and Wealth in a Globalizing World

Thomas D. Lairson and
David Skidmore

NEW YORK AND LONDON

Published 2017
by Routledge
711 Third Avenue, New York, NY 10017

and by Routledge
2 Park Square, Milton Park, Abingdon, Oxon, OX14 4RN

Routledge is an imprint of the Taylor & Francis Group, an informa business

© 2017 Taylor & Francis

The right of Thomas D. Lairson and David Skidmore to be identified as authors of this work has been asserted by them in accordance with sections 77 and 78 of the Copyright, Designs, and Patents Act 1988.

Library of Congress Cataloging in Publication Data
Names: Lairson, Thomas D., author. | Skidmore, David, 1958- author.
Title: International political economy : the struggle for power and
    wealth in a globalizing world / Thomas D. Lairson, David
    Skidmore.
Description: New York, NY : Routledge, 2017. | Earlier edition:
    2003. | Includes index.
Identifiers: LCCN 2016027236| ISBN 9781138228122 (hardback) |
    ISBN 9780415829618 (pbk.) | ISBN 9780203648926 (ebook)
Subjects: LCSH: International economic relations—History. |
    Globalization—Economic aspects.
Classification: LCC HF1359 .L35 2017 | DDC 337—dc23
LC record available at https://lccn.loc.gov/2016027236

ISBN: 978–1–138–22812–2 (hbk)
ISBN: 978–0–415–82961–8 (pbk)
ISBN: 978–0–203–64892–6 (ebk)

Typeset in Sabon
by RefineCatch Limited, Bungay, Suffolk

Visit the eResources: www.routledge.com/9780415829618

MIX
Paper from
responsible sources
FSC
www.fsc.org   FSC® C014174

Printed and bound in the United States of America by Sheridan

Table of Contents

Preface

The present volume is the product of collaboration between the authors dating back a quarter-century.* Between 1992 and 2003, we produced three editions of a successful textbook on international political economy. After a lengthy hiatus, we once again took up the challenge of explaining the workings of the global political economy to students who are new to the topic. The result is the current book, which represents not just an updating of our previous work, but a rethinking of how to present the field of international political economy under conditions of advanced globalization. The designation of the present volume as a first edition reflects this thorough reorganization and our new collaboration with Routledge Press.

A number of important themes and objectives carry over from our earlier work. We strive for clarity and readability without sacrificing sophistication or rigor. We recognize the difficulties that students face in mastering a subject that lies at the intersection of two complex fields – political science and economics. We address this challenge in several ways. First, we devote a full chapter to basic concepts in each discipline. Second, we review, compare, and work to move beyond basic theoretical perspectives in international political economy, including liberalism, realism/statism, and Marxism. Third, we offer historical depth through a review of the uneven path of globalization over the past 200 years. We believe that the resulting volume is accessible enough to be used as a supplement in an introductory course on international relations, but challenging enough to be assigned as a main textbook for upper-level courses.

Topically, the present volume has been fully updated to reflect recent events and policy debates. In particular, our book:

- considers the new forms and structures of globalization;
- examines debates over the reach and significance of globalization;

---

* For the record, Professor Lairson is the primary author of Chapters 2, 4, 5, 7, 8, 9, and 12; Professor Skidmore is the primary author of Chapters 1, 3, 6, 10, and 11.

- explores alternative models for how globalization should be governed;
- examines the sources of global financial instability;
- explores the origins and consequences of global inequality;
- compares various strategies of development and state roles in competitiveness;
- discusses the role of key international economic institutions;
- examines the impact of the rise of China on the global economy and the potential for war and peace; and
- examines collective efforts to fight hunger, disease, and environmental threats.

Throughout the volume, we call attention to the primacy of politics. Even under conditions of increased globalization, states continue to play central roles in steering management of the global economy, national development paths, and economic outcomes. In sum, our aim is to offer students a deep understanding of how globalization affects their lives and those of people around the world.

The text includes a number of useful pedagogical features, including numerous graphs and illustrations, key concepts for each chapter linked to a glossary, discussion questions and annotated bibliographies at the end of each chapter, and a list of acronyms. A website related to the text offers additional resources, including a list of links to international political economy-related web pages.

We thank the editors at Routledge for their assistance in guiding the book to completion. Also, we appreciate the suggestions provided by the following reviewers: Francis Adams, Gregory C. Dixon, Roxanne Lynn Doty, Orfeo Fioretos, Robert J. Franzese, Jr., Steven Hall, Sandra Joireman, George Shambaught, Martin Staniland, Kenneth P. Thomas, and Gregory White. Finally, we each thank our spouses, Sally Lairson and Charlene Skidmore, for their patience and support.

Thomas D. Lairson and David Skidmore

Acronyms

AFTA	ASEAN Free Trade Agreement
AID	Agency for International Development
AIG	American International Group
ARPA	Advanced Research Projects Agency
ASEAN	Association of Southeast Asian Nations
BITs	bilateral investment treaties
CAP	Common Agricultural Policy
CDOs	Collateralized Debt Obligations
CDSs	Credit Default Swaps
CFCs	chloroflourocarbons
CGIAR	Consultative Group on International Agricultural Research
CIMMYT	Centro Internacional de Major-amiento de Maiz y Trige
CIS	Commonwealth of Independent States
DARPA	Defense Advanced Research Projects Agency
DoD	Department of Defense
EC	European Community
ECB	European Central Bank
ECU	European Currency Unit
EEC	European Economic Community
EFTA	European Free Trade Area
ELI	Export-Led Industrialization
EMS	European Monetary System
EMU	Economic and Monetary Union
ERM	Exchange Rate Mechanism
EU	European Union
FDI	Foreign Direct Investment
FRBNY	Federal Reserve Bank of New York
FTA	Free Trade Agreement
G–7	Group of Seven
G–8	Group of Eight
G–20	Group of Twenty
GATT	General Agreement on Tariffs and Trade
GDP/GNP	Gross Domestic Product/Gross National Product

GFCF	gross fixed capital formation
GMOs	Genetically Modified Organisms
GPN	global production network
GPTs	general purpose technologies
GRPNs	Global and Regional Production Networks
HCFCs	hydrochlorofluorocarbons
HDI	Human Development Index
HFCs	hydroflourocarbons
IBM	International Business Machines
IBRD	International Bank for Reconstruction and Development
ICP	International Comparison Program
ICTs	information and communication technologies
IDA	International Development Agency
IFC	International Finance Corporation
IGOs	international government organizations
IMF	International Monetary Fund
INGOs	international non-governmental organizations
IPCC	Intergovernmental Panel on Climate Change
IPE	international political economy
IRRI	International Rice Research Institute
ISI	Import Substitution Industrialization
ITO	International Trade Organization
M&A	merger and acquisition
MDGs	Millennium Development Goals
MFN	Most Favored Nation
MIT	Massachusetts Institute of Technology
MITI	Ministry of International Trade and Industry
MNC	Multinational Corporation
NAFTA	North American Free Trade Agreement
NASA	National Aeronautics and Space Administration
NATO	North Atlantic Treaty Organization
NGOs	non-governmental organizations
NIC	newly industrializing country
NIH	National Institutes of Health
NIST	National Institute of Standards and Technology
NSF	National Science Foundation
NTBs	Non-Tariff Barriers
ODA	Official Development Assistance
OECD	Organization for Economic Cooperation and Development
OEM	original equipment manufacturer
OEP	Open Economy Politics
OPEC	Organization of Petroleum Exporting Countries
PEPFAR	The President's Emergency Plan for AIDS Relief
PPP	Purchasing Power Parity
PTAs	Preferential Trade Agreements

QE	Quantitative Easing
R&D	Research and Development
RCEP	Regional Comprehensive Economic Partnership Agreement
RMB	Renminbi
RTAs	regional trade agreements
RTAA	Reciprocal Trade Agreements Act
SARS	Severe Acute Respiratory Syndrome
SDGs	Sustainable Development Goals
SEZs	Special Economic Zones
SOEs	state-owned enterprises
SWFs	Sovereign Wealth Funds
TNC	transnational corporation
TPP	Trans-Pacific Partnership
TRIPs	Trade Related Aspects of Intellectual Property
TTIP	Transatlantic Trade and Investment Partnership
UNCED	United Nations Conference on Environment and Development
UNDP	United Nations Development Program
WCED	World Commission on Environment and Development
WHO	World Health Organization
WTO	World Trade Organization

Part I
Politics and Economics

1 International Political Economy

As Jill catches the morning news before rushing to work, she learns of violence in the Middle East, protests against budget cuts in some debt-riddled European country, and new export data from China. The latest numbers from financial markets in New York, London, Frankfurt, and Singapore scroll across the bottom of the screen. On her morning commute, she fills up her car – a South Korean brand – with gasoline that originated in Venezuela. At the office, she hears rumors about jobs in the firm being outsourced to India. Jill spends the morning banging away on an office computer that was assembled in Guangdong, China, but that includes components from a dozen different countries. A conference call during the afternoon brings together marketing directors from Brazil, South Africa, Italy, and Indonesia. On the way home, she stops to pick out a toy produced in Vietnam for her son's birthday. The take-out dinner she enjoys that night was prepared by a chef who recently emigrated from Hong Kong. As Jill catches up on Facebook before bed, she scrolls through wall posts updating her on the lives of friends from half a dozen different countries.

Such is a typical day in a globalizing world. While it is easy to take for granted the degree to which our lives have become intertwined with those of peoples beyond our country's borders, globalization is, in reality, the product of a complex and rather extraordinary set of political and economic dynamics. Globalization is neither automatic nor inevitable and its consequences are far-reaching and varied. Understanding how the global economy works – and for whom – is a challenging task but essential to comprehending the world.

This book draws upon the relatively young field of international political economy to explore the causes and consequences of globalization. Although its intellectual roots can be traced back much earlier, the contemporary field of international political economy was born in the early 1970s as a hybrid between the disciplines of economics and political science.[1] Scholars began to appreciate that the growth of international interdependence – a phenomenon later called globalization – could not be adequately grasped by either economists or political scientists working in isolation. Rather, the political and economic dimensions of globalization must be analyzed in conjunction with one another.

While at one level, this may seem an obvious statement, in fact popular discourse in the media and among politicians and pundits often obscures or oversimplifies the relationships among politics, economics, and international interdependence. The financial crisis of 2008 offers a case in point. The near-collapse of the US financial system cut the net worth of American households by half while pitching the US economy into a lasting recession that cost millions of jobs. Media commentary on the crisis sought to fix blame on greedy bankers, crooked mortgage brokers, profligate borrowers, incompetent credit agencies, and lax regulators. Often overlooked was the role played by America's imbalanced relationship to the global economy. In other words, the international dimensions of the crisis were often not fully appreciated.

In the years leading up to the crisis, large US trade deficits left major trading partners in possession of huge pools of American dollars. These dollars made their way back into the US economy as loans or investments. Combined with lax US monetary policy, the effect of these inflows of capital was to push down interest rates. Access to cheap loans encouraged home buying, pushing up housing prices. As the value of their homes shot up, Americans borrowed against the equity in their homes to finance expanded consumption. For their part, investors sought higher returns in a low interest rate environment by lowering lending standards and accepting greater risk. All of this fed a speculative bubble in the housing market that finally burst in 2008 as homeowners began to default on inflated mortgages. While much of the drama played out on Wall Street, in Washington, DC and in communities across the United States, the international roots of the financial crisis lay in Americans' growing dependence upon foreign borrowing to finance excess consumption.

In other cases, the economic motivations for a new policy initiative may be evident, but the political dynamics are unclear. Why, for instance, did the United States give such priority to the recently completed Trans-Pacific Partnership (TPP), a multilateral agreement that will remove many barriers to trade among countries in Asia and the Americas that border on the Pacific Ocean? The economic motivation is easiest to spot. The TPP represents a step toward freer markets, as prescribed by economists. Participating states will each realize gains as greater international specialization creates expanded openings for trade and profit.

From another perspective, however, the TPP is also about power politics. The terms of the agreement require that participating states adopt free market policies that favor private over state-owned enterprises (SOEs). This effectively excludes China, whose economy remains heavily dependent upon state guidance and state-owned enterprises. As a result, the TPP, should it be successful, will likely enhance US political and economic influence in Asia at China's expense. The terms of the agreement will also serve to discourage other Asian countries from emulating China's statist economic model, instead locking them into the kind of pro-market policies that the United States favors.

While China's exclusion thus offers relative gains for the United States, the United States will also gain should China someday join the Partnership. China's participation would require it to abandon some of the state economic controls that the United States finds most objectionable. Either way, the TPP serves American political, as well as economic, purposes.

Finally, there are cases where international political disagreements hide underlying economic factors. China, Vietnam, the Philippines, Brunei, Malaysia, and Taiwan each claim sovereignty over all or part of the small islands and surrounding waters of the South China Sea. Untangling the competing legal and historical claims has been rendered all the more complicated by the economic stakes. The area not only straddles key shipping lanes and fishing grounds, but is also thought to contain large underwater oil reserves that each nation is eager to exploit.

As these examples suggest, understanding how states manage international interdependence requires that we draw upon theories and concepts from the fields of both economics and political science. As is typical in the social sciences, there is no universally accepted theoretical approach to the study of international political economy. Rather, there exist a number of competing perspectives, each of which conceptualizes the relationship between political and economics in distinct ways. This chapter examines these contending theoretical approaches to international political economy. Since these perspectives differ in how they understand globalization and its impacts, mastering the underlying logic of each will help us navigate policy debates over how globalization should be managed.

Understanding anything as complex as international political economy requires, somewhat paradoxically, that we make it simpler. This is usually done by developing ideas about how the system works by focusing on one main factor that affects outcomes. In the study of international political economy, three of these broad perspectives have been important. One perspective focuses on markets, one on states, and the third on class power. Each seeks to explore the implications and effects of a given factor for international political economy. The assertions of each perspective come in two main forms. First is a policy preference that emphasizes how choices in political economy should be made. Second is a claim about how we should study international political economy, which comes down to asserting the primacy of one causal force over others.

Three Perspectives on International Political Economy

The study of international political economy has been shaped by three overarching perspectives: liberalism, realism/statism, and Marxism.

These sets of ideas about political economy function at two levels. First, they structure social scientific research programs that arise from collaboration among communities of like-minded scholars. Second, these ideas also work as ideologies that are employed by political actors whose interests are served by the growing influence of particular ideas over others. While we will describe liberalism, realism, and Marxism as these perspectives are understood and employed by scholars, it is important to keep in mind that ideas are seldom neutral or disinterested, but instead reflect certain values and interests and are employed by political actors in service of their particular goals.

Liberalism

Liberal scholars focus on the role that markets play in providing for the efficient exchange of goods, services, and labor among individuals and firms. Liberals make two very important assertions: first, that unimpeded markets provide the greatest economic welfare for the largest number of people; and second, that market operations define the political choices of governments and individuals.[2] Thus, liberals assert the correct way to study and analyze international political economy is through the role of markets, thereby attributing little independent force to politics itself.

Liberalism can be traced to the writings of eighteenth-century Scottish philosopher Adam Smith and the later work of early nineteenth-century economist David Ricardo.[3] With respect to international economics, Smith sought to counter the dominance of mercantilist thinking, which prescribed that states simultaneously protect their economies from imports while promoting exports so as to earn growing reserves of gold through trade. Smith argued instead that free trade was the superior path to wealth, even where other states continued to practice protectionism. Ricardo elaborated upon this thesis by demonstrating that trade was desirable and beneficial for both states, even in cases where one party was the low-cost producer across all categories of goods (i.e., the theory of comparative advantage, explained in Chapter 2).

This defense of free trade – later expanded to encompass the free movement of capital across borders – continues to serve as a core belief for liberal economists. It is grounded in the view that unimpeded markets serve as the most effective mechanisms for allocating resources to their most efficient uses and therefore maximize overall social welfare. Competition among private firms driven by the profit motive both pushes down costs and ensures that production is directed toward the satisfaction of consumer wants. Modern economic theory recognizes a variety of exceptions to this generalization, some warranting corrective action by states. Nevertheless, the work of mainstream economists is mostly focused on ways to perfect markets and to extend their reach.

Within the field of political science, liberal scholars focus on the political arrangements most likely to promote international economic openness. While markets are thought to maximize overall social welfare, not all individuals and groups gain equally. In particular, growing exposure to international trade creates both winners and losers within society. Scholars have developed models for identifying which groups will gain from the removal of barriers to trade and which groups will be harmed. Those business firms and workers who stand to lose from lower-priced imports often organize to lobby government for protection from competition. Whether such interests succeed in gaining protection depends upon a variety of factors, including the counterpoising efforts of free trade interests, the ideological views of policymakers, and the legal and institutional design of electoral systems, legislatures, and bureaucracies that have influence over trade policy.

As an example, agricultural interests in the United States, Europe, and Japan have succeeded in lobbying for government subsidies that harm consumers and taxpayers in these countries while also curtailing export opportunities for lower-cost producers in the developing world. This pattern is partly rooted in electoral systems that give disproportionate voting power to rural residents. Liberals have suggested a variety of means to dampen the influence of protectionist interests, such as insulating the policymaking process from protectionist pressures or compensating those groups who stand to lose from open trade.[4]

Another set of potential obstacles to realizing international economic openness arises from the anarchic and competitive nature of the international state system. There exists no higher authority at the global level to impose openness to trade upon independent states. Openness must thus arise through voluntary cooperation among states. Such cooperation may be difficult to arrange, particularly since, as we have seen, states face domestic resistance from groups that stand to lose from freer trade. Moreover, cooperation among as many as 200 independent states raises collective action problems. States may seek to push burdens onto others rather than carry their fair share of the costs, or may cheat upon agreements in an effort to gain short-term advantage. The growing discord that surrounds global trade negotiations illustrates these obstacles.

One way in which states overcome such impediments is by creating institutions, or sets of rules and norms, that ease collective action problems through sharing information, bundling issues, establishing norms of behavior, defining and monitoring cheating, and specifying mechanisms for dispute resolution and enforcement. Liberal scholars have developed theories that explain the demand for international economic institutions and prescribe their most effective design for various purposes.[5]

From a liberal perspective, globalization is a logical and nearly inevitable process driven by the gains to be had by extending markets beyond the borders of national economies. While globalization is accompanied by painful adjustments on the part of some groups, the benefits are thought to far outweigh the losses. Markets serve as the driving force underlying globalization, while states face a rather simple choice between adapting policies to the needs of the global marketplace or allowing opportunities for growth and prosperity to slip from their grasp.

Realism and Statism

Like liberals, realists/statists make assertions about what matters the most in international political economy and this leads them to conclusions about policies and methods of analysis. Though related, realism and statism emphasize different aspects of this subject, with realists focused on the relations among states and statists keen to consider how governments and markets should be related.

Realists[6] focus on the competition among states for power and security within an anarchic international order. In this sense, international political economy is treated as a subfield within international relations. For liberals, the principal goal for states in their economic relations with one another is to maximize their own society's wealth. Wealth is an absolute good in the sense that all states can grow wealthier (or poorer) together. Moreover, liberal economic theory claims that international cooperation in the form of coordinated movement toward freer trade is an important mechanism for gaining wealth. Thus, the independent pursuit of wealth by individual states readily leads to cooperative efforts to achieve this goal.

Realists, on the other hand, argue that states value power above all else. In an anarchic self-help international system, states must be concerned about survival in the face of possible aggression by other states. Power is critical to security and survival, as well as more ambitious goals. While wealth is an important prerequisite for power, the two are not identical goals for states. Unlike wealth, power is a relative good. Power has to do with a state's ability to prevail in a contest for influence with other states (even up to the point of war). More power for one state necessarily means less power for some other state. From a realist perspective, international relations is therefore an inherently competitive game.

This is no less true of economic relations than in the spheres of political and military relations. Realists therefore interpret international economic institutions in a very different manner than liberals. Among great powers, states will be reluctant to enter into any ongoing economic relationship that promises to shift the balance of power in an unfavorable direction. This may mean foregoing an opportunity for absolute gains if a state calculates that a potential rival will gain more in relation to the initial power balance. During the Cold War, for instance, the United States passed up opportunities to gain from trade and investment with the

Soviet Union out of fears that such exchanges would contribute to the relative growth of Soviet political and military power.

Moreover, realists assert that states will be reluctant to rely upon international markets to supply certain strategic goods that are considered necessary on security grounds. For instance, states may wish to protect their ability to supply essential foodstuffs or energy from their own resources even if doing so is costlier than importing the same goods from other states. Similarly, resources, industrial capacities, and technologies considered critical to military defense may be shielded from foreign control.

While for liberals the key criterion in judging a proposed international economic relationship is whether it promises to enhance a nation's wealth, realists believe that states also consider the effects of international interdependence upon their power and autonomy. One consequence is that international economic institutions are unlikely to be designed in ways that maximize overall global welfare. Instead, they will reflect and preserve an existing distribution of power among the participating states. Unless states are convinced that the gains from international exchange will be distributed roughly proportional to the hierarchy of power, then agreement will prove impossible because states that stand to lose in a relative sense will decline to participate.

From a realist perspective, international economic institutions are first and foremost venues through which power relations are enacted and only secondarily, if at all, instruments for realizing the liberal goal of free trade. Indeed, some institutions serve to restrict and constrain markets more than to expand or enhance them. Realists do not reject the reality of globalization, but instead treat it as a competitive process driven by states rather than markets. Globalization, from a realist perspective, reflects rather than displaces the struggle for power among states. It is also contingent rather than inevitable. Globalization can – and has in the past – become victim to intensifying power struggles among great powers. Markets are thus subordinate to politics.

Statism is distinct from but closely related to realism. While realists focus mostly on relations among states, statists examine the relationship between states and markets. In particular, statists take issue with the liberal view that markets function best when the role of the state in the economy is limited to a few essential functions (e.g., protecting private property, issuing currency, providing public goods, etc.). Instead, statists advocate a far more expansive role for the state in steering economic growth, especially in the early stages of development. Statists point out that, historically, few, if any, successful developers followed liberal free market prescriptions. Far more commonly, states actively intervened in markets, often through public–private partnerships. This is true, for instance, throughout East Asia, which has been the most rapidly growing region of the world in the past half-century.[7]

States in successful developing societies have protected infant indus-tries, selectively managed the flow of foreign investments, allocated credit and foreign exchange to targeted industries, supported the development and acquisition of new technologies, set product and industrial stan-dards, retained direct ownership over firms in strategic sectors, and pursued tax and financial policies that boosted the rate of national savings. Through so-called "industrial policies," states have not been content to allow the market to determine their nation's areas of compar-ative advantage in international trade, but have instead acted to shift underlying factor endowments so as to create new and more rewarding areas of comparative advantage.

Statists argue that such strategies are often effective because they involve state action to correct market failures – cases where markets acting alone produce inefficient or suboptimal outcomes. Markets fail under a number of conditions: when a few buyers or sellers hold power over prices, when negative externalities are high, when some market participants possess private information, when entry barriers are high, and when there exist increasing returns to scale. Statists argue that market failure is far more common than liberal economists acknowledge and that such conditions create both the need and opportunity for corrective action by states.

Marxism

A third perspective on international political economy is inspired by the work of nineteenth-century German political economist Karl Marx. Marx developed a wide-ranging critique of capitalism centered on the notion of class and the power relations that result from these social divisions. In the simplest terms, capitalist societies are divided between those who own or control the means of production and those who engage in wage labor. Power and wealth are concentrated among owners, or capitalists, who extract value from the labor of those under their employ. This conflict of interest between the capitalist class and the working class constitutes the core insight of Marxist thought.[8]

From a Marxist perspective, the state in a capitalist society serves the interests, first and foremost, of business. The state is neither the neutral referee of liberal thought nor the active promoter of a singular national interest as realists would have it, but instead an instrument of class rule. This does not mean that labor unions or other groups have no influence or representation. It does mean that the state seeks above all to preserve capitalism and is particularly responsive to the desires of the largest banks and business firms, whose decisions directly impact the health of the overall economy.

While Marx did not develop a theory of international relations, thinkers influenced by Marx's work have sought to do so. Writing in 1902, English economist John Hobson argued that late nineteenth-century imperialism was the product of a tendency for capitalist economies to overproduce and underconsume. The concentration of wealth meant that the invested savings of the wealthy fueled industrial expansion beyond the limited capacity of the working classes to absorb at profitable prices. Falling profits at home prompted investors to seek overseas outlets for their capital and goods. European governments used colonialism as a method for securing such markets.[9]

Russian revolutionary Vladimir Lenin argued that the expansionist imperatives identified by Hobson would inevitably lead to rivalry among the imperialist powers as each state's efforts to avoid economic collapse through colonization produced intensifying territorial disputes. Lenin saw capitalism's tendencies toward imperialism and war as a key contradiction that would lead eventually to the system's demise.[10]

The 1960s and 1970s brought a wave of Marx-inspired dependency and world-systems theories that sought to explain the vast inequalities among countries and regions in the global economy (discussed in greater detail in Chapter 6). Immanuel Wallerstein argued that the class divisions within capitalist societies are mirrored by the hierarchical division of the world economy into core, semi-peripheral, and peripheral zones.[11] Wallerstein thus took direct aim at liberal modernization theories, which posited a singular path to development; one first blazed by today's rich countries but which was available to those poor countries who emulated earlier developers and pursued integration into the world economy. Wallerstein instead argued that the wealth gap between core and peripheral countries was both permanent and functional from the perspective of the core states. Northern wealth depended in crucial ways on surplus value extracted from semi-peripheral and peripheral countries. In turn, the poverty of the majority of the world's people was a product of exploitation by core countries. While individual countries might move upward or downward in this hierarchy, the overall structure that privileged a wealthy core over subordinate peripheries was a permanent feature of the world capitalist economy.

While Lenin believed that the main contradiction within global capitalism pitted rival imperialist states against one another and Wallerstein emphasized the conflict between core and periphery, the recent work of William Robinson has returned to the class conflicts that stood at the heart of Marx's own thought.[12] Robinson argues that a transnational capitalist class has emerged that seeks to create global rules and institutions for the management of globalization. In previous eras, the production networks of capitalist firms seldom extended much beyond the nation-state. Products were manufactured within one country and traded for products wholly produced within other countries. As a result, even large business firms had a largely national character. Their profits depended upon production within the home country and they developed strong ties with home country governments, who guarded the interests of "national champions."

Today, by contrast, production networks may extend across many countries, with particular segments of the production chain located wherever the greatest efficiencies can be found. The largest multinational firms are denationalized – their ownership, management, production, and distribution are all highly transnational in scope. This weakens the dependence of such firms on given countries and states. Instead, transnational business has an interest in strengthening global rules and institutions that ensure corporate rights across the many national domains in which they operate. The national imperial rivalries of Lenin's day give way to a global political order in which states are incorporated as subordinate actors. For Robinson, the central contradictions within capitalism pit transnational capital on the one hand against workers and smaller firms that remain local or national in scope on the other hand. The labor forces of different countries are forced to compete for the investment of transnational firms, thus bidding down wages and weakening unions. Smaller nationalist business firms are also disadvantaged by the competition to which they are exposed as protectionist barriers and national regulations are dismantled. For Robinson, globalization is a process managed by large transnational firms against resistance from labor movements and smaller national firms around the world.

Other Perspectives

Beyond liberalism, realism, and Marxism, the study of international political economy has expanded to incorporate a number of newer intellectual approaches in recent years, including constructivist, feminist, and ecological perspectives. As with all perspectives, these focus on different (and, they would say, neglected) features of international political economy. Constructivist theories draw upon concepts from the field of sociology to explore the ways that ideas, norms, identities, and roles shape the behavior of political and economic actors and their interactions. In seeking to understand the influence of international institutions such as the International Monetary Fund (IMF) or the World Bank, a constructivist scholar would be interested not only in the size of the financial resources controlled by such institutions, but also the role that they play in both creating and disseminating ideas and norms concerning appropriate responses to debt crises, which public interventions to combat poverty are likely to be most effective or other policy questions of concern to developing country governments. From a constructivist perspective, ideas are systems of meaning that both steer the behavior of various actors and serve as sources of social power within the global economy.[13]

Feminist approaches to international political economy focus upon the ways that global economic structures reflect and reproduce underlying gender disparities and systems of patriarchy. In some societies, for instance, immigrant domestic workers – overwhelmingly female – lack effective legal protections against exploitation and mistreatment. The low pay and poor working conditions common among workers in segments of the highly globalized textile industry are possible in part because the largely female workforce lacks alternative economic opportunities or political representation in many countries. Young women from impoverished circumstances are often victimized by human trafficking networks operating across national borders, and by the spread of sex tourism. By exploring these problems, as well as the policies adopted by international institutions and aid programs toward issues such as birth control, the economic empowerment of women and female educational opportunities, feminists seek to uncover the gendered nature of globalization.[14]

An ecological approach to international political economy begins with recognition that virtually all economic activity is dependent upon the extraction and processing of finite resources from nature. Drawing upon biology, ecological international political economy employs such concepts as carrying capacity, the global commons, and ecological footprints to examine whether the combination of historically unprecedented population growth and massive industrialization of the past two centuries is sustainable. Many ecological studies have concluded that the present global economy has already breached the natural carrying capacity of the earth and that radical changes in lifestyles and processes of production and exchange are inevitable. Ecological international political economy explores the ways in which various political and economic features associated with globalization exacerbate resource strains and distribute ecological risks unequally across societies and populations.[15]

Major Themes: The Primacy of Politics

In this book, we do not adopt any singular perspective, but instead draw ideas from various schools of thought. From liberalism, we take the key insight that markets are powerful mechanisms for enhancing efficiency and growth. Also, liberalism helps us understand how and why international economic institutions are created. Realism, however, is necessary to understand the more competitive aspects of international economic relations, especially under circumstances where states have particular reason to be concerned about power and security. Statism offers a useful corrective to limited liberal understandings of the ways that state action can promote growth and development. And Marxist perspectives help us better understand the sources of inequality by underlining the power of capital and the ways that the rules of the international economic system reflect the interests of core states and transnational business.

Throughout this book, we emphasize the primacy of politics. Politics shapes globalization and the international economic order in several senses.

First, all economic activity takes place within a set of legal and institutional structures created by states. Indeed, markets could not function without states to ensure property rights and enforce contracts. Moreover, all firms operate within the jurisdictions and legal regimes of those states in whose territory they do business. State primacy ultimately rests in its monopoly over the means of legitimate coercion.

Second, markets do not serve as the last word for actors who are dissatisfied with the outcomes of market competition. Business firms, banks, labor unions, and other economic actors have the option of overturning, altering, or compensating for market outcomes by appealing for state action.

Third, politics has a logic of its own that is distinct from economic logic. Liberal economists often assume that states that have created institutions or pursued policies that appear irrational from an economist's point of view do so out of simple ignorance. They therefore write reports or visit foreign capitals with the expectation that once the proper advice is given, the government will alter course and pursue pro-growth policies. But political actors often have good reasons, from the perspective of their own power, survival, and enrichment, to pursue policies that benefit themselves at the expense of particular groups or even the society as a whole. Even where political leaders wish to serve the public interest, they cannot afford to prioritize economic efficiency over political stability. When a country accumulates too much international debt, for instance, economists often insist upon harsh austerity policies. If, however, such policies lead to strikes, street riots, and the downfall of any government that pursues them, the prospects for their success and sustainability are poor.

Beyond our emphasis on the political foundations of international economic order, a number of important themes shape our perspective on globalization in the world economy:

- While globalization continues to strengthen bonds of mutual dependence among societies, the process of global integration is uneven and incomplete.
- Globalization has important distributional consequences within and among nations. Globalization creates opportunities for some and risks for others.
- While the global integration of markets is driven by economic incentives that drive the behavior of firms, the degree, shape, and impact of globalization are also profoundly shaped by the political interests of states and the rules that states together devise for governing the world economy.

- There is no single path to development but rather multiple paths that are shaped by varying mixes of resource endowments, historical legacies, institutional contexts, and societal values.
- The center of economic and political power in the world economy is shifting from West to East, with the rise of China and other emerging powers gradually eroding the traditional dominance of the United States and the European Union.
- The simultaneous rise in global population levels and per capita consumption is placing enormous strains on the natural environment upon which all economic activity depends. In particular, the global economy in this century will be profoundly shaped by global warming and the transition toward a post-fossil fuel future.

Organization of the Book

This book is divided into three parts. Part I provides background on politics and economics that readers will find essential to understanding the remainder of the text. The present chapter addresses the relevance of international political economy and reviews the key theoretical perspectives that have defined debates within the field. Chapter 2 introduces the basic economic and political concepts that are most commonly employed in the study of international political economy. Chapter 3 assesses trends in the globalization of the world economy and outlines three alternative perspectives on global governance. Chapter 4 focuses on the rise, demise, and reemergence of liberal economy order and the roles that two hegemonic powers – Great Britain in the nineteenth century and the United States in the post-World War II period – played in laying the conditions necessary for a more open and stable international economic order during their periods of dominance.

Part II turns our attention to the competitive dynamics of contemporary globalization. Chapter 5 examines international trade and the growth of globalized production networks. Chapter 6 explores empirical and theoretical perspectives on divergent patterns of wealth and poverty in the global economy. Chapter 7 focuses on the international financial system. Chapter 8 examines the ways that states and firms maneuver to gain advantage with respect to one another. Chapter 9 examines the rapid rise of Asia – especially China – to a central role in the global economic order and the consequences of this shift in political and economic power for the system's future.

Part III addresses questions related to the sustainability of globalization and the economic order upon which it is based. Chapter 10 explores the challenges of providing the food and health care for a global population that is simultaneously growing and aging. Chapter 11 focuses on environmentally sustainable development and cooperative efforts to combat threats to the global commons. The concluding chapter considers various alternative futures for globalization in the world economy.

Conclusion: Competing Perspectives

Globalization is an ongoing historical process that is reconfiguring relationships among states, firms, and markets on a global scale. International political economy is an interdisciplinary field of study that provides useful concepts and analytic tools for understanding globalization. Scholars working within the international political economy tradition represent varied theoretical schools, each offering a different perspective on the relationship between politics and economics in the global economy. Chief among these schools of thought are liberalism, realism/statism, and Marxism. This book draws upon all three theoretical perspectives while stressing throughout the primacy of politics in guiding the process of globalization.

Key Concepts (see Glossary)

Class	Marxism
Dependency	Neoliberalism
Free Trade	Protection(ism)
Imperialism	Realism
Liberalism	State
Market Failure	Statism
Markets	World Systems Theory

Discussion Questions

1   In our local community, which economic groups benefit most from globalization? Which groups are hurt most by globalization?
2   From a liberal perspective, what role do international institutions play in overcoming the collective action problems that otherwise impede the development of free market exchange across national borders?
3   Which kinds of state intervention in markets might be advocated by realists or statists even if they are objectionable from a liberal point of view?
4   We often think of globalization as an economic phenomenon. But in what ways is globalization a process also influenced by political factors?
5   From William Robinson's perspective, how has the globalization of production networks altered the principal political cleavages within the global economy?
6   What does each of the three main perspectives on international political economy – liberalism, realism/statism, and Marxism – contribute to our understanding of globalization?

Notes

1   For an overview, see Benjamin J. Cohen, *International Political Economy: An Intellectual History*, Princeton: Princeton University Press, 2008.

2 This relates to the Open Economy Politics (OEP) theory, which reduces political choices to the economic preferences of groups and omits any state interests independent of these groups. For a review of OEP, see David Lake, "Open Economy Politics: A Critical Review," *Review of International Organizations*, 4 (2009) 219–44.

3 Adam Smith, *The Wealth of Nations*, New York: Simon & Brown, 2013; David Ricardo, *The Principles of Political Economy and Taxation*, Mineola, New York: Dover Publications, 2004.

4 Michael J. Hiscox, *International Trade and Political Conflict: Commerce, Coalitions, and Mobility*, Princeton: Princeton University Press, 2001; Ronald Rogowski, *Commerce and Coalitions: How Trade Affects Domestic Political Alignments*, Princeton: Princeton University Press, 1990; Helen V. Milner, *Interests, Institutions and Information*, Princeton: Princeton University Press, 1997.

5 See Robert O. Keohane and Joseph S. Nye, Jr., *Power and Interdependence*, New York: Pearson, 4th ed., 2011; Robert O. Keohane, *After Hegemony: Cooperation and Discord in the World Political Economy*, Princeton: Princeton University Press, Classic ed., 2005; and Stephen Krasner (ed.), *International Regimes*, Ithaca: Cornell University Press, 1983.

6 Among the chief realist works within international political economy are Albert Hirschman, *National Power and the Structure of Foreign Trade*, Berkeley: University of California Press, 1981; Stephen Krasner, *Defending the National Interest: Raw Materials Investments and U.S. Foreign Policy*, Princeton: Princeton University Press, 1978; Robert Gilpin and Jean M. Gilpin, *Global Political Economy: Understanding the International Economic Order*, Princeton: Princeton University Press, 2001; and David Allen Baldwin, *Economic Statecraft*, Princeton: Princeton University Press, 1985. For a review of realist international political economy, see Jonathan Kirschner, "Realist Political Economy: Traditional Themes and Contemporary Challenges," in Mark Blyth (ed.), *Routledge Handbook of International Political Economy: IPE as a Global Conversation*, New York: Routledge, 2010, 36–47.

7 Robert Wade, *Governing the Market: Economy Theory and the Role of Government in East Asian Industrialization*, Princeton: Princeton University Press, 2003; Atul Kohli, *State-Directed Development: Political Power and Industrialization in the Global Periphery*, Cambridge: Cambridge University Press, 2004; Peter B. Evans, *Embedded Autonomy*, Princeton: Princeton University Press, 1995.

8 Karl Marx, Friedrich Engels, and Robert C. Tucker, *The Marx–Engels Reader*, New York: W.W. Norton & Company, 2nd ed., 1978.

9 John Atkinson Hobson, *Imperialism: A Study*, New York: Cosimo Classics, 2005.

10 V.I. Lenin, *Imperialism: The Highest Stage of Capitalism*, Eastford, CT: Martino Fine Books, 2011.

11 Immanuel Wallerstein, *World Systems Analysis: An Introduction*, Durham, NC: Baltimore: Duke University Press, 2004.

12 William I. Robinson, *A Theory of Global Capitalism: Production, Class and State in a Transnational World*, Baltimore: The Johns Hopkins University Press, 2004.

13 Rawi Abdelal, "Constructivism as an Approach to International Political Economy," in Mark Blyth (ed.), *Routledge Handbook of International Political Economy: IPE as a Global Conversation*, New York: Routledge, 2010, 62–76; Andre Broome, "Constructivism in International Political Economy," in Ronen Palen (ed.), *Global Political Economy: Contemporary Theories*, New York: Routledge, 2nd ed., 2012, 193–204.

14 Kate Bezanson and Meg Luxton (eds), *Social Reproduction: Feminist Political Economy Challenges Neo-liberalism*, Montreal: McGill Queens University Press, 2006.
15 Herman E. Daly and Joshua Farley, *Ecological Economics: Principles and Applications*, Washington, DC: Island Press, 2003; Simon Dalby, Ryan Katz-Rosene, and Matthew Paterson, "From Environmental to Ecological Political Economy," in Ronen Palen (ed.), *Global Political Economy: Contemporary Theories*, New York: Routledge, 2nd ed., 2012, 219–31.

Further Reading

Benjamin J. Cohen, *International Political Economy: An Intellectual History*, Princeton: Princeton University Press, 2008.
Cohen surveys the intellectual evolution of the field of international political economy over the past half-century, focusing on the ideas of leading scholars. He argues that the field can be divided into distinct American and British schools of thought.

Robert W. Cox and Timothy J. Sinclair, *Approaches to World Order*, Cambridge: Cambridge University Press, 1996.
An examination of multilateralism and global political economy from a Gramscian perspective.

Robert Gilpin and Jean M. Gilpin, *Global Political Economy: Understanding the International Economic Order*, Princeton: Princeton University Press, 2001.
This volume serves as an update of Robert Gilpin's classic 1987 book *The Political Economy of International Relations*. Gilpin approaches international political economy from a realist perspective.

Robert O. Keohane, *After Hegemony: Cooperation and Discord in the World Political Economy*, Princeton: Princeton University Press, 2005.
Keohane examines why and how international economic institutions arise and why they are likely to persist even under conditions of waning hegemony.

Robert O. Keohane and Joseph S. Nye, Jr., *Power and Interdependence*, New York: Pearson, 4th ed., 2011.
This seminal early text laid the essential conceptual groundwork for much later work on international political economy from a liberal perspective.

Atul Kohli, *State-Directed Development: Political Power and Industrialization in the Global Periphery*, Cambridge: Cambridge University Press, 2004.
This offers a statist perspective on economic development.

Nicola Phillips and Catherine Weaver (eds), *International Political Economy: Debating the Past, Present and Future*, New York: Routledge, 2010.
This volume collects essays written in response to Benjamin Cohen's review of the history of international political economy. The authors seek to identify commonalities and differences among various theoretical and methodological approaches.

John Ravenhill (ed.), *Global Political Economy*, Oxford: Oxford University Press, 4th ed., 2014.
A set of authoritative surveys of various subfields within international political economy written by leading scholars.

William I. Robinson, *A Theory of Global Capitalism: Production, Class and State in a Transnational World*, Baltimore: The Johns Hopkins University Press, 2004.
Writing from a Marxist perspective, Robinson describes the development of a transnational state that has emerged to serve the needs of the transnational capitalist class.

Immanuel Wallerstein, *World Systems Analysis: An Introduction*, Durham, NC: Duke University Press, 2004.
This volume provides a concise introduction to Wallerstein's influential account of the development and spread of capitalism as a world system over the past 500 years.

2 Basic Concepts for International Political Economy

All specialized fields of study must create a terminology and language used to communicate among those engaged in research. These ideas emerge from discussion, debate, and consensus among scholars. New students wanting to enter into study of this field will need to understand these terms if they want to become part of this conversation. The study of international political economy is both an old and a new field; two centuries ago, political economy was a commonly used term, but only in the past forty years have scholars regularly and systematically examined international political economy.[1]

This "newness" can be both exciting and frustrating as scholars continue to debate many of the basic ideas and consensus among them has often been elusive. Complicating matters further, many people operating in the political and economic world have very strong economic and ideological interests in promoting one way of thinking over another and this can affect how scholars reach conclusions as well.[2] Even so, there are many basic ideas in international political economy accepted by most scholars and you will need to understand them. Our goal in this chapter is to provide students with one place to learn about many of these terms and ideas.

International political economy is especially hard because it involves an interdisciplinary subject, bringing the study of economic and political systems together. There is a prima facie case for such study. Clearly, virtually all parts of the world are organized into somewhat sovereign nations, all of these nations have economic systems, and virtually all engage in trade and monetary transactions with each other. Economic transactions with and among nations are deeply affected by the political entities that compose the system.

How can we begin to understand the differences between politics and economics? One useful distinction between political and economic systems is the latter is primarily a distributed system and the former is a centralized system. The exchange of goods and services usually occurs between people who arrange the terms of the transaction themselves and each will hopefully be better off as a result; political relationships are typically based on power and are hierarchical, in which rules are defined for a group and various forms of coercion can be used to enforce these rules. Of course, power often enters economic relationships as one party to an exchange may have more money or information or even political power. And voluntary features of politics can result from gaining support and legitimacy for the rules. One version of political economy asserts that governments and markets must be kept separate, with as little influence by governments as possible. But in real life these two realms of human activity have very large effects on each other and the globalization of economic and political relationships is very advanced, hence the need to study international political economy.

Our task here is to introduce some basic ideas about capitalism, markets, and political systems. We consider the nature of economic markets and advance into particular features of international markets. Trade and financial flows are two of the most important kinds of international markets, and you will learn how trade works and how we measure international transactions. What are some of the arguments for and against letting markets work without restrictions, having "free" markets for money, goods, and services? When trade takes place across borders, currencies from different nations must be used. How can this work and how does it affect trade? All advanced nations have governments that play a large role in overall economic management, known as macroeconomic policy. This includes monetary policy and fiscal policy along with policies relating to maintaining economic growth, high employment, and overall price stability.

We also examine several concepts from international politics and economics. This includes the state, domestic politics, and international power relations, global economic strategies, globalization, international economic regimes and institutions, public goods, and economic welfare. Each concept helps to convey various dimensions of involvement in economic life by governments around the world. Taken together, these ideas form the backbone of our discussion of international political economy in this book.

The Nature of Markets and Economies

Markets are both simple and extraordinarily complex human systems. At the most elementary level, a market is a group of people buying and selling. So, when I go to a "farmer's market" and purchase some fresh vegetables I see other buyers and sellers who may have grown the food or they may have purchased it from others who grew it. I pay money and get the food – a pretty simple and visible system.

When we probe into this a bit, things get much more complicated. And as we probe this simple market system, we can see some of the history of the development of markets. Perhaps most important is the medium of exchange we use – *money* – which requires that some governmental entity take on the responsibility for creating, maintaining, and gaining widespread acceptance for this money so I can use it and the seller will readily accept it.[3] For most of human history, this has been a very uncertain process. Only in the last century or two have governments been capable of providing a common, stable, and widely accepted currency. An even more recent feature of markets comes if I get sick from eating contaminated food. I may decide to sue the seller for damages or expect the government to do more to inspect the food. This requires an effective legal system and an effective inspection agency, both of which mean an effective government. Moreover, a food seller may want to purchase insurance against losses, which requires another firm able to provide such insurance at reasonable rates.

Even the simple farmer's market is more complicated than it seems. The farmer's market is linked to a web of other markets for the various inputs to growing food, such as fertilizer, land, and water, and to complementary and competing products in other foods such as processed and frozen food. The price I pay is related to the effects of these other markets and the prices there.

Once we begin to talk about prices, our examination of markets turns more analytical and abstract because we can begin to think about the broader economic consequences of markets. Aggregating and averaging the prices paid over many transactions and over time tells a great deal about the relationship between the *supply* of and the *demand* for this product. A *price* is simply the amount one pays for a product, but it also represents crucially important information to market participants. The movement of prices provides signals to buyers and sellers about the overall market – the broad system of supply and demand – for the product and this is used to make future decisions about production and purchases. Thus a market is a system of production, sales, and prices across many buyers and sellers, but it is also a system of *information* that directs the behavior of market participants.

Markets are also bottom-up or *distributed systems* in which individuals and firms pursue their own economic interests, and these interactions generate an aggregate or collective system of supply, demand, and prices. Without any central control, this system has some rather remarkable properties. Most important, if we make some qualifying assumptions, such a market can flexibly and effectively allocate resources for production to the best possible use.[4] The most important value of a free market is this ability to generate good decisions from market players about production and investment that benefit the entire society: the ability to coordinate production and distribution across the multitude of complex linkages of inputs and outputs is a remarkable feat. To be able to do so with no direct control from the top and result in a highly *efficient* and flexible use of resources is indeed quite astonishing.

Even so, there are important qualifications to this conclusion. Market players are often in a position to affect prices because they are so big; a market composed of a few large firms and many buyers is very different from one with many small buyers and sellers. When the power of a producer is large – when it is big and has much better information than buyers – it can exploit these advantages and distort market outcomes. The term *oligopoly* is used to describe a market dominated by a few large sellers. Markets work well when there is a high level of competition, but firms prefer to have less competition because this increases their power and profits.

Also sometimes problematic is the reliance on consumer preferences as the basis for defining and determining efficiency and "best" use. Markets will reallocate resources ruthlessly based on these preferences and this generates high flexibility. One famous economist, Joseph Schumpeter, called this a process of "*creative destruction*." This makes change a constant feature of capitalist market economies. But we should remember these resources being reallocated are people and firms that will lose their livelihood and often will call on governments for help. There are other instances when markets don't reallocate fast enough. In instances where there are large positive benefits or negative consequences from markets and these cannot be priced in products, reallocation will not take place. Consider air pollution from industrial production and product use: this very negative effect will not show up in the prices of industrial activity and so will not be a basis for resource allocation. Much of the study of political economy is about finding the "right" relationship between allowing free markets to operate and the restrictions and supports we decide to place on these markets.

Discussion of markets leads easily to a consideration of the most important of market economies: *capitalism* and its seeming antithesis, *socialism*. Capitalism is an economic system involving an organized set of institutions for accumulating wealth as liquid capital and directing those resources toward investment in the production of goods and services based on profits. Capitalist systems historically are based on a market economy and a very large role for private enterprise, with profits flowing to investors. Thus, capitalism has provided large rewards to those entrepreneurs able to develop and market goods and services effectively in a competitive market. In a capitalist economy, successful firms receive increasing investment and non-successful firms fail to survive. The rewards are disproportionately large for owners of capital and typically much smaller for workers in a capitalist firm.

Socialism is a system in which private ownership and control of economic activity is significantly restrained, with arrangements designed to direct much more of the gains from the economy to workers and the poor. Much higher levels of resources are devoted to income maintenance programs, access to health care, and retirement benefits in a socialist economy. These costs are usually paid for with high tax levels on the wealthy. In addition, many of the most important industries are owned by the government and operated for the public welfare instead of for private gain.

This discussion of capitalism and socialism can easily lead to an effort to define rigid rules for determining which is which. Thus, we sometimes hear that a socialist economy is one that contains any deviation from pure capitalism. If health care is mandated by a nation's government, then this must be a socialist economy. However, this position quickly breaks down when we try to examine real nations and compare them. Adopting this viewpoint leads to the conclusion there are no capitalist economies in the world. Instead, we should work to develop a continuum that identifies degrees of capitalism and socialism.

This is because almost all advanced economies are a mixture of capitalism and socialism; it is hard to identify a society that accepts a system in which economic gains are tilted completely toward the owners of capital and in which markets are left to sort out all economic gains and losses. In reality, virtually all advanced governments have a major economic role in affecting economic distribution and other outcomes; only in the United States is there a major political movement to disband the state and most of the welfare systems provided by the state. One area of significant difference among advanced capitalist states is the role played by finance, that sector of a capitalist economy engaged in making investments and allocating credit. All advanced nations guarantee this part of the economy against systemic collapse, and thus will protect the largest banks and investment groups against failure. Some, such as the United States and Great Britain, give very wide latitude to financial firms to take risks and control the allocation of capital. Others, such as Japan and Germany and even more so, China and Korea, place much tighter controls on the financial and investment sectors of the economy, with the government often being active in allocating credit.

International Trade

International trade is a special case in the study of markets. In a market with few restrictions on the movement of goods, such as inside a nation, trade occurs freely; but international trade takes place across national boundaries and that often results in large barriers to the movement of goods, services, people, and even capital. So international markets are usually shaped dramatically by the rules adopted by nations affecting these exchanges.

Two of the most important questions we will consider about international markets for goods and services are first, why should international trade happen at all, and second what, if any, restrictions should be imposed on international trade? *Free trade* refers to a policy adopted by a nation that places few, if any, restrictions on the process of importing goods and services into a nation. Free trade is often contrasted with a policy of *protection(ism)*, in which restrictions and barriers are placed on importing goods.

The study of international trade has developed a very sophisticated body of research and evidence. Much of this analysis focuses on the merits of free trade, which is perhaps the best supported and also the most controversial of ideas from economics. Put simply, *the key idea of free trade is that when restrictions on trade are removed production will take place where it is most efficiently done and the resulting trade will benefit all trading nations.* The efficiency of allocation of resources to production is the standard used to evaluate free trade by economists and is based on maximizing the gains from lower prices and wider selection for consumers.

Others may use different standards. When your job or business must move to another country so the global allocation of resources can be the most efficient, you may want to measure the disruptive and negative consequences of free trade. In political terms, only a particular combination of domestic and *international political order* can lead to free trade. This is because organizing and maintaining a policy of free trade requires control of governments by those groups who consistently win from free trade combined with an international political order in which nations cooperate with each other to achieve this end. Free trade requires that groups that are consistently disadvantaged by free trade cannot gain political control of a nation; otherwise they will create barriers to trade. In practice, the nature of domestic and international political orders will be mixed, resulting in some compromise between free trade and protection.

Another long-standing way of thinking about international trade is to see buying goods from abroad as a bad thing. Some even believe selling goods and services abroad should be avoided, based on the view this makes a nation dependent on such trade. These somewhat eccentric but popular views see trade as an involuntary act: self sufficiency in everything needed should be the prime goal and international purchases should be tightly restricted. A variation of this view was dominant in Europe between 1500 and 1850 and is known as *mercantilism*. Here national leaders saw trade as a weapon in the struggle for power among nations and sought to maximize national gains and penalize other nations. By pushing sales abroad and eliminating purchases from abroad, a nation could build up its own resources (especially precious metals) and reduce the resources of others. This notion of trade as comparative enrichment in a world of conflict has frequently defined thinking. Unclear from this approach is whether and how a nation loses by closing off its borders. The analysis of self-sufficiency in this book finds this a wildly unrealistic goal in the twenty-first century for almost all nations. Achieving this is near impossible and attempting this condemns a nation to high-cost and low-quality products.

The Economic Case for Free Trade

Proponents of free trade have been able to measure the gains from trade and assert quite convincingly that nations can almost always achieve mutual gains from trade. This is because nations differ in the ability to produce goods. If one nation is better than another in producing a particular good, as measured by the cost of production, then it should be able to sell that good abroad and benefit other consumers. This kind of advantage is an *absolute advantage* and with some simplifying assumptions we can see how nations can gain from trade. Imagine just two nations – A and B – and two goods – wheat and iron, and each nation has an absolute advantage over the other in one of the goods.

	Wheat (bushels/worker)	Iron (tons/worker)
Nation A	100	250
Nation B	200	150

Clearly, Nation A has an absolute advantage in iron (producing one and two-thirds times as much per worker as Nation B). And Nation B has an absolute advantage in wheat (producing twice as much per worker as Nation A).

To see the gains from trade, we need to compare a situation of no trade to one of free trade. So, assume each nation has 200 workers and we use 100 for production of each product.

	Wheat (bushels)	Iron (tons)
Nation A	10,000	25,000
Nation B	20,000	15,000
Total Output	30,000	40,000

If Nation A and Nation B adopt a policy of no trade, together they can produce 30,000 bushels of wheat and 40,000 tons of iron.

Now assume each nation specializes in the production only of the good in which it has a comparative advantage. This means Nation A will use all its workers to produce iron and Nation B will use all its workers to produce wheat. By itself, Nation A can produce 50,000 tons of iron and Nation B can produce 40,000 bushels of wheat. This yields a relative price for these two products and we assume trade will take place at the ratio of four bushels of wheat for every five tons of iron.

The amount of trade depends on how much of each good is needed. For simplicity's sake, assume Nation A and Nation B are willing to trade

16,000 bushels of wheat for 20,000 tons of iron. This leads to the following outcome from specialization and trade:

	Wheat (bushels)	Iron (tons)
Nation A	16,000	30,000
Nation B	24,000	20,000
Total Output	40,000	50,000

Specialization by nations in an area of absolute advantage combined with trade yields a situation in which all nations are better off. Not only has total production increased, but almost certainly the price of each product has declined. You should take note that it is the gains to consumers that count here, while whatever losses might be incurred by producers are ignored.

The situation in which a nation possesses an absolute advantage is the easy case for demonstrating the merits of free trade. Much more demanding is a situation where a nation has no absolute advantage in any product. In this case, can free trade benefit this nation and others with whom it trades? Economists make a very persuasive case for a positive answer: as long as a nation is not equally disadvantaged in its production capabilities – that is, as long as it has a *comparative advantage* in at least one product – then specialization and trade are beneficial for all.

We can see this if we modify the previous situation with one of the nations having an absolute disadvantage in both products but a comparative advantage in one.

	Wheat (bushels/worker)	Iron (tons/worker)
Nation A	300	1200
Nation B	100	200

In this situation, Nation B had an absolute disadvantage in both wheat and iron, but this disadvantage is not the same. The ratios of productivity between the workers of the two nations are different for wheat (3:1) and iron (6:1); that is, Nation B has a comparative advantage in the production of wheat. Notice also that the ratios for transferring resources for the production of one good to another are different as well: 4:1 for Nation A and only 2:1 for Nation B. It is this comparative advantage that can be used to make trade beneficial for both nations.

The easiest way to show these benefits is to examine the difference between the cost of producing the good at home or buying it from abroad. If it costs less to buy the good from another nation, specialization and trade would be the best option. We can measure the price of the product by the ratio of production capabilities. For Nation A the cost of producing wheat is four units of iron, but for Nation B the cost of producing wheat is only two units of iron. Nation A can buy wheat from Nation B at this price and will be much better off than producing it at a cost of four units of iron. Similarly, Nation B can produce iron but at a cost equal to two units of iron for each unit of wheat, whereas Nation A can produce four units of iron for each unit of wheat. Nation A is better off buying its wheat from Nation B while Nation B is better off buying its iron from Nation A; comparative advantage is sufficient to make trade beneficial for each nation, even for Nation B which has an absolute disadvantage in both goods. Typically, many nations will have an absolute advantage in some product(s). At the same time, demonstrating the benefits of free trade in a situation of comparative advantage makes a very strong case for free trade.

However strong the argument for free trade, the assumptions made to develop this conclusion can be questioned. The person who first made this analysis was *David Ricardo*, one of the greatest of economists, writing early in the nineteenth century. He assumed a world of small national firms where none has significant cost advantages over others, that the factors of production – land, labor, and capital – were largely fixed in attachment to a nation, and that trade consisted of exchanging manufactured goods for agricultural goods. How valid are these assumptions in a world of complex and rapidly changing technology, large transnational firms, widespread governmental involvement in firms and markets, and international trade defined mostly by manufactured goods and globally traded services? This raises many important questions about free trade that we will consider throughout the book. For now, at least one major qualification must be to allow for new ways of thinking about the sources of comparative advantage. Fixed national endowments are now less important than the ability to create productive advantages through new technology, skills, and innovation. Further, such capabilities may derive from matters of governmental policy affecting the national and international environment in which firms operate.[5]

The Political Economy of Free Trade

The analysis of free trade has been based on the benefits of free markets for consumers. But consumers are also producers and they live in nations that are affected in significant ways by trade. These considerations can alter the conclusions about free trade. Specialization and free trade may not always produce the level and kind of economic development a nation prefers. If a country specializes in food and raw materials and the price of these goods is falling relative to manufactured goods over time, it will invariably fall behind industrial nations in economic development. Likewise, a nation concentrating on low wage/labor-intensive products will miss out on the gains in income and social development to be had from advanced technology production. In addition, certain kinds of goods are essential to national security, such as an advanced system of technological capabilities. Specialization can expose nations to dependence on external supplies of such goods and thereby compromise security and other international goals.

The politics of free trade usually hinges on the effects of free trade on people as producers instead of their position as consumers. Adopting a policy of free trade exposes a nation to the effects of global markets and of comparative advantage. When a nation's resources – capital and labor – are employed in industries where a comparative advantage does not exist, these resources must be shifted to areas and industries where such an advantage does exist. Some firms will go out of business and people will lose their jobs as a consequence of free trade. From an economic perspective, this boosts efficiency and keeps the prices of goods low for consumers; but from a political perspective these changes can have very negative consequences for those who must bear the burdens of changing jobs and industries. These costs are not usually measured by markets and cannot easily be incorporated into the analysis of free trade.

Political implications of free Market

Adopting a policy of free trade by many nations will result in widespread reallocation and in the end there will likely be net gains for all societies. But this process generates gains and losses – winners and losers – and the political process that is responsible for making the decision about free trade will be affected. The international political economy of free trade must consider the position and power of the winners and losers from free trade in order to determine the policies likely to be adopted. We can begin to do this by trying to determine what kinds of economic resources will usually have a comparative advantage or disadvantage in global trade.

Comparative advantage can be traced to the unevenness of the distribution of a factor of production around the world. A nation will have a comparative advantage in goods whose main *factor of production* (land, labor, and capital) is nationally plentiful relative to that factor's availability throughout the world. By contrast, a nation will have a comparative disadvantage producing a good based on using a factor that is nationally scarce relative to the rest of the world. An abundant factor will be less expensive in that nation, whereas scarce factors will be more expensive in that nation. From this we can see that free trade will allow those groups controlling a relatively *abundant factor* to gain and will lead to losses for groups whose economic position is based on a relatively *scarce factor*. Though free trade helps consumers it does not help all producer groups, actually harming some.

This pattern of gains and losses sets up a political conflict between winning and losing groups over whether the nation should have free trade or protectionism. For example, assume a nation in which labor is scarce relative to the rest of the world and capital is plentiful. This means products that are labor intensive will be more expensive and the nation will have a comparative disadvantage in these products. Those goods associated with financial capital will be more competitive and the nation will have a comparative advantage. Labor groups will prefer a policy of protection, as that will prevent globally competitive goods from forcing down wages rates. Owners of capital will prefer a policy of openness, at home and abroad, to permit them to advance their interests around the world. The policy actually adopted will depend on the political strength of labor versus capital.[6]

Measuring Global Economic Exchange: The Balance of Payments

One of the most important concepts for understanding and measuring global economic activity is the *balance of payments*, which focuses on a particular nation and measures its transactions with the rest of the world. This accounting technique records the movement of goods, services, and money across national boundaries for some period of time (month, quarter, year). The notion of "balance" here is somewhat misleading, for although this statistic always balances (because of the requirements of double-entry bookkeeping), we really care most about the imbalances that inevitably appear in the balance of payments.

In many ways, the parts of the balance of payments are more important than the whole. The purpose of the system is to measure all of a nation's transactions with the rest of the world. This is a complicated task and requires many different accounts. For our purposes, we will simplify things by focusing on eight major categories. An important way to think about the balance of payments is to determine whether a transaction results in a payment to the nation (a credit or positive number) or a payment by the nation to a foreigner (a debit or negative number). Typically, each of the categories is a summation of the credits and debits and a "balance" for each as a surplus or deficit is recorded.

Major Components of the Balance of Payments

1 **Merchandise Exports and Imports**
   This refers to tangible goods produced at home and sold abroad – *exports* – and tangible goods produced abroad and sold at home – *imports*.
2 **Services exports and imports**
   Services are less tangible and refer to such things as transportation costs for goods and people, consulting, insurance,

information, satellite transmissions, and banking. The totals for merchandise and services are sometimes combined to produce the most familiar item in the balance of payments, and this is referred to as the *balance of trade*.

3 **Investment Income and Payments**

An investment abroad is usually made in expectation of receiving a return, in the form of dividends or interest. This item measures these payments by foreigners to citizens of the home country and by the home country to foreigners.

4 **Government Exports/Imports and Foreign Aid**

The government of a nation may be engaged in buying or selling or buying goods and services abroad. Additionally, the government may give or receive foreign aid.

5 **Balance on *Current Account***

This is a summary measure of items 1–4 (Merchandise, Services, Investment Income, and Government). This is the most commonly used overall measure of a nation's transactions with the rest of the world.

6 ***Capital Account***

This records the actual making of investments abroad and by foreigners in the home country. A distinction is usually made between investments with a maturity of less than one year (short term) and longer than one year (long term). When a Chinese bank purchases US government debt that matures in 180 days, this is a short-term item; when a US firm purchases a factory in Shenzhen, China, this is a long-term item.

7 **Official Reserves**

The central bank of a nation holds reserves of foreign exchange and gold that can be used to conduct transactions with central banks abroad and can be used to intervene in foreign exchange markets. These transactions are often used to offset imbalances in other parts of the balance of payments.

8 **Statistical Discrepancy**

The measurement of the balance of payments is an inexact process, owing to its complexity and to the fact that many international transactions are concealed (illicit drugs and movement of funds to tax havens). This item is used to estimate the amount of such activity and to bring the overall system into balance.

The basic categories of the balance of payments are much easier to understand if we work through a hypothetical example of a nation over time (see "Major Components of the Balance of Payments" above). We will focus especially on how imbalances in one area tend to be offset by other parts of the system. The analysis of the balance of payments focuses on the relationships among the various major components. One of the most important is the relationship between the current account and the capital account, as imbalances in the trade and investment accounts tend to be offset by the capital account. A current account surplus permits a nation to make investments abroad, or, to put it another way, permits the accumulation of assets abroad. A nation with a current account surplus gets paid with ownership of the assets of foreign countries.

We can see this through an examination of Table 2.1 (notice the data in Table 2.2 are in year 3 of Table 2.1). A first cut is to compare the categories over the four years: exports rise but imports rise faster; the nation consistently pays out more in investment income than it makes; the capital account fluctuates somewhat dramatically. Closer inspection shows a fluctuation in rates of change in trade and investment income lead first to a current account deficit, then to a surplus, and then back to a deficit. Generally, the current account and capital account tend to mirror each other, though not very precisely. The capital account shows a net inflow of funds corresponding to a current account deficit, and a net outflow of investment funds corresponds to a current account surplus.

Major issues can arise when imbalances persist for many years. For example, suppose the current account deficit continues for a decade or more. This will usually mean other nations will continue to invest and

Table 2.1 Hypothetical Nation A's Balance of Payments Over Four Years

	YEAR			
	1	*2*	*3*	*4*
Goods/Services				
Exports	102.2	156.7	164.3	191.4
Imports	119.9	140.1	129.6	227.5
Investments				
Income	3.2	3.7	14.6	20.2
Payments	8.4	11.9	21.4	23.1
Government (net)	1.5	11.8	10.2	8.1
Current Account Balance	−21.4	20.2	39.9	−30.9
Capital Account				
Exports	12.2	32.6	58.4	27.7
Imports	26.8	29.1	31.7	50.3
Capital Account Balance	14.6	−3.5	−26.7	22.6
Reserve Account	3.2	−11.0	−7.0	4.1
Statistical Discrepancy	3.6	−5.7	−6.2	4.2

Table 2.2 Hypothetical Balance of Payments for Nation A (billions $US)

	Credit (+)	Debit (–)	Balance
Merchandise			
Exports	164.3		
Imports		129.6	
Services			
Exports	21.1		
Imports		19.3	
Trade Balance			+36.5
Investment Income and Payments			
Income	14.6		
Payments		21.4	
Government			
Exports	13.5		
Imports		2.6	
Aid (net)		.7	
Balance on Current Account	213.5	173.6	+39.9
Capital Account			
Exports (LT/ST)		58.4	
Imports (LT/ST)	31.7		
Balance on Capital Account			–26.7
Official Reserves		7.0	
Statistical Discrepancy		6.2	

that is certainly good. But, increasing investment also means increases in investment income payments to foreigners. This cannot go on forever and the adjustments can be unpleasant. One possibility is to curtail the balance of payments deficit by restricting imports. If unchecked, foreigners may at some point refuse to make additional investments – remember, they are not compelled to do so. When this happens, often suddenly, the nation may need to default on its debts, thereby damaging its credit position internationally for some time.

The balance of payments is most important for what it reveals about imbalances, especially persistent ones in the current account.[7] The processes of global exchange in the balance of payments affect a nation's overall prosperity and financial position, and various policy options exist to try to correct imbalances. To understand this, we need to consider monetary, fiscal, and exchange rate policies.

Macroeconomic Policy

Over the twentieth century, governments in all advanced nations have expanded greatly their role in affecting the overall level of the national economy. The effort by the national government to manage the process of economic growth is usually referred to as *macroeconomic policy*. The two most established areas of macroeconomic policy are *fiscal policy* and *monetary policy.* Fiscal policy refers to decisions about governmental spending, taxes, and borrowing, whereas monetary policy refers to efforts by a nation's central bank to manage the *money supply, interest rates, and inflation.* Of the two, monetary policy has the longest tradition, is the most insulated from national politics, is the most institutionalized, and is the most effective. Fiscal policy, by contrast, tends to be much more politicized because interest groups are easily able to identify the benefits and costs and act to influence decisions. The result is fiscal policy has a checkered legacy as a tool of macroeconomic policy.

Central Banks and Monetary Policy

The United States created a modern *central bank* – the *Federal Reserve* – in 1913. The United States was very late in creating a central bank: Great Britain did so in the 1840s, Germany in the 1870s, and even upstart Japan in the 1880s.

The combination of repeated large-scale banking and financial instability and the demonstrated stabilizing features of other nations' central banks convinced even conservative leaders to support establishment of the Federal Reserve System. One of the recurring features of capitalism and financial markets is a boom–bust cycle, involving a panicked loss of confidence in financial markets resulting in a large and rapid drop in the prices of financial assets.[8] The ravages of these cycles can be very damaging to economic systems and central banks were often created to reduce their frequency and severity. A central bank can act as a *"lender of last resort"* in situations of economic and financial distress in order to restore stability.[9] In recent years, the severity of financial crises has brought central banks like the Federal Reserve to the forefront again as the key player in both stopping the economic hemorrhaging during the crisis and providing the resources to mitigate or control the crisis.

Central banks differ in purpose. All central banks have the goal of promoting financial stability, but the two other main goals are somewhat contradictory. One goal is enhancing economic growth, which usually involves stimulating the economy; the other is controlling *inflation,* which often means placing restraints on economic growth. Economic growth is an indication that the production of goods and services in a nation has increased from year to year, which usually leads to rising incomes and employment. Some central banks use monetary policy to create the conditions that enhance economic growth. Inflation is a measure of changes in the prices of goods and services. Some low level of inflation – 1 percent to 2 percent – is thought to be consistent with economic growth and is acceptable. Beyond this level, inflation is considered an impediment to growth, as incomes may not keep up with rising prices and inflation can debase the value of a nation's currency. Inflation is especially disliked by banks and other lenders, as the dollars used to repay a debt are worth less than the dollars used to make a loan. This means lenders and creditors represent a natural political constituency highly motivated to oppose inflation.

Central banks also differ with respect to the level of independence of political control. Often thought to have the greatest independence was the German Bundesbank, with the Bank of England and the Banque de France generally following a policy established by the government. The Federal Reserve falls somewhere in between, able to act on its own but also often responding to political pressure to expand the money supply or lower interest rates.[10] The European Central Bank, now more than a decade old, is supposed to be somewhat independent of political pressure, and operates with a singular focus on maintaining low inflation. Other central banks have been given the role of promoting economic growth. The emphasis on controlling inflation or expanding growth involves some of the main contradictions in the making of monetary policy.

The US central bank, or Fed as it is commonly known, has two major tools for managing the *money supply* and the economy: *open market operations* and the *discount rate*.[11] The purpose of each is to affect the availability of credit – that is, the willingness of banks to make loans and of individuals and corporations to borrow. Increasing the supply of money tends to increase borrowing and hence economic activity; decreasing the money supply has the opposite effect and can be used to lower inflation rates.

When banks lend money to their customers, whether to buy a house, a computer, a boat, or an office building, this expands the money supply and economic activity. The production of goods and services to meet this demand boosts employment, and these additional workers spend their new incomes and perhaps borrow money themselves. The process also works in reverse: when banks contract lending, purchases of goods and services shrink, employment declines, and additional decreases in spending result.

The Fed affects the money supply through its relationship with the large number of private banks that are members of the Federal Reserve system. The Fed is connected to these member banks (private banks) in several ways: it determines the proportion of bank assets that must be held as reserves; it engages in regulation of bank lending practices; it lends money to member banks; and the Fed engages in transactions with these banks and with all holders of US government securities. The most commonly used method for influencing the money supply is something known as open market operations, which involves buying or selling US government securities in the market maintained for this. The Fed is either pumping funds into or withdrawing funds from the banking system. When the Fed purchases these securities (a typical transaction involves billions of dollars), the sellers will now deposit money into the banking system; when the Fed sells these securities, the opposite occurs. The increased deposits from buying securities adds to the ability of banks to make additional loans, and when funds are used to pay the Fed for securities this reduces the ability to lend.

Federal Reserve *open market operations* are coordinated with and affect the level of *interest rates* in the economy.[12] Three interest rates are commonly used as measures of overall interest rates: the *discount rate*, the *Fed Funds* rate, and the *ten-year rate* on US government bonds. The discount rate is the interest rate charged by the Fed when it loans money to member banks. When the Fed increases or decreases the discount rate, it is affecting the price of borrowing money, both directly for banks and indirectly for those who borrow money from banks. The Fed Funds rate is the price banks pay to borrow money from other banks, usually for very short time periods. This rate is managed by the Fed and is used as a kind of anchor rate for the whole economy. The ten-year US government bond rate is the price the government pays when it borrows money with a ten-year maturity period, and is established in auctions of the bonds. Each of these interest rates is closely watched and usually affects other interest rates, such as for mortgages, credit cards, and auto loans. Various forms of actions by the Fed work to influence especially the Fed Funds rate and thereby interest rates generally, and through this the money supply and the rate of economic growth.

The leaders of the Federal Reserve pay close attention to indicators of economic growth, contraction, and inflation. When the evidence indicates growth is too fast and inflation may be increasing, the Fed will act in a coordinated way to withdraw liquidity from the banking system with a monetary policy of contraction. This could include sales of securities in open market operations and efforts to push up the Fed Funds rate. This kind of policy was especially evident during the 1978–83 period, when inflation was especially high. By contrast, when economic indicators are declining the Fed can act to boost liquidity through open market purchases and efforts to lower the Fed Funds rate. This expansionary monetary policy was especially clear for much of the time after 2001, when the US economy suffered several bouts of economic difficulty.

In addition to efforts to manage the economy through monetary policy, the role of central banks since about 1980 has increasingly returned to efforts to contain the effects of financial crises. Over the last three decades, financial crises have increased in frequency and severity. Because of the ability to act quickly using their substantial monetary resources, central banks have assumed primary responsibility for countering the rapid and large declines in the availability of credit in a financial crisis. Acting as the lender of last resort, central banks provide direct loans to financial institutions and inject large amounts of funds into banking systems. Central banks also operate to manage the effects of or even prevent the bankruptcies of especially large financial institutions that can exacerbate the crisis.

During and after the recent financial crisis beginning in 2008, the Fed took the lead in preserving many of the large financial institutions threatened by the rapid declines in the availability of credit, and took the lead in stimulating the US economy and much of the world economy, by purchasing government securities with money the Fed was able to create.[13] This process, known as *Quantitative Easing* (QE), requires a bit of clarification. The Federal Reserve has the ability to create money, both by printing it but more typically by simply making a computer entry on its own balance sheet. This money – US dollars – is then used to enter global bond markets for US government bonds and purchase those bonds. This process meant the Fed had injected large amounts of money into the economy and provided resources for consumption and the purchase of various assets, such as stocks. The Fed then would hold these government bonds on its balance sheet. For long periods of time, the Fed through several rounds of QE was injecting as much as $85 billion per month into the US and the global economies. This was a very controversial policy, which some monetary conservatives warned threatened to produce massive global inflation. Others were concerned about what would happen when QE ended, the monetary stimulus declined, and interest rates began to rise.[14]

Fiscal Policy

The management of the overall economy – macroeconomic policy – includes not only the monetary policy of the central bank but also the spending and taxing policy of the government, known as *fiscal policy*. The basic ideas of fiscal policy can be traced to a prominent British economist, John Maynard Keynes, who was engaged in understanding efforts to boost economic activity during the Great Depression of the 1930s. Keynes argued that policies relating to government spending and taxes could be used to push up economic activity during times of depression. Heretofore, most had argued that governments should seek to restrict spending to an amount equal to tax revenues, yielding a *balanced budget*. Keynes and others asserted that fiscal policy need not, and should not, be tied to the orthodoxy of a balanced budget. Instead, fiscal policy should be more flexible and could be used during times of economic downturn to avoid the extreme declines of recession and depression.[15]

Keynes focused on the benefits of deficit spending, in which the government deliberately spends more than its revenue, borrowing the difference from those who have funds to lend. (A *deficit* in the government accounts occurs when spending exceeds tax revenues; a *surplus* occurs when revenues exceed spending.) There was great resistance from many conservatives to Keynes's ideas, feeling the government would gain too much power over business and business would lose its predominant position in controlling the society and economy.[16] However, during the period from 1940–60, *Keynesianism* – as Keynes's ideas came to be known – was more and more accepted as government policy. The theory supporting deficit spending was that selling bonds and using the revenues to expand government spending worked to expand the economy by returning unused savings into the spending and income stream. During the Kennedy Administration, in the early 1960s, these ideas were adjusted to include cutting income taxes while maintaining or even increasing government spending to boost the economy. Recipients of tax increases were expected to spend their increased income to accomplish the same effect on the economy. In the 1980s, conservatives eager to cut taxes for the more affluent twisted this idea to include using tax cuts for boosting the willingness of the owners of capital to invest and take risks. The theory here, much less accepted, is that investors and entrepreneurs require higher returns in order to have sufficient incentives to take risks and drive economic growth. Tax policy is being used to increase returns to the wealthy and these "bottom line" profits will act to "incentivize" these behaviors.[17]

Fiscal policy in Western democracies has become much less effective as a means of macroeconomic management. This is because, unlike monetary policy, fiscal policy is enacted by elected officials. Rather than fine-tuning the size of spending and taxes to the needs of the economy, these decisions are often used to win votes. Whether the matter is welfare spending, retiree benefits, or the tax levels for the wealthy, these choices invariably affect electoral prospects. The cumulative and consistent policy effect has been to raise spending and reduce taxes because each is a winning political strategy. The result, at least in the United States, has been persistent deficits in government accounts and a rising level of government debt. Also undermining the effectiveness of fiscal policy after about 1990 has been the withering relationship between growth in production and growth in employment. Firms can increase production without necessarily a proportionate increase in hiring because of rising productivity from technology. This means economic growth can come without the previous gains in employment, thereby reducing the overall effect of economic stimulus.

Nonetheless, fiscal policy does happen and these actions raise numerous policy questions about fairness and appropriateness. For example, fiscal deficits are no longer the major issue, but instead the debate centers on whether tax cuts are the source or increasing spending is the source of the deficit. Conservatives accept and liberals reject deficits resulting from tax cuts, while the positions are reversed when increases in spending for food stamps or unemployment benefits lead to the deficit. An important set of strategic choices in fiscal policy relates to what activity should be taxed in order to provide the "right" kinds of economic incentives. Should we

Table 2.3 Effective Tax Rates for Incomes of $100,000 (Income Tax plus Social Security)

Country	Tax as % of income of $100,000 (2011)
Australia	25
Belgium	48
Brazil	39
Britain	31
China	26
Czech Republic	29
Denmark	41
France	43
Germany	44
Greece	44
Japan	28
Russia	13
UAE	5
United States	25

Source: Data from *The Economist*, October 1, 2011, www.economist.com/node/21531016.

enact laws that tax wealth or income or consumption or capital gains or some combination? And major issues of ideology and policy result from the class basis that defines much of the debate on fiscal policy. In particular, a vast asymmetry in special benefits is asserted for the social and economic value of "jobs creators," who must receive special treatment and benefits as compared to the rest of society, particularly workers, in order to perform their job as risk takers and job creators. This form of naked elitism is unlikely to work for very long and is a shallow basis for national policy.

Comparison of the effects of tax policy is also revealing, though these differences rarely seem to affect policy decisions. There is significant variation in the level of taxation across advanced economies. This can be seen in Table 2.3. When we add income taxes and the employee contributions to social security, we can see a range from about 25 percent of income in the United States (near the lowest among advanced states) to Belgium, where 48 percent of income is paid in taxes. These differences are substantial and reflect very different systems of political economy, class relations, and political conflict.

Exchange Rates and Trade

One of the most important forms of international economic exchange is trade. For trade to occur, money must change hands and it must be in a form the seller is willing to accept and the buyer can use. But, of course, international trade occurs across national boundaries with different kinds of money. This means one nation's money must be exchanged for another and the rate of this exchange has significant consequences for the value of the goods and services being bought and sold. You need to remember that a product produced in the United States – with costs paid in dollars – and exported to and sold in Japan, will be priced and sold in yen. Moreover, the way the exchange of currencies takes place – whether in free markets or some other more controlled setting – affects trade as well. We will discuss how foreign exchange trading takes place and how exchange rates can affect trade, consider how and why governments might seek to control this process, and explore the reasons for fluctuations in foreign exchange rates for a currency.

The exchange rate for a currency is simply how much of another country's currency can be purchased with a specified amount of your currency. The price of a currency is usually but not always established in large global markets where the currency is traded on business days of the week. Between 2011 and 2014, the exchange rate of the US dollar and the euro fluctuated between .7 and .8 dollars per euro. In early 2014, the price of a US dollar was .7319 euros (or a euro would buy 1.3662 US dollars).[18] Other important prices included $1 = 104.08 Japanese yen (1 yen = $.0096) and $1 = 6.0523 Chinese Renminbi (RMB) (1 RMB = $.1652).[19] It is the fluctuation of exchange rates that provides the opportunity for traders to profit but also creates significant benefits and losses for those who buy and sell goods in international trade.

The global trading system for foreign exchange involves those who need to exchange currencies relating to trade in goods and services, but even more persons and institutions trade foreign exchange for purposes of speculation. The exchange rate, or price, of a currency is determined by the demand for and supply of one currency in relation to another. Trade generates a considerable part of this supply and demand, as sellers in foreign markets (exporters) seek to exchange their buyers' currency for their own. Speculators make estimates of future directions for currencies in order to profit from these changes. On a daily basis, foreign exchange trading is certainly the largest organized global market system in the world, with volume totaling more than $5 trillion dollars, and more than three-fourths concentrated in the exchange of dollars, yen, euros, and British pounds.[20] By contrast, equities trading in the United States on one day totals about $300 billion, or less than one-tenth of foreign exchange trading.

Exchange rates can fluctuate considerably. For example, see Figures 2.1 and 2.2. The data in the first Figure calculates exchange rates as an index, which shows percentage changes from the base point of January 2000 to September 2011.

Notice how much change in percentage terms can occur. Sometimes, as in 2006–9, changes come in opposite directions; in other periods, changes in exchange rates come in the same direction but in different degrees. Remember this when we discuss exchange rates systems and the impact of exchange rates on the prices of exports and imports.

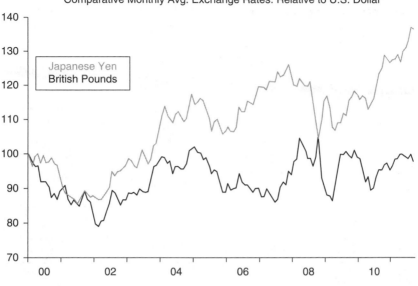

Figure 2.1 Index of US Dollar Exchange Rates with British Pound and Japanese Yen.

Source: Data from © 2011 by Prof. Werner Antweiler, University of British Columbia, Vancouver BC, Canada. Reprinted by permission. Time period shown in diagram: 1/Jan/2000–9/Sep/2011.

The data in Figure 2.2 – US dollar and the Chinese RMB – permits us to discuss different kinds of exchange rate systems. Essentially, a nation's government has some choice as to whether its currency fluctuates freely in global markets or whether it will place restrictions on that trading. The status of a currency's convertibility refers to the degree to which it can be exchanged in global markets for other currencies.

Notice how the fluctuations in the Chinese RMB are quite different from those of the dollar, pound, or yen, which are freely convertible. Instead, the RMB is a pegged currency that is only partly convertible. The Chinese government places restrictions on holding RMB outside of China and additionally links, or pegs, its currency's exchange rate value to an average value of a group, or basket, of other currencies. For a time, the RMB was pegged to the value of the US dollar. As we can see, during the time from 2000–5 the value of the RMB in terms of the dollar did not change, at 8.27RMB = $1.[21] Then, between 2005 and 2008, the value changes when the Chinese government loosened controls to let the value of the RMB against the dollar rise from 8.27 to 6.8.[22] This same policy happened between 2010 and 2014. The Chinese government allowed the RMB to slowly float upward to the new level.[23]

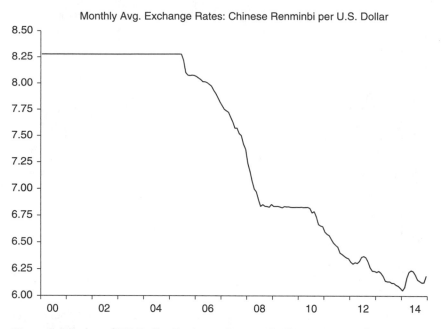

Figure 2.2 Index of US Dollar Exchange Rate with Chinese Renminbi.

Source: Data from © 2011 by Prof. Werner Antweiler, University of British Columbia, Vancouver BC, Canada. Reprinted by permission. Time period shown in diagram: 1/ Jan/2000–9/Sep/2011.

One of the most common ways to measure exchange rate fluctuations is to create an average of exchange rates of one currency in terms of the currencies of its major trading partners. Typically the average is weighted for each nation's currency by the size of trade with that country. Figure 2.3 provides such a measure for the US dollar exchange rates over several years. As you can see, there is substantial variation in the value of the dollar, even as an average. A rise of as much as 20 percent followed by a decline of an equal amount happens several times. We now need to understand how such fluctuations can affect trade.

How Exchange Rates Affect Trade

The relation between exchange rates and trade is a result of the fact that different currencies are being used in trade and the ultimate price of a good sold abroad is affected by the exchange rate between these currencies. Exporters must price their goods in the currency of the market where they sell, though they eventually want to exchange the money received for their home currency. This is why exchange rates matter.

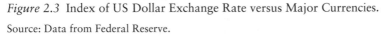

Figure 2.3 Index of US Dollar Exchange Rate versus Major Currencies.

Source: Data from Federal Reserve.

To see this in action, consider the following simplified examples. A Japanese producer of high-definition televisions is selling these in the United States. In order to cover costs and make a small profit, this firm needs to sell the TVs for the equivalent of 100,000 yen. If the exchange rate between the yen and the dollar is $1 = 100 yen, this company needs to sell its TV in the United States for $1,000, which when converted back to yen will yield 100,000 yen. Now, assume the exchange rate changes to $1 = 120 yen, which means the dollar has appreciated in value (it brings more yen) and the yen has declined (it now takes more yen to get a dollar).

How does the rising dollar and falling yen affect the price of Japanese TVs in the United States? Keeping the price at $1,000 means the Japanese firm can reap a whirlwind profit of 20,000 yen ($1,000 now equals 120,000 yen). Another option for the Japanese firm would be to lower its price from $1,000 in order to increase the volume of sales. The depreciating yen permits (but does not require) the Japanese exporter to lower prices and become more competitive in foreign markets.

By contrast, suppose the yen appreciates to an exchange rate of $1 = 80 yen. Now the Japanese exporter has little choice but to raise prices in the United States. The $1,000 now will yield only 80,000 yen, far less than is needed. Thus, a rising currency penalizes exporters. You should also consider how these changes would affect US exporters.

These examples help us understand how government exchange rate policy might be used to affect its trade balance. Remember, governments often intervene in foreign exchange markets to affect the price of the currency. One reason to do so is if the nation is experiencing a large and persistent trade deficit. A drop in the value of the currency would give the exporters of the nation an opportunity to lower prices and perhaps increase volume by more than the drop in prices. Conversely, the declining currency means the currencies of other nations are rising relative to that currency, which somewhat compels those nations' exporters to raise prices and suffer a decline in volume. This relationship is depicted in Figure 2.4. Here we consider the expected effects of a decline in the value of the dollar on the US trade deficit. These effects work through the consequences of the dollar decline for the prices of exports and imports, the effects of prices on demand for exports and imports, and the resulting effects for the volume of exports and imports.

Our chart shows a decline in the value of the dollar should lead to a decline in the price of exports and a rise in the price of imports, resulting in a rise in the demand for exports and a decline in the demand for imports, with the volume of exports rising and the volume of imports decreasing. The overall effect is to reduce the trade deficit, with exports rising and imports falling. Perceptive students will note this relationship depends on the relationship between price and demand and assumes the percent change in demand is greater than the percent change in price. Economists refer to this as an elastic demand, with the change in demand greater than the change in price. Inelastic demand would be a situation in which the change in demand falls short of the change in price.

The ultimate effects of exchange rates on a nation's trade balance are much more complicated than the simple chart. Neither producers nor consumers may behave as expected. Transnational firms, which dominate international trade, have capabilities and interests in many nations and make decisions on pricing and production based on many factors other than the exchange rate of one nation. Consumers of oil, as in the United States, have few if any substitutes for oil and its byproducts and may well change their purchases little as a result of price increases. And governments often use various trade rules to affect the price and volume of trade to undermine the effects of exchange rates. Consider Figure 2.5, which displays the US dollar–Japanese yen exchange rate over twenty years. The clear overall trend of the dollar is down against the yen, by a large percent,

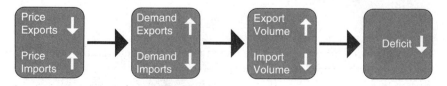

Figure 2.4 How Exchange Rates Affect Trade.

Monthly Avg. Exchange Rates: Japanese Yen per U.S. Dollar

Figure 2.5 US Dollar–Japanese Yen Exchange Rate, 1990–2011.

Source: Data from © 2011 by Prof. Werner Antweiler, University of British Columbia, Vancouver BC, Canada. Reprinted by permission. Time period shown in diagram: 1/ Jan/1990–9/Sep/2011.

although for about five years the dollar rose substantially against the yen. We would expect this overall decline to lead to a significant improvement in the US trade balance versus Japan. <u>And yet, in every year from 1990 to 2010 the United States has run a deficit in trade in goods with Japan,</u> a deficit that had increased steadily until the global recession of 2008.[24] And the overall US deficit in goods and services has expanded substantially over the same period, rising from about $39 billion in 1992 to about $700 billion in each of the four years from 2005–8.[25] As we will see in subsequent chapters, there are many mostly political factors that help us understand why the expected changes in trade balances did not happen.

Economic Growth and Sustainable Development

For the greatest part of the time when humans have lived in groups – about 10,000 years – *economic growth* was tiny in per-person terms. Most economic growth came because people figured out ways to produce more food and over time the rise in food production was followed by a growth in population. Unfortunately, the rise in population negated the rise in per person growth. Humans have always been subject to changes in climate or just to bad luck, and starvation was common. There were situations when human short-sightedness led to exploitation of the environment beyond sustainable levels and the human society simply collapsed, and even more situations in which bad decisions led to a variety of social breakdowns and pathologies.[26] Most societies had very little surplus to fall back on in difficult times.

This long trend of low growth and extreme human vulnerability was broken for some people about two centuries ago, when the capacity to produce goods and food began to grow over long periods, even faster than population, and human wealth per person began to rise.[27] First concentrated only in a few areas of Europe and North America, the process of economic growth expanded to other areas, such as Japan during the nineteenth century and in the twentieth century to parts of the Americas and Asia. Global inequality increased dramatically, as many areas achieved very little economic growth while others surged ahead.[28]

This rare phenomenon of economic growth occurs when an economic system increases the ability to produce goods and services. Not only does the quantity of output increase, but over time the nature of what is produced changes as a result of economic growth. Thus, the US economy of 1950, with electricity, air travel, televisions, automobiles, and a vast array of consumer products, was fundamentally different than the US economy of 1900, where most production was in agriculture and raw materials. This comes as competitive processes drive firms toward making improvements and innovation in products and processes that change the very nature of the composition of production.

Economic output and growth is measured by a calculation known as *Gross Domestic Product* (GDP), which is the sum of all the goods and services produced in a nation over a period of time, usually one year. When the value of GDP rises from one year to the next, economic growth has taken place. However, there are some important qualifications to this statement. The measurement of GDP needs to be reduced by the level of *inflation*, because increases in the measure of production just from an increase in prices should not count as growth. This means GDP should be measured in inflation-adjusted terms, or *real terms*. Furthermore, growth resulting from higher population is less valuable than growth shared by all. So, often GDP will be calculated in per person, or *per capita*, terms measured by dividing production totals by population. Economic growth per capita then gives a better sense of improving ability to produce and not just increases in the number producing. One other qualification comes from comparing GDP levels across nations. The prices of products can be very different from one nation to the next, and therefore using local prices will understate production in low-price nations relative to high-price nations. Another kind of GDP calculation attempts to adjust for this problem by defining GDP in terms of *purchasing power parity* (PPP), or equalizing prices relating to measuring GDP. This means making an adjustment to low-price nations based on establishing a standard set of prices based (arbitrarily) on prices in the

United States. This new measure is GDP (PPP), which calculates an average price ratio relative to US prices and raises the value of the GDP for low-price nations by a ratio equal to the relationship of prices in the United States.[29] Conversely, a nation whose prices are, on average, above those in the United States will find its GDP (PPP) reduced in value because the higher prices overstate the value of its GDP.

Economic growth and the consumption of goods produced has historically been very resource intensive, with a host of negative consequences for the air, water, and land, and the continuing growth in many societies has begun to put very serious strains on natural resources, health, and the quality of life. Perhaps nowhere is this clearer than to a visitor to China, where the air and water are very polluted from the immense economic growth there.[30] Further, Chinese economic growth has begun to affect the global availability of many natural resources, with prices of many rising dramatically due to the demand pressures on supplies.

China helps illustrate a point about the costs of economic growth and how the term "*sustainable development*" has come to influence changes in thinking about economic growth. This term focuses on how present-day production and consumption can limit the ability of future generations to enjoy the same benefits and quality of life. This is because increasing pollution and using scarce but essential resources can harm the interests and capabilities of those living in even the near future.[31] The extraordinarily rapid growth in China clearly shows how growth today can harm as well as benefit the quality of life today, but it also threatens the ability to grow and possibly even survive tomorrow. At a very practical and not theoretical level, the Chinese case shows the need to conserve resources, protect the environment, and limit sharply the effects of rampant economic growth. This point about the practicality of conserving resources has been taken up in the West by many corporations and other organizations, often as a way to control the costs of production. Thus, considerable effort in the largest global firms is now directed to managing the firm so as to enhance sustainability.[32] At the same time, many carbon resource firms – coal, oil, and natural gas – and their ideological allies have resisted efforts to think in terms of sustainable development.

The Politics of International Political Economy

The political dimensions of international political economy focus on the role of states, *international cooperation* and *institutions, interest groups* and *political coalitions, power relationships*, and the *collective interests* and concerns that define the nature of political entities. Political systems operate within, affect, and are affected by economic systems. The importance of economic growth and technological capabilities for a nation guarantees deep involvement by governments in economies. And economic systems cannot function well without effective systems of order and rules and sometimes even support by political systems. But political systems are not the same as economic systems and have different, even if sometimes complementary, ways of thinking and acting.

The *state* is a centralized system of power that organizes a society and provides order within and protection from without. Typically, this system of power is based on various forms of organized support from groups within the society. States claim to monopolize the use of legitimate force within a society and also develop considerable physical power to defend the society from external threats and attacks. The interaction of states creates a large part of what we think of as *international relations*, including efforts by states to affect the economic success of the nation at home and abroad. *International political economy* focuses much attention on the political and economic forces that define states and their capabilities and choices, and on how the political, ideological, and military relations among states relate to economic activity within and between states. We will provide here a brief overview of the ways these arrangements have been studied.

States as we know them today can be traced to the events of the seventeenth century, when, following the Thirty Years' War, the Peace of Westphalia helped establish the concept of sovereign states with exclusive control over territory. Over the next several centuries the bureaucratic, political, military, and economic capabilities of states expanded considerably and this form of political organization has come to dominate the entire globe. States are far from the only important actor in global political and economic affairs, but they possess resources that give them a dominant role in many areas. States have *sovereignty*, which means they control territory and make the rules that define how people interact within that area. States also possess the military forces needed to enforce those rules and the combination of territory and military makes it difficult for actors other than states to challenge this power. Though states seem to be a homogeneous form of political organization, they are far from alike in capabilities. Only a small number of states combine high levels of economic and military power and this high level of differentiation creates a very complex system of international relations.

The leaders of states have a very keen interest in the level of economic development within their nation and in the economic capabilities of other nations. A defining feature of sovereignty is the ability to create, enforce, and manage a single currency accepted throughout the nation. Control of the monetary system permits states to influence economic relationships throughout the nation. Likewise, a system for the efficient administration and collection of taxes is essential for an effective state to operate. These capabilities can take many decades or longer to develop. For many societies, the development of state capacities was deeply connected to the requirements for fighting and preparing to fight wars.[33]

One of the main goals of studying international political economy is to understand the domestic and foreign economic policies of states and the ways these policies aggregate into a system of states. This is because these policies have such a large effect on the economic fate of nations and on economic exchange across borders. For a social scientist, "understanding" policy means figuring out why choices were made. Three main ways of doing this can be found in studying international political economy: the relationship of state interests to the external environment of states, the political coalitions that frame the state, and the ideas and ideologies commonly accepted by political elites.

The external environment of a nation can influence its choices about economic policy in several ways. Likewise, state choices can influence the overall structure of the system of states.[34] The external environment can sometimes be composed of one dominant state with the capacity and the interests in developing a global system of free trade and free capital movement. Such a state can open its economy to imports and invite others to do likewise, or it can even provide other benefits as an enticement. By contrast, the external environment can be composed of a multitude of states engaged in fierce competition and acting to control territory and restrict trade in this area. Any given nation within these two quite different systems confronts a very different set of *incentives* relating to domestic and foreign economic policy. The effect of these external environments can be different depending on the size and power of a nation. Moreover, states have a generalized set of interests in increasing their power, promoting their economy, and worrying about social stability. The varying degree of these circumstances can intersect with the external environment to influence policy choices. The distribution of the characteristics of state – the proportion of large and small, weak and strong – can affect the overall external structure of the system. A large number of small and highly developed states will likely result in an open system of international trade, whereas a small number of heterogeneous states will likely lead to a closed system of trade.

The political leadership of a state, even when the government is not democratic, usually depends on obtaining the support of important groups within society, which usually can be understood as coalitions of interests. Various groups in a society may be situated economically in different ways and will have policy preferences based on their economic position. Those groups gaining from a policy will support it and those losing will oppose it. Understanding economic policy can be linked to the structure and composition of the political coalitions in a society and to the institutions in a society that aggregate and organize interests. Key complexities in this approach relate to just how a group's position in the economy defines its interests and policy preferences and how political institutions structure political power and choices.[35] Additionally, changes in a nation's external environment can influence the economic and political fate of domestic interests and thereby national policy. For example, globalization in terms of a rapid growth in global trade and in global financial flows can alter the actual or potential incomes of many groups and thereby change their interests and political alliances.

One last area for political analysis in international political economy is the nature, origins, and consequences of global institutions, which are formal and informal organizations and rules that affect the ways economic exchange takes place in the global economy. In the nineteenth century, the *gold standard* was the most important international institution, structuring global trade and finance and even the domestic economies of many nations. However, there were very few other institutions affecting exchange on a global scale. In the second half of the twentieth century, this changed dramatically with the creation by governments of a multitude of international organizations and the emergence of an even larger number of international organizations not connected to governments.

One reason for this development was the powerful political response to the ravages of two world wars and a global depression between 1914 and 1945. The capitalism operating across national borders requires clear rules for trade and mechanisms to adjust the imbalances that develop. Many of the institutions developed after 1945 were designed to provide these arrangements for the global economy. Each of these institutions was the result of cooperation among nations to create, fund, and promote them. One of the key issues in international political economy is to explain how and why this cooperation takes place and the effects of institutions on the global political and economic interactions. Perhaps the clearest results have been for international trade, where rules regarding the level and forms of trade barriers have been established and modified greatly in favor of freer trade. These rules are the result of considerable negotiation, with a framework of rules for negotiating established through international cooperation. The result has been an explosion of trade in the six decades after World War II.

Not as clear in the results has been the development of a range of less formal and even tacit rules and assumptions about the way international relations should operate. These regimes are themselves usually associated with international organizations. One important and disputed proposition is that even if the institutions change, many of the regimes will persist and continue to affect national behavior. Examples of tacit regimes include a preference for multilateral negotiation to achieve outcomes that are to be managed by an international organization.

Conclusion: Conceptual Tools

This chapter provides an overview of many of the ideas, concepts, and relationships that comprise the study of international political economy. Understanding the political and economic arrangements that make up global and national economic systems across the entire planet is a formidable task. The first step is developing a vocabulary that allows you to enter the conversation about the global economy. We have worked to describe the many economic and political terms associated with the study and analysis of international political economy.

But, just understanding the concepts is insufficient. Most of these terms, especially those linked to policy, are intensely debated and these debates are closely related to the political and economic interests of various groups. In subsequent chapters, we will consider the major questions and issues of policy in relation to the ideas, hypotheses, and conclusions of international political economy. Reaching judgments about the validity of this form of analysis will be your task. We believe this chapter has given you many of the tools you will need.

Key Concepts (see Glossary)

Macroeconomic Policy
Autarchy
Central Bank
Discount Rate
Economic Growth
Federal Reserve Bank
Fed Funds Rate
Fiscal Policy
Gross Domestic Product
  (GDP)
Inflation
Interest Rates
Lender of Last Resort
Monetary Policy
Money Supply
Open-Market Operations
Per Capita
Prime Rate
Purchasing Power Parity (PPP)
Quantitative Easing
Real Terms

Trade
Absolute Advantage
Balance of Payments
Budget Deficit/Surplus
Capital Account
Comparative Advantage
Creditor Nation

Currency Appreciation/
  Depreciation
Currency Convertibility
Current Account
  Deficit
  Surplus
Debtor Nation
Dirty Float
Exchange Rate Systems
  Fixed
  Floating
  Dirty Float
Free Trade Agreement
Specialization
Trade Surplus/Deficit

Political Analysis
Capitalism
Collective Interests
Interest Groups
International Cooperation
International Institutions
Political Coalitions
Power Relationships
Regime
Socialism
Sovereignty
State
Sustainable Development

Basic Definitions
Collective Goods
Efficiency
Elasticity
Factor of Production
Free Trade

Gold Standard
Keynesianism
Liquidity
Markets
Oligopoly
Protection(ism)

Discussion Questions

1 What are some of the most important complexities of the operation of markets? Are markets always effective in solving economic problems?

2 Explain how the concept of comparative advantage can be used to make an especially strong economic case for all nations to adopt a policy of free trade.

3 Are there winners and losers from trade? How and why?

4 Explain how changes in exchange rates for currencies affect exports and imports.

5 Consider the balance of payments. What is the relationship between the current account and the capital account?

6 How does a fiscal stimulus operate to boost the economy?

7 What are the different kinds of policies adopted by central banks to manage the money supply?

8 Compare the distinctions between capitalism and socialism and analyze the reasons why all advanced economies are a mixture of the two systems.

Notes

1 For a history of international political economy, see Benjamin Cohen, *International Political Economy*, Princeton: Princeton University Press, 2008.

2 An award-winning film, "Inside Job," describes how some economists examining financial markets had their conclusions affected by the vast resources available to financial firms promoting free markets.

3 The Internet has changed many things, and money may be one of them. The digital money, bitcoin, is an attempt to bypass the state's role in establishing a medium of exchange. *The Economist*, "The Trust Machine," October 31, 2015,www.economist.com/news/leaders/21677198-technology-behind-bitcoin-could-transform-how-economy-works-trust-machine

4 These assumptions include: buyers and sellers must be many in number and small in size and unable to affect overall prices; buyers and sellers must be able to see prices across the whole market; inputs such as labor and capital must be able to move to new uses; and "best use" is determined by the preferences of consumers for products.

5 For a detailed discussion of many of the complex issues related to relaxing the simplifying assumptions of free trade, see Elhanan Helpman, *Understanding Global Trade*, Cambridge, MA: Belknap/Harvard, 2011.

6 Ronald Rogowski, *Commerce and Coalitions: How Trade Affects Political Alignments*, Princeton: Princeton University Press, 1989.

7 The balance of payments is a measurement system focusing on transactions between one nation and another. One important process missed or even distorted involves a multinational firm from one nation that sets up production in another nation, where it sells all this output. Only the initial investment in production facilities will show up in any of the balance of payments; this production and sales will not because nothing crosses a national boundary. Even more complex are global production networks that involve multiple firms, countries, investments, and locations for production and sales. Balance of payments systems do poorly in measuring the results of this kind of global activity.

8 Charles Kindleberger and Robert Aliber, *Manias, Panics and Crashes: A History of Financial Crises*, New York: Wiley, 2005; Carmen Reinhart and Kenneth Rogoff, *This Time is Different: Eight Centuries of Financial Folly*, Princeton: Princeton University Press, 2009.

9 Richard Timberlake, *The Origins of Central Banking in the United States*, Cambridge, MA: Harvard University Press, 1978.

10 John Wooley, *Monetary Politics: The Federal Reserve and the Politics of Monetary Policy*, Cambridge: Cambridge University Press, 1984.

11 The Global Financial Crisis of 2008–11 has led the Fed to expand its activities for managing the economy. We will discuss these new tools in Chapter 7.

12 Interest rates refer to the cost of borrowing money, expressed as a percent of the loan. A 10 percent interest rate would require the payment of $10 per year in interest for every $100 in loan remaining.

13 In addition, financial crises have become much more of a global phenomena, thereby requiring coordination among central banks and a willingness of a nation's central bank to provide help to foreign financial institutions operating in that country. During 2011, the Fed and the central banks of Britain, Japan, and Switzerland provided loans to the European Central Bank, which in turn provided loans to European banks that were threatened by a possible default by countries in the European Union.

14 Matt Boesler, "A Complete History of Quantitative Easing in One Chart," *Business Insider*, January 25, 2014, www.businessinsider.com/quantitative-easing-chart–2014–1

15 Robert Skidelsky, *John Maynard Keynes, Vol. 2: The Economist as Savior, 1920–1937*, New York: Macmillan, 1994.

16 Robert Collins, *The Business Response to Keynes*, New York: Columbia University Press, 1981.

17 One important issue typically not discussed is the implications for the vitality of capitalism in a society where investors are unwilling to invest and take risks except for government profit subsidies.

18 The price of one currency is simply the reciprocal of the other.

19 Exchange rates are easy to find on the Internet. One of many sites is www.oanda.com/currency/converter/

20 Bank for International Settlements, *Survey of Foreign Exchange and Derivatives Markets*, April 2007, 5–7.

21 But the RMB would change in value in relation to other currencies, in direct proportion to the changes in value of the US dollar in relation to those currencies.

22 Understanding the rise and fall of currencies can be a bit confusing. Notice that in 2005, 8.27 RMB were needed to get $1; in 2008, only 6.8 RMB were needed. The RMB has increased versus the dollar and the dollar has declined in terms of the RMB.

23 Few countries with as large an international trading sector as China can control the value of their currency so tightly. One important reason is China

has massive reserves of foreign currencies and can intervene in foreign exchange markets to supplement its legal controls on convertibility.

24 www.census.gov/foreign-trade/balance/c5880.html
25 Bureau of Economic Analysis, US International Trade in Goods and Services, 1992–2010, www.bea.gov/international/index.htm
26 See the contrasting views of Jared Diamond, *Collapse: How Societies Choose to Fail or Succeed*, New York: Penguin, 2011, and Patricia McAnany and Norman Yoffee, *Questioning Collapse: Human Resilience, Ecological Vulnerability and the Aftermath of Empire*, Cambridge: Cambridge University Press, 2009.
27 See the discussion of economic growth in Chapter 4.
28 Elhanan Helpman, *The Mystery of Economic Growth*, Cambridge, MA: Harvard, 2004; Gregory Clark, *A Farewell to Alms*, Princeton: Princeton University Press, 2007; Paul Collier, *The Bottom Billion*, Oxford: Oxford University Press, 2007.
29 Thus, if prices in the low-price nation are half those in the United States, the GDP (PPP) for that nation would need to be doubled to make the purchasing power of its citizens equal to that in the United States.
30 Visiting China in 2015 is a lot like visiting the United States in 1970, before the passage of much of the environmental legislation mandating changes in pollution by industry and consumers.
31 Peter Rogers, Kazi Jalal, and John Boyd, *An Introduction to Sustainable Development*, New York: Routledge, 2012.
32 Carol Sanford, Rebecca Henderson, and Chad Holiday, *The Responsible Business: Reimagining Sustainability and Success*, New York: Jossey-Bass, 2011.
33 Charles Tilly, *Coercion, Capital and European States, AD 90–1990*, Oxford, Basil Blackwell, 1990; Matthew Lange and Dietrich Rueschemeyer (eds), *States and Development: Historical Antecedents of Stagnation and Advance*, New York: Palgrave, 2005.
34 Stephen Krasner, "State Power and the Structure of International Trade," *World Politics*, 28.3 (April 1976) 317–47.
35 David Lake, "Open Economy Politics: A Critical Review," *Review of International Organizations*, 4 (2009) 219–44.

Further Reading

Ha-Joon Chang, *Economics: The Users Guide*, London: Bloomsbury, 2015.
Basic economics from a very unorthodox perspective.

Benjamin Cohen, *International Political Economy*, Princeton: Princeton University Press, 2008.
Cohen surveys the intellectual evolution of the field of international political economy over the past half-century, focusing on the ideas of leading scholars. He argues that the field can be divided into distinct American and British schools of thought.

Robert Heilbroner, *The Worldly Philosophers*, New York: Touchstone, 1999.
A highly readable, even lively, introduction to economics through the lives and ideas of the greatest economists.

John Ravenhill (ed.), *Global Political Economy*, Oxford: Oxford University Press, 4th ed., 2014.
A set of authoritative surveys of various subfields within international political economy written by leading scholars.

3 Globalization and Governance

In this chapter, we review the major trends that have shaped the path of globalization and compare perspectives on how globalization should be governed. A good place to begin is with the term "globalization" itself, which has come into widespread academic and popular use only since the early 1980s.[1] In fact, globalization has rapidly come to be viewed as a central motif of modern life, whether for good or for ill depending upon one's perspective. One indicator of the growing ubiquity of globalization in intellectual and popular discourse is that the number of books focusing upon globalization has risen from less than 600 in 1980 to over 38,000 today.[2]

The contemporary fascination with globalization – and especially the sense that it is something fundamentally new and transformative – is puzzling from several angles. The first humans originated in Africa and have since gradually migrated to every habitable continent, forming diverse cultures and civilizations in the process. If we are considering exchange across distinct populations, flows of people, goods, and ideas began to link the great civilizations of China and the West across the Silk Roads over two millennia ago. The Age of Exploration, by which European seafarers made their way to Africa, Asia, and the Americas, setting the stage for both commerce and conquest, dates back more than six centuries. And the modern political economy, based upon the liberal precept of trade as a process of mutually beneficial exchange to be encouraged, rather than tightly controlled, by governments, can be traced to the lifting of British tariffs on corn in the 1830s. Clearly, globalization has a long history that precedes the popularity of the word itself.[3]

A second puzzling aspect of what has come to be called the globalization debate is that the meaning of the term is so broad, varied, and nebulous as to ensure confusion and misunderstanding. One academic blogger, Eric Beerkins, has assembled a lengthy list of quotes that attempt to define, affirm, dismiss, or pass judgment over globalization.[4] Skimming through the list, it becomes apparent that authors are referring to quite different phenomena, ranging from cultural homogenization to intensifying information networks, to the growth of global civil society, to threats to the global commons, to the thickening of global governance, and to the quickening movements of goods, services, money, and people across national borders. This raises the question of whether a term that refers to so many different things is too imprecise to have meaning.

A final puzzle is why globalization has become such a source of intense controversy. The first major popular demonstration with a specifically anti-globalization agenda took place at the 1999 meeting of the World Trade Organization (WTO) in Seattle, Washington. Protesters had a variety of complaints about how trade liberalization and intensifying flows of goods and finance affected their lives. Some highlighted growing inequality. Others underlined threats to the global environment. Others pointed to the undemocratic character of the global institutions that increasingly set the rules governing globalization. Among the 40,000 demonstrators, a small number skirmished with police in the streets, a somewhat larger number engaged in acts of peaceful civil disobedience, while the great majority marched under the slogan – aimed at the WTO – "Fix it or nix it."[5] In the aftermath of Seattle, meetings of the WTO, the International Monetary Fund (IMF), and the World Bank face the prospect of large protests, with one result that conference organizers now often schedule such meetings in remote or undemocratic settings where large-scale demonstrations can be avoided.

Of course, globalization also has ardent defenders. Indeed, pro-globalizers coalesced in the 1990s around a set of economic and political prescriptions for development offered by economist John Williamson that came to be called the Washington Consensus. While we will put off detailed discussion of the Washington Consensus until later in this chapter, the major thrust was an unapologetic embrace of free markets, free trade, and a reduced government role in economic management. Advocates of globalization associated it with growing prosperity, the spread of democratic government, and a more peaceful world built around mutually beneficial webs of commerce.

Popular perceptions of globalization are mostly positive. A spring, 2011 survey by the PEW Global Attitudes Project reveals that two-thirds or more of respondents in all twenty-one countries surveyed felt that international trade and business ties were very good or somewhat good for their country.[6] In most cases, this figure exceeded 80 percent. Americans were the most skeptical, with only 18 percent convinced that international trade and business were "very good" for the United States. With the exceptions of Japan, Argentina, and Indonesia, majorities in the remaining countries surveyed agreed that people are better off in free market economies (see Figure 3.1).

Nevertheless, an earlier PEW survey (2009) also suggested that nationalism continues to influence economic thinking in most countries.[7] Amidst the greatest global economic downturn since the 1930s, large majorities in twenty-five countries agreed that their own governments

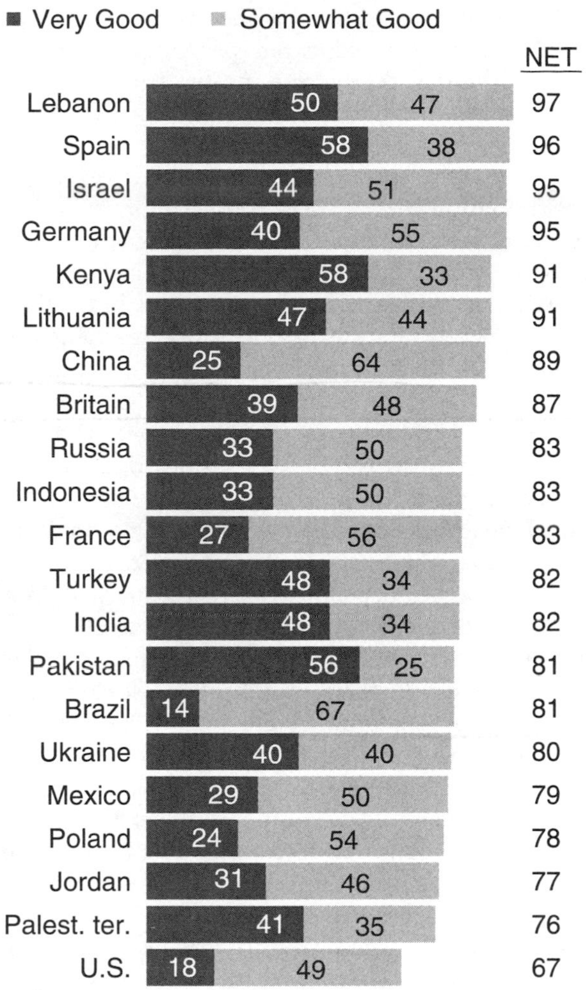

■ Very Good   ▨ Somewhat Good

		NET
Lebanon	50 · 47	97
Spain	58 · 38	96
Israel	44 · 51	95
Germany	40 · 55	95
Kenya	58 · 33	91
Lithuania	47 · 44	91
China	25 · 64	89
Britain	39 · 48	87
Russia	33 · 50	83
Indonesia	33 · 50	83
France	27 · 56	83
Turkey	48 · 34	82
India	48 · 34	82
Pakistan	56 · 25	81
Brazil	14 · 67	81
Ukraine	40 · 40	80
Mexico	29 · 50	79
Poland	24 · 54	78
Jordan	31 · 46	77
Palest. ter.	41 · 35	76
U.S.	18 · 49	67

Figure 3.1 Trade and Business Ties.

Source: Data from "China Seen as Overtaking U.S. as Global Superpower," PEW Global Attitudes Project, chapter 5, July 13, 2011, www.pewglobal.org/2011/07/13/chapter-5- economic-issues/

should act to protect their own country economically, even if other countries object. There was similar majority support across all countries for the statement: "Our way of life needs to be protected against foreign influence." Also, majorities in twenty-two of twenty-five countries surveyed supported stricter immigration controls. Faith in free markets has also been on the wane in recent years. Between 2007 and 2012,

PEW surveys showed erosion in the belief that people are better off in a free market economy in thirteen of the fifteen countries included in both years. The decline exceeded ten percentage points in seven of these countries. Nevertheless, the free market still drew the support of 50 percent or more of respondents in thirteen of the twenty countries surveyed in 2012.[8]

To make better sense of these conflicting perspectives and to rescue the concept of globalization from the conceptual morass into which it has sunk, we approach the topic with several precepts in mind. First, we focus in particular on the political economy of globalization. From this angle, globalization refers to the intensification over time in the flows of goods, services, money, people, and ideas among nations as compared with such flows within nations. Globalization is thus not an end state, but a gradually unfolding process of growing international interdependence.

It is also relative. For instance, trade and investment flows across national borders might increase, but if they do so less quickly than the rate of growth in domestic transactions, then we would conclude that globalization of the world economy had actually contracted over the relevant time period. In other words, the average person in such circumstances would become less dependent, in relative terms, upon economic exchanges across borders as compared with exchanges within the borders of one's own country. Since there in fact have been periods when this has been the case (most recently during the 2008–9 Global Financial Crisis), we know that globalization is not irreversible.[9] One reason for emphasizing the relative intensity of economic flows within and among states is that it is the balance between them that is most relevant to political debates over globalization.

Considered in this way, the world economy as a whole has experienced a gradual process of globalization over at least the past two centuries, although with significant reversals during particular periods. The pace of globalization has generally accelerated over the past several decades. Yet we also conclude that the globalization process remains very much incomplete. In all but a handful of smaller countries, most people depend far more heavily upon economic exchange taking place within the domestic economy than they do upon international transactions. Globalization is quite uneven across societies, institutions, and various types of exchange. The emergence of global civil society is, at best, nascent. International economic institutions remain largely the creations of states and pose only a limited challenge to the power and authority of national governments. Globalization is neither inevitable nor irreversible. It is largely a product of political decisions and has in the recent past shifted into reverse gear, at least for a time.

In general, we argue that it makes little sense to cast blankets of praise or blame over a phenomenon as complex and multi-faceted as contemporary globalization. Indeed, globalization is too often treated as a cause or cure for problems that have little to do with globalization as such and that must be approached through a more fine-grained analysis.

This chapter does not attempt to review the full breadth of the globalization debate. Particular aspects of it, such as financial stability, or inequality or protecting the global commons, are addressed at various points in other parts of the book. Our goals in this chapter are twofold.

First, we review the major trends related to globalization in the world economy. We find that globalization is real, significant, and ongoing. At the same time, globalization is also an uneven process and its pervasiveness and effects are often exaggerated.

Second, we examine three perspectives on how the global economy should be governed. We adopt this approach, rather than toting up globalization's pros and cons, because governance focuses on the locus and processes by which decisions over how to deal with both the benefits and drawbacks of globalization are made. This draws our attention to those aspects of the globalization debate that are most relevant to a book on political economy – how interested groups work through institutions to shape political and economic outcomes. Another advantage of this approach is that questions of governance allow us to move beyond popular punditry to address the relevant theoretical literatures that shed light on such choices.

Globalization can take varied forms with quite different outcomes depending upon how the rules of the game are structured. We focus on three possible governance arrangements: market-led globalization, nation-state-led globalization, and (international) institution-led globalization. Obviously, these are not mutually exclusive. Any global system is likely to include markets, states, and international institutions. The question is where the balance among these entities is to be struck and how regulation is to be managed: by market participants themselves, by individual states, or by overarching global rules and institutions.

Trends in Globalization

We begin by charting some of the key trends and features that have shaped the evolution of the global economy.

Governments have lowered legal and political barriers to the movement of goods, services, and finance across borders

The General Agreement on Tariffs and Trade (GATT), signed in 1947, established a process designed to gradually lower tariffs, quotas, and other government-imposed impediments to trade. The core principals guiding the multiple negotiating rounds carried out over subsequent decades were reciprocity (concessions by one country should be matched by trading partners), non-discrimination (imports from all member countries should receive the same treatment and local firms should not be favored over foreign firms), transparency (trade regulations and statistics should be openly shared), and liberalization (the process as a whole should reduce barriers to trade over time). Over time, the membership of GATT grew in number, the scope of trade barriers addressed broadened (including so-called non-tariff barriers, such as discriminatory subsidies and regulations), and, with the transition to the WTO in 1995, the rules governing global trade became more formal while dispute resolution and enforcement mechanisms became more clearly defined and legally binding.

The global trading order served to virtually eliminate the use of quotas and brought average tariff levels down from 13 percent in the late 1940s to roughly 4 percent today. Barriers to trade in manufacturing goods fell the most during the early rounds of GATT negotiations. More recently, restrictions on trade in textiles, previously allowed under the GATT, have been largely eliminated and some progress has been made in liberalizing trade in services. Liberalization has made the least progress in agriculture, which remains heavily subsidized by many governments and encumbered by rules restricting both imports and exports as well as differing standards for food safety and quality.

Nevertheless, further progress toward global trade liberalization has stalled in recent years. The WTO-sponsored Doha Round of negotiations dragged on for over a decade and resulted in a weak, face-saving agreement.[10] The reasons for slower progress on the global front are several: with a growing membership, the requirement that any WTO agreement be adopted by consensus has become a more significant hurdle; negotiations have come to address deeper and more sensitive issues traditionally considered domestic in nature; differences between developed and developing nations have widened over some issues; and the more formal and binding character of WTO commitments leaves governments less flexibility in building domestic consensus in favor of liberalization among affected interests.

Another sort of barrier arises from policies that discriminate against foreign investors as compared with domestic investors or that create uncertain legal protections for all investors, whether domestic or foreign. These kinds of risks discourage otherwise profitable movements of foreign direct investment. There is no global regime that governs such policies, aside from some very general and rather weak commitments built into the WTO. As a result, governments seeking fair and equal treatment for their firms that invest abroad have entered into bilateral investment treaties (BITs) with one another. The 1990s represented a peak in the number of new BITs arrived at. In general, the past two decades have brought a growing cumulative number of BITs, reaching over 2,900 by 2016.[11]

Such agreements lower the risks to foreign investment and facilitate the transnationalization of production into complex networks that spread various tasks, such as product design and engineering, extraction of raw materials, fabrication of parts, final assembly, marketing, and sales, across multiple national economies and involving layers of suppliers and sub-contractors. As a result, the transnational corporation has become the preeminent agent of globalization. In 2005, 77,000 transnational corporations controlled 770,000 foreign affiliates, employed 62 million workers, and sold goods and services roughly equal to 54 percent of global GDP (although the latter figure falls to 11 percent on a value added basis).[12]

The declining costs of international transportation and communication have facilitated globalization

Government-imposed tariffs and quotas constitute one form of impediment to international trade. Another is simply distance. Shipping goods across vast oceans or continents adds to the final cost of the product. Similarly, globe-spanning communications infrastructures are costly to construct and maintain. Over time, however, one of the major contributing factors to global economic integration has been the rapidly declining cost of international transportation and communication, due to improved technologies and infrastructure investments (see Figure 3.2).

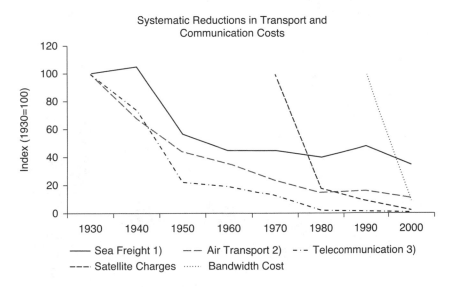

Figure 3.2 Costs of Transportation and Communications.

Source: Adapted from Minet Schindehutte, *Rethinking Marketing: The Entrepreneurial Imperative*, 1st ed. (2008), Upper Saddle River, New Jersey: Pearson. Data for graph from Georg Hufbauer, "World Economic Integration: The Long View," *Economic Insights*, vol. 30 (1991), 26–7; Bernhard Fisher, "Globalisation and the Competitiveness of Regional Blocs," *Intereconomics*, 4 (1998); Matthias Busse, "Tariffs, Transport Costs and the WTO Doha Round: The Case of Developing Countries," *Journal of International Law and Trade Policy*, vol. 4, no. 1 (2003), 15–31.

One key innovation was containerization of non-bulk goods, which began in the 1950s. Bulk goods, such as corn or oil, can be stored in a ship's hull. But prior to the 1950s, consumer goods had to be lashed down on a ship's deck during transport. Containerization entailed packing non-bulk goods in boxes that could be loaded and off-loaded from semi-trailers or cargo trains. This allowed containers to be moved more quickly and stacked upon one another, while also packing together goods bound for the same destination. Containerization reduced transport time by 85 percent and costs by 35 percent.[13]

Cheaper transportation combined with rising incomes have also led to increased international mobility, as illustrated in the growth of tourism. Global tourist arrivals have risen from less than 200 million in 1970 to 1.2 billion in 2015[14] (see Figure 3.3).

The laying of trans-Atlantic and trans-Pacific cables allowed almost instantaneous telegraph and, later, telephone and Internet communication among major cities. Satellites have further enhanced the speed and lowered the cost of sending words, images, and data across long distances. In 1930, a three-minute phone call from New York to London cost several hundred of today's dollars. Today, through voice-over-Internet protocols, the cost of an international phone call has been reduced to pennies per call. The rapid spread of mobile phones and computers has produced exponential increases in communication via

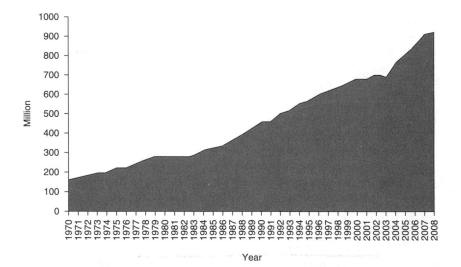

Figure 3.3 International Tourist Arrivals.

Source: Data for 1970–99 from Worldwatch Institute. Data for 2000–8 from World Tourism Organization. Adapted from graph by Tom Hale, July 2003; updated by Leila Farahani, February 2009, Global Policy Forum, www.globalpolicy.org/globalization/tables-and-charts-on-globalization/27543-international-tourist-arrivals.html

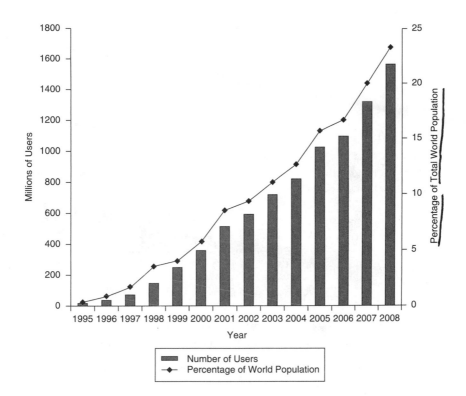

Figure 3.4 Number of Internet Users Worldwide, 1995–2008.
Source: Data from Internet World Stats. Adapted from graph by Tom Hale, July 2003; updated by Leila Farahani, February 2009, www.globalpolicy.org/component/content/article/109/27518.html

email, the Internet, and social media. The number of Internet users worldwide has more than tripled in the past decade, to a total of 3.1 billion[15] (see Figure 3.4).

Most types of international economic exchange have outpaced growth of national economies

It is relatively easy to describe the overall pattern of globalization. Trade has grown faster than national income. Over the long term, the growing weight of international trade is evident in the fact that exports rose from 1 percent of global GDP in 1820 to a peak of 29 percent in 2008.[16] Among traded goods and services, those characterized as knowledge-intensive (e.g., engineering, pharmaceuticals) have grown more rapidly than those that are capital- or labor-intensive.[17] Despite long-term growth, trade flows have leveled out in recent years, casting doubt on whether this facet of globalization will continue to intensify[18] (see Figure 3.5).

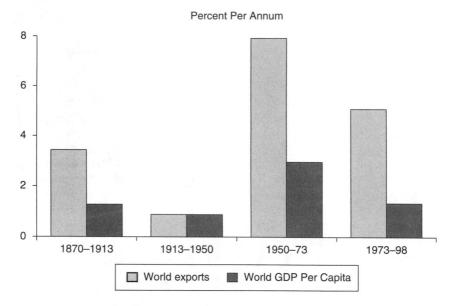

Figure 3.5 Growth of Exports and World GDP Per Capita.

Source: Adapted from graph by Angus Maddison, 2001. Data from The Treasury, New Zealand, www.treasury.govt.nz/publications/research-policy/wp/2007/07–05/03. htm. Data from http://theunbrokenwindow.com/Development/MADDISON%20The%20 World%20Economy—A%20Millennial.pdf

Yet trade is only a part of the globalization story. Over the past two decades, foreign direct investment has grown more quickly than either trade or national income. In turn, other types of financial transactions, such as bank lending, stock and bond purchases, and exchanges of currency have grown even more quickly than foreign direct investment. In 1989, for example, the average daily turnover in foreign currency exchanges was $590 billion. By 2013, this figure had risen to $5.3 trillion.[19] Cross-border banking external assets have risen from 13.7 percent of world GDP in 1980 to 47.9 percent in 2010. The cross-border stock of bank loans and deposits has grown from 13.9 percent of world GDP in 1980 to 34.9 percent in 2010.[20] As these figures suggest, finance, rather than trade, is the leading edge of globalization in the world economy (see Figure 3.6).

In short, market participants have responded to lowered political and technological barriers by seeking profitable opportunities abroad, though the pace of integration has varied across economic sectors.

Small countries have benefited from globalization more than large countries

The benefits of free trade are especially pronounced for small countries. This is because roughly one-third of industries experience increasing

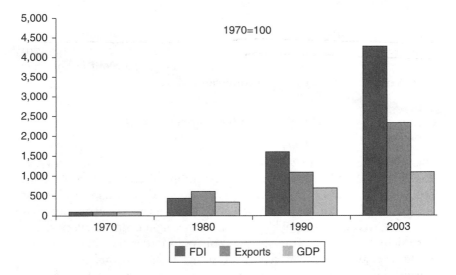

Figure 3.6 World GDP, FDI, and Export Indices.

Source: Adapted from graph by The Treasury, New Zealand, www.treasury.govt.nz/publications/research-policy/wp/2007/07–05/03.htm/#ref5

returns to scale.[21] In other words, the unit cost of a good goes down as the volume of production goes up. Only at high volumes can producers of such goods achieve favorable economies of scale, which allow profits at low and globally competitive prices. Confined to service only national markets with limited consumer demand, producers in small countries cannot achieve maximum economies of scale. Consumers thus pay a premium for domestically produced goods. Assuming comparative advantage, the same producers can increase volumes, lower prices, and increase profits if given access to global markets. Likewise, consumers in small countries will enjoy lower prices and greater variety of choice if given the opportunity to purchase goods produced beyond their nation's borders. In large countries, by contrast, local producers may achieve economies of scale even if limited to servicing the national market alone. While large countries still benefit from trade, they therefore do so less than small countries. For this reason, small countries are typically far more dependent upon trade than large countries.

The different dependence upon the global economy for small and large countries is evident in the country rankings produced by the KOF globalization index. For 2012, the top ranked countries in terms of economic globalization are Singapore, Luxembourg, Ireland, Malta, and Belgium – all small and thus heavily exposed to global markets. By contrast, large countries tend to rank well down the list – the United States is 79th among 208 countries, Russia comes in at 98th, Brazil ranks

100th, China appears in the 107th position, and India is the 129th most globalized economy.[22]

One consequence of a more open global economy is that small political units become economically viable. This is perhaps one factor helping to explain the growth in the number of independent states from seventy-five after World War II to over 200 countries today.[23]

Contemporary globalization is neither unprecedented nor irreversible

The period of 1870 to 1914 witnessed levels of global economic integration that rival and in some cases exceed those of recent years. Finance and labor, in particular, moved easily and in great quantities across borders. While levels of trade protection varied across countries, international trade grew more quickly than national income almost everywhere. Yet this golden age of globalization collapsed under the weight of two world wars and the Great Depression of the 1930s. By mid-century, the world economy was again fragmented into a series of largely self-contained national economies. Viewing this circumstance as not only economically irrational, but also politically dangerous given perceptions that economic nationalism had set the stage for World War II, the United States and its allies met at Bretton Woods, New Hampshire in July 1944 to create a new set of rules and institutions designed to serve as the foundation for a new era of global integration. Out of this conference emerged the major international economic organizations of the post-World War II era: the GATT, the IMF, and the World Bank.

The experience of the interwar period suggests that globalization cannot be taken for granted. Under the right (or wrong) political circumstances, political leaders may face overwhelming domestic pressures to cut economic ties with other countries. Business firms themselves may retreat from international exposure during periods of financial instability or economic downturn. Thus, the Global Financial Crisis of 2008–9 brought sharp, though temporary, disruptions to international trade and finance, along with limited, but nevertheless worrisome, protectionist responses on the part of national governments.[24] Indeed, some measures suggested that the world was less globally connected in 2012 than in 2007.[25] Nor is globalization the only form that international economic integration can take. Indeed, as our next trend suggests, it is unclear whether the current period is dominated by globalization or regionalization.

The global economy has become increasingly segmented into a series of regional economies

In place of global trade agreements, recent years have brought an explosion of bilateral and regional trade deals that lower barriers selectively.

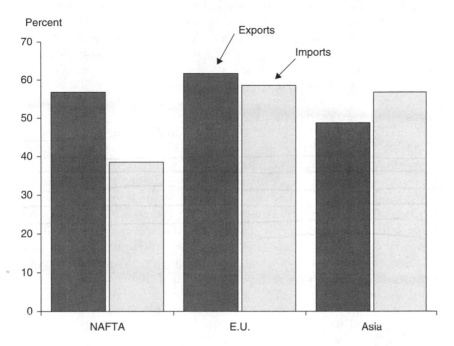

Figure 3.7 Regional Trade Areas: Intra-Regional Share of Exports and Imports, 2002.

Source: Data from Government of Canada, Foreign Affairs, Trade, and Development Canada, "NAFTA & 10: A Preliminary Report, Economic Analysis Division (EET), DFAIT; IMF, Direction of Trade Statistics, www.international.gc.ca/economist-economiste/analysis-analyse/research-recherche/10_pre.aspx?lang=eng

among small groups of countries. The WTO has received notification of 511 regional trade agreements (RTAs), most concluded over the past two decades.[26] The two largest are the European Union (EU) and the North American Free Trade Agreement (NAFTA). Cross-regional agreements are also emerging. Simultaneous negotiations are currently underway to create a Transatlantic Trade and Investment Partnership (TTIP) and a Trans-Pacific Partnership (TPP). Whether this trend represents a deepening of globalization is uncertain. Some argue that the growth of RTAs undercuts incentives for progress in global negotiations (see Figure 3.7).

Moreover, whether the lowering of tariffs and other barriers among members of an RTA creates more trade or merely displaces trade from non-members to members is an empirical question, the answer to which varies across cases. What seems evident is that the proliferation of RTAs and bilateral trade deals introduces greater legal complexity into the global trade order, complicating the calculations of business firms and possibly introducing incentives that distort markets.

States in North America, Europe, and Asia conduct more than half of their trade with other states within their own region. The concentration of FDI flows is less marked, but still exceeds one-half of outward-bound FDI for members of the European Union. Among Fortune 500 companies, 71 percent of equity affiliates are located within the home country or the nearby region.[27] Overall, global figures on trade and investment thus mask an underlying trend toward regionalization: most countries trade most intensively with their closest neighbors. This is due to lower costs of transportation, the geographic concentration of production networks, greater congruence in consumer tastes among culturally similar societies, fewer language barriers, and the preferential incentives created by regional trade agreements that favor trade among member states over trade with non-member states[28] (see Figure 3.8).

Where commonalities such as geographic proximity, cultural and linguistic similarity, past colonial ties, and closeness in political regime type are lacking, economic ties are generally slow to form. In this

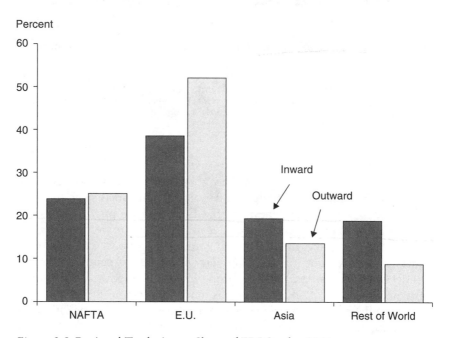

Figure 3.8 Regional Trade Areas, Share of FDI Stocks, 2001.

Source: Data from Government of Canada, Foreign Affairs, Trade, and Development Canada, "NAFTA & 10: A Preliminary Report, Economic Analysis Division (EET), DFAIT; IMF, Direction of Trade Statistics, www.international.gc.ca/economist-economiste/analysis-analyse/research-recherche/10_pre.aspx?lang=eng; www.international.gc.ca/economist-economiste/analysis-analyse/research-recherche/10_pre.aspx?view=d

sense, markets are products of the social systems in which they are embedded.

The organizational density of transnational connections has risen

The number of formal international government organizations (IGOs), addressing issues as disparate as health, trade, weapons proliferation, international justice, and environmental problems, grew from thirty-six to 7,350 over the course of the twentieth century. Moreover, one study counted 1,600 international treaties created between 1976 and 1995, giving rise to 100 new international organizations. The growing density of global civil society has been even more explosive. The number of international non-governmental organizations (INGOs) mushroomed from 176 in 1900 to 51,500 in 2000.[29]

Collectively, this thickening in the organizational architecture of international cooperation represents a substantial investment in global problem-solving capacity. Within most governments, virtually every major bureaucratic agency finds itself drawn into regularized communication, information-sharing, and problem-solving with counterpart agencies in other governments. Among civil society actors, transnational coalitions have developed along many issue-areas, creating political struggles that cut across traditional national lines.

The global penetration of local and national economies is uneven and often exaggerated

Despite the declining costs of moving goods, people, and information across borders, it remains striking the degree to which most people remain dependent upon local and national economies. Only 1 percent of letters physically mailed each year cross a national border. Only 2 percent of telephone call minutes connect people across an international border. From 2006–8, only 17–18 percent of Internet traffic crossed a national border. Only 21 percent of US news reporting deals with international topics and one-half of that coverage focuses on US foreign relations. Despite growth in the numbers of students who study abroad, the overall number of students enrolled outside of their home country remains only 2 percent.[30]

The limits of globalization are also evident in so-called "border effects." This term refers to the dampening effects of political borders between two countries on the intensity of economic exchange even where formal protectionist barriers have been removed. Despite the absence of tariffs or other formal restrictions on trade between the United States and Canada, for instance, trade among Canada's provinces is somewhere between five and ten times as intense as trade between those provinces and the United States. Price differentials also remain significant.

Borders still serve to inhibit economic exchange even in the absence of protectionist barriers for several reasons. The need to exchange currencies imposes added costs on cross-border exchange. Administrative and regulatory differences – everything from labeling requirements to health and safety standards – force manufacturers in one country to make costly adjustments in products and processes when selling into a neighboring market. Even differences in language and culture make it easier and less costly to market goods in one's home country as compared with another country.[31]

Immigration illustrates the limits of contemporary globalization. First generation immigrants to the United States have risen from 4.7 percent of the resident population in 1970 to 12.5 percent in 2009, fueling a backlash against the supposed cultural and economic costs of large-scale immigration. In fact, however, the present level of immigration only mirrors earlier such movements in American history. Between 1860 and 1920, immigrant levels fluctuated between 13 percent and 15 percent of the US population. At that time, immigrants required no visa to enter the United States and were typically turned away only in cases where an individual was considered to pose a threat to public health or safety.[32] Today, by contrast, immigration to the United States and most other countries is highly regulated and sharply restricted.

On a global basis, only 3 percent of people live outside of the country of their birth – about the same as in 1910 – and one-half of immigrants return to their home country within five years of their initial move. Sixty percent of international migrants move from one developing country to another developing country, with most staying within their home region.[33] Those who move instead from a developing country to an already developed country will, on average, experience a tripling of real income. The relatively few who move from one of the least developed countries to a developed country typically enjoy a fifteenfold increase in income, a doubling of educational enrollment, and a sixteenfold decrease in child mortality.

Given such incentives, the fact that immigration remains so modest is testimony to the effectiveness of state controls on the movement of people across borders, the inability of the very poor to afford the costs and risks of travel to distant places, and the depth of attachments to culture, place, and family that discourage displacement. Indeed, 90 percent of the world's population will never leave the country of their birth.[34]

Most economists agree that the freer mobility of labor across countries would do far more to spur aggregate growth in the global economy than further decreases in already low barriers to the movements of goods and capital. Economist Dani Rodrik has estimated that a temporary work visa scheme that allowed an expansion of the rich country labor force of 3 percent through increased immigration from developing countries would add $360 billion annually to the global economy, a sum that dwarfs any expected benefits from further reductions in tariffs from their already low levels.[35] The fact that governments have instead opted to sharply increase impediments over the past century illustrates that globalization is not an autonomous process but one that depends upon the selective willingness of states to open or close their borders to various types of exchange.

Illicit globalization is growing

Globalization has a dark side that even states have found difficult to control. The same quick and efficient transportation and communications networks that permit us to enjoy legal goods and services from around the world also facilitate transnational organized crime. The variety and scope of illicit globalization is immense. Shipments of cocaine and heroin to North America, Europe, and Russia amount to $105 billion in value per year. Europe imports over $8 billion in counterfeit goods annually, while the smuggling of undocumented immigrants from Latin America to the United States brings $6.6 billion per year to criminal organizations. Other major types of illicit globalization include human trafficking, maritime piracy, trade in counterfeit medicines, identity theft, child pornography, shipments of ivory and exotic species, and illegal timber exports. Even human organs have become a focal point for illegal international trade.[36]

Although Interpol[37] and other information-sharing efforts connect police forces from around the world, the same measures that ease the movement of legal goods, service, finance, and information in a more globalized world also create spaces through which transnational organized crime can thicken connections and evade control.

The globalization of production networks has shifted manufacturing and growth from the developed to the developing world

Over most of the past two centuries, the story of globalization was connected to the industrialization of the Western world and the growing gap between these economies and the rest of the globe. The rise of the West was both cause and consequence of the colonization of much of Latin America, Africa, and Asia. Developing countries were relegated to the production of raw materials for export to Europe, North America, and a few other high-income industrial countries while manufactured goods flowed in the other direction, as well as among the developed countries themselves. (See Table 3.1.)

Table 3.1 Relative Shares of World Manufacturing Output: 1750–1900 (in percentages)

	1750	1800	1830	1860	1880	1900
Europe	23.2	28.1	34.2	53.2	61.3	62.0
United States	0.1	0.8	2.4	7.2	14.7	23.6
Japan	3.8	3.5	2.8	2.6	2.4	2.4
Global South	73.0	67.7	60.5	36.6	20.9	11.0

Source: Data from Paul Bairoch, "International Industrialization Levels from 1750 to 1980," *Journal of European Economic History*, 11, 1982, 296.

Circumstances have changed dramatically in recent decades. Globalization has facilitated the shift of manufacturing production from the mature, high-wage countries of Europe and North America to East Asia and, to a lesser extent, other regions of the developing world. The share of global GDP accounted for by developing countries has risen from 30 percent in 1950 to well over one-half today.[38] Much of this shift is related to the relocation of manufacturing, which rose from 31.4 percent of developing country exports in 1980 to 68.1 percent of such exports in 2005. The developing country share of world manufacturing exports has doubled in the short space of a quarter-century, as has the developing country share of capital spending.[39] Between 1995 and 2010, the percentage of Fortune 500 companies headquartered in the developing world rose from 4 percent to 25 percent.[40] Particularly striking is the shift to high-speed growth in the world's two most populous countries: China and India. Between 1983 and 2003, India's per capita income more than doubled while in China per capita income quadrupled.[41] Indeed, by one measure, overall economic output in China surpassed that of the United States in late 2014, placing China as the world's largest economy as well as the largest exporter.[42] Over the long term, the world has witnessed striking movements in the global economic center of gravity. The westward shift of the nineteenth through the mid-twentieth centuries is now being reversed in equally dramatic fashion and over a shorter timescale (see Figure 3.9).

A Partially Globalized World

Globalization is more than just hype. The world economy is knitted together from ever-tighter networks of production, finance, and information flows. Yet the process is far from complete. International connections are uneven in both sectoral and geographic terms. Most people's economic livelihoods depend more heavily upon local and national markets than upon global markets. States remain powerful and relevant actors and business firms operate within rules set by political authorities.

Figure 3.9 Shifting Shares in Global Economic Output: 1980–2015

Note: Area indicates size of global economy.

Source: Adapted from IMF, Consensus Forecast, HM Treasury, The Treasury, New Zealand, www.treasury.govt.nz/publications/research-policy/wp/2007/07–05/07.htm

The world is, at best, "semi-globalized," to use a term offered by Pankaj Ghemawat.

Debating Global Governance

Among mainstream scholars and commentators, the crucial question is not whether to globalize but how to manage the process in a way that best serves the values prioritized by the author, whether these be economic efficiency, global equity and sustainability, or the preservation of democracy and national autonomy. In other words, the globalization debate has much to do with questions of governance – who gets to participate in making the rules that govern global and national economies and through what sort of institutions?

Three alternatives present themselves. Advocates of market-led globalization prioritize efficiency and output. From this perspective, the role of governments and international institutions is to clear away those obstacles that prevent self-regulating global markets from functioning more effectively.

Another set of authors believes that markets cannot and should not be self-regulating. Markets must be embedded within some set of rules and institutions capable of ensuring that social values and interests beyond mere economic efficiency are considered. Advocates of state-led governance argue that globalization must be subordinated to national autonomy and the participatory mechanisms of democratic states. This approach calls for a "thin globalization" that regulates international commerce for the common good and preserves the ability of societies to adopt varying paths to development.

A third perspective agrees that markets must be regulated in order to serve broader purposes beyond efficiency, but doubts that the nation-state is capable of serving this function under conditions of capital mobility and international economic openness. Advocates of institution-led governance thus argue that international institutions must be strengthened, absorbing some of the market-regulating functions previously undertaken at the nation-state level.

Market-Led Governance *neoliberal*

In his 1999 book, *The Lexus and the Olive Tree*, best-selling author Thomas Friedman used the metaphor of a "Golden Straightjacket" to illustrate the constrained economic choices available to governments: "If your country has not been fitted for one," Friedman wrote, "it will be soon."[43]

In Friedman's view, the ability of capital to flow easily across national borders meant that governments that adopted policies considered unfavorable by investors would quickly be punished by financial markets as capital fled to friendlier locales. Whereas in the past states had the power to force private actors to adjust their behavior in order to serve public ends, Friedman asserted that globalization now reversed this relationship: states had to adjust to markets or risk losing access to the capital needed to finance growth. What made the straightjacket imposed by global markets "golden" was that states going along with this new reality would be rewarded with growth and prosperity. In short, Friedman envisioned a world in which the task of governing globalization was largely left to markets, which, through the decentralized power of an "electronic herd" of investors and currency traders, endorsed some policy choices and vetoed others.

Friedman's celebration of market-led globalization captured the spirit of the 1980s and 1990s; decades when free market enthusiasts gained the upper hand in intellectual and policymaking circles.[44] The post-World War II era had brought the rise of the welfare state and more interventionist government regulation of economic activity. The backlash against such policies began with the electoral triumphs of Ronald Reagan and Margaret Thatcher, respectively, as president of the United States and prime minister of the United Kingdom in 1979. Harking back to nineteenth-century concepts of laissez faire – a French phrase meaning "hands off" or "let them be" – Reagan, Thatcher, and their supporters celebrated the wonders of free markets while seeking to rein in the power of states to regulate economic decision making. In the United States and Great Britain, the Reagan and Thatcher years brought reduced taxes on corporations and top income earners, privatization of public enterprises and services, deregulation of certain industries, and efforts to weaken the power of labor unions.

These ideas – sometimes labeled neoliberalism – represented an updating of liberal economic thought that stretched back to eighteenth-

and nineteenth-century thinkers such as Adam Smith, Jeremy Bentham, and John Stuart Mill. Neoliberalism is based upon the notion that markets function best to maximize efficiency of production and satisfy consumer demands when free of government interference. The neoliberal concept of a "self-regulating market" refers to the equilibrating qualities of uninhibited exchange within a market system: the price mechanism serves to ensure that the collective but decentralized decisions of thousands or millions of producers and consumers result in a balance between supply and demand. In this sense, the market "governs" itself.

This does not mean that government is superfluous from a neoliberal perspective. Governments are necessary to provide for the common defense, define and enforce property rights, supply legal currency, provide public goods that would be undersupplied by markets, issue patents and copyrights to encourage innovation, offer a social safety net for individuals who are temporarily or permanently unable to effectively compete in the labor market, and compensate for market failures, such as the negative externality of pollution, through appropriate regulatory policies. Governments should not, however, compete with the private sector, set prices, subsidize production or consumption, impose taxes that discourage investment, or inhibit competition.

It follows from these neoliberal precepts that governments should also refrain from interfering with the transnational movement of goods, services, money, and people, unless there exist compelling public rationales for doing so that trump considerations of maximizing efficiency and income (such as, for instance, national security). Neoliberals recognize that states have in fact historically engaged in costly protectionist policies, whether due to erroneous economic doctrines, the political clout of special interests, or the competitive nature of the nation-state system. In order to curb such behavior, liberals favor global institutions, such as the WTO, that encourage the removal of such barriers and punish states that engage in protectionism.

These ideas gained wide currency during the 1980s and 1990s. The eclipse of the state in favor of an increasingly globalized marketplace seemed to be confirmed most dramatically by the collapse of communism in Eastern Europe and the Soviet Union and the introduction of market reforms by surviving communist party rulers in China and Vietnam. Indeed, many observers began to argue that globalization tended to force countries in the direction of convergence around a single model of state–society relations.

In 1990, for example, economist John Williamson, reflecting upon the lessons from a decade of policy reform in Latin America as countries in that region grappled with international debt, developed what he dubbed the "Washington Consensus."[45] This was a set of policies that others, if not Williamson himself, soon embraced as a universal formula for economic development. The original list included:

- fiscal discipline;
- reorientation of public expenditures;
- tax reform;
- financial liberalization;
- unified and competitive exchange rates;
- trade liberalization;
- openness to FDI;
- privatization;
- deregulation;
- secure property rights.

Largely endorsed by the International Monetary Fund and the World Bank, this formula served as a template for the conditions that these institutions attached to the loans they made to troubled debtor countries.

In short, neoliberals expected states to converge around a free market approach to economic development and governance under the combined influences of economic logic (i.e., the persuasiveness of neoliberal ideas), the pressures exerted upon states by transnational capital markets, and the rules and norms embodied in the major international economic institutions.

The convergence thesis has been criticized from a number of angles. Economist Pankaj Ghemawat argues that the world economy is far less globalized than has often been assumed.[46] This finding leads him to three conclusions: first, the forces of globalization are too weak to compel states to adopt policies that they otherwise find objectionable; second, the success or failure of economic growth in any given country is principally due to domestic factors; and third, there remain enormous efficiency gains to be had from reducing the considerable obstacles that continue to inhibit transnational economic integration.

Some scholars have questioned both the empirical and the causal claims of convergence. State behaviors with respect to fiscal, monetary, tax, regulatory, and labor policies remain quite diverse and show little evidence of converging around a single standardized model. For example, the most successful developing economies of recent decades – those of East Asia – have not followed neoliberal prescriptions, but have instead featured strong states which actively direct the accumulation and allocation of capital toward national development goals. These hybrid systems that combine market mechanisms with state ownership and regulation have generated rapid growth in China and other East Asian countries and thus pose a major challenge to neoliberal thinking about the proper relationship between state and society.

Nor is there compelling evidence that investors have strong and fixed preferences for particular policy mixes. Some studies find that capital is likely to flee economies where loose fiscal and monetary policies raise the risks of inflation. But the size of government (as opposed to whether revenues and expenditures are in rough alignment) does not appear to dissuade investment. Nor does investment behavior appear strongly correlated with government policies with respect to labor, the environment, or government support for targeted industrial sectors.[47]

Indeed, fears among some globalization critics that capital mobility would lead to a "race to the bottom" as corporations and investors sought havens from taxation, strong labor movements, and strict environmental regulations appear to be exaggerated.[48] While some kinds of labor-intensive or polluting industries may gravitate toward investment sites that offer these sorts of advantages, there exist other industries where firms are attracted by the lure of healthy, skilled workforces, ample infrastructure, public support for research, development and education, and close proximity to high-income consumers. In such cases, corporations may be willing to tolerate high tax rates and strong protections for labor and the environment. Indeed, those countries most open to the global economy also tend to have larger public sectors.[49]

Another criticism of neoliberal prescriptions has to do with financial globalization. During the 1980s and 1990s, the IMF and rich-country governments encouraged developing countries to deregulate their financial sectors and open their economies to international financial flows. While many countries in Latin America and East Asia did so, the results were not as expected. Destabilizing flows of short-term investment capital led to asset bubbles and inflation, eventually triggering financial crises even in those countries that otherwise pursued cautious fiscal and monetary policies. The Asian financial meltdown of 1997–8 produced a severe, if temporary, economic downturn across much of the region, eventually spreading to Russia, Brazil, and Argentina. China, which retained controls on international capital flows, was spared the economic pain experienced by its neighbors. Roughly a decade later, financial deregulation was blamed by many observers for the massive banking crisis that hit the United States in 2008–9, followed soon by the Euro crisis.

Although certainly not vanquished, the neoliberal vision of market-led globalization has lost ground over the past decade in the debate over the future of globalization. Neoliberals such as Friedman exaggerate the depth of globalization and the degree to which world economic integration compels governments to converge upon a single, standardized recipe for growth and development. Indeed, as the fastest growing economy of the past three decades, China offers a sharp counterpoint to the Washington Consensus, as that country has managed to combine market incentives with continuing state dominance over the Chinese economy. Finally, the financial crises of the late 1990s and 2008 have offered reminders that markets do not police themselves, but work best within a framework of regulation and governance that considers the broader public good.

If global markets require some form of oversight and regulation, then which institutions – national governments or global organizations – are better suited to set relevant rules and norms? It is to this question that we now turn.

State-Led Governance

Economist Dani Rodrik has offered perhaps the most comprehensive critique of what he labels "hyper-globalization" – the pursuit of wholesale global integration as an end in itself. Rodrik argues that hyper-globalization requires the sacrifice of either democracy, as under market-led globalization in which free-flowing capital exercises veto-power over government choices, or national autonomy, as under institution-led globalization in which supranational institutions set global rules to which individual states must conform.[50]

Rather than surrender choices over the character and direction of economic development to markets or global institutions, Rodrik advocates a "thin globalization" that removes those protectionist barriers that mainly serve narrow interests, while nevertheless preserving the capacity of states to regulate cross-border flows of capital and labor, to pursue varied development strategies, including different levels of state intervention in markets, and to set different standards of regulation with regard to health, safety, the environment, and consumer rights. According to Rodrik, a more modest path of globalization mediated by strong and capable states would avoid the imposition of a singular economic model while enhancing both democracy and national autonomy. In his words: "Democracies have a right to protect their social arrangements, and when this right clashes with the requirements of the global economy, it is the latter that should give away."[51]

This argument rests upon historical precedent. The liberal economic order of 1870–1914 arguably represented the first era of hyper-globalization. Although successful in its time, this European-centered effort to build an international economy based upon the principles of laissez faire proved unsustainable, giving way to imperialism, two world wars, protectionism, class conflict, the rise of communism and fascism, and the Great Depression. The great social theorist Karl Polanyi attributed this descent of European society into war and barbarism to

> the measures which society adopted in order not to be, in its turn, annihilated by the action of the self-regulating market. . . . the conflict between the market and the elementary requirements of an organized social life provided the [nineteenth] century with its dynamics and produced the typical strains and stresses which ultimately destroyed that society.[52]

The post-World War II international order embodied hard-won lessons from the earlier failure of laissez-faire liberalism. Liberals of the post-World

War II era had no intention, of course, of abandoning the market or international economic exchange. They did, however, seek to circumscribe the social space in which markets, both domestic and international, operated and to embed the market in a social compact among the state, capital, and labor. Capitalism had to be tamed to render it compatible with social peace and international stability. John Gerard Ruggie has referred to these arrangements as "embedded liberalism," in contrast with the "disembedded" or supposedly self-regulating markets of the late nineteenth century.[53]

Domestically, the postwar order was built upon social democracy within the advanced industrial democracies, which entailed Keynesian macroeconomic management, the creation of the welfare state, progressive taxation, public ownership of key industries, regulation of big business, and recognition of labor unions and collective bargaining. Internationally, commitments to multilateralism and the gradual lowering of trade barriers were coupled with mechanisms designed to insure against the transmission of negative economic shocks from one nation to another, including exchange controls, protection for strategic and politically sensitive sectors, restrictions on international capital flows, and safeguards against import surges that threatened established national producers. These arrangements created the basis for a substantial degree of class peace, social stability, economic growth, and the consolidation of liberal democracy in the advanced industrial world.

The postwar order depended, however, on the maintenance of some degree of national economic autonomy, particularly in terms of financial flows. The economist John Maynard Keynes argued that social democracy was compatible with free trade, but not with the uncontrolled flow of capital across national borders, which undermined state control over a country's macroeconomic fundamentals.[54] Yet large corporations and banks chafed at the restrictions on their freedom to invest abroad. When the economic troubles of the 1970s hit, business leaders argued that it was time to unleash capital from the confines of the national market and loosen the regulatory grip of states. As previously mentioned, these appeals found a receptive audience with the elections of Ronald Reagan and Margaret Thatcher, thus ushering in an era of neoliberalism.

The political effect of this development, according to Ruggie, has been to disrupt the social pact that lay at the core of the social democratic order in Europe and North America.[55] The balance among the state, labor, and capital has shifted decidedly in favor of the latter. With capital controls and other sorts of restrictions lifted, capital has become internationally mobile to a greater degree than ever before. The same is not true of labor, whose movement across national borders remains heavily regulated, or of states, which remain territorial entities. The unilateral capacity of capital to exit the national economy produces an asymmetry. As capital is a key ingredient of economic growth, business can pit workers and states in different countries against one another in a bidding war for investment. As a result, labor movements everywhere have lost clout and the ability of states to regulate capital in the public interest has been compromised. Under existing arrangements, for instance, one study estimates that competition from low wage countries has reduced the annual wages of American workers with only a high school education by over $1,800.[56]

Building upon the work of Ruggie and others, Rodrik argues for a return to the state-led globalization path of the post-World War II era, which focused on the liberalization of trade rather than finance, allowing states to better balance the power of capital. International institutions and rules should not inhibit developing countries from experimenting with varied economic models.[57] The international economic order should be designed in such a way as to strengthen, rather than weaken, national autonomy and the ability of citizens to express choices over economic policy through democratic institutions.

The path of state-led globalization does not entail a return to protectionism, but it does prioritize diversity, democracy, and national autonomy over the efficiency gains to be had through unencumbered markets. It would also require the weakening of international economic institutions. Advocates of institution-led globalization argue that this vision underestimates both the dangers of renewed protectionist pressures at the national level and the pitfalls of fragmented governance in a world that has already achieved high levels of international independence. We now examine the argument for strengthened global regulation of the international economy.

Institution-Led Governance

Advocates of institution-led governance – whom we will refer to as globalists – support a robust set of rules, norms, and institutions for managing the global economy. They agree that markets can only function fairly and effectively if embedded within a framework of law and regulation. But they also believe globalization has undermined the effectiveness of regulation that is limited to the nation-state level. Neither markets nor individual nation-states acting alone can provide the global public goods, such as an effective response to climate change, that are required to maintain a stable and growing international economy. A global economy thus necessitates global governance.

Few globalists foresee the emergence of a single world government or the passing away of the nation-state. Instead, this vision would entail the strengthening of an array of global and regional institutions, as states voluntarily agree to common sets of rule, norms, and procedures for managing the global economy and gradually transfer certain powers and resources to international institutions. The result would be a "multi-level polity" through which sovereignty is shared and dispersed across governing institutions of varying functional and geographic scope.

The most important example of transnational governance is the European Union, which encompasses twenty-eight countries. The scope of the European Union extends far beyond the removal of border controls on the movement of goods, services, people, and money among member states. In varying degrees, the European Union coordinates national policies with respect to areas such as trade, finance, energy, agriculture, immigration, infrastructure development, investment, research and development, foreign aid, and even foreign policy. The European Union has a president, a parliament, a Court of Justice, and a bureaucracy based in Brussels. National governments delegate some powers to EU institutions, share governance in other areas, and retain national control over still other issues. The European Union has expanded in membership over the years and has generally succeeded in promoting peace, prosperity, democracy, and global influence among its member states.

Despite the successes of the European Union, no other group of states has sought to emulate the degree of transnational governance represented by Europe's example. Nor has the European Union itself been uniformly successful. Critics argue that the gradual shift in decision-making powers from the national to the supranational levels of governance has produced a democratic deficit, in which European citizens feel that distant technocrats, rather than local political parties and politicians, are increasingly empowered to make choices that impact upon their own lives.

Moreover, the recent European financial crisis may have revealed weaknesses in the halfway house of shared national and supranational governance in which Europe finds itself. Financial integration around a common currency among the seventeen EU states that have adopted the euro exposed the entire group to the financial mismanagement of its weakest members. Yet the still limited authority of the European Central Bank, the lack of strong EU controls over national fiscal policies, and the reluctance of the stronger countries of the Eurozone to bail out weaker members have hampered the ability of European political and financial elites to respond quickly and effectively to contain the economic damage from the crisis. Arguably, the financial problems of Greece, Italy, Spain, and Ireland might have been better managed under either full national financial autonomy or full European governance. Shared authority, on the other hand, created opportunities for confusion and the buckpassing of responsibility.

While the European Union serves as a showcase for both the strengths and weaknesses of transnational governance, no mainstream globalists have suggested that the world is ready to adopt such far-reaching institutional reform on a global scale. Rather, there have been a number of more modest proposals for strengthening the reach and authority of international institutions in the interest of a fairer, more inclusive, and more stable system of global governance. A shortlist of proposals that have received serious consideration include:

- a small tax on international financial transactions designed both to discourage speculative capital flows and to raise money for fighting world poverty;
- the creation of procedures to manage sovereign bankruptcy – allowing states, like private firms and individuals, some means for escaping unsustainable debt obligations in a legal and orderly fashion;
- an agreement governing the rights and responsibilities of foreign direct investors and pledging states to forego policies that either favor or discriminate against foreign investors;
- the inclusion of minimum standards for labor and the environment in trade agreements so as to discourage states from using labor repression or lax pollution laws as sources of competitive advantage;
- the creation of a binding global cap on greenhouse gas emissions.

These and other global agreements and institutions would exist within and alongside the already significant set of international organizations that provide a measure of global economic management. These include the International Monetary Fund, the World Bank, the World Trade Organization, the Group of 20, the United Nations and its various agencies, the Basel Accords, and many others at both the global and regional levels.

The political challenges of strengthening global governance are considerable. As the number of independent states has mushroomed from seventy-five after World War II to more than two hundred today and political and economic power has become more dispersed across a larger number of significant players, the difficulty of reaching consensus around major new initiatives in global governance has also grown.

Moreover, there is the fundamental question of which perspectives and what interests will be represented through institutions of global governance. As decision-making moves from the national to the global level, it also shifts further away from the direct control and participation of average citizens. International organizations are created and controlled by governments, some, but not all, of whom may be democratic. But even once an elected government makes commitments through a formal treaty, all succeeding governments are bound by those legal obligations, even if the preferences of voters in that country may have changed during the interim.

Also, existing international institutions often lack full transparency and may be subject to the direct influence, or at least the shared worldviews, of powerful private actors. Nobel prize winner Joseph Stiglitz – himself formerly the chief economist of the World Bank – has argued that international institutions such as the International Monetary Fund and the World Bank are "dominated not just by the wealthiest industrial countries but by commercial and financial interests in those countries."[58] The principal purposes of existing international economic institutions to date have been to promote open markets and to strengthen legal protections for financial and corporate interests as they move beyond their home markets.

Nevertheless, many critics of the existing order who seek a globalization that is fairer, more democratic, more environmentally sustainable, and more inclusive reject Rodrik's solution of reasserting the primacy of nation-states on the grounds that globalization has progressed too far to turn back the clock. Rather than attempting to corral footloose capital back under national control, globalists would prefer to create a global version of the New Deal by crafting strong global regulations that can restore some balance among competing classes and nations of varying size, power, and levels of development. Only in this way can the benefits of globalization be retained and global public goods be provided, while still responding to a broader array of interests and values.

Stiglitz himself has offered guidelines for lessening the democratic deficit that plagues global governance. These include greater transparency, increased participation by developing countries in decision making, increased voice for non-governmental organizations, and mechanisms for greater accountability.[59] Without such reforms, institutions of global governance will suffer from a continued crisis of legitimacy and would seem incapable of assuming a deeper role in guiding globalization along a path acceptable to the wide array of affected interests.

One response to perceived deficits in global governance is to move away from formal, universal, and legally binding institutions as represented by the United Nations and similar organizations. Instead the World Economic Forum has advocated, through its Global Reform Initiative, less formal types of voluntary cooperation among diverse groups of willing stakeholders encompassing states, international organizations, non-governmental organizations, and corporations. The purpose is to bypass the protracted and often fruitless negotiations that often accompany efforts to reach legally binding rules through universal membership bodies. Voluntary public–private partnerships are thought by their advocates to be more flexible and quicker to bring results. By their very nature, however, such arrangements lack the legitimacy and binding character of more formal institutions. Also, major players who – by choice – lack representation in such partnerships may serve as spoilers, seeking to derail unwelcome outcomes from outside.[60]

What seems clear at present is that existing international institutions are too weak to supplant states in managing the global economy. Major investments of resources and political commitment would be required to empower international institutions with sufficient clout to steer the process of globalization.

Conclusion: Governing Globalization

Globalization is a pervasive reality, even if its novelty and reach have been subject to excessive hype. International economic integration has altered the context in which national politics and policymaking are conducted, necessitating increased coordination among states and reconfiguring political bargains at both the national and transnational levels. The growth of global networks of production and finance along with increasingly significant layers of transnational governance make for a more complex and integrated system of political economy.

The central debates over globalization revolve on questions of governance. Can and should markets govern themselves? Or should they be subject to democratic control and regulation through strong nation-states? Are individual states sufficient managers of economic systems in light of globalization? Or must we seek to shift greater degrees of authority to global institutions? While overly simplified, this schema helps to make sense of the many and complex debates that have swirled around globalization over the past several decades. With this conceptual map in mind, we now turn to a more detailed and nuanced account of the historical evolution of the global economy over the past two centuries.

Key Concepts (see Glossary)

Border Effects	Interdependence
Embedded Liberalism	International Institutions
Foreign Direct Investment (FDI)	Market-Led Globalization
Free Trade	Regionalism
Globalization	State-Led Globalization
Institution-Led Globalization	Washington Consensus

Discussion Questions

1 Should we be more impressed with how much or with how little globalization has progressed?
2 Why is finance the most globalized sector of the world economy?
3 Is globalization reversible? What conditions are most likely to slow or reverse the trend toward greater globalization?
4 Is regionalization an endpoint in itself or a stepping-stone toward global integration?
5 How do national borders serve to impede economic transactions even where tariffs and quotas have been removed?
6 What differences does it make in whether global governance is centered upon markets, states, or international institutions?
7 Is there a tradeoff between free markets and democracy? Or do the two naturally go together?

8 How much autonomy should states enjoy in managing a country's relationship to the global economy? Are we better off in a world with stronger global institutions or one with more independent states?

Notes

1 Paul James and Manfred B. Steger, "A Genealogy of 'Globalization': The Career of a Concept," *Globalizations*, 11(4) (2014) 417–34, http://dx.doi.org/10.1080/14747731.2014.951186

2 Mauro Guillén's Indicators of Globalization, 1980–2010, www-management.wharton.upenn.edu/guillen/2010-docs/Global-Table–1980–2008.pdf

3 For a comprehensive overview of these historical movements, consult Ian Morris, *Why the West Rules – For Now: The Patterns of History and What They Reveal about the Future*, New York: Farrar, Straus, and Giroux, 2010, and Jared Diamond, *Guns, Germs and Steel, The Fate of Human Societies*, New York: W.W. Norton & Company, 2005.

4 Eric Beerkinds, "Globalisation: Definitions and Perspectives," 2006, www.beerkens.info/files/globalisation.pdf

5 Janet Thomas, *The Battle in Seattle: The Story Behind and Beyond the WTO Demonstration*, Golden, CO: Fulcrum Publishing, 2000.

6 PEW Research Global Attitudes Project, July 31, 2011, chapter 5, www.pewglobal.org/2011/07/13/chapter–5-economic-issues/

7 PEW Research Center Global Attitudes Project, "Confidence in Obama Raises U.S. Image Around the World," July 23, 2009, chapter 5, www.pewglobal.org/2009/07/23/chapter–5-views-on-trade-and-globalization/

8 PEW Research Center Global Attitudes Project, "Pervasive Gloom About the World Economy," July 12, 2012, www.pewglobal.org/2012/07/12/pervasive-gloom-about-the-world-economy/

9 Indeed, some argue that we have entered a period of deglobalization. See Joshua Kurlantzick, "The Great Deglobalizing," *Boston Globe*, February 1, 2015.

10 "W.T.O. Reaches First Global Trade Deal," *New York Times*, December 7, 2013.

11 UNCTAD, 2016, http://investmentpolicyhub.unctad.org/IIA

12 David Held and Anthony McGrew, *Globalization/Anti-Globalization: Beyond the Great Divide*, Cambridge, England: Polity, 2nd ed., 2007, 111. Pankaj Ghemawat, *World 3.0: Global Prosperity and How to Achieve It*, Boston, MA: Harvard Business Review Press, 2011, 211.

13 Michael T. Bohlman (September 2001) "ISO's Container Standards are Nothing but Good News," *ISO Bulletin* (Geneva: International Standards Organization), 12–15.

14 Donald Wood, "International Tourist Arrivals Reach Record-Breaking 1.184 Billion in 2015," *Travel Pulse*, January 20, 2016.

15 Statista, 2016, www.statista.com/statistics/273018/number-of-internet-users-worldwide/

16 Pankaj Ghemawat, *World 3.0: Global Prosperity and How to Achieve It*, Boston, MA: Harvard Business Review Press, 2011, 10, 27–8.

17 Neil Irwin, "Growth in Global Trade Is In Ideas, Not Stuff," *New York Times*, April 29, 2014.

18 John W. Schoen, "Why the Days of Booming World Trade May Be Over," *CNBC*, May 29, 2014.

19 "Table – Global FX Volume Reaches $5.3 Trillion in 2013 – BIS," *Reuters*, September 5, 2013.

20 Mauro Guillén's Indicators of Globalization, 1980–2010, www-management. wharton.upenn.edu/guillen/2010-docs/Global_Table_1980–2010.pdf
21 Ghemawat, *World 3.0*, 70.
22 KOF Index of Globalization, 2012, www.kof.ethz.ch/static_media/filer_ public/2012/09/16/rankings_2012_1.pdf
23 Ghemawat, *World 3.0*, 220.
24 Annie Lowrey, "An Increase in Barriers to Trade is Reported," *New York Times*, June 22, 2012.
25 "Going Backwards," *The Economist*, December 22, 2012. In 2012, for instance, cross-border capital flows remained at 60 percent of their 2007 peak. Susan Lund, Toos Daruvala, Richard Dobbs, Philipp Härle, Ju-Hon Kwek, and Ricardo Falcón, "Financial Globalization: Reset or Retreat?" McKinsey & Co., March 2013, www.mckinsey.com/insights/global_capital_ markets/financial_globalization
26 World Trade Organization, "Regional Trade Agreements," www.wto.org/ english/tratop_e/region_e/region_e.htm
27 Pankaj Ghemawat, "Are Multinationals Becoming Less Global?" HBR Blog Network;   http://blogs.hbr.org/2013/10/are-multinationals-becoming-less-global/?utm_source=feedburner&utm_medium=feed&utm_campaign=Feed %3A+harvardbusiness+%28HBR.org%29, October 28, 2013.
28 Ghemawat, *World 3.0*, 58.
29 David Held and Anthony McGrew, *Globalization/Anti-Globalization: Beyond the Great Divide*, Polity, 2nd ed., 2007, 22–3.
30 Ghemawat, *World 3.0*, 26–7.
31 Ghemawat, *World 3.0*, 42–8.
32 Aaron Terrazas and Jeanne Batalova, "Frequently Requested Statistics on Immigrants in the United States," *Migration Policy Institute*, October 2009.
33 Ghemawat, *World 3.0*, 27.
34 Ghemawat, *World 3.0*, 27, 174, 179.
35 Dani Rodrik, *The Globalization Paradox*, New York: W.W. Norton & Company, 2011, 268.
36 Patrick Di Justo, Adam Rogers, and Allison Davis, "Organized Crime: The World's Largest Social Network," *Wired Magazine*, January 31, 2011, www. wired.com/magazine/2011/01/ff_orgchart_crime/
37 Interpol (www.interpol.int/).
38 Matthew O'Brien, "Emerging Power: Developing Nations Now Claim the Majority of World GDP," *The Atlantic*, June 4, 2013.
39 David Held and Anthony McGrew, *Globalization/Anti-Globalization: Beyond the Great Divide*, Polity, 2nd ed., 2007, 77.
40 "Why the Tail Wags the Dog," *The Economist*, August 6, 2011.
41 Charles Kenny, *Getting Better: Why Global Development is Succeeding – And How We Can Improve the World Even More*, New York: Basic Books, 2011, 19.
42 Michael Forsythe and Neil Gough, "By One Measure, China Set to Become Largest Economy," *International New York Times*, April 30, 2014.
43 Thomas Friedman, *The Lexus and the Olive Tree*, New York: Anchor Books, rev. ed., 2000.
44 Other works that offer generally positive appraisals of market-led globaliza- tion include Martin Wolf, *Why Globalization Works*, New Haven, CT: Yale University Press, 2005; Jagdish Bhagwati, *In Defense of Globalization*, Oxford, England: Oxford University Press, 2nd ed., 2007; and Michael Spence, *The Next Convergence: The Future of Economic Growth in a Multispeed World*, New York: Farrar, Straus, and Giroux, 2011.

45 John Williamson, "What Washington Means by Policy Reform," in John Williamson, *Latin American Adjustment: How Much Has Happened?* Washington, DC: Institute for International Economics, 1990.
46 Ghemawat, *World 3.0.*
47 Layna Mosley, *Global Capital and National Governments*, Cambridge, England: Cambridge University Press, 2003.
48 Daniel Drezner, "Globalization and Policy Convergence," *International Studies Review*, vol. 3, no. 2, 2001.
49 Dani Rodrik, "Why Do More Open Economies Have Bigger Governments?" *Journal of Political Economy*, vol. 106, no. 5, 1998.
50 Rodrik, *The Globalization Paradox.*
51 Rodrik, *The Globalization Paradox*, xix.
52 Karl Polanyi, *The Great Transformation: The Political and Economic Origins of Our Time*, New York: Farrar and Rinehart, 1944, 249.
53 John G. Ruggie, "International Regimes, Transactions and Change: Embedded Liberalism in the Postwar Economic Order," in Stephen Krasner (ed.), *International Regimes*, Ithaca: Cornell University Press, 1983.
54 Once World War II was concluded, Keynes feared that "Loose funds may sweep round the world disorganizing all steady business." To obviate this possibility, Keynes felt that "Nothing is more certain than that movements of capital funds must be regulated – which in itself will involve far-reaching departures from *laissez-faire* arrangements." Cited in D.E. Moggridge, *Maynard Keynes: An Economist's Biography*, London: Routledge, 1992, 673.
55 John G. Ruggie, "Trade, Protectionism and the Future of Welfare Capitalism," *Journal of International Affairs*, Summer 1994.
56 David Andrews, "Capital Mobility and State Autonomy: Toward a Structural Theory of International Monetary Relations," *International Studies Quarterly*, June 1994.
57 On the argument for diversity rather than standardization in models of development, see Dani Rodrik, *One Economics, Many Recipes: Globalization, Institutions and Economic Growth*, New York: Princeton University Press, 2008; Josh Bivens, "Using Standard Models to Benchmark the Costs of Globalization for American Workers without a College Degree," Economic Policy Institute, March 22, 2013.
58 Joseph Stiglitz, *Globalization and Its Discontents*, New York: W.W. Norton & Company, 2002, 18.
59 Joseph Stiglitz, *Making Globalization Work*, New York: W.W. Norton & Company, 2006, 282–4.
60 Harris Gleckman, "Will Global Voluntarism Supersede Rule of Law?" *Policy Innovations* (Carnegie Council), March 22, 2013.

Further Reading

Jagdish Bhagwati, *In Defense of Globalization*, Oxford University Press, 2nd ed., 2007.
Bhagwati takes on globalization's critics, especially in defending the benefits of open trade. He is more cautious about the risks of liberalizing finance.

Paul F. Diehl and Brian Frederking (eds), *The Politics of Global Governance: International Organizations in an Interdependent World*, Boulder, CO: Lynne Rienner Publishers, 4th ed., 2010.
A balanced collection of essays on global governance.

Thomas Friedman, *The Lexus and the Olive Tree*, New York: Anchor Books, rev. ed., 2000.
Thomas Friedman, *The World is Flat: A Brief History of the Twenty-first Century*, New York: Farrar, Straus, and Giroux, 2005.
Two best-selling tributes to globalization by a leading journalist.

Pankaj Ghemawat, *World 3.0: Global Prosperity and How to Achieve It*, Boston, MA: Harvard Business Review Press, 2011.
Ghemawat argues that the current reach of globalization has been exaggerated. At best, the world economy is "semi-globalized." He also contends that the gains from deeper globalization are considerable, but must be pursued under the umbrella of strengthened regulatory systems.

David Held and Anthony McGrew, *Globalization/Anti-Globalization: Beyond the Great Divide*, Cambridge, England: Polity, 2nd ed., 2007.
The authors argue for a globalization guided by the principles of cosmopolitan social democracy.

Robert Keohane and Helen Milner (eds), *Internationalization and Domestic Politics*, Cambridge, England: Cambridge University Press, 1996.
Explores the various ways that international interdependence shapes both domestic politics and policymaking within nation-states.

Layna Mosley, *Global Capital and National Governments*, Cambridge, England: Cambridge University Press, 2003.
Mosley argues that states continue to possess the capacity to pursue distinct national economic models and to mediate the domestic impacts of globalization. She rejects the idea that globalization necessitates a "race to the bottom."

Dani Rodrik, *The Globalization Paradox*, New York: W.W. Norton & Company, 2011.
Rodrik argues that globalization presents us with a "political trilemma." National autonomy, democracy, and global free markets are all goods to be valued, but we cannot enjoy all three at once. Instead, we must trade off any two against the remaining good.

Michael Spence, *The Next Convergence: The Future of Economic Growth in a Multispeed World*, Farrar, Straus, and Giroux, 2011.
Spence argues that we have entered a period of "catch up," in which high-speed growth in the developing world will close the gap between rich and poor countries over the coming decades. Globalization will facilitate this process of convergence.

Joseph Stiglitz, *Globalization and Its Discontents*, New York: W.W. Norton & Company, 2002.
A Nobel Prize winning economist, Stiglitz lends his expertise and authority to many popular critiques of globalization. He argues that in its present guise, globalization is rigged against workers, less developed countries, and the environment.

Joseph Stiglitz, *Making Globalization Work*, New York: W.W. Norton & Company, 2006.
In this follow-up to his 2003 volume, Stiglitz offers policy prescriptions for reforming the international rules and institutions that govern globalization. He suggests that a reformed globalization can produce a fairer and more sustainable global economy.

Martin Wolf, *Why Globalization Works*, New Haven, CT: Yale University Press, 2005.
A journalist for the *Financial Times*, Wolf marshals a defense of globalization, arguing that governments, not markets, are responsible for many of the present ills that plague the global economy.

Daniel Yergin and Joseph Stanislaw, *The Commanding Heights: The Battle for the World Economy*, New York: Free Press, rev. ed., 2002.
An historical review of the intellectual and political battles over the proper balance between state and market power and how the 1980s and 1990s shifted the balance in favor of markets.

4 The Political Origins of a Global Economy

Power and Markets

A global economy is an astonishing thing to behold. It involves the production, transportation, and exchange of goods, services, and knowledge among billions of people, over thousands of miles, and across national boundaries and oceans, often including investments and the movement of money over equal distances. Perhaps less obvious, a global economy involves arrangements for the coordination of economic activity as it crosses distances, boundaries, and currencies. Making economic exchange work can mean following the rules established by one dominant political entity, or from cooperation among different powers, or from ad hoc rules negotiated by traders. Further, these activities can have enormous consequences for people's lives. This can influence the division of labor on a global scale, meaning what is produced and where; incomes may follow this division; goods from afar can improve people's lives or disrupt their livelihoods; and knowledge, technology, and military power frequently come along with goods and services.

Did a global economy always exist, at least as long as humans have lived in settled groups? Are all global economies the same? What criteria can we use to identify and classify global economies? These are some of the basic questions we consider in this chapter, as a global economy provides much of the subject matter of international political economy. Determining when a global economy exists is related to the purposes of the inquiry. For us, we are interested in the following criteria, as they define a type of global economy that emerges from a particular kind of political–economic system.

There are three main criteria for locating a global economy. First, we focus on the proportion of global trade in relation to domestic economies. We are interested in those situations in which global trade is truly global in scope and is relatively large in relation to economic activity that takes place within nations. Second, we want to consider situations in which industrial production generates a large part of the goods and services involved in world trade. This allows us to examine much more dynamic global economies, in which economic advantages among nations can change and in which the cost of production and transportation can rapidly decline. Third, we are concerned with systems in which there is a wide scope for consistency of the rules affecting exchange. Widespread use of similar rules makes it easier to see the processes of exchange arising from comparable circumstances. Using these criteria – large role for trade, goods arising from industrial production, and consistent rules – sharply reduces the space for discussion to about the past two centuries or so.

What have we left out? We can find several examples of large trading systems, especially in one or more regions of the world. The Roman Empire in and around Europe, and China in and around East and Southeast Asia were the centers for extensive trade in the distant past and some rules existed to govern that exchange. But there was little industrial production and trade was mostly confined to a relatively small portion of the world. A second important era, in which trade emerged on a global scale over the Eurasian landmass, followed the global military victories of the Mongols in the thirteenth and fourteenth centuries. Perhaps the most important period left out is between 1500 and 1800, when trade on a more global scale emerged. Connected to the new capabilities in trans-ocean sailing by Europeans and the resulting links to North America and Asia, this was a time when a new world system of capitalism was created by guns, ships, and trade. The world economy during this time was the object of control by national governments, which frequently engaged in war and expanded domestic taxes to support these efforts.[2] The trading systems during these times were confined mostly to luxury goods, and although trade growth was especially rapid in the eighteenth century, it remained relatively small as a proportion of overall economies.[3]

The time from 1750–1850 produced changes unprecedented in human history, created by the fundamental break in economies brought on by industrialization in Great Britain. Previously, whenever economic growth occurred this was followed by a rise in population that would negate the gains in per capita incomes. This changed when the gains from industrialization prompted additional economic and technological changes that spurred growth even faster than the growth in population. Not only did growth expand, but so too did inequality. In 1500, the ratio of richest to poorest region was 2:1; 1800 saw 3:1; but by 2001 this ratio had expanded to 18:1.[4]

The locus of industrialization and trade was in Britain, already a major military, colonial, and economic power. The creation of new industries in the eighteenth century led to rapidly expanding output resulting from rapidly falling costs of production, which meant these products were competitively priced all across the globe. Between the 1730s and 1790s, a series of technological innovations emerged mainly in Britain and revolutionized the production and weaving of cotton yarn. The cost of production fell dramatically; before these innovations, by hand 50,000 person-hours were required to process 100 pounds of cotton; by 1790, only 300 hours were needed. In spite of the general restrictions on international trade at the time, increases in British exports of cotton goods were dramatic after the end of the Napoleonic Wars in 1815. Moreover, Britain became the center for importing raw materials and semi-finished goods and re-exporting these and other products to Europe. As the world's greatest imperial power, Britain exchanged manufactured goods for raw materials with its colonies. By mid-century, Britain dominated the pig iron and railroad industries and exported locomotives, rail cars, and finished rails to much of the world. During the period from about 1790–1860, a new kind of economy was created around a much greater pace and scale of industrial capabilities, technological improvements, and economic growth. This quickly spilled into new forms of global trade and the beginnings of a new global economy.[5]

The political economy of this new system began to take shape over the nineteenth century, with forms that increasingly resemble the political economy of the present. The nature of specialization based on factor endowments and chains of complementary forms of international specialization linked by trade began to emerge. Winners and losers from international trade created a series of domestic political struggles over trade policy and a set of international negotiations designed to define an international trading space followed. International capital flows deriving from large accumulated profits developed to support trade. International knowledge flows through communication and migration supported and sustained rapid technological improvements. And international monetary relations and negotiations based on a multilateral system of arrangements designed to support trade also developed.

Why Britain and Not China?

During the eighteenth century, there was little difference between the poorest nations and the richest nations in per person incomes, as all economies were predominantly based on agriculture. The China of 1750 was not all that different from Europe, save in population size. This meant China was by far the largest economy in the world; even in 1820 the Chinese economy accounted for one-third of the entire global economy. Moreover, China had been the source of great inventiveness over the previous millennia with gunpowder, the printing press, and the greatest ships in the world, and was the main producer of ceramics, silk, and fine cotton for export to Europe.[6] So why did the Industrial Revolution happen in Britain and not in China, or somewhere else?

This is a question of great practical import, as the new economic world after 1750 came increasingly to separate nations in terms of incomes and growth. These differences frequently cumulate and carry into today, with only some nations able to participate in global growth and with astonishing income and wealth gaps across the globe. Clearly we need to

understand how industrialization has so divided nations and made them less alike.

Fortunately, this question has generated considerable investigation and discussion.[7] Though no firm consensus exists, several broad conclusions can be offered. These focus on first, the special combination in Britain of the investigation of nature based on scientific criteria, significant knowledge of mechanics across the nation, and an internationally engaged commercial society with considerable investment capacity. Unlike most societies across the world, including China, economic knowledge in England developed with modern science and was distributed over a dense network of like-minded "tinkerers."[8] Second, Britain and more generally Europe possessed a special and privileged access to the resources of the New World won as a result of global advantages in military technology. In a world where natural resources placed sharp limits on growth, access to the vast resources of the New World was a large advantage for England and Europe over China.[9]

At this point, the analysis of economic growth becomes much more controversial. A very important thesis comes from neoclassical economics focusing on the institutional basis for the creation of efficient markets.[10] Such markets arise when governments provide the rule of law for the nation but withdraw from other forms of involvement in economic life. In this environment, entrepreneurial investors will supply capital to the best use and markets for land, labor, capital, and protected knowledge will result that continually reallocate resources efficiently. According to this view, efficient markets will then produce economic growth. If this theory is correct, we would expect the institutions in England and China to be quite different, thereby leading to quite different levels of market efficiency, and this would account for the origins of industrialization in Britain and not China.

There were differences in the institutions relating to property rights and individual rights between China and England in the mid-eighteenth century, with the property holders in the latter better able to control use of their property.[11] However, a detailed examination of the market systems of these areas does not reveal clear differences in levels of efficiency. Several measures of market operations provide conflicting indicators of only small degrees of advantage; there is certainly no conclusive or even significant evidence of greater market efficiency in England. Moreover, England in the eighteenth century had a relatively high tax rate undermining the notion of a night watchman state.[12] Though institutions seem to have an intuitively obvious role in affecting economic growth, the process is more subtle and complex than we yet understand.

The Nineteenth-Century Global Economy

The progression of industrialization within England quickly led to international consequences and over the century after 1800 helped to create a

Table 4.1 Per Capita Levels of Industrialization During the Nineteenth Century

Country	1800	1860	1913
Belgium	10	28	88
France	9	20	59
Germany	8	15	85
Russia	6	8	20
Spain	7	11	22
Switzerland	10	26	87
United Kingdom	16	64	115
Japan	7	7	20
China	6	4	3
India	6	3	2

Source: Data from Paul Bairoch, "International Industrialization Levels from 1750 to 1980," *Journal of European Economic History*, 11 (1982) 281.

global economy unlike any that had existed before. Industrialization and economic growth not only continued across the century but, even more important, the rate of growth increased and spread to many nations in Europe, North America, and to Japan in Asia. Many other nations began to participate in the global economy through the export of primary products and raw materials. Technological change cumulated and expanded with a host of new inventions, products, processes, and innovations that dramatically altered economic and social life during this time. At least in urban areas, real wages began to increase and rose substantially over the century.

Some sense of the changes from industrialization can be seen in Table 4.1. Notice that in 1800 most nations were at about the same level, with the distance between England and China not that large and between England and other European states even smaller. After sixty years some nations had surged ahead, some had changed only a little, and some had even regressed. By 1913, just before World War I, the gaps had increased with those between China and India on the one hand and the United States at over 40:1 (see Table 4.2).

The differences in industrialization had profound consequences. Not only did this directly affect the levels of per capita income across nations, but the capacity for military power was also a result of industrial capabilities. As a result, in 1913 India remained under the control of England, and China had succumbed to Western imperialist dominance and seen its millennia-long dynastic system collapse. Japan, by contrast, had emerged from a position of subservience to Western domination and established a position of imperialist strength in Asia.

Associated with the dynamic transformations in industrial capabilities was the creation of new global patterns of trade and investment. The leading edge industry for the early years of British industrialization was

Table 4.2 Real GDP Per Capita Growth Rates, 1820–1996

Nation	1820–70	1870–1913	1913–50	1950–73	1973–96
UK	1.2	1.0	0.8	2.5	1.6
US	1.3	1.8	1.6	2.4	1.6
Germany	1.1	1.6	0.3	5.0	1.8
France	0.8	1.3	1.1	4.0	1.5
Russia	0.6	0.9	1.8	3.4	-1.2
Japan	0.1	1.4	0.9	8.0	2.5
China	0.0	0.6	-0.3	2.1	5.4
India	0.1	0.4	-0.3	1.6	2.9
Brazil	0.2	0.3	1.9	3.8	1.4
Korea			-0.2	5.2	6.8
Singapore				4.3	6.1

Source: Data from Nicholas Crafts, "Globalization and Growth in the Twentieth Century," IMF Working Paper, WP/00/44, March 2000, 14, www.imf.org/external/pubs/cat/wp1_sp.aspx?s_year=2000&e_year=2000&brtype=default

cotton goods and textiles, which subsequently became an important part of industrial development for many nations. Exports of these products rose significantly as a proportion of the English economy, marking a new role for exports in creating economic growth. For England, this industry required the import of raw cotton produced largely in the southern United States on plantations using slave labor. By mid-century, England was importing fifty times the raw cotton from the United States as in the 1780s and nearly 70 percent of US exports were produced by slave labor.[13] This pattern of purchasing raw materials and food from abroad – especially from nations operating within the orbit of British imperialism – was linked to sales of manufactured goods and increasing outward investment by Britain.

The Turn to Freer Trade

At least from the time of the creation of modern nation-states in the seventeenth century, economic relations were largely seen as a weapon in gaining advantages and even dominance in international relations. A very large part of what we call international trade was really a form of imperialism, with one nation gaining exclusive control over an area rich in resources and then excluding other nations from these opportunities. The products of that area, if in sufficiently high demand, would be sold at especially high prices and the imperial nation would pocket the extra profits. Gold, silver, furs, spices, and silk – mostly luxury goods for the rich – were especially coveted and used to build the resources of the national treasury. Trade in such products was awarded exclusively to a national trading company (the British East India Company is an example) and transport could only occur in ships operating under a national charter

(British Navigation Acts had this purpose). Not surprisingly, war was often the means to gain and secure control of these resources. A vicious cycle was common, involving a victorious war for resources, which led to special gains for one nation that sparked another war with other nations seeking to take these gains away. The system, known as mercantilism, was one in which trade and war were part of the same process.

The creation of an international economy based on industrial production led to new forms of thinking and some changes in national economic policy. The intellectual leadership for this came from the new economic philosophers such as Adam Smith and David Ricardo, who argued that mercantilism was bad for all and even for individual nations.[14] In particular, Ricardo asserted that rather than being caught in the trap of a zero-sum game, nations could mutually gain from policies of free trade and specialization. (See Chapter 2 for details.) Slowly, over the first half of the nineteenth century British liberals began to espouse these ideas and the growing political power of rising entrepreneurs gave political weight to this view. The expansion of voting rights in 1832 was especially important in altering the composition of the House of Commons, and the cost of expensive food in England provided additional reasons to question the value of protection of English landowners.

Traditionally, as part of its mercantilist policy Britain had protected agriculture with tariffs and other restrictions – commonly known as the Corn Laws – and based this in the interests of its landowning aristocracy. But the dynamic economic changes of the nineteenth century led to new interests, including those of manufacturers, financiers, and political leaders who saw the Corn Laws as damaging to Britain. Industrial exporters were especially adamant that the Corn Laws kept food prices artificially high, thereby reducing the ability of other nations to sell British food and then buy British manufactured products. Some suggested a British move to freer trade could induce other nations to likewise lower barriers and thereby prompt a new international division of labor, with Britain purchasing raw materials and food and selling manufactured goods. Others were concerned about the ability of Britain to feed its rising population and the implications for political instability. A key feature of decisions was the imposition of an income tax, which reduced the need for the revenues from tariffs. Combined with the shock of the Irish potato famine, the views of liberalism triumphed in 1846 with repeal of the Corn Laws and soon thereafter of the Navigation Acts. Tariffs on manufactured goods were also reduced.[15]

The unilateral move toward free trade by the British government is of profound significance for understanding the development of the global economy. The new system of sustained economic growth via industrialization and trade had altered the basic structure of economic interests and thereby the political arrangements in the nation. The new economic class of manufacturers/exporters created by globally competitive industry was able to increase its political power and press for a new trade policy. Indeed, even landowners became investors in the manufacturing economy and diversified their interests.[16] The British government developed a strategy for promoting its economic interests in free trade; by acting unilaterally, they hoped to entice other nations to follow by adopting free trade as well, based on a recognition of the common interests in the gains from free trade. However, the British strategy had more of a long-term effect on the global economy than on overall tariff levels.

Over the next quarter-century, Britain was able to induce many other European nations to adopt some version of freer trade. Much of this was through a series of bilateral trade treaties that were given wider effects from a clause known as "most-favored-nation." With this process, a nation engaged in a trade treaty with another nation agreed to extend to all other nations with whom it had treaties the most favored terms it had with any one nation. By the 1860s, the first era of relatively free trade had been arranged through this process.[17] Equally important, a new system of multilateral trade and capital flows emerged, centered on Britain, to form a world economy of substantial proportions.

But this system of free trade was a politically and economically fragile one and beginning in the 1870s and over the next twenty years was largely dismantled when most European nations and the United States reversed course and raised protectionist tariffs. Only Britain and the Netherlands retained an absolute commitment to free trade. This meant Britain, as the most important trading nation, was unable to retaliate against defecting nations and, as a result, was powerless to halt the reversal of free trade. Nonetheless, global trade continued to rise. The combination of British retention of free trade and the dramatic declines in the cost of transportation propelled the growth of trade in spite of the increasing protectionism in most nations.

The era from 1850–1914 also produced a new surge of imperialism that affected trade. Most of the African continent came under direct European control, as did large parts of coastal China and Southeast Asia, along with areas of today's Middle East. Latin America was subject to varying levels of economic influence through investment and trade and North America was populated by force with support by the US government. Thus, successful efforts by Western nations to control territories abroad included both conquest and control and intimidation and control. But one main purpose was to open these societies to trade with the imperial nation; this was usually exclusive in cases of direct control, and open to all in cases of indirect control. Examples of direct control include the British in India and the French in Indochina; examples of indirect control include Western influence in Japan and Argentina.[18] In terms of trade, a global division of labor emerged with colonial areas selling raw materials and primary products to imperial controllers in return for manufactured products.[19]

Globalization: The First Wave

The creation of a global economy during the nineteenth century was a result of globalization, which refers to a systemic change in which national economic systems interact based on increasingly greater weight for international transactions in overall economic activity.[20] Transactions involving the production of goods for export – cotton, grain, iron ore – count as international. But so does the purchase of the bonds of one nation by investors in another. And the movement of people, both those on holiday and those moving permanently, must be seen as international transactions. One of the best indicators of globalization is the creation of global markets for money, goods, services, and labor. Instead of local market prices that differ substantially from one place to another, the integration of markets leads to a convergence of prices. This increasingly came to happen over the nineteenth century.

Perhaps ironically, it was the globalization of trade – especially the growth of trade in grains – that spurred the nineteenth-century protectionist backlash. The combination of the railroad, steam ships, and the telegraph provided the technological basis for dramatic declines in the cost of transporting food and the ability to manage the operation of firms over long distances. Especially after 1870, grains grown in the central United States could be shipped overland to eastern ports, loaded on ships, and sent across the Atlantic to Europe at a very low cost.[21] The productivity and price advantages of the vast and fertile American land led to significant declines in grain prices that overwhelmed European farmers, who could not compete but who increasingly could vote. In rapid order, European nations began to raise tariffs on grain to protect the economic interests of farmers but often extended those tariffs to manufactured goods.[22] Well before 1913, liberal trade policies had become the exception rather than the rule. Even so, the declining cost of transport helped promote a global restructuring of production, capital, and people of substantial proportions and led to a vast expansion of global markets.[23]

Changes in global production and trade led to a significant convergence of prices across much of the world in the nineteenth century. Before this new global economy, factor prices and the costs of production were much more localized and could vary dramatically from place to place. Comparative and absolute advantages in production across much of the globe began to affect local producers in ways that were previously impossible. The large profits available from agricultural production in land-rich areas were only possible by increasing tillage of this land, which required large investments in roads, railroads, and distribution systems but also more people. This process built on and accelerated globalization in spite of the rising protectionism. In addition to goods, capital and people began to move in large numbers, with capital-rich and densely populated areas moving money and people to resource- and land-rich areas.

Between 1820 and 1913, about 26 million persons left Europe to migrate abroad, or about 10 percent of the total European population of 1850. This massive movement of people was sustained by an equally impressive system of global investment, the largest part of which issued from Britain. The growth and aggregate size of this investment can be seen in Table 4.3.

Clearly, in the four decades before World War I international financial transactions were large and growing. Investments rose from $8 billion in 1870 to $45.45 billion in 1914, with nearly half or more coming from Britain. The purchase of securities from other nations was common throughout Europe, where few regulations or restrictions existed to limit these transactions.[24] The greatest part of this investment went for infrastructure such as railroads, roads, and sewage systems for areas expanding their production of raw materials and food. One of the remarkable features of the new global economy was the eagerness of investors in rich nations to supply the capital to increase the competitive capabilities of other parts of the world.[25]

Of course, trade itself expanded in substantial, if less dramatic, ways. Remember, we partly define a global economy in terms of the proportion that trade represents in relation to national economic production. Table 4.4 demonstrates the significant growth of this measure over the long nineteenth century.

Table 4.3 Overseas Investments of the Major Economic Powers, 1870–1914 (millions $US)

	1870	1900	1914	% of world in 1914
Great Britain	4,900	12,000	20,000	44.0
France	2,500	5,800	9,050	19.9
Germany	—	4,800	5,800	12.8
United States	100	500	3,500	7.8
Other nations	500	1,100	7,100	15.5

Source: Data from Sidney Pollard, "Capital Exports, 1870–1914: Harmful or Beneficial?" *Economic History Review*, 38.4 (November 1985) 492.

Table 4.4 Trade/Global Production (Exports + Imports/World GDP)

1800	1870	1900	1913	1929	1938
2%	11%	19%	22%	15%	9%

Source: Data from Antoni Estevadeordal, Brian Frantz, and Alan Taylor, "The Rise and Fall of World Trade, 1870–1939," *Quarterly Journal of Economics*, 118.2 (May 2003) 359–407.

Table 4.5 Global Trade in the Long Nineteenth Century (millions $US of exports + imports)

Nation/Region	1876–80	1913
UK	2,569	5,708
Europe	5,975	19,264
US + Canada	1,220	5,268
Latin America	NA	3,056
Africa	NA	1,464

Source: Data from Ronald Finlay and Kevin O'Rourke, *Power and Plenty*, Princeton: Princeton University Press, 2007, 412.

Table 4.5 shows both the increases and the enormous dominance of Europe in the global trade system preceding World War I. Even in 1913, global trade remained concentrated in primary products. Only 36 percent of trade that year was in manufactured goods.

Facilitating the globalization of finance and trade was the gold standard, which operated to stabilize currency values and thereby established a favorable economic environment. The gold standard as the basis for an international monetary system arose from the creation of a gold standard for the domestic currencies of a significant number of nations and the ability of gold to move freely between nations. This meant a nation's currency could be exchanged for a certain fixed quantity of gold and this relationship created an exchange rate between two different currencies. If currency "A" was worth 10 ounces of gold and currency "B" was worth 5 ounces of gold, then the exchange rate was fixed at one "B" = two "A." In effect, the gold standard made all currencies operating on this basis a form of international money and made this money a fixed standard of value. In effect, the fixing of domestic currencies to gold created a fixed exchange rate system between currencies.

This certainty of value promoted global trade and investment by reducing the risk that currencies would change value. But, the gold standard had several very negative economic consequences that meant it could only be sustained by a particular political system. The gold standard required a political order such as existed in Europe in the late nineteenth century, one very heavily weighted toward the economic interests of economic elites. In particular, the gold standard tended to drive down the price of goods and of labor and thereby increase the value of productive assets and investments.[26] In particular, such a system rewarded creditors and penalized those who had to borrow money. By fixing the amount of a nation's currency to the amount of gold it held, the currency itself became the scarcest of assets and the inflation of money was very difficult. Moreover, governments operating on the gold standard were very constrained in their ability to affect the economy through any monetary policy. Sustaining such a system that harmed the economic interests of the majority of the society was possible only when elections were restricted to a small number of voters. Not surprisingly, it was these same economic elites who vigorously advocated the gold standard. For them, it was the clearest indicator of an effective economic system and government. The late nineteenth-century political order offered wide latitude to economic elites to preserve this system.[27]

Knowledge and Economic Growth: Germany and Japan

The development of the global economy in the nineteenth century eventually came to resemble that of later times, especially in the growing role of knowledge in the production of industrial goods.[28] Though initially confined to a small number of industries, "knowledge-intensive" production became increasingly important by the end of the century. More generally, the nature of industrial society came to be based on a widening arc of knowledge about technology, the management of firms, and the operation of finance. This became a wellspring of knowledge capabilities for poor nations in an effort to catch up with rich nations. But gaining access to this knowledge was only an option for those poor nations also exceptionally well organized for this task.

Economic knowledge is a structure of ideas informing activities used to provide goods and services. This kind of knowledge builds on and influences other forms, such as scientific knowledge used to understand the causes and consequences of the physical and social worlds. Knowledge linked to technology has always been at the root of economic life, from the technology of agriculture that served as the basis for living in organized communities, to the bronze and iron that affected warfare, to the printing press that dramatically lowered the cost of making books and transmitting information, to the computer and Internet that altered the scope, speed, and cost of information on a global scale. What makes knowledge so interesting is not only the ability to create new products and ways of making and delivering products, often at prices much lower than before; equally significant, knowledge can be reused over and over by many people at low cost and without using it up. The knowledge I have and use does not diminish your knowledge; most likely, it can actually increase yours. Thus, economic knowledge drives economic growth by generating cumulating and expanding economic reasons for investment and consumption. Though the marginal cost of reusing knowledge is low and even falling, it is not zero. This means there is a barrier to its use: you (and your economy) must have already invested in learning and knowledge sufficient to understand and act on this knowledge.

Even as knowledge and technology have always been central to economic growth, for millennia changes and improvements were very slow and were transmitted very poorly. As a result, the ability to reuse knowledge and its ability to spawn innovation were usually quite limited.

This meant economic growth was mostly limited to the rate of population growth and the benefits from increases in the size of markets. This changed with the Industrial Revolution, which was to lead to continuing, cumulating, and much more rapid advances in economic knowledge and thereby to an increasing role for knowledge in economic life. And, as knowledge became more important, the dynamics of competition among nations was also changed.

Germany and Global Competition in Synthetic Dyes

An early example of this effect is the creation of the chemical industry in the mid-nineteenth century, which arose from the ability to develop new kinds of synthetic dyes for clothing and textiles.[29] The industry first developed in England in the mid-nineteenth century when an entrepreneur/inventor developed a method for making synthetic dyes from coal tar and then devised methods for efficient manufacture in 1857. Based on this advantage and with patent protection, British synthetic dye firms were globally dominant. This was to last little more than a decade. By 1870, German firms had captured 50 percent of the global market and in 1900 controlled an 85 percent global market share. Only in 1914, in the midst of World War I and based on government intervention to build a domestic industry, did Britain and the United States establish a viable position in this industry.

How did this rapid shift take place and persist over time? Why, in spite of its great advantages, did Britain quickly lose its position in the synthetic dye industry? First, the knowledge content of this product and its production was very high, with raw materials being only a small part of the value of the product. And, because knowledge is inherently social, it leaks, in this case very quickly. Once the basic information about the synthetic dye process became known, chemists across Europe quickly moved to duplicate this achievement. Through a process known as reverse engineering, others learned how to duplicate the product and the manufacturing process, mainly by working backward from the end product through the constituent steps involved. Equally important, knowledge from reconstructing product and process provided a basis for inventing new dyes and improving existing ones. Once new firms had been established, the competitive process shifted to one of innovation in product and process; that is, the capacity for developing new knowledge became the basis for business success. And the ability of firms to achieve innovation was closely related to the institutional environment in which they operated. German firms became globally dominant because Germany was the location of the largest numbers of chemists with advanced university training; the largest pool of specialized knowledge workers provided German firms with a continuing stream of new ideas and innovators. German firms established large and sophisticated research and development (R&D) labs and these labs were closely linked to additional research occurring in universities. Moreover, the R&D process for synthetic dyes led to many other products (aspirin is an example) that produced additional profits.

The story of the global synthetic dye industry is very important. It requires that we begin to modify our notions of global economic competition. Any comparative advantage based in knowledge can be very ephemeral and subject to efforts by others to reproduce or even steal this knowledge. So, why didn't German firms also quickly lose their advantages? The answer lies in the German government, which was much more prepared than the liberal British government to spend large sums on education. And education provided much of the basis for creating a comparative advantage in synthetic dye knowledge and continuing innovation. In 1900, just the largest German state – Prussia – spent twenty times more than all of Britain on universities.[30] Unlike the weather as a basis for producing wine in Portugal, universities are subject to human control. The basis for competition in knowledge is a result of creating institutions such as firms and universities that are subject to human intervention.

Japan and State-Led Economic Growth

The German ability to make rapid gains by emphasizing education and knowledge in special industries was reflected in different ways by Japan. We have seen how most poor nations in the nineteenth century made limited gains in industrialization, with economic growth limited to the export of primary products. Japan is the most important exception to that pattern. Japan was forced to open its society and economy as a result of US and British military threats in the 1850s and experienced revolutionary changes in its government in the 1860s. The resulting Meiji Restoration led to a major effort to strengthen the government, which acted to transform both the social order in Japan and build an industrial economy. Engaging in a trial and error process, the Japanese government came to understand the importance of gaining knowledge from abroad by building national firms and institutions able to find and apply this knowledge.

Japan entered this period with a semi-feudal society and government, unable to protect itself from the incursions of the West. Though its economy had become more developed in terms of trade in markets and there were considerable crafts skills and small-scale technological innovations, Japan was by almost any measure a very poor and undeveloped society. Less than fifty years later Japan had become a semi-industrial state with considerable production for global markets of textiles and with the most modern and powerful military in Asia.

Fortuitous for Japan, Western imperialists were satisfied with access and not direct control, leaving Japan with high levels of domestic political autonomy. Japan is unique among poor nineteenth-century nations in that it came to have a strong, capable, and internally autonomous central government and capable local governments.[31] Western nations never gained the physical concessions they had in China, nor the indirect or certainly direct control in areas such as Indochina or the Philippines. Western troops did not occupy Japan and destroy its political order. But, Western treaties with Japan did force on them a free trade regime in which Western goods were imported with few restrictions. The effect was to put great pressure on Japanese production, which was usually unable to compete with these products. The combination of pressure plus political autonomy was what left Japan mostly free to fashion a response of its own making. The Japanese succeeded because the government was able to organize a national system of technological borrowing and direct the process of economic development.

The most active role for the government in creating and controlling a modern economy came during the first decade or so after the Restoration. This was a time for the creation of the infrastructure – hard and soft – of a modern economic system. Put in our terms, the Japanese needed to create not merely the physical infrastructure of roads, rails, and telegraph lines but equally important were the institutions to carry out and sustain a dynamic capitalist system. This included creating competitive firms able to hold their own against the firms from advanced states operating at will in Japan. And competitiveness meant the ability to organize and manage such firms, using knowledgeable managers and skilled workers able to work with and adapt advanced technologies and supported by external monetary, financial, and educational institutions.[32]

Initially, central government ministries operated to gain and apply knowledge for economic production and the development of advanced military capabilities. The agencies were directly responsible for the rail and telegraph construction projects, using many foreign advisers, and hired many foreign companies to aid the effort to import technology and knowledge related to mining, iron manufacturing, shipbuilding, and lighthouse networks. Parallel efforts were directed toward channeling the activities associated with technology, knowledge, production, and infrastructure toward military strength. State-owned arsenals helped define and build much of this infrastructure and often had a large impact on the sales and profits of emerging private firms. Direct procurement by the military provided a substantial stimulus to production, and some machines produced for the military, such as steam engines, were also used by textile firms.[33]

Japanese leaders worried about the potential for dependence on foreigners as sources of knowledge and development. This led to a determination to make sure this technology and knowledge were developed for Japan. Japanese leaders, in the national as well as local governments, understood the value of building Japanese capabilities in knowledge and technology as a basis for capturing additional knowledge and development of an indigenous knowledge and technology capability. Foreign firms operating in Japan and foreigners brought to Japan were used as a source of knowledge transfer to Japanese. Many Japanese were sent abroad to learn about Western technology and training centers and universities were established in Japan. A variety of expositions of foreign technology were used to diffuse awareness and understanding. Considerable attention was devoted to reverse engineering and then adapting foreign technology and ideas to Japanese conditions, thereby promoting additional national knowledge and technology capabilities.[34]

The initial Japanese companies during the Meiji era were owned and directed by the government, often operating experimentally for purposes of trial and error learning in military-related areas such as iron and steel. Much of the products and processes of new manufacturing in the Meiji era were dual-use, for both military and civilian purposes. This can be seen in shipbuilding and steel, but also in motors for textile looms, in machine tools, in optical equipment, and in power generation. Further, the creation of state firms and the new infrastructure, technology, and knowledge required new complementary institutional capabilities in finance and generated new state and organizational capabilities from the new systems of communication, education, and transport. With this process, the Japanese government developed an institutional basis for a modern capitalist economy.[35]

Most of these state firms were not profitable and after 1881 were sold off to newly established private firms. This process became a partial basis for the creation of the special Japanese form of firm, the *zaibatsu*. These *zaibatsu* came to be especially large and diversified firms (for a poor nation), and were usually closely related to large banks as a source of capital. The foundations of several *zaibatsu* – such as Mitsui, Furukawa, and Mitsubishi – were laid with the sales of government firms. The "private" firms received assets and operations at bargain rates and a trained and knowledgeable workforce with many established links to Western firms for continued flows of knowledge and inputs of machinery.[36] The creation of *zaibatsu* was a state project that helped define and also nurture new capabilities. And as "private" firms *zaibatsu* were themselves able to develop and build on state help, since most were not yet globally competitive.

The emerging form of Japanese capitalism did not operate on the Western concept of a sharp separation of government and markets; rather, the Japanese established a complementary system of collaboration between state and firm that continues to develop even after the "privatization" process. For example, after 1895 the central government expanded its role in economic and technological change via new efforts in creating a modern military force, using in particular its links to the emerging *zaibatsu*. The pattern of government establishment of firms and development of knowledge and technology later passed on to private firms continued in areas directly related to national security. The Mitsubishi *zaibatsu* owed much of the development of its shipping industry to military considerations in providing government subsidies, training, special treatment, and outright gifts.[37]

The Japanese and German cases illustrate in different ways that a variety of paths to economic growth existed in the late nineteenth century. Through understanding and drawing on the expanding pool of global knowledge accumulating through economic and scientific expansion, both Japan and Germany were able to make rapid leaps in economic development. In both cases, the governments of each nation played a central role in the expansion of knowledge capabilities. The national and state governments in Germany spent heavily on education, especially scientific education, and thereby created a new form of competitive advantage: a large pool of science-based knowledge workers able to advance and sustain product and process innovation. In Japan, governments at all levels were central to gaining, diffusing, and applying foreign knowledge and to building an expanding pool of educated workers. The Japanese government helped to create, expand, and nurture the demand for foreign knowledge. Further, the development of production facilities and of capable firms can be linked to government efforts. The role of competent and effective governments in economic growth is demonstrated, even in the nineteenth century, by Germany and Japan.

British Power and the Global Economy

Complex and large economic systems require a political base in order to operate effectively. Arrangements to protect property rights and contracts, provide a medium of exchange, invest in infrastructure and physical security, establish rules for the terms of exchange across borders, and generally protect the interests of investors are some of the basic political goods needed for markets to function.[38] If true, this should mean that a large and complex global economy requires a similar set of arrangements. However, international relations are typically defined by a fractured system of political sovereignty, which provide a barrier to the supply of these political goods across the system. Two alternative sources are a potential substitute: cooperation among nations or one dominant nation, a hegemon.[39]

The political arrangements supporting markets, especially global markets, were only dimly understood in the nineteenth century. International cooperation in managing international security was an accepted element of statecraft, but this did not generally extend to international economic policy.[40] The alternative could possibly come from a hegemon, a nation with the power to shape the global economy and the interests in a stable and expanding global economy to justify the effort and cost of such an undertaking.[41] Over the century, British policymakers began to understand the importance of political efforts to sustain economic systems and used the nation's economic position to support and sustain the global economy. However, the British position of power from which to supply these goods was weakening as this understanding developed, leaving it less able to act effectively.

The most important contributions of nineteenth-century British hegemony were to develop and sustain international capital markets, contribute to a loosely organized international monetary system based on gold, and maintain open markets during a time of increasing protectionism. British power in monetary affairs derived primarily from the importance of the City of London, with its short-term financing of international trade, the role of sterling as a near international currency, and from the vast sums of capital that flowed abroad into long-term foreign investments. These areas of power permitted London bankers to influence interest rates around the world, provide international liquidity during times of crisis, and finance the balance of payments deficits of a variety of countries without harsh adjustments.[42] In addition, the gold standard required some management provided by the Bank of England and was accompanied by a constant outflow of British capital.[43]

But on the whole, Britain acted primarily as a passive hegemon, reflecting the laissez-faire political economy of the age and restricting itself to a persuasion by example form of leadership. Moreover, British power advantages – military, economic, and political – were never all that large over other major states and these advantages began to wane considerably after 1870. During this period, the British diversified their economy into financial-based services but also turned increasingly to the empire as a basis for economic relations. British leadership by example in conducting policies of imperialism was at least as strong as in free trade, and the nineteenth century was ultimately as much about imperialism and the search for exclusive control over territory as about the creation of a liberal trading order. The global competition for colonies intensified late in the nineteenth century along with global economic competition in trade and investment. The political position of Britain at the center of this imperial struggle undermined its ability to act as a creator of global economic rules.

The British experience of global dominance in the nineteenth century provides a limited case for understanding the role of political power in fashioning a global economy. British power advantages were relatively limited and fleeting, given the unprecedented changes in economic life. At the time, there was little intellectual analysis and understanding of how such systems and relationships might operate. Moreover, the legacy of mercantile thinking focusing on imperialism remained strong throughout the world, thereby undermining the ability to focus on mutual gain. The British did little to articulate an understanding of the global economy other than to emphasize the benefits of laissez faire, which asserts only a negative role for political involvement in economic life. Thus, the shaping of the global economy in the last decades of the nineteenth century was defined by the political rules of imperialism and growing antagonism as much as by trade and financial investment. Interdependence was certainly high, but the political underpinnings of the global system were framed around competitive political struggle, even if goods, money, and people moved freely over borders.

The Global Economy and World War I

The century preceding the outbreak of World War I in 1914 led to an unprecedented transformation of the global economy: economic growth dwarfed that of any century before; the processes of production and the industrial goods produced were categorically different; and the level of interdependence across the world was much higher than ever. A finer brush allows us to see an even more complex system of global economic relations.

During this same period, much wider gaps began to develop in the level of economic development among nations. These gaps were the result of large differences in the ability of nations to engage in industrial development. Some nations, largely in Europe and North America, were somewhat quickly able to emulate British industrial capabilities and begin a process of catching up or even surpassing the British. Others were hobbled by imperialism and had existing industrial capabilities destroyed. A once-vibrant Indian textile industry was unable to compete with cloth and yarn produced by much more advanced industrial techniques in Britain. Because its markets were held open by British imperial control, 75 percent of the domestic Indian textile market was made up of imported goods.[44] Many other nations found their gains from the new global economy limited to the sale of primary products to industrial nations. Japan is the main exception to this pattern, driven to industrialization by the enhanced capabilities of its revolutionary government.

Among advanced nations, interdependence advanced dramatically through increased trade, finance, and migration. Rapidly falling transportation costs mostly overwhelmed the rise of protectionism. One nation, the United States, rose to industrial supremacy behind the walls of high tariffs while benefiting greatly from exporting primary products. Of course, the high tariff policy was a government intervention in the free market that altered prices in the United States, such that domestic manufacturers were able to develop and compete with foreign producers. Notwithstanding the rise of tariffs, trade levels grew much faster than output and by 1913 merchandise exports represented 13 percent of the GDP of advanced nations. Global financial investment also advanced, primarily through the purchase of the government bonds of developing nations by private investors in rich nations. By 1913, annual international capital flows were 5 percent of the GDP of advanced nations. The globalization of finance also led to frequent financial crises, which were quickly transmitted across borders and demonstrated the size of the ties connecting nations.

Missing from the global economy in 1913 were effective systems of international cooperation embedded in international institutions and capable of managing this emerging interdependence. Theoretically, the gold standard was supposed to regulate trade and financial imbalances by forcing automatic declines in prices, wages, and employment by deficit nations. Not surprisingly, the losers in this process resisted these changes. Moreover, the gold standard had little effect in preventing financial crises. Perhaps the greatest weakness in the global economy was the failure of global elites in understanding the nature and consequences of increased interdependence. The national leaders of most advanced nations continued to see trade and investment as a weapon in international competition. Seizing territory and establishing an exclusive economic area was a common objective of foreign policy, a pattern legitimized by the ethos of imperialism. The ideas of mutual gain from interdependence found in liberal notions of trade were in retreat in the years before 1913. Consequently, the substantial ties of interdependence did little to stop the impending disaster of 1914.[45]

The Economic Consequences of War

The global war that began in August 1914 was partly a result of a failure to find security and prosperity within a context of increasing global interdependence. Equally important was an extraordinary restructuring of the global economy as a result of the war: trade and financial flows were dramatically rearranged, economic power was redistributed, and political relationships were fractured. Further, the era from 1919–39 is defined by largely unsuccessful efforts to reorganize a world economy, but is also a time when the pattern of increasing interdependence was disrupted.[46] This era provides a case study in the importance of political management of a global economy and the terrible consequences when these efforts fail.

Global economic stability faced three major impediments after 1919, all the result of political failures. First, most governments lacked the political strength or acumen to design and carry out a managerial role in their domestic economies and were even less able to design such systems for the global economy. Missing especially were institutional mechanisms for transferring capital from surplus to deficit countries, especially during times of economic distress. Private firms, the only alternative to government, lacked the size, incentives, and the ability to act in a crisis. Second, the United States, as the world's largest economic power, failed to accept a leadership role, largely because its political system was too immature to assume this responsibility. Third, the ferocity of the global depression in 1929 actually exacerbated these weaknesses and nations turned to autarchy and protectionism to defend their domestic economies.

We can see these difficulties by concentrating on global economic relationships in the two decades after 1919. The political economy of World War I helps to understand many of its consequences. The United States initially declared its neutrality, but quickly became the main supplier of war-related goods to the British and French. The United States entered the war in 1917, and before that the Allies purchased these goods by liquidating their considerable international investments and by borrowing from private US banks. After the United States' entry, the lending process was continued by the US government. At war's end in 1918, Britain and France had accumulated $10 billion dollars in debts owed to the United States. Equally important, fighting the war led to a deterioration of European productive capabilities and provided an opening to nations like the United States and Japan to build up their industrial positions. The war left European nations much less competitive in the global economy and saddled with significant debts.[47] In addition to the economic difficulties of the victors, the defeated Germany also faced significant problems. The terms of the Versailles peace treaty imposed on Germany required the payment of war reparations to Britain and France. German ability to pay was in considerable doubt, as the funds had to come either from an unlikely current account surplus or from even less likely foreign loans.[48] The combination of trade imbalances, restructured competitiveness, and war debts made for potential instability in the global economy. Many hoped, with little reason, that repayment of British and French war debt would be financed by German reparations. The disintegration of this deeply flawed system into depression, authoritarianism, and war demonstrates the terrible consequences of shortsighted and simplistic thinking about the global economy.

A Failure of Political Vision

Effective solutions to these problems were impeded by the failure of political thinking to keep up with the changes wrought by the war. Statesmen (all were men) and informed publics expected to return easily to the world of 1914, and for the global economy this meant the gold standard, fixed exchange rates, and monetary stability. Perhaps the most shortsighted policy was the United States' insistence on repayment of all war debts. This was based on a narrow-minded business logic that ignored the ability to pay, the massive asymmetries in the death and destruction from the war, and the negative effects on global recovery. The much richer and undamaged United States could have absorbed a process of partial or complete debt forgiveness with some increase in taxes, but political leaders were unable to think in such a long-term fashion. Additional problems were created when US tariffs were increased in 1922, further undermining the ability of Europeans to earn the foreign exchange needed to pay for debts.[49]

The result was the British and especially the French pressed the Germans to pay war reparations, which led to an international financial and political crisis in 1923. Following French military actions to collect reparation and the near financial and economic collapse of Germany, US officials were forced to act. Operating out of the public eye, government officials collaborated with private bankers to negotiate the Dawes Plan. This called for a reduction in annual reparations payments by Germany coupled with private bank loans from the United States to Germany. For five years these loans were available to permit Germany to make reparations payments and achieve an uneven economic recovery.[50]

A second and equally problematic attempt to restore stability was the British effort in 1925 to reestablish the pound–gold prewar rate and through this return to the gold standard. This decision failed to reflect the considerable inflation from the war and the weakening of Britain's competitive position. This meant Britain was likely to experience a chronic current account deficit, which would lead to selling pounds for gold and a continuing drain of gold from London to New York and Paris. A second weakness of the restored gold standard was the need to provide assured mechanisms for capital flows from surplus to deficit nations. The British were unable to provide this essential service and, though able, the domestic focus by the United States made it unreliable as a source of funding. Beginning in 1928, US imports (which provide funds to foreign export nations) and foreign lending contracted. The strain on the global financial system was too great and it collapsed in 1929.[51]

International Political Economy and the Great Depression

Although the imbalances from World War I and the patchwork efforts at resolution did not directly cause the global depression, they played a key role in producing the hurricane of deflation and unemployment that made it much worse. The US Federal Reserve moved in 1928 to restrict credit in order to contain the intense speculative excesses. This resulted in a decline in US banking lending, a drop in US production, and the bursting of the stock market bubble in 1929. The associated decline in US international lending contributed to an economic downturn in Europe and a decline in global commodity prices and stock prices.[52]

Interdependence meant nations had to be much more sophisticated in managing their economies or face very negative consequences. The economic decline in one major country quickly led to declines in others. In 1930, US manufacturing fell by 20 percent and exports by 35 percent, while unemployment in Britain rose from 10 percent to 16 percent and in Germany from 13 percent to 22 percent.[53] Governments, operating on the long-standing conservative precept that once prices had fallen far enough this would prompt private investors to return, did little to stem the tide. Only in 1931, when facing a "complete collapse of Germany's credit structure within a day or two" and the disintegration of the reparations system of the Dawes Plan, did President Herbert Hoover grant a moratorium on reparations payments. When this failed, Hoover again retreated into inaction. The German government then closed all banks and placed severe restrictions on foreign exchange transaction, which had the effect of freezing all foreign assets in Germany.[54]

Belatedly, as the crisis now began to focus on London, President Hoover reversed the ten-year US policy of refusing official participation in European affairs. Over several months in 1931, attempts were made to develop an international plan to preserve the British ability to redeem pounds for gold. The credits to achieve this were exhausted in September 1931, and the British government decided to abandon the gold standard. The next day the United States suffered massive gold withdrawals and by the end of October the first of a series of bank failures.[55] By now, the world was locked into a spiral of self-perpetuating decline: collapses in trade and domestic production; falling prices, profits, and investment; and rising loan defaults and bank failures. By early 1933, the banking system in the United States was perilously close to complete collapse. Only a decision by the newly elected President Roosevelt to close and rebuild the entire banking system averted this outcome.[56]

The global depression led many nations to attempt to cope by cutting themselves off from the world economy.[57] In 1930, Congress passed and President Hoover signed the much-maligned Smoot–Hawley tariff, which substantially increased US protectionism and triggered a series of retaliatory tariff increases around the world.[58] In 1931, Japan invaded Manchuria in China in an effort to gain exclusive control over markets and resources.[59] Once Britain left the gold standard, the pound fell by 30 percent, helping to promote devaluations from other nations. Britain also moved to organize a trading bloc of nations tied together by the use of sterling, mostly composed of colonies and former colonies. France responded by organizing a bloc of nations remaining on the gold standard. Germany, under the new Nazi government, used a vicious form of national economic planning, deficit spending, conscription, and arms production to spark a recovery. And in 1933, President Roosevelt took the United States off the gold standard to permit a depreciation of the dollar, rejected international cooperation, and focused on reorganization of the domestic economy.[60]

Notwithstanding these inward turns, the depression eventually led some nations to engage in cooperative efforts to rebuild the global economy. The first indications of a larger and more responsible international role for the United States came only one year after a strongly nationalistic recovery program. In June 1934, the US Congress adopted the Reciprocal Trade Agreements Act (RTAA). Unlike the British in the nineteenth century, the United States was prepared to negotiate reciprocal reductions in tariffs with other nations. Although many agreements did occur and tariffs fell on many goods, the RTAA is important for marking a shift away from a narrow nationalist–protectionist tariff policy dating back to the nation's founding. Also reflecting this change was the Tripartite Monetary Agreement of 1936 among the United States, France, and Great Britain. The purpose was to stabilize currency fluctuations and end the process of competitive devaluation. Unfortunately, the scope of the agreement was limited and currency stability remained an elusive goal.[61] A more thoroughgoing and effective organization of the international financial relations would come after World War II.

The Political Economy of American Hegemony, 1938–45

The three decades following the end of World War II in 1945 produced dramatic, even epoch-making changes in the global economy. Unprecedented prosperity, the development of new international economic institutions, rapid expansion of trade, and an extraordinary expansion of international cooperation were key elements in this new international economic order.

How did this happen? We posit the critical factor was political change in the United States brought on by the traumas of global depression and war. American leaders, who previously were hamstrung by public preferences rooted in isolationism, redefined US security and prosperity in terms of investing substantial American resources in global stability and economic growth. The vast economic, military, and political capabilities of the United States were devoted to rebuilding the global economy, blocking any advances by communist states and promoting international cooperation. This era marks a fundamental change in the nature and operation of global economic and political relations, a change directly attributable to the actions and interests of the dominant state. Perhaps most interesting is the liberal base of these actions, namely the view that global institutions needed to create the opportunity for mutual gains even as these arrangements also provided large benefits to the United States. The international political economy of this era is rich in details that raise important theoretical and empirical questions. We focus here on the strategy of hegemony, the nature and effects of new global institutions, and the weaknesses within and changes in the underpinnings of hegemony.

The Strategy of Hegemony

The concept of hegemony is a somewhat strange idea that may seem to be a bundle of contradictions. It is rooted in the notion of dominance and control, perhaps even exploitation of the weak by the strong. But hegemony is also closely linked to the ideas of order and even stability. Perhaps most bizarre is the connection to interests and to mutual gains. Hegemony is all of these things and more, as it takes on different meanings when seen in historical terms but also depending on where it is discussed. In the nineteenth century and before, a key feature of hegemony was the somewhat matter-of-fact forms of domination and control, indeed exploitation, by powerful states over weaker nations and peoples. Britain had few qualms about naked and even brutal control over India, and these policies and views were widely shared by the leaders and citizens of France, Russia, Germany, and the United States before 1940.

But something happened, exactly what is unclear, but mostly it was the ability of the weak to fight back and sometimes win but always impose large costs on the powerful. Beginning especially in the second half of the twentieth century, powerful, even hegemonic, states began to change in recognizing the need for fixing the rules so that even poor states and peoples can gain along with the rich and powerful. The ideas of mutual gains, global stability, and preventing the strong from using force to take over the weak began to appear as part of the definition of the interests of the strongest. New rules and institutions were created by the powerful that were built around mutual gains for all. Later, even poor and exploited nations, previously very hostile to the global system of powerful capitalist states and capitalist firms, began to join in this same system and experience substantial economic gains. Hegemony is the term we in international political economy use to understand this process, perhaps incompletely, but nonetheless with powerful effects.

World War II left the United States as the dominant power in the world and over time the US government developed a commitment to using this power to preserve global stability and for remaking the global economic and political system.[62] Though the Soviet Union and later China would resist and even challenge the United States, they did so from a much weaker position of power. The strategic elements of fighting World War II were framed around bringing overwhelming military power against Germany and Japan. This placed great importance on the productive capabilities of war, and in this area the United States had enormous advantages. Not only did the United States possess the largest economy, but its productivity – output per unit of input – was also far higher than any other nation. By 1944, the United States was producing 40 percent of the world's armaments, and its productivity was twice that of Germany and five times that of Japan. The US economy grew in real terms from $88.6 billion in 1941 to $135 billion in 1945.[63] Much of German, Japanese, and Soviet industrial capacity was destroyed by the war.

The depression and war from 1929–45 created significant psychological and political scars that affected the economic choices and overall strategy of the United States. The fear of recurrent depression was strong and pressed governments to act much more vigorously in promoting domestic prosperity. Between 1944 and 1950, the United States was determined to promote not only economic growth at home but also in Europe and even in Germany and Japan. Initially, this focused on financing the global imbalances left from the destruction and disruption of the war. This meant providing the funds to sustain a US current account surplus, which began with a large loan to Britain in 1946.[64] Continued economic deterioration across Europe led in 1947 to a much more systematic arrangement for capital transfers in the Marshall Plan. Provided not as a loan but rather as an outright capital transfer, the Marshall Plan was linked to rebuilding the European economy – including Germany – in order to stabilize that area, gain support for liberal capitalism, and undermine the political appeal of communism and the Soviet Union. Extending from 1947–51, the Marshall Plan provided more than $12 billion dollars to Europe and helped promote the idea of European economic integration. A similar but less visible policy, known as the Dodge Plan, was adopted for Japan in 1948, with the goal of rebuilding the economy and establishing Japan as a barrier to Soviet expansion in Asia.[65] The long-term effects of the injection of US capital into Europe and Asia were to jump-start economic growth, help bind these nations to the US vision of global order, and clearly enshrine the US dollar as the world's key currency. That is, the dollar became the primary medium for international payment, with the currency serving as the store of value throughout the world.[66]

The effort to provide capital to deficit nations and rebuild economies operated in parallel to an effort to create new international institutions designed to promote stability for the global economy. This included formal and informal institutions. Formal institutions are typically the result of deliberate negotiations and result in a set of written rules and regular decision-making processes. By contrast, informal institutions require more tacit and even nuanced arrangements that usually involve acquiesce instead of open agreement. In this instance, formal institutions include those devised in 1944 at an international conference in Bretton Woods, New Hampshire. These included the International Monetary Fund and the International Bank for Reconstruction and Development – the World Bank. Developed a bit later was the General Agreement on Tariffs and Trade. Informal institutions included such things as the arrangements for an international oil regime based on creating a global market for oil. These new institutions had the broader purpose of regularizing and stabilizing the processes of trade and finance, thereby removing the deep uncertainties that had damaged the system in the recent past and reversed globalization since 1914.

Beyond the immediate economic difficulties were many political and security problems that affected efforts to rebuild the global economy. Perhaps the most important was persuading the leadership and populations of many countries to participate in a new liberal world order. This depended on developing confidence in the United States and its willingness to commit its resources to security and prosperity. After all, the United States had withdrawn into isolationism after 1919, had engaged in economic nationalism in the 1930s, and was very late becoming involved in the recent global wars. This became an especially acute issue when the Soviets, already in occupation of central Europe, engaged in threatening actions in Germany in 1948. US leaders believed the success of the postwar system rested on US power and preventing the use or threat of force from affecting the shape of international politics. One important result was the creation of the North Atlantic Treaty Organization (NATO), which involved a standing US commitment to defend Western Europe against attack. In 1950, the United States moved toward a large military buildup in response to the Korean War and signed a peace treaty with Japan, which also included a security guarantee. These actions provided a security base that would permit development of such institutions as European economic and political integration, as well as support long-term investments that would promote global economic growth.

Growth of the Global Economy

International trade and economic growth grew faster during the three decades after 1945 than in any previous time, resuming the upward trends of the nineteenth century disrupted by the era from 1914–45.

As we can see from Table 4.6, per capita growth rates accelerated after 1950 and growth rates for merchandise exports increased even faster. After 1973, growth rates for both GDP and exports declined but exports continued to grow much more rapidly than GDP. As a result of these trends, exports as a percent of GDP doubled from 1950–73 and more than tripled between 1950 and 1998.

Global Institutions and Management of the Global Economy

One of the most distinctive and important features of the post–1945 world was the creation of a set of new formal and informal international institutions for managing the global economy. With these actions, global leaders, especially in the United States, reversed much of the economic thinking of the nineteenth century and acknowledged the economic significance played by political arrangements to manage markets. During the 1920s, an array of mostly informal institutions, often relying on actions by private firms, had been created to deal with economic complexities.[67] The new institutions of the Bretton Woods era were the result of a coordinated effort by the United States to organize international negotiations and sustain cooperation. These institutions had formal rules, a competent and well-paid staff, and significant monetary resources. The values and preferences of these institutions were defined by the United

Table 4.6 World Trade and Economic Growth, 1870–1998 (real terms, based on 1990 $US)

	1873–1913	1913–50	1950–73	1973–98
World per capita GDP growth rates	1.30%	0.91%	2.93%	1.33%
World merchandise Exports growth rates	3.4%	0.9%	7.9%	5.1%

	1870	1913	1950	1973	1998
World Exports (billion 1990 dollars) Merchandise	50	212	296	1,691	5,817
Exports % GDP	4.6	7.9	5.5	10.5	17.2

Sources: Data from Angus Maddison, *The World Economy*, Paris: OECD, 2006, 265, 361; Ronald Findlay and Kevin O'Rourke, *Power and Plenty*, Princeton: Princeton University Press, 2007, 510.

States and included convertible currencies, lowering trade barriers, fixed exchange rates, and the promotion of a multilateral system of trade and payments.

The belief in fixed exchange rates was based on the value of stability in international transactions and the largely negative experience with floating rates in the 1930s. Leaders were also remembering the "golden age" of fixed rates under the gold standard. The fixed exchange rates under Bretton Woods were embodied in the IMF and were based on a gold exchange system in which the US dollar was fixed in price to gold at $35 per ounce and the US government committed to redeem gold for dollars at that price, but *only* for foreigners. Then, other nations would fix their currencies to the dollar and intervene in foreign exchange markets to keep the currency value within a narrow band around the fixed rate. This worked because the United States held the vast majority of the gold in the world, more than enough to meet all private traders of the time.[68] This system would ultimately fail in the 1970s, when private traders got too big. The global management of the system of fixed exchange rates was assigned to the new International Monetary Fund. Resources for the operation of the IMF came from payments of gold and national currencies from member states. The United States provided 31 percent of IMF resources and thereby had the largest share of the voting power.

The main original purpose of the IMF was to provide short-term loans to nations experiencing a current account deficit. Nations would use the funds to support their fixed exchange rate and, as a condition of the loan, would be required to adopt national economic policies designed to eliminate the deficit. This usually meant some combination of reducing government spending, lowering money supply growth, and restricting wage increases. The goal of this "belt tightening" was to induce an economic downturn, higher unemployment, and lower inflation. The reduction in relative prices would hopefully make the nation more competitive, and with exports rising and imports falling the current account deficit would disappear. The IMF took on the role of enforcing the conservative views of the US financial community. During that era, current account deficits were seen as a result of domestic profligacy and reductions in domestic prices were necessary to restore trade competitiveness.[69] Should a nation's current account deficit be more serious – a structural and not temporary deficit – the IMF would permit a devaluation of the exchange rate. The fixed rate would be changed so the currency would decline against other currencies.

The second major institution created at Bretton Woods was the International Bank for Reconstruction and Development, or the World Bank. Its purpose was to supply longer-term capital via loans in order to support the recovery of war-torn nations. However, the capita deficiency of Europe and Japan, especially in face of the Cold War need for rapid development, was too large for the new and fledgling World Bank. Over the first decade of its existence, the bank played only a marginal role in the postwar reconstruction process. By the late 1950s, there was considerable interest in economic development for the Third World. The World Bank became an important source of capital, with over $1 billion annually in new loans.[70]

The third member of the Bretton Woods institutions is the General Agreement on Tariffs and Trade, which has a more complex lineage. GATT was not directly a result of Bretton Woods, though the sentiments for free trade through multilateral negotiation of tariff reductions was a core element of the thinking there. But achievement of free trade was a more difficult nut to crack in the wake of the protectionism of the 1930s and the worry by many that US productivity would swamp their economy. Concurrent negotiations from 1946 to 1948 yielded a treaty on processes and procedures for future negotiations on free trade – GATT – and an international organization to manage the process – the International Trade Organization or ITO. However, the ITO could not gain ratification from the US Senate because it called for treating the United States as a special case for purposes of trade. The ITO never came into existence, and after 1950 GATT emerged as the institutional base for negotiating and managing free trade. In 1994, negotiations led to transforming GATT into the new World Trade Organization.[71]

For forty-six years GATT served as the primary international organization for trade, providing a forum for negotiating reductions in tariff and other trade barriers. Over a series of negotiating "Rounds," GATT led to a substantial decline in tariff rates.[72] In the decades prior to 1945, US tariffs averaged between 30 percent and 45 percent of dutiable imports. By 1955, these had been cut to 15 percent and by 1970 to 12 percent.[73] This data helps to illustrate a key fact about GATT and US trade objectives: US leaders wanted to lower tariffs to achieve *freer* trade. However, for much of the postwar era they were not seeking free trade, as this was politically unattainable. Although tariffs on manufactured goods fell substantially, trade in services and agricultural products were largely excluded from GATT negotiations. Only in the 1970s and 1980s did negotiations advance to non-tariff barriers to trade and to agriculture and services.[74]

The Bretton Woods institutions did contribute substantially to rule-making for the global economy and to the expansion of trade and global markets. Also helping to sustain economic growth was the availability of oil on global markets at stable prices. As we can see from Table 4.7, inexpensive, but imported, oil became the primary energy source supporting the growing global economy. This was especially true for Europe and Japan. Between 1950 and 1970 Western Europe increased its use of oil from 14.3 percent to 55.6 percent of total energy needs, while Japan

Table 4.7 World Energy Consumption by Source, 1950–72 (% of total)

Source	1950	1960	1965	1972
Coal	55.7	44.2	39.0	28.7
Oil	28.9	35.8	39.4	46.0
Natural Gas	8.9	13.5	15.5	18.4
Electricity	6.5	6.4	6.2	6.9

Source: Data from Joel Darmstadter and Hans Landsberger, "The Crisis," in Raymond Vernon (ed.), *The Oil Crisis*, New York: Norton, 1976, 19.

increased its oil consumption from 5 percent to 68.8 percent of its energy used. From 1962 to 1972 imports of oil by Europe and Japan rose from 6.17 to 18.84 million barrels per day.[75]

The role of the corporation in creating the new global economy was considerable. The privately owned, limited liability corporation was the dominant form of economic institution in advanced nations by the turn of the twentieth century. Some of these firms, especially in areas such as distribution, had begun to operate across national borders. In the first era of globalization, there was considerable global investment, most of it in bonds and portfolio investment. By contrast, foreign direct investment (FDI), which involves the purchase of foreign assets in order to operate a business, has become the dominant form of global investment in the twentieth century. The East India Company is a very early example of this strategy, but large numbers of such enterprises emerged in the twentieth century mainly in areas such as oil and raw materials. The greatest expansion of firms with production and/or distribution facilities in at least two nations – multinational corporations – has come in the years after 1945.[76]

The process of foreign direct investment in the years to 1973 was overwhelmingly an American phenomenon and helped to demonstrate the new forms of global production. About one-half of all FDI by the early 1970s was by US firms, which produced $172 billion of goods and services abroad. By contrast, only $43.5 billion in goods were produced in the United States for export. That is, production abroad by US firms was four times larger than US exports.[77]

This growth was focused in a wave of FDI by US firms in Europe after 1958, the result of a confluence of political and economic circumstances. The European Economic Community (EEC) (discussed in the next section) in 1958 created lower tariff rates for those inside the EEC than for those operating outside; that is, tariffs discriminated in favor of firms operating within the six nations of the EEC. The US government was prepared to tolerate this discrimination, but only if members of the EEC would permit US firms to locate there and be treated as if they were European firms.[78]

Why would US firms want to do this, especially given that operating abroad requires new capabilities and creates new risks? The answer lies in the basic nature of most multinational corporations (MNCs): typically MNCs of this era are large firms with an oligopolistic position in their markets. These firms have large fixed costs and need a substantial share of the overall markets for their products to sustain profits. Moving abroad to nations with a relatively wealthy population is an essential strategy for maintaining market share. Such firms also seek to differentiate their products, often through creating a brand by sophisticated marketing. This and similar advantages permit expanding profits by operating in new markets. Further, the products of a firm and the technologies of production had matured to the point where a firm operating in another nation can compete successfully with a domestic firm. The initial strategy of producing at home and exporting may have become inadequate and the firm may need to move abroad to take advantage of lower costs or develop foreign resources to compete with a foreign producer. This "product cycle" theory of the multinational firm may be especially relevant to understanding US firms in the 1950s and 1960s. A combination of factors pushed US firms abroad: they were facing competition from rising European firms moving into markets pioneered by US firms; US firms wanted to maintain market share and exploit special brand advantages; and many feared the effects of discriminatory tariffs on their exports. Of course, in the background defining the ability to make these calculations was the new global economic order created by US power, which permitted these calculations relating to long-term investment in foreign lands.[79]

Perhaps the clearest and most important indicator of the success of American hegemony was the creation of the European Economic Community, with the signing of the Treaty of Rome in March 1957, just twelve years after the end of World War II.[80] The EEC was to develop into perhaps the most important international institution, with the expansion of membership and the achievement of considerable political and economic integration. There were several factors at work. The United States consistently encouraged efforts for integration in the Marshall Plan and later. The French government was a strong advocate, anxious to bring German industrial power under international supervision and wanting a strong Europe able to deal with the Soviet Union and the United States on equal terms. Interestingly, the US concept of world order could accommodate the idea of an independent Europe, at least one also closely allied to the United States. The EEC also emerged out of negotiations among the Europeans that led to smaller-scale customs unions. In 1955, negotiations began to create the EEC, reaching fruition with the 1957 Rome treaty.[81]

The agreement established a timetable for the reduction of tariffs and quantitative restrictions on trade. Generally, this schedule was met or exceeded, with tariffs slashed dramatically and quotas eliminated entirely. Full currency convertibility was established among fourteen European nations in 1958, facilitated by resources from the IMF.

Nature and Effects of International Institutions

Formal and system-wide institutions for the purpose of managing the global economy are a unique feature of the past eighty years, and especially during the time after World War II. Perhaps more remarkable, not only have these institutions persisted, they have expanded membership and function. Today, membership in the IMF and WTO includes nearly all economically relevant nations,[82] and the WTO has much greater powers than were ever imagined at the birth of GATT. Formal international organizations whose membership is composed of governments (IGOs) number in the dozens. The number of international non-governmental organizations (INGOs) is in the hundreds. How do we explain the massive proliferation of international institutions, many of which start before the beginnings of recent globalization? What effects do these institutions have?

First, we should recognize the wide variety of international organizations, along with an increasing role for MNCs, also create a variety of new actors in international politics. Though many of these actors are connected to nations, the resources and effects cannot be reduced to nations. Included in the examination of institutions are the many less formal arrangements of international economic relations.[83] Our focus should thus be on the broader category of international regimes, which refers to a process for the convergence of elite actors' expectations about the principles, norms, rules, and procedures related to deciding about international economic and political issues. Thus, we need to understand the underlying and often tacit common thinking related to formal and informal international institutions, as well as the operations of the institutions themselves.[84] Second, at the core of understanding the origins of IGOs and INGOs is the matter of explaining the sources of cooperation. Third, the consequences of international institutions can be linked to the ability of IGOs, INGOs, and MNCs to alter the structure of choices made in global affairs.[85]

Much of this can be reduced to the answers and issues related to two questions: (1) Why would nations want to create regimes, especially as formal institutions? (2) What consequences do regimes have for the global economy? One key element of the first question includes consideration of the timing: why the proliferation of regimes and institutions after 1945? The timing of the development of a much richer institutional order in the global economy can be linked to the events of the first half of the twentieth century. The confluence of two horrific global wars and debilitating global economic collapse, all in a context of global information and communication systems, was more than sufficient to focus minds on the dangers in international affairs. Coupled with the postwar power of the United States, cooperation among nations for the development of institutions to prevent more war and depression is a likely outcome.

More general arguments for the presence of regimes and institutions relate to the calculations of gains and losses by state and economic leaders. Broadly, leaders recognize that markets frequently work poorly and can have negative consequences. Regimes and institutions help to plug those gaps usually by creating standards for exchange and interaction. For example, markets contain considerable uncertainty and regimes can operate so as to reduce uncertainty. Regimes provide rules that affect the behavior of states and firms and thereby reduce uncertainty related to future planning. Regimes can also supply information that permits market participants to make better decisions. For example, the WTO requires nations to organize their economies according to certain rules as a condition of membership. Joining the WTO provides information to existing and potential investors about the future rule systems for a nation. Regimes can also provide information to other states that reduce uncertainty about future behavior. Regimes also reduce the costs associated with interacting in global affairs, for states and firms. Large parts of the terms for economic exchange are established by regimes, thereby facilitating trade. For example, most of the various potential barriers to trade have been redefined by the rules of regimes and are not subject to renegotiation each time a transaction takes place.

The effects of regimes and institutions are more difficult to measure, but research frequently provides evidence that nations and firms comply with the rules. This is not surprising, given the gains from compliance. What about the penalties for non-compliance? If frequent, such non-compliance will lead states and firms to shun this nation as untrustworthy and remove it from the benefits of participation in the global economy. Further, once the costs of creating a regime have been paid, continuing interaction based on the terms of a regime creates benefits that reinforce the value of the regime.[86]

Challenges to US Hegemony: Money and Oil, 1971–3

The global economy and global political relations are subject to considerable flux; change is endemic to this system. Such was true for the position of the United States atop the system as hegemon. Acting as leader for a liberal global system contributed to the dissipation of US power and/or to the relative increase in the power of other states and even of multinational firms. Over time, the position of the United States has changed in important ways as a result of shifts in power relations.

The 1970s brought important changes in the global economy reflecting and confirming this alteration in power. We will consider two arenas where this happened. The link between the dollar and gold, the very basis for the system of fixed exchange rates, came apart. And the ability to rely on a secure and inexpensive source of energy – oil – was seriously weakened. How and why these changes took place and the results are of considerable importance.

The Collapse of Fixed Exchange Rates

The dollar as the key currency was a vital element in US hegemony and this conveyed enormous benefits: the rest of the world was prepared to accept the dollar in payment for goods and services sold to the United States. The burdens of hegemony were considerable in the 1960s, which meant more and more dollars ended up in foreign banks as the United States expended its money to fight foreign wars and pay for goods and services. The stabilizing force was always thought to be the tie between the dollar and gold. But this depended on the ratio of US gold to the amount of dollars in foreign, and increasingly private, hands. The costs of hegemony, combined with expansion of the global economy resulting from US hegemony, ultimately brought down the gold–dollar link and the system of fixed exchange rates.

The economic growth of Europe and Japan, a weakening of the US balance of trade, and the rapid growth of international capital markets spelled doom for the Bretton Woods system of fixed exchange rates and the role of gold. As early as 1960, the liabilities created by foreign-held dollars exceeded the US supply of gold. That same year, the price of gold in private markets (remember, the United States maintained a fixed price for gold at $35 ounce, though gold continued to trade outside that arrangement) reached $40 dollars an ounce. Over the decade of the 1960s, the gold–dollar link became less and less tenable.[87]

The economic recovery of the rest of the capitalist world, a major goal of US policy, proceeded apace after 1960. Combined with the weakening of US competitiveness in global trade and the continuing drain for global military engagement, dollars accumulated abroad in larger amounts. Between 1960 and 1972, US exports as a percent of world exports fell from 18 percent to 13 percent. This is not surprising, with the recovery of other nations. But more negative were the trends in the overall US balance of payments. Tables 4.8 and 4.9 provide data on these momentous trends.

These data help to identify the specific areas of US weakness in its balance of payments. The 1960 balance of trade surplus and investment income shown in Table 4.8 were large enough to offset the outflows from military commitments and external investment. But by the early 1970s, the trade balance had slipped into deficit, while military and capital

Table 4.8 US Balance of Payments, 1960–72 (billions $US)

Year	Exports	Imports	Net	Military	Invest Inc.	Current Act. Bal.	Capital Act. Bal.	Error	Net Liquidity Bal.
1960	19.7	14.8	4.9	-2.8	2.8	1.8	-3.0	-1.1	-3.7
1965	26.5	21.5	5.0	-2.1	2.1	4.3	-6.1	-0.5	-2.5
1970	42.0	39.8	2.2	-3.4	6.4	0.4	-3.4	-1.2	-3.9
1971	42.8	45.5	-2.7	-2.9	8.9	-2.8	-6.8	-10.8	-22.0
1972	48.8	55.7	-6.9	-3.6	9.8	-8.4	-1.5	-3.5	-13.9

Source: Data from John Odell, *U.S. International Monetary Policy*, Princeton: Princeton University Press, 1982, 203–5.

Note: Some items in the balance of payments have been omitted.

Table 4.9 US Trade in Manufactured Goods, 1960–71 (billions $US)

	1960	1965	1971
Low-Tech Goods			
Exports	3.57	4.41	6.23
Imports	4.49	7.35	14.55
Balance	–0.92	–2.94	–8.32
High-Tech Goods			
Exports	9.01	13.03	24.19
Imports	2.37	3.89	15.90
Balance	6.64	9.14	8.29

Source: Data from Robert Gilpin, *U.S. Power and the Multinational Corporation*, New York: Basic Books, 1975, 193.

outflows continued. The overall balance fell deeply into deficit in 1971 and 1972 due to unreported outflows of funds that show up in the "error" account.

Table 4.9 helps narrow the problem to an expanding deficit in low-technology products while the surplus in high-technology products grew much less. The result was a widening trade deficit. Much of the problem stemmed from a weakening of US global competitiveness as a result of rising US prices and wages. The consumer price index, a measure of price levels, rose from 1.7 percent in 1965 to nearly 6 percent in 1970 and over 6 percent in 1973. Because productivity increases did not keep pace, prices of US products became less competitive abroad. The result was a rapid rise in imports of low-tech products, a relative flattening in exports of these products and a rapid rise in the importation of all products. By 1971, the surplus of a decade earlier had vanished.

The outflow of dollars from trade, investment, and foreign policy created a cumulating pressure against the link between the dollar and gold.[88] The only way the United States could ever match the gold it held with the dollars in foreign hands was to raise the price of gold a lot, thereby devaluing the dollar. Anticipating this outcome, global financial speculators were betting against the dollar by selling dollars for gold, which created additional pressure on the United States to act. Having rejected finding a cooperative solution, on August 15, 1971 President Nixon unilaterally announced a new policy. The United States suspended indefinitely the commitment to redeem dollars for gold (remember, only foreign central banks could do this), imposed domestic wage and price controls, demanded a devaluation of the dollar against other currencies, and placed a 10 percent tariff surcharge on imported goods. This policy amounted to a unilateral rejection of many of the basic rules and values of the international monetary system largely created by the United States and demanded that US military and economic allies adjust their economic systems to solve this problem. This was an audacious act and marked the beginning of a much more unilateral and nationalist economic policy by the United States.

Over the next eighteen months, negotiations among the great capitalist states focused on the future of the gold–dollar link, fixed exchange rates, the rates of exchange, and which nations would make the largest adjustments. Conflict between the United States and the French and Japanese was particularly intense, especially over the effort to transfer some of the cost of US international commitments. A temporary deal was reached in December 1971 at the Smithsonian Institutions in Washington. The United States devalued the dollar in terms of gold, but made no future commitment to redeem dollars for gold. The other major capitalist states agree to a devaluation averaging 8 percent (Japan's was 16.9 percent) and adjusted their currencies with each other. There was no agreement on trade issues. For the moment, fixed exchange rates returned.

But the US payments deficits continued and in early 1973 prompted renewed selling of the dollar and another currency crisis. The United States responded by unilaterally devaluing the dollar by 10 percent and threatened another similar devaluation unless the Japanese and West Europeans agreed to let their currencies float against the dollar. By March 1973, the system of fixed exchange rates had collapsed in the advanced capitalist world. This element of the Bretton Woods system disintegrated for two reasons. First, fixed rates cannot work in an environment of substantial global economic change. When changes take place, the rate system must change too; that had not happened. The US shift from surplus to deficit in its payments balance made adjustment necessary; the link to gold was undermined by the limited quantity of US gold and an expanding supply of dollars to the world.

The second reason was the substantial growth of international financial institutions and the capital they controlled. Much of this can be traced to the development of the Eurocurrency market. The outflow of dollars over the 1960s began to accumulate in foreign banks. London bankers, an ingenious lot, chose to lend out these dollars rather than return them to the United States. Banks in the United States saw the profits associated with lending in this new and unregulated market and began following MNCs to Europe. The rise of the Eurocurrency market and the expansion of US MNCs and international banks were linked together by the late 1960s. This unregulated market developed into a system of bank credit, a Eurobond market (bonds denominated in dollars but sold outside the United States), and a large volume of funds moving across borders in search of higher yields. In 1970, the Eurocurrency market approached $70 billion and in three years would grow to over $200 billion. This was almost nine times the size of US foreign exchange reserves and was capable of overwhelming even coordinated government action to preserve a fixed exchange rate.[89] In the early 1970s, the new global actors – MNCs and international banks – lost confidence in the system of fixed exchange rates. By March 1973, the governments of the capitalist world had little choice but to accept the end of this system and usher in a new era of flexible exchange rates.[90]

Loss of Control Over Oil

Concurrent with the dramatic changes in the international monetary order was an equally significant structural change in the global regime for oil. Several fundamental shifts in power relationships converged in the early 1970s to produce an end to Western control of oil. These included changes in the political and military relationship of the United States and Britain to Middle Eastern states, shifts in the demand and supply of oil, the ability of several developing nations to gain physical control over oil within their borders, and the 1973 Yom Kippur War. US domination of the global oil regime, operating through large multinational oil companies, came to an end as prices skyrocketed and an embargo demonstrated American vulnerabilities.

From the 1930s onward, the discovery and exploitation of vast oil reserves in the Middle East (especially the Persian Gulf) fueled the expansion of the world economy. In the early decades, however, these reserves and the profits they generated were controlled not by local governments but by seven large Western oil companies (dubbed the Seven Sisters), which indirectly benefited the United States and Great Britain. Under the concession system, private firms controlled all aspects of the industry while paying modest royalties to the states from whose territory the oil was extracted.[91] Chafing under these arrangements, five major oil exporters formed the Organization of Petroleum Exporting Countries (OPEC) in 1960 to bargain for greater control over their own resources.[92]

Against resistance from Western firms and governments, little was accomplished in the first decade of OPECs' existence. But a shifting configuration of global power and markets opened the door to important change. Between 1968 and 1971, as part of a global military retrenchment, Great Britain withdrew its military forces from the Middle East, leaving a military and political vacuum it had filled for more than a century. At this same time, the United States was mired in the Vietnam War, which restricted its ability to use military force anywhere else in the world. These developments undermined the ability to defend the international oil regime based on cheap and plentiful oil.[93]

During the years after 1945, the rich world became much more dependent on oil from the Middle East. This was a result of declining production in the United States and rapid increases in demand by much of the world. From 1957–72, oil production peaked in the United States and the proportion of total global oil supplies from the United States declined from 43.1 percent to 21.1 percent. At the same time, global production totals from the Middle East increased from 19.4 percent to 41 percent. Necessarily, the United States was forced to increase its oil imports from 11 percent to 35.5 percent of consumption. Even as these shifts in the distribution of production and consumption were occurring, the basic global relationship of supply and demand shifted toward shortages. Supplies from all sources could not keep up with rising demand, making price increases very likely.[94]

The mostly poor nations where oil was located were historically in little control over the amount of oil produced or the price charged. The changing circumstances in oil led the leaders of several of these nations to challenge control over these decisions by the large multinational oil companies. Beginning in Libya in 1970, and soon spreading to other states, governments used various forms of intimidation to increase their take, the level of ownership of the oil, and even the decisions about price. The tightening of global supplies accelerated the process, as countries began leapfrogging each other in terms of demands for control over production and price. The devaluations of the dollar in 1971 and 1973 also prompted additional price increases, as oil was priced in dollars. When the United States was forced to lift import quotas for oil in 1973, this signaled the beginning of a new round of negotiations.[95]

The shifting relations of oil, markets, money, and military power were further upset when Anwar Sadat, president of Egypt, launched an October 1973 attack on Israel that began the Yom Kippur War. Continuing support for Israel by the United States led the Middle East dominated Organization of Petroleum Exporting Countries to unite around a large increase in oil prices (from $3.01 to $5.12 per barrel) and, with less agreement, to impose an oil embargo. This consisted of a production cutback and a ban on shipments of oil to the United States and the Netherlands. By January 1974, oil prices had risen to $11.65 a barrel and the United States was confronted by a shift in power relations that, in Secretary of State Henry Kissinger's words, "altered irrevocably the world as it had grown up in the postwar period."[96]

Conclusion: British and American Hegemony Compared

In the famous inaugural address by President John Kennedy in 1961, he asserted the United States was prepared to "pay any price, bear any burden, meet any hardship, support any friend, oppose any foe, in order to assure the survival and the success of liberty." Some might wonder, why did the United States adopt the burdens and the costs of hegemony? And others might ask, what were the consequences for the global economy of US hegemony? Yet others might want to know how the experience of the United States and Great Britain help us understand the political origins of a global economy? For make no mistake, economic systems always depend on political systems.

Understanding motives can be very hard, and so it is for the United States. Was the United States acting to provide a set of generalized benefits to the global community, even as it sacrificed short-term gains for itself? Or did the United States provide the collective benefits to the rest of the world because it was able to achieve gains greater than any other state, perhaps by forcing others to pay much of the costs? The evidence for a combination of both perspectives is strong. The United States was clearly the nation that bore the greatest part of the costs of creating and sustaining international order. The United States provided billions of dollars in direct grants to nations to promote economic recovery, spent far more on the military and global deployment of US troops, and did a disproportionate part of the fighting and dying. The result was substantial economic gains and relative peace, enjoyed by most nations in the US-defined sphere. In terms of gains, the US economy grew rapidly until 1973, but many countries in Europe and Asia grew even faster. Under US hegemony, there was considerable economic catch-up. The strongest case for special US benefits is in the effects of the dollar as key currency. These gains were more evident after the end of fixed exchange rates, but the United States was able to pay its international obligations with its own currency because other nations continued to accept payment in dollars.[97]

The key to understanding US purposes in sustaining global stability is political and less purely economic, and can be found in the beliefs of US leaders about the military and political costs from the dissolution of world order. The experience of depression and war convinced a broad spectrum of American elites that US prosperity and security depended on prosperity and peace abroad. And the rise of Soviet communism came to convince even conservative US elites of the necessity of major global efforts. Failing to block the acts of aggressive and hostile states and/or failing to protect and enhance the system of global capitalism would doom full employment and free enterprise in the United States. If a hostile power were to gain control over the resources of Europe and Asia, this would make necessary a garrison state in the United States and lead to another world war. In an important sense, the benefits of a liberal world order were great and the costs of foregoing that order were unacceptable.[98]

Comparing the periods of British and American dominance helps to answer questions about the consequences and the political economy of hegemony.[99] There are important differences in the patterns of international political economy in the nineteenth and twentieth centuries.[100] Many of these differences can be related to differences in the political roles played by Britain and the United States. The British effort to establish a system of free trade was focused in the 1846–70 period. This consisted largely of leading by example, while expecting others to follow through enlightened self-interest. Beyond this, the British government devoted little political effort to organizing and directing global policy and practice. The system of free trade arose largely from bilateral treaties, made multilateral by MFN, in combination with Britain's unilateral free trade commitment. Britain was certainly the key player in promoting free trade, but was unable to stop the reversal of free trade policies during the 1870s and after. This system of free trade lacked a clear commitment of British power to its creation and preservation, but such was the nature of global economic policy in the nineteenth century. Britain even refused any direct help to its own investors or businesses operating abroad, believing this was not a governmental responsibility. The international monetary system was also largely informal, with states able to opt in and opt out somewhat easily and with the British defining the gold standard for all simply through its own monetary policy. This came not out of a sense of responsibility for systemic stability, but instead from calculations of national interest.[101]

In the twentieth century, US strategy was much more disciplined and organized, with formal international institutions and a formal multilateral system of negotiations. The twentieth-century global economy is based on explicit political organization through formal and expanding systems of state cooperation. This is true for GATT/WTO and the IMF. Why the differences? The power position of the United States in relation to the rest of the system in the twentieth century is much greater than for Britain in the nineteenth century. Two other factors matter: the Victorian state was much less organized and was mostly incapable of domestic economic management, much less global economic management. The relatively laissez-faire world of the nineteenth century is mostly a result of weak political capabilities by states, with the inability to intervene rationalized by appeals to the benefits of free markets. Moreover, the high-spending and high-tax state of the late eighteenth century provided a negative model for those in the mid-nineteenth century. At the same time, large parts of the global economy of 1900 were organized politically through the relationship of imperialism, direct and indirect.[102]

By contrast, the twentieth-century US state was bolstered by decades of growing capabilities for economic management and by the broad commitments to the welfare of all citizens. Further, the complexities of a global economy and the consequences of a lack of political management were much less evident in the 1870s than in the 1970s. War and depression provided stark evidence of the effects of failing to act. And, by that point nations could draw on considerable systems of economic management and apply those capabilities for global management. Moreover, the mobilization of large parts of an attentive public connected together by real-time communications systems – and working from memory of past economic collapse – produced substantial incentives for political management of the global economy.

The concept of structural power helps illuminate both the process and politics of hegemony. Structural power refers to the ability to define the context for and the parameters within which political and economic choices will take place. This occurs because the resources controlled by a nation or group are so substantial that others must take them into account in making decisions. For example, in a capitalist society, control over the investment resources of the nation by firms and banks gives them great influence over economic growth. One indicator of structural power is the ability to persuade others to adopt the preferred form of action, rather than being coerced. Hegemons and other political leaders prefer persuasion to military force, because this is much more efficient.

In the nineteenth century, the British had a strong preference for persuasion and used it almost exclusively as the form of exercising power over other advanced states. Unilateral efforts to promote free trade are an example. The United States also used persuasion in relation to the advanced parts of the "free world," reserving coercion for poor communist states. But this form of structural power, often expressed in terms of freedom and democracy, was bolstered by the provision of military security, large capital and technology flows, and other forms of tangible benefits. There were clear collective gains for large parts of the world and this greatly enhanced US structural power and thereby its persuasiveness.

The sticking power of the US global order has been substantial, a result of the gains being generated. Remarkably, the breakdown of the Bretton Woods international monetary system and Western control over oil in the early 1970s did not lead to an international economic breakdown. The basic institutions of the global economy continued to operate as before. Though economic instability followed as growth slowed and inflation increased, after about a decade of adjustment, growth resumed based on new relationships between states and firms. In the midst of the large instability during the late 1970s, the Chinese Communists chose to join this system and wager their political survival on this decision.

By contrast, the weakening of Britain in the 1920s and 1930s coupled with the United States' failure to contribute to global stability was primarily responsible for the depression and war that followed.[103] Perhaps we are now seeing the effects of a real weakening in US power with global financial and economic crises. The debate over the effects of the United States' weakening and China's strengthening is a topic we will reserve for later chapters.

Key Concepts (see Glossary)

Bretton Woods System
Corn Laws
Dawes Plan
Eurocurrency (Eurodollar)
European (Economic)
    Community (EC, EEC)

General Agreement on Tariffs
    and Trade (GATT)
Global Economy
Gold Standard
Hegemony
Interdependence

International Monetary Fund (IMF)

Knowledge-Intensive Production

Marshall Plan

Mercantilism

Most Favored Nation (MFN)

Organization of Petroleum Exporting Countries (OPEC)

Regime

Reverse Engineering

Smoot–Hawley Tariff

Discussion Questions

1 What are the most important defining features of a global economy?

2 How is the emergence of a global economy related to the Industrial Revolution?

3 Why did the Industrial Revolution emerge in Britain and not in China?

4 How does the expansion of the Industrial Revolution and the globalization of trade affect the relationship of China and UK and the United States from 1813–1913?

5 How do scholars of international political economy explain the rise of free trade in the mid-nineteenth century? How is the approach of free trade different from the political economy of trade in the past? How active was Britain in promoting free trade with other countries?

6 What happened to the free trade movement in Europe and the United States over the nineteenth century? What led to a protectionist backlash against free trade? How did the declining cost of transportation offset the effects of rising tariffs? How did price convergence after 1870 push nations to resist globalization?

7 How did the gold standard facilitate the globalization of trade and finance? How did the domestic political economy of the gold standard reflect differences in political power in that era?

8 Did the pattern of economic growth achieved by Germany and Japan reflect new patterns for national success in the global economy? How does German development of a new synthetic dye industry relate to the special role of knowledge in production? Explain this statement:

> knowledge from reconstructing product and process provided a basis for inventing new dyes and improving existing ones. Once new firms had been established, the competitive process shifted to one of innovation in product and process; that is, the capacity for developing new knowledge became the basis for business success. And the ability of firms to achieve innovation was closely related to the institutional environment in which they operated.

9 Does a knowledge-based industry change the way we think about the sources of comparative advantage?

10 What was the economic development strategy adopted by the United States?
11 Why do large and complex economic systems, such as a global economy, require a significant effort by political forces to provide public goods that support such an economy? What political processes can provide public goods for a global economy?
12 Did Britain, acting as a hegemon, provide the public goods for the global economy?

- Global finance in interest rates and crisis lending? Finance balance of payments deficits?
- Limits of laissez-faire thinking?

13 Why did the globalization of the nineteenth century expand the inequality among nations?
14 How did World War I affect the global economy and the process of globalization? Most nations experienced significant economic damage from the war. Did any nations benefit economically?
15 Were the ideas of laissez faire government and economic nationalism appropriate to the problems of the global economy after 1919?

- War debts?
- Great depression?

16 What happened to the gold standard? Why not bring it back?
17 How did the US strategy of hegemony create new characteristics for the global economy from 1945–75?
18 How did the meaning of hegemony change after World War II?
19 What are the major components of US hegemony?
20 How and why did the regimes for oil and exchange rates collapse in the 1970s? What are the effects of these changes?
21 Compare and contrast Britain and the United States as hegemons.

Notes

1 Having referred to "nations" also confines us to a world where bounded political entities exist and can be readily identified.
2 An exceptionally useful and recent discussion of world economic relations during the Mongol Empire and the European-centered trade system is Ronald Findlay and Kevin O'Rourke, *Power and Plenty: Trade, War, and the World Economy in the Second Millennium*, Princeton: Princeton University Press, 2007, 101–310. Another important source for this era and for trade in general, is William Bernstein, *A Splendid Exchange: How Trade Shaped the World*, New York: Grove Press, 2008.
3 For example, in 1800 world trade was only about 2 percent of all economic activity. A century later, world trade now made up about 17 percent of all global economic activity. Elhanan Helpman, *Understanding Global Trade*, Cambridge, MA: Harvard University Press, 2011, 6. For a review of previous

eras of "globalization," see Kevin O'Rourke, *Politics and Trade: Lessons from Past Globalisations*, Brussels: Bruegel, 2009.

4 Oded Galor, "From Stagnation to Growth: Unified Growth Theory," in Philippe Aghion and Steven Durlauf, *Handbook of Economic Growth*, Amsterdam: Elsevier, 2005, 171–293, with data at 174. Another estimate sees the ratio of richest to poorest nations in 1820 as 3:1 and in 1992 as 71:1. Branko Milanovic, *Worlds Apart,* Princeton: Princeton University Press, 2005, 46.

5 Findlay and O'Rourke, *Power and Plenty*, 318–28.

6 Angus Maddison, *Contours of the World Economy, 1–2030*, Oxford: Oxford University Press, 2007; Jack Goldstone, *Why Europe? The Rise of the West in World History*, Boston, MA: McGraw Hill, 2009. There is a considerable debate about the evidence for whether China was even wealthier than Europe in the eighteenth century.

7 The many recent studies framed around this basic issue testify to its importance. See: Findlay and O'Rourke, *Power and Plenty*; Gregory Clark, *A Farewell to Alms*, Princeton: Princeton University Press, 2007; Angus Maddison, *Growth and Interaction in the World Economy*, Washington, DC: AEI Press, 2005; Giovanni Arrighi, *The Long Twentieth Century*, London: Verso, 2010; Joel Mokyr, *The Gifts of Athena*, Princeton: Princeton University Press, 2002; William Easterly, *The Elusive Quest for Growth*, Cambridge, MA: MIT Press, 2002; Kenneth Pomeranz, *The Great Divergence*, Princeton: Princeton University Press, 2000; and David Landes, *The Wealth and Poverty of Nations*, New York: Norton, 1999.

8 This is emphasized in Goldstone, *Why Europe?*, 132–61; and generally in Mokyr, *The Gifts of Athena*.

9 This point is emphasized in Pomeranz, *The Great Divergence*.

10 Douglas North, *Institutions, Institutional Change and Economic Performance*, Cambridge: Cambridge University Press, 1990; Douglas North, *Understanding the Process of Economic Change*, Princeton: Princeton University Press, 2005.

11 The relationship between secure property rights and economic growth in England is doubtful. Gregory Clark, "The Political Foundations of Economic Growth: 1540–1800," *Journal of Interdisciplinary History*, 26.4 (Spring 1996) 563–88.

12 See Pomeranz, *The Great Divergence*; and Clark, *A Farewell to Alms*. The tax rates in late eighteenth-century England may have been as high as 20 percent. By contrast, the Chinese government at the same time was as much as 8 percent. Findlay and O'Rourke, *Power and Plenty*, 348–57.

13 See the discussion in Findlay and O'Rourke, *Power and Plenty*, 316–45, with data at 334 and 343.

14 A wonderful introduction to economists and economics is in Robert Heilbronner, *The Worldly Philosophers*, New York: Touchstone, 1999.

15 P.J. Cain and A.G. Hopkins, "The Political Economy of British Overseas Expansion, 1750–1914," *Economic History Review*, 33.4 (November 1980) 474–81. There is considerable recent work on the political economy of the Corn Laws. Paul Rohrlich, "Economic Culture and Foreign Policy: The Cognitive Analysis of Economic Policy Making," *International Organization*, 41.1 (Winter 1987) 61–92; Scott James and David Lake, "The Second Face of Hegemony: Britain's Repeal of the Corn Laws and the American Walker Tariff of 1846," *International Organization*, 43.1 (Winter 1989) 1–29.

16 Cheryl Schonhardt-Bailey, "Specific Factors, Capital Markets, Portfolio Diversification, and Free Trade: Domestic Determinants of the Repeal of the Corn Laws," *World Politics*, 43.4 (July 1991) 545–69.

17 Charles Kindleberger, "The Rise of Free Trade in Western Europe, 1820–1875," in Kindleberger (ed.), *Economic Response: Comparative Studies in Trade, Finance, and Growth*, Cambridge, MA: Harvard University Press, 1975, 54–6. For an analysis of the effects of most-favored-nation in negotiations to construct a free trade area, see Robert Pahre, "Most-Favored-Nation Clauses and Clustered Negotiations," *International Organization*, 55.4 (Autumn 2001) 859–90. For a different view of most-favored-nation clauses, see Bryan Coutain, "The Unconditional Most-Favored-Nation Clause and the Maintenance of the Liberal Trade Regime in the Postwar 1870s, *International Organization*, 63.1 (Winter 2009) 139–75.

18 An excellent recent discussion of imperialism is Niall Ferguson, *Empire*, New York: Basic Books, 2002.

19 By 1913, tariffs were high in most of Europe and very high in North and South America; in Asia (except for Japan), the Middle East, and for some European nations such as Britain they were very low. See Findlay and O'Rourke, *Power and Plenty*, 403.

20 There are many definitions of globalization. This one emphasizes the changes in national economies – their internationalization. The effects of this process may, or may not, lead to fundamental global changes or to changes in the nations themselves.

21 Ocean freight rates were roughly constant in the century before 1840, but dropped by 70 percent from 1840–1910. See Findlay and O'Rourke, *Power and Plenty*, 381.

22 Peter Gourevitch, *Politics in Hard Times*, Ithaca: Cornell University Press, 1986, 71–123.

23 Mette Ejrnaes and Karl Perrson, "The Gains From Improved Market Efficiency: Trade Before and After the Transatlantic Telegraph," *European Review of Economic History*, 14 (2010) 361–81.

24 Michael Edelstein, *Overseas Investment in the Age of High Imperialism*, New York: Columbia University Press, 1982. As much as 25 percent to 33 percent of the national savings of Britain and France was funneled into foreign investment. Barry Eichengreen and Peter Temin, "The Gold Standard and the Great Depression," *Contemporary European History*, 9.2 (2000) 187.

25 Lance Davis and Robert Huttenback, *Mammon and the Pursuit of Empire: The Political Economy of British Imperialism, 1860–1912*, New York: Cambridge University Press, 1986.

26 During World War I, when the gold standard was suspended and labor became scarce, wages rose. In order to reestablish the gold standard after the war, wages and other social benefits in Britain had to be reduced to that of competitors. Economic and political elites were the advocates of a restoration of the gold standard: it provided direct economic benefits and served to control the gains to others in society that provided costs to the owners of capital.

27 Eichengreen and Temin, "The Gold Standard" offers an excellent discussion of the political requisites for the gold standard. Also see, Jeffry Frieden, "Monetary Populism in Nineteenth-Century America: An Open Economy Interpretation," *Journal of Economic History*, vol. 57.2 (1997) 367–95.

28 For analysis of the role of knowledge in economic growth, see Philippe Aghion and Stephen Durlauf, *Handbook of Economic Growth*, Amsterdam: Elsevier, 2005, and David Warsh, *Knowledge and the Wealth of Nations*, New York: Norton, 2007. Also provocative is Jack Goldstone, "Efflorescences and Economic Growth in World History: Rethinking the 'Rise of the West' and the Industrial Revolution," *Journal of World History*, 13.2 (Fall 2002) 323–89.

29 This story is ably told in Johann Peter Murmann, *Knowledge and Competitive Advantage*, Cambridge: Cambridge University Press, 2003. A much shorter version is in Landes, *The Wealth and Poverty of Nations*, 288–91.

30 Murmann, *Knowledge and Competitive Advantage*, 165.

31 The literature on the Meiji era is enormous. Two important sources include: Kozo Yamamura (ed.), *The Economic Emergence of Modern Japan*, Cambridge: Cambridge University Press, 1997; Richard Samuels, *Rich Nation, Strong Army*, Ithaca: Cornell University Press, 1994.

32 The tasks of late development have been expressed by many scholars. One is Samuels, *Rich Nation, Strong Army*, 14. Similar ideas come from the "big push" thesis, which stresses the problems of establishing, at roughly the same time, a broad set of complementary institutions. Some of this might happen over many years from markets, but rapid creation of institutions almost surely must come from government action. A contrary view is Randall Morck and Masao Nakamura, "Business Groups and the Big Push: Meiji Japan's Mass Privatization and Subsequent Growth," *Enterprise and Society*, 8.3 (September 2007) 489–542. This view rests on the erroneous notion that Japan's *zaibatsu* in the late nineteenth century operated independently of the state. A theoretically and empirically more accurate interpretation sees a network of related institutions, including state and *zaibatsu*. See Morris-Suzuki, *The Technological Transformation*, 71–104.

33 The Japanese government ministries were known as Kobusho – 1870–85 (Ministry of Industry/Engineering/Construction) and Hyobusho – the Ministry of Military Affairs. Eric Pauer, "Review of *Kobusho to Sono Jidai*," in Suzuki Jun (ed.), *Social Science Journal Japan*, 7.2 (October 2004) 289–92. Samuels, *Rich Nation*, 84–5.

34 Samuels, *Rich Nation*, 42–8. Samuels makes clear that the Japanese attitude to nation and technology was also commonplace in the West in the nineteenth century. Morris-Suzuki, *Technological Transformation*, 73–7.

35 Samuels, *Rich Nation*, 90–1.

36 Samuels, *Rich Nation*, 40.

37 Samuels, *Rich Nation*, 85–6.

38 There is considerable debate about whether the benefits in a system are public goods, which are available to all whether or not they contribute to the creation, or political goods, which benefit primarily a particular group and can be confined to such a group. See John Conybeare, "Public Goods, Prisoners' Dilemmas and the International Political Economy," *International Studies Quarterly*, 28.1 (March 1984) 5–22; and Joanne Gowa, "Rational Hegemons, Excludable Goods, and Small Groups: An Epitaph for Hegemonic Stability Theory?" *World Politics*, 42.3 (April 1989) 307–24.

39 Charles P. Kindleberger, "Dominance and Leadership in the International Economy: Exploitation, Public Goods, and Free Riders," *International Studies Quarterly*, 25(2) (June 1981) 242–54. For discussion of cooperation as a source of the political goods sustaining markets, see Robert Keohane, "The Demand for International Regimes," *International Organization*, 36.2 (Spring 1982) 325–55.

40 Paul Schroeder, *The Transformation of European Politics, 1763–1848*, Oxford: Clarendon Press, 1994.

41 The nature of the power exercised by a hegemon can range from military force, a large market, technological leadership, control over credit and finance, and ideological attractiveness. See, Patrick K. O'Brien and Geoffrey Pigman, "Free Trade. British Hegemony and the International Economic Order in the Nineteenth Century," *Review of International Studies*, 18 (1992) 89–113.

42 Robert Skidelsky, "Retreat from Leadership: The Evolution of British Economic Policy, 1870–1939," in Benjamin Rowland et al. (eds), *Balance of Power or Hegemony: The Interwar Monetary System*, New York: New York University Press, 1976, 152–63.

43 Barry Eichengreen, "Conducting the International Orchestra: Bank of England Leadership under the Classical Gold Standard," *Journal of International Money and Finance*, 6 (March 1987) 5–29. As we will see, financial markets are built on confidence and are especially prone to high levels of instability that can threaten the prosperity of all. The political and business components of the British financial system were prepared, up to a point, to provide liquidity to prevent development of a systemic crisis. Charles Kindleberger, "International Public Goods without International Government," *American Economic Review*, 76.1 (March 1986) 1–13; and Barry Eichengreen, "Hegemonic Stability Theories of the International Monetary System," NBER Working Paper No. 2193, 1987.

44 Paul Bairoch, *Economics and World History*, Chicago: University of Chicago Press, 1993, 88–90.

45 For an excellent analysis of the reaction of the United States to the war, especially the potential advantages to the United States, see William Silber, *When Washington Shut Down Wall Street: The Great Financial Crisis of 1914 and the Origins of America's Monetary Supremacy*, Princeton: Princeton University Press, 2008.

46 For discussion of the economies of the major combatants in the war, see Stephen Broadberry and Mark Harrison (eds), *The Economics of World War I*, Cambridge: Cambridge University Press, 2009.

47 Kathleen Burk, *America and the Sinews of War, 1914–1918*, Boston, MA: Allen and Unwin, 1986; Derek Aldcroft, *From Versailles to Wall Street, 1919–1929*, Berkeley: University of California Press, 1977.

48 The size of reparations was never fixed, but could have been as high as $33 billion. Aldcroft, *From Versailles to Wall Street*, 81.

49 Joan Hoff Wilson, *American Business and Foreign Policy, 1920–1933*, Boston, MA: Beacon Press, 1971, 70–133.

50 William McNeil, *American Money and the Weimar Republic*, New York: Columbia University Press, 1986; Melvyn Leffler, *The Elusive Quest: American Pursuit of European Stability and French Security, 1920–1933*, Chapel Hill: University of North Carolina Press, 1979.

51 Aldcroft, *From Versailles to Wall Street*, 168–86; Robert Skidelsky, "Retreat from Leadership," 168–73.

52 Aldcroft, *From Versailles to Wall Street*, 231–84.

53 Leffler, *The Elusive Quest*, 231–2; Charles Kindleberger, *The World in Depression, 1929–1939*, Berkeley: University of California Press, 1973, 128–45.

54 Leffler, *The Elusive Quest*, 238–46; Kindleberger, *The World in Depression*, 146–53.

55 Stephen Clarke, *Central Bank Cooperation, 1924–1931*, New York: Federal Reserve Bank of New York, 1967.

56 Susan Kennedy, *The Banking Crisis of 1933*, Lexington: University of Kentucky Press, 1973, 152–223.

57 Harold James, *The End of Globalization: Lessons from the Great Depression*, Cambridge, MA: Harvard University Press, 2001; Barry Eichengreen and Douglas Irwin, "The Slide to Protectionism in the Great Depression: Who Succumbed and Why?" *Journal of Economic History*, 70.4 (December 2010) 871–97.

58 Leffler, *The Elusive Quest*, 195–202.

59 Michael Barnhart, *Japan Prepares for Total War*, Ithaca: Cornell University Press, 1987, 22–58.

60 Kindleberger, *The World in Depression*, 162–81, 247–64. Skidelsky, "Retreat from Leadership," 178–88. Albert Romano, *The Politics of Recovery: Roosevelt's New Deal*, New York: Oxford University Press, 1983.

61 Stephan Haggard, "The Institutional Foundations of Hegemony: Explaining the Reciprocal Trade Agreements Act," *International Organization*, 42.1 (Winter 1988) 91–119; Skidelsky, "Retreat from Leadership," 186–8.

62 Examination of the economies of the major nations in the war is in Mark Harrison, *The Economics of World War II*, Cambridge: Cambridge University Press, 2000.

63 Alan Milward, *War, Economy and Society, 1939–1945*, Berkeley: University of California Press, 1977, 63–8.

64 In the four years after 1945, the US government and other sources provided more than $28 billion to sustain the US surplus with the rest of the world. W.M. Scammell, *The International Economy Since 1945*, New York: St. Martins Press, 2nd ed., 1983, 21.

65 Michael Hogan, *The Marshall Plan*, Cambridge: Cambridge University Press, 1989; John Lewis Gaddis, *Strategies of Containment*, Oxford: Oxford University Press, 2005.

66 Barry Eichengreen, *Exorbitant Privilege*, Oxford: Oxford University Press, 2011. Hogan, *The Marshall Plan*.

67 Michael Hogan, *Informal Entente*, Columbus: University of Missouri Press, 1977. The main formal institution of this era was the Bank for International Settlements, which still exists and served as a precursor for the World Bank and the IMF. See Frank Costigliola, "The Other Side of Isolationism: The Establishment of the First World Bank," *Journal of American History*, 59 (December 1972) 602–20.

68 Benjamin Cohen, *Organizing the World's Money*, New York: Basic Books, 1977, 95 reports the level at 75 percent. David Calleo, *Beyond American Hegemony*, New York: Basic Books, 1987, 227 sets the figure at 60 percent.

69 Alfred Eckes, *A Search for Solvency: Bretton Woods and the International Monetary System, 1941–1971*, Austin: University of Texas Press, 1975; Fred Block, *The Origins of International Monetary Disorder*, Berkeley: University of California Press, 1974.

70 Edward S. Mason and Robert Asher, *The World Bank since Bretton Woods*, Washington, DC: Brookings Institution, 1973; Katherine Marshall, *The World Bank: From Reconstruction to Development to Equity*, New York: Routledge, 2008; Ngaire Woods, *The Globalizers: The IMF, the World Bank and Their Borrowers*, Ithaca: Cornell University Press, 2007.

71 Robert Pastor, *Congress and the Politics of Foreign Economic Policy*, Berkeley: University of California Press, 1980; Soo Yeon Kim, *Power and the Governance of Global Trade: From the GATT to the WTO*, Ithaca: Cornell University Press, 2010.

72 The GATT Rounds include: 1947, Geneva; 1949, Annecy; 1950–1, Torquay; 1955–6, Geneva; 1959–62, Geneva (Dillon Round); 1963–7, Geneva (Kennedy Round); 1973–9, Tokyo; 1986–93, Uruguay.

73 Pastor, *Congress*, 78.

74 For detailed information about tariff levels, see WTO, *World Tariff Profiles, 2010*, Geneva: WTO, 2011. See Chapter 5 for more details about trade negotiations.

75 Joel Darmstadter and Hans Landsberger, "The Crisis," in Raymond Vernon (ed.), *The Oil Crisis*, New York: Norton, 1976, 19.

76 Mira Wilkins, "The History of Multinational Enterprise," in Alan M. Rugman (ed.), *The Oxford Handbook of International Business*, Oxford: Oxford University Press, 2010, 3–38. Also see, Alfred Chandler and Bruce Mazlish (eds), *Leviathans: Multinationals and the New Global History*, Cambridge: Cambridge University Press, 2005. On the East India Company, see Ann M. Carlos and Stephen Nicholas, "Giants of an Earlier Capitalism: The Chartered Trading Companies as Modern Multinationals," *The Business History Review*, 62.3 (Autumn 1988) 398–419.

77 Robert Gilpin, *U.S. Power and the Multinational Corporation*, New York: Basic Books, 1975, 15.

78 Gilpin, *U.S. Power*, 107–8, 124–5, 154–5.

79 For theoretical discussion of the sources of FDI by MNCs, see John Dunning, "The Eclectic Paradigm of International Production: A Restatement and Some Possible Extensions," *Journal of International Business Studies*, 19.1 (1988) 1–31; Lorraine Eden, "Bringing the Firm Back In: Multinationals in International Political Economy," *Millennium*, 20.2 (1991) 197–224; Raymond Vernon, "The Product Cycle Hypothesis in a New International Environment," *Oxford Bulletin of Economics and Statistics*, 41.4 (November 1979) 255–67.

80 The six original members were France, the Federal Republic of Germany (West Germany), Belgium, Luxembourg, Italy, and the Netherlands. The EEC went into effect on January 1, 1958.

81 Examination of the sources of European integration is in Andrew Moravcsik, *The Choice for Europe*, Ithaca: Cornell University Press, 1998; and Ben Rosamond, *Theories of European Integration*, New York: Palgrave, 2000.

82 In 2011, the IMF had 187 members. See, www.imf.org/external/np/sec/memdir/members.aspx©tal. The WTO has 153 members and 31 observer governments. See, www.wto.org/english/thewto_e/whatis_e/tif_e/org6_e.htm

83 Helen Milner and Andrew Moravcsik (eds), *Power, Interdependence, and Nonstate Actors in World Politics*, Princeton: Princeton University Press, 2009.

84 Stephen Krasner (ed.), *International Regimes*, Ithaca: Cornell University Press, 1983.

85 Details about the range of international organizations can be found in the *Yearbook of International Organizations*, 2011–2012, vols 1–6, Leiden: Martinus Nijhoff, 2011.

86 A short but useful review of the literature on regimes is found in Benjamin Cohen, *International Political Economy: An Intellectual History*, Princeton: Princeton University Press, 2008, 100–8.

87 An excellent discussion of this period is in Barry Eichengreen, *Exorbitant Privilege*, Oxford: Oxford University Press, 2011, 39–63.

88 The next paragraphs rely on John Odell, *U.S. International Monetary Policy*, Princeton: Princeton University Press, 1982, 188–291; Joanne Gowa, *Closing the Gold Window: Domestic Politics and the End of Bretton Woods*, Ithaca: Cornell University Press, 1983; Frank Gavin, *Gold, Dollars, & Power: The Politics of International Monetary Relations, 1958–1971*, Chapel Hill: University of North Carolina Press, 2004; and Eichengreen, *Exorbitant Privilege*, 57–68.

89 Jeffry Frieden, *Banking on the World: The Politics of American International Finance*, New York: Harper & Row, 1987, 79–85; Benjamin Cohen, *In Whose Interest? International Banking and American Foreign Policy*, New Haven: Yale University Press, 1986, 19–33.

90 John Odell, *U.S. International Monetary Policy*, 229–305. The system was not one of floating rates; rather it was a "dirty" float. Governments continued

to intervene in foreign exchange markets to keep price movements within an acceptable range.

91   For readable accounts concerning the relationship between the major oil firms and producing countries, consult Anthony Sampson, *The Seven Sisters: The Great Oil Companies and the World They Created*, London: Coronet, rev. ed., 1988; Daniel Yergin, *The Prize: The Epic Quest for Oil, Money and Power*, New York: Free Press, 2008; and John Blair, *The Control of Oil*, New York: Pantheon, 1976.

92   The original five members of OPEC were Venezuela, Iran, Iraq, Saudi Arabia, and Kuwait. Today OPEC members also include Qatar, Libya, the United Arab Emirates, Algeria, Nigeria, and Angola.

93   Yergin, *The Prize*, 543–633.

94   Joel Darmstadter and Hans Lansberg, "The Crisis," in Raymond Vernon (ed.), *The Oil Crisis*, New York: Norton, 1976, 31–3.

95   Yergin, *The Prize*, 577–87.

96   Yergin, *The Prize*, 588.

97   The range of views about US motives can be found in Charles Kindleberger, *The World in Depression*, Berkeley: University of California Press, 1973; Gilpin, *U.S. Power*; Bruce Russett, "The Mysterious Case of Vanishing Hegemony, Or, Is Mark Twain Really Dead?" *International Organization*, 39.2 (Spring 1985) 207–31; John Conybeare, "Public Goods, Prisoners' Dilemmas, and International Political Economy," *International Studies Quarterly*, 28 (March 1984) 5–22.

98   Waldo Heinrichs, *Threshold of War*, New York: Oxford University Press, 1988; Gaddis, *Strategies of Containment*.

99   David Lake, "British and American Hegemony Compared: Lessons for the Current Era of Decline," in Michael Fry (ed.), *History, the White House and the Kremlin: Statesmen as Historians*, London: Pinter, 1991, 106–22.

100   Time periods don't correspond exactly with centuries. By the nineteenth century, we refer to the period from about 1820–1939; the twentieth century extends from 1939–2014.

101   Patrick K. O'Brien and Geoffrey Pigman, "Free Trade, British Hegemony and the International Economic Order in the Nineteenth Century," *Review of International Studies*, 18.2 (April 1992) 89–113.

102   Peter Cain, "British Free Trade, 1850–1914: Economics and Policy," *Refresh*, 29 (1999) 1–4.

103   David Calleo, *Beyond American Hegemony*, New York: Basic Books, 1987.

Further Reading

William Bernstein, *A Splendid Exchange: How Trade Shaped the World*, New York: Grove Press, 2008.
A delightful and even entertaining story of global trade.

Alfred Chandler and Bruce Mazlish (eds), *Leviathans: Multinationals and the New Global History*, Cambridge: Cambridge University Press, 2005.
An essential source on the development of multinational firms.

Barry Eichengreen, *Globalizing Capital: A History of the International Monetary System*, Princeton: Princeton University Press, 2008.
An exceptionally lucid and comprehensive history of international monetary relations over the past two centuries.

Barry Eichengreen, *Exorbitant Privilege*, Oxford: Oxford University Press, 2011.
A detailed and insightful examination of the dollar as key currency.

Ronald Findlay and Kevin O'Rourke, *Power and Plenty: Trade, War, and the World Economy in the Second Millennium*, Princeton: Princeton University Press, 2007.
An extraordinary examination of trade and war in the creation of a global economy during the last millennium.

John Lewis Gaddis, *Strategies of Containment*, Oxford: Oxford University Press, 2005.
Provides a detailed history and analysis of the Cold War.

Robert Gilpin, *U.S. Power and the Multinational Corporation*, New York: Basic Books, 1975.
An early but important source on US globalization.

Robert Gilpin, *War and Change in World Politics*, Cambridge: Cambridge University Press, 1981.
One of the most important sources on US hegemony.

Michael Hogan, *The Marshall Plan*, Cambridge: Cambridge University Press, 1989.
A classic study.

Harold James, *The End of Globalization: Lessons from the Great Depression*, Cambridge, MA: Harvard University Press, 2001.
The story of how the global depression stopped globalization.

Kenneth Pomeranz, *The Great Divergence*, Princeton: Princeton University Press, 2000.
A defining study of nineteenth-century growth differences in Europe and Asia.

Ngaire Woods, *The Globalizers: The IMF, the World Bank and Their Borrowers*, Ithaca: Cornell University Press, 2007.
A very useful study of international organizations and globalization.

Daniel Yergin, *The Prize: The Epic Quest for Oil, Money and Power*, New York: Free Press, 2008.
An essential and readable story of the international oil regime.

Part II
Contemporary Globalization

5 The Political Economy of Global Production and Exchange

Over the past two centuries, the geography of global production and exchange has experienced two large swings, resulting in radical changes in the relative prosperity of nations and regions. In 1820, the dominant economic power in the world – measured by the size of economies – was China. What followed was an industrial revolution concentrated in the West and largely missing from most of the rest of the world, especially China. For nearly a century after 1820, the rapid globalization of trade and financial flows accompanied industrialization. Changes in the technology of production interacted with changes in the technology of communication and transportation to give those nations developing and adopting new capabilities enormous economic and even military advantages over those that did not. In 1820, China's gross domestic product (GDP) was about one-third of global GDP and that of the British and United States combined was about 7 percent; by 1950, this same figure for China was near 4 percent and for the United Kingdom plus United States was about 34 percent.[1]

The second great swing in the global geography of production began in the 1970s and continues to the present. In 1973, China's proportion of global GDP remained low at 5 percent and the United States and United Kingdom remained high at more than 25 percent. A second great wave of industrial transformation and globalization, again driven by technological change, was underway and also continues today. The effect was to radically shift the locus of global production and trade, and the result was to transform many previously poor nations into global economic powers. By 2003, China had quadrupled its global GDP share to 16 percent and the United States and United Kingdom had dipped slightly to 24 percent. By about 2020, the Chinese economy is expected to equal and then surpass the US economy in size and by 2030 to exceed the United States by as much as 30 percent.[2]

Expanding our view to include all emerging economies gives an even more striking sense of the significant changes in the global structure of production in the last three decades. These relatively poor nations are labeled as emerging because they have moved toward rapid economic

growth, even as the growth rates in rich nations were somewhat stag-
nating. Emerging economies typically had recent growth rates of three or
four times that of rich nations, and this compounding over time led to
rapid catch-up. Some comparisons make this clear. In 1990, rich nations
held 80 percent of global GDP and poor nations (some of which are
emerging economies) only 20 percent. Just two decades later, in 2011,
this ratio had shifted to 60–40 percent. Projecting into the near future, by
2018 the ratio will be 50–50 percent, a stunning shift in global economic
relations in less than thirty years.[3]

During the recent period, when the global geography of production
has changed so much, one of the main drivers has been the rapid expansion of global trade. Much of the growth of emerging economies can be
traced to the ability to export more and more products to wealthy
nations. One of the core features of globalization is this process and its
connection to the creation of global and regional production networks.

This chapter examines in detail the nature, sources, and consequences
of the globalization of production and exchange. We will review much of
the data on global trade, which provides a clearer picture of what is
produced, where it is produced, and the patterns of exchange and global
imbalance. Equally important are the global actors that facilitated and
pressed this process forward. These include dominant economies like the
United States and Europe, but also include smaller emerging economies
such as Korea, Taiwan, and Saudi Arabia, and larger nations such as
China. Trade growth comes from the ability of nations to change the
rules for trade and even create institutions to manage and adjudicate
these rules. The General Agreement on Tariffs and Trade (GATT) and its
transformation into the World Trade Organization (WTO) are essential
sources in the expansion of trade. Regional trade arrangements, especially the European Union (EU), have propelled trade increases and
transformed the locus of production. The immediate agents of global
trade have become multinational corporations. These firms invest across
the world in facilities for production, organize and integrate globally
distributed supply chains, and then market these products on a global
scale.

The interactions among states, firms, and global institutions created
the new patterns of global markets and led to the existing and projected
shifts of production and prosperity. The expansion of global trade has
substantial and differential effects for nations and for various groups
within nations. And the creation of such a system of relatively free trade
can only happen when the political processes and economic policies of
nations are willing to support and sustain it. Put simply, but accurately,
the winners from global trade must somehow prevail politically over the
losers from global trade. Understanding the patterns of winners and
losers and the political processes associated with expanding global trade
is a key feature of this chapter.

Patterns of Global Trade

We begin with some basic information about the patterns of global trade. This includes the role of trade in globalization, where trade takes place, the regions and nations that dominate global trade, the openness of nations to trade (Goods + Services Trade/GDP), and the imbalances in global trade (see "Components of Global Trade" below).

Components of Global Trade

Merchandise Trade
One general division of merchandise trade is among manufactured goods, agricultural products, and fuels and mining. **Manufactures** cover a vast range, such as steel and iron, automotive products, high technology such as telecom equipment, computers and communication devices and integrated circuits, chemicals and pharmaceuticals, and clothing and textiles. **Agricultural products** are similarly diverse, with food and various derivative products such as palm oil. **Fuels and mining** include oil and a large variety of minerals such as copper, magnesium, and rare earth minerals.

Commercial Services
A second major category of global trade consists of **commercial services**. This typically includes non-tangible but valuable products that both support merchandise trade and provide value for transactions. Such items as **transportation, communication** and **telecommunications, insurance, financial,** and **computer** services are significant categories in international trade.

Table 5.1 Distribution of Global Trade, 2010

Total Global Trade	100%
Merchandise Trade	80.6
Commercial Services	19.4

Source: Data from WTO, *World Trade Report*, 2011, 24.

Throughout the post-World War II era, the connection between global merchandise and services trade and global prosperity has been a close one. And for almost every year, growth in trade has been higher than growth in GDP, a clear indication of the expanding globalization of trade in relation to domestic economic activity. Between 2001 and 2011, global trade as a proportion of global GDP rose from 23.8 percent to 29.7 percent.[4] However, severe economic downturns such as in 2008–10 do result in a larger decline for trade than for overall economic activity, a sort of de-globalization. So, in 2009 trade fell by 12 percent as economies declined on average by 2.5 percent. An important feature of this decline is the centering in developed nations, especially the United States. The result has been a somewhat differential pattern of decline and recovery, with developed nations having a sharper decline and a slower recovery than developing nations. This has also been true for trade.[5]

The Triad of Global Production

There are three great poles of global trade: Europe, Asia, and North America.

Not only is global trade dominated by three areas, as we see in Table 5.2, but the trade of these areas is regionally defined, as a nation's trade partners are predominately those in its geographic region. This is true for the greatest poles of trade in Europe, Asia, and North America but far less true for nations that account for a much smaller proportion of global trade, as seen in Table 5.3.

A small number of nations dominate global exchange. The top fifteen nations (Table 5.4) in global merchandise trade account for 63 percent of all such trade. Table 5.5 reveals important information about the composition of global trade. First, is the overall dominance of manufac-

Table 5.2 Global Trade (Merchandise and Services) by Region, 2008 (billions $US)

	Total (M+S)	Merchandise	Services
Global Trade	19,943	16,117 (80.8%)	3,826 (19.2%)
North America (% total)	2,638 (13.2%)	2,035 (12.6%)	603 (15.8%)
United States	1,805	1,287	518
Canada	522	456	66
Mexico	290	272	18
Europe	8,440 (42.3%)	6,469 (40.1%)	1,971 (51.5%)
Belgium	557	472	85
France	782	616	166
Germany	1,702	1,446	256
Italy	661	543	118
Netherlands	740	638	102
United Kingdom	745	460	285
Asia	5,601 (28.1%)	4,726 (29.3%)	875 (22.9%)
China	1,577	1,431	146
Hong Kong China	462	370	92
Japan	929	782	147
Korea	498	422	76
Singapore	435	338	97

Source: Data from WTO, *International Trade Statistics*, 2010, 181–4, 189–91.

Table 5.3 Regional Merchandise Trade Flows

Region	% Total Trade with Regional Partners
North America	37.9
Europe	70.9
Asia	57.8
South and Central America	27.4
CIS	27.9
Africa	11.5
Middle East	20.9

Source: Data from WTO, *International Trade Statistics*, 2010, 10.

Table 5.4 Top Fifteen Nations in Global Trade, 2009 (billions $US) (Merchandise + Services Trade)

Nation	Exports (M+S)	Imports (M+S)	Exports (M+S)/GDP
United States	1530	1936	11%
Germany	1353	1191	41
China	1331	1164	27
Japan	707	699	13
France	627	686	23
Netherlands	589	530	69
United Kingdom	585	643	28
Italy	507	528	24
Belgium	449	426	73
Korea	421	398	50
Hong Kong	415	396	195
Canada	374	408	29
Singapore	357	327	200
Russian Federation	344	251	28
Mexico	245	263	28

Source: Data from WTO, *International Trade Statistics*, 2010, 180–94. World Bank Data, http://data.worldbank.org/indicator/NE.EXP.GNFS.ZS

tured goods in global merchandise trade. However, this statement masks the considerable variation in the role of these goods in the exports of many nations, which is related to some level of regional specialization. Though manufactures comprise over 77 percent of Europe's exports, these total only 19 percent of Africa's, 24 percent of the CIS, and 27 percent of Middle East and South and Central America's exports. Second, agriculture represents almost a third of the exports of South and Central America but only 2 percent of the Middle East. Manufactured goods are an even more important part of the exports of Asian nations.

For most of the last two centuries of global trade, the dominant pattern was for poorer nations to export agricultural goods and raw materials to

Table 5.5 Distribution of Global Merchandise Trade, by Region (% Global Trade)

Region	Manufacture		Agriculture		Mine/Fuel	
	EX	IM	EX	IM	EX	IM
World	68.6	68.6	9.6	9.6	18.6	18.6
North Am.	70.5	73.0	11.2	7.0	13.6	17.5
South/Cent. Am	27.4	68.8	30.5	10.0	38.9	18.3
Europe	77.3	70.9	10.5	10.7	9.6	15.6
CIS	24.1	72.6	8.7	14.0	62.9	12.0
Africa	19.2	69.5	10.2	14.3	64.0	13.5
Middle East	27.3	77.0	2.6	11.2	68.0	9.0
Asia	79.7	62.8	6.3	8.6	10.8	26.0

Source: Data from WTO, *International Trade Statistics*, 2010, 45–6.

Note: Figures show the % of manufacturing, agricultural, and mine/fuel for each area.

richer nations, which in turn exported manufactured goods to each other and to poorer nations. Only in the last forty to fifty years have less developed nations become major exporters of manufactured products. This division of labor, a legacy of colonialism, generally relegated developing countries to less dynamic and profitable roles in the world economy.

Global Imbalances

Because trade takes place among nations with different currencies, the relation of inflows and outflows of goods and money matters. Under most circumstances, a nation obtains the ability to purchase imports by selling its products abroad and gaining foreign exchange. Of course, nations also gain foreign exchange from inflows of investment and loans from abroad and this can serve to offset a balance of trade deficit.[6] Thus, on a global level, large and persistent imbalances in trade can call forth adjustments in financial flows, in the form of loans and investment. But such imbalances are difficult to sustain through time, because other nations' investors and lenders are not likely to continue such behavior indefinitely. Long-term imbalances in trade can also reveal important imbalances in competitive advantage among nations.

The global trading system after 1945 was in many ways a creation of the United States and its preferences, policies, and power. An essential feature of this power – the role of the US dollar as key currency – creates the major exception to the patterns just described. Unlike most nations, the dollar as key currency has meant the United States could purchase goods from abroad with dollars and need not exchange its currency for another. Indeed, the dollar has effectively functioned as a global currency for many transactions. Most nations were eager to hold dollars as the largest part of their foreign exchange reserves for this reason. This has permitted the United States to operate with a persistent current account deficit for decades, with a variety of nations holding and using the dollars they accumulated.[7]

The economic crisis of the 1970s led to larger and larger global imbalances over time, largely driven by US policies.[8] Flexible exchange rates and rising oil prices led to large trade deficits, and slow economic growth often yielded larger budget deficits in many advanced nations. Market-based and policy-based decisions relating to shifting away from manufacturing and toward services and finance created large opportunities for the growth of manufacturing in several Asian nations. Rising government spending and lower taxes led to ever-increasing budget deficits. The result was a secular trend toward increasing trade deficits and budget deficits, especially by the United States.

The key measurement of global imbalances is current account deficits and surpluses, especially when these are concentrated between certain nations or regions (see Chapter 2 for details). For more than a decade beginning in 1980, adding together current account surpluses and deficits totaled an average of 2 percent of global GDP. In the mid-1990s and until the global financial crisis of 2008, this measure rose almost continuously to an average of 6 percent of global GDP. These imbalances were very much concentrated in surpluses by Germany, Japan, oil exporters, and China and in deficits by the United States.[9] The US current account deficit peaked in 2006 at more than $800 billion or 1.3 percent of global GDP. Of this, more than a half was with Asia as a whole and one-third with China alone.[10] Thus, from 1980 to the present global imbalances expanded dramatically and remained focused in a small number of states. Because of the dollar's role as key currency and because nations such as China, Japan, and Korea wanted to preserve the trade surplus with the United States, the dollars used to purchase these goods were held by these nations and used to buy US debt. The system of financing trade and budget deficits suffered a major setback with the global financial crisis but persists at a much lower rate in subsequent years.

Explaining the Expansion of Global Trade

The Political Economy of Free Trade

However much free trade can be shown to produce mutual gains for nations, achieving free trade always involves a deep web of political relationships operating within nations and between them as well. This is because free trade is a political choice about the rules for economic interaction with the rest of the world.[11] Moreover, the gains from trade are not evenly distributed and almost always involve relative and even absolute losses for some groups and for the interests of some governments. The economist's retort that reallocating resources produces efficiencies for all is generally correct but masks the reality of lost jobs, lost profits, the burdens of retraining, and the strategic importance of some products and goods. A policy of free trade in a democratic society requires mechanisms for choosing rules that will invariably help some and hurt others. In non-democratic societies, free trade is more closely linked to the strategic calculations of political leaders but gains and losses still exist. Further, we should consider the possibility that political leaders, even in a democracy, may see the potential of free trade and engage in the political mobilization of groups that could benefit from this policy.

Creating a system of free trade also requires that nations cooperate to develop and define the specific rules about how trade relations will work. Even with a specific set of rules and standards, some nations may be tempted to defect from a general preference for free trade. This possibility can be reduced through some sort of international institution, which functions to enforce these rules. Further, even when support for free trade is widespread across nations this will be uneven, especially across different industries, and this will affect the precise wording of the rules that might be adopted. The actual process of cooperation will require considerable negotiation and bargaining among nations. More generally, we can say that free trade requires a system of political relations within and among nations that will support and sustain free trade, by emphasizing the gains and minimizing the losses, combined with global institutions to interpret and enforce the rules.[12]

So it is for the system of free trade that developed in the decades after 1945 and which was a result of the power and preferences of the United States and its ability to construct a global free trade regime. During the period until about 1965, achieving freer trade was a project promoted domestically and internationally by the United States, primarily with its major allies in the Cold War, namely Europe and Japan. And freer trade quickly merged with and sometimes competed with the goal of rebuilding the economies of these nations as bulwarks in the struggle against the Soviet Union. This led US officials to tolerate asymmetrical free trade rules, with Europe and Japan engaging in significant policies of protection and the United States maintaining a relatively open market for the exports of these nations. Negotiated agreements within GATT usually permitted much higher tariff barriers for US allies than for the United States and typically excluded products with high levels of political sensitivity.[13] The ability of the United States to negotiate freer trade depended on a domestic political relationship that involved a commitment to protect the incomes and economic position of groups adversely affected by international trade. This arrangement of "embedded liberalism," whereby liberalization of trade was sustained by efforts to maintain economic growth and welfare policies, received widespread support across the political spectrum.[14] This system began to break down, at least with respect to working classes, in the 1970s.[15]

Thus, international cooperation for freer trade rested on a political base of US global power and international and domestic political commitments, combined with bargains that decidedly benefited US allies. The negative effects on some US producers were ignored and this was managed politically through appeals to the demands of the Cold War conflict. The various agreements on trade under GATT were successful in lowering tariffs but also excluded significant areas of trade and rules affecting trade. The real goal was freer trade, not free trade. And yet, tariff levels did fall and trade rose by 7 percent per year on average from 1948–90.[16] Perhaps the most important political basis for freer global trade was domestic economic growth in the United States and abroad, which ameliorated the negative effects of trade liberalization on uncompetitive sectors and generated widespread gains to smooth the transition.[17] Over time, this growth in trade served to mobilize and engage the interests of the beneficiaries of trade in the United States and abroad.

International Institutions and Global Trade

A central proposition of neoliberal thinking about international political economy is that high levels of interdependence promote cooperation among nations, which is regulated through the creation of international institutions and regimes, which themselves further affect future cooperation. The specific forms and rules found in international institutions and regimes typically reflect the bargaining power and position of the states constructing the arrangements. We consider the global and multilateral institutions of GATT/WTO, regional trade institutions such as the European Union, and preferential trade institutions. Our interest is the manner and degree to which these institutions affect global economic exchange.

The primary institution involved with global trade is the General Agreement on Tariffs and Trade, which in 1995 was morphed into the World Trade Organization. GATT's ability to affect trade issues in the global economy was greatly hampered by its weak institutional position. In effect, GATT was primarily a forum for the negotiation of trade agreements with some limited capacity to deal with trade disputes and interpret the rules for trade. In important ways, GATT reflected the economic and domestic political interests of a small number of major economies, which did not always lead to the promotion of freer trade. Put simply, for decades after 1945 the political economy of global trade was very much mixed in its affinity for free trade and this placed important limits on GATT and on the political process for designing global trade rules.[18]

Specifically, this meant negotiations under GATT focused on obtaining reciprocal deals between nations on a "product-by-product" basis among goods traded by main suppliers – that affected major trading nations with similar factor endowments in selected areas of trade. Among those major economies, the GATT can be seen to have augmented trade.[19] These effects were quite large for a small number of nations but also quite small for most nations. Even with the application of "most-favored-nation" rules, the deals reached were of little value to most nations.

Negotiations Under GATT and Creation of the WTO

The negotiation of meaningful agreements for international trade did not really begin until after the creation of the European Economic Community (EEC) in 1958, for only after that could the then six members of the EEC deal with the United States as an equal. Between 1963 and 1967, in the Kennedy Round, negotiations yielded both significant tariff reduction (if only on a limited set of products) and new forms of legal rules governing trade. The next set of negotiations, the Tokyo Round from 1973–9, focused again on tariff reduction but also produced important innovations in addressing non-tariff barriers (NTBs) and some of the special problems created by the rise of developing nations in global trade.[20]

By the 1990s, the expansion of global trade, decades of economic growth, and the GATT process led to a substantial convergence of trade policies, practices, and preferences for major parts of the world. This convergence was embodied in the set of GATT negotiations called the Uruguay Round, with agreements signed in 1994 that led to the creation of the WTO in 1995. There were substantial obstacles to the eventual achievements of the Uruguay Round and the WTO. These were rooted in the role that protectionism played in the politics of many nations and the political difficulties associated with reducing or eliminating these benefits so as to reduce or eliminate these restraints on trade. Many nations, especially Japan and in Europe, have long won and sustained political support for ruling parties through subsidies to farmers, who on a global scale were not really economically competitive. Similar arrangements existed for textile producers and workers, who needed to be shielded from competition coming from emerging economies. New issues relating to the protection of intellectual property and defining rules for trade in services presented obstacles to agreement. After more than a decade of negotiation, agreement was reached on tariff reductions, new rules for agriculture and textiles, and, most important, a new global institution for the management of trade, the WTO.

The WTO is a significant step in the process of global cooperation and in establishing effective rules and rules enforcement arrangements. The

GATT was an institution designed to facilitate the negotiation of agreements and had a very limited capacity to adjudicate disputes and enforce the rules. The WTO is a much more formal and robust institution created to do just what the GATT could not. Members of the WTO now are obliged to treat the agreements as a whole and are not free to pick and choose what to abide by. Further, members are required to remake their domestic laws so as to conform to the WTO rules. And when one nation chooses to bring a dispute over compliance with WTO rules, the other nations involved are obliged to submit to the process of adjudication and to accept the decision in effect as final. The very existence of the WTO as an outcome of decades of trade negotiations is testament to the emerging global consensus on the value of a common set of effective rules to govern trade relations and a willingness to cede some measure of control over that process to an international body.[21]

The Domestic Political Economy of Trade

The rules developed under WTO and various other trade agreements and institutions have increasingly come to be affected by firms powerful enough to insert their preferences into agreements via the positions of governments.[22] This suggests we examine how domestic politics leads to certain kinds of global economic policies by states with a focus on the role of the interests of domestic actors and the institutions within which these interests are expressed and related to policy choices. At the same time, international trade and finance serve to engage and even help to formulate domestic interests.[23] The expansion of global trade can lead existing firms and interests to press harder for free trade and even bring other firms' interests into the free trade camp. And the political institutions of a society may be able to link interests across sectors. Here firms focused on trade and other firms focused on finance may have their interests linked through political parties, ministries, and political entrepreneurs. Global institutions such as the WTO create penalties for rules violation that encourage interests in an affected nation to lobby domestically in favor of free trade.

An important form for the analysis of the political economy of trade is to link the interests of different business groups to their position in the overall economy, attempting to predict interests on the basis of economic position as defined by the distributional consequences of policies of free trade and protection. That is, analysts want to predict reliably how business groups will gain or lose from free trade based on their economic position and then link these patterns to political conflict over this policy. From this pattern of gains and losses, interests and political conflict, scholars hope to explain why some nations act to create an open economy and others choose to erect barriers to trade, while others adopt a more mixed system.

An early model of trade politics links interests to the basic ideas of comparative advantage. This theory is based on the relative distribution of the factors of production (land, labor, capital) within and among nations. Business groups in a society that use intensely those factors plentiful in the nation but scarce globally will have globally competitive advantages and should support a policy of free trade. By contrast, those groups using factors scarce in the nation but plentiful globally will be at a competitive disadvantage and should back a policy of protection.[24] This analysis is often better at understanding broad patterns of trade politics rather than the specifics of which groups of economic factors will align for and against policies.

Another approach has been to examine the factors of production in a more finely grained manner, primarily by seeing them as politically affected more by industry. This view asks whether these factors are closely tied to a specific industry or whether they can move somewhat freely from one industry to another. Here, all the factors in an industry with competitive global advantages are thought to align together and with other like industries to favor free trade, whereas these same factors more closely tied to industries lacking these advantages will align over policies of protection. Not only do these ideas often help to explain trade politics, but similar thinking can be used to examine policies relating to exchange rates, foreign direct investment, and global finance more generally.

Of course, understanding preferences of various groups alone is insufficient to understand political choices and outcomes. Equally important is the characteristics of the political institutions in which these preferences are embedded. One interesting result of studies is the difficulty in determining the precise nature of institutional characteristics that matter. For example, it is not clear that democratic nations tend to develop dramatically distinct patterns of outcomes than autocratic nations.[25] In particular, autocratic nations can often be seen to follow along behind more democratic (and advanced economies) with policies that mimic but do not exactly duplicate the tendencies toward openness. However, it is much easier to examine the more transparent democratic systems and we often find various structural reasons for outcomes as much as institutional reasons. For example, it is much easier to organize politically around a policy of protectionism – especially in societies like the United States and Japan, which emphasize local interests – than around a policy of free trade. This is because the benefits of protection flow to a very specific group, which maintains its incomes as a result of such policies. The gains from free trade are much more diffuse and more difficult to identify, flowing mostly to consumers in the form of lower prices and more plentiful products. The gains may be large but are less concentrated and therefore less politically relevant.[26]

The Impact of Transnational Firms

Global Trade and Transnational Firms

The central actor in the globalization of production and trade has been the transnational corporation (TNC).[27] There are many different kinds of transnational firms, with significant differences in the degree to which they operate internationally. Broadly, these are corporations engaged in the production and/or distribution of goods and services that span multiple nations, but it also can include firms that simply operate a business in two or more nations.[28] Such activities usually require these firms to make investments in production and/or assembly facilities abroad, but may include using contract manufacturers for production. Facilities abroad can also include product development, testing, and marketing operations in the various markets where they sell. In some cases, TNCs have established research and development operations abroad to take advantage of specialized knowledge capabilities. Frequently, such firms will have operations abroad that are larger than those in their home countries. The cumulative effect of these investment, production, and knowledge transfer actions has been the globalization of production and trade.

The operations of transnational firms take on a complex variety of interrelationships among these firms, and we will focus especially on international production, offshore outsourcing of production and services, fragmentation of the value chain, global and regional production networks, and a myriad of forms of contractual relationships by which production, sales, and distribution are organized and controlled. Thus, transnational firms are responsible not only for production and sales, but also for massive global investment flows, the globalization of product and process technology and knowledge, and for much of the restructuring of global economic relationships. The economic prospects of much of the world are intensely affected by the calculations and actions of these corporations, which include both privately owned and state-owned firms. Many nations now devote considerable resources to developing national capabilities – an educated and trained workforce, significant infrastructure for production, communication and transportation, and cooperative and supportive policies – to attract and retain transnational firms. A considerable part of the surging role for emerging economies as a proportion of the global economy is a consequence of the investment and knowledge transfer policies of transnational firms.[29]

Foreign Direct Investment and Global Production

There are various mechanisms by which corporations create and operate a global enterprise. Traditionally – before about 1965 – most production was done by a single firm and within the home nation of that firm.

Internationalization consisted of exporting some part of that production to other nations, which may have required establishing a marketing and distribution operation in other nations. The growth and importance of the European Economic Community and the European market led many US firms to establish some production facilities inside the EEC, largely to avoid the tariffs and other barriers imposed on imports. Creating production, marketing, and distribution facilities in a foreign nation requires foreign direct investment (FDI). This refers to an investment in another nation to acquire assets that provide effective control over the operation of a business in that nation. Thus, the purpose of FDI is to create or obtain a business to be used to make a profit and therefore establishes a long-term position for that company in this nation. Once the investment has been made, it cannot be sold easily. A distinction is often made between a greenfield investment, when a firm sets up a new business operation in another country, and activities such as buying an existing firm in another nation in what is called a merger and acquisition (M&A) process.

An example of a greenfield investment helps define this process. In 1972, a very new company named Intel, making computer memory and seeking to control the costs of manufacturing, established a facility on the small island of Penang that is part of Malaysia. Intel paid for the facilities and the machinery, hired 100 employees and began production by air shipping nearly complete memory chips to Penang. These were assembled with the housing, tested for any errors, and then shipped out to Intel's customers. Over the next forty years, Intel has expanded these facilities, increased dramatically the complexity of the operations in Penang, and is now employing 8,000 workers there (see Photo 5.1). The money invested in Penang is an example of foreign direct investment.

Foreign direct investment has become of increasing importance as a source of business investment in many nations and as a main engine of economic growth and development. However, flows of foreign direct investment are both highly volatile and highly skewed toward some nations, specifically those where transnational firms expect the greatest benefits. This can be because a nation or region has a special combination of worker skills, low costs, high-quality infrastructure, specialized suppliers, and knowledge resources. Or, this can result from large and expanding markets with a particular value from being close to customers. Nations lacking in special production resources or important markets are not large recipients of FDI. This can be seen in Table 5.6. This data demonstrates the remarkable growth in FDI, along with its volatility and substantial redistribution over these twenty years. From 1990 to the peak in 2007, FDI increased by a factor of nearly ten. But for several nations in Europe, the decline from 2007–10 was more than two-thirds. Though developed nations were major beneficiaries of FDI across this period, poorer nations were proportionally much bigger gainers. In 1990, the

Table 5.6 Global FDI Inflows, 1990–2010 (billions $US)

Nation/Region	1990	1995	2000	2005	2006	2007	2008	2009	2010
World	207.5	342.4	1,403	982.6	1,462	1,971	1,744	1,185	1,244
EU	97.3	132.0	698.3	496.0	581.7	850.5	488.0	346.5	304.7
France	15.6	23.7	43.3	84.9	71.8	96.2	64.2	34.0	33.9
Germany	3.0	12.0	198.3	47.4	55.6	80.2	4.2	37.6	46.1
UK	30.5	20.0	118.8	176.0	156.2	196.4	91.5	71.1	45.9
US	48.4	58.8	314.0	104.8	237.1	216.0	306.4	152.9	228.3
China/Hong Kong	6.8	43.7	102.7	106.0	117.8	137.9	167.9	147.4	174.6
South/Central Amer.	8.1	29.0	77.4	72.2	69.8	108.7	126.2	75.8	111.1
CIS	0.04	3.9	5.4	26.2	44.6	78.2	108.4	63.8	64.1
Africa	2.8	5.7	11.0	38.2	46.3	63.1	73.4	60.2	55.0

Source: Data from UNCTAD Annex Tables, No. 1, www.unctad.org/en/Pages/DIAE/World%20Investment%20Report/Annex-Tables.aspx

Photo 5.1 The Intel Factory in Penang, Malaysia.
Source: Tom Lairson.

European Union plus the United States received 70 percent of all FDI, while China/Hong Kong, South and Central America, the CIS, and Africa together received less than 1 percent. In 2010, the European Union plus United States totaled 43 percent of global FDI while the emerging economies in our chart received 33 percent of this much larger total (see Table 5.7).

Table 5.7 Distribution of FDI, 1990–2 and 2007–9 (billions $US)

Sector	1990–2 (%)	2007–9 (%)
Total	175.8	1,633
Primary	14.9 (8.0)	164.3 (10.0)
Manufacturing	53.6 (30.0)	393.0 (24.0)
Services	92.6 (53.0)	1,025 (63.0)

Source: Data from UNCTAD Annex Tables, No. 26, www.unctad.org/en/Pages/DIAE/World%20Investment%20Report/Annex-Tables.aspx

Note: Remaining FDI is unspecified by sector.

This chart helps to show how FDI is flowing into primary products and services and less into manufacturing over this two-decade period.

Table 5.8 Smallest Recipients of FDI, 2005–10 Average

Nation	Population (millions)	Average FDI 2005–10 (millions $US)	Average FDI Per Capita (2005–10)
Pakistan	187.3	3,654	$19.51
Bangladesh	158.6	833.7	$5.26
Burma	54.0	615.3	$11.40
Tanzania	42.7	627.0	$14.68
Kenya	41.1	195.2	$4.75
Uganda	34.6	701.5	$20.27
Afghanistan	29.8	218.8	$7.23
Nepal	29.4	13.3	$0.45
Ghana	24.8	1,211	$48.84
Yemen	24.1	515.2	$21.38
Haiti	9.7	79.8	$8.23
By comparison:			
US	313.2	207,570	$662.74
Singapore	4.7	24,050	$5,117
China	1,337	89,614	$67.03

Source: Data from CIA World Factbook (for population data), www.cia.gov/library/publications/resources/the-world-factbook/; UNCTAD Annex Tables, No. 1, www.unctad.org/en/Pages/DIAE/World%20Investment%20Report/Annex-Tables.aspx

There are enormous gaps in the level of FDI, with some nations receiving very large absolute amounts and in proportion to GDP and population, and some with tiny amounts. Table 5.8 shows some of the lowest recipients of FDI in relation to population. Nations such as Nepal, Haiti, Afghanistan, and Bangladesh, collectively with a population about that of the United States, receive miniscule amounts of FDI, especially when we measure this in per capita terms. For comparison, the United States receives roughly sixty times as much FDI, China about ten times as much, and Singapore almost 1,000 times as much in per capita terms.

Why is this? The answer is TNCs are looking always to improve profits through FDI and seek locations that provide a special advantage to them in this effort. Sometimes this means natural resources, but at least as often TNCs are looking for a combination of high-quality infrastructure, a somewhat skilled workforce willing to accept lower wages, and specialized firms that complement their business. They may also look for a regulatory environment that is lax as a way of further reducing costs. Much about the presence and attractiveness of a particular location comes from efforts by national governments willing to make the investments to create and support these capabilities. Nations at the bottom of the list for FDI have usually been unable or unwilling to improve their ability to attract FDI by making the needed investments (see Table 5.9).

Table 5.9 FDI Flows by Type of Nation (billions $US)

Type of Nation	Inflows of FDI			Outflows of FDI		
	2011	2012	2013	2011	2012	2013
Developed Nation	880	517	566	1216	853	857
Developing Nation	725	729	778	423	440	454
Transition Economies	95	84	108	73	54	99

Source: Data from UNCTAD, *World Investment Report, 2014*, xiv.

One measure of the importance of FDI is the ratio of the stock of FDI[30] to GDP. In 1990, for the world as a whole, FDI represented 9.6 percent of global GDP, with developed nations receiving an average of 8.9 percent of their GDP and developing nations receiving 13.4 percent of their GDP. Not surprisingly, there was considerable variation across nations, with some, such as Hong Kong, at more than two and a half times GDP and many, such as India, at 0.5 percent. In 1990, the United States saw FDI coming into the United States at 9.3 percent of GDP, while China saw inward FDI at only 5.1 percent of GDP. In 2010, FDI across the world represented 20.2 percent of global GDP, even with more than a doubling of GDP levels two decades earlier. Developed nations now received FDI totaling 30.8 percent of GDP and developing nations received 29.1 percent. The United States now saw this measure soar to 23.5 percent, while China experienced a rise to 9.9 percent of GDP.[31]

Transnational Firms and the Global Economy

TNCs are very important actors in the global economy. States provide a geographic, political, infrastructure, knowledge, and worker base for production of goods and services. But firms, and especially transnational firms, actually engage in production, making decisions about what, where, and how to produce and typically retaining the profits. The growing scale of TNCs can be seen from some basic data. Though a large number of states contain an aggregate of economic strength of enormous size, many firms generate and control very large economic resources as well. Of course, the economies of states are composed of millions of economic actors while firms involve some significant centralized control over the resources of the firm.

Here is some data that allows us to compare the economic resources of states and firms. In 2013, world GDP was $74.2 trillion (see Table 5.10). The concentration of economic power can be seen from just the largest five nations, which together amount to $43 trillion or 58 percent of global

Table 5.10 Largest Twenty Nations by GDP (2013) 2010 (trillions $US)

Nation	GDP
1. US	16.72
2. China	13.39
3. India	4.99
4. Japan	4.73
5. Germany	3.23
6. Russia	2.55
7. Brazil	2.42
8. UK	2.39
9. France	2.28
10. Mexico	1.85
11. Italy	1.81
12. South Korea	1.67
13. Canada	1.52
14. Spain	1.39
15. Indonesia	1.28
16. Turkey	1.17
17. Australia	1.00
18. Iran	.99
19. Saudi Arabia	.93
20. Taiwan	.93

Source: Data from CIA World Factbook, www.cia.gov/library/publications/resources/the-world-factbook/

Note: The data for GDP are in terms of purchasing power parity (PPP), adjusted to prices in the United States.

GDP. If we count only the United States and the twenty-seven nations of the European Union, which together represent 10 percent of the world's population, these nations represent 44 percent of global GDP.

Measuring the size and importance of global firms can be done using a variety of metrics. In Table 5.11 we measure global financial firms in terms of assets and non-financial firms in terms of revenues. Comparing the size and influence of TNCs and nation-states is a very tricky venture, as these are quite different entities. Nonetheless, no matter which metric we use, TNCs represent large and important actors in international political economy. Clearly, the total resources of some nations, based on the entire economic output of a nation, dwarf that of TNCs. However, note this is true for only four or five nations; BNP Paribas, a global financial institution originating in Europe but with operations in eighty nations and with 200,000 employees, is one of the five or six largest economic entities in the world. Firms similar to BNP Paribas – global financial firms – control enormous resources as assets and have very large effects on nations and firms through their investment and lending behavior. Notice there are ten financial firms with economic resources that approx-

Table 5.11 World's Largest Transnational Corporations (Financial and Non-Financial) Listed by Assets or Revenues

Financial TNCs	Assets (trillions $US)	Non-Financial TNCs	Revenues (2008) (billions $US)
BNP Paribas	2.949	Exxon	477.4
Royal Bank Scotland	2.682	Royal Dutch Shell	458.4
HSBC	2.364	Wal-Mart	404.3
Bank of America	2.339	BP	365.7
Japan Post Bank	2.320	Chevron	273.0
Deutsche Bank	2.261	Conoco-Phillips	240.8
Barclays	2.237	Total	234.6
Credit Agricole	2.232	PetroChina	221.6
Mitsubishi	2.184	China Petroleum	220.4
JP Morgan	2.135	Toyota	204.0
ICBC	2.044	General Electric	182.5
Citigroup	2.002	Volkswagen	166.5
Bank of Tokyo	1.841	Eni Group	158.2
ING	1.673	General Motors	149.0
Mizuho	1.672	Ford Motor	146.3
China Construction	1.642	Daimler	140.3
Sumitomo Mitsui	1.600	E.On	126.9
Bank of China	1.588	ArcelorMittal	124.9
Lloyds	1.575	Hewlett-Packard	118.4
Agr. Bank of China	1.570	Fiat	116.0
Banco Santander	1.546	Siemens	116.0
Societe Generale	1.467	Thyssenkrupp	114.3
Unicredito Italiano Spa	1.331	Samsung	110.3
UBS	1.290	IBM	103.6
UniCredit	1.245	Honda	99.5
Wells Fargo	1.244	GDF	99.4
Commerzbank	1.145	Metro AG	99.4
Credit Suisse	1.022	Hitachi	99.4

Source: Data from UNCTAD Annex Tables, Nos 26 and 28, www.unctad.org/en/Pages/DIAE/World%20Investment%20Report/Annex-Tables.aspx; author's calculations from various annual reports.

imate those of Germany, Russia, Brazil, the United Kingdom, and France. And there are twenty-six financial TNCs with economic resources greater than Indonesia (population 245 million), Turkey, or Australia. Though these firms have little military force and do not control territory, they are able to augment their resources with the ability to operate throughout much of the world.

Transnational firms are more diverse than might be expected. Though most TNCs are private firms, meaning the ownership of the shares is in the hands of private individuals and institutional investors, an increasingly important set of TNCs is owned, in part or whole, by governments.

An especially important group of state-owned enterprises (SOEs), which operate globally as TNCs, are in the energy business. Indeed, the very largest global energy firms are state-owned.[32] These include firms such as Saudi Aramco, Petrobras (Brazil), and China National Petroleum Company, which dominate much of the production of oil around the world.[33] Many of these firms, especially those from China, operate across the world looking for, producing, and distributing energy products. Another important category of state-owned TNCs is financial firms. From China, where state-owned covers a multiplicity of forms, to a variety of nations benefiting from global trade, many nations have created investment firms to leverage their large holdings of foreign reserves. These are referred to as sovereign wealth funds (SWFs). Many nations have built up a very large financial surplus from trade relations and have chosen to establish a unit of the government to invest these funds. From China, with its gargantuan 4 trillion dollar holdings of foreign reserves, to a collection of several energy surplus nations (Saudi Arabia, UAE, Abu Dhabi, Kuwait), to nations with large trade surpluses (Taiwan, Korea, Japan), there are many very large and important sovereign wealth funds.[34] Perhaps the most successful example is in Singapore, where the government owns two large SWFs with assets totaling about $400 billion. The goals of the Singapore SWFs are related to enhancing the economic capabilities of the government and the economy, with an exemplary record of accomplishment. Though there is increased concern about the potential impacts of SWFs, the real and unanswered question is whether state investments will operate any differently from private funds.[35] A broader conception permits us to see beyond the categories of private and public to understand the deeper partnership between governments and firms in the management and governance of the global economy.[36]

Why do firms engage in FDI? The commonly understood answer – to gain access to lower wages and easier sets of business rules – is correct but misleadingly narrow and incomplete. Because labor is a declining proportion of production costs, there are increasingly more complex reasons for operating abroad and especially for operating a globally dispersed business. There is now a vast array of global resources located in a wide variety of nations, and TNCs typically seek to gain competitive advantage from a unique organization of those resources.

Perhaps one of the most surprising reasons for global TNC investment is that emerging economies contain not only many workers but many consumers as well. Economic growth brings higher wages and incomes and an expanding middle class. TNCs want to sell their products where markets are growing rapidly. Increasingly, this means production, distribution, and marketing capabilities to serve these emerging markets. An example is the auto market in China – now the largest in the world – and in which the German firm Volkswagen and the US firm General Motors produce and sell more cars than in any other market. Though these markets usually require new kinds of products specialized for different tastes, the ability to spread costs, risks, and demand fluctuations over a new set of consumers provides a compelling incentive for FDI.

But surely the most important purpose for TNC investment in recent years is to gain access to specialized capabilities in a particular environment. Global production is increasingly knowledge-intensive and specialized knowledge is now widely distributed across the world. The competitive advantage of a firm now often rests on the ability to assemble a unique set of global resources. This means developing a sophisticated global scanning and knowledge-gathering capability. Then, it must act organizationally to develop a product mix and innovation capacity and distribute its production facilities – inside and outside the firm – to those locations with the kinds of specialized resources to enhance the efficiency and effectiveness of the system. For example, in 2006 one of the world's great firms – IBM – relocated a critically important part of its entire business operation from the United States to China. The process of procurement – the purchasing of all the resources IBM uses to operate its business – was moved to the southern Chinese city of Shenzhen. This was not much related to the costs of labor in China but rather to the tremendous concentration of knowledge workers in procurement in the Shenzhen area. It was not the low wages of these workers but the cluster of knowledge capabilities they collectively create that drew IBM halfway across the world.[37] Another example comes from India, which has provided IBM and other software services firms with low-cost but highly skilled software engineers. But, as with procurement in China, IBM has various operations that allow it to gain access to complementary skills in numerous locations around the globe, and much of its global competitive advantage comes from the ability to organize and combine these knowledge resources.[38] Put simply, low wages is of declining importance for the operation of global firms and specialized knowledge resources of rising importance in explaining global FDI patterns.[39]

Global/Regional Production Networks

The extraordinary expansion of emerging market economies, described at the beginning of this chapter, is linked in part to new forms of relationship among transnational firms, national and local governments, and local firms in these nations. Moreover, this set of relationships reflects the creation of various forms of local but globally specialized assets sought out by TNCs in their FDI activities. The global and regional production network (GRPN) is a new system of production and involves the partnership of TNCs, states, and local firms to reorganize the scale and geography of production based on the capabilities of information technology.

Understanding the global production network requires that we consider how the production of goods takes place. An important concept is the value chain, which refers to the various elements and activities that are involved in production. Consider the value chain of a computer. It must be designed so all the components – the solid state drive, memory, the microprocessor, the different kinds of software, the LCD screen, and other related components – work effectively together. The various components must be manufactured, and sometimes rapidly improved, so they work together and with a high level of reliability; the parts must be assembled in one place; the computer must be sold, perhaps online and in a retail store; it must be marketed, with ads in various kinds of media; it must be delivered; it must be serviced if something goes wrong; and the entire process must be organized and managed. Collectively, these make up the value chain. Though an automobile is much more complex in the number of parts and the design, it too has a comparable value chain.

In the 1960s and earlier, a very large part of the value chain of a computer (then a mainframe, as there were no PCs) was organized within the direct control of a single firm, largely because of the information and communication difficulties and costs of controlling production. It was usually better to make it yourself than to find some other firm. For example, IBM integrated production of most of the parts and the software within IBM, and most of this took place within the United States. This was common for most large companies. Even when subcontractors were used for production of certain components, almost always these firms were located within the home country of the buyer of these parts.

Interestingly, it was computers – personal computers – and the ability to link these computers together inexpensively that changed this process and gave us the global production network. The rapid improvement in the processing power of personal computers, at a falling price, coupled with the ability to network computers and communicate directly with each other, have had a vast impact on the globalization of production.[40] Quite simply, the globalization of production (and finance) has been made possible by the long-term and exponential declines in the cost of creating, manipulating, and distributing information, even on a global scale. The changes wrought by this are truly stupendous. Consider the comparison of an advanced desktop personal computer from 1982 with an iPhone 6 of 2014. The iPhone 6 has a processing power that is 350 times that (1.4Ghz versus 4Mhz) of a $2,500 1982 desktop and costs one-fifth that of the same desktop (even less in real dollars). When you add in the fact the iPhone 6 weighs about one-hundredth of the desktop, is a global phone, connected to a global Internet, takes high-quality photos and HD video, and you can talk to it and it answers back, and the differences are nothing less than miraculous.

When connected to the system of production, these information and communication technologies have altered dramatically the location and the process of the production of goods and services. One of the first changes relating to computers was the containerization of global shipping, with vast ships loaded with large container modules full of a diversity of products. The containers were quickly loaded and unloaded and switched to a truck or train for delivery. Keeping track cheaply of the goods and their destinations was through computers and linked to a specialized and sophisticated port infrastructure usually built by the government.[41] In addition, rapidly falling costs of information and communication removed many of the managerial barriers to operating production around the world.

Firms are constantly looking to achieve competitive advantages by lowering costs and therefore the prices of their products. There are large gaps in wage levels between rich and poor nations that offer significant potential for lowering costs, but achieving these gains was very difficult because of several problems that were solved in the years after 1965. One was the continuing decline in tariffs, not only in the markets of rich nations but also in poor nations. A second was the weak infrastructure and business systems in many poor nations. Several nations in Asia began upgrading these capabilities, sometimes in a focused area known as a "special economic zone," and making commitments to continuous upgrading for the future. The third was the large difficulties in managing firms at long distances. Computers and networks changed that by continuously lowering the costs of creating, applying, and distributing information.

The result was to shift much of the production and assembly part of the value chain from the rich home country of a firm to nations where costs were lower and then to independent firms operating in those nations that specialized in those parts of the value chain. Sometimes referred to as the "fragmentation" of the value chain, this meant breaking up various elements of the value chain and offshore outsourcing them to an independent firm operating in another nation. Major sources for this offshore outsourcing from the 1970s onward were Singapore, Taiwan, Hong Kong, Korea, Malaysia, Thailand, Vietnam, and especially China. New specialized firms emerged, operating in these nations to provide the production processes and services outsourced by global firms who would retain control over the design, branding, and marketing of the products. For example, throughout the period after 1984, Apple has designed and created many new computer products, music players, phones, and tablets. Apple has many suppliers that operate factories around the world, none of which is owned by Apple. One of the most important is Foxconn, a company from Taiwan that operates numerous very large production and assembly facilities in southern China and elsewhere.[42] Apple is an example of a "global network flagship" firm, a TNC organizing and coordinating production of their products through a variety of suppliers that often are themselves global firms.[43] Many other firms, such as Cisco, Nike, GAP, and even Disney for its toys, operate the same way.

The rise of global production networks fueled much of the spectacular economic growth of nations able to attract and/or create firms related to this process. And, GPNs served to affect dramatically the overall structure of global trade and the global economy. A large part of what we call globalization – especially the globalization of trade – is really the global diffusion of production. The process of shifting production abroad to take advantage of cost advantages requires TNCs either to set up a production facility abroad or to engage in offshore outsourcing to an independent firm. This can mean a Western firm – such as Flextronics – establishes production facilities abroad and engages in production for a flagship firm. Or a local firm – such as Taiwan Semiconductor Manufacturing or Samsung (Korean) – establishes these facilities and obtains contracts for production. Such a system often means different parts of a product are manufactured in different countries and then brought together for assembly in yet another nation (often China). The result is a set of global or regional trade networks that follow the geography of global production. One outgrowth of this process is the emergence of regional trade agreements, which are specialized trade arrangements among nations to reduce tariffs and other trade barriers and thereby facilitate this kind of trade. The production capabilities of nations, combined with the benefits of a regional trade arrangement, represent a competitive advantage for attracting and locating additional production.[44]

At the same time GPNs enhanced the economic capabilities of some nations, this new system also had measurable effects on the global economic system as a whole. Perhaps most important, GPNs were central in creating new global economic structures. The most important processes of economic relationships in the global economy have shifted from trade among nations to the interactions among firms and between firms and states. Global production is now far more important than exchange that simply crosses borders, and both global production and trade depend on the partnerships between TNCs and states for developing the industrial ecology that supports both processes.[45] These partnerships, especially in more knowledge-intensive industries, are built around continuing flows of FDI and of technology and knowledge leading to long-term changes in the diffusion of knowledge and to the potential for continuing economic upgrading.[46] The very capacity for building manufacturing systems, and for innovating those systems, has been shifted in great measure from rich nations to emerging economies. Increasingly, firms from emerging markets have leveraged their knowledge and technology resources into the much more lucrative design and product development part of the value chain, especially as this relates to production processes. Even the most advanced parts of innovation are now being done in the same emerging nations.[47]

Regions of Production, Trade, and Investment

The European Union

An important question for thinking about the trends in global political economy is whether we should examine globalization as a process sweeping across much of the world and providing for unifying and integrating processes, or whether we should see the world fragmenting into separate and distinct regions.[48] Do special trade agreements framed around geographic regions – some call these preferential trade agreements – have the effect of enhancing trade among nations or simply diverting trade from one place to another?[49] The viability and effectiveness of systems of regional trade can be examined as a first step by considering the most important, the European Union, now more than fifty years old.

Though certainly not the first preferential trade agreement, the European Union is surely the most important, as it encompasses twenty-seven countries with a total population of 500 million and a combined GDP equal to that of the United States. Europe dominates global trade as a result mostly of very high levels of exchange within this region. Moreover, the European Union has become much more than a Preferential Trade Agreement (PTA), with a complex system of political processes and its own currency, the euro. As such, the European Union is the most far-reaching effort at international cooperation, consistently seeking to expand its membership as well as the issues under its jurisdiction.

The European Economic Community or Common Market, as today's EU was once called, was established in 1958. The original six members[50] sought to use the creation of a common tariff area as a means of resolving some of the lingering political conflicts that had troubled Europe for the preceding seventy-five years. This Common Market would provide important new markets for the products of individual nations and the increased level of interdependence was expected to promote enhanced levels of political cooperation. In addition, the economic and political successes of the original six served to draw other European nations into the system as well.[51]

The expansion of membership in the EEC was accompanied by an enlargement of political capabilities and a deepening of economic interdependence within the European Community. In 1985, agreement was reached on moving beyond the removal of tariff barriers to the elimination of non-tariff barriers as well. In addition, the community sought to establish common standards across the members on a wide range of trade-related matters in order to facilitate the free movement of goods, money, and people. The process of political decision making on EEC issues was shifted much more to a majority vote, with much less of a possibility for any one member to veto a decision. In 1991, at Maastricht, the Netherlands, the members of the European Community reached agreement on the goal of much greater integration through an economic and monetary union. Adopting the name, European Union, was linked to a series of arrangements to deepen multilateral decision making, a common foreign and security policy, and establish a common currency.

Creating the common currency – the euro – between 1999 and 2002 was certainly the most significant form of economic and political integration, one that forced the greatest sacrifice of sovereignty.[52] Though the decision for a common currency permitted some nations in the European Union to opt out, there were compelling reasons to move in this direction. Most important was that closer integration in trade made for closer integration in money. This was first recognized in the 1970s when the community adopted mechanisms to link exchange rates, supported by procedures to coordinate monetary and fiscal policies. The success of this effort helped prompt decisions to permit the unhindered movement of money, community-wide branch banking, and an integrated market for financial services. Once money began to move freely, large benefits and costs were associated with developing a single monetary unit that would operate across this geographic area (see Figure 5.1).

Notwithstanding the powerful reasons for a single currency, there are also strong countervailing arguments. Creating the money for a nation and managing the money supply are core features of modern national sovereignty. A single currency for the European Union negates many of the prerogatives of the nation-state, not least of which was the ability to influence economic growth through monetary policy. Nations often differ substantially in their domestic commitment to a loose or tight monetary policy, that is, whether or not the nation will expand its money supply to boost growth. Within Europe, one nation had historically provided a strong anchor for a tight money policy, working to restrain the inflationary effects of too rapid a growth in the money supply: Germany. Differences among Eurozone nations about monetary policy have been greatly exacerbated by the global financial crisis. Operating a single currency successfully would mean a real sacrifice of fiscal policy as well, with all nations conforming to a unitary standard based on Germany. What's more, a single currency obscures the reality that different countries in the European Union have very different levels of competitiveness and operate with wide variations in their balance of trade, some with significant deficits and some with large surpluses. Adjusting these imbalances now is somewhat disconnected from the value of the euro and must rest primarily on wage levels.

Notwithstanding the monetary difficulties of the euro, trade relationships of the European Union have been spectacularly successful. However, the economic growth in Europe associated with the creation of the euro contained numerous structural problems that ultimately threatened the

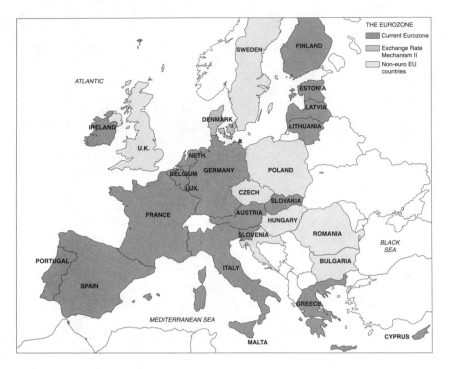

Figure 5.1 The European Union and the Eurozone.

Sources: Adapted from Balaam and Dillman, *Introduction to Political Economy*, 6th edn. Taylor & Francis (2014), p. 294, Figure 12–1, and Evan Centanni, www.polgeonow. com/2015/01/eurozone-gains-new-member-country.html

European Union once the global financial crisis struck in 2008. In the years preceding the crisis, the economy of production and trade and the economy of finance failed to produce balanced growth. Much like the United States, financial speculation combined with a rapid expansion of debt (government and private) to create widespread vulnerabilities across much of Europe.

Between 2000 and 2010, EU external exports rose by 58.7 percent to 1.349 trillion; in the same time, external imports to the European Union rose by 52 percent to 1.509 trillion. The composition of this trade changed substantially in terms of the weights of various trading partners over time. These changes can be seen in Table 5.12.

The United States remains the preponderant market for EU exports, but has declined substantially along with Japan in favor of China and Russia. In the area of EU imports, the position of the United States has declined more substantially, with China and Russia the major beneficiaries of selling in the European Union.

Table 5.12 Composition of EU External Trade, 2000–10 (% of total EU exports or imports)

Exports				
Trading Partner	2000	2006	2008	2010
United States	28.0	23.2	19.1	18.0
China	3.0	5.5	6.0	8.4
Switzerland	8.5	7.6	7.5	7.8
Russia	2.7	6.2	8.0	8.4
Turkey	3.8	4.3	4.1	4.5
Japan	5.4	3.9	3.2	3.2
Imports				
Trading Partner				
China	7.5	14.4	15.8	18.7
United States	20.8	13.0	11.9	11.3
Russia	6.4	10.4	11.4	10.6
Switzerland	6.3	5.3	5.1	5.5
Japan	9.3	5.7	4.8	4.4

Source: Data from *External and Intra-EU Trade, A Statistical Yearbook*, 2011, 31–2.

The Rise of Preferential Trade Agreements[53]

The European Union may be the most important preferential trade agreement but it is far from being the only important one. Indeed, there is reason to believe the increasing openness in the global system resulting from the GATT/WTO process actually contributes to the creation of PTAs. Such arrangements can provide important forms of bargaining leverage within the negotiating processes of the larger multilateral systems.[54] And the success of the EU project has contributed to creating other regional agreements as a competitive response to the European Union. In many ways, the creation of the North American Free Trade Agreement (NAFTA) in 1994 can be seen in these terms. And, NAFTA can be seen as a stimulus for MERCOSUR in Latin America and ASEAN-AFTA in Asia. And a recent wave of bilateral trade agreements and even cross-regional agreements has also been a response to this growing trend of negotiations. One estimate is that by 2008, as much as $5.9 trillion in trade (a bit more than one-third of global trade) took place among nations engaged in these kinds of agreements.[55]

The relationship of the WTO system and the emerging PTA system is a complicated one. The GATT/WTO system is based on multilateralism, non-discrimination, and a commitment to most-favored-nation, which have the effect of spreading new rules quite widely. By contrast, regional trade agreements (RTAs), Free Trade Agreements (FTAs), and Preferential Trade Agreements (PTAs) are based on bilateral or restricted multilateralism and preferential terms that discriminate against non-members. As a consequence, PTAs represent a significant challenge to the WTO-based system of trading rules that has evolved over the past six decades. For the past two decades, PTAs have expanded considerably and have come to define much of the direction for trade. Though many PTAs have a strong regional cast, about an equal number operate across regional boundaries. The rules in many PTAs extend significantly beyond those embodied in the WTO and the complex and differentiated system of rules for those inside and outside of PTAs undermines the broadly multilateral system created by the WTO. Measuring the impact of PTAs on overall global trade is difficult, but basic indicators suggest that most global trade remains associated with the multilateral rules established by the WTO system.[56]

PTAs have become much more important as a vehicle for advancing free trade in the past twenty years.[57] Figure 5.2 displays this growth and the diversity of PTAs during this period, especially the increasing importance of such agreements for free trade and economic integration. Nonetheless, many observers have worried about the exclusionary character of PTAs and fear the potential for large PTAs to turn into regional trade blocs threatening to undermine the multilateral trading order that has defined the post-1945 era. This concern has deepened, as the WTO process has seemed to break down with no new agreements in two decades. Perhaps more troubling has been the move by some of the largest emerging economies – China and Russia – as well as the United States and Europe to embrace large PTAs as a substitute for the WTO.[58] The

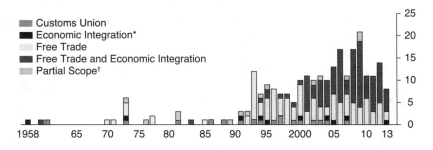

Figure 5.2 The Growth and Diversity of Preferential Trade Agreements.

Source: Adapted from *The Economist*, October 12, 2013, www.economist.com/news/special-report/21587380-multilateral-trade-pacts-are-increasingly-giving-way-regional-ones-my-backyard

* Includes joint customs union and partial-scope agreements
† Covering only certain products

limited agreement achieved at Bali in the Doha round of WTO trade talks may well extend the importance of PTAs and the worries over the results for multilateralism.

In 2015, three mega groups of PTA negotiations were being conducted across the globe:

1. Trans-Pacific Partnership (TPP), the United States, Australia, Brunei Darussalam, Canada, Chile, Japan, Malaysia, Mexico, New Zealand, Peru, Singapore, and Vietnam
2. Transatlantic Trade and Investment Partnership (TTIP), the United States and the European Union
3. Regional Comprehensive Economic Partnership Agreement (RCEP), Brunei, Myanmar, Cambodia, Indonesia, Laos, Malaysia, the Philippines, Singapore, Thailand, and Vietnam are the ASEAN members negotiating with six other nations with which ASEAN has FTAs: Australia, China, India, Japan, Korea, and New Zealand.

The outcomes for each mega-negotiation remain uncertain, with each somewhat dependent on the other two.

The expansion of PTAs – especially the array of massive deals focusing on China, India, the European Union, and the United States – calls into question the role of the WTO as the primary institution for defining the rules for global trade. For nearly two decades the WTO has been stalled in an effort to reach new agreements on trade rules that will close the divide between developed and developing nations on new trade rules. However, in December 2013 an agreement was reached under the Doha Round of negotiations conducted by the WTO. This agreement focused on trade facilitation procedures and subsidies for agriculture.[59] Though the agreement is a substantive success, the dynamism in PTAs seems to have surpassed the WTO. But this can only come true if these large PTAs reach fruition.

Conclusion: Evaluating the Gains and Losses from Trade

Few topics generate more conflict in political analysis than trade. This is surely because trade is a double-edged sword: it can lead to large gains from lower costs and more variety in goods, but also can produce large losses from the effects on wages, jobs, and even profits. In addition, the gains and losses are unevenly distributed, especially for those who find their earnings and life prospects severely affected. One way to focus our thinking on this topic is to examine the trade relationship between the United States and China. This is one of the largest bilateral trading relationships in the world and one of the most controversial. There is considerable conflict between the United States and China over this issue, with

Table 5.13 Global Imbalances/Asian Imbalances, 1999–2012 (US Current Account Balances)

Year	US Current Account – Total (millions $US)	US–Asia Current Account (millions $US)	US–China Current Account (millions $US)	US–China % Total	US–Asia % of Total
1999	−301630	−216071	−72743	24.1	71.6
2000	−417426	−246690	−88043	21.1	59.1
2001	−398270	−225945	−88658	22.3	56.7
2002	−459151	−249558	−109899	23.9	54.3
2003	−521519	−260713	−131825	25.3	50.0
2004	−631130	−325465	−172343	27.3	51.6
2005	−748683	−377908	−219196	29.3	50.5
2006	−803547	−437434	−259490	32.3	54.4
2007	−726573	−452594	−293105	40.3	62.3
2008	−706068	−430534	−306849	43.7	61.0
2009	−376551	−338602	−263548	70.0	89.9
2010	−470898	−381118	−300348	63.8	80.9
2011	−465926	−395296	−315033	67.6	84.3
2012	−440417	−424376	−329475	74.8	96.4

Source: Data from Bureau of Economic Affairs, www.bea.gov/international/bp_web/ simple.cfm?anon=71&table_id=10&area_id=35; author's calculations.

regular calls from the US Congress for efforts to punish China for its unfair behavior, and much resentment in China over what they view as unfair treatment.

Over the years after 2000, trade between the United States and China has grown rapidly in size and the imbalances in this relation have grown even faster. Table 5.13 gives details. As we can see, with the entire world the United States has run a very large and mostly expanding current account deficit in recent years. Perhaps the best that can be said is the current account deficit in 2012 had declined by half and had declined as a percent of GDP. Analyzing US trade problems cannot simply focus on China or even Asia alone, even though China and Asia represent a very large, and for China growing, proportion of US trade.[60] Examining these numbers requires an important qualification. If we measure Chinese exports to the United States in terms of value added in China, the US deficit specifically with China would decline. This is because most of the components for much of the final goods are manufactured elsewhere (mostly in Asia) and the value added by China is the result of assembling the product in China. This is only a small part of the value added. Nonetheless, such a value-added approach would also shift the value of components produced to other Asian nations and would also reflect the fact that many US firms capture much of the profits from these products.

Chapter 2 discussed how the most important gains from trade come from the ability to specialize in goods where a nation has at least a comparative advantage. The exchange of these goods for those produced by a nation with a different comparative advantage allows both nations to consume at higher levels than either could by producing each of the goods alone. But, as we have also seen, this comes at a cost for workers who were previously employed in areas where specialization was less effective and must now shift their work to industries where the comparative advantage and specialization yield the highest benefits. This transition from one industry to another entails some costs and only works to the extent that all workers can make this transition. Otherwise, the benefits of specialization must be offset by the costs of economic restructuring. To this calculation one must also add the benefits trade can have on the dynamic quality of an economy. Trade can produce incentives to improve the capacity to produce from investments in new equipment, in additional worker training, in more research and development, and generally in innovative activities. Shifting from static to dynamic ways of analyzing comparative advantage suggest that trade can promote a more innovative and adaptable economic system. At the same time, the process of restructuring over part of the value chain can potentially damage other parts of that value chain that depend on the segment lost to foreign competition.

How can we apply these ideas to the case of United States–China trade? There is considerable evidence that this trade relationship has led to adjustment costs that must be offset against the gains from lower prices for goods imported from China. One important study looked at measures by US counties for exposure to Chinese trade and of changes in manufacturing jobs and overall employment. Not surprisingly, those counties most heavily exposed to Chinese goods were hit much harder in employment than those less exposed. For example, counties at the 75th percentile – with more exposure to Chinese imports than three-quarters of all counties – saw their manufacturing employment fall by one-third more than counties at the 25th percentile and also saw the non-manufacturing employment and wages fall more than in those counties less exposed. Further, the rise in unemployment caused government payments for unemployment insurance, food stamps, and disability payments.[61]

Much of this impact can be traced to the speed of China's rise as an export power, with most of the effects coming in the decade after 2000. Low-income countries (mostly China) accounted for a rapidly rising share of US manufacturing imports, increasing from 2.9 percent in 1991 to 5.9 percent in 2000 to 11.7 percent in 2007, and by that year 4.6 percent of all US spending was on goods imported from China.[62] Chinese imports were especially significant in luggage, rubber and plastic footwear, games and toys, and die-cut paperboard, and substantial in apparel, textiles, furniture, leather goods, electrical appliances, and jewelry. When the gains from trade are compared to the increased welfare costs from the resulting unemployment, as much as two-thirds of the gains are wiped out even without trying to measure the individual costs of being unemployed and finding another job. Though China trade still has a net gain for the United States as a whole, the losses from trade are substantial and sobering.

There are other gains to be had from trade, and also other losses that must be considered in tallying the effects. An important feature of the gains and losses comes from the ways firms respond to the competitive effects of imports from nations such as China. Some firms can fail to act, others may choose to relocate part or all of production abroad – offshoring – and others can invest in new products and processes and innovate in effective ways to gain competitive advantage. Recent studies confirm some of the losses from Chinese imports, finding falling prices, lower demand for unskilled workers, declining profitability, and failing firms. But there are also gains from trade competition that drive surviving firms to engage in significant technological upgrading:

> Firms facing higher levels of Chinese import competition create more patents, spend more on R&D, raise their IT intensity, adopt more modern management practices, and increase their overall level of TFP (total factor productivity).[63]

The positive consequence of this process is a stronger economy, with firms and workers better able to compete in global markets and also deliver higher quality and lower prices domestically.

There are yet more complexities to this story. Though trade does press domestic firms to innovate, it may also lead to other less favorable consequences. Trade certainly did lead to adaptation and adjustment in the US economy, but some of these adjustments may have pernicious consequences. Focusing on the industrial restructuring and shifts in employment in the United States over the two decades after 1990, we see employment shifting from tradeable sectors (goods that can be traded in the global economy, such as manufactured goods) to the non-tradeable sectors (such as health care, government, construction, and hotels and food service), which experienced almost all of the US growth in employment after 1990. Much of the growth in construction employment to 2007 was a result of the creation of a bubble of investment in housing that was unsustainable and collapsed in the global financial crisis beginning in 2008. Moreover, non-tradeable sectors have experienced lower wage levels than tradeable sectors and the large growth in employment here is associated with increasing income inequality.[64] Rapid declines in manufacturing employment were associated with the ability of firms to maintain levels of production, primarily by investing in machines and technology. The offshore outsourcing of large parts of the value chain produced a rather stark process of specialization that led to rising wages for the shrinking number of persons remaining in manufacturing.

Equally troubling has been the erosion of the capacity for innovation as a result of the process of offshore outsourcing. The sharp division of labor in this process – develop, design, and innovate in the United States combined with manufacture components and assemble abroad – often cannot work because of the deep connections between innovation and manufacturing. These two parts of the value chain are connected through the concept of an industrial ecology, thought of as a complex flow and exchange of knowledge and expertise that nourishes both parts. Innovation requires the presence of the knowledge and expertise associated with manufacturing, which has been systematically moved offshore and used by firms there to upgrade their capabilities over time.[65] When companies like Kodak gave up manufacturing cameras, this damaged their ability to design and innovate with the very digital camera they invented. This was because the industrial ecology for this kind of manufacturing was gone and this absence was a barrier to innovation.

So, how does the complex thicket of gains and losses net out? In one very important sense this is a political and not just an economic question. How a nation sees the net effects of trade depends greatly on the political configuration of the various groups who are affected in differentiated ways. Though there are almost always important costs associated with the gains from trade, whether these costs are recognized and actions taken to ameliorate them is the result of a political process and therefore inconsistent from one nation to the next. Systems of political economy will act to reap certain gains because of the political strength of those groups positioned to obtain these gains. Costs are recognized when those who are hurt have the political leverage to get them recognized. The policies adopted in relation to trade often are best understood as a political balancing act designed to balance gains against losses in political terms. Making a coherent national trade strategy is sometimes undermined by the cacophony of vested interests focused only on what gains or losses they will experience.

Consider agricultural production. Food is a vital resource, is often produced domestically, the producers (farmers) often have the ability to express their political interests, and food imported from abroad can enhance the quantity and quality of domestic consumption. Because of the political power of agricultural interests, many nations have chosen to provide various forms of payments to these interests in order to maintain their incomes in the face of market pressures to lower prices. Some of this can surely be justified on the grounds of food security, so as to guarantee domestic food production even if this is not economically feasible. But the largest part of agricultural subsidies comes from the political leverage of those groups that benefit.

After 1995, subsidies by Japan and the European Union have generally declined from very high levels, but in 2010 still totaled over $50 billion for Japan and $100 in the European Union. In the United States agricultural subsidies in 2010 totaled $26 billion.[66] Each of these societies has determined politically that subsidies to promote domestic food production are worth billions of dollars. However, many nations reach very different conclusions about supporting workers whose jobs have been eliminated by trade. The value of forcing workers to adjust – often under very difficult circumstances – is thought to be high and the political strength of displaced workers is somewhat less than for owners of farms. Over time, this can lead to dramatic declines in support for free trade and to intensified political struggles.

Key Concepts (see Glossary)

ASEAN Free Trade Agreement (AFTA)
Association of Southeast Asian Nations (ASEAN)
Commercial Services
Emerging Economies
European Union (EU)
Eurozone
Foreign Direct Investment (FDI)
Fragmentation of the Value Chain
Global Production
Global and Regional Production Networks (GRPNs)
Global Network Flagship Firm
Greenfield Investment
Merchandise Trade
Merger and Acquisition (M&A)
Non-Tariff Barriers (NTBs)

Offshore Outsourcing
Preferential Trade Agreements (PTAs)
Regional Comprehensive Economic Partnership Agreement (RCEP)
Sovereign Wealth Fund (SWF)
Special Economic Zone (SEZ)
State-Owned Enterprises (SOEs)
Transatlantic Trade and Investment Partnership (TTIP)
Transnational Corporations (TNCs)
Trans-Pacific Partnership (TPP)
Triad of Global Production
World Trade Organization (WTO)

Discussion Questions

1 Explain the structural features of global trade:

- Triad of trade
- Regionalization of trade

- Regional specialization
- Concentration of trade
- Global imbalances.

2 What do we mean by the political economy of trade? Here are some statements that can be discussed to help understand this idea:

- Explain the statement: "free trade is a political choice about the rules for economic interaction with the rest of the world."
- Explain the statement: "free trade requires a system of political relations within and among nations that will support and sustain free trade, by emphasizing the gains and minimizing the losses, combined with global institutions to interpret and enforce the rules."
- Explain the various ways to predict how economic interests are affected by trade.

3 How should we describe the actions to reduce trade barriers in the twenty years after World War II? Was this based on a clear commitment to free trade?

4 Explain how the emerging system of trade rules based on RTAs, FTAs, and PTAs poses a threat to the system based on the WTO.

5 Explain the political economy of how nations respond to the gains and losses from trade by discussing the following statements:

Though there are almost always important costs associated with the gains from trade, whether these costs are recognized and actions taken to ameliorate them is the result of a political process and therefore inconsistent from one nation to the next. Systems of political economy will act to reap certain gains because of the political strength of those groups positioned to obtain these gains. Costs are recognized when those who are hurt have the political leverage to get them recognized.

At the same time, international trade and finance serve to engage and even help to formulate domestic interests. The expansion of global trade can lead existing firms and interests to press harder for free trade and even bring other firms' interests into the free trade camp. And the political institutions of a society may be able to link interests across sectors. Here firms focused on trade, and other firms focused on finance may have their interests linked through political parties, ministries, and political entrepreneurs.

It is much easier to organize politically around a policy of protectionism – especially in societies like the United States and Japan, which emphasize local interests – than around a policy of free trade. This is because the benefits of protection flow to a very specific group, which maintains its incomes as a result of such policies. The gains from free trade are much more diffuse and more difficult to identify, flowing mostly to consumers in the form of lower prices and more plentiful products. The gains may be large but are less concentrated and therefore less politically relevant.

6   How do we explain the very large gaps in the amount of FDI received by different nations?
7   How valid is the effort to compare nations and firms in terms of the size of economic resources? What conclusions can we reach about the power of TNCs?
8   What are the objectives of TNCs in engaging in FDI?
9   Explain the special features of a global/regional production network (GPN). How is a GPN different from production systems in the past?
10   What are some of the most important consequences of GPNs?
11   Discuss the partnership relationship between governments and firms in creating GPNs.
12   Explain the nature of a preferential trade agreement and the effects this can have on economic and political relations among nations.
13   Discuss the gains and losses from trade and some of the policy implications that flow from how we measure these quantities.

Notes

1   Data in this and the next paragraph are from: Angus Maddison, *Chinese Economic Performance in the Long Run*, Washington: OECD, 2nd ed., 2007, 44; Giovanni Arrighi, "China's Market Economy in the Long Run," in Ho-fung Hung (ed.), *China and the Transformation of Global Capitalism*, Baltimore: Johns Hopkins University Press, 2009, 23.
2   James Miles, "China: Rising Power, Anxious State," *The Economist*, June 23, 2011, www.economist.com/node/18829149
3   *The Economist*, "Emerging vs. Developed Economies," August 4, 2011, www.economist.com/blogs/dailychart/2011/08/emerging-vs-developed-economies
4   *The Economist*, "All in the Same Boat," September 10, 2011, 82.
5   Both exports and imports for developed nations declined more in 2009 and recovered less in 2010 than for developing nations. World Trade Organization, *World Trade Report*, 2011, Table 1, 7, 22. Available at www.wto.org/english/res_e/publications_e/wtr11_e.htm
6   Review Chapter 2 if you don't remember what this means.
7   This special ability is discussed in Barry Eichengreen, *Exorbitant Privilege*, Oxford: Oxford University Press, 2011.
8   These events will be discussed in much greater detail in Chapter 6.
9   Bank for International Settlements, *Annual Report 2011*, 35.
10   Data from author's calculations based on Bureau of Economic Affairs, www.bea.gov/international/bp_web/simple.cfm?anon=71&table_id=10&area_id=35

11 Helen Milner, "The Political Economy of International Trade," *Annual Review of Political Science*, 2 (1999) 91–114.

12 Kevin O'Rourke, "Politics and Trade: Lessons from Past Globalisations," *Bruegel Essays and Lecture Series*, 2009, who traces the patterns of global trade to a "military or political equilibrium among contending powers."

13 Judith Stein, *Pivotal Decade*, New Haven: Yale University Press, 2011, 215–376.

14 John Gerard Ruggie, "International Regimes, Transactions, and Change: Embedded Liberalism in the Postwar Economic Order," *International Organization*, 36.2 (1982) 379–415.

15 Layna Mosley, *Global Capital and National Governments*, Cambridge: Cambridge University Press, 2003.

16 Dani Rodrik, *The Globalization Paradox*, New York: Norton, 2011, 71.

17 Charles Maier, "The Politics of Productivity: Foundations of American International Economic Policy after World War II," *International Organization*, 31.4 (Autumn 1977) 607–33.

18 Judith Goldstein, "Creating the GATT Rules: Politics, Institutions, and American Policy," in John Ruggie (ed.), *Multilateralism Matters*, New York: Columbia University Press, 1993, 201–32; Joanne Gowa and Soo Yeon Kim, "An Exclusive Country Club: The Effects of the GATT on Trade, 1950–94," *World Politics*, 57 (July 2005) 453–78; Eric Reinhart, "Adjudication Without Enforcement in GATT Disputes," *Journal of Conflict Resolution*, 45.2 (April 2001) 174–95.

19 Gowa and Kim, "An Exclusive Country Club" and Arvind Subramanian and Shang-Jin Wei, "The WTO Promotes Trade, Strongly but Unevenly," *Journal of International Economics*, 72 (2007) 151–75. A contrary conclusion about the effects of GATT/WTO on global trade is Andrew Rose, "Do We Really Know That the WTO Increases Trade?" *American Economic Review*, 94.1 (2004) 98–114. Also see, Michael Tomz, Judith Goldstein, and Douglas Rivers, "Do We Really Know that the WTO Increases Trade? Comment," *American Economic Review* (2007) 2005–18. For additional evidence of a larger WTO effect, see Judith Goldstein, Douglas Rivers, and Michael Tomz, "Institutions in International Relations: Understanding the Effects of the GATT and the WTO on World Trade," *International Organization*, 61 (Winter 2007) 37–67.

20 Gilbert R. Winham, *The Evolution of International Trade Agreements*, Toronto: University of Toronto Press, 1992.

21 Winham, *The Evolution*; John H. Barton, Judith Goldstein, Timothy Josling, and Richard Steinberg, *The Evolution of the Trade Regime*, Princeton: Princeton University Press, 2006.

22 Alan Deardorff, "Who Makes the Rules of Globalization?" in Elias Dinopoulos, Pravin Krishna, Arvind Panagariya, and Kar-yiu Wong (eds), *Trade Globalization and Poverty*, New York: Routledge, 2008, 173–86.

23 Jeffry Frieden and Lisa Martin, "International Political Economy: Global and Domestic Interactions," in Ira Katznelson and Helen V. Milner (eds), *Political Science: State of the Discipline*, New York: Norton, 2002, 118–46. Robert Putnam, "Diplomacy and Domestic Politics: The Logic of Two-Level Games," *International Organization*, 42.3 (Summer 1988) 427–60.

24 For a comprehensive discussion of the political economy of trade, see Michael Hiscox, *International Trade and Political Conflict*, Princeton: Princeton University Press, 2002.

25 Edward Mansfield, Helen Milner, and Peter Rosendorff, "Free to Trade: Democracies, Autocracies, and International Trade," *American Political*

Science Review, 94.2 (June 2000), 305–21; Xinyuan Dai, "Political Regimes and International Trade: The Democratic Difference Revisited," *American Political Science Review*, 96.1 (March 2002), 159–65.

26 Hiscox, *International Trade*.

27 One estimate is that 25 percent of global GDP is composed of the activities of transnational corporations. See UNCTAD, *World Investment Report, 2011*, New York: United Nations, 2011, 25.

28 John Dunning and Sarianna Lundan, *Multinational Enterprises and the Global Economy*, Cheltenham: Edward Elgar, 2nd ed., 2008, 3–12.

29 The discussion of transnational financial firms will be concentrated in Chapter 7.

30 Economists distinguish between stock and flow for FDI. The flow refers to the amount in any single year. The stock of FDI is an accumulation of FDI investments made over a period of time and attempt to measure the total FDI in a nation.

31 Source: UNCTAD Annex Tables, No 7, www.unctad.org/en/Pages/DIAE/FDI%20Statistics/World-Investment-Report-(WIR)-Annex-Tables.aspx

32 *The Economist*, "Big Oil's Bigger Brothers," October 29, 2011, 75–6.

33 Ian Bremmer, "State Capitalism Comes of Age," *Foreign Affairs*, 88.3 (May/June 2009); UNCTAD, *World Investment Report, 2011*, 28–38; Adrian Woolridge, "The Visible Hand," *The Economist*, January 21, 2012.

34 SWF Institute, www.swfinstitute.org/; *The Economist*, Foreign Reserves, January 12, 2012, www.economist.com/node/21542831; Ian Bremmer, *The End of the Free Market*, New York: Portfolio, 2010, 69–77.

35 Daniel Drezner, "Sovereign Wealth Funds and the (In)security of Global Finance," *Journal of International Affairs*, 62.1 (Fall 2008) 115–30.

36 Giselle Datz, "Governments as Market Players: State Innovation in the Global Economy," *Journal of International Affairs*, 62.1 (Fall 2008) 35–49; Brad Setser, "A Neo-Westphalian International Financial System," *Journal of International Affairs*, 62.1 (Fall 2008) 17–34.

37 Edward Tse, "The China Challenge," *Strategy+Business*, 58 (Spring 2010) 3–4.

38 Steve Lohr, "Global Strategy Stabilized IBM During Downturn," *New York Times*, April 19, 2010.

39 John Dunning (ed.), *Regions, Globalization, and the Knowledge-Based Economy*, Oxford: Oxford University Press, 2000; Thomas Murtha, Stefanie Lenway, and Jeffrey Hart, *Managing New Industry Creation*, Stanford: Stanford Business Press, 2001; Barry Jaruzelski, Kevin Schwartz, and Volker Stack, "Innovation's New World Order," *Strategy+Business*, Issue 81, Winter 2015, www.strategy-business.com/feature/00370?gko=e606a

40 Personal computers improve at a rapid and somewhat predictable rate and have done so for more than fifty years. About every eighteen to twenty-four months the processing power doubles at a constant cost. This is commonly known as "Moore's Law," named after Gordon Moore, a founder of the microprocessor firm Intel. Moore identified this pattern in the mid-1960s.

41 Marc Levinson, *The Box*, Princeton: Princeton University Press, 2006. Also see, Peter Dicken, *Global Shift*, New York: Guilford, 5th ed., 2007, 73–105.

42 Nick Wingfield and Charles Duhigg, "Apple Lists Its Suppliers for First Time," *New York Times*, January 13, 2012, www.nytimes.com/2012/01/14/technology/apple-releases-list-of-its-suppliers-for-the-first-time.html?_r=1&scp=1&sq=apple%20suppliers&st=cse; Charles Duhigg and Keith Bradsher, "How the U.S. Lost Out on iPhone Work," *New York Times*, January 21, 2012, www.nytimes.com/2012/01/22/business/apple-america-

and-a-squeezed-middle-class.html?hp. Foxconn employs as many as 1 million workers in China.

43 Dieter Ernst and Linsu Kim, "Global Production Networks, Knowledge Diffusion, and Local Capability Formation," *Research Policy*, 31 (2002) 1417–29.

44 Wilfrid Ethier, "The New Regionalism," *Economic Journal*, 108 (1998) 1149–61; Peter Katzenstein and Takashi Shiraishi (eds), *Beyond Japan: The Dynamics of East Asian Regionalism*, Ithaca: Cornell University Press, 2006; Martin Kenney and Richard Florida, *Locating Global Advantage*, Stanford: Stanford Business Books, 2004. Importantly, some of these agreements have begun to include nations outside of a geographic region.

45 Steven Brooks, *Producing Security*, Princeton: Princeton University Press, 2005, 16–46. The largest part of "trade" is actually exchange between the various units of TNCs, the geography of which is defined by the investment actions of these TNCs and the production networks they organize.

46 Shahid Yusuf, Anjum Altaf, and Kaoru Nabeshima (eds), *Global Production Networking and Technological Change in East Asia*, Washington: World Bank, 2004.

47 Xiaolan Fu and Yundan Gong, "Indigenous and Foreign Innovation Efforts and Drivers of Technological Upgrading: Evidence from China," *World Development*, 39.7 (2011) 1213–25; *The Economist*, "The Next Big Bet: Samsung," October 1, 2011, www.economist.com/node/21530976

48 Amitav Acharya, "The Emerging Regional Architecture of World Politics," *World Politics*, 59.4 (July 2007) 629–52.

49 WTO, *World Trade Report, 2011*, 40–197.

50 France, Germany, Italy, Belgium, Luxembourg, and the Netherlands.

51 Between 1973 and 1995, nine new members joined: Denmark, Ireland, the United Kingdom, Greece, Spain, Portugal, Austria, Finland, and Sweden. Then, from 2004–13 thirteen new members joined: Bulgaria, Croatia, Czech Republic, Cyprus, Estonia, Latvia, Lithuania, Hungary, Malta, Poland, Romania, Slovakia, and Slovenia.

52 The membership of the Eurozone is not identical to the membership of the EU; some of the latter have chosen not to participate in the Eurozone. The nineteen members of the Eurozone in 2015 include: Austria, Belgium, Finland, France, Germany, Ireland, Italy, Luxembourg, the Netherlands, Portugal, and Spain in 1999; Greece in 2001; and in the designated year, Slovenia (2007), Cyprus (2008), Malta (2008), Slovakia (2009), Estonia (2011), Latvia (2014), and Lithuania (2015).

53 See Chapter 8 for additional discussion of PTAs as a strategy of competitiveness.

54 Edward Mansfield and Eric Reinhardt, "Multilateral Determinants of Regionalism," *International Organization*, 57 (Fall 2003) 829–62.

55 WTO, *World Trade Report, 2011*, 66 and generally 52–71, www.wto.org/english/res_e/publications_e/wtr11_e.htm

56 WTO, *World Trade Report, 2013*, Geneva, 2013. A thorough review of the development and impact of PTAs can be found in WTO, *World Trade Report, 2011*, Geneva, 2011. Also important is Edward Mansfield and Jon Pevehouse, "The Expansion of Preferential Trading Arrangements," *International Studies Quarterly*, 57 (2013) 592–604.

57 Mansfield and Pevehouse, "The Expansion of Preferential Trading Arrangements."

58 Greg Ip, "The Gated Globe," *The Economist*, October 12, 2013, www.economist.com/news/special-report/21587384-forward-march-globalisation-has-paused-financial-crisis-giving-way. The United States is negotiating with

several Asian and Latin American nations in the Trans-Pacific Partnership (TPP) and with the EU in the Transatlantic Trade and Investment Partnership (TTIP).

59 The government of India had refused to ratify the agreement, but a subsequent negotiation with the United States may have cleared the way for a final agreement.

60 This is a long-standing issue for the United States, extending back at least thirty years to a similar problem with Japan and other Asian nations. Steve Lohr, "Maybe Japan Was Just a Warm-up," *New York Times*, January 21, 2011, www.nytimes.com/2011/01/23/business/23japan.html?_r=1&scp=1& sq=steve%20lohr%20Maybe%20Japan%20Was%20Just%20a%20Warm-Up&st=cse

61 David H. Autor, David Dorn, and Gordon Hanson, "The China Syndrome: Local Labor Market Effects of Import Competition in the United States," *American Economic Review*, 113.6 (2013) 2121–68; Justin Lahart, "Tallying the Toll of US–China Trade," *Wall Street Journal*, September 27, 2011.

62 Autor, Dorn, and Hanson, "The China Syndrome," 1.

63 Nicholas Bloom, Mirko Draca, and John Van Reenan, "Trade Induced Technical Change? The Impact of Chinese Imports on Innovation, IT and Productivity," CEP Discussion Paper No. 1000, January 2011.

64 Michael Spence and Sandile Hlatshwayo, "The Evolving Structure of the American Economy and the Employment Challenge," Council on Foreign Relations Working Paper, March 2011; Michael Spence, "The Impact of Globalization on Income and Employment: The Downside of Integrating Markets," *Foreign Affairs*, 90.4 (July/August) 2011, 28–41.

65 David Rotman, "Can We Build Tomorrow's Breakthroughs?" *Technology Review*, February 2012, 36–45; Gary Pisano and Wally Shih, "Restoring American Competitiveness," *Harvard Business Review* (July–August 2009), 2–13; Charles Duhigg and Keith Bradsher, "How the U.S. Lost out on iPhone Work," *New York Times*, January 21, 2012, www.nytimes.com/2012/01/22/business/apple-america-and-a-squeezed-middle-class.html?hp; Stephanie Overby, "IT Outsourcing: How Offshoring Can Kill Innovation," *CIO*, July 22, 2011, www.cio.com/article/686597/IT_Outsourcing_How_Offshoring_Can_Kill_Innovation?source=rss_offshoring&utm_source=feedburner&utm_medium=feed&utm_campaign=Feed%3A+cio%2Ffeed%2Fdrilldowntopic%2F3197+%28CIO.com+-+Offshoring%29

66 *The Economist*, September 24, 2011, www.economist.com/node/21530130

Further Reading

John Dunning (ed.), *Regions, Globalization, and the Knowledge-Based Economy*, Oxford: Oxford University Press, 2000.
An important examination of the role of knowledge in the global economy.

John Dunning and Sarianna Lundan, *Multinational Enterprises and the Global Economy*, Cheltenham: Edward Elgar, 2nd ed., 2008.
One of the most important recent studies of multinational firms.

Deborah Elms and Patrick Low (eds), *Global Value Chains in a Changing World*, Geneva: WTO, 2013.
A series of excellent articles.

Michael Hiscox, *International Trade and Political Conflict*, Princeton: Princeton University Press, 2002.
A lucid and comprehensive examination of the domestic political economy of trade.

Martin Kenney and Richard Florida, *Locating Global Advantage*, Stanford: Stanford Business Books, 2004.
Analysis of the process by which TNCs seek to create global competitive advantage.

Thomas Murtha, Stefanie Lenway, and Jeffrey Hart, *Managing New Industry Creation*, Stanford: Stanford Business Press, 2001.
A very useful analysis of the complexities of developing and producing a rapidly changing high technology product.

UNCTAD, *World Investment Report, 2013: Global Value Chains*, New York: United Nations, 2013.
A comprehensive analysis of FDI and the relationship to global value chains.

Shahid Yusuf, Anjum Altaf, and Kaoru Nabeshima (eds), *Global Production Networking and Technological Change in East Asia*, Washington, DC: World Bank, 2004.
An excellent collection of readings on GPNs in Asia.

6   Wealth, Poverty, and Inequality

Like a dumbbell, the global distribution of income is strikingly bifurcated. In the year 2011, 70 percent of the world's population lived in countries with average per capita incomes (PPP) below $7,500 per year while 14 percent resided in countries with average per capita incomes (PPP) exceeding $26,000 per year. Only 1 percent of the world's population lived in countries with average per capita income (PPP) falling between $17,000 and $26,000. Robert Wade has referred to this as the "missing middle."[1] This level of international social and economic inequality is historically unprecedented. Before the past century, living standards had never diverged so widely across different countries and regions of the world.

This development gap raises moral questions about the fairness and legitimacy of the international order that has given rise to such disparities in life prospects. A recent multi-country survey of global elites found that respondents ranked inequality number two on a list of the world's most urgent challenges for 2014.[2] As another measure of concern about the topic, economist Thomas Piketty's 700-page tome on inequality – *Capital in the Twenty-First Century* – rocketed up the best-seller lists in the spring of 2014.[3] The persistence of gross inequities reduces the chances for agreement among rich and poor countries about the management of international trade and finance. Scholars face the challenge of explaining how the division of the world into rich and poor arose and what might be done to promote greater equity.

This chapter addresses these issues in five parts. First, we review various indicators of economic development and human welfare. This is a necessary first step if we are to accurately measure levels of global inequality. Second, we examine empirical data to better understand the dimensions of the development gap and trends over times. Third, we compare three major theoretical perspectives on why and how a relatively few rich countries diverged in economic well-being from the rest of the world over the past two centuries. Fourth, we survey the development strategies that Southern states have pursued in order to lift their economic prospects. Fifth, we shift focus from inequality to the question of whether and how foreign aid might serve as a tool for addressing the needs of the poor.

Before tackling these topics, we offer a note on terminology. For much of the past century, the rich countries of the world consisted of much of Europe, the United States, Canada, Australia, New Zealand, and Japan. It became common to refer to this group of high-income countries as the "North" since most, though not all, were located in the Northern Hemisphere. Lower- and middle-income countries came to be referred to as the "South," since many, though again not all, were located in the Southern Hemisphere (moreover, some formerly developing countries have since joined the ranks of the high-income economies, further complicating matters). Although imprecise and unsatisfactory in some respects, we will on occasion use this terminology as a matter of convenience.

Indicators of Development

Economists have long sought a single, simple measure of economic development and human welfare. This sort of yardstick should, ideally, provide some sense of how far a society has progressed over time and how different nations compare with one another in economic performance. This is, however, an inherently difficult task. The concepts of "development" and "human welfare" are multidimensional and subject to varying interpretations. Overall averages calculated for societies as a whole tell us nothing about the status of particular groups or individuals and may hide gross inequities in the distribution of resources. Economic figures cannot capture the psychological, spiritual, cultural, or other nonmaterial aspects of human welfare.

Even after a given measure has been selected, its meaningfulness can be called into doubt by the difficulty of collecting accurate and reliable data, particularly for developing countries where mechanisms for gathering economic information are less developed than in rich nations. Such problems are particularly acute across much of Africa. Statistical offices in many countries are underfunded. A great deal of economic activity takes place outside of the formal economy and is therefore difficult to measure. Political considerations sometimes distort reported data. Civil strife can disrupt data collection. The three main indices of national economic data (the World Development Indicators, the Penn World Tables, and the datasets of economist Angus Maddison) rely upon differing assumptions and statistical techniques in coping with these complexities and uncertainties. As a result, there is little agreement across datasets. While the World Development Indicators pegged average income per person in Mauritius at $4,104 in 2009, for instance, the Penn World Tables gave a figure of $15,121 – almost four times higher. The author of the most exhaustive study of the accuracy and reliability of African economic statistics bluntly concludes: "we do not know very much about income and growth in Africa."[4]

Because, however, governments, international agencies, and businesses require clear and comparable measures of development for planning and decision-making purposes, the issue cannot be easily sidestepped despite the difficulties involved. The most commonly cited statistical measure of economic development is per capita income. This figure is calculated by adding up the value of all of the market transactions conducted within a given society over the course of a particular year and dividing by total population. Because inflation can appear to boost income without any real change in the standard of living, its effects are typically canceled out by recalculating income figures in terms of a given base year. To make comparisons over time in "real," inflation-adjusted income, measurements from years prior to the chosen base year are raised by the amount of intervening inflation, and figures for later years are lowered.

To allow for international comparisons, income figures for any given country are stated in terms of US dollars. One way to accomplish this is to use exchange rates in the conversion. At the end of 2011, for instance, the average annual income of Mexicans was roughly 80,600 pesos per person while the rate of exchange was 13 pesos per US dollar. Dividing 80,600 by 13, we arrive at an annual Mexican per capita income of $6,200.

Using exchange rates to accomplish the conversion of income figures from local currencies into dollars does, however, introduce important distortions. Exchange rates may vary significantly, even over brief periods of time. These gyrations produce artificial and misleading shifts in comparative calculations of national income when exchange rates serve as the basis for conversion. When the value of the dollar falls vis-à-vis the Japanese yen, for instance, the same yen will be able to purchase more dollars than before. Although Japan's per capita income level may not change at all – when calculated in yen – it will appear to rise when translated into dollars at the new exchange rate.

Also, local price levels vary significantly from country to country. Exchange rate-based income comparisons tell us, in effect, how well the average person from another country could live if all of his or her income were converted to dollars and spent in the United States on American goods and services. In reality, a haircut that costs $30 in the United States may cost only a fraction of that amount in most developing countries due to lower labor costs. In other words, a given income level, stated in dollars, will go much further in a developing country, where the overall price level is much lower, than it would in the United States. This distortion tends to understate the living standards of most developing countries when comparisons with the North are accomplished via exchange rate conversions.

Economists have developed an alternative measure of per capita income that attempts to correct for these problems. This method of calculating income levels is called purchasing power parity (PPP). Income figures are adjusted to account for differences in local price levels. When PPP conversion is used to compare income, the gap between developed and developing countries, while still large, noticeably narrows. In particular cases, the different estimates produced by these two methods for calculating average national income can be striking. As previously mentioned, Mexico's per capita income in 2011 using exchange rate conversion was around $6,200. But Mexico's per capita income in 2011 was roughly $17,500 when measured with the PPP method. This astounding difference stems from lower price levels in Mexico as compared with the United States. Overall, developing countries accounted for 38 percent of global output in 2010 using market exchange rates. But this figure jumps to 54 percent using PPP measures, which take into account price differentials.[5]

PPP estimates of national income depend upon accurate data about relative prices across countries. This data is gathered through price surveys carried out by the International Comparison Program (ICP) roughly every ten years. As relative prices change over time, adjustments to income estimates must be made following each survey. These adjustments can greatly alter our picture of how national economies compare in size.

The 2005 ICP, for instance, led to major changes in estimated per capita incomes in many developing countries. In some cases, overall price levels were higher than previously estimated, leading to a lower per capita income figure when expressed in PPP. Estimated per capita income for Bangladesh fell by almost one-half. In other cases, the new price estimates were lower than previous calculations. This led to upward adjustments in PPP per capita, as in the case of Nigeria, which witnessed a jump of 26.7 percent (see Table 6.1).

Table 6.1 New GDP Per Capita Compared to the "Old" WDI (World Development Indicators) Data (Thirteen Most Populous Countries in the World; Year 2005; PPPs Year 2005)

	GDP Per Capita Based on "Old" PPPs	GDP Per Capita Based on "New" PPPs	Revision (in percent)
Vietnam	3106	2143	−31.0
Philippines	4991	2956	−40.8
Mexico	10356	11387	+10.0
Japan	31262	30290	−3.1
Nigeria	1200	1520	+26.7
Bangladesh	2025	1068	−47.3
Russian Federation	11053	11858	+7.3
Pakistan	2437	2184	−10.4
Brazil	8854	8474	−4.3
Indonesia	3898	3209	−17.7
United States	42454	41813	−1.5
India	3536	2222	−37.2
China	6666	4088	−38.7

Source: Data from Branko Milanovic, "Global Inequality Recalculated and Updated: The Effect of New PPP Estimates on Global Inequality and 2005 Estimates," *Journal of Economic Inequality*, 13 (November 16, 2010), www.gc.cuny.edu/CUNY_GC/media/CUNY-Graduate-Center/PDF/Centers/LIS/Milanovic/papers/2012/milanovic_JOEI.pdf

Note: Both GDPs per capita are expressed in 2005 international dollars.

Some of the adjustments proved controversial. In 2005, for instance, Chinese authorities permitted ICP surveys only in a limited number of urban areas.[6] This resulted in a PPP estimate of China's GDP that understated reality. A new and more comprehensive price survey in 2011 resulted in a 20 percent upward adjustment of China's GDP as measured by PPP, leading to predictions that China was, by this indicator, poised to surpass the United States to become the world's largest economy (see Table 6.2).

Whichever conversion method is used, however, per capita income has a number of disadvantages as a measure of development or welfare. It reflects only current income, not the amount of wealth accumulated over previous years (while, by PPP measures, China may have already surpassed the United States in annual GDP, for instance, US net worth stands at four times China's total[7]). It provides us with no clue as to how equitably or inequitably income is distributed across the population. It does not reflect the value of goods and services that are not exchanged for money in the legal economy. Thus, for instance, household work, barter, illegal exchange, and subsistence production (for one's own use) are typically not measured by income figures.[8] Because all market transactions are treated the same, purchases of staple foods and housing are given the same weight as the money spent on cigarettes, junk food, or tanks, even though most people would agree that these various items make very different contributions to human welfare. The environmental costs of economic activity are ignored, no matter how real. The sale of timber obtained by clear-cutting a forest shows up as an addition to total income even if one result is to impose costs on nearby communities in the form of flooding during rainy

Table 6.2 Percentage of GDP to US GDP (PPP-based) for Twelve Largest Economies, ICP 2011 and ICP 2005

Economy	Percentage of GDP to U.S. GDP (PPP-based), ICP 2011	Percentage of GDP to U.S. GDP (PPP-based), ICP 2005
United States	100.0	100.0
China	86.9	43.1
India	37.1	18.9
Japan	28.2	31.3
Germany	21.6	20.3
Russian Federation	20.7	13.7
Brazil	18.1	12.8
France	15.3	15.0
United Kingdom	14.2	15.4
Indonesia	13.2	5.7
Italy	13.2	13.1
Mexico	12.2	9.5

Source: Data from *Purchasing Power Parities and Real Expenditures of World Economies*, International Comparison Project, The World Bank, 2014, Table 7.2, 81.

seasons.[9] Economist Simon Kuznets, who invented the concept of gross domestic product, commented that: "The welfare of a nation can scarcely be inferred from a measurement of national income."[10]

The Human Development Index (HDI) was devised by researchers at the United Nations (UN) Development Program as a means for capturing some of the social dimensions of a nation's socioeconomic development that are neglected by income measures alone.[11] The HDI includes three components of human development: longevity (measured by life expectancy), knowledge (measured by a combination of adult literacy and mean years of schooling), and standard of living (measured by per capita GDP, adjusted for the local cost of living by means of PPP conversion) (see Table 6.3).

Table 6.3 Measures of Development: Selected Countries

	Human Development Index 2012 (HDI rank)	Real GDP Per Capita (PPP$) 2012
United States	0.937 (3)	48,688
Korea, Republic of	0.909 (12)	28,231
Hong Kong	0.906 (13)	45,598
Saudi Arabia	0.782 (57)	22,616
Cuba	0.780 (59)	5,539
Costa Rica	0.773 (62)	10,863
Brazil	0.730 (85)	10,152
China	0.699 (101)	7,945
Egypt	0.662 (112)	5,401
Philippines	0.654 (114)	3,752
Botswana	0.634 (119)	13,102
Indonesia	0.629 (121)	4,154
Vietnam	0.617 (127)	2,970
Nicaragua	0.599 (129)	2,551
Ghana	0.558 (135)	1,684
India	0.554 (136)	3,285
Congo	0.534 (142)	2,934
Kenya	0.519 (145)	1,541
Pakistan	0.515 (146)	2,566
Tanzania	0.476 (152)	1,383
Zambia	0.448 (163)	1,358
Zimbabwe	0.397 (172)	424
Guinea	0.355 (178)	941
Mozambique	0.327 (185)	906
Very high human development	0.905	33,391
High human development	0.758	11,501
Medium human development	0.640	5,428
Low human development	0.466	1,633
World	0.694	0,184

Source: Data from United Nations Development Program, *Human Development Report, 2013*, United Nations Development Program, 2013, Table 1, 144–7.

For each component, a nation's rating is determined along a scale ranging from zero to one. Zero represents the lowest possible measure for that component, and one represents the highest. So, for instance, a country with an adult literacy rate of 75 percent would score .75 on that component of the HDI. The scores from all three components are then averaged to produce an overall measure of human development that can be compared across countries (see Table 6.4).

The HDI is a useful way to compare the overall quality of life across different countries. Life expectancy, for instance, reflects on a country's overall nutrition level, the quality of its health care, and the type of sanitary conditions under which people live. Adult literacy and mean years of schooling capture both the quality and the breadth of a nation's educational system. The HDI can reveal cases where relatively high income levels fail to translate into a commensurate quality of life, or, conversely, where the population of a country with a relatively low per capita income nevertheless enjoys relatively good health and education. Cuba, for instance, roughly equals Saudi Arabia on the HDI scale even though Saudi Arabia enjoys a per capita income level more than four times that of Cuba.[12]

Another way to measure development is to focus on wealth rather than on income. Traditionally, wealth has been measured by estimating the market value of a nation's physical capital, including such things as factories, machinery, and buildings. This figure provides some sense of the size of the productive base upon which future economic returns depend. Yet a nation's future economic potential rests upon more than these so-called "produced assets." Both natural resources and the level of human skills possessed by members of a society are as important, and often more so, than the available stock of machines and factories.

For this reason, researchers at the World Bank have compiled a broader measure of national wealth that includes natural and human resources alongside manufactured capital.[13] For each nation, the World Bank attaches estimated monetary values to a set of natural resources, such as land, minerals, water, and forests. Much the same is done for human and social resources, including education, skills, and institutions such as legal systems. By this means, researchers can estimate the relative proportions of a nation's or region's wealth accounted for by natural capital, produced assets, and so-called intangible capital (human, social, and institutional resources) (see Table 6.5).

This method for calculating wealth shows that, on a global basis, the value of the world's natural resources exceeds the total value of all manufactured wealth and that both of these together are far outweighed by the combined economic value of the world's human and social resources. This suggests that, from the standpoint of maximizing long-term economic health, nations are better served by focusing on ways to preserve and exploit scarce natural resources on a sustainable basis and on investing in

Table 6.4 HDI and Components, by Region and HDI Group, 2012

Region and HDI group	HDI	Life Expectancy at Birth (Years)	Mean Years of Schooling (Years)	Expected Years of Schooling (Years)	Gross National Income Per Capita (2005 PPP $)
Region					
Arab States	0.652	71.0	6.0	10.6	8,317
East Asia and the Pacific	0.683	72.7	7.2	11.8	6,874
Europe and Central Asia	0.771	71.5	10.4	13.7	12,243
Latin America and the Caribbean	0.741	74.7	7.8	13.7	10,300
South Asia	0.558	66.2	4.7	10.2	3,343
Sub-Saharan Africa	0.475	54.9	4.7	9.3	2,010
HDI group					
Very high human development	0.905	80.1	11.5	16.3	33,391
High human development	0.758	73.4	8.8	13.9	11,501
Medium human development	0.640	69.9	6.3	11.4	5,428
Low human development	0.466	59.1	4.2	8.5	1,633
World	0.694	70.1	7.5	11.6	10,184

Source: Data from *Human Development Report, 2013: The Rise of the South: Human Progress in a Diverse World*, United Nations Development Program, 2013, Table 1.1, 25.

Note: Data are weighted by population and calculated based on HDI values for 187 countries. PPP is purchasing power parity.

Table 6.5 Total Wealth and Share by Type of Asset and Income Group, 2005

Income Group	Total Wealth (US$ billions)	Intangible Capital (%)	Produced Capital (%)	Natural Capital (%)
Low income	3,597	57	13	30
Lower middle income	58,023	51	24	25
Upper middle income	47,183	69	16	15
High income OECD	551,964	81	17	2
World	673,593	77	18	5

Source: *The Changing Wealth of Nations: Measuring Sustainable Development in the New Millennium*, Washington, DC: World Bank Publications, 2011, Table 2.1, 28.

Note: Figures are based on the set of countries for which wealth accounts are available from 1995 to 2005, as described in annex 2.1. High-income oil exporters are not shown.

human resources, such as education, than by placing sole priority on enhancing the nation's stock of factories, machines, and other hardware.

The relative weight of these different sources of wealth varies considerably from one set of countries to another. In India, China, and the countries of East and Southeast Asia, an overwhelming majority of wealth is accounted for by human resources while these countries are relatively poorer in natural capital. Africa's wealth, by contrast, is heavily dependent upon natural capital while its human resources contribute far less to the overall total. Latin America falls in between these extremes. The richest countries rely very little upon natural capital, with human and social resources representing the lion's share of wealth. Overall, high-income countries account for 82 percent of total wealth worldwide and 17 percent of total population. These differences in the composition of wealth have important implications for each country's development strategy and help to determine where a nation's comparative advantage lies in world trade.

This way of measuring wealth also underlines the need for sustainable development strategies. Countries that rapidly deplete their mineral resources, cut down forests, or undermine the value of their land through shortsighted agricultural practices may increase their income in the short run or even translate revenues from these activities into physical capital. This will, however, only create the illusion of greater wealth. In the long term, such a pattern of development cannot be sustained and will erode the environmental basis for economic activity.

Measuring the Development Gap

Many people adopt a fatalistic attitude toward the enormous development gap between rich and poor on the assumption that such disparities have always existed and therefore always will. Yet Latin America, Africa, and Asia have each served as the home of civilizations that once rivaled or surpassed European society in science and technology, culture, and economic productivity. In fact, the present concentration of global wealth and income is of quite recent origin.

The North developed a lead that continued to expand through the nineteenth century and well into the twentieth century. In the process, the structure of economic inequality shifted in dramatic ways. At the beginning of this period, differences in average income across countries were modest while gaps between rich and poor within countries were large. Social status mattered more than country of birth in determining one's fate. Calls for transnational worker solidarity in confronting the ills of capitalism seemed plausible, since the material circumstances of laborers in various countries differed less than the gulf between workers anywhere and their capitalist masters. In today's world, by contrast, domestic inequality is dwarfed by the vast gulf between rich and poor countries. Individuals at the bottom of the income distribution in rich countries are still vastly better off than all but a tiny proportion of the residents of poor countries. And those who are well off compared with their compatriots in a poor country would rank near the bottom in a rich country.[14]

Just how large are the income gaps between rich and poor countries? Have incomes continued to diverge over recent decades or has the gap begun to close? The most widely used measure of inequality is the Gini coefficient. This measure ranges from zero (representing perfect equality) to one (representing perfect inequality – one actor monopolizes all resources). World Bank economist Branko Milanovic has applied the Gini coefficient to three sets of data representing differing conceptions of global inequality[15] (see Figure 6.1).

The first measure – Concept 1 – compares average per capita income across countries. Each country is weighted equally, regardless of population. Concept 2 also compares average per capita income across countries, but adjusts the weight given to each score according to the country's population level. In other words, India is given more weight than Botswana, for example, in order to reflect India's much larger population. Concept 3 dispenses with country averages entirely and instead ranks individuals against one another on a global level.

The unweighted comparison among countries – Concept 1 – shows a growing gap between rich and poor countries over the last half of the twentieth century. In other words, the richest countries continued to build their lead over the poorest countries. If we adjust for population levels, however, we instead see very high but relatively stable levels of inequality for much of this period, followed by a substantial decline in inequality beginning around 1990. Both measures, however, witness a shrinking gap between rich and poor countries during the first decade of the twenty-first century.

The differences between the two measures arise because the two most populous countries in the world – China and India – have experienced very rapid income growth over the past quarter-century. Since these

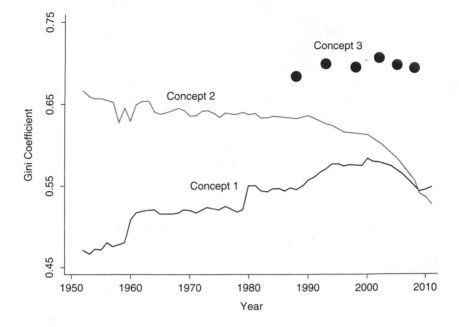

Figure 6.1 International and Global Inequality, 1952–2011.

Source: Adapted from Branko Milanovic, "Global Income Inequality by the Numbers: in History and Now," The World Bank, Development Research Group, Poverty and Inequality Team, November 2012, 6.

countries count more heavily in Concept 2 than in Concept 1, the former reflects this shift while the latter does not. Were we to remove China and India from our Concept 2 dataset, we would find that inequality actually rose among the remaining countries through the end of the twentieth century.

While global inequality among nations may be shrinking in relative terms according to some measures, the absolute gap between rich and poor countries continues to widen. To see why, consider an example. Average per capita income in the United States is $45,403 while the figure for India is $3,285. If, over the period of one year, India's per capita income grows by 6 percent while that of the United States grows by 2 percent, then the relative gap between average incomes in the two countries will have fallen in some small measure. But the absolute difference would actually have widened: the average income in the United States would grow by $974 during the year while India's average income would expand by only $197, despite its higher rate of growth.

In order to measure inequality among individuals (Concept 3) as opposed to countries, Milanovic uses household survey data which is only available from the 1980s onward. This measure shows very high levels of inequality that waver over the past quarter-century, but display a modest decline during the most recent period. Overall, however, inequality remains higher today than in the mid-1980s.

As mentioned, the greater part of global inequality is due to differences across countries rather than within countries. As long as India and China are included, all three of the measures discussed by Milanovic – Concepts 1, 2, and 3 – show declining overall inequality in the past decade. The world's two most populous countries plus a handful of others have begun to "catch up" with the already rich countries.

Yet this obscures a contrary trend with respect to domestic inequality. Virtually all high-income countries have witnessed growing gaps between rich and poor within these societies over the past four decades. In the United States, for instance, the top 1 percent of income earners captured 60 percent of all economic growth between 1977 and 2007.[16] The same 1 percent captured 20 percent of national income in 2000–10 compared with only 9 percent in the 1970s.[17] Growing inequality in Northern countries is due to increased concentration of wealth in fewer hands, a growing gap between the returns to capital and overall economic growth, and an expansion of wage inequality associated with skill level and education.[18]

Similar trends hold for much of East Asia, which was once admired for its ability to reconcile rapid growth with a relatively egalitarian income distribution.[19] China has experienced the most striking shift. In 1988, the average income of the top 10 percent of earners exceeded the average income of the bottom 10 percent by a ratio of 7.3 to 1. By 2007, this ratio had risen to 23 to 1.[20] More than 80 percent of the world's population lives in countries where income differentials are widening.[21] The major exception is Latin America, where previously extreme income gaps have begun to narrow.[22] Growing inequity within countries can be a recipe for political instability. A recent multi-country survey found that more than one-half of respondents in thirty-one of thirty-nine countries identified inequality as a major problem. A majority of respondents in thirty-five of the thirty-nine countries surveyed believed that inequality was rising.[23]

Considering individual wealth rather than income, global disparities are glaring. The eighty-five richest people on earth control wealth equal to that of the 3.5 billion people who constitute the bottom half of the distribution.[24] The wealthiest .1 percent of adults on the planet (4.5 million out of 4.5 billion adults) account for 20 percent of all global wealth while the top 1 percent (45 million out of 4.5 billion) control 50 percent of global assets.[25]

If we examine the development gap by looking not at income or wealth, but instead more direct measures of welfare, the differences are less extreme and the trend over time is toward convergence. In 1950, for instance, the average lifespan of people who lived in the bottom 20 percent of the world's countries (by income) was only one-half of that in the top 20 percent of the world's countries. By 1999, however, lifespans in the poorest countries rose to two-thirds of those in the richest countries.[26] In 1990, adult literacy in the developing world was 67 percent compared with 99 percent in the developed countries. By 2011, the already high literacy rate of rich countries remained the same while rising to 80 percent for developing countries.[27]

One interesting question that has generated much debate is whether the intensified globalization of the past three decades has worsened or ameliorated global inequality. The evidence is mixed. Comparing rich and poor countries, two very populous countries – China and India – narrowed the gap with the rich world while most other countries fell further behind. Since 2000, a more broad-based movement toward reduced inequality among nations appears to have emerged while inequality within countries has grown in most places. How to explain these movements – and to what degree they can be attributed to globalization – remains a contested issue among economists. Even with recent evidence of modest narrowing, however, what remains uncontested is that present levels of global inequality are troublingly high by any historical standards.

Contending Perspectives on Development

Scholars disagree over both the sources of the development gap and the likelihood that it can be narrowed in the future. There is also extensive debate over whether the South benefits from its extensive economic ties with the North. These disagreements revolve around much more than how to interpret the data. Fundamentally, they stem from differing assumptions about the nature of the development process itself. Here we identify and compare three contrasting theories about the problems of Third World development and North–South political economy.[28]

Geoeconomics

The earliest complex agrarian societies developed in the Fertile Crescent area of the Middle East and the Yellow River basin of China. The civilizations that spread from these starting points surpassed societies elsewhere in the world in terms of material abundance (though the differences were modest if compared to those of today's world).

Jared Diamond attributes these disparities to geographic and biological factors.[29] The most nutritious and high-yielding species of grain were native to Eurasia. Of the fourteen species of domesticated animals, thirteen could be found in Eurasia, only one in South America, and none in other regions of the world. Moreover, the East–West axis of Eurasia meant that agricultural innovations could easily move from Europe to Asia or vice versa across relatively similar climatic latitudes. Africa and the Americas, by contrast, featured North–South geographic axes, making it difficult for productive plant species to spread from North to

South given the radical climate differences as one moved from temperate to tropical zones.

By living in close proximity to domesticated animals for thousands of years, Eurasians developed a measure of immunity to diseases that were transmitted from animals to humans. Once these diseases moved from Europe to the Americas, however, inhabitants of the latter region had no resistance and died in their millions. While European settlers in South America and Africa were plagued by the tropical diseases found there, these diseases could not take hold in Europe itself since they were typically borne by insects that could not survive Europe's cold winters. This asymmetry in the exchange of germs strongly favored Europeans.

Although both Europe and China enjoyed inherent geographic advantages, it was Europe that pulled away from all other societies, including China, beginning in the nineteenth century. One reason is that Europe was closer to the Americas than China, thus allowing Europeans the opportunity to exploit the natural resources and labor made available through colonization. Europe's complex geography also resulted in political fragmentation and incessant warfare. The political insecurity of European states prompted investments in military technology that China's rulers found unnecessary. This technology provided Europeans with decisive advantages in the campaigns of conquest that they conducted around the world.

Climate and geography remain relevant in today's world. Ninety-three percent of the combined population of the world's thirty richest countries lives in temperate and snowy climate zones. Of the forty-two least developed countries, on the other hand, thirty-nine are located in tropical or desert climactic zones.[30] Overall, tropical countries had an average per capita income only one-third that of temperate zone countries in 1995.[31] A tropical climate is less well suited than a temperate climate for many kinds of agricultural production and is given to extremes of heat and weather. Moreover, tropical countries are plagued by diseases not typically experienced in temperate climates. Ninety-five percent of all malaria cases, for instance, occur in the tropics. Tuberculosis is also more prevalent in the developing world.[32] Because these societies are so poor, however, drug companies devote few resources to developing vaccines and other treatments for topical diseases. Of the 1,223 new drug compounds launched between 1975 and 1997, for instance, only eleven were designed to fight tropical diseases.[33]

Unlike Asia, Africa does not enjoy the extensive river plains that are necessary to support irrigated agriculture. The high-yielding wheat and rice strains that the Green Revolution brought to Asia in the 1960s onward depended upon regular and ample inputs of fertilizer and water, neither of which were available in much of Africa. Africa's soils are also poor and lacking in nutrients as compared with most temperate zone countries. Transportation systems in Africa are also weak, due in part to political fragmentation. Africa's many landlocked countries face especially high transportation costs and find it difficult to access global markets.[34]

Geography is not always destiny. Some tropical zone countries have become wealthy (e.g., Singapore and the oil-rich states of the Persian Gulf) and technological advancements can reduce some of the disadvantages faced by farmers in tropical zone countries. Moreover, geography cannot explain why South Koreans are so much wealthier than North Koreans or why the residents of El Paso have higher incomes than those in neighboring Juarez. Clearly, political and economic institutions also matter in determining a country's development trajectory.

Modernization Theory

Modernization theory views the obstacles to Southern development through the prism of the North's own development experience. The North grew rich, according to this theory, not by exploiting the South, but rather by discovering the secrets of sustained economic growth. The cultural values and social, political, and economic institutions that provided the keys to Northern development are embodied in the notion of modernity. The modernization of Europe involved the gradual shedding of traditional ways of organizing society. Although little of this process was planned, simultaneous trends in a number of different spheres of social life converged to create the basis for dynamic economic growth and industrialization.

What are the principal elements of modernity? The list of traits provided by different authors varies enormously.[35] But among the most commonly cited are secularization (or the declining centrality of religion in social and cultural life), urbanization, the rise of science and technology, increased social mobility, a system of social rewards based upon merit rather than upon inherited status, a tolerance for social innovation and intellectual diversity, the limitation of controls placed by political authorities on social and economic life (i.e., the emergence of a "private" sphere), the ascendance of rule by law, and the development of an extensive division of labor within society. All of these traits complement the development of modern market-based economies in which economic decision making is decentralized among large numbers of producers, consumers, and laborers and is relatively free of direct control by political or religious authorities.

Traditional societies are dominated by religious authority, revolve around rural life, lack the capacity to generate scientific and technological discoveries, suffer from rigid social structures allowing little mobility, distribute social rewards based upon inherited status rather than upon merit, discourage innovation and new ideas, place few controls on the arbitrary exercise of political authority, and feature little social differentiation.

The economies of traditional societies often rest upon either subsistence agriculture – in which extended families produce only for their own needs – or feudal or semi-feudal landholding arrangements, in which relatively small numbers of large landowners live off of the surplus produced by an indentured peasantry. Northern societies were once characterized by the traits associated with traditionalism, but they gradually made the transition to modernity over a period of centuries. According to modernization theorists, many Southern societies continue to be dominated by traditional values and institutions, though most have begun to embrace some elements of modernity.

The most critical element in the transition from a traditional society to a modern one, from the standpoint of economic development, is the emergence of a system of rewards for innovation. The society must not only come to expect and welcome change and to embrace the notion of progress, but also willingly tolerate the inequalities that result from allowing individuals to reap handsome private returns for innovations that have high social value. For this to be possible, the state must devise means of organizing and protecting private property. By property, we refer not just to material possessions, but also to the propriety that innovators must have over their own original ideas if others are not to profit from them instead. Although the state must protect property rights, it must at the same time allow economic decisions to be made in at least partial autonomy from political oversight and intervention. This is necessary because innovation is most likely to occur if decision making is decentralized through competitive market arrangements that encourage and reward new ideas while punishing inefficiency and stagnation. As this discussion suggests, the development of capitalist institutions lies at the heart of modernization, although the rise of capitalism in the North would not have been possible without the simultaneous transformations already mentioned in the noneconomic spheres of society.

Economists cite other factors, besides the rate of innovation, that may influence a country's potential for economic development. These factors include overall rates of savings and investment, the skill level of the workforce, the relative abundance of natural resources, and the degree to which market prices are allowed to steer available resources to their most efficient uses.[36] Even more crucial is the development of political institutions that provide public goods, such as education, infrastructure, and health care, in a relatively efficient, inclusive, and transparent manner. Democratic states are more likely to meet these criteria of good government than authoritarian states.[37]

Modernization theorists suggest that before sustained and self-generating economic growth can become possible in the South, developing societies must undergo the same transition from traditionalism to modernity previously undergone by the North. The path to development thus lies through emulation of the North. The principal obstacle to modernization arises from the persistence of traditional cultural values and institutions in the South that are incompatible with economic growth and industrialization.

Adherents to this school of thought disagree over just how likely it is that Southern societies will progress smoothly toward modernity. A majority believes that the modernization of the South is an inevitable process. The agents of progress, in this view, are many. They include the modernizing political elites (often Northern educated) to be found in many Southern countries. Multinational corporations serve as transmitters of modern skills and values while also providing close-up examples of modern forms of economic organization. Exposure to international trade offers Southern societies incentives to embrace reform and change if they are to compete effectively. The penetration of Southern societies by European or US culture through books, films, advertising, consumer products, and the media also helps Southerners to assimilate modern values, beliefs, and knowledge.

North–South economic interdependence is to be valued, according to modernization theorists, not simply for the mutual gains that routinely flow from market transactions, but also for the beneficial impact that such ties have in helping to erode and undermine the traditional social values and structures that hold back development. Over time, both external and internal pressures will tend to shrink the traditional sector of the economy and society while the growth of the modern sector proceeds apace. Globalization produces the diffusion of knowledge, which is perhaps the most crucial driver of economic growth. Evidence of these trends at work, according to modernization theorists, can be found in growing urbanization, the development of a wage labor force, and broadened educational opportunities.

A minority of modernization theorists accepts the distinction between traditionalism and modernity but questions the assumption that Southern societies will necessarily modernize over time, leading eventually to a convergence between the social and economic structures of North and South. These authors instead see traditionalism as deeply embedded in the cultures and institutions of many Southern countries. Change may come slowly and not necessarily in the direction of a European-inspired ideal of modernity. Others who question the inevitability of modernization and convergence between North and South go further to suggest that economic development may well be possible in societies that embrace some elements of modernity but not others. There may be, in other words, multiple paths of development.

Modernization theory has been criticized on a number of grounds. The concept of traditionalism is quite nebulous. In practice, the traditional label has been applied to virtually any social practices and institutions that are not modern, or in other words, not characteristic of present-day

European and North American societies. To bundle all of the many varied Southern cultures that do not meet the criteria for modernity under the label "traditional" perhaps serves to obscure more than to illuminate.

Some critics also charge that modernization theory springs from an ethnocentric viewpoint. Certainly it is not difficult to deduce that most modernization theorists consider modernity good and traditionalism bad. This obviously reflects a Eurocentric bias. Whatever the merits of Northern societies, they are certainly not above reproach, and Southerners who embrace modernity in a general way may well hope to avoid some of the less-appealing aspects of Northern societies even while seeking to match Northern living standards. Moreover, modernization theorists may be too dismissive of traditional societies, ignoring the possibility that they might contain redeeming traits worth preserving.

Some critics point out that modernization theory incorrectly assumes that the obstacles to Third World development lie solely in the persistence of the traditional sector of the society. This ignores the possibility that the modern sector itself may be subject to contradictions and distortions that slow growth. Moreover, the movement from traditionalism to modernity is likely to be anything but smooth. Modernization in Europe proceeded in fits and starts, and the process often generated enormous dislocations such as war, revolution, unemployment, mass immigration, and class conflict. There is little reason to expect modernization to be any less disruptive as it transforms developing societies.

Modernization theorists are quite sanguine about the benefits of North–South economic exchange for Southern development. Whether it is true in general that links with the North spur modernization, most modernization theorists ignore the potential conflicts of interest between North and South. This is apparent in their tendency to downplay the North's potential economic power over the South. As we will discuss, the South's dependence upon the North offers the latter with political leverage that can be used to capture a disproportionate share of the benefits flowing from North–South economic exchange.

Despite these criticisms, modernization theory offers important insights into the development experience of the North. It would be surprising indeed, despite the changed context, if these insights did not hold useful lessons for those seeking to promote Southern development. Perhaps the most important of these is that capitalism, as a distinctive way of organizing economic relationships within a society, is a powerful mechanism for producing wealth. The development of capitalism, in turn, is dependent upon the evolution of supportive social, political, and cultural institutions in the noneconomic spheres of society. Whether these innovations can be successfully transplanted to a society from without or whether they must evolve indigenously is a crucial question in assessing the prospects for capitalist-led development in the South. This is, in fact, the central question raised by dependency theory, our second perspective on Third World development.

Dependency Theory

Dependency theorists reject modernization theory's optimistic prediction that Southern states that imitate the cultural attitudes, institutions, and policies of the North can follow the same path toward development previously trod by present-day rich countries.[38] They point out that the international context facing developing societies today is vastly different from that which confronted the early industrializers. Capitalism developed largely indigenously in Europe, and the first wave of industrializers faced no competition from already developed rivals. Moreover, industrialization in Europe was helped along by the access that conquest provided Europeans to the raw materials and cheap labor of colonized lands.

Present-day developing countries face an entirely different set of international realities. Southern efforts to industrialize must cope with the formidable competition provided by earlier developers. Moreover, the infrastructure needed to support scientific and technological innovation is overwhelmingly located in the North. In general, capitalism was introduced to Southern societies from the outside on terms largely set by, and favorable to, Northern governments, merchants, and investors. Many Southern economies remain heavily dependent upon external trade with the North, and Northern multinational corporations often dominate the most dynamic industries in developing countries.

Dependency theorists contend that these differences (and others) between early and late developers mean that the development experiences of the North hold little relevance for assessing the present-day prospects for Southern development. These distinctions are considered so important, in fact, that dependency theory locates the primary obstacles to development in the international system rather than in the domestic political, cultural, and social characteristics of particular states. In other words, the international system, rather than the nation-state, is viewed as the appropriate unit of analysis.

Capitalism is the most important defining feature of the contemporary international system, according to dependency theorists. Capitalism is a distinct set of economic relations defined by the private ownership of property, wage labor, and market exchange. The capitalist world system, which some dependency theorists believe has existed since the sixteenth century,[39] involves two sets of exploitative relationships. Within firms, the owners of capital exploit workers by profiting from their labor. The second relationship of exploitation, and the more relevant one from our standpoint, exists between core and peripheral states in the world economy. Capitalism does not develop evenly. Instead, it tends to concentrate development in certain areas, called the core, which are

characterized by advanced industrialization, rapid technological development, and high wage rates and living standards. Peripheral areas, which
constitute the geographic bulk of the world economy, instead feature
limited industrialization, little technological innovation, and relatively
low wages and living standards.

The development of core countries is linked to the underdevelopment
of the peripheral countries. The workings of the capitalist world system
tend to perpetuate and reinforce economic inequalities among countries.
As two prominent advocates of dependency put it: "Both underdevelopment and development are aspects of the same phenomenon, both are
historically simultaneous, both are linked functionally and, therefore,
interact and condition each other mutually."[40]

Third World countries were drawn into the capitalist world economy
through colonialism as well as through the expansion of European trade
and investment. European countries used their political domination to
create and enforce a division of labor that reserved the most dynamic
segments of the world economy for themselves. North–South trade was
built around the movement of manufactured goods from North to South
and the transfer of primary products, including minerals, raw materials,
and agricultural goods, from South to North. Moreover, whereas
Northern countries traded extensively with one another, Southern countries traded almost exclusively with the North. Colonialism left the economies of Southern countries geared more toward the needs of Northern
markets than the domestic needs of their own societies. This set of
economic relationships, dependency writers point out, outlived colonialism itself.

This position of Southern subordination to, and dependence upon, the
North is captured in Theotonio Dos Santos's widely cited definition of
dependency: "Dependency is a situation in which a certain number of
countries have their economy conditioned by the development and
expansion of another . . . placing the dependent country in a backward
position exploited by the dominant country."[41]

Dependency theorists offer a number of mechanisms by which dependency hampers Southern development. Some cite changes in relative
export prices as the primary means by which Northern societies extract
surplus wealth from the South. The prices of goods exported by the
South, it is argued, tend to decline over time relative to the prices of the
goods that Southern societies import from the North. A country that
finds itself in this situation – where, over time, a given quantity of the
country's exports can purchase fewer and fewer of the imports it desires
– is said to be suffering from declining terms of trade. Those developing
countries that export primarily manufactured goods and those that
mainly export raw materials and agricultural goods have each experienced declining terms of trade. Moreover, the prices of primary goods,
such as raw materials and agricultural goods, tend to fluctuate more

widely than do the prices of manufactured goods – a pattern that leads to cycles of feast or famine for countries that depend upon only a few primary products for the bulk of their exports.

Northern multinational corporations are also viewed as instruments of exploitation. Foreign firms bring inappropriate technology, use their mobility and transnational links to evade taxes and regulations, drive out local competitors, manipulate Southern governments, and repatriate their profits rather than invest them locally. Dependency theory asserts that these forms of Northern exploitation, along with others such as foreign aid, commercial bank lending, and the influence of multilateral lending agencies, hinder Southern industrialization and development.

Dependency theorists differ over how severe and universal are the constraints that dependence places on Southern development. Some, especially among the early writers, argued that dependence allowed little latitude for development and was likely to continue to produce growing misery and poverty among most Southerners. The principal beneficiaries of dependence in the South would be a "compradore" class of elites who benefited from their privileged ties with the North, whether they be political or economic, and who acted as the local agents of imperialism.

Some dependency authors concede that dependency is not incompatible with economic growth and development, even including a degree of industrialization. Moreover, some countries are likely to progress further than others. These authors nevertheless maintain that dependence constrains development in most Southern countries, rendering economic growth and industrialization slower and less substantial than might otherwise be the case. They also generally argue that the overall relative position of the periphery in comparison with the core is unlikely to improve even where absolute gains are made.

A third set of authors argues that although dependency is sometimes compatible with vigorous economic growth, it nevertheless produces a myriad of undesirable "distortions" that are peculiar to dependent Southern societies and economies. Among these distortions are growing income inequality, wasteful consumption, cultural degradation, and political repression. The main concern of these authors is not with whether "development" is occurring, but rather with the type of development produced under conditions of dependence.

Dependency theorists differ widely over the appropriate remedy for Third World dependence upon the North. Some favor inwardly directed development strategies that emphasize production for the domestic market. This would imply a curtailment of economic ties with the North through high protectionist barriers designed to nurture domestic industry and the strict regulation of foreign investment.

Others advocate some form of collective bargaining strategy, whereby Southern states pool their political and economic resources to press for reforms in the international economic order, much as trade unions attempt to ameliorate capitalist exploitation of workers. This can take the form of resource cartels, such as the Organization of Petroleum Exporting Countries (OPEC), which are designed to reverse the declining terms of trade, or broad coalitions that demand Northern assent to various specific reforms such as the lowering of Northern protectionist barriers to Southern manufactured goods, commodity stabilization plans, or mandatory codes of conduct for multinational corporations. Those who advocate this strategy often stress the importance of improving economic ties, including the development of regional common markets, among Southern countries as a means of lessening dependence upon the North.

In short, although modernization theory asserts that Southern economic ties with the North are desirable because they transfer needed technology and skills, foster efficiency through competition, and break down cultural and institutional barriers to development, dependency theory views Northern economic and political penetration of the South as exploitative, producing a transfer of resources from the poor to the rich.

In order to evaluate dependency theory, we must distinguish between two lines of argument, each of which can be found, together or separately, in the writings of different authors. The first strain of dependency theory focuses primarily on economics. The concern here is with the way in which Southern states have been incorporated into the world capitalist system and the effects this process has had on their prospects for development. The second strain of dependency theory explores the asymmetries in power and interdependence that influence bargaining between North and South over the rules of the international economic system. Although both the economic and political dimensions of dependency theory derive from the same body of thought, each deserves separate treatment in any effort to assess the strengths and weaknesses of the dependency approach to Southern development and North–South relations.[42]

The economic dimension of dependency theory revolves around the suggestion that dependent capitalism, introduced to the South via Northern colonialism, trade, and investment, differs from the home-grown variety. The dependence of Third World economies on trade and investment with the North and their subordinate position in the international division of labor constrain the prospects for Southern development and lead to imbalances and distortions.

Critics of dependency theory have pointed to several difficulties with these claims.[43] One of these is that many of the features that are associated with dependency, such as penetration by multinational corporations and heavy reliance on external trade and technology, are also characteristic of many developed countries. Canada, for instance, is more dependent upon foreign direct investment (FDI) than is India. Moreover, as any reader of Dickens can surmise, the extreme social and economic inequalities that are painful features of most developing countries today were not unknown to the European societies of 150 years ago. This suggests that some of the inequities and distortions that have been attributed to external dependence may instead be characteristic of the early stages of capitalist development more generally.

Multinational corporations often hold superior bargaining positions vis-à-vis Southern host states. This allows them to extract considerable benefits from their operations in developing countries and to escape some forms of regulation. Yet this does not establish that foreign direct investment stymies Southern development. The economic benefits that multinational corporations bring developing countries vary depending upon the nature of the investment. Manufacturing investments likely offer the host state more than do extractive investments, such as mining or agricultural production. Yet the package of assets foreign firms bring to the country, including capital, technology, managerial expertise, and global marketing networks, often cannot be matched by local firms, whether private or state-owned. In any case, the ability of Southern countries to maximize the benefits of foreign direct investment while minimizing the negatives varies across countries and across time.

Perhaps dependency theory's greatest shortcoming is that it has trouble explaining the enormous diversity of development experiences. Whereas many Southern countries remain locked in poverty and show few signs of narrowing the gap with the North, a growing handful of countries have displayed impressive economic dynamism. Located primarily in East Asia, these so-called newly industrializing countries (NICs) have grown at rates far exceeding those in the North. They have also developed diversified economies that rest increasingly upon the production and trade of manufactured goods. Some have also become the originators of new technology.

Moreover, these countries have succeeded not by asserting greater autonomy from the North, but rather by integrating themselves ever more thoroughly into the international economic system. Although the strategies pursued by these countries do not necessarily suggest a blueprint for success by other Southern nations, it does seem clear that the nature of the international economic system does not preclude the possibility of development for all Southern countries. Indeed, because the external constraints faced by the newly industrializing countries did not differ radically from those facing many other Southern states, these cases of success should shift our attention toward those internal or domestic characteristics that can account for such different outcomes. This requires close attention to factors that are not typically included in dependency analysis.

The other strain of dependency theory emphasizes the disparities in political power between North and South. Northern leverage depends principally upon asymmetries in the relations of economic interdependence between North and South. Simply put, asymmetrical interdependence exists when two countries depend upon trade, investment, and other economic ties with one another, but one country is significantly more dependent upon the relationship than is the other. If the relationship were for some reason suddenly cut asunder, the more dependent trade partner would be hurt far more than the less dependent partner. The less dependent country can play upon the weakness and vulnerability of the more dependent country as a source of power or leverage.

A hypothetical case may help to clarify this point. Let us imagine that two countries, A and B, engage in trade with one another. For country A, its trade with country B constitutes only a small share of its overall trade with all countries and a much smaller proportion of its total national income. Were trade between A and B to be curtailed, country A would be only marginally hurt and could probably substitute for the losses by expanding its trade with alternative partners. Country B, however, is much smaller and less well developed than country A. Trade with country A constitutes a large portion of country B's overall trade and a significant increment of its national income. The loss of trade with country A would be devastating to country B's economy. Moreover, as a less developed nation dependent upon a narrow range of exports, country B might find it difficult to locate alternative buyers for its goods. This, in extreme form, is a relationship of asymmetrical interdependence. Country B's vulnerability to a rupture in trade provides country A with a source of power over B. Should political or commercial conflicts arise between the two countries, country A can reliably compel concessions from country B by threatening to withhold trade.

Dependency theorists point out that this hypothetical case conforms rather closely to the actual realities of economic ties between many Northern states and many Southern states. As a result, the North's interests dominate in bargaining between the two.[44]

Dependency theorists are on much firmer ground with this line of argument than with their critique of dependent capitalism. Southern dependence upon the North may not pose an insuperable obstacle to development, but it does clearly give rise to disparities in power and influence both in relations between particular states and in collective negotiations over the rules and institutions of the international economic order.

Before we embrace these conclusions, however, several caveats are in order. It should be noted that the recognition that power flows from asymmetrical interdependence is not unique to dependency theory. Indeed, the concept of asymmetrical interdependence can, with appropriate modifications, be applied to the analysis of power in many different spheres of social, political, and economic life. Moreover, asymmetries exist not just between North and South but also among Northern countries themselves, although the resulting disparities in power are unlikely to be as wide in the latter instances as in the former. Finally, power relationships among states are not static. OPEC, for instance, managed to turn the tables on the North during the 1970s when it took advantage of the industrial world's enormous dependence on a particularly crucial resource. As the world's second largest economy, China today possesses strong bargaining power, even though Chinese per capita income remains well below that of Northern countries.

What seems clear from our overview of geoeconomic, modernization, and dependency theories is that none provides an entirely adequate, overall understanding of the problems facing Southern countries as they attempt to close the development gap with the North. Geoeconomics gives too little weight to the influence of political and economic institutions on a country's growth prospects. Modernization theory ignores some of the less appealing aspects of economic development under capitalism. It is also vague on some key theoretical points, such as the concept of traditionalism. Moreover, modernization theory overlooks the importance of power disparities between the North and the South. Dependency theory has weaknesses as well, especially in its tendency to exaggerate the constraints that the international system places on development. The concept of dependence is vague, and the links between it and underdevelopment are tenuous. Dependency theory also provides us with few means for understanding why some Southern countries are rapidly developing while others are falling further behind. These shortcomings in the principal alternative perspectives on development are perhaps a measure of the limits to our knowledge about the complex process of economic development.

Nevertheless, each of these theoretical perspectives offers useful insights. Geoeconomics correctly emphasizes that geography and material resources matter. Modernization theory provides a convincing account of the factors that contributed to the development of the North, and it points to a number of present-day obstacles to development in the cultures and institutions of Southern societies. It also makes a strong case for the proposition that the spread of capitalism and the incorporation of Southern states into the international economic system provide an overall positive contribution to Southern economic development. Dependency theory, on the other hand, reminds us that great power disparities flow from Southern dependence upon the North.

In general, we suggest that modernization theory is closer to the mark in contending that the gains to the South from North–South economic ties outweigh the losses. Indeed, as one might expect from market exchanges, both North and South tend to benefit. Yet this does not imply that both sides benefit equally. The gains from mutual trade and investment may accrue to both North and South, yet not in equal proportions. As dependency writers point out, market relations are not free from the exercise of power. Asymmetrical interdependence provides the North with leverage over the South. The use of this leverage can allow the North to bend the rules of the game in its favor to ensure that the benefits of

North–South economic relations flow disproportionately its way. The South has been attracted toward greater involvement with the world economy by the promise of economic gain and accelerated modernization through exchange with the North. Yet it has also been repelled due to the dangers posed by overreliance upon the North and the risk that this dependence holds for exploitation.

Although modernization and dependency remain the principal general perspectives on development and North–South political economy, recent years have brought a shift in the terms of debate. New questions are being raised. Increasingly, scholars are turning to comparative studies that ask why countries facing similar international circumstances pursue differing development strategies. These policy choices, in turn, are seen as critical to economic outcomes.

Neither dependency theory nor modernization theory is well adapted to answering these sorts of questions. Dependency theory's emphasis on external constraints rules out domestically generated variation across countries. Modernization theory does look at domestic factors but emphasizes broad social and cultural traits that change slowly and are only loosely connected to specific policy choices. The newer literature, by contrast, pays close attention to the roles that political coalitions, as well as bureaucratic, institutional, and political structures, play in determining which development path a particular state is likely to choose. These sorts of factors are used to help explain, for instance, why the large countries of Latin America, including Brazil and Mexico, have generally pursued inward-looking development strategies stressing autonomy, whereas a number of successful East Asian countries, such as South Korea and Taiwan, have opted for outward-looking strategies based upon export expansion.[45] The next two sections trace the development choices between resource and industrial and between inward and outward strategies.

Strategies of Development

Resource Cartels

For most of the last two centuries of global trade, the poorer nations exported agricultural goods and raw materials to richer nations, which in turn exported manufactured goods to each other and to poorer nations. This division of labor, a legacy of colonialism, generally relegated developing countries to less dynamic and profitable roles in the world economy.

The major exceptions have been the oil exporting countries. Unlike other resource commodities, oil plays a central role in modern industrial economies and has at times provided a handful of oil-rich countries with the leverage needed to extract economic rents through trade.

From the 1930s onward, the discovery and exploitation of vast oil reserves in the Middle East (especially the Persian Gulf) fueled the expansion of the world economy. In the early decades, however, these reserves and the profits they generated were controlled not by local governments but by seven large Western oil companies (dubbed the Seven Sisters). Under the concession system, private firms controlled all aspects of the industry while paying modest royalties to the states from whose territory the oil was extracted.[46]

Chafing under these arrangements, five major oil exporters formed OPEC in 1960 to bargain for greater control over their own resources.[47] Against resistance from Western firms and governments, little was accomplished in the first decade of OPEC's existence. During the 1970s, however, an expanded OPEC took advantage of tighter oil markets to nationalize the assets of foreign firms and engineer two major price hikes that raised the cost of a barrel of oil from $3 to $36. This was accomplished in part through a quota system that allocated each OPEC country a ceiling on production. In other words, OPEC members set out to create a resource cartel. By collaborating to reduce the supply of oil on the market, OPEC succeeded for a time in pushing up prices and profits. This was possible because OPEC members in 1970 accounted for 90 percent of world oil exports. Overnight, a handful of lightly populated Persian Gulf producers became fabulously wealthy.[48]

The limits of OPEC's success, however, became apparent during the 1980s. Oil importing countries undertook conservation efforts and switched from oil to alternative energy sources, both of which served to curb demand. Also, investments in exploration brought major new flows of oil from non-OPEC sources, such as the North Sea, the Soviet Union, and Alaska. Finally, OPEC countries were themselves divided over pricing strategies and the quota system broke down. Indeed, two of the largest OPEC producers, Iraq and Iran, spent much of the decade at war with one another.

The combined effects of slackening global demand and more abundant supplies exacted a fearsome toll on OPEC countries. Between 1979 and 1988, per capita income fell by 27 percent among OPEC countries taken together, while imports shrank by half.[49] Saudi Arabia's oil revenues, which peaked at $19,000 per person in 1980, fell precipitously to $3,000 per person by 1994.[50]

Over the past quarter-century, oil prices have gyrated up and down, depending upon the balance between supply and demand and periodic market disruptions brought about by political uncertainty. In recent years, for example, the price of oil rose from $20 per barrel at the beginning of the century to over $100 per barrel in 2011 before falling again to less than $50 per barrel as of this writing. While still an important player, OPEC no longer has the power to dictate prices or overall supply.[51] Technological advances have allowed profitable exploitation of nonconventional oil resources, including deep-water offshore reserves, shale-based oil and hydraulic fracturing. Due to these innovations, the United States is well on its way to relative energy independence.[52]

While, moreover, oil exports have brought riches to a small number of Persian Gulf producers, the economic benefits to other oil exporting countries have been mixed. Indeed, economists refer to dependence upon a single commodity export – even one as critical as oil – as the "resource curse." For countries such as Nigeria, oil exports force up the value of the national currency, thereby forestalling the development of competitive manufacturing industries. As a result, resource-based economies lack diversity and resilience. Government budgets become dependent upon highly variable oil revenues, rendering long-term public investments difficult to plan or sustain.

Perhaps most important are the political effects of the resource curse. State-owned firms today account for 90 percent of global oil revenues.[53] Where oil dominates an economy, control over the state thus constitutes the only effective route to power and riches. Politics becomes a zero-sum game, rendering democratic institutions unviable, while struggles for political power take on an all-or-nothing quality. Despite vast oil or mineral wealth, countries such as Nigeria or the Congo are paradoxically laggards when it comes to economic development or political stability: the country is rich, but the people are poor.

OPEC's example led some observers during the 1970s to predict that resource cartels would proliferate, allowing developing countries to turn the tables on their former colonial masters. This never came to pass. Despite numerous efforts, no other group of commodity exporting countries managed to exert control over prices in the way that OPEC did during the 1970s. OPEC's own success has been quite variable and for some members excessive dependence upon oil revenues may have foreclosed more promising and sustainable paths to development.[54]

Industrialization

Lacking the advantages and disadvantages of large oil reserves, many developing countries have looked instead to industrialization as a path to prosperity. In the wake of World War II, a number of developing countries, particularly in Latin America, experimented with Import Substitution Industrialization (ISI). The goal was to nurture domestic manufacturing industries producing goods for consumption in the home market.

The difficulty in pursuing such a course was that Southern firms were generally too small and inexperienced to withstand direct competition from Northern exporters. In an effort to nurture these infant industries and to substitute domestic production for previously imported goods, Southern governments raised protectionist barriers to stymie foreign competition. The first industries to be offered protection were producers of consumer goods because the technical barriers as well as the capital requirements to this sort of production were lower. Due to the lack of experienced entrepreneurs, these firms were often created and owned by the state. Besides tariff protection, the new firms were offered other forms of assistance, including subsidized financing and preferential access to foreign exchange with which to purchase imported inputs. Where domestic industry lacked the knowledge or the capital to engage in certain types of production, Northern multinational corporations were encouraged to jump protectionist barriers and to serve local markets through domestic production rather than through exports.

Other policies were associated with ISI. Local currencies were kept overvalued. This cheapened the price of imported inputs such as oil, raw materials, and capital goods for ISI industries. Wage rates were allowed to rise, and social spending increased so as to encourage the growth of a domestic market for the consumer goods produced by ISI industries. Although the export of cash crops remained necessary in order to secure the foreign exchange needed for imported industrial inputs, the agricultural sector was generally squeezed. Investment was shifted from agriculture to industry, and surplus rural labor was channeled toward urban areas.

ISI produced impressive growth and industrialization during the 1950s in much of Latin America and elsewhere.[55] Yet by the 1960s ISI began to run out of steam due to contradictions inherent to the strategy. After the potential for further growth in the consumer goods sector slackened, governments began to pursue the "deepening" of ISI by encouraging the development of manufacturing capabilities in basic and intermediate industries such as steel and capital goods. For the most part, these investments involved larger-scale commitments of capital and more-sophisticated technologies than had been the case in the consumer goods industries. This required foreign borrowing or massive government spending. Moreover, because the domestic market for such goods remained small in many countries, new factories could not operate at efficient economies of scale, leading to high prices and large government subsidies.

These were not the only problems encountered by countries pursuing ISI. The justification for protecting the initial ISI industries from foreign competition was that they needed a breathing spell until they attained sufficient size and experience to compete successfully on their own. In fact, many firms became dependent on protectionism and lobbied hard against lifting barriers. With little effective competition, moreover, these firms had few incentives to maximize efficiency or to carry out innovation. They were also free to charge monopoly prices.

Financial difficulties also characterized the late stages of ISI. Government subsidies to industry and high social spending led to large budget deficits. Foreign borrowing, the repatriated profits of multinational corporations, and the discouragement of exports due to overvalued currencies also led to external deficits and a growing debt, despite the substitution of domestically produced goods for imports. Growing wage levels, large budget deficits, and the high prices associated with inefficient and monopolistic ISI industries created severe inflationary pressures.

Among development experts, ISI is now largely in disrepute. Although ISI may once have played a necessary role in jump-starting the process of industrialization in Latin America and elsewhere, many observers concluded that the rigidities and inefficiencies that ISI policies produce served to hinder growth and development in its later stages. The past four decades have brought great interest in an alternative path to development often referred to as export-led industrialization (ELI). This strategy entails an emphasis on the growth of manufacturing production aimed at the international market, in contrast to ISI, which focused on producing for the domestic market. ELI is rooted in theories of international trade that emphasize that countries are best off specializing in those goods for which they possess a comparative advantage while opening their economies to the import of goods that can be produced more cheaply elsewhere. Although the goal of ISI was to develop a well-rounded and relatively self-sufficient industrial economy, the goal of ELI is to exploit a country's particular advantages by finding a narrower, but profitable, niche in the world economy.

The most successful examples of export-led industrialization can be found in East Asia. Japan led the way in the 1950s and 1960s, followed by the "Four Tigers" – South Korea, Taiwan, Singapore, and Hong Kong.[56] Southeast Asia, including Malaysia, Indonesia, Thailand, and Vietnam, has jumped on the bandwagon as well. The largest and most consequential country to successfully pursue export-led industrialization has been China. East Asian industrialization has shifted the center of gravity in world manufacturing and lifted hundreds of millions of people from poverty.

Many of these countries have shared certain characteristics in common: strong, interventionist states, skilled bureaucracies, high rates of savings, weak landowning classes, low rates of labor mobilization, an emphasis on broad-based quality education, and aggressive efforts to cultivate technological advancement. There have been strong linkages among these economies as regional production networks have arisen.

Whether the export-led successes of East and Southeast Asia can be replicated in other parts of the developing world at a time when rich country markets are slowing will depend upon the ability of other countries to match the ensemble of competitive strengths that have come together across much of Asia.

Foreign Aid and Poverty Alleviation

While the sources of the development gap between North and South remain a matter of debate, much of the focus in recent years has turned to the question of whether and how the world's wealthy countries can help in alleviating extreme poverty around the world. Though inequality is, by definition, a relative concept, extreme poverty can be measured in absolute terms. The World Bank currently classifies any individual whose purchasing power falls below $1.25 per day as suffering from absolute poverty.

In contrast with global inequality, where the picture is mixed, progress toward reducing the worst forms of poverty has been rapid. In 1990, 43 percent of the world's people lived under conditions of extreme poverty. By 2010, that figure had fallen by more than half to 21 percent. Seventy percent of this reduction was accounted for by China alone, where sustained and rapid economic growth pulled 680 million people from poverty.[57] As the examples of China and much of East Asia attest, overall economic growth remains the best antidote to poverty. Overall, developing country GDP growth rose from 4.3 percent per year in 1960–2000 to 6 percent per year in 2000–10.[58] Growth generates jobs and provides governments with the resources necessary to expand schooling, improve health care, and offer other social services designed to enhance welfare.

Nevertheless, sustained economic growth has proven elusive in many countries. Moreover, growth may fail to benefit the poor where it is accompanied by worsening inequality and corrupt or unresponsive governance. In highly unequal societies, a 1 percent increase in GDP yields .6 percent reduction in poverty, whereas in the most equal societies the same increment of growth reduces poverty by 4.3 percent.[59] Today, roughly 1.3 billion people remain mired in poverty.[60] The great majority of the poor are located in Southern Asia (India, Pakistan, Bangladesh, and Nepal) and sub-Saharan Africa.

For more than a decade, governments, foundations, non-governmental organizations (NGOs), and academic experts have sought to accelerate poverty eradication through a set of targeted interventions aimed at the conditions that give rise to poverty. The focal point for these efforts has been the Millennium Development Goals (MDGs), which were promulgated by 189 member states at a UN Summit in 2000. Each of the ten MDGs focused on a particular dimension of human and environmental welfare. Each was connected with a set of concrete and measurable targets to be achieved by the year 2025. Wealthy donor countries and developing country government pledged to direct additional resources toward meeting these standards through coordinated effort.

The Millennium Development Goals:

1   To eradicate extreme poverty and hunger
2   To achieve universal primary education
3   To promote gender equality and empowering women
4   To reduce child mortality rates
5   To improve maternal health

6   To combat HIV/AIDS, malaria, and other diseases
7   To ensure environmental sustainability
8   To develop a global partnership for development

Official Development Assistance (ODA) provided by member states of the Organization for Economic Cooperation and Development (OECD) to developing countries amounted to $125 billion in 2012.[61] While this amount paled in comparison with the $703 billion in FDI received by developing countries in that same year,[62] much of ODA is directed toward poor countries that attract little commercial investment. In particular, major donor countries pledged a doubling of aid to sub-Saharan Africa at the 2005 Group of 8 summit meeting at Gleneagles, Scotland. For at least sixteen African countries, ODA represents more than 10 percent of annual national income.[63]

Despite much effort, progress toward meeting the MDGs has been mixed,[64] leading to debate over the underlying premises of the MDG project and the prominent role played by foreign aid. A leading voice calling for increased foreign aid to fight poverty is economist Jeffrey Sachs, who directs the Earth Institute at Columbia University. Sachs argues that many who languish at the bottom of the global income distribution are caught in a "poverty trap."[65] Whatever the original sources of poverty, conditions of destitution themselves serve as insuperable handicaps as the poor attempt to improve their own circumstances.

Insufficient income leads to hunger and malnutrition. These conditions render the poor vulnerable to illness and make it difficult to engage in prolonged physical labor. Without capital or access to credit, poor farmers cannot afford high-yielding seeds or the fertilizer and irrigation that are necessary to improve agricultural productivity. Lack of education precludes well-paid employment. Poverty thus feeds upon itself and perpetuates misery across generations.

Poverty traps can only be overcome, according to Sachs, through targeted interventions by external actors aimed at clearing away the obstacles to sustained improvements in income and welfare. Once hunger, ill health, illiteracy, and lack of access to credit and modern technology have been addressed, then individuals and communities begin to benefit from a virtuous cycle of self-sustaining economic improvement that frees them from poverty's deadly embrace. Sachs and others contend that the scale of the problem is manageable. Although overly simplistic, one estimate suggests that cash transfers amounting to 1 percent of global GDP per year would be sufficient to raise incomes above $2 per day for those currently experiencing extreme poverty.[66]

National governments, of course, must play lead roles in providing the resources needed to unleash the human potential of the poor. Brazil's Bolsa Familia (Family Allowance) program, for instance, has made great progress toward eliminating extreme poverty in that famously inequitable society through cash transfers to families conditioned upon vaccinating children and keeping them in school.[67] But among the least developed countries, governments often lack the financial means, the knowledge and organization, and perhaps the will to implement effective anti-poverty programs.

For these reasons, Sachs advocates expanded foreign aid programs aimed at providing those resources that neither the poor nor their governments can provide for themselves. Focusing on rural poverty in Africa, Sachs has spearheaded the creation of Millennium Villages in twenty African countries.[68] These pilot projects attempt to implement a comprehensive development model that tackles food security, health, education, environmental sustainability, and agricultural productivity as a package. Over a fixed period of time (originally five years and now ten years) and within defined spending constraints, the Millennium Villages project seeks to show that local interventions can set rural communities on a self-sustaining path to greater welfare and prosperity. By demonstrating the effectiveness of this kind of external support, Sachs hopes that governments and international donors will step forward with the resources necessary to scale up such projects to all of rural Africa.

The ultimate success or failure of the Millennium Villages project remains to be seen.[69] Nevertheless, many development experts remain skeptical about the utility of massive new investments in foreign aid. William Easterly points out that many low-income countries have remained dependent upon foreign aid for decades without shifting to a path of sustained and high-speed growth, while a number of countries that have made major strides, such as China, were never themselves major aid recipients. Economist Dambisa Moyo and journalist Andrew Mwenda argue that aid fuels corruption, leads to bloated state bureaucracies, and orients political leaders toward meeting the demands of external aid agencies rather than those of their own constituent. Critics charge that the priorities of aid agencies are distorted by bureaucratic interests or those of donor governments. The terms and conditions of foreign aid constantly change as intellectual fads influence the elusive search for the right formula for overcoming poverty.[70]

Sachs's approach in particular has been criticized for applying a one-size-fits-all solution that may conflict with local realities and the desires of the poor themselves. Even if the right inputs are provided at the village level, any gains can be easily swept aside if the national government pursues unwise macroeconomic policies or political violence intrudes.

While Sachs offers a supply-side approach to fighting poverty that emphasizes marshaling new resources for development, Easterly and others offer demand-side prescriptions that prioritize market incentives. Easterly rejects the idea of a poverty trap, pointing to examples where once desperately poor countries have become wealthier without the intervention of Marshall Plan-type infusions of aid. In China, for instance, the breakup of agricultural communes and the restoration of individual market incentives produced large gains in agricultural productivity and farmer incomes in the 1980s. From this perspective, improvements in welfare are a consequence of economic growth rather than a prerequisite for it. By focusing the attention of economic planners on MDG goals rather than the creation of commercial opportunities, foreign aid agencies may in fact retard economic progress.

Debates over the role of aid in fighting global poverty often turn on one's ideological perspective. One cleavage pits those who believe in the superiority of unfettered markets against others who argue that vigorous government intervention can improve economic outcomes. A second debate concerns whether growth or redistribution should have priority as vehicles for alleviating poverty.[71]

Some economists seek to cast aside ideological preconceptions in favor of scientific tests built upon empirical evidence. The Abdul Latif Jameel Poverty Action Lab (J-Lab) was created in 2003 at the Massachusetts Institute of Technology for the purpose of carrying out experimental trials – similar to those used to test the efficacy of new drugs – aimed at testing hypotheses concerning the effectiveness of various anti-poverty measures.[72] Typically, two population samples are compared – one that has been the subject of a policy intervention and a control group that has similar characteristics. As an example, researchers interested in finding out the most effective way to distribute bed nets meant for fighting malaria provided one set of villagers with free nets but attached a small fee to the nets distributed to a second set of villagers. They found that villagers value the nets more and are more likely to use them when they come at some cost. In this way, researchers hope to accumulate a body of empirically driven knowledge that can drive more cost-effective and meaningful policy interventions. The key question of this approach is not whether aid is good or bad but how it can be made to work better.[73]

Conclusion: An Inequitable World

Inequality, both within and across countries, has become a potent political issue, spurring protest movements from the Arab Spring to Occupy Wall St. Within market economies, some degree of inequality can serve the positive roles of rewarding hard work and promoting innovations that benefit the society at large. Inequality can also, however, arise from concentrations of political and economic power that entrench the status quo, undercut social mobility, and sunder the relationship between risk and reward. While the rise of China and India may have attenuated the development gap between North and South in recent years, the present degree of global inequality remains near its historical peak even as the gap between rich and poor within most societies continues to grow. It is perhaps understandable, then, that groups perceiving themselves as disadvantaged by the present order have coalesced to demand change.

Those at the bottom of the distribution of wealth and income are concerned less with relative position and economic fairness than with the more pressing concerns arising from absolute deprivation. The good news is that overall economic growth combined with greater access to education and the spread of public health measures have allowed hundreds of millions to escape the worst forms of poverty over recent decades. Yet one in six people on the planet continue to endure a day-to-day struggle for survival. Motivated by both moral and self-interested concerns, governments in both the North and the South, along with international organizations, NGOs, and private foundations, have devised various types of interventions aimed at ameliorating poverty and its afflictions. As we have seen, however, knowledgeable observers differ in their assessments of such efforts.

Key Concepts (see Glossary)

Absolute Gains
Asymmetrical Interdependence
Dependency
Export-Led Industrialization
   (ELI)
Geoeconomics
Gini Coefficient
Gross Domestic Product (GDP)

Human Development Index
   (HDI)
Import Substitution
   Industrialization (ISI)
Modernization
Poverty Trap
Purchasing Power Parity (PPP)
Resource Cartels

Discussion Questions

1 What are the advantages and disadvantages of various measures of social and economic development?
2 Why and how did the North gain such an economic advantage over the rest of the world during the nineteenth and much of the twentieth centuries?
3 How do different measures of global inequality differ and how does the choice among these measures influence the conclusions we draw about overall trends?
4 Are economic disparities larger among individuals within countries or among populations across countries?
5 Why should we care about inequality?
6 How are economic growth and economic inequality related to one another?
7 How do geoeconomic, modernization, and dependency theories differ in accounting for disparate outcomes in economic development? Which view is most persuasive?

8   What role can and should foreign assistance play in overcoming absolute poverty?

Notes

1   Robert Hunter Wade, "Globalization, Growth, Poverty, Inequality, Resentment and Imperialism," in John Ravenhill (ed.), *Global Political Economy*, Oxford, England: Oxford University Press, 3rd ed., 2011, 315.
2   Richard Wike, "The Global Consensus: Inequality is a Major Problem," PEW Research Center, November 15, 2013, www.pewresearch.org/fact-tank/2013/11/15/the-global-consensus-inequality-is-a-major-problem/
3   Thomas Piketty, *Capital in the Twenty-First Century*, Cambridge, MA: The Belknap Press of Harvard University Press, 2014.
4   Morten Jerven, *Poor Numbers: How We are Misled by African Development Statistics and What to Do About It*, Ithaca, New York: Cornell University Press, 2013.
5   "Why the Tail Wags the Dog," *The Economist*, August 6, 2011.
6   Kevin Rafferty, "Is China Already the No. 1 Economy?" *South China Morning Post*, March 1, 2011. Table 6.2: Percentage of GDP to US GDP (PPP-based) for Twelve Largest Economies, ICP 2011 and ICP 2005.
7   See Credit Suisse, *Global Wealth Databook 2014*, October 2014, https://publications.credit-suisse.com/tasks/render/file/index.cfm?fileid=25EC6CF2-0407-67D9-AAEAAE8BDFEDE378
8   As a result, income figures for some developing countries may be misleadingly low because some developing economies rely more on barter or subsistence production than do developed countries.
9   For an interesting discussion of the deficiencies of GDP measures and alternative ways to measure economic welfare, see Clifford Cobb, Ted Halstead, and Jonathan Rowe, "If the GDP is Up, Why is America Down?" *Atlantic Monthly*, October 1995.
10 "Rising GDP Not the Answer to Equitable Growth," *South China Morning Post*, March 11, 2011.
11 For a description of how the HDI is compiled, see United Nations Development Program, *Human Development Report, 2013*, United Nations Development Program, 2013, 141–2. The Social Progress Index represents a similar effort to offer a broader and multidimensional measure of human welfare, but includes more numerous and diverse indicators than the HDI. See www.socialprogressimperative.org/data/spi
12 Other efforts to measure well-being include the World Happiness Index (http://unsdsn.org/resources/publications/world-happiness-report-2013/) and the Happy Planet Index (http://www.happyplanetindex.org/about/).
13 World Bank, *The Changing Wealth of Nations: Measuring Sustainable Development in the New Millennium*, 2011.
14 Branko Milanovic, "Global Income Inequality by the Numbers: In History and Now," The World Bank, Development Research Group, Poverty and Inequality Team, November 2012, 17–20.
15 Milanovic, "Global Income Inequality by the Numbers," 3–11. Also, see Branko Milanovic, *The Haves and the Have Nots*, New York: Basic Books, 2011.
16 Piketty, *Capital in the Twenty-First Century*, 297.
17 Piketty, *Capital in the Twenty-First Century*, 296.
18 Piketty, *Capital in the Twenty-First Century*, 296.
19 Frederic Neumann, "Asia's Perilous Inequality," *International Herald Tribune*, March 6, 2012.

20 Mark O'Neill, "The New Class Struggle in China and Why It Threatens Economic Progress," *South China Morning Post*, March 13, 2011. Also see Victor Shih, "China's Highly Unequal Economy," *The Diplomat*, February 2011. China's Gini coefficient, which measures income inequality, has risen from .3 in 1980 to .55 in 2010 (the scale runs from 0 – perfect equality – to 1, which would indicate perfect inequality). Dexter Roberts, "China's Income–Inequality Gap Widens Beyond U.S. Levels," *Bloomberg Businessweek*, April 30, 2014.

21 *2007 Human Development Report* (HDR), United Nations Development Program, November 27, 2007, 25.

22 "Latin America: Gini Back in the Bottle," *The Economist*, October 13, 2012.

23 Wike, "The Global Consensus."

24 Based upon an Oxfam study reported in Kim Hjelmgaard, "In Global Wealth, 85=3,500,000,000," *USA Today*, January 21, 2014.

25 Piketty, *Capital in the Twenty-First Century*.

26 Charles Kenny, *Getting Better: Why Global Development is Succeeding – And How We Can Improve the World Even More*, New York: Basic Books, 2011, 76.

27 UNESCO Institute for Statistics, Adult and Youth Literacy: National, Regional and Global Trends, 1985–2015, 2013, Annex I, Table 1, 27.

28 For a review of these theories, see Nicola Phillips, "Globalization and Development," in John Ravenhill (ed.), *Global Political Economy*, Oxford, England: Oxford University Press, 3rd ed., 2011, 416–49.

29 Jared Diamond, *Guns, Germs, and Steel: The Fates of Human Societies*, New York: W.W. Norton & Company, 1999. Also see Gordon C. McCord and Jeffrey D. Sachs, "Development, Structure and Transformation: Some Evidence on Comparative Economic Growth," NBER Working Paper No. 19512, October 2013.

30 Jeffrey Sachs, "Helping the World's Poorest," *The Economist*, August 14, 1999, 18.

31 Ricardo Hausmann, "Prisoners of Geography," *Foreign Policy*, January/February 2001, 46.

32 Sachs, "Helping the World's Poorest," 19.

33 "Balms for the Poor," *The Economist*, August 14, 1999, 63.

34 Jeffrey Sachs, "Challenges of Sustainable Development Under Globalization," *International Journal of Development Issues*, vol. 4, no. 2 (2005) 1–20.

35 A partial list of works in the modernization tradition would include: Alex Inkeles and David H. Smith, *Becoming Modern: Individual Change in Six Development Countries*, Cambridge, MA: Harvard University Press, 1974; David McClelland, *The Achieving Society*, Princeton: Van Nostrand Co., 1961; Henri Avjac, "Cultures and Growth," in Christopher Saunders (ed.), *The Political Economy of New and Old Industrial Countries*, London: Butterworth's, 1981; Kalman Silvert, "The Politics of Social and Economic Change in Latin America," in Howard Wiarda (ed.), *Politics and Social Change in Latin America: The Distinct Tradition*, Amherst: University of Massachusetts Press, 1974; Myron Weiner (ed.), *Modernization: The Dynamics of Growth*, New York: Basic Books, 1966; Cyril Black, *The Dynamics of Modernization*, New York: Harper & Row, 1966; Gabriel Almond and James S. Coleman, *The Politics of Developing Areas*, Princeton: Princeton University Press, 1960; and Daniel Lerner, *The Passing of Traditional Society*, New York: Free Press of Glencoe, 1958. For a critique of the modernization school, see Alajandro Portes, "On the Sociology of National Development: Theories and Issues," *American Journal of Sociology* (July 1976). More recent works that echo themes from this earlier literature

are David S. Landes, *The Wealth and Poverty of Nations: Why Some are So Rich and Some So Poor*, New York: W.W. Norton & Company, 1999; and Daron Acemoglu and James Robinson, *Why Nations Fail: The Origins of Power, Prosperity, and Poverty*, New York: Crown Business, 2012.

36 For a brief but accessible discussion of neoclassical growth theory and some of its recent variants, see "How Does Your Economy Grow?" *The Economist*, September 30, 1995, 96. For scholarly works exemplifying so-called new or endogenous growth theory, see Paul Romer, "Increasing Returns and Long-Run Growth," *Journal of Political Economy* (October 1986); Paul Romer, "Endogenous Technological Change," *Journal of Political Economy* (October 1990); and Paul Romer, "The Origins of Endogenous Growth," *Journal of Economic Perspectives* (Winter 1994).

37 Acemoglu and Robinson, *Why Nations Fail*.

38 Among the major works in the dependency school are Theotonio Dos Santos, "The Structure of Dependence," in K.T. Fann and Donald Hodges (eds), *Readings in U.S. Imperialism*, Boston, MA: Porter Sargent Publisher, 1971; Fernando Henrique Cardoso and Enzo Falleto, *Dependency and Development in Latin America*, Berkeley: University of California Press, 1979; Fernando Henrique Cardoso, "The Consumption of Dependency Theory in the United States," *Latin American Research Review*, vol. 12, no. 3 (1977); Susanne Bodenheimer, "Dependency and Imperialism," *Politics and Society* (May 1970); Samir Amin, *Accumulation on a World Scale*, New York: Monthly Review Press, 1974; Andre Gunder Frank, *Capitalism and Underdevelopment in Latin America*, New York: Monthly Review Press, 1967; Andre Gunder Frank, *Latin America: Underdevelopment or Revolution*, New York: Monthly Review Press, 1969; C. Furtado, *Development and Underdevelopment*, Berkeley: University of California Press, 1964; A. Emmanuel, *Unequal Exchange*, London: New Left Books, 1972; Paul Baran, *The Political Economy of Growth*, New York: Monthly Review Press, 1957; and Immanuel Wallerstein, *The Modern World-System: Capitalist Agriculture and the Origins of the European World-Economy in the Sixteenth Century*, New York: Academic Press, 1976.

39 For an interpretation concerning the origins of the capitalist world system, see Wallerstein, *The Modern World-System*.

40 Quoted in J. Samuel Valenzuela and Arturo Valenzuela, "Modernization and Dependency: Alternative Perspectives in the Study of Latin American Underdevelopment," in Heraldo Munoz (ed.), *From Dependency to Development: Strategies to Overcome Underdevelopment and Inequality*, Boulder: Westview Press, 1981, 25. Translated from Osvaldo Sunkel and Pedro Paz, *El Subdesarrollo Latinoamericano y la Teoria del Desarrollo*, Mexico City, DF: Siglo Veinteuno Editores SA, 1970, 6.

41 Quoted in Valenzuela and Valenzuela, "Modernization and Dependency," 25–6. Also see Dos Santos, "The Structure of Dependence."

42 Our discussion of these two strains in dependency theory draws upon a similar distinction made in James Caparaso and Behrouz Zare, "An Interpretation and Evaluation of Dependency Theory," in Heraldo Munoz (ed.), *From Dependency to Development: Strategies to Overcome Underdevelopment and Inequality*, Boulder: Westview Press, 1981, 44–5.

43 For critical reviews of dependency theory, some more sympathetic than others, see David Ray, "The Dependency Model of Latin American Underdevelopment: Three Basic Fallacies," *Journal of Inter-American Studies and World Affairs* (February 1973); Sanjaya Lall, "Is Dependence a Useful Concept in Analyzing Underdevelopment?" *World Development* (November 1975); Richard Fagen, "Studying Latin American Politics: Some Implications

of a Dependencia Approach," *Latin American Research Review* (Summer 1977); Raymond Duvall, "Dependence and Dependencia Theory: Notes Toward Precision of Concept and Argument," *International Organization* (Winter 1978); Tony Smith, "The Underdevelopment of the Development Literature: The Case of Dependency Theory," *World Politics* (January 1979); and Bill Warren, "Imperialism and Capitalist Industrialization," *New Left Review* (September–October 1973). For an effort to subject dependency propositions to empirical testing, see Vincent Mahler, *Dependency Approaches to International Political Economy: A Cross-National Study*, New York: Columbia University Press, 1980.

44 For a seminal discussion of how asymmetries in economic dependence can provide one party with potential power over another, see Albert Hirshman, *National Power and the Structure of Foreign Trade*, Berkeley: University of California Press, 1969.

45 Two examples of research in this vein are Stephan Haggard, *Pathways from the Periphery: The Politics of Growth in the Newly Industrialized Countries*, Ithaca: Cornell University Press, 1990; and Sylvia Maxfield, *Governing Capital: International Finance and Mexican Politics*, Ithaca: Cornell University Press, 1990.

46 For readable accounts concerning the relationship between the major oil firms and producing countries, consult Anthony Sampson, *The Seven Sisters: The Great Oil Companies and the World They Created*, London: Coronet, rev. ed., 1988; and Yergin, *The Prize*, New York: Simon & Schuster, 1991.

47 The original five members of OPEC were Venezuela, Iran, Iraq, Saudi Arabia, and Kuwait. Today, OPEC members also include Qatar, Libya, the United Arab Emirates, Algeria, Nigeria, and Angola.

48 On the origins and evolution of OPEC, see Ian Skeets, *OPEC: Twenty-Five Years of Prices and Politics*, Cambridge: Cambridge University Press, 1988.

49 "The Cartel That Fell Out of the Driver's Seat," *The Economist*, February 4, 1989.

50 Agis Salpukas, "Long-Term Oil Strain Seen," *New York Times*, October 31, 1994.

51 Thijs Van de Graaf and Aviel Verbruggen, "Saving OPEC: How Oil Producers Can Counteract the Global Decline in Demand," *Foreign Affairs*, December 22, 2014.

52 See Clifford Krauss, "New Technologies Redraw the World's Energy Picture," *New York Times*, October 25, 2011; Amy Myers Jaffe, "The Americas, Not the Middle East, Will Be the World Capital of Energy," *Foreign Policy*, September/October, 2011; Clifford Krauss, "Can We Do Without the Mideast?" *New York Times*, March 30, 2011.

53 Joshua Kurlantzick, "The Rise of Innovative State Capitalism," *Bloomberg Businessweek*, June 28, 2012.

54 For a relatively up-to-date account of the role of oil in the world economy, see Daniel Yergin, *The Quest: Energy, Security and the Remaking of the Modern World*, New York: Simon & Schuster, rev. ed., 2012.

55 For a discussion of Latin America's experience with ISI, see Robert Alexander, "Import Substitution in Latin America in Retrospect," in James L. Dietz and Dilmus D. James (eds), *Progress Toward Development in Latin America: From Prebisch to Technological Autonomy*, Boulder: Lynne Rienner, 1991, and other essays in the same volume.

56 For general treatments of the East Asian NICs, see Richard P. Appelbaum and Jeffrey Henderson (eds), *States and Development in the Asia Pacific Rim*, Newbury Park: Sage Publications, 1992; Ezra Vogel, *The Four Little Dragons: The Spread of Industrialization in East Asia*, Cambridge, MA: Harvard

University Press, 1991; Bela Balassa, *Economic Policies in the Pacific Area Developing Countries*, New York: New York University Press, 1991; and Jon Woronoff, *Asia's "Miracle" Economies*, Armonk: M.E. Sharpe, 2nd ed., 1992.

57 "How Did the Global Poverty Rate Halve in 20 Years?" *The Economist*, June 2, 2013.

58 "Towards the End of Poverty," *The Economist*, June 1, 2013.

59 "Towards the End of Poverty," *The Economist*, June 1, 2013.

60 "Whose Problem Now? Awkward Questions about How to Best Help the Poor," *The Economist*, September 30, 2010.

61 "Aid to Poor Countries Slips Further as Governments Tighten Budgets," OECD, www.oecd.org/dac/stats/aidtopoorcountriesslipsfurtherasgovernmentstightenbudgets.htm

62 UNCTAD *World Investment Report, 2013*, ix, http://unctad.org/en/publicationslibrary/wir2013_en.pdf

63 United Nations Development Program, *Towards Human Resilience: Sustaining MDG Progress in an Age of Economic Uncertainty*, 2011, 160.

64 For a progress report broken down by region, see "Millennium Development Goals: 2013 Progress Chart," United Nations, 2013, www.un.org/millenniumgoals/pdf/report-2013/2013_progress_english.pdf

65 Jeffrey Sachs, *The End of Poverty: Economic Possibilities of Our Time*, New York: Penguin Books, 2006. Paul Collier expands upon the concept of poverty traps in *The Bottom Billion: Why the Poorest Countries are Failing and What Can Be Done About It*, Oxford, England: Oxford University Press, 2008.

66 Andy Sumner, "Dumb-bell or Emerging Middle?" *The Economist*, September 24, 2013.

67 "Brazil's Rousseff Says Extreme Poverty Almost Eradicated," *New York Times*, February 18, 2013.

68 For information on the Millennium Villages project, go to: http://millenniumvillages.org

69 For one assessment, see Nina Munk, *The Idealist: Jeffrey Sachs and the Quest to End Poverty*, New York: Doubleday, 2013.

70 William Easterly, *The Tyranny of Experts: Economists, Dictators and the Forgotten Rights of the Poor*, New York: Basic Books, 2014; William Easterly, *The White Man's Burden: Why the West's Efforts to Aid the Rest Have Done So Much Ill and So Little Good*, New York: Penguin Books, 2007; Dambisa Moyo, *Dead Aid: Why Aid is Not Working and How There is a Better Way for Africa*, New York: Farrar, Straus, and Giroux, 2009. Also see Ted Talk by Andrew Mwenda: "Let's Take a New Look at African Aid," 2007, www.youtube.com/watch?v=RfobLjsj230

71 Gardiner Harris, "Rival Economists in Public Battle Over Cure for India's Poverty," *New York Times*, August 21, 2013.

72 See www.povertyactionlab.org/about-j-pal

73 An accessible summary of key J-Lab research findings is Abhijit Banerjee and Esther Duflo, *Poor Economics: A Radical Rethinking of the Way to Fight Global Poverty*, New York: PublicAffairs, 2012.

Further Reading

Daron Acemoglu and James Robinson, *Why Nations Fail: The Origins of Power, Prosperity, and Poverty*, New York: Crown Business, 2012.
Makes the case that the right political institutions are the key to successful economic development.

Abhijit Banerjee and Esther Duflo, *Poor Economics: A Radical Rethinking of the Way to Fight Global Poverty*, New York: PublicAffairs, 2012.
Presents the results of poverty research utilizing experimental models similar to those employed in drug trials.

Cyril Black, *The Dynamics of Modernization*, New York: Harper & Row, 1966.
A widely cited statement of modernization theory.

Fernando Henrique Cardoso and Enzo Falleto, *Dependency and Development in Latin America*, Berkeley: University of California Press, 1979.
An important study of Latin American political and economic development from a dependency perspective.

Paul Collier, *The Bottom Billion: Why the Poorest Countries are Failing and What Can Be Done About It*, Oxford, England: Oxford University Press, 2008.
An empirically driven study of those factors that hold back economic growth in the least developed countries and how to overcome such obstacles.

Jared Diamond, *Guns, Germs, and Steel: The Fates of Human Societies*, New York: W.W. Norton & Company, 1999.
A sweeping examination of how geography has influenced social and economic development across the course of human history.

William Easterly, *The White Man's Burden: Why the West's Efforts to Aid the Rest Have Done So Much Ill and So Little Good*, London: Penguin Books, 2007.
An influential critique of foreign aid and of the assumptions underlying it.

Morten Jerven, *Poor Numbers: How We are Misled by African Development Statistics and What We Can Do About It*, New York: Cornell University Press, 2013.
A detailed examination of the severe inaccuracies and distortions that afflict economic data in African countries.

David S. Landes, *The Wealth and Poverty of Nations: Why Some are So Rich and Some So Poor*, New York: W.W. Norton & Company, 1999.
Offers an historical perspective on the roles that culture and technological innovation have played in economic development across various societies.

Branko Milanovic, *The Haves and the Have Nots: A Brief and Idiosyncratic History of Inequality Around the Globe*, New York: Basic Books, 2012.
An information-rich examination of changes in global inequality over time, including readable historical vignettes.

Ian Morris, *Why the West Rules – For Now: The Patterns of History, and What They Reveal About the Future*, London: Picador, 2011.
A sweeping comparison of social, political, and economic development in East and West across several millennia.

Dambisa Moyo, *Dead Aid: Why Aid Is Not Working and How There Is a Better Way for Africa*, New York: Farrar, Straus, and Giroux, 2009.
A searing critique of the ways that foreign aid has failed Africa.

Douglass C. North and Robert Paul Thomas, *The Rise of the Western World: A New Economic History*, Cambridge, England: Cambridge University Press, 1976.
An interpretation of European economic history that stresses the importance of property rights and institutional change for economic growth.

Thomas Piketty, *Capital in the Twenty-First Century*, Cambridge, MA: The Belknap Press of Harvard University Press, 2014.
An exhaustive and data-driven analysis of the sources and evolution of inequality within developed countries over the past two decades.

Jeffrey Sachs, *The End of Poverty: Economic Possibilities of Our Time*, New York: Penguin Books, 2006.
An optimistic discussion of how relatively inexpensive interventions can improve the lives of the poor and spur development.

Amartya Sen, *Development as Freedom*, New York: Anchor, 2000.
A philosophical examination of the concepts of inequality, development, and ethics.

Immanuel Wallerstein, *The Modern World-System I: Capitalist Agriculture and the Origins of the European World-Economy in the Sixteenth Century*, Berkeley: University of California Press, 2011.
A seminal text on world-systems theory, which is closely related to dependency theory.

7 The Political Economy of Global Finance
States, Firms, and Markets

Exchanging money for money isn't the same as exchanging money for goods and services. This is because money has many differentiated uses: as a fungible and tangible source of purchasing products; as a store of value; as a commodity used for trading; as a commodity used for lending; the choices made by the owners of financial resources affect the nature and level of economic growth; and as a mechanism for leveraging itself. The globalization of trade and production involves the creation of production sites and communication systems across the world. The globalization of finance involves the increasing exchange of and movement of money across national boundaries. But these systems of financial exchange are often coupled together by loans and the purchase of other assets, which increase the potential for volatility in markets when the changing value of one asset affects the value of connected financial assets.

The connections among financial markets are frequently defined by credit. Financial markets usually operate with a large dose of borrowed money and large debts link the fates of creditors and borrowers together. This also generates a significant psychological element to markets, as lenders depend on confidence in the ability of borrowers to repay debts. The normal functioning of financial markets requires confidence that the flow of funds in credit markets will continue to operate; when this confidence breaks down, lending stops and creditors demand payment, creating a potentially catastrophic crisis. And, because financial markets are tightly connected to the production of goods and services, this breakdown can have systemic economic consequences. The larger the scope and scale of financial markets, the greater the risks of systemic instability.

Financial markets require special study because of the interdependencies with each other and the links to broader forms of economic activity. Put another way, the operation of financial markets is an essential feature of all capitalist economies and this special quality of finance confers significant power in capitalist societies. This peculiar aspect of finance, especially the link to the creation and allocation of money, leads governments everywhere to develop a special relationship to financial firms and operations. Historically, free markets for finance and money are very unusual and some form of governmental control and management is far more typical. Even in cases where markets appear to be "free," underlying arrangements of management are almost always at work. Moreover, money in its varying forms is a fungible asset and this conveys considerable political power to its holders. Because money is issued by national agencies, there is no "international" money; at the same time, there is. Global economic preeminence – as possessed by the United States – promotes the US dollar to the role of "key currency," which means it functions like a global currency. And this status conveys numerous privileges on the US government that it has frequently exploited.

This chapter examines the international political economy of global finance, focusing mainly on the political arrangements for managing money in the global economy. The most important development in international finance over the past sixty years is the reversal of policy and preferences from a system of controlled finance in the two decades after World War II – known as the Bretton Woods system – to one of a state-supported system of globally free markets for investment in the period after about 1970. This transformation was the result of a long series of political decisions and of a political process, reflecting shifts in political power linked to an economically aggressive finance industry, operating mainly in the United States. At the same time, the political process was linked to the ability of financial firms to escape the control of governments and operate in self-created markets.

The system that followed was based on the expansion of finance on a domestic and a global scale. The financialization of the US economy involved an escalating role for financial firms in the overall economy, especially in the generation of profits. The expansion of credit as a percent of the overall economy, coupled with the deregulation of finance, increased the number and size of financial firms and the relative weight of these firms in generating profits and political power. The second process was the globalization of finance, with financial firms extending their operations to a global scale. Global financialization was associated with the shifting of political power toward the largest financial firms in New York and London, and was sustained through the use of US political power to press nations to liberalize their financial systems and to open them to global – meaning largely US and British – financial firms.

The operation of this new system of financialization and globalization resulted in many important consequences and problems. Newly floating exchange rates based on semi-free markets operated in ways that resulted in periodic intervention by governments and even in the creation of a new monetary unit in Europe. Domestic macroeconomic policies in the United States generated large domestic and global imbalances that both spurred and destabilized globalization. And, most important, the system of globally free markets for money generated numerous financial crises that required government intervention and management. In this chapter, global debt crisis of 1982, the Asian Financial Crisis of 1997–8, and the global financial crisis of 2008–12 receive detailed examination. We conclude the chapter with an examination of the consequences of the system of globalized finance.

The Structural Power of Finance in a Capitalist Economy

In terms of the political economy of a capitalist society, money is different from goods and services. In a capitalist economy, capital is the lifeblood of economic activity; the ability to borrow and the terms for borrowing provide an essential element for the day-to-day operation of the economy and for economic growth. The ability to make decisions about who receives loans and investment capital, and on what terms, conveys enormous power over the distribution of gains but also the overall fate of an economy. In many ways, even though the allocation of finance is a private good in that it can be withheld from some and provided to others, in other ways finance is like a public good in the overall impact on the economy and on the economic fate of most people. Thus, the organization of the system of finance carries great weight.

To this vital economic role of finance is added the intense interdependence of the institutions and markets of a financial system. The extension of credit is the essential link in a financial system, and because virtually every financial institution operates on credit, they are themselves linked together very tightly. Because banks are tied together by the mutual granting of credit, the loss of confidence in repayment not only can lead banks to stop lending but also can produce a broad lack of confidence in banks themselves. The result is a systemic crisis. It is this essential role of banks and the potential for small events to have much bigger consequences that makes banks such frequent recipients of bailouts. When this central role for banks in managing the economy is accompanied by frequent large errors in judgment about investment, bailouts increase. Even in the face of moral hazard, governments are unwilling to take the political and economic risks of large negative consequences from a banking collapse.

Beyond the essential role of finance is a set of complementary capabilities that add to its political and economic power. The financial industry experiences very high levels of profit and is a major contributor to political campaigns, with the highest absolute level of all industries. Moreover, the financial industry has spent lavishly to support academic institutions to insure a favorable intellectual climate for financial interests.[1] At least in the United States, finance is one of the most globally competitive of industries, making it a very desirable asset for the nation. The finance industry also acts as an allocator of resources and in this role has the capacity to organize and direct industrial restructuring. In some ways, the position of the financial industry allows it to operate as a partner of the state and as such presents itself as an alternative source of political and social governance.

The public goods-like quality of finance in a capitalist economy strongly suggests the need for a large governmental role in making sure decisions relating to these public goods are not abused, nor that the power potential deriving from control of this resource is not excessively exploited. An additional argument can be made that the achievement of public purposes by the state requires significant control over the financial system in order to achieve these goals. The American pattern of free markets for money reflects the political power of financial interests and the ideological preferences for private profits over public purposes. By contrast, the financial systems in other nations reflect other patterns of political power and a different relationship of political purpose and private action. In Germany and Japan, the effort to achieve economic growth in the nineteenth and twentieth centuries took on considerable overtones of national security. Consequently, the key role of credit allocation was partly assumed by the national government through institutional arrangements that gave considerable discretion to government officials. In the twentieth century, these tendencies were likewise found in the rapidly growing economies of East and Southeast Asia. Korea, Taiwan, Singapore, and most certainly China are nations that established very direct and extensive control over their financial systems, with the state as the dominant partner in a system of credit creation and allocation.

Banks, Markets, and Governments: The Evolution of Capitalist Financial Systems

A large part of the political economy of finance turns on the degree to which financial capital is harnessed to the political ends of the state or whether financial capital is freed of these controls and is able to leverage its structural power to move the political order to serve its ends. This key relationship was at the center of the major developments in political economy during the global capitalist era beginning in the nineteenth century. This includes the political order of the nineteenth-century gold standard, the post-World War I political struggles over returning to the gold standard, the period of the 1930s to 1960s with political elites able to exert control over finance, and from the 1970s to the present with a substantial elimination of political controls on finance and a subsequent and proportional increase in the political power of finance.[2]

The breakdown and collapse of the liberal financial order of the gold standard in the 1930s came as a result of the disintegration not only of the global economy but also of the political power of financial interests resulting from the effects of the Great Depression. The Depression proceeded much like the global financial crisis of 2008, except the process of cumulating collapse continued for four years in the 1930s but for less than one year in the most recent case. The financial collapse fed on itself by completely freezing the credit system and bank lending, leading to additional financial collapse by many cut off from credit, including several waves of banks themselves. As this happened, previously financially stable firms and banks were dragged down by the collapsing economy now being adversely affected by the disintegrating financial system. This cycle continued until a large intervention by the US government beginning in 1933 stemmed the collapse.[3]

Bretton Woods and State Control of Finance

The massive economic collapse in the 1930s had substantial political consequences. The political and economic views of previously dominant bankers "were increasingly replaced at the levers of power in the industrial world by a new coalition of social groups that included industrialists, labor leaders, and Keynesian-minded state officials."[4] The result was the creation of a new set of political controls on finance, including a system of controls on capital movement across national boundaries coupled with restraints on the economic flexibility and power of finance. These controls were extended into the postwar era with the creation of the Bretton Woods system and "embedded liberalism."[5] From the 1940s to the 1960s, the US financial industry was embedded in a new set of political relationships defined by preferences that would subordinate financial interests to broader political goals. This was true in both domestic and international terms. Substantial controls on the movement of capital internationally – capital controls – were enacted, along with an array of regulations limiting the ability of financial firms to operate. Perhaps most important, the political leadership of the US government asserted control over domestic and international monetary policy through control over the Federal Reserve. This system of political economy was one of "embedded liberalism," in which the liberalization of trade and national policies for equitable economic growth were given preference over the freedom of finance.[6]

All forms of order in international political economy rest on political processes of development and political relationships of interests and power. In the case of the postwar order of embedded liberalism, the political processes are found in the struggles associated with the Great Depression and global war, which had the effect of deeply damaging the political power of finance, elevating the political power of producing industries, and greatly raising the power of the state in the management of the economy and in the achievement of national security. These outcomes always encountered fierce political opposition from groups such as finance, whose power and economic position were disadvantaged by these changes. At the same time, the system of embedded liberalism was accepted as appropriate and legitimate by the general public and by most elites. In the United States, the key force holding together a political coalition supporting embedded liberalism was the Cold War and the threat to capitalism posed by global communism. The result was a domestic and international financial order based on significant state power directed toward engineering a system of fixed exchange rates and restraints on capital movement, the expansion of global trade, the use of a coordinated fiscal and monetary policy to promote economic growth and low unemployment, along with a rising state role for preserving incomes during a crisis and for the retired. The result was significant rates of economic growth in developed nations and rising incomes across most economic classes.

This system began to break down economically and politically from the early 1960s and especially by the 1970s. Remember, the Bretton Woods system was based on fixed exchange rates of various national currencies to the US dollar, coupled with the dollar fixed in value to gold. The system depended on stringent capital controls, which prevented the movement of capital across borders and on two contradictory relationships for the dollar. The US dollar was the key currency and the growth of dollars in global circulation was necessary for the expansion of global trade. At the same time, the gold–dollar link depended on keeping the quantity of dollars in global circulation to an amount less than the value of the gold held by the United States.[7] Over time, the US balance of payments deficits persisted, increasing the volume of dollars in global circulation. And several internationally oriented banks began to find ways to globalize their financial activities, in spite of capital controls.

State actions were often responsible for the new opportunities for international banks. Policies that promoted change included the widespread adoption of currency convertibility in the late 1950s and the loosening of capital controls in the 1960s. Each step had the effect of creating new profit opportunities for finance, especially as it operated on an international plain. In the midst of these developments, the Euromarket emerged as an embryonic system of international financial liberalization and a precursor to the changes of the next several decades. London bankers, with centuries of experience in international finance, decided to lend the dollars accumulating in their banks rather than return them to the United States. The British government, eager to reestablish London's position in international finance, actively encouraged this innovation and avoided any effort at regulation.

Over time, the Euromarket system became an unregulated supply of international money, with a system of deposits of dollars and other currencies, bank credit, and a Eurobond market of dollar-denominated bonds issued outside the United States. Other states also abjured regulation, in part because Euromarket funds were often used to provide financing to nations experiencing a balance of payments deficit. During the 1960s, because of the unremitting outflow of dollars the United States tightened capital controls even as it encouraged US banks and multinational firms to use the Euromarket. By 1970 this market approached $70 billion dollars in size and would triple in the next three years.[8] Perhaps more significant, the loosening of international financial operations opened the way for the crisis in and ultimate collapse of the gold–dollar standard that stood at the center of the Bretton Woods international monetary system. This is because the emergence of a more liberal environment for finance led quickly to speculative attacks on currencies and ultimately to systemic breakdown.

The speculative attacks focused on the British pound and US dollar and were linked to the growing imbalance between the holdings of gold and the value of US dollars held abroad. In this circumstance, the growing inability of the United States to redeem dollars with gold foretold a near certain depreciation of the dollar against gold. Anticipating this, speculators would sell dollars today in hopes of repurchasing them at a lower rate in the future. Thought to be the weaker currency, traders first attacked the British pound, leading to its devaluation in 1967. Attacks against the dollar often were associated with events that pointed to an increase in the US balance of payments deficit and/or increasing inflation. These attacks culminated in 1971–3 with the decisions to end the gold–dollar link and to end the system of fixed exchange rates.[9]

The Neoliberal Transformation of Domestic and Global Political Economy

The 1970s brought the beginnings of a set of dramatic changes in the political, economic, and strategic arrangements that had governed the relationships of domestic and international systems for three decades. Détente with the Soviet Union and the new relationship between the United States and China were perhaps the most dramatic changes. The end of the Bretton Woods system and the massive rise in oil prices were economic changes of equal import, and together these economic developments were connected to substantial changes in the political economy within the United States. The system of embedded liberalism, with its commitment to broadly rising incomes and support for an expanded welfare system sustained by an activist government, deteriorated as support from various elites began to erode. This was the result of a confluence of economic and political relations that tore apart the fabric of this consensus on political economy. Labor costs, rising significantly since the 1950s, accelerated in the 1970s and confronted a large slowdown in productivity. Energy costs exploded with the newfound leverage of oil producers on global prices. And a self-reinforcing cycle of inflation in products, a declining dollar, and rising wage rates propelled inflation to unprecedented levels at the end of the 1970s. Economic recessions, previously short and mild, became for a while more frequent and intense.[10] The political resurgence of business interests was driven by these developments and led to much greater support for neoliberal policies.[11]

The result was the creation of a new system of global political economy, premised on the globalization of production facilitated by the globalization of finance and directed by the ideology of neoliberalism. This new system involved a restructuring of the relationship of the state and economic markets, especially financial markets. Rather than operating to control finance and tie these interests to the ends of state policy, governments shifted to the role of subordinate partner, deregulating financial firms, promoting global opportunities for financial firms, and providing financial support when frequent financial crises developed. State policy in relation to financial markets remained extensive in managing the money supply, interest rates, and exchange rates, but policymakers often hid this role behind celebrations of the efficacy of markets.

This shift in economic strategy was a result of the interaction of several factors: the growing power of markets and market players in relation to government resources; the appeal of neoliberal ideology; and the adoption of a new strategy of hegemony based on freer markets as a pathway to preserving the structural power of the United States and as a means to expand policy flexibility in global and domestic economic issues.[12] The outcome of this new system was nearly three decades of surging globalization, a return to economic growth by rich nations, combined with extraordinarily rapid growth by those nations best able to adjust to the globalization of finance, production, and knowledge. And this growth was punctuated by increasingly frequent and more severe financial and economic crises that culminated in the crisis of 2008–12.

This section will review the political economy of the events and processes leading to a new system of global relations. We are especially interested in the explosive growth of financial markets and firms and the role of finance in economic life. Moreover, this process of financialization was closely connected to the globalization of money and production. And, various economic changes in oil prices, inflation, government deficits, and exchange rates all contributed much to domestic and global financial expansion. We will discuss how and why this happened and how governments both participated in and reacted to these very important changes. The most powerful governments were typically helping to create global finance and to manipulate these changes for political advantage. Much of the operation and many of the problems of contemporary economies can be traced to these changes.

Financialization

The mutually reinforcing processes of financialization and globalization advanced on a series of fronts over the period from 1971–2008. The

domestic policy impetus came mainly from actions to reduce and/or eliminate various forms of financial regulations imposed during the 1930s.
Financial deregulation in the 1970s consisted mainly of eliminating price
controls on credit and savings. As part of the process of controlling
finance extending from the 1930s, the amount banks could pay for
deposited funds was controlled by governments, and similarly, the rates
banks and other lenders could charge for credit were also controlled.
Between 1970 and 1982, most of these controls were lifted, primarily due
to the conflicts over credit allocation brought on by higher inflation. In
the 1980s and 1990s, deregulation took the form of increasing the opportunities for banks to operate in a multitude of financial markets. This
contrasted with the restrictions on bank activity enacted in the 1930s.[13]

A second domestic process leading to greater financialization came
from macroeconomic policy, on the part of the Federal Reserve and in
terms of taxing and spending policy by the government as a whole.
Further, these domestic policies spilled into the global arena and contributed greatly to the globalization process. The consequence of slashing
taxes in the early 1980s and early 2000s, in combination with massive
current account deficits, led to an enormous increase in global purchases
of US government securities, which are sold to cover the rising fiscal deficits. And efforts to control inflation by the Federal Reserve, especially the
actions by Paul Volcker, operated to restore confidence in the monetary
integrity of the US government.

Sustaining economic growth depended more heavily on governmental
and private debt and on innovation in financial operations. Profits for
firms came to depend on cutting costs in domestic operations and
expanding production to lower cost sites abroad. But profits also came
increasingly to involve the financialization and securitization of traditional assets held by firms and individuals. Many firms, with profits from
normal operations waning, turned to financial investments to bolster
profits. Thus, financialization also includes the shifting of corporate
behavior toward investing in financial rather than productive assets and
the governance of firms shifting from managers with significant autonomy
to one of shareholder value and financial markets as the primary focus of
management decisions.[14] One important measurable result was the explosion of banking assets as a percent of Gross Domestic Product (GDP). In
Britain, between 1966 and 2006, banking assets as a percent of GDP
rose from 35 percent (approximately the level since 1880) to more than
550 percent.[15]

Globalization of Finance

At the global level, the first great wave of financial globalization took
place as a result of the growth of foreign exchange trading, the expansion
of lending by global banks to governments, and the massive shift in

financial resources resulting from rising oil prices. This happened in the decade or so after the collapse of the Bretton Woods system. Accompanying these processes was a decline in the value of the US dollar, significantly slower economic growth in rich nations, and a rapid increase in the level of inflation. The United States took the policy lead in ending capital controls in the mid-1970s, followed soon thereafter by Great Britain. US political pressure on other advanced nations to adopt a similar policy on capital controls combined with rising global market activity to induce other states to end controls. A constant impetus to greater foreign exchange trading was the digitization of communication and expanding computerization, which lowered transaction costs dramatically across borders.[16] As exchange rates came to operate with less direct state controls, efforts expanded to use cooperation among the major powers to manage the volatility and negative consequences of these markets.[17] And the volatility of exchange rates and the disruptive effects on the competitiveness of traded goods led many nations to cooperate in adopting various forms of monetary unions as a way to restore stability.

Ending Capital Controls

The elimination of capital controls, a key element of the Bretton Woods system, was driven by decisions in the United States which had the effect of shifting even more US dollars onto the rest of the world, thereby increasing substantially the size of global financial markets. The effects of these markets could be seen in exchange rates and in markets for government bonds. Under the system of embedded liberalism of Bretton Woods, nations could increase government spending (and budget deficits) without great concern for the effect on their currency and assume the capital could be raised in their domestic markets. With the newly globalized financial markets, governments could take these actions only when global financial markets were supportive of such policies. Otherwise, money could simply flee to another location on the globe, leaving the exchange rate and bond prices declining. These markets, now composed mostly of globally oriented investors (banks, investment firms, and individuals), acted as a daily vote on the viability of government policy.[18]

In the period from 1974 to about 1990, governments in advanced nations faced the choice of preserving capital controls and effectively withdrawing from the world economy or loosening or lifting these controls in order to preserve access to the world economy. Throughout this period, global markets expanded at an exponential rate, which increased the pressure on governments and expanded the power of global markets and the largest firms operating in these markets. The United States and Great Britain took additional steps to liberalize their securities and banking markets so as to attract international funds, thereby adding to the pressure to end capital controls by other nations. One-by-one, countries such as Japan, France, Germany, New Zealand, Australia, and Denmark lifted controls on capital, thereby increasing the pressure on other advanced capitalist nations to do likewise.[19]

Oil and Money

A second major contributor to the globalization of finance came from the financial consequences of the rapid rise of oil prices in the 1970s. The increase in oil prices, in current dollars from about $3 to over $30 per barrel, placed great stresses on the global economy, including the United States. We can think of this as like a tax imposed by producers on consumers, which led to a massive transfer of wealth from rich nations to oil producing nations. Many oil producing nations preferred keeping these funds in dollar-denominated accounts held in Western banks (the most secure and liquid institutions in the world). The presence of these newfound deposits meant banks needed to find new investment and lending options in order to make profits from these deposits. Western economies were generally in recession, so the banks turned to the governments of developing nations, which were eager to borrow. The "recycling of petrodollars" meant money had been globalized into international trade and into international banks and borrowers. During the 1970s, the debt of developing nations grew sixfold, from $100 billion to $600 billion, most of this in the form of loans and bond purchases provided by large banks in rich nations.[20]

In making the decision to hold dollars in Western banks in payment for oil, the producers of oil were responding to the structural power of the financial system of the United States and to the dollar's role as the key currency. The financial system in the United States was very strong, with very liquid financial markets and very strong banks. Moreover, the debt instruments of the US government were viewed as extremely safe and could be sold quickly in these markets if necessary. And the US dollar as a global key currency was accepted in payment everywhere. As such, the structural power of the United States meant it was able to pay for the massive trade deficit created by rising oil prices with its own currency. This pattern of offsetting a US trade deficit with investment capital from trade surplus nations was to continue over the entire era of financial globalization and helps explain many of the features of this process.

Other important patterns can be seen from the 1970s expansion of lending to developing nations. These countries were forced to borrow in dollars and pay back in dollars, which made their debt closely tied to their balance of payments. The ability to service this debt (pay it back) was dependent on the ability to produce a trade surplus and thereby accumulate dollars. Further, most loans from Western banks to developing nation governments in this period carried a variable interest rate.

This meant the interest rate on the loan was dependent on interest rates in rich nations – mostly in the financial centers of New York and London. If interest rates rise, the amount of repayment rises as well. The combination of rapidly rising debt, variable rates, and loan repayment in dollars created a financial train wreck waiting to happen.

The Global Debt Crisis of 1982

The first great postwar debt and banking crisis came into the open in 1982, when several Latin American nations were unable to make regular payments on their debt. This was a result of the combination of increased costs for oil imports for some, falling exports as a result of economic recessions in the rich nations, and extremely high interest rates resulting from Federal Reserve policies to reduce inflation.[21] For the indebted nations, their ability to repay the debt had been reduced by each of these events. The resolution of the crisis was organized by the International Monetary Fund (IMF), which worked out a combination of restructured debt payments and additional loans from both the IMF and the US government, in effect acting to bail out both the banks and the government borrowers.

This debt crisis raises numerous questions about the operation and consequences of the globalization of finance. The answers given often reflect the ideological and political biases that dominate thinking about international political economy.[22] The most important relate to two main issues. First, is questions about the ability of those making decisions about lending (and investing) to make prudent choices, such that crises do not result from resources being allocated in ways that lead to bad outcomes. Can financial markets work to produce the efficient allocation of resources to borrowers able to use these resources and pay them back? The second group of questions relate to the role of governments in resolving the crisis. Why should public funds be committed to fixing problems created by lenders and borrowers operating in a private business transaction?

Those who are proponents of free markets as the most effective and efficient allocators of resources – neoliberals (economists and bankers) – argue the crisis was a result of government policies in oil, money, and economic mismanagement. Without the actions of oil exporters and the Federal Reserve, borrower nations could have repaid the debt and no crisis would have ensued. However, many neoliberals are a bit more divided on the role of government actions to resolve the crisis with funds for bailouts. The preponderant view is that global and national economic systems are very vulnerable to financial breakdowns and allowing large financial institutions to go bankrupt presents an unacceptable risk to the entire global economic system. In a financial crisis such as the one in 1982, an additional concern is for the economic consequences for the borrower nations and the implications for all of a debt default. A minority view holds that bailouts for poor decisions by bankers create a "moral hazard" that actually encourages highly risky actions in the future by such bankers. By letting banks collapse and enduring the pain (admittedly horrific) this would cause, we would reduce the chances of similar events in the future.[23]

The positions of neoliberals are countered by a heterogeneous collection of critics. An important argument sees significant flaws in financial markets, which are thought to be inherently unstable. Such markets are prone to overshooting prudent levels of lending, as success by a few banks leads to a herd effect with other banks seeking similar profits. This leads to a deterioration of lending evaluation criteria and therefore to loans of lower quality. Moreover, when the crisis comes these same banks will act in near unison to cut off additional lending by freezing new credit, thereby exacerbating the crisis. Those who reject the free market mantra are also critical of the actions to bail out banks and foreign governments, because these actions are rarely extended to those in the middle and lower classes, whose financial positions are destroyed by the actions of these banks and governments.[24]

Deficits and Debt

Center stage in the global debt crisis of 1982 were the effects of economic policies in the United States, with various parts of the US government attempting to deal with the economic problems resulting from the continuing difficulties of inflation and recession in the 1970s. On the one hand was the Federal Reserve, headed by Paul Volcker, committed to wrenching inflation from the US economy and using a policy of extremely tight money that had the effect of pushing up interest rates to record levels. On the other was the new administration of President Ronald Reagan, which was determined to respond to the intense anti-tax sentiments in much of the electorate, but especially among the wealthy. In 1981, Reagan persuaded Congress to lower income tax rates substantially. This action was supported by the false theory that cutting tax rates would provoke so much economic growth that tax receipts would ultimately rise and make up the initial losses. The actual consequence was a massive increase in the federal budget deficit. Ironically, the combination of high interest rates and massive budget deficits would play a major role in financial globalization.

Inflation is anathema to those whose wealth is held mainly in financial assets, especially those who provide loans and hold debt. This is because inflation represents a decline in the value of money relative to other assets, such as houses and gold. The rising rates of inflation in the 1970s engaged the interests of those with financial assets and many others unable to keep incomes rising faster than inflation. The disruptive effects of oil prices, technological change, and government policies in the 1960s and 1970s generated considerable inflation. Between 1973 and 1979, inflation in the United States, as measured by the Consumer Price Index, averaged nearly 10 percent per year, and peaked at 12 percent in 1975 and at 14 percent in 1980.[25] This produced a determined political response to inflation in late 1979, when Paul Volcker was appointed chairman of the Federal Reserve. In adopting a policy to squeeze out growth in the money supply, Volcker was prepared to let interest rates go up as far as was necessary. And they did rise to unprecedented levels. By 1982, the typical interest rate for the best borrowers from banks was 21.5 percent and interest rates remained exceptionally high for many years. But inflation was reduced and generally has remained low since the early 1980s.[26]

Reviving economic growth after the problems of the 1970s was both more difficult and more politicized. Neoliberal views gained politically as economic conditions failed to improve and came to focus on a strategy of cutting tax rates by dramatic amounts as the path to prosperity. Though this plan was a version of the Keynesian approach to spurring growth tried by the Kennedy Administration in the 1960s, it was justified as an effort to improve incentives for entrepreneurship. In addition to reducing tax rates, the Reagan Administration adopted a policy of rapid expansion of defense spending. The most important and predictable consequence of reducing fiscal revenues and raising expenditures was a massive increase in the budget deficit to far higher levels than previously in peacetime. With the US government borrowing money at record levels, there were fears this would push interest rates much higher and choke off a recovery. But, miraculously, this did not happen, largely because of the globalization of finance and the structural power associated with the US global financial position.[27]

Keep in mind our discussion of the balance of payments in Chapter 2, and remember that a current account deficit must be balanced by an inflow of funds into the deficit nation. Supporting this process, the high real interest rates in the United States throughout the 1980s worked to pull investment into the United States. In particular, foreigners were eager to purchase US government debt, which was expanding dramatically as a result of the large and growing US fiscal deficits. Moreover, US consumers were increasingly ready to borrow more to purchase goods made in Asia that flowed into US markets.[28] So economic growth resumed, generated by the stimulus from deficit spending financed by foreign investment that permitted larger US consumer borrowing to purchase foreign-made goods. All the while, financialization and the globalization of finance proceeded apace. Large deficits, large global borrowing, and increasing debt by firms, governments, and households all operated to expand the importance of financial firms in the US economy and the integration of global financial markets.

Managing Floating Exchange Rates: Market Intervention

The freeing of exchange rates from the controlled world of Bretton Woods was a necessary step toward the globalization of finance. Exchange rates based on market processes of supply and demand provide the flexibility to permit large movements of money across national boundaries. At the same time, fluctuations in exchange rates generate substantial effects on the profits of those engaged in international trade, as well as on the profits and losses from international investment.[29] Even though national governments acquiesced in and even encouraged the development of a new system of flexible exchange rates, these same governments have repeatedly intervened in these markets to manipulate the price of their currency. Governments have often needed to protect themselves from negative consequences of flexible exchange rates, and after the demise of Bretton Woods fluctuations were often much greater and more volatile than expected.[30] Because foreign exchange markets are so large, cooperation among nations in these efforts is usually needed for intervention to work. In some cases, cooperation was ad hoc and intermittent; in other instances, nations were prepared to establish formal arrangements to create monetary unions for managing exchange rates.

The imbalances generated by US fiscal and trade deficits in the 1980s had important but contradictory links to exchange rates. Normally, a nation experiencing a large trade deficit would find its currency falling in value against other currencies. On the other side, the high interest rates and large supply of government debt resulting from the fiscal deficit attracted substantial investment into the United States. In order to purchase US government bonds, a foreign buyer first needs to purchase US dollars.[31] The result was a large increase in the demand for US dollars and the US dollar rose substantially, even as the current account deficit ballooned. In relation to the Japanese yen, the dollar rose by about 25 percent and against a collection of other currencies rose by as much as 60 percent. The paradoxical effect of the rising dollar was to expand the trade deficit, as US exports became more expensive and US imports less expensive. The effect was to engage the interests of US exporters, who became increasingly less competitive in global markets. These firms pressed the Reagan Administration hard for a solution.[32]

One option, admittedly a difficult one, would be to raise taxes and cut spending to reduce the budget deficit and to direct domestic investment toward improving global competitiveness. This would have produced long-term gains but significant short-term pain. Political leaders in a democracy face elections on a short-term cycle and they are reluctant to implement policies that can lead to electoral defeat, even if these are needed for future improvements. Because the Reagan Administration had staked its political position on tax cuts and increased defense spending, they largely ignored the effects of these policies on exchange rates until after the 1984 election. Moreover, the policy of "benign neglect," as this was known, placed great pressure on US economic partners to make adjustments to US policies and preferences. However, in 1985, the Reagan Administration shifted gears and a policy of reducing the dollar while preserving existing tax and spending policies was adopted.[33]

The new Secretary of the Treasury James Baker and his deputy Richard Darman worked to organize an international effort to lower the value of the dollar. In a meeting at the Plaza Hotel in New York, the finance ministers and Central Bank heads of the United States, Germany, Japan, France, and Great Britain orchestrated a cooperative effort to boost the value of the mark, yen, franc, and pound in relation to the dollar. Known as the Plaza Agreement, this was to be accomplished through coordinated governmental efforts to intervene in foreign exchange markets. To be clear, this was a policy adopted by two governments, the United States and Great Britain, otherwise expressing a strong commitment to free markets.[34]

Although originally designed to produce a 10 percent decline in the value of the dollar, the operation had much larger consequences and led to considerable conflict among these nations. The effort at intervention worked only too well and the outcome suggests the manipulation of markets provoked a market psychology that fed a constantly falling dollar. By 1987, after the United States repeatedly rejected pleas to intervene in the market to buy dollars, the dollar stood at roughly 60 percent of its value in 1985 against the yen and mark. In February 1987, at the Louvre in Paris, the United States agreed to an intervention designed to stabilize the dollar. The somewhat wild currency swings during the 1980s, in particular the declining dollar after 1985, contributed to only a modest improvement in the current account deficit. Interestingly, the falling dollar also illustrates the great structural power of the US economy. The falling dollar/rising foreign currencies did lead to much greater foreign investment in the United States, with foreigners able to use their much higher-valued currency to buy US assets. US firms responded to the effects of declining competitiveness in global markets by shifting abroad significant portions of the value chain for products formerly produced in the United States. Often, these products would now be produced abroad and sold in the United States, thereby enlarging the current account deficit.

The impact of the rising yen/falling dollar on Japan was even more dramatic. The Japanese stock market and markets for real assets exploded in price. This was a result of the combination of financial liberalization in Japan and the rising yen, which led banks to seek borrowers using real assets as collateral. The rising yen also led many Japanese exporters, now facing a loss of competitiveness, to send foreign direct investment (FDI) abroad to establish new production facilities in lower-cost locations across Asia.[35] In places such as Malaysia, where costs were much lower, Japanese firms began to produce parts of the value chain formerly made in Japan as a way of reducing costs. This, of course, not only boosted international trade, but also led to the internationalization of the Japanese banking system. In several ways, the currency interventions contributed considerably to the globalization of finance but did little to moderate the global imbalances of this period.

Managing Exchange Rates through Monetary Unions

Flexible exchange rates can have beneficial effects on the global economy, mainly by permitting market-based adjustments to imbalances in the current accounts of nations. However, this assumes the currency values in these markets reflect trade relations. Unfortunately, this is far too simple. Exchange rates are the result of giant global markets dominated by speculators and the market behavior of these actors is driven more by relative interest rates and market psychology. Foreign exchange markets are vastly bigger than the currency exchange needed to sustain global trade; the overwhelming bulk of trading is by speculators. Because currency fluctuations are so large and have very important consequences for firms, some nations have created monetary unions as one way to moderate these effects. Europe, with many nations already committed to economic integration, has been at the forefront of these efforts.

Following the collapse of the Bretton Woods system, European nations began exploring mechanisms for reestablishing stability in exchange rates, at least among themselves. In 1979, most members of the European Economic Community (EEC) (Britain was the main exception) created the European Monetary System (EMS). This was an arrangement to establish a weighted average of currencies – the European Currency Unit (ECU) – with each individual currency having a pegged value to the ECU, and with small room for fluctuation (+ or – 2.25 percent). Over the next decade, the EMS worked to stabilize exchange rates. This facilitated trade expansion and investment planning by multinational firms, and supported economic growth.

The EMS also contributed to efforts to bring European nations into an even closer economic union. As part of the creation of the European Union (EU) in 1986, nations agreed to provide for free capital movement, effectively ending the capital controls that had sustained the EMS. With the end of the Cold War in 1991, the idea of a single currency to enhance economic integration gained support. And the signing of the Maastricht Agreement in 1992 committed these nations to a single currency to replace their national currencies. Between 1999 and 2002, the euro was created and functioned as the one currency for all of the members of the Euro Area. Currently, nineteen nations use the euro, with several others having their currency pegged to the euro, and with yet others, such as Turkey, permitting euros in widespread circulation.[36]

The euro is supported by the European Central Bank (ECB), which was established in 1998. The ECB is modeled on the German Bundesbank

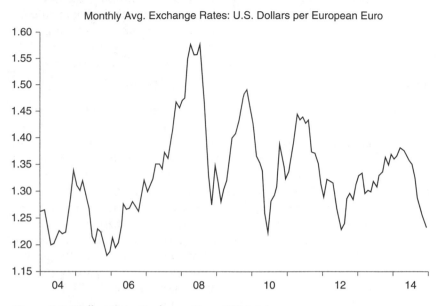

Figure 7.1 Dollar–Euro Exchange Rate, 2004–14.

Source: Data from © 2015 by Prof. Werner Antweiler, University of British Columbia, Vancouver BC, Canada. Reprinted by permission. Time period shown in diagram: 1/Jan/ 2004–31/Dec/2014.

and is located in Frankfurt. Following the German tradition, the ECB has one primary focus: preserving price stability. In addition, the terms for participating in the euro call for adoption of certain macroeconomic standards, with limits on the size of the budget deficit, total governmental debt, and inflation rates. However, in the time since the creation of the euro, several nations in Europe have failed to meet these criteria.

Among the nations using the euro, it clearly promotes monetary stability among those nations and the euro has taken on a significant status in the global economy. It has reserve currency status and plays a large role in global foreign exchange trading. However, the value of the euro in relation to other currencies still fluctuates substantially. Figure 7.1 provides a chart of the US dollar–euro exchange rate from 2004–14.

As you can see, short-term swings of 10 and even 20 percent are common and demonstrate anything but stability. This was true even before the 2008 financial crisis.

Evidence for Financialization and Globalization

The essence of a capitalist economy is capital accumulation, in the form of a stock of productive assets managed to create goods and services but also in the form of investible resources available to firms to create business or to be invested in productive activities. The decades after 1980 have witnessed revolutionary increases in the process of capital accumulation on a global scale. Both the size of capital as investible resources has expanded and its global dispersal through global flows has grown in truly historic terms. This section provides data to document these developments.

The sheer size of global financial transactions and holdings of assets has exploded in the decades after 1980. One estimate of the stock of FDI, equity holdings, and debt held as foreign assets increased almost eleven-fold between 1980 and 2004.[37] Another measure of total global financial assets includes equity securities, government debt, private debt, and bank deposits. This indicates an increase from $48 trillion in 1990 to $194 trillion in 2007. More important, the ratio of global financial assets and global GDP is shown in Table 7.1.

The absolute rise of global financial assets – capital accumulation – from $48 trillion to $194 trillion in seventeen years is breathtaking. But Table 7.1 demonstrates how much faster capital accumulation growth is taking place in relation to the growth of global GDP.

Measuring global financial assets is difficult because of the exotic nature of some of these financial instruments. Perhaps the most unusual for the uninitiated is the derivative, which is one of several ways financiers engage in a form of leverage and thereby magnify the ability to make money from money. Leverage typically involves making an investment using a large amount of borrowed funds. This permits an investor to make profits on the total investment but use personal funds for only a small part, thereby increasing the percent return on those personal funds. A derivative elevates this process to another level by creating a financial instrument whose value is a function of the value of some other financial security, index, or other asset. This value relationship is usually structured in such a way as to leverage the price of the derivative. Thus, a small change in the value of the underlying security – say 2 percent – can lead to a much bigger change in the value of the derivative – say 20 percent. Derivatives can be seen in many different kinds of markets, for example in stock markets with options known as puts and calls, or in foreign exchange markets with currency options. But large

Table 7.1 Ratio of Global Financial Assets to Global GDP, 1990–2007

1990	2000	2007
2.26	3.03	3.42

Source: Data from Charles Roxburgh, "Global Capital Markets: Entering a New Era," McKinsey Global Institute, September 2009, 9.

global banks have put this to use by taking existing securities – such as mortgages on houses – and bundling them together to create a new security based on these mortgages – a derivative – and selling this to investors. The total value of these securities – sold all over the world – is difficult to measure but numbers in the hundreds of trillions of dollars.[38]

The global distribution of financial assets is much wider than in the past, with even emerging market nations now operating as major players in debt and foreign exchange reserves.[39] Though the United States, the Eurozone, and Great Britain remain dominant, the financial holdings of Japan, plus China and emerging Asia, nearly match those of the Eurozone, with emerging economies globally representing about one-quarter of all financial assets. And the stock market capitalization of emerging economies represents more than one-third of the global total. These same emerging economies hold more than three-fourths of all foreign exchange reserves.[40] Table 7.2 provides data on the largest holdings of foreign reserves.

This global distribution of foreign exchange represents two main factors: first, those nations with large trade surpluses tend to have large holdings of foreign reserves; and second, many Asian nations have worked to build up their foreign reserves following the Asian Financial Crisis (see discussion in this chapter). This was designed to permit them to protect the value of their currencies from attacks by speculators.

The financialization of the US economy took place over an extended time period, essentially taking more than fifty years, with perhaps the most dramatic changes taking place beginning in the mid-1980s. Evidence for financialization usually points to changes in the ratio of financial economic activity in relation to the entire economy. Here are three important measures. The first is the ratio of financial assets to GDP in the United States. Between 1950 and 1980, this ratio was essentially unchanged, with financial assets at 200 percent of GDP, or about two times GDP. By 2008, just at the beginning of the Global Financial Crisis,

Table 7.2 Holdings of Foreign Reserves (January 2012)

Nation	Foreign Reserves (billions $US)
China	3,202
Japan	1,270
Eurozone	863
Saudi Arabia	542
Russia	463
Taiwan	386
Brazil	350
South Korea	309
Hong Kong	285
United States	148

Source: Data from *The Economist*, January 12, 2012, www.economist.com/node/21542831.

this ratio had grown from 200 percent to 442 percent, or nearly 4.4 times GDP.[41] A second major indicator is debt as a ratio to GDP. The ratio of total US debt, public and private, between 1980 and 2012 is depicted in Table 7.3.

Thus, in 2012, Americans had borrowed $2.50 for every $1 of GDP whereas in 1980 they had borrowed only $1.30 for every $1 of GDP. Importantly, it was US households that generated the greatest increase in debt in the period from 2000–8, far more than government or business.[42] The rapid growth of debt in the United States was more than matched by debt growth in many other nations. Indeed, in Europe, Great Britain, Spain, Italy, and France all exceeded the United States in level of debt as a percent of GDP.[43]

A third major indicator of the financialization of the US economy comes from corporate profits. Although financial, insurance, and real estate firms grew very modestly as a sector in terms of employment between 1950 and 2001, this group of industries essentially doubled its proportion of output from 12–24 percent of US GDP during the same period. Even more astonishing, this same set of industries increased the proportion of the profits of all industries from 10 percent to more than 40 percent over the same fifty-one years. In 2001, this financial, insurance, and real estate group employed about 7 percent of US workers, contributed a little less than 24 percent of US output, but made nearly 44 percent of all profits.[44]

Shifting our focus back to the global level, the flow of financial assets in various forms across borders provides a clearer indication of the globalization of finance. One measure adds together all FDI, global transactions in foreign equities and debt securities, and cross-border lending and deposits. This total is displayed in Table 7.4. This astonishing growth is a

Table 7.3 US Debt to GDP, 1980–2012 (Total Debt/GDP)

1980	1995	2012
1.3	1.8	2.5

Source: Data from Bloomberg, www.bloomberg.com/news/2012–06–18/dear-mr-dimon-is-your-bank-getting-corporate-welfare-.html

Table 7.4 Annual Global Capital Flows, 1980–2007, as % of Global GDP (trillions $US)

1980	1990	2000	2007
0.5	1.0	5.3	10.5
4.5%	4.5%	6.5%	11.9%

Source: Data from Charles Roxburgh, "Global Capital Markets: Entering a New Era," McKinsey Global Institute, September 2009, 14.

Table 7.5 Average Daily Foreign Exchange Trading – 1989–2013 (trillions $US)

1989	1992	1995	1998	2001	2004	2007	2011	2013
.543	.789	1.23	1.55	1.31	1.93	3.12	4.70	5.30

Sources: Data from Morten Bech, "FX Volume During the Financial Crisis and Now," *BIS Quarterly Review* (March 2012) 36; Dagfinn Rime and Andreas Schrimpf, "The Anatomy of the Global FX Market Through the Lens of the 2013 Triennial Survey," *BIS Quarterly Review* (December 2013).

powerful indicator of the globalization of finance. At the same time, the Global Financial Crisis that began in 2008 demonstrated the volatility of financial flows and the devastating consequences of this particular crisis. In 2007, global financial flows were $10.5 trillion; in 2008 these flows collapsed to $1.9 trillion.

Perhaps the most striking indicator of financial globalization is the growth of trading in foreign exchange. The size of these markets dwarfs the markets for all other financial activity and indeed dwarfs the size of global production and trade. The vast bulk of this market activity is from speculators, individuals, and financial institutions hoping to profit on the fluctuations in currency values. Only a small portion of the market for currencies is related to buying and selling currencies in relation to trade in goods and services.[45] We can see from Table 7.5 that daily foreign exchange trading rose about tenfold from 1989–2013. Over the 250 trading days for an entire year, foreign exchange trading will total about $1.325 quadrillion or about eighteen times global GDP and sixty-five times global trade.

The integration of markets resulting from globalization can be measured by the co-variation of price movements in different markets and this itself serves as a measure of increasing financial globalization and increasing interdependence. This can be seen from the correlation of stock prices in a large number of stock markets in different nations over a three-decade period from 1982–2011. There is a long-term increase in the correlation of prices, with significant variation, from a correlation coefficient of .5 in 1982 to above .8 from 2008–11.[46] The explanation for this rising correlation comes from the role of large institutional investors, which tend to follow the leader, and from the increasing role of global investors in global markets.

Global Financial Crises, 1997–2015

The extensive financialization of the economic systems of several advanced economies and the rapid globalization of finance generated increasingly frequent and more severe financial crises during the 1980s, 1990s, and 2000s. These crises occurred in both advanced and emerging economies and culminated (at least for now) in a very difficult crisis centered in Asia in 1997–8 and in the most damaging financial crisis since in the 1930s centered in the United States and the Eurozone from 2008–15. In addition, the United States experienced a very serious stock market collapse from 2000–2. Over the period from 1980–2008, financial crises of varying severity happened about every three years.[47]

Globalization and financialization represent not just processes of economic change but also engage very important economic and political interests. Any sector that achieves over 40 percent of the corporate profits in the United States is certain to have many people with very strong interests in protecting and promoting this position. Not surprisingly, many analysts and commentators, not to mention political leaders, can find their objectivity colored or even purchased by this level of wealth. This makes analysis and explanation of financial crises especially difficult, because this process is itself deeply affected by these interests.[48]

Financial interests and the academic analysts of finance are the strongest advocates of the neoliberal theory of markets: market efficiency, markets always get the price right, markets are self-correcting, and markets fail only when governments intervene. These ideas were in the ascendency, politically and economically, in the three decades before 2008 but have been called seriously into question after that.[49]

What is a Financial Crisis?

There is, however, a tradition of analysis of financial crises and panics, because these events have a long and somewhat repetitive history.[50] A financial crisis can take many forms, resulting from the default of governments on sovereign debt, the inability of private borrowers to repay debts leading to a banking and credit collapse, or the collapse of stock markets. All have in common a severe overextension of lending or of investment in some kind of financial instrument and the financial crisis typically begins when the value of these financial instruments collapses, leading to losses for others in markets that are linked together. Financial crises are thus various forms of cascading collapses in the value of financial instruments that are linked together across several financial markets. The most severe financial crises come when a market collapse is linked to large banks, whose ability to make and repay loans is compromised. Thus, financial crises represent a threat to entire financial systems because the collapse of one market leads to collapse in other markets and together these lead to the collapse of banking and credit systems.[51] The rapid decline in lending reflects the loss of confidence and contributes to even more of a loss of confidence. The 2008–9 financial crisis provides a clear example. In the years leading up to the crisis, bank lending in the United States and Europe regularly expanded by 10 percent per year or more.

But in 2009–11, banking lending plunged to an annual decline of 5–10 percent.[52]

Why and how are markets so interdependent that prices in one can drastically affect prices in others? Typically, there are two main ways financial markets are linked together: one is psychological, and the other is based on lending. Much of the activity in financial markets is based on making predictions about the future and placing money at risk based on these predictions. A loan is made based on a prediction that it will be repaid and/or if needed the collateral can be sold to repay the loan. An investment is based on predictions about the future value of the investment. The process of making predictions involves considerable uncertainty and depends in many cases on confidence in the borrower or recipient of an investment. Financial markets are linked together through the psychology of confidence, which can be subject to large and rapid changes based on circumstances. The well-known "run on the bank" is a form of cascading loss of confidence that itself makes the bank collapse. A second psychological factor in financial crises is the propensity to believe the history of financial crises no longer applies: "this time is different." This can lead to much greater confidence in the solidity of financial markets than is warranted.[53]

These same financial markets are often linked in more tangible ways, as when money is borrowed from a bank to make an investment or even another loan. This is referred to as leverage, in which an investor borrows a large part of the funds for an investment in order to magnify the percentage rate of return on the equity part of the investment. In this case, changes in the value of the investment can threaten the value of related loans, which can threaten the solvency of a bank, which can affect the bank's capacity to make future loans, which can affect the economy as a whole. Financial crises can quickly metastasize in circumstances where confidence is connected through significant tangible forms of market interdependence to transmit changes in one market to many others. These forms of interdependence help us understand how a seemingly small event like the collapse of one large firm can threaten and even undermine the stability of entire financial systems.

Moreover, the intense interdependence of financial markets combines with the typical behavior of players in financial markets to create high levels of inherent instability, which make financial crises occur with some frequency. Neoliberals assume market players possess complete information and act on that information in a dispassionate manner, thereby producing high levels of rationality. Those who study actual market players find this assumption to be little better than a caricature. Much more likely is herd-like behavior, usually based on observation of other market players and attempting to duplicate their successes or follow their lead.[54] This produces frequent price bubbles in assets where leverage is available and these bubbles contribute greatly to financial crises. If the availability of loans is interrupted, then the rising price of the asset, on which the value of the loans depends, can begin to fall. This engages the herd behavior operating in the opposite direction and produces a panic of selling. Many of those who borrowed money will be unable to repay, placing banks at risk and leading to a broader crisis of confidence.

The Asian Financial Crisis, 1997–8

The neoliberal perspective asserts that severe financial crises are most likely in emerging economies, for it is here that poorly developed banking systems and bad government policies lead to a high potential for destabilizing events. The Asian Financial Crisis of 1997–8 was one of global proportions and certainly was centered in emerging economies. But, as we shall see, presumably sophisticated banks in developed economies were key actors in the process. This crisis provides a fascinating case study of the benefits and costs of the globalization of finance and of the political efforts used to stabilize the global economy. Once again, we are confronted by the great importance of political processes as a vital feature of market relations, especially financial crises that threaten many nations.

The principal nations involved in this crisis were Thailand, Korea, Malaysia, Indonesia, Russia, and Brazil, though Japan and the United States played important roles as well. In the period from 1965–97, economic growth in Asia was the fastest in the world, transforming previously very poor nations such as Korea, Taiwan, and Malaysia into much richer nations. The accelerating globalization of finance and investment parallel these developments and especially after 1985 are connected very closely. This was the year of the Plaza Agreement (discussed earlier in this chapter), which resulted in a significant rise in the value of the Japanese yen against the US dollar. This had two important consequences: first, the rising yen became ever more valuable for purchasing foreign assets, and second, the rising yen also made manufacturing production for export much more expensive for Japanese-based firms. This generated large incentives for Japanese manufacturers to find new sites for production in less expensive nations, and many did so across Asia.[55] Much of this investment was directed toward Southeast Asian nations, such as Thailand and Malaysia. In the decade before the crisis, this rush of Japanese firms was followed by a similar rush of Korean and Taiwanese firms, and economic growth in Southeast Asia soared.[56]

This accelerating investment and growth turned Asia into a "hot" area for global investors, attracting funds from many nations looking to match the returns achieved by others, and reflecting the herd behavior already described. To facilitate this process, the United States urged nations in the area to liberalize their capital accounts and to liberalize their domestic banking systems. An additional measure designed to attract foreign capital was linking the exchange rate of the local currency to the US dollar, which removed an important source of uncertainty for investors. In the twelve years from 1985–97, Thailand, Indonesia, and Malaysia joined the ranks of major global exporters, as multinational firms built plants and produced for export. But after 1990, with these nations now much more closely integrated into global finance, money began to flow in like a tidal wave. Perhaps most important, the nature of the investments shifted from relatively long-term FDI to much shorter-term stock market investments and short-term loans. Remember, FDI involves purchasing assets to operate a business, making liquidation and removal of the funds somewhat difficult. By contrast, portfolio investments and short-term loans make removing the funds much easier.

This process of globalizing the economies of East Asia developed on a very shaky basis and could be sustained only as long as nothing went wrong. Several of these nations operated with a current account deficit, not unusual for an emerging economy. This meant the investment coming in from abroad was essential for sustaining the imports of technology, production equipment, and manufacturing inputs. The newly liberalized domestic banking systems in these nations led to the creation of many new local financial institutions with little lending experience and inadequate regulation by the government. In actual practice, liberalization meant:

> locals could open foreign bank accounts; banks could extend credit in foreign currencies in the domestic market; nonbank financial institutions and private corporations could borrow abroad; foreigners could own shares listed by national companies on domestic stock markets; foreign banks could enjoy wider freedom of entry into the domestic banking sector; and offshore banks could borrow abroad and lend domestically.[57]

Global investors seeking a fast return increasingly provided short-term loans, and especially in Thailand this resulted in funding to build office centers and apartments. In 1995, about one-half of Thailand's $83 billion foreign debt had a maturity of one year or less.[58] Ending capital controls meant governments had little influence over the flow of money, but the system was heavily dependent on this flow and was vulnerable to any interruption.

Into this arena of uncertainty came the global foreign exchange traders – the 800-pound gorillas of international finance, at least when their trading decisions work together. A combination of events exposed the weaknesses of the Asian system of globalization: the dollar–yen exchange rate reversed and the dollar began to rise. Because many Asian currencies were pegged to the dollar, this increased their export costs and expanded their trade deficit. The Thai stock market and property markets began to sink in value. Sensing the peg between the Thai baht and the dollar could not be preserved, foreign exchange traders began in the spring of 1997 to speculate on a currency devaluation by Thailand. This means currency traders would sell the baht in hopes of its decline and then repurchase it at lower prices. To prevent this from happening, the Thai government needed to intervene in foreign exchange markets to buy baht with dollars or some other highly convertible currency. However, the government had only a limited amount of foreign reserves, and when these were exhausted in July 1997 the baht–dollar peg was ended and the baht fell precipitously in value. The Thai government then turned to the IMF for help in stabilizing its currency.

The IMF, an international institution whose values have long been closely in line with the United States' financial interests, stands ready to help nations such as Thailand with loans to support its currency and economy. But these loans come at a price, with the IMF imposing conditions on the receiving nation that usually result in significant economic difficulty. Thailand and the IMF negotiated an agreement for a $17 billion loan and in return Thailand was required to close many of its banks, cut government spending and raise taxes, make reductions in its current account deficit, and open its economy to foreign ownership of its firms. These terms – fiscal austerity, better government oversight, and greater international openness – represent the basic liberal perspective of the IMF on economic policy.[59]

Though the IMF agreement did help to stabilize Thailand, it largely failed in preventing the crisis from spreading to other nations. The Thai government's decision to float the baht shifted the focus of foreign exchange traders to other Asian nations, and attacks on currencies and stock market declines spread across much of the region. This "contagion effect" resulted from common interdependencies in financial markets: psychological and tangible relationships that link markets together. The rapid decline in the baht raised large doubts about the ability of other nations to maintain the value of their currencies. Further, in a more tangible sense, the declining baht reduced the prices of Thai exports, virtually forcing other nations to follow this or lose the competitiveness of their exports. The cumulative effects were to produce additional panic and speculative selling. For more than a year after the crisis began in Thailand, other nations such as Malaysia, Indonesia, South Korea, Taiwan, Hong Kong, and the Philippines experienced much the same crisis conditions: volatile declines in currency, real estate, and stock market values. Price declines of 25–90 percent were typical. Perhaps the most radical and most effective response to the crisis came from Malaysia, which re-imposed capital controls and fixed the Malaysian ringgit to the US dollar. Foreign exchange traders then moved on to other currencies.[60]

For several months the US government relied on the IMF to manage the crisis. Republicans in Congress were critical of any plan that led to direct use of US funds to bail out nations, but were less critical of the indirect path through the IMF. However, the crisis deepened when the IMF agreement with Korea failed to prevent a seemingly imminent loan default and this pushed the US government into action. International bankers were refusing to renew Korea's considerable short-term debt even though default could threaten a much broader systemic crisis. This led to a series of dramatic Christmas-time meetings among the Korean government, the US Treasury, the US Federal Reserve, the IMF, and international bankers in New York. An agreement was reached to speed up the flow of IMF funds, obtain a Korean government guarantee of bank debt, and renew existing short-term loans.

Stemming the losses in Korea did little to end the crisis, as currency speculation now shifted to Indonesia. Saddled with a very large short-term debt, a substantial current account deficit, and a mountain of non-performing loans, Indonesia was a vulnerable target. Its currency, the rupiah, and its stock markets suffered as much as 80 percent declines as a result. Over a five-month period of negotiations, the IMF and the Indonesian government maneuvered for advantage, with the IMF pressing the government to accept very harsh conditions for receiving loans. Once this agreement was finalized and austerity was imposed, riots and demonstrations forced the Indonesian leader of more than thirty years – Suharto – to resign.

Even so, the crisis was still not finished, as the focus shifted away from Asia and now centered on Russia and Brazil. Russia faced turmoil because of its large budget deficit (caused by the inability to collect taxes) and high levels of short-term debt from foreign banks. A preemptive loan of $22.6 billion from the IMF designed to permit Russia to meet its loan payments failed to reassure financial markets and Russia too slid into crisis with a collapsing currency and large-scale capital flight. The Russian banking system essentially disintegrated as banks ceased to loan money. What followed was more than a year of economic collapse, largely ineffectual governmental efforts to cope with the crisis, and an IMF refusal to provide more funds. Only when a rigorous set of conditions were accepted did a new IMF loan pave the wave for Russia to renegotiate its debts with Western banks and governments.

At about the same time, the crisis spread to Brazil, which faced the familiar problems of a huge budget deficit, massive international debt and short-term debt payments, and capital flight as rich Brazilians sent their money out of the country. Under IMF pressure, Brazil announced a tough austerity package to try to defend the fixed value of the currency – the real. Even when coupled with a $41.5 billion IMF loan, the efforts failed and Brazil was forced to float the real, leading to a quick 15 percent drop in value. Once more, currency markets linked economies together as Argentina's position was affected by the competitiveness consequences of the real's decline. The Argentine peso, fixed in value to the US dollar, could not fluctuate to adjust for this problem and Argentina's exports dropped, leading to 15 percent unemployment and a large current account deficit. Argentina turned to the IMF and received a loan in return for austerity conditions. Financial chaos, public protest, and political instability continued for more than one year. Ultimately, Argentina was forced to cut the link of the peso to the dollar and effectively defaulted on its debt.

Perhaps the most indelible effect of the Asian Financial Crisis is the political trauma created among Asian leaders. The role of the IMF is extremely intrusive and disruptive and even humiliating for national leaders. Indeed, national sovereignty and freedom of action are lost when a nation must turn in desperation to the IMF for help. Events that threaten and even topple long-standing regimes can have major consequences. Many Asian nations altered their economic policies so as to protect themselves from this situation in the future, and they did so by building up foreign reserves. With a large store of resources, foreign exchange traders could be deterred from a currency attack.

Why did the Asian Financial Crisis happen and what were the consequences? The clearest cause was the many bad decisions by global investors and lenders compounded by the high-risk policies adopted by many governments. Investors and lenders often failed to engage in due diligence, and therefore failed to understand the risks associated with the economies in which they were placing money. These investors and lenders were seeking large and fast returns and many governments were quite willing to partner in this process. The accumulation of short-term loans invited a crisis given the typical fluctuations in the capacity for repayment. Fixed exchange rates combined with high-risk macroeconomic policies invited attacks by foreign currency traders.

In many ways, this was also a systemic failure. The newly globalized financial order encouraged and facilitated high levels of global financial flows, but the money that enters a nation can oftentimes leave very fast and with devastating consequences. And foreign currency traders were ready and willing to exploit weaknesses and often were the precipitating force in the crisis. The events of the Asian Financial Crisis demonstrate the inherent instability of financial markets and the way interdependence in these markets can transfer a crisis from a small to a systemic problem. Perhaps most important, financial markets would wreak far more damage on economic systems were it not for government institutions – domestic and international – that stand ready to serve as a lender of last resort and limit the contagion processes that come from large market collapses.

The Global Financial Crisis, 2008–15

Maybe the really important result of the Asian Financial Crisis was the dog that did not bark: political leaders, bankers, and economic analysts in developed nations took no heed of the threat of financial crises, and not only did not backtrack from financialization and globalization but pressed ahead even faster with liberalization.[61] When we examine many of the indicators of globalization, the curve bends up even steeper after 1998 than before. This reluctance to reexamine the processes of financial expansion came from the now ascendant power of the financial community and its ability to deliver enormous and growing profits. Economic experts repeatedly asserted the effectiveness of free markets in generating the best economic outcomes and in managing risk. Very few predicted a catastrophe and very few paid attention to those anticipating such an outcome. This section provides an overview of the Global Financial Crisis that struck the United States and many advanced nations and left the economic systems of these nations severely damaged.

Deregulation and Derivatives

The increasing weight of finance in the US economy and the global expansion of finance provide a key backdrop for the development of the instabilities that led to the Global Financial Crisis. The policies of the US and British governments, particularly those involving the deregulation of finance, contributed directly to the development of market relations that proved profoundly destabilizing. For these policies opened the way for the expansion of very exotic financial instruments that played a central role in the subprime crisis that turned into a Global Financial Crisis.

We have already reviewed the growth of financial operations around the world in the years after 1973 and the political role in facilitating this process. Beginning even in the 1960s, the postwar regime of embedded liberalism, including the policies designed to control financial capital, was being dismantled. During the 1980s, regulations in the United States for some banks were relaxed dramatically, leading to a financial crisis related to savings and loan banks late in that decade. In Great Britain and Japan, significant steps were taken to liberalize the banking system and its openness to international competition. Perhaps the culmination of this process of deregulation and liberalization came in 1999 in the United States, with the Gramm–Leach–Bliley Act, which eliminated the restrictions on banks dating back to the 1930s.[62] Now banks were able to operate both as traditional commercial and consumer lending institutions and also as investment banks. Banks became much more complex institutions in this new environment, able to operate in new business environments and on a global scale. They became very innovative in finding ways to develop new business through lending and investment operations.[63]

Enamored by the concepts of neoliberalism, governments in the advanced world engaged in deregulatory competition as a way of attracting the business operations of global banks – a kind of race to the bottom of regulatory requirements.[64] The regulation of financial institutions also takes place on an international scale, through a process known as the Basel Accords. These have established levels of reserves banks must hold in relation to loans to insure themselves against losses – a kind of crisis insurance. Further, regulatory rules in the pre-1980 era were based on defining the riskiness of bank assets and modifying the reserve requirements accordingly. But, consistent with the regulatory ethos of the age of globalization, both the reserves needed to be held by banks and the evaluation of the riskiness of bank assets were relaxed considerably. The new reigning assumption advocated by bankers and government officials was that bankers themselves, operating in competitive markets, were the best judges of the riskiness of their actions. Financial markets were believed to be self-regulating. Financial analysts and economists developed quantitatively precise measures of risk and used these tools to make decisions about making investment and lending with little or no regulatory oversight.[65]

Into this new world of deregulation and globalization came the immensely profitable and innovative investment bankers, no longer conservative and reserved but sitting atop a global capital glut, armed with quantitative analysis and certified by the ideology of free markets. They did not invent the derivative but instead expanded its use dramatically.[66] And derivative markets played a central role in the Global Financial Crisis.[67] Two of the most common and significant derivatives were Collateralized Debt Obligations (CDOs) and Credit Default Swaps (CDSs). And there were even derivatives in which a CDS was linked to a CDO. We should understand that derivatives are typically used to manage risk, such as in buying a futures contract on foreign exchange. A firm may want to reduce the risk from changes in exchange rates in the future and does this by purchasing a futures contract that locks in a future exchange rate today. But the massive expansion of the derivatives market – made possible by the deregulatory actions of the late 1990s – operated in ways that obscured the risks. This is because these shadow markets, with little transparency and public visibility, obscured the exposure of individual firms. With no external regulation and dependent on self-regulation of the risk, the derivatives market produced a classic case of herd mentality.

What do these terms for the more exotic derivatives mean and why might they have negative consequences? A CDO is a type of security with several characteristics: it has collateral behind it, usually fixed-income assets such as house mortgages; the fixed income assets are bundled together, with a variety of risk and therefore returns; and those who purchase the CDO are usually very large investors looking for higher returns and willing to accept varying amounts of risk. By purchasing a CDO, investors are providing liquidity into the market for the fixed income assets, such as home mortgages. Theoretically, in the worst case the CDO holder can recover their investment by selling the collateral, either the mortgage or the house, which is collateral for the mortgage. So, as long as house prices are stable or rising, the CDO owner is safe. And, typically, the CDO is safe because the risk of default is spread over so many people.

The difficulty in the financial crisis came when many CDOs were backed by more and more subprime mortgages, that is, mortgages made when the borrower has weak credit and purchases a house that may not be good collateral for the mortgage. The crisis really began when rising interest rates threatened the ability of these subprime borrowers to make their mortgage payments and many houses were sold in foreclosure, thereby driving down the value of houses below that of the value of the mortgage. At this point, the value of the CDOs came into question. Remember how important confidence is in financial markets, and the situation in 2007–8 led to very shaken confidence. The crisis of confidence was brought on by the huge number of CDOs (a number that could not be determined with precision) and the fact that many big global banks were large owners of CDOs. When, in 2007, some of the world's largest investment banks began reporting huge losses from CDOs, the crisis began to unfold.

A second important derivative is the Credit Default Swap, which is much like an insurance policy against the possibility of a fixed-income security default, that is, a failure to pay. The buyer of a CDS makes payments during the lifetime of the insured security to the company that sells the CDS and in the event of a default, the seller agrees to make good on the debt. You probably have guessed that, among other things, CDSs were used to insure against the risk that CDOs would default. This created a new layer of interdependence in financial markets and a new layer of debt obligation that was only as good as the entity (bank, hedge fund, etc.) issuing the CDS. Because the CDS system was unregulated (remember, neoliberals opposed government regulation and were certain markets would self-regulate), many CDSs were not adequately capitalized against losses. This means losses on CDOs were magnified by derivative losses in CDSs and the system of interdependent debt failed, thereby producing a massive Global Financial Crisis.[68]

Origins of the Global Financial Crisis

The threat posed by derivatives came from the immense size of the investments in these securities, the leverage relationships associated with derivatives, the potential instability of the values of the underlying assets, and the deep interdependence among many of the derivatives markets. This threat became evident in 2008, when two of the largest and most important investment banks – Bear Sterns and Lehman Brothers – were forced into bankruptcy as a result of losses from derivatives trading. Each firm operated with extensive leverage, meaning they had very big debts, usually to banks and other investment firms. The bankruptcy of one big firm threatens the solvency and portends the bankruptcy of many other firms. In normal market conditions, firms are able to recycle their debts by paying off debt with more debt. But in a crisis, credit markets freeze, as lenders are loath to make more loans in a panicked environment. This means companies that are solvent in normal circumstances become insolvent in a crisis, thereby compounding the problem. Financial panics feed on themselves, as some losses cascade into much bigger losses and soon the entire financial system and even the entire economy are placed at risk.

It is this fundamental set of relationships that must be understood: a financial crisis can quickly threaten entire economies with massive losses; and the crisis always pushes governments – any government – into efforts to prevent a collapse of the economy. All governments will act to prevent the destruction of their economy. Even those most enamored of neoliberal ideology – such as the Bush Administration in 2008 – will act.[69] And acting means taking steps to save the largest firms from collapse and thereby producing an uncontrollable downward spiral. So, it is entirely predictable that when Bear Sterns faced bankruptcy, the US government – primarily the Treasury Department and the Federal Reserve – provided funding to enable another firm to buy Bear Sterns and assume its liabilities. When, a few months later in September 2008, Lehman faced bankruptcy and the Bush Administration faced the possibility of using government funds to save the firm, they flinched and let it go broke. It was this decision that produced the financial panic that made the Global Financial Crisis.[70] Within days, the US government reversed its position as the dominoes began to fall. In a panic themselves, the highest government officials acted to obtain the funding to save other banks and financial firms.[71]

The crisis deepened in economic terms for another six months, with the presidential election preventing additional governmental action. With the election of President Obama and a new government, additional coordinated actions between the Administration and the Federal Reserve became possible. The Fed used its resources to provide loans directly to banks and other firms unable to receive credit in the worst days of the crisis. Moreover, the Fed launched a program to purchase large amounts of US government securities to pump liquidity into the economy and drive interest rates much lower. And the US government approved a large stimulus package that operated as a cushion for an economy in free fall to prevent a repeat of the 1930s collapse. These actions prevented an economic disaster of much greater proportions in the United States and a global disintegration that could have many unwanted consequences.

The costs of the financial crisis in the United States, even with the muting of its impact by government intervention, were staggering. Declines in the stock market, measured from the top in 2007 to the bottom in 2009, were roughly 65 percent, wiping out large parts of the investments and retirement funds of millions. The US economy suffered its most severe downturn since the 1930s, with unemployment as officially measured rising from 4.4 percent in 2007 to 10 percent in October 2009, placing millions into significant financial distress. Commitments of government funds to deal with the crisis totaled in the trillions of dollars, which include congressionally appropriated funds for bank bailouts, funds for the stimulus program, and the largest part coming from the Federal Reserve to provide assistance to banks and to purchase US government debt. Perhaps as many as 12 million homes received foreclosure notices as a result of the financial and economic crisis, and millions of other families saw the value of their homes decline precipitously. One estimate is the losses in home values and real estate investments came to $28 trillion.[72] The average net worth of Americans shrank by 40 percent from 2007–10. It is difficult to square the idea of efficient markets with the massive misallocation of funds that are represented by these costs.

The question of reforming the financial system in order to reduce the likelihood of another financial crisis remains mired in continued political struggle over the nature of markets and is embedded in the power of financial interests to promote a system of very limited regulation. One avenue of concern is the large and expanding role played by non-state actors in the process of regulating actions and outcomes. Private firms engaging in the rating (and therefore certification of value) for debt instruments have a significant effect on choices made by investors. And yet, the accuracy and autonomy of the ratings agencies are sometimes in doubt.[73]

A second arena of interest is the widening arc of national players in defining the rules for global markets. In the midst of the crisis itself, international cooperation efforts expanded from the set of seven or eight main nations – the G–7 or G–8 – to the G–20, which include Brazil, India, and most importantly, China.[74] Composed mainly of finance ministers and the heads of central banks, this group engages in coordination and cooperation efforts for managing global crises. China's presence can have the effect of reducing the importance of US preferences for liberal solutions to global problems. A third venue for regulation and political management of finance is Basel, a forum for the coordination of regulatory rules among the most advanced nations.[75] The primary decisions involve setting a minimum reserve requirement for banks. This is a proportion of assets that must be set aside and not lent or invested to serve as a pool of money available to support the bank in a crisis. Few expect this process of coordination to be effective in reducing global financial risks.

Indeed, the capacity of the international community to address effectively the sources of financial crises and work together to reduce the risks of future crises has been held hostage by the ability of global financial interests to affect the decisions needed to achieve these goals. One way this can be seen is the recognized need to alter the governance of the IMF, the organization most central to providing resources to many nations caught up in a financial crisis. The financial crisis of 2008 prompted a decision in the G20 to expand the voting power of those nations holding large pools of financial assets and able to contribute resources to stabilization efforts.[76] This decision, formalized in 2010 at the IMF but subject to member ratification, called for the expansion of member contributions and a restructuring of voting shares. These changes, which fall far short of reflecting the relative size of national economies, primarily benefit China, but still leave the United States with 2.71 times the voting power of China.[77] However, even this somewhat marginal change is being blocked by the refusal of the US Congress to ratify the changes and expand the United States' contribution. A combination of ideological resistance to any government role in managing financial crises, nationalism, and opposition from financial interests has stymied these changes. Similar resistance to change can be seen in making reforms to control over the World Bank[78] and in achieving regulatory reform.[79]

The Eurozone Financial Crisis, 2009–14

The financial crisis that originated in the United States could not be contained there. The globalization of finance meant many of the same financial imbalances appeared elsewhere, particularly the penchant for deficits and debt. The essence of the Eurozone financial crisis came from serious problems resulting from having a single currency for many nations, who retain the right to operate independent spending, taxing, and borrowing policies but lack central banks. Compounding these difficulties is the participation of Eurozone private banks in the same sort of derivatives activity that brought down so many US institutions. The near-collapse of the US banking system spilled over into Europe and led to a similar, if smaller-scale, bailout of banks there.[80] To recall the extent and complexity of the Eurozone, refer back to the map in Figure 5.1.

Distinguishing the Eurozone is the connection between government debt and banks, in which the threat of sovereign default carries with it large damage to banks holding this debt. Private banks across Europe, and across the world, hold this sovereign debt.[81] Several of the most indebted nations lack the resources to save themselves and the banks under their jurisdiction, forcing them to turn to other Eurozone nations and to the European Central Bank for help.[82] The tight interdependencies among nations and among banks mean that small-scale problems can quickly become a globally systemic crisis. But because the Eurozone has weak collective mechanisms for bailouts and some nations in the Eurozone have resisted bailouts, a recurring threat of default and contagion hangs over Europe and the world.[83]

Perhaps the key source of the Eurozone's financial troubles lies in the contradictions between having a European Central Bank establishing interest rates throughout the Eurozone and the ability of very different governments in very different economic positions to borrow money at the same rate. This means economically weak Greece can borrow money trading on the economic strength of Germany. And, this has led some nations, and also private banks, to borrow far more than their economic situations could justify. Not surprisingly, the economically strongest members of the Eurozone are reluctant to commit their resources to saving the economically weakest members. Eurozone nations certainly have the capacity to make up the potential losses, but they will do so only grudgingly, and this persistent hesitation creates the uncertainty that intersects with the fears of default and contagion to fuel the crisis. Hanging over the outcome of the financial crisis is the ultimate fate of the euro. The possible withdrawal of Greece and other nations from the monetary union or even a German-engineered breakup of the union could be the result of a bad resolution of the crisis.[84] Though Britain is not a Eurozone member, the crisis has increased the possibility of a British exit from the European Union.[85]

Compounding the financial problem are the effects of the adoption of the euro on the economic strategy and competitiveness of different nations in the Eurozone.[86] One group of nations mimicked the economic strategy of the United States, and pumped up their economies with debt – public and private – at the expense of investment in hard and soft infrastructure. Soon, the ability of these nations to compete in the global economy had diminished greatly. Other Eurozone states followed Germany in controlling costs while sustaining investment in competitive resources, such as labor skills. Indeed, some commentators assert the essential issue for Europe is whether as an economic entity it can adjust to the structural transformations of the world economy brought on by globalization. The financial crisis is simply a symptom of Europe's failure to this point.[87] The crisis reveals just how divided are Europeans over this question, with many preferring to attempt to escape from globalization and international competition.

The central player in this drama is Germany, the largest and most competitive economy in the Eurozone, with its strong and historic commitment to a very restrictive monetary policy. From the perspective of Germans, this is a crisis about profligacy and a refusal to participate in the moral hazard associated with bailing out profligates. Further, Germans prefer the burdens of aid to fall primarily on the banks that bought the debt, rather than on German taxpayers. The crisis has continued so long primarily because Germans resist providing aid to one profligate nation (Greece) when there are others waiting for a handout too. Additionally, German leaders hope to pressure nations receiving aid into substantial economic reforms. At the same time, waiting has led to deeper recession, thereby exacerbating the problem by widening budget deficits. Unemployment in 2012 in Greece and Spain exceeded 20 percent (unemployment among young adults is over 50 percent), with Portugal, Latvia, and Ireland approaching 15 percent. By contrast, Dutch and German unemployment hovers at 5–6 percent.[88]

The outcome of the Eurozone crisis remains uncertain. One possibility is the withdrawal of Greece or other states from the euro, which, combined with an even more severe financial crisis, would lead to the demise of the euro. This could have unpredictably bad consequences for the global economy, with massive uncertainty, loss of confidence, and economic disruption. Should this happen, something like the Eurozone could be reformed around northern European nations with more similar systems of political economy.

At the same time, the economic case for the European Union remains stronger than ever, with the single integrated market the most important competitive advantage for most European nations.[89] The fragmentation of the European Union could leave all of Europe much worse off. A political resolution that leaves the Eurozone and euro intact hinges primarily on the willingness of the German government to craft a compromise position that effectively restructures the debt of those nations in trouble and reorganizes the autonomy of individual governmental borrowing. This will almost certainly involve significant inflation of the money supply in the Eurozone to absorb part of these costs, something the Germans abhor. The likely form for this action will come from the European Central Bank, supported by Germany, engaging in systematic purchases of the government debt of threatened nations. Even so, reforms in these same nations will also involve a significant challenge to the sovereignty of these states. How the Germans will see the value of preserving the Eurozone in relation to this inflation, as well as the political reaction of other member states, remains unclear.

Conclusion: Analyzing the Globalization of Finance

The transformation of the systems of domestic and global political economy in the past thirty to forty years has produced many large and important consequences. And it may be a century or more before we can begin to reach a judgment on the balance of positive and negative. This section briefly and tentatively considers three of the most important issues in the study of global finance. One is the political power and political role of states, a second is the role of the United States in the process of globalization, and a third is the redistribution of global economic capabilities and power.

States and Global Finance

It is somewhat commonplace to assert that globalization undermines the power of states, a view that sometimes expresses the wishes of its advocates. At one important level, this position seems unchallengeable: states in the 1950s and 1960s were in a much better position to manage their economies without interference from outside economic forces.[90] Today, macroeconomic management still exists but as a partnership between states and global firms and market forces. One important issue is whether states can use spending to ameliorate the negative effects of globalization. The answer is yes, because global financial markets now make it much easier to sell government bonds for deficit spending. Of course, this is a partnership of states and global bond markets, and in times when the markets withdraw their cooperation – as in the Eurozone crisis – the capabilities of states are constrained. Over the period of intense globalization, from 1970–2016, there is little evidence that states were generally constrained in their spending by global markets. Between 1970 and 2009, the thirteen richest nations raised spending from about 32 percent of GDP to 48 percent.[91] Global financial markets seem to have been willing and even eager partners in the use of debt to expand state spending.

A dispassionate examination of the operation of the global economy reveals a deepening role for states in managing the volatility associated with globalization. Much of this comes through cooperative efforts and is seen most clearly in financial and economic crises. Nations frequently pull and push on exchange rates, which can become misaligned by the operation of markets based overwhelmingly on speculation. Central banks are often the main actors in international monetary cooperation. The use of swap agreements, in which currency reserves are used to stabilize currency fluctuations, or lending arrangements to preserve liquidity across several national banking systems are common examples of this process.[92]

The recent Global Financial Crisis provides another take on the partnership of financial systems and states. Clearly, unregulated globalizing financial systems are not capable of delivering stable growth and in times of systemic crisis will threaten economic systems as a whole. Only states have the concentrated resources and decision-making power to control the tide of economic disintegration that comes from these crisis events. Quite simply, the global financial system would have broken down long ago without the support system provided by states.[93]

The United States and the Globalization of Finance

Has the globalization of finance and the financial crisis altered the structural power of the United States in the global economy? One area with measurable results is in the role of the dollar as a key currency. The dollar's position has been an essential feature of the United States' ability to leverage its power for economic benefit. If we measure the role of the dollar through its weight in foreign exchange trading, the answer to the question is no. More than 80 percent of all currency trades include the US dollar, which is double the role of the euro.[94] Indeed, the US dollar remains the dominant – or key – currency in many ways. The criteria for key currency status help us to compare the position of the US dollar and the Chinese RMB. These criteria and the status of each nation's currency are shown in Table 7.6.

Though China has made some progress in the globalization of its currency, the priority given to the state control of its financial system makes operation as a global key currency impossible. The dollar retains its preeminent position in global finance.[95] At the same time, the "extraordinary privilege" of key currency status and the United States' dominance of the global economy have led to serious difficulties and raise important questions about the overall viability of the US global economic order.

For many decades US political and economic leaders have consistently seen the creation of a liberal world order as providing enormous structural power to the United States. The globalization of finance is really possible only in a liberal world. Less clearly recognized but equally valid, a liberal world offers substantial gains to other states – Europe, Japan, China, Korea, and many more – so these states will frequently cooperate in important ways to achieve and sustain this order. In financial terms, the first version of a semi-liberal world – the embedded liberalism of Bretton Woods – failed. This led to a recalibration of US liberal preferences – such an order must have the intense support of the dominant power. The United States dropped much of the welfare-regarding features of Bretton Woods and pressed forward with a much purer version of liberalism. Secondary states worked to carve a niche for themselves in this world even as they acquiesced to the restructuring wanted by the United States: the assertiveness by the United States in promoting financial liberalism was accepted in return for the openness of the US market, which itself is a massive source of structural power.[96]

Table 7.6 Key Currency Criteria – United States and China

	US	China
Foreign confidence in macroeconomic stability	recovered	moderate
Deep and liquid capital markets	dominant	low
Capital account convertibility	very high	low
Flexible exchange rate	very high	very low
International medium of exchange in trade and finance	dominant	low
Foreign central banks as hedge against financial crises	dominant	some

Out of this relationship emerged, in succession, three primary supporters of the US global system: Germany, Japan, and China.[97] These nations became the major holders of US dollars and US governmental debt and, as such, supported the United States' capacity for providing global security and economic benefits. Moreover, these nations were the major beneficiaries of selling their products into the US market. The ability to maintain this openness, in spite of the costs to US workers, came from the nature and restructuring of the US domestic political order. Initially based on a system of embedded liberalism, the system during and after the 1970s morphed into one based on suppressing the power of workers and emphasizing the power of financial interests.[98] This adaptation was linked to the shift of global political economy away from the Bretton Woods order and toward the neoliberal era of globalization. It consisted of liberalism abroad linked to at least the threat of protectionism for the US home market combined with strong pressure on trading partners to open up their markets for US goods and especially for US finance.[99]

The United States has used its great structural power to force adjustments on its trading partners, such as in the Plaza Agreement, based on its ability to act unilaterally and cause considerable economic dislocation. The attractions of preserving a liberal world, with access to markets for goods, money, and resources, were enough to bring nations such as Germany and Japan to accept US preferences for adjustment of the system.[100] After the end of the Cold War in 1991, the United States adopted an even more assertive policy pressing for free and open markets and adoption of US-style capitalism. Creation of the World Trade Organization (WTO) and the structural pressure on even Communist China to join was an indication of this new emphasis. Moreover, the United States, often through the World Bank and IMF,[101] aggressively pressured developing nations in East Asia and in Eastern Europe to open their financial markets to international finance.[102]

The enormous imbalances in the global economy that dominate the era of financialization and globalization are a direct result of the economic policies of the United States.[103] By 2008, China had replaced Japan and Germany as the principle US partner in creating and sustaining these imbalances. Furthermore, these imbalances were a direct result of policies that promoted the financial industry of the United States domestically and internationally and shifted the locus of global manufacturing to Asia. But the United States needed cooperative partners, providing goods to its consumers and financing this by lending dollars to the United States. After 2001, China surged forward in economic growth driven by producing and selling to the United States and secondarily to Europe. And its holdings of US debt and foreign reserves generally surged in tandem with this trade relationship.[104]

After the Global Financial Crisis, the origins of which rest squarely with the United States and its economic policies of the past three decades, the United States has reverted to form and attempted to control the process of adjustment and coerce its economic partners into making changes that prevent any painful choices by the United States:

> U.S. officials will accelerate demands that their Asian partners open their markets, appreciate their currencies, and take on a greater share of the cost of providing international public goods—while allowing the United States to manage its monetary, fiscal, and foreign policies as it sees fit.[105]

However, this is much more uncertain a strategy than in the past. China is not in remotely the same strategic position of dependency as Germany and Japan and thus far has resisted much of US pressure. Moreover, the United States cannot simply close its market to China, as it has few alternative sources of goods and is in no position to produce these goods at home. And the use of pressure on China to make adjustments to the US advantage will engage a nation with equally credible options to inflict damage on the US economy. The result of this strategic conundrum is the potential for rebalancing of the global economy and a new direction for international political economy.

The Redistribution of Global Economic Power

Financial globalization, especially without regulatory processes, has generated considerable losses and misallocation of resources. The price of free markets is almost certainly periodic financial panics and economic downturns, with very large costs for millions. At least within the developed world, rising economic inequality is associated with this process. So the benefits of liberalized financial globalization go increasingly to a very small group and the costs must be borne by an increasingly large group. This is not politically sustainable.

One option for change is to reintroduce some kind of capital controls through a cooperative global agreement, the effect of which would be to tame the levels of speculation in exchange rates. There is little real economic value in allocating trillions of dollars every day to this activity. Exchange rates could reach market-based values with less volatility if markets were one-tenth this size. This would also remove much of the incentive for nations to simultaneously engage in currency manipulation to push their exchange rate down as a competitiveness strategy.[106] And many nations, especially those in Asia, would be able to reduce their massive foreign exchange reserves, freeing these resources for better use.

The reintroduction of a more controlled system of international finance will depend on the continued redistribution of global economic resources and global economic power, a process that has been facilitated by globalization itself. This process has resulted in the remarkable economic growth and development of many nations, especially in Asia: what we now refer to as emerging markets. Some of this growth has been a result of rising energy prices, but the greatest part has come as a result of the massive global transfer of money, technology, knowledge, and manufacturing capabilities to previously poor nations able and willing to capture and use these resources.[107] This process of catch-up has gone a long way toward reversing the enormous advantages rich nations have had over (many) poor nations for two centuries and carries huge implications for the distribution of global economic power in the coming decades. Now, with much faster growing economies and seemingly better prospects for the future, emerging market nations are poised to surge past rich nations. China stands ready to overtake the United States as the world's largest economy and emerging market nations are close to equaling and then surpassing rich nations in economic size. This has already happened using purchasing power parity (PPP) measures of GDP and will happen using exchange rate measures in the next decade or less.[108] This epochal transformation has happened largely in the last forty years and is a direct result of liberal globalization.

But the Global Financial Crisis may have landed a death-blow to this form of globalization. How will the adjustment and adaptation to this event change the global economy? This is a core element in the relationships of global economic competition, to which we now turn our attention.

Key Concepts (see Glossary)

Capital Accumulation	Financialization
Capital Controls	Foreign Exchange Reserves
Collateralized Debt Obligations (CDOs)	Key Currency
	Leverage
Credit Default Swaps (CDSs)	Moral Hazard
Derivative	Structural Power
Embedded Liberalism	Systemic Crisis
European Central Bank (ECB)	

Discussion Questions

1 How is money different from goods? Discuss the political and economic effects of the structural power of finance on domestic and international systems.
2 Explain the structural power of finance in a capitalist economy. Why is this important?
3 How does the extension of credit, especially to banks, create an intense level of interdependence in a capitalist economy?
4 What was the political relationship between the state and banks under the Bretton Woods system? How did that break down in the 1960s and 1970s?

5 Discuss the concept and process of financialization and the impact this had on global political and economic relations.

- How was the globalization of finance related to the emergence of the Euromarket; changes in the system of exchange rates, capital controls, tax policy, and fiscal deficits; global markets for US government debt; deregulation; petrodollars and global lending?
- How was the Global Debt Crisis of 1982–3 a result of the complexities of managing the global effects of interest rates policies of the Federal Reserve?
- How did the effort to mange exchange rates between 1985 and 1987 contribute to the globalization of finance?
- Discuss the effort to manage exchange rates in the European Union.

6 Analyze the conditions in markets that can lead to a financial crisis. Explain how systemic crises emerge. What does a financial bubble look like?
7 To what extent did these conditions exist in the Asian Financial Crisis of 1997–8?
8 What are the main features of the regulation of banks?
9 Discuss the role of the deregulation of finance, the expansion of exotic financial securities, and the ideology of free markets in the Global Financial Crisis of 2008.
10 How does financialization promote increased risks of systemic crises?
11 Evaluate the alternatives for US government leaders when large investment firms began collapsing.
12 How did the financial crisis in the Eurozone develop? Evaluate the European Union's ability to resolve this crisis.
13 Consider the evidence relating to the impact of the globalization of finance on the autonomy and power of states.
14 What is the likelihood for the US dollar to lose its status as the key currency?

Notes

1 David Kocieniewski, "Academics Who Defend Wall Street Reap Reward," *New York Times*, December 27, 2013, www.nytimes.com/2013/12/28/business/academics-who-defend-wall-st-reap-reward.html?hp&_r=0
2 Eric Helleiner, *States and the Reemergence of Global Finance*, Ithaca: Cornell University Press, 1994. These differences are reflected in political choices, institutions, and processes. See Peter Gourevitch, "The Macropolitics of Microinstitutional Differences in the Analysis of Comparative Capitalism," in Suzanne Berger and Ronald Dore (eds), *National Diversity and Global Capitalism*, Ithaca: Cornell University Press, 1996, 239–59.
3 Our discussion of the most recent financial crisis will detail how the government acted more quickly with massive injections of credit and spending and broke the collapse of confidence in early 2009.

4 Helleiner, *States and the Reemergence of Global Finance*, 27. One key feature of this political process of change was the partnership arrangement between the major financial firms in New York and the Federal Reserve Bank of New York (FRBNY). When the responsibility for international monetary policy was transferred from the FRBNY to the US Treasury during World War II, this marked a reversal of political fortune for the New York financial community.

5 See Chapter 5 for details.

6 John Gerard Ruggie, "International Regimes, Transactions, and Change: Embedded Liberalism in the Postwar Economic Order," *International Organization*, 36.2 (Spring 1982) 379–415; Helleiner, *States and the Reemergence of Global Finance*, 26–50.

7 This contradiction is known as the Triffin Dilemma or Paradox, in honor of Robert Triffin, who first pointed to this in 1947. Barry Eichengreen, *Exorbitant Privilege*, Oxford: Oxford University Press, 2011, 50.

8 Helleiner, *States and the Reemergence of Global Finance*, 81–100; Jeffry Frieden, *Banking on the World*, New York: Harper and Row, 1987, 79–85.

9 Barry Eichengreen, *Globalizing Capital*, Princeton: Princeton University Press, 1996, 125–34.

10 On a global scale, economic growth declined from 3.5 percent per year in the 1960s to 1.8 percent in the 1970s and 1.3 percent in the 1980s. For the same periods, growth in rich nations declined from 4.4 percent to 2.6 percent and 2.5 percent. Niall Ferguson, "Crisis, What Crisis?" in Niall Ferguson, Charles Maier, Erez Manela, and Daniel Sargent (eds), *The Shock of the Global: The 1970s in Perspective*, Cambridge, MA: Harvard University Press, 2010, 9.

11 The story of this political and economic transformation is told in Thomas Ferguson and Joel Rogers, *Right Turn*, New York: Hill and Wang, 1986; Jacob Hacker and Paul Pierson, *Winner-Take-All Politics*, New York: Simon & Schuster, 2010. A comparative examination of the neoliberal transformation is Monica Prasad, *The Politics of Free Markets*, Chicago: University of Chicago Press, 2006.

12 Martijn Konings, "The Institutional Foundations of U.S. Structural Power in International Finance," *Review of International Political Economy*, 15.1 (2008) 35–61; Helleiner, *States and the Reemergence of Global Finance*, 101–45; Greta Krippner, *Capitalizing on Crisis*, Cambridge, MA: Harvard University Press, 2011, 58–85.

13 Krippner, *Capitalizing on Crisis*, 58–85. For a review of deregulation in the United States from 1980–2008, see Fiona Tregenna, "The Fat Years: The Structure and Profitability of the U.S. Banking Sector in the Pre-Crisis Years," *Cambridge Journal of Economics*, 33 (2009) 610–11. An overview of the movement toward deregulation in the United States, including finance, is by Joshua Green, "Inside Man," *The Atlantic*, April 2010, www.theatlantic.com/magazine/archive/2010/04/inside-man/7992

14 Gerald Davis, *Managed by the Markets*, Oxford: Oxford University Press, 2009.

15 Andrew Haldane and Piergiorgio Alessandri, "Banking on the State," *BIS Review*, 139 (2009) 14.

16 Carlota Perez, *Technological Revolutions and Financial Capital*, Cheltenham: Edward Elgar, 2002.

17 Yoichi Funabashi, *Managing the Dollar: From the Plaza to the Louvre*, Washington, DC: Institute for International Economics, 1989.

18 Helleiner, *States and the Reemergence of Global Finance*, 102–12, 123–45.

19 Francis Rosenbluth, *Financial Politics in Contemporary Japan*, Ithaca: Cornell University Press, 1989, 50–89; John Goodman and Louis Pauly,

"The Obsolescence of Capital Controls: Economic Management in an Age of Global Markets," *World Politics*, 46.1 (October 1993) 65–70; Helleiner, *States and the Reemergence of Global Finance*, 152–66.

20 David E. Spiro, *The Hidden Hand of American Hegemony: Petrodollar Recycling and International Markets*, Ithaca: Cornell University Press, 1999.

21 For data on interest rates, see Manuel Pastor, "Managing the Latin American Debt Crisis: The International Monetary Fund and Beyond," in Gerald Epstein and Julie Graham (eds), *Creating a New World Economy*, Philadelphia: Temple University Press, 1993, 295.

22 For a discussion of the politics of the questions and answers, see Miles Kahler, "Politics and International Debt: Explaining the Crisis," *International Organization*, 39.3 (Summer 1985) 357–82.

23 We will see this debate played out again in the discussion of the recent Global Financial Crisis and the decisions by the pro-market administration of George Bush about whether to bail out investment banks such as Lehman Brothers and Bear Sterns in 2008. Remember, the President in 1982, at the time of the bailout of banks and developing nations, was the pro-market Republican Ronald Reagan.

24 The argument for bailouts of financial firms based on the structural power of finance is a pragmatic one related to the demonstrable consequences for everyone should a systemic collapse of the financial system take place. It is not a moral argument about the deservedness of those receiving support. Put another way, this is a reflection of the structural power of capitalists in a capitalist economy. We can also see this structural power expressed in the constant refrain of Republicans in the United States about the need to provide special incentives to "job creators."

25 Source: St. Louis Federal Reserve.

26 Krippner, *Capitalizing on Crisis*, 114–37.

27 The US experience with budget deficits was unusual for the United States as compared with the period before the 1960s, but many advanced economies also found themselves operating in the red. Between 1978 and 2011, the US average budget deficit was 3.9 percent of GDP. Here are comparable figures for other nations: France 3.3 percent, Britain 3.7 percent, Japan 4.1 percent, Canada 3.5 percent, Sweden 1.4 percent. By contrast, over the same period Korea achieved an average budget surplus of 2 percent. See *The Economist*, May 8, 2012, www.economist.com/blogs/graphicdetail/2012/05/daily-chart–4

28 Krippner, *Capitalizing on Crisis*, 86–105.

29 J. Lawrence Broz and Jeffry Frieden, "The Political Economy of International Monetary Relations," *Annual Review of Political Science*, 4 (2001) 317–43.

30 For indicators of volatility, see Barry Eichengreen, *Globalizing Capital*, Princeton: Princeton University Press, 1996, 142.

31 The step was unnecessary for nations operating in a current account surplus with the United States. These nations accumulated dollars through trade, but rather than selling them for another currency or converting them to their own currency they could choose to purchase US assets. This process also supported a rising dollar.

32 I.M. Destler and C. Randall Henning, *Dollar Politics*, Washington, DC: Institute for International Economics, 1989, 17–25.

33 Yoichi Funabashi, *Managing the Dollar*, Washington, DC: Institute for International Economics, 1989.

34 Intervention works by having the government become a player in foreign exchange markets, using foreign exchange reserves to purchase or sell currencies in a large enough quantity to move prices. In the case of the Plaza

Agreement, each country would use dollars to purchase one of the other currencies, thereby increasing the supply of dollars and increasing the demand for other currencies.

35 Japanese auto makers and their suppliers built new plants in the United States during the 1980s, though this was partly a response to threats of tariff increases and other protectionist measures from Congress.

36 The nineteen nations include: Austria, Belgium, Cyprus, Estonia, Finland, France, Germany, Greece, Ireland, Italy, Latvia, Lithuania, Luxembourg, Malta, the Netherlands, Portugal, Slovakia, Slovenia, and Spain.

37 The total rose from an average of $7.124 trillion in 1980–4 to an average of $76.133 trillion in 2000–4, with the absolute total in 2004 approaching $100 trillion. M. Ayhan Kose, Eswar Prasad, Kenneth Rogoff, and Shang-Jin Wei, "Financial Globalization: A Reappraisal," IMF Working Paper 06/189, August 2006, 54, 63.

38 These derivatives, already leveraged in the price relationship, were usually purchased with mostly borrowed money. For estimates of the global values of the derivatives market, see the Bank for International Settlements, www.bis.org/statistics/derdetailed.htm. See the section in this chapter on the Global Financial Crisis for discussion of the importance of derivatives.

39 Holdings of foreign exchange reserves can by tracked at the following website: www.tradingeconomics.com/countries

40 Charles Roxburgh, Susan Lund, and John Piotrowski, "Global Capital Markets: Entering a New Era," McKinsey Global Institute, September 2009, 27; *The Economist*, "Power Shift: Emerging Versus Developed Economies," August 4, 2011, www.economist.com/blogs/dailychart/2011/08/emerging-vs-developed-economies

41 Roxburgh, Lund, and Piotrowski, "Global Capital Markets," 8.

42 Roxburgh, Lund, and Piotrowski, "Global Capital Markets," 21.

43 Susan Lund, Charles Roxburgh, and Tony Wimmer, "The Looming Deleveraging Challenge," *McKinsey Quarterly* (January 2010) 3.

44 Greta Krippner, "The Financialization of the American Economy," *Socio-Economic Review*, 3 (2005) 177–81; also see Krippner, *Capitalizing on Crisis*, 27–57.

45 Morten Bech, "FX Volume During the Financial Crisis and Now," *BIS Quarterly Review*, March 2012, 35, provides a useful description of the types of foreign exchange transactions:

- Spot transactions are single outright transactions that involve the exchange of two currencies at a rate agreed to on the date of the contract for value or delivery typically within two business days.
- Outright forwards involve the exchange of two currencies at a rate agreed to on the date of the contract for value or delivery at some time in the future.
- Foreign exchange swaps involve the exchange of two currencies on a specific date at a rate agreed to at the time of the conclusion of the contract, and a reverse exchange of the same two currencies on a future date at a rate agreed to at the time of the contract.
- Currency swaps involve the exchange of fixed or floating interest payments in two different currencies over the lifetime of the contract.
- Currency or foreign exchange options are contracts that give the right to buy or sell a currency with another currency at a specified exchange rate during or at the end of a specified time period.

46 *The Economist*, "All in the Same Boat: Why Global Stockmarkets Have Become More Correlated," September 10, 2011, www.economist.com/node/21528640

47 For a timeline of financial crises from 1973 onward, see Thomas D. Lairson, "The Global Financial Crisis: Governments, Banks and Markets," in Ralph Carter (ed.), *Contemporary Cases in US Foreign Policy*, Washington, DC: CQ Press, 5th ed., 2013, 273–315.

48 Charles Ferguson, "Inside Job," a film, provides considerable perspective on thisprocess.Seewww.npr.org/blogs/monkeysee/2010/10/01/130273644/-inside-job-director-charles-ferguson-taking-aim-at-wall-street

49 For contrasting views on the efficacy of markets, see Patric Hendershott and Kevin Villani, "The Subprime Lending Debacle," *Policy Analysis*, 679 (June 20, 2011), www.cato.org/pub_cat_display.php?pub_cat=2&page=all, and John Cassidy, *How Markets Fail*, New York: Farrar, Straus, and Giroux, 2009.

50 There are two classic studies of the history of financial crises: Charles Kindleberger and Robert Aliber, *Manias, Panics, and Crashes: A History of Financial Crises*, New York: Wiley, 2005; Carmen Reinhart and Kenneth Rogoff, *This Time is Different: Eight Centuries of Financial Folly*, Princeton: Princeton University Press, 2009.

51 An interesting exercise is the bank failure simulation, using actual banking and finance officials, and provided by *The Economist* at www.economist.com/node/21536514

52 *The Economist*, September 10, 2011, 83, www.economist.com/node/21528677

53 Reinhart and Rogoff, *This Time is Different*, xxxix–xlv, 15–20.

54 Knowledge@Wharton, "Efficient Markets or Herd Mentality? The Future of Economic Forecasting," November 25, 2009, http://knowledge.wharton.upenn.edu/article.cfm?articleid=2383

55 Japanese firms also moved production facilities to the United States and Europe to improve their competitive position.

56 Walter Hatch and Kozo Yamamura, *Asia in Japan's Embrace*, Cambridge: Cambridge University Press, 1996.

57 Robert Wade, "The Asian Crisis and the Global Economy: Causes, Consequences and Cure," *Current History* (November 1998) 362.

58 Wade Bello, "The End of a Miracle: Speculation, Foreign Capital Dependence and the Collapse of the Southeast Asian Economies," *Multinational Monitor*, 19.1–2 (January–February 1998).

59 Axel Dreher, "IMF Conditionality: Theory and Evidence," *Public Choice*, 141.1–2 (2009) 233–67.

60 T.J. Pempel, *The Politics of the Asian Financial Crisis*, Ithaca: Cornell University Press, 1999.

61 Knowledge@Wharton, "Why Economists Failed to Predict the Financial Crisis," May 27, 2009, www.knowledgeatwharton.com.cn/index.cfm?fa=viewArticle&Articleid=2041&languageid=1

62 James R. Barth, Dan Brumbaugh, Jr., and James Wilcox, "The Repeal of Glass–Steagall and the Advent of Broad Banking," *Journal of Economic Perspectives*, vol. 14, no. 2 (Spring 2000) 191–204.

63 For an effective visual telling of this story, see PBS Frontline, "Money, Power and Wall Street," www.pbs.org/wgbh/pages/frontline/money-power-wall-street/

64 Knowledge@Wharton, "A 'Race to the Bottom': Assigning Responsibility for the Financial Crisis," December 9, 2009, http://knowledge.wharton.upenn.edu/article.cfm?articleid=2397

65 Daniel K. Tarullo, *Banking on Basel: The Future of International Financial Regulation*, Washington, DC: Peterson Institute, 2008; "Base Camp Basel," *The Economist*, January 23, 2010, 66–8; Felix Salmon, "Recipe for Disaster: The Formula that Killed Wall Street," *Wired* (February 23, 2009), www.wired.com/techbiz/it/magazine/1703/wp_quant?currentPage=all

66 See earlier in this chapter for the discussion of derivatives. An introduction to derivatives is by Randall Dodd, "Derivatives Markets: Sources of Vulnerability in U.S. Financial Markets," in Gerald Epstein (ed.), *Financialization and the World Economy*, Cheltenham: Edward Elgar, 2005, 149–80. A more sophisticated review is by Robert C. Merton, "Observations on the Science of Finance in the Practice of Finance," MIT World, http://mitworld.mit.edu/video/659. An analysis of financial innovations is by Saskia Sassen, "Mortgage Capital and Its Peculiarities: A New Frontier for Global Finance," *Journal of International Affairs*, vol. 62, no. 1 (Fall 2008), 187–212.

67 For data on derivative markets, see Bank for International Settlements, "Detailed Tables on Semiannual OTC Derivatives Statistics at End-June 2009," www.bis.org/statistics/derdetailed.htm. See specifically Table 19: "Amounts Outstanding of Over-the-Counter (OTC) Derivatives." See also Dore, "Financialization of the Global Economy," 1099, and "The Changing Face of Investors," *Finance and Development*, vol. 44, no. 1 (March 2007).

68 American International Group (AIG) was especially involved in issuing CDSs, perhaps as much as $400 billion. This firm's financial position disintegrated during the financial crisis when the losses on these contracts exceeded the ability to pay.

69 The behavior of the Reagan Administration in the debt crisis of 1982 and the savings and loan crisis of 1988, and the actions of the Clinton Administration in the exchange rate crisis of 1994 are consistent with this generalization.

70 Acting to save Lehman might have delayed and even diminished the crisis, but probably would not have prevented it. The global financial system was too unstable and unbalanced to be saved without a massive contraction in values.

71 For a more detailed description and analysis of the crisis, see Thomas D. Lairson, "The Global Financial Crisis: Governments, Banks and Markets," in Ralph Carter (ed.), *Contemporary Cases in US Foreign Policy*, Washington, DC: Congressional Quarterly Press, 5th ed., 2013, 273–315. Also see, Frederic Mishkin, "Over the Cliff: From the Subprime to the Global Financial Crisis," *Journal of Economic Perspectives*, 25.1 (Winter 2011) 49–70.

72 Roxburgh et al., "Global Capital Markets," 7.

73 Timothy J. Sinclair, *The New Masters of Capital: American Bond Rating Agencies and the Politics of Creditworthiness*, Ithaca: Cornell University Press, 2005.

74 The G–20 existed before the financial crisis, but the events of 2007–9 undermined the position of rich nations, especially the United States. The use of the G–20 was acknowledgment of that fact and of the large financial resources of nations like China, Saudi Arabia, and South Korea.

75 Daniel K. Tarullo, *Banking on Basel: The Future of International Financial Regulation*, Washington, DC: Peterson Institute, 2008.

76 Jacob Vestergaard and Robert Wade, "The West Must Allow a Power Shift in International Organizations," *DIIS Policy Brief*, February 2014, http://pure.diis.dk/ws/files/62484/the_west_must_allow_a_powershift_for_webfinal3.pdf; Robert Wade and Jacob Vestergaard, "The IMF Needs a Reset," *New York Times*, February 4, 2014, www.nytimes.com/2014/02/05/opinion/the-imf-needs-a-reset.html?hpw&rref=opinion&_r=1

77 Vestergaard and Wade, "The West Must Allow a Power Shift." The United States would retain 16.47 percent of the votes and China would move up to 6.07 percent.

78 Jacob Vestergaard and Robert Wade, "Protecting Power: How Western States Retained the Dominant Voice in the World Bank's Reforms," *World Development*, 46 (2013) 153–64.

79 Eric Helleiner and Stefano Pagliari, "Towards a New Bretton Woods?" *New Political Economy*, 14.2 (June 2009) 275–87.

80 Interestingly, those nations that retained tight financial regulations, and prevented their banks from participating in the extreme levels of investment in derivatives, were largely able to avoid the worst effects of the Global Financial Crisis. Canada is an example.

81 An excellent graphic depicting these relationships is Bill Walsh, "It's All Connected: An Overview of the Euro Crisis," *New York Times*, October 22, 2011,www.nytimes.com/interactive/2011/10/23/sunday-review/an-overview-of-the-euro-crisis.html?ref=europeansovereigndebtcrisis; Liz Alderman and Susanne Craig, "Europe's Banks Found Safety of Bonds a Costly Illusion," *New York Times*, November 10, 2011, www.nytimes.com/2011/11/11/business/global/sovereign-debt-turns-sour-in-euro-zone.html?pagewanted=1&_r=1&sq=alderman%20sovereign&st=cse&scp=1

82 *New York Times*, "Understanding the European Crisis Now," June 14, 2012, www.nytimes.com/interactive/2012/06/14/business/global/understanding-the-european-crisis.html?ref=global

83 Peter Boone and Simon Johnson, "Europe on the Brink," Peterson Institute for International Economics, Policy Brief PB 11–13, July 2011.

84 For an excellent discussion of the crisis in relation to the overall euro project, see David Marsh, *The Euro: The Battle for the New Global Currency*, New Haven: Yale University Press, 2009.

85 Stephen Castle, "European Union Exit? Concerns Grow for Britain," *New York Times*, October 27, 2012, www.nytimes.com/2012/10/28/world/europe/european-union-exit-concerns-grow-for-britain.html?hp

86 Uri Dadush, *Paradigm Lost: The Euro in Crisis*, Washington, DC: Carnegie Endowment for International Peace, 2010, especially 93–9.

87 Edward Carr, "Staring into the Abyss: Europe and Its Currency," *The Economist*, November 12, 2011, www.economist.com/node/21536872

88 *The Economist*, "What Germany Offers the World," April 14, 2012, www.economist.com/node/21552567

89 Robert Gogel et al., "The Business Case for the European Union," *Strategy+Business*, July 23, 2012, www.strategy-business.com/article/00123?gko=c50 2d&cid=20120724enews

90 An important analysis of this relationship is Susan Strange, *The Retreat of the State*, Cambridge: Cambridge University Press, 1996.

91 John Micklethwait, "Taming Leviathan," *The Economist*, March 19, 2011, www.economist.com/node/18359896

92 www.newyorkfed.org/markets/fxswap/fxswap.cfm

93 Charles Calomiris and Stephen Haber, *Fragile by Design*, Princeton: Princeton University Press, 2014.

94 *The Economist*, "Reserve Currencies: Climbing Greenback Mountain," September 24, 2011, www.economist.com/node/21528988

95 A thorough discussion of the dollar as key currency is Eric Helleiner and Jonathan Kirshner (eds), *The Future of the Dollar*, Ithaca: Cornell University Press, 2009. Eswar Prasad and Lei Ye, "The Renminbi's Role in the Global Monetary System," Brookings Institute, February 2012.

96 Konings, "The Institutional Foundations of U.S. Structural Power in International Finance."

97 Several other nations played an important supporting role, such as Korea, Taiwan, Singapore, and Saudi Arabia. For Germany and the political economy of keeping US troops in Europe, see Michael Mastanduno, "System Maker and Privilege Taker: U.S. Power and International Political Economy," *World Politics*, 61.1 (January 2009) 131–6.

98 Thomas D. Lairson, "The Global Financial Crisis and the Restructuring of the Global Economy," *Fudan American Review*, 2011 (in Mandarin) 24–47; Hacker and Pierson, *Winner-Take-All Politics*.

99 Mastanduno, "System Maker and Privilege Taker," 137–8.

100 Mastanduno, "System Maker and Privilege Taker," 141–3.

101 Howard Stein, "Financial Liberalisation, Institutional Transformation and Credit Allocation in Developing Countries: The World Bank and the Internationalisation of Banking," *Cambridge Journal of Economics*, 34 (2010) 257–73.

102 Much of this pressure derived from the structural power of US finance. Richard Deeg and Mary O'Sullivan, "The Political Economy of Global Finance Capital," *World Politics*, 61.4 (October 2009) 731–63; Martijn Konings, "The Institutional Foundations of U.S. Structural Power in International Finance," *Review of International Political Economy*, 15.1 (2008) 35–61; Martijn Konings, "The Construction of U.S. Financial Power," *Review of International Studies*, 35.1 (2009) 69–94.

103 Stephen D. Cohen, "The Superpower as Super-Debtor: Implications of Economic Disequilibria for U.S.–Asian Relations," in Ashley Tellis and Michael Wills (eds), *Strategic Asia 2006–07: Trade, Interdependence, and Security*, Seattle: National Bureau of Asian Research, 2006, 29–63.

104 Stephen Cohen and J. Bradford DeLong, *The End of Influence: What Happens When Other Countries Have the Money*, New York: Perseus, 2010.

105 Mastanduno, "System Maker and Privilege Taker," 149.

106 David Smick, "Taming the World's Crazy Currency System," *Foreign Policy*, 191 (January/February 2012) 69–70.

107 John O'Sullivan, "A Game of Catch-Up," *The Economist*, September 24, 2011, www.economist.com/node/21528979

108 *The Economist*, "Power Shift: Emerging Versus Developed Economies," August 4, 2011, www.economist.com/blogs/dailychart/2011/08/emerging-vs-developed-economies

Further Reading

Barry Eichengreen, *Exorbitant Privilege*, Oxford: Oxford University Press, 2011.
Offers a detailed analysis of economic and political gains from the dollar as the key currency.

Gerald Epstein (ed.), *Financialization and the World Economy*, Cheltenham: Edward Elgar, 2005.
A global analysis of the process of financialization.

Andrew Gamble, *Crisis Without End: The Unraveling of Western Prosperity*, Basingstoke: Palgrave Macmillan, 2014.
Considers the financial crisis as but one episode in the decline of economic growth in the West.

Eric Helleiner, *States and the Reemergence of Global Finance*, Ithaca: Cornell University Press, 1994.
An exceptional analysis of the relationship of states and the financial industry.

Eric Helleiner and Jonathan Kirshner (eds), *The Future of the Dollar*, Ithaca: Cornell University Press, 2009.
A thorough discussion of the dollar as the key currency.

Charles Kindleberger and Robert Aliber, *Manias, Panics, and Crashes: A History of Financial Crises*, New York: Wiley, 2005.
The classic history of financial crises.

Jonathan Kirshner, *American Power After the Financial Crisis*, Ithaca: Cornell University Press, 2014.
Examines the impact of the Global Financial Crisis on the legitimacy of US ideas and preferences for the global financial order.

Greta Krippner, *Capitalizing on Crisis*, Cambridge, MA: Harvard University Press, 2011.
A stimulating reconceptualization of the relationship of states and finance.

Carmen Reinhart and Kenneth Rogoff, *This Time is Different: Eight Centuries of Financial Folly*, Princeton: Princeton University Press, 2009.
Provides an extraordinary comparative historical analysis of financial crises.

Timothy J. Sinclair, *The New Masters of Capital: American Bond Rating Agencies and the Politics of Creditworthiness*, Ithaca: Cornell University Press, 2005.
A critical analysis of the misuse of power by bond-rating agencies.

8 States and the Dynamics of Global Economic Competition

Our ability to understand the dynamics of competition within global political economy depends much on the ability to comprehend the role of technology and its effects on this system. The developments in technology over the past forty years affect systems of global political economy in at least four related ways. First, technological capabilities are at the heart of the pace and size of economic growth, which affects the global distribution of economic, military, and political power. Second, technologies affect what can be done at a particular price in shaping the human and physical environment and consequently alter where and how production takes place, the quality and speed of communication and interaction, and the ability to create and apply power. Third, the distribution of technology across and within nations, combined with the relative size of barriers to accessing knowledge and technology, dramatically affect the ability of nations to catch up or fall behind in relative capabilities. Finally, technologies interact with political and economic institutions to influence the character of economic production and the nature and degree of economic interdependence among nations. Technology alone does not determine these outcomes, but interacts with political and economic institutions to shape processes related to power, wealth, and modes of global interaction. This chapter is designed to help students comprehend and analyze these processes.

The interactions among firms, and among nations, and among nations and firms within global markets lead to an extraordinarily complex and dynamic system of relationships and change. Much of the global economy is now defined by a global system of production, investment, trade, and innovation linking firms, nations, and markets. All at the same time, these actors cooperate, compete, mutually gain, and receive substantially different gains and losses. Nations and firms, from many locations, are constantly engaged in efforts that improve the capabilities and processes for production of goods and services and often improve the very nature of these goods and services. These processes can lead to dramatic, even historically unprecedented, changes in the relative positions of firms and of nations in the global economy and in the strategic military relations among nations. In the space of a few decades, desperately poor nations can achieve rapid economic growth and ascend to global prominence.

Nations have distinctive kinds of institutions, firms, systems of capital formation, and allocation that add up to different forms of capitalism. At the same time, nations compete to attract the operations of global firms, to be the locus for the production of goods and services, and to serve as a center for innovation in processes and products. Firms compete through costs, marketing, production, and innovation and have distributed their activities across nations as part of these efforts. Much of this dynamism can be traced to the effects of technology, as it constantly restructures the nature of products and processes, as well as what can be produced, where it can be produced, how it can be produced, the nature and costs of communication and production, and the gains from production and exchange.

This chapter examines this dynamism from the prism of the competitive relationships in the global economy, a competition driven by but not confined to technology. We take some time to examine the concept of competitiveness, define it, consider how it can be measured, and determine some of its effects. We then shift our attention to technology and its effects on global economic competition. This comes from a discussion of general purpose technologies (GPTs), which ripple through economies and change basic structures. Information and communications technologies are the most recent GPTs and these have operated to create a particular environment for global competition, most importantly through new products, processes, radical changes in relative prices, and the creation of global production networks. These new capabilities have dispersed knowledge across the world, contributed much to the extraordinarily rapid rise of emerging economies, generated new forms of competition and innovation, and distributed the gains from production and trade in new ways. We examine some of these outcomes through four case studies of the varying roles played by governments in promoting competitiveness. Three of these consider how states can affect the production and use of knowledge: the Defense Advanced Research Projects Agency in the United States, the efforts of the Israeli government to promote high-technology industries, and the efforts of Finland to expand research and development (R&D) investment by private firms. The fourth case focuses on using structural power to enhance competitiveness with the negotiation of the Trans-Pacific Partnership (TPP) as a means to advance US exports. We conclude with a consideration of the debate about the proper role of government in promoting competitiveness.

What is Competitiveness?

That firms and nations and even local areas within nations compete is relatively obvious, though there are important qualifications to this point.

The essence of competition is the existence of a significant form of zero-sum relationship in the pursuit of common goals. Two agents are each attempting to achieve related goals and the success of one in some way undermines or detracts from the success of the other. Notice the zero-sum element of the interaction does not define the entire relationship; various forms of cooperation are always important. Such is the case in the competitive relationship of firms and of nations. For example, the competitive process among firms and nations is possible only in a context in which the rules for trade and investment have been created and maintained through political cooperation. In addition, firms engaged in competition frequently engage in cooperation to develop products. For example, Apple and Samsung have a series of strategic alliances even as they compete fiercely for global markets in smartphones and tablets. The point is that competition and cooperation are not mutually exclusive.

The competitiveness of nations and of firms, though related, is not quite the same. A nation's competitiveness can be understood as the ability to achieve economic growth and a rising standard of living when substantially exposed to the global economy through trade and capital flows. This ability is the result of certain characteristics of a nation's economic, social, and political institutions, including its firms. The competitiveness of a firm can be defined as the ability to achieve profitability through its efforts in global markets in relation to other firms. This ability is the result of various strategies adopted by the firm in an effort to sell its products and/or services. There are two main measures used to determine the competitiveness of nations and of firms. For nations, the rate of increase in its productivity is typically used to analyze the degree of its competitiveness. For firms, various measures of profitability such as profit margin or return on equity are used. Typically, the enhancement of the productivity of a nation leads to an increase in the profitability of its firms.[1]

The concept of competitiveness, especially as applied to nations, is a contentious one and tends to divide economists from political economists. The latter emphasize the potential conflicts that arise from economic growth, while economists focus on the mutual gains from economic growth and reject the idea of an economic zero-sum relationship among nations. Political economists assert that conflict can frequently emerge from differential rates of economic growth, which can affect the military and political strength of a nation and its influence in global affairs. Moreover, national governments have a distinct bias in preference for the success of their own firms over the success of those of other nations. This can include taking steps to have a larger portion of high value-added firms and industries located within their territory. At the same time, economic growth based on increasing productivity and enhanced capabilities of one nation can actually lead to gains for other nations through trade. Other nations can potentially sell more goods and services to this growing nation and can also buy its goods and reap some of the consumption benefits from the rise in another nation's productivity. Another side benefit of improvements in one nation for another nation is the ability to imitate and gain from a clearer path to economic success.[2]

In this chapter we take both positions seriously, but recognize the realities of international political economy. Today, almost all important nations are significantly connected to the global economy and understand the mutual gains available from this participation and the importance of preserving this system. Though there are different levels of engagement with the global economy, very few important nations engage in intense efforts to close off their economy and reap the possible gains from autarchy. At the same time, most of these same nations engage in policy efforts to boost the capabilities of the firms and populations in their territory. In doing so, they act to improve the competitiveness of their nation – typically to enhance productivity and thereby growth and incomes – even if this also works to the benefit of other nations as well. In this sense, we see contemporary competitiveness not as a purely zero-sum relationship but as an effort to reap the mutual gains from efforts increasing national productivity across the global economy. The actions taken by nations matter – often a lot – for economic competitiveness; a few seconds comparing the firms of the United States and Vietnam make this abundantly clear. Nonetheless, though both Vietnam and the United States can achieve mutual gains from trade, this should not obscure the competitive dimensions of this relationship.

Measuring Competitiveness

For the moment, we will focus our attention on measuring competitiveness for nations and later turn to considerations for firms. Most of the major efforts to measure competitiveness include but do not limit themselves to productivity. One important effort in measuring competitiveness develops a differentiated measure based on the stage of a nation's development.[3] Nations are divided into three groups: developing nations that rely mainly on the existing factor endowments in their nations; a second group of nations capable of achieving growth through enhanced efficiencies; and a third group able to achieve growth through innovation.

The first set of components of the measure focuses on nations that depend primarily on the relative endowment of production factors such as low wage labor and natural resources. The competitiveness of these nations will depend on the ability to develop a basic economic system sufficient to operate effectively in the global economy (see "Basic Requirements for Factor-Driven Economies" below).

Basic Requirements for Factor-Driven Economies

Institutions

Property rights, intellectual property, corruption, low waste in government spending, transparency of government policymaking, level of crime and violence, reliability of corporate information

Infrastructure

Transportation, energy, telephony

Macroeconomic environment

Government budget balance, savings, inflation, interest rate spread, government debt, national credit rating

Health and primary education

Incidence of disease, infant mortality, life expectancy, primary education enrollment rate

---

A second stage of development emphasizes those arrangements that enhance the efficiency of a nation (see "Efficiency Enhancers for Efficiency-Driven Economies" below).

Efficiency Enhancers for Efficiency-Driven Economies

Higher education and training
Goods market efficiency
Labor market efficiency
Financial market development
Technological readiness
Market size

The most advanced economies develop competitiveness based on more complex and difficult systems (see "Innovation and Sophistication Factors for Innovation-Driven Economies" below).

Innovation and Sophistication Factors for Innovation-Driven Economies

Business sophistication
Innovation

The cumulative measure of competitiveness involves weighting the set of three broad capabilities according to a nation's level of development.[4] The results of this effort yield interesting and important data. The rankings of the top six nations and the bottom five nations on competitiveness are displayed in Table 8.1. Clearly, the measures of competitiveness reflect important differences in nations.

The trends found over time also suggest important relative shifts in competitiveness between advanced and emerging economies and between the United States and other advanced economies. Figure 8.1 shows that over just a seven-year period we can see a closing of the gap that previously existed between the United States and other advanced economies, mainly owing to the decline of the United States. At the same time, those same seven years witnessed a significant rise in the competitiveness of China and a smaller but noticeable increase by other emerging economies.

More broadly, the competitiveness measure tracks closely to overall levels of development, as measured by gross domestic product (GDP) per

Table 8.1 Top Six and Bottom Five in Competitiveness

Top Six	
Country	*Overall Competitiveness Score*
Switzerland	5.70
Singapore	5.65
United States	5.54
Finland	5.50
Germany	5.49
Japan	5.47
Bottom Five	
Country	*Overall Competitiveness Score*
Angola	3.04
Mauritania	3.00
Yemen	2.96
Chad	2.85
Guinea	2.79

Source: Data from World Economic Forum, *The Global Competitiveness Report, 2014–2015*, Geneva, 2015, 16–17.

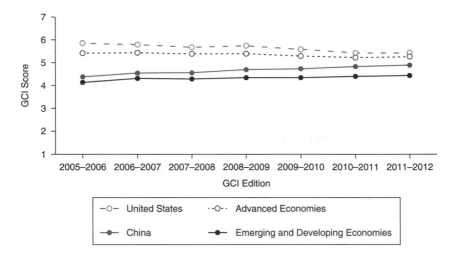

Figure 8.1 Competitiveness Trends, 2005–11.

Source: Data from World Economic Forum, *The Global Competitiveness Report, 2011–2012*, Geneva, 2012, 23.

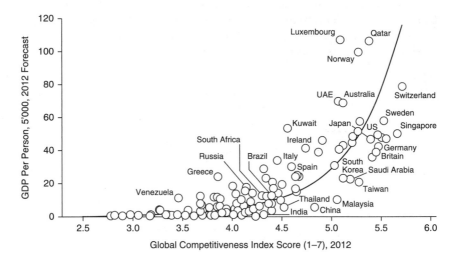

Figure 8.2 Competitiveness and GDP Per Capita.

Source: Adapted from *The Economist*, "The Wealth of Nations," September 8, 2012, www.economist.com/node/21562228

capita, as we see in Figure 8.2. The idea of competition among nations and among firms is intuitively powerful and can be measured in ways that fit with our sense of its effects. Now we need a clearer understanding of why it matters and how it relates to broader processes of global change.

Technology, Competitiveness, and Growth Strategies

The competition of nations and firms is defined and even directed by the environment for technology, production, and markets. In the contemporary world, this is a system defined by the following elements:

- intense global interdependence based on established rules operating through highly legitimate international organizations;
- competition among advanced states and among advanced firms based on innovation in applying knowledge to products;
- new forms of competition from emerging economies and the firms located there;
- a rapidly increasing scale and intensifying pace for innovation;
- new global systems of specialization for production;
- high turbulence in markets;
- rapid and even epochal shifts in the rates of economic growth;
- wrenching changes in the distribution of gains across nations and individuals;
- all leading to unprecedented complexity and dynamism in global economic systems.[5]

Consider a comparison of the contemporary world with that of a century ago. In the early twentieth century, the forefront of technological change and innovation was in electricity and dynamos, communication, the internal combustion engine, the construction of large battleships, and the creation of organizations able to manage national systems for the mobilization of human and material resources for war. By contrast, in the early twenty-first century, the frontier of technological change focuses on the application of information technology to a range of sciences such as biology to accelerate new knowledge in genetics, in robotics and autonomous machines, in developing new materials, in creating new forms of manufacturing, managing information systems over widely dispersed physical spaces, and in formulating plans for defending against and making war against the computers of other nations.

A century ago, production was by national firms largely in heavy industries, with the need for relatively massive amounts of capital and large inputs of raw materials. Today, global production is concentrated in large transnational firms operating across a wide variety of nations and is organized by specialized firms emphasizing the application of knowledge to products and processes. Global markets in 1913, though somewhat open, were mostly defined by tariffs that had been rising for thirty years and by the various barriers created by imperialism. Today, global markets are not only open but operate in a pattern of greater opening and rules for trade defined by global institutions and international agreements. The competitive environment for nations and firms is largely the result of efforts to create and reap the gains from new technologies. A century ago, this mostly meant amassing national-level capabilities in production, energy development, managing organizations, and communication. Today, the focus is on developing global-scale systems for producing, scanning for, and applying a vast expansion of knowledge across a multitude of disciplines.

General Purpose Technologies

The current technological environment of competition can be best understood with the concept of general purpose technologies (GPTs) and by appreciating the effects these have in fostering dynamic economic systems.[6] A GPT is a set or system of related technologies that provide significant improvements in a wide range of products and processes, usually through simultaneously lowering the costs and significantly enlarging the capabilities of products and processes. The most important GPTs induce large and continuing changes in costs and capabilities. In addition, for a GPT to have really big consequences it must be an input to and/or have an impact on a wide variety of additional technologies and on products, processes, and even organizational arrangements, thereby transferring the gains from lower costs and improved capabilities across the economy as a whole. The gains from costs and capabilities also need to continue and expand for a considerable period of time, effectively cascading across the economy and generating benefits in quantity, quality, and capability of products, processes, organizations, productivity, and innovations.[7]

There are multiple examples of GPTs and the impact these have had on economic growth and transformation. One of the earliest GPTs was the domestication of plants and animals roughly ten thousand years ago. This led not only to a giant increase in the size and consistency of caloric intake for humans, but also prompted living in cities, the development of complex political systems, and the economic surplus needed to engage in war. The combination of electricity, the internal combustion engine, and the dynamo in the late nineteenth century led to new forms of energy applied across a wide spectrum of products and processes and to new forms of production.[8] And, most recently, the emergence of an array of information and communication technologies (ICTs) has propelled dramatic changes in the ability of individuals and groups to create, manipulate, and transmit information on a global scale at rapidly falling costs. Further, this set of capabilities from digitization has been applied to an expanding range of products, processes, and new organizational forms.[9]

Information and communication technologies are very important products in and of themselves. The invention of the transistor in 1947, the integrated circuit in 1958, and the microprocessor in 1971 led to an extraordinary process of miniaturization, improvement in capabilities, and reduction in costs associated with the ability to store and manipulate information. The development of the Internet in 1969 and of the World Wide Web (via hypertext) in 1991, and the rapid improvement in connectivity and speed, led to the ability to transmit rich and complex information from computer to computer across the globe. The digitization of almost all forms of information permitted new kinds of information transfer over new ICT networks, and this has opened the way to a new set of products and even industries such as digital pictures and smartphones.[10]

The profound effect of GPTs is twofold. First, these technologies create very large and complex forms of new economic value, providing new products, production processes, organizational relationships, and dramatic changes in relative prices for economic inputs, thereby altering what, where, and how production and distribution of valued things can take place. Second, and even more important, these changes cumulate. This comes as new forms of economic value affect each other to create additional forms of value. The GPT affects many, even most, industries through new products, processes, and organizational forms.[11] One or more forms of value can be recombined with existing capabilities to create new capabilities, which can spawn new organizational forms to reap new gains, which alter relative prices yet again and thereby proffer additional opportunities. These processes call forth an explosion of new investment and rapidly rising increases in productivity that propel economic growth.

Moreover, what the economist Joseph Schumpeter called "creative destruction" takes place, in which technology makes changes that eliminate firms, industries, and jobs and creates new firms, industries, and jobs.[12] And further, these changes can relocate where the industries and jobs will be. As a result, extraordinary changes can take place in incomes and wealth across different nations and regions based on how and whether these areas participate in these technological developments. In the nineteenth century, the complementary effects of steam power, steel, telegraph, railroads, finance, organization, and management were scale intensive, which permitted some nations and regions to adapt and gain from these new capabilities. However, the large-scale dimension to the new technologies served as a barrier to many nations and regions unable to amass the scale of finance and organization able to build such systems. For a variety of reasons, the ICT revolution has lowered barriers to participation in production of advanced products and opened up opportunities for many previously poor nations to participate successfully in the global economy.

Information and Communication Technologies and the Global Economy

Significant changes have taken place in the global economy as a result of ICTs and changes in production: knowledge has become much more important as a basis for adding value in production; knowledge has become much more widely distributed across the planet; global production networks have become a predominant form for the production of a larger and larger number of goods and services; and as a result of these developments, the barriers to entry into the global economy have declined, opening the door to the rise of emerging economies.[13] Equally profound, the environment for global economic competition has been transformed by the cumulative effects of ICTs on the global economy. The focus of competition has shifted to innovation in product, process, and organization, the pace of innovation has accelerated, and the turbulence in global markets has expanded.

The Dispersion of Knowledge

The globalization of knowledge becomes apparent by examining the process of knowledge development and exchange in the core knowledge-intensive industry, semiconductors and software. Figure 8.3 plots the emerging networks of jointly authored scientific papers in these fields to provide one indicator of the global distribution of leading-edge knowledge in these areas.

What do these charts in Figure 8.3 reveal about the dynamics of global knowledge capabilities? For semiconductors we see a somewhat diminished but still central role for the United States, a diminished role for Japan, and a significantly expanded role for a range of secondary actors, such as Belgium, the Netherlands, Taiwan, and Korea, along with the emergence of new actors such as Singapore, Norway, and China. This global expansion and deepening of semiconductor knowledge production reflects the diffusion of knowledge and the abilities of national firms and universities to capture, harness, and build on this knowledge.

The development of semiconductor devices has seen a very substantial geographic diffusion between 1996 and 2011, as shown by the emergence of a much larger and more dense network of producing nations. Likewise, in the development of software applications and programming systems, a massive expansion and deepening of national actors closely linked to the United States has occurred. In addition, the appearance of networks of capabilities among some of these secondary actors suggests a greater complexity of knowledge relationships for these knowledge arenas. In our case studies, we will examine two nations – Israel and Finland – that have developed national strategies for participating in and gaining from this global knowledge dispersion.

Global Production Networks and the Rise of Emerging Economies

Previous chapters have discussed the predominant developmental strategies of poor nations in the years after World War II. Most of these nations

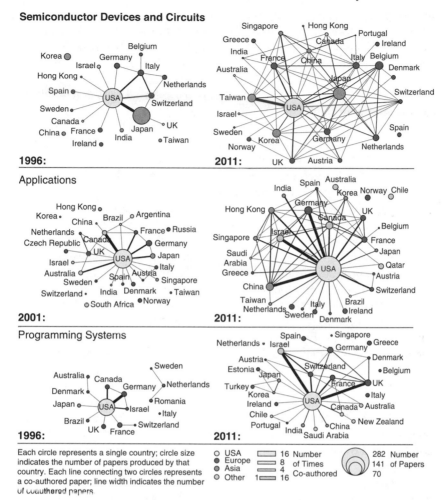

Figure 8.3 The Distribution of Knowledge Formation in Knowledge-Intensive Industries.

Source: Adapted from *The New Global Ecosystem in Advanced Computing*, Washington, DC: National Academies Press, 2012, 20, by permission of the National Academies Press, Washington, DC.

in the 1950s and 1960s chose to restrict imports and foreign direct investment (FDI) in order to boost the opportunities for domestic firms. To some extent, this began to change in the 1960s, as a few Asian nations adopted a strategy based on exports to rich nations. By the 1970s, new technological capabilities began to alter the way production of many products took place. In particular, knowledge about manufacturing techniques became more globally dispersed, as advanced firms not only operated abroad but required local firms in poor nations to participate in production by supplying simple inputs and components. At first, simple supply chain networks developed around plants, but as knowledge about production cumulated these capabilities expanded over time to include wider regions and even across national boundaries. The emergence of regional and even global production networks, based on the new information and communication technologies, led to new opportunities for poor nations.

The creation and proliferation of global production networks (GPNs) represent the most transformative feature of the post-1980 global economy. These are complex systems of production, knowledge flows, and investment organized among firms and nations. The role of global/regional production networks in the diffusion of knowledge and in lowering the barriers to entry for many poor nations is very significant. We have previously examined the origins and development of GPNs in relation to trade in Chapter 5. Briefly, global production networks are systems of production, investment, trade, and knowledge exchange typically among a set of companies and nations organized around a major global brand or set of brands. The GPN is created as the value chain for a product is split up into activities that can be outsourced to specialized firms, which typically cluster in a single region. The coordination of this system usually comes from a single "global flagship" company engaged in the design, development, and branding of the product(s), often in conjunction with contract manufacturing firms able to organize and coordinate the product design with production and assembly. The GPN system has been concentrated in Asia and is directly related to the rapid growth of many nations in this region.[14] The combination of new technologies, the creation of the complex systems of trade, production, investment, and knowledge represented in GPNs, and the policies of liberalization of trade have produced a dramatic set of opportunities for poor nations to create the conditions for rapid economic growth.

The global/regional production network has been an essential feature in the diffusion of knowledge from developed states to emerging economies that accompanied the rapid expansion of FDI and the building of production facilities in these societies. And this system of knowledge and investment created vast opportunities for exporting by these same emerging economies to the markets of developed nations. The industrialization of previously poor nations and the resulting rapid economic growth has reversed the patterns for global distribution of GDP over nearly two centuries. As we see in Figure 8.4, the proportion of global GDP accounted for by the richest seven nations increased dramatically and with no interruption from 1820 until the late 1980s, peaking in 1988. Since then it has fallen quite dramatically with the rise of emerging economies.

G7 share of world GDP, 1820–2010

Figure 8.4 The Shifting Distribution of Global GDP.

Source **Overall Competitiveness Score**: Adapted from Richard Baldwin, "Global Supply Chains: Why They Emerged, Why They Matter, and Where They Are Going," Fung Global Institute, Working Paper FGI–2012–1, 2012, 8, with permission from Richard Baldwin.

If we focus on the GDP ratios of developed and developing nations over just the past quarter-century, an astonishing transformation has taken place. In 1990, developed nations generated 80 percent of global GDP and developed nations just 20 percent, a distribution that had persisted since the beginning of the twentieth century. But by 2015, the ratio is very close to 50:50.[15] No change of this speed and magnitude has ever happened before; as we see from Figure 8.4, in the nineteenth century such a comparable shift required eighty years, from 1820–1900.

How did this happen? In our terms, the expansion of GPNs led to the dispersion of competitive capabilities and through knowledge diffusion built a base for the upgrading of capabilities among an expanding number of poor nations. In a broader sense, the production of a good has become the result of a complex system of global and regional economic exchange based on organizing a complementary system of competitive capabilities distributed across many nations.

In another sense, the rapid and large-scale impact of GPNs, focused on the development of poor nations, reflects a new basis for global economic competition. Knowledge has become the primary source for adding value to products and services, for increasing productivity, and for achieving innovation. As such, knowledge creation, diffusion, sharing, and application across global knowledge networks connected to global production networks have become the most important source of global competitiveness. The remarkable speed with which emerging economies have gained a prominent global position demonstrates the effects of the ability of these nations to create local infrastructure that compliments low wages, attract FDI, and build industrial capabilities. Subsequently, these nations have been able to leverage existing knowledge to upgrade those capabilities and achieve sustainable growth. Not only have trends of the last two centuries been reversed, but nations that were quite poor in 1990 have collectively reached a rough equality in share of global trade and soon will achieve parity in proportion of global GDP.

These changes can also be seen in rates of economic growth displayed in Figure 8.5, which demonstrate an equally significant deviation from past patterns. As we see, developed and developing nations experience declining rates of economic growth after 1950, which persist for developed states until 2010. And the rate of growth for developing nations remains below that for developed states until the mid-1980s. At that point rates of growth for these nations surge upward and now stand much above those of developed states.

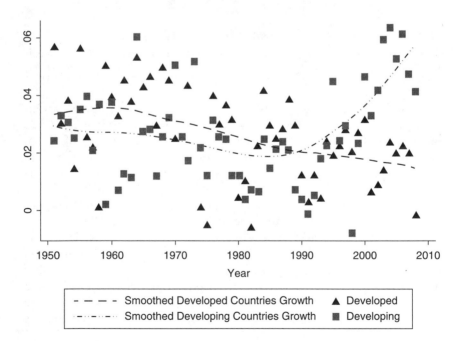

Figure 8.5 Rates of Economic Growth, Developed and Developing Nations 1950–2010.

Source: Adapted from Richard Baldwin, "Trade and Industrialisation after Globalisation's Second Unbundling," NBER Working Paper 17716 (December 2011) 2, with permission from Richard Baldwin.

The Global Competitive Environment

These changes in the global economy significantly affect the competitive environment for states and for firms. Much of the global economy has been altered with new and complex arrangements for the division of labor and the distribution of gains from trade. The fragmentation of supply chains and the distribution of value added from this system have produced a new set of global structures. GPNs shift transactions and exchange that previously took place within firms and factories and certainly within nations, and split them up into separate transactions among different firms and simultaneously disperse these operations and transactions around the world. The process of global trade has shifted from a traditional exchange of physical goods across borders to a complex system of transactions involving parts and components, various forms of FDI, new private and public systems of infrastructure for exchange such as logistics, port services, training for workers, educational systems, trade-related finance, bargains between firms and nations regarding the terms of production, and knowledge flows generated directly and indirectly by this system. Contemporary trade involves continuous, multidirectional, globalized flows of things, people, training, investment, and information that used to take place within national factories and offices. A very significant outcome of this form of globalization is the generation of interdependence that is deep and complex and different from the interdependence in the past.

The new forms of globalization have important consequences for the processes of global competition. The goods produced in the past were the result primarily of the capabilities of one nation – the comparative advantages of the nation and the competitive advantages of the nation's firms. The production of goods and services is now the result of the ability to combine various "packages of *many nations*" productive factors: technology, infrastructure, wage levels, human capital, knowledge institutions, social capital, and governance capacity. In many ways, a nation's trade pattern is now inseparable from its position in the global supply chain.[16]

Flowing across these networks, in addition to the goods being produced, is investment capital, knowledge, technology, and opportunities for firms and nations. Global production networks rest on a set of nations and national policies that created environments in which these networks can flourish, usually in partnerships with global firms. The governments of many nations were prepared to devote the resources required for the hard and soft infrastructure needed to attract foreign direct investment: roads, electric power systems and grids, water systems, communication systems, transportation systems, airports, education systems, legal systems, and credible government commitments to maintain and expand these capabilities through time. Very often these governments were essential in supporting and even providing the entrepreneurial capabilities to develop local firms and organize the local business systems needed to sustain a transnational firm's operations. These same governments were also frequently engaged in strategies that propelled their nations into new and higher value-added capabilities, providing the investment capital and the incentives, and obtaining the technology and knowledge required. It was these nations that make up the major winners among emerging economies.

This new system of political economy alters substantially the environment for competition by nations and firms. Increasingly today, the level of productivity growth of one firm, locality, or region derives from the ability to assemble a set of complementary resources from all over the world that generate new and/or enhanced capabilities. This is a system involving the globalization of competitiveness and it has significant consequences for the nature and speed of economic change.

The dynamics of economic change affecting emerging and developed economies can be seen in different forms at the level of firms, regions, and individuals. From the position of a firm, the speed and scale of competition has accelerated and expanded geographically. The rate of technological change has increased significantly and the sources of competitive advantage have shifted toward a global scale of capabilities, with the result that most forms of competitive advantage for firms are temporary. A product's life cycle has shortened because even a significantly new product will rapidly encounter strong competitors from firms all over the world pursuing a fast-follower strategy. And this new product must be produced quickly, requiring a globally competitive supply chain – composed of the set of competencies of companies and countries across the world – to reap the gains available for only a short time.[17]

Various observers frequently comment on the experience of rapid change, a kind of Moore's Law applied to the pace of economic change.[18] The result is an equally rapid rise and fall for firms in global competition. For examples, we need only look at the impact of Wal-Mart on the fates of traditionally important retail discount stores such as K-Mart in the 1980s and 1990s. More recently, Amazon has had devastating effects on the price discounting stores such as Best Buy and book retailers such as Borders. And Apple's iPhone quickly took down the previously dominant smartphone, Blackberry.[19] The pace of innovation and technological change has accelerated so much it has led to a rising turbulence in markets, so the number and relative positions of firms in global market share rise and fall quickly and with much greater variation, a result of hyper-competition.[20] Nations that fail to take aggressive efforts to sustain competitive improvements find themselves quickly falling behind.

Global systems of production have permitted and even encouraged rapid and significant growth by previously poor nations. But the actual distribution of gains from these systems – as revealed by the locus of value added – is decidedly skewed in favor of the global flagship firm and the nations with such firms. The distribution of gains across the value chain is highly differentiated and unequal, with owners of knowledge-intensive resources gaining the most while owners of unskilled labor benefiting the least. Figure 8.6 shows a shifting distribution of value added across supply chains comparing the 1970s and the early twenty-first century. The manufacturing stage has seen a significant decline, owing primarily to declines in the wages for low-skilled workers in that stage, while the knowledge-intensive stages of product, concept, design, and marketing have seen a relative value-added rise proportionately.

These highly important changes can also be illustrated in the supply chain of individual firms. Apple has enjoyed remarkable success over the past fifteen years in developing and marketing new products and this success is measured by its very high profit margins. Like almost all advanced electronics firms, Apple operates with a fragmented supply chain with the design, development, and research and development of its products located in the United States while the various components of its devices and the assembly are outsourced to a multitude of firms in Asia.[21] When we sort out the location of production and the value added to the final product from this activity, we can see the starkly different distribution of the gains from global production.

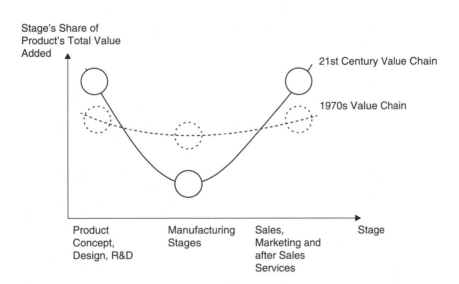

Figure 8.6 The "Smile Curve" of Changing Value Added Across the Supply Chain.

Source: Adapted from Richard Baldwin, "Global Supply Chains: Why They Emerged, Why They Matter, and Where They Are Going," Fung Global Institute, Working Paper FGI–2012–1, 2012, 18, with permission from Richard Baldwin.

These differential distributions can be seen in the Apple iPod. Profits to Apple represent 30 percent of the total value of the iPod, the distribution and retailing yield 15 percent of the value added, while labor costs in China and elsewhere represent only 7 percent of the value of the iPod.[22] The same patterns can be seen in the production of more recent products, such as an iPhone and iPad.[23] At the same time, the gains represented in the value chain are decidedly tilted toward knowledge workers in the United States, there is an even larger imbalance in the global distribution of employment. Apple directly employs 43,000 persons in the United States and another 20,000 outside the United States, but those firms operating in Apple's supply chain employ another 700,000 workers in other countries.[24]

The global competitive environment has been dramatically affected by new technologies, new forms of production, and by the extraordinary rise of emerging economies. Global exchange relationships have become immensely more complex, composed of networks of exchange of closely related components produced in many nations. This system of value added creates a new distribution of gains and losses, and itself reflects underlying networks of investment, knowledge flows, complementary production capabilities, and political bargains. This system also has evolved over time, as the pace of change and innovation accelerates and the turbulence in markets affects firms and nations. The depth and complexity of interdependence arising from this system binds nations into new sets of relationships. We turn now to a consideration of the nature and effectiveness of competitiveness strategies adopted by nations and firms within this environment.

Strategies of Competitiveness

The leaders and citizens of all nations have a distinct preference for which places succeed the most in the global economy. As a consequence, the policies and political economy of policymaking regarding the economy usually involve a set of calculations about the effects on prospects for growth, jobs, and innovation.[25] This section will review the array of actions taken by nations in the expectation of creating economic gains.

There is a remarkably large number and diversity of such actions and policies. Nations are constantly engaged in efforts to shape markets in their favor and boost the capabilities of particular industries and even firms, and often seek to anticipate markets by investing in future trends. Strategies for the adjustment of the national economy to the demands of the global economy are commonly asserted and enacted. However, often such efforts draw criticism from neoliberal analysts, who consistently assert these policies will lead to negative economic outcomes. We will review a large sample of the kinds of policies adopted and consider the effectiveness of such efforts.

The Variety of State Policies and Actions

States vary considerably in the ability to act effectively in designing and implementing strategies and policies to promote competitiveness.[26] A considerable part of these differences comes from the historical legacies of state capacities and the political abilities of leaders. The political struggle to reduce state capacities during the nineteenth and twentieth centuries has been most intense in the United States and Great Britain, where advocates of limited government have often successfully worked to undermine and block an active state. By contrast, in many nations state prerogatives derive from long traditions of significant state power. Japan and China present two examples of nations where the state has long enjoyed an extensive and largely unchallenged role in society and economy. Also influencing state policies is the presence or absence of large amounts of natural and social resources. Saudi Arabia and Venezuela have options for economic policy owing to large amounts of oil, a situation quite different from Singapore or Finland. At the same time, large populations combined with large markets create options for complex specialization unavailable to a small nation.

There is no standard set of competitiveness policies and strategies, so we will invent appropriate categories for purposes of organization (see "Competitiveness Policies" below).[27] Perhaps surprisingly, the list is quite long.

Competitiveness Policies

Macroeconomic Policies

> Monetary and Fiscal Policy
> Tax policies
> Welfare
> Interest Rate and Exchange Rate policies
> Trade policies
> Regulatory policies
> Inward and Outward Foreign Investment policies
> Labor policies
> Intellectual Property
> Innovation and innovation ecosystem

Investment Policies

> Education and Human Resource policies
> Infrastructure policies

Science and Technology Basic Research
Knowledge production and certification
Government relationship to national financial system
Specialized investment agencies – DARPA, ITRI, EDB
Industrial policies
Differentiation of various policies by sector and even by firm
Government Ownership of Economic Enterprises

Global Economy Strategies

Press for multilateral policies on opening or closing the global
  economy
Create or modify global institutions
Regional rules and agreements on systems of exchange such as
  FTAs/RTAs

Macroeconomic policies are frequently developed and implemented to enhance the competitive qualities of a nation. One long-standing goal of macroeconomic policy is price stability, which if achieved can help to ensure that market forces will operate correctly. In addition, a significant strategy focuses on the cost of labor as a key input to the cost of production. Several macroeconomic policies, such as welfare benefits, labor rules, tax, and regulatory policies have considerable effects for the cost of labor. Financial policies in the regulation and ownership of financial firms influence greatly the nature of capital allocation in a nation. Recently in the United States, financial firms were given much greater latitude and freedom based on the belief that more markets would lead to better decisions on lending and investment and promote the growth of this industry.

It is in the area of investment where the largest differences in nations appear. This is not surprising, given the critical importance of capital allocation for the effectiveness of a capitalist economy. Nations have quite different traditions and ideas on the degree of control and direction needed by government policy over the financial sector. And these differences often affect the kinds of investment and the amount of investment that takes place in a nation. In Table 8.2, we see measures of gross fixed capital formation, which includes expenditures on improvements for land, plant, equipment and machinery, roads, bridges, schools, hospitals, offices, and residential housing. This level of investment is often linked to rates of economic growth, as it represents resources devoted to building and improving the productive assets of a nation.

The data suggest important differences among the sample of nations and somewhat over time for each nation. The richest nations tend to have the

Table 8.2 Gross Fixed Capital Formation (GFCF) (Average % of GDP, 1993–2011)

Country	1993–1997	1998–2002	2003–2007	2008–2011
Australia	24%	24%	27%	28%
Brazil	19%	17%	17%	20%
China	41%	37%	42%	47%
France	17%	19%	20%	20%
Germany	22%	21%	18%	17%
Indonesia	31%	19%	25%	31%
Japan	28%	24%	23%	21%
Korea	37%	29%	30%	29%
Mexico	22%	23%	25%	25%
United States	18%	20%	19%	16%
Vietnam	26%	30%	36%	38%

Source: Data from the World Bank, http://data.worldbank.org/indicator/NE.GDI.TOTL.ZS

lowest level of gross fixed capital formation (GFCF) and generally tend to have much higher expenditures for consumption. Poorer nations, needing to build basic infrastructure, tend to have higher levels of GFCF. And, the Asian nations in this group, whether rich or poor, tend to have much higher levels than all other nations. These differences are the result of different national policies and have large consequences for national competitiveness.

There are also significant differences in how financial allocation decisions are made and the kinds of investments that result. Some forms of capital investment are more productive and enhance competitiveness more than others. For example, residential housing, though certainly a positive force for growth, has less positive effect on productivity than investment in capital equipment, education, or in research and development. In a mostly market-driven financial system, the price signals for investment will be driven by consumers and preferences for consumption. If those preferences favor housing over education or R&D, then investment allocation will flow in that direction. At the same time, very few societies are willing to let investment choices be driven entirely by market forces. Rather, taxes are imposed on citizens and the state engages in considerable investment on military preparation, basic science, education, and infrastructure, much of which would not take place in a purely market- and profit-based environment. What distinguishes nations is the degree and manner in which the state affects investment choices.

This can come in many ways. One is to affect the way decisions about consumption and savings are made. In a society such as the United States, where credit is easy for making consumer purchases, saving is discouraged. However, in many Asian nations, where building national savings was essential to accumulating the capital needed for economic development, consumer debt is discouraged and saving is encouraged. By requiring high levels (or low levels) of down payments for housing purchases, governments can greatly affect savings rates. Additionally, providing effective welfare safety nets can reduce the incentives for savings. The ability of a government to adopt such measures may be a result of its strength or autonomy from domestic business interests.[28] Generally, savings rates are higher where governments have a large role in the financial system, such as in owning or heavily influencing investment allocation policies. In China, the central government holds a controlling interest in the major banks of the nation and frequently issues directives to these banks to make certain kinds of investment decisions. In many ways, China has followed in the footsteps of Japan, Singapore, and Taiwan in establishing this financial system (see "Chinese Infrastructure" below).[29] This has permitted extraordinary high levels of investment as a primary driver of productivity and economic growth in China. Look at Table 8.2 and you will note the very high levels of investment by China. One important consequence has been the ability to rapidly transform a very poor nation into one with quite good infrastructure.

Chinese Infrastructure

The large expenditures for capital investment by China are often easily visible in the buildings, subways, and fast trains. Such infrastructure creates physical spaces that attract business investment and operate to enlarge and integrate markets.

Photo 8.1 The Iconic Skyline of Pudong in Shanghai.
Source: Picture taken by Sally Lairson.

Photo 8.2 Travelers on the Shanghai Subway.

Source: Picture taken by Sally Lairson.

Note: In a city of more than 20 million, you can go from any point to any other point for 3 RMB, or about 50 US cents. The effect is to integrate many markets in and around the city. On one day in 2010, more than 7 million persons rode the Shanghai subway.

Photo 8.3 The Fast Train Ready to Leave Beijing.

Source: Picture taken by Sally Lairson.

Note: At about 180 MPH (300 KPH), these trains travel to Shanghai very quickly. The one-way cost is about $55 US.

For much of the post-World War II era, Germany and Japan have stood out from the United States in the way their financial systems operate. There, corporations received financing mainly from banks, in the form of loans. This is unlike the United States, where financing has been more from investors willing to own stock. These differences mean that banks coordinate the investment process in Germany and Japan, whereas in the United States, stock markets have a much more prominent role. For example, banks in Germany and Japan often place their officials in management positions in firms receiving loans. The governments of these nations have operated in something of a partnership relationship with these banks in providing strategic direction to the Japanese and German economies. A main outcome of these systems has been a stronger tendency to provide "patient" finance to firms, with a propensity to adopt a longer-term perspective, as opposed to the somewhat "impatient" capital drawn from equity investors and even from banks in the United States.[30] The result is to create a capitalist system in Germany and Japan that emphasizes longer-term payoffs to investment; but in the United States the financial incentives push managers to maximize short-term profits.

National Systems of Competitiveness

In considering the range and array of policies and institutions for competitiveness that nations adopt, scholars have examined the effectiveness of different forms of economic–political–business systems with different competitive strengths and weaknesses. Thinking about how nations might create distinctive forms of competitiveness has led to consideration of how national policies interact with patterns of business and economic relationships. One widely used approach sees the competitiveness of a nation and its firms as closely connected, with the capabilities of a firm resulting from the national environment in which it develops. Broadly, the competitive advantages of a nation derive from the interaction of the business strategies of its firms, the demands of its markets for high-quality products, the strengths of the firms and their capabilities, and the quality of the labor force, financial system, and infrastructure. The competitive position of firms in national and global economies is a result of the opportunities and resources created by the combination of national policies and the strengths generated by firms and markets.[31] This approach asserts a complex relationship among a variety of influences rather than simply one kind of action or policy. The competitive advantages of firms and of nations interact and cumulate to build a competitive system.

The systems approach to competitiveness also carries into studies of different kinds of capitalism and the innovation systems that develop in different nations. Much of this research has focused on specifying and analyzing the relationships among firms, institutions, and national policies, as these affect the competitive and innovative capacities of firms and nations. One frequent form of analysis divides the systems of political economy in advanced capitalist nations into three categories: liberal market economies, coordinated market economies, and state-managed economies.[32] An important topic for this research is to understand how a particular configuration of institutions – labor, financial, governmental, and firms – leads to institutional and comparative advantages in the production and development of certain kinds of goods and services. This area of investigation has also led to a focus on how different institutional systems can be more and less effective at innovation. And a broader concern has examined the various ways capitalist systems change in relation to each other and as a result of changes in the global economy.[33] Work on national innovation systems has concentrated on understanding how institutional systems learn, diffuse information and knowledge, and sustain firms in efforts to innovate. The levels of R&D investment, the nature and effectiveness of educational systems, and the incentives for long-term over short-term and for higher-risk investment are examples of capabilities examined.[34]

The Developmental State and State Capitalism

Perhaps the most challenging form of analysis of the role of government activity in economic growth and competitiveness comes from the examination of the policies and capabilities of several Asian nations over the past several decades. This discussion has focused on the concept of the developmental state and more recently has shifted to a consideration of state capitalism. Each perspective sees a pattern of very significant state direction of the economy linked to the spectacular economic success of many Asian nations over the past forty years.

A developmental state is a particular kind of governmental strategy for achieving rapid economic growth based on significant engagement with the global economy and continuing efforts to upgrade the competitive capabilities of the nation and (at least some of) its firms.[35] The term was initially used to analyze the Japanese economy from the 1930s to the 1970s and was later applied to understand the effectiveness of Korea, Taiwan, and Singapore from the 1960s to the 1990s and beyond. Some have found the Chinese achievement of rapid growth a result of the actions and policies of the Chinese state, in all its complexities, though others find the concept of state capitalism more appropriate for understanding China.

The main element of a developmental state is a high governmental commitment to achieving rapid economic growth, typically in order to enhance the security position of the nation.[36] Accomplishing this goal involves an extensive array of state policies and actions designed to push growth forward. Sometimes this involved state ownership of firms

(Singapore, China, and Taiwan) but more typically direct state involvement in accumulating and allocating capital (Korea, Singapore, and China). The state also acted to manage economic relations with the rest of the world through tariffs but also with efforts to attract FDI (Singapore and China) or attract technology and knowledge (Korea and Taiwan). The state often created special economic zones (SEZs) within the nation that combined high-quality infrastructure and low tariffs as production platforms for foreign investors. The multinational corporations (MNCs) engaging in FDI in these SEZs were often required by the state to share technology and knowledge with local firms. Frequently, local firms would receive various forms of protection from foreign competition and also be required to enter global competition through exports. Government efforts were often of central importance for the creation of firms and the encouragement of entrepreneurial activities. Developmental states saw high levels of investment in mandatory and universal education as essential to building the capacity for improving the competitive position of local firms and the ability to attract and absorb technology and knowledge. Very often, local firms were strongly encouraged to develop the capabilities to enter new markets and product spaces. And governments were active in creating specialized bureaucracies to manage the development process, including the ability to gain access to important knowledge (semiconductors in Taiwan) and disseminate this to local firms.[37]

In short, developmental states were engaged in nothing less than the creation of an entire national competitiveness system. The early developmental state success stories were focused on several small Asian nations exceptionally able to engage in exports of manufactured goods.[38] The economic rise of China both seemed to confirm and expand the conceptual boundaries of the developmental state. The initial developmental states were thought to have a coherent and centralized organizational apparatus consisting of a unified executive and an effective bureaucracy able to define and implement developmental policies. Though elements of this characterization have some merit, much more of the policymaking was based on a trial and error process and significant divisions in the state often appeared.[39]

The Chinese state does not conform well in structural terms to the typical notion of the developmental state.[40] Contrary to many expectations about China, the Chinese state is composed not only of the central party-state apparatus but also multiple layers of provincial and local party-state organizations with considerable degrees of latitude and capacity for initiative in policy implementation. It is more accurate to characterize the Chinese state as a plurality of "states," an arrangement that can be analogized to federal systems in many respects.[41] The binding glue for the Chinese states is the Chinese Communist Party, which operates a parallel set of monitoring and governing structures alongside the various levels of the Chinese state.[42]

Though the complexity of the Chinese system produces many examples of conflicting and even contradictory actions and outcomes, the cumulative result of Chinese state policy is both deeply economic and developmental in effect. The Chinese states are organized so as to promote economic growth, with the structure of party-state incentives directed toward engaging in entrepreneurial actions to raise economic growth. An important statement of "Sino-capitalism" describes this relationship as one with a "a unique duality that combines top-down state-led development with bottom-up entrepreneurial private capital accumulation."[43] The multiplicity of entrepreneurial relationships among the various layers of the state and the emerging private systems produces a degree of dynamism to Chinese political economy somewhat distinctive from traditional developmental states. However, given these arrangements and economic outcomes, there can be little doubt that China conforms in many important ways to the developmental state(s) process.

Other scholars have begun to characterize China and other nations with the term "state capitalism," a concept that widens the perspective about the role of national governments in terms of influencing overall economic activity in general and competitiveness in particular.[44] State capitalism involves a system of political economy in which the state strategically influences market relations for purposes of national and even global economic and political gain. This approach focuses on the role of states like China not only in controlling financial accumulation and allocation, but also in developing state investment agencies – sovereign wealth funds – able to use the funds for national and global investments. If we add together the assets of the largest seven of the sovereign wealth funds (Table 8.3), these total an investment pool of over $4 trillion in 2012. The total of all Sovereign Wealth Funds (SWFs) in 2012 was $5,283 trillion.[45] An additional feature of state capitalism is the large role of state-owned enterprises (SOEs), especially in what government leaders define as strategic industries, such as energy and telecommunications,

Table 8.3 Largest Sovereign Wealth Funds, 2012

Country	Assets (trillions $US)
China	1.185
UAE – Abu Dhabi	.745
Norway	.716
Saudi Arabia	.533
Singapore	.405
Hong Kong	.298
Kuwait	.296
Total	4.180

Source: Data from Sovereign Wealth Fund Institute, www.swfinstitute.org/fund-rankings/

and usually managed by professionals. Somewhat surprisingly, many of the Chinese SOEs have engaged in selling partial ownership to private shareholders and take on many of the features of a private firm even as they retain aspects of state ownership and control.[46]

In addition to the analysis of countries like China and state capitalism, this concept can also embrace a system in which the state operates in a partnership with private finance to press for financial opening in other societies, deregulates finance to attract global capital, and intervenes in markets with bailouts in times of systemic crisis. This description fits the United States and suggests the variety of state capitalism, especially when the focus of analysis is on competitiveness. Analogously, in China many nominally private firms have significant political, social, and economic links to the state, which often act as a partner in promoting growth.

Case Studies of Competitiveness Strategies

There is considerable variety to the ways governments act to improve the competitive position of firms and economies. We offer now several case studies to help illustrate this variety. These case studies include efforts by three nations to bolster their positions in high technology and an effort by one, the United States, to design new rules for trade.

The US Government in the Knowledge Value Chain

The leading edge of global competition is concentrated in innovation in a variety of high-technology industries, where the basis of competition is the ability of firms to leverage existing and new knowledge into new products, processes, and organizations. In areas such as biotechnology, new materials, advanced information technology, new energy sources, and advanced manufacturing such as 3D printing, significant resources are devoted to basic science in universities and research labs, followed by additional R&D in corporate labs focused on developing new products. In related industries, such as automobiles and robotics, advances in software related to artificial intelligence and in hardware related new kinds of microprocessors – with important links to advances in basic research – lead to new products, new capabilities for existing products, and new forms of manufacturing.[47]

For decades, scholars and policymakers have understood that knowledge-intensive industries have a complicated value chain that often requires a quite direct role for government agencies. This is because advanced knowledge typically has an uncertain link – in time and in application – to new products. This leads to very limited investment by profit-oriented firms in the creation of new and especially advanced knowledge. In the United States, significant investment in the creation of advanced and basic knowledge, often with no apparent link to profitable products, came during

World War II and the Manhattan Project. After 1945, this investment widened to include an ongoing and significant investment in university-based and corporate research by the US government in many scientific fields. The National Science Foundation (NSF), the National Institutes of Health (NIH), the National Institute of Standards and Technology (NIST), the Atomic Energy Commission (now part of the Department of Energy), the National Aeronautics and Space Administration (NASA), and a variety of agencies in the Defense Department – in particular, the Defense Advanced Research Projects Agency (DARPA) – were created to finance and direct basic research and other efforts to increase the production and application of scientific knowledge. These organizations, and others, were central to the massive expansion of government funding for knowledge creation, diffusion, and application. In 2012, the combined expenditures by NIH and NSF were about $38 billion,[48] while the entire R&D budget for the US government in 2012 was $140.8 billion.[49] From 1953–2008, in real dollars the US government spent $1.2 trillion for research and contributed mightily to the development of world-class universities and the commercial powerhouse in Silicon Valley.[50]

The role of the US government in boosting R&D is not unusual. Moreover, the source of spending on R&D across nations varies considerably. In relation to GDP, Israel is the global leader in R&D spending at more than 4 percent of GDP. The German and South Korean governments are major sources of R&D spending, as compared with other top nations and the OECD averages. However, for all top nations, the dominant source of R&D has come from business. The ability to translate these expenditures into patents also varies considerably, with Switzerland, Japan, and Sweden generating patents at a much higher rate than nations such as Canada and Australia.[51]

In the United States, perhaps the most interesting of the government agencies engaged in knowledge production and application is the Defense Advanced Research Projects Agency. Created in 1958, in the wake of the Sputnik crisis, DARPA has been an essential player in the development of some of the most important technologies of the past half-century.[52] Because its mission is to advance the military capabilities of the United States, DARPA has taken on an entrepreneurial role in defining important directions for research, by assuming responsibility for assembling knowledge resources from government, industry, and education to develop new technologies, and even by funding the development of the knowledge infrastructure for new industries. These actions are a result of the special mission given to DARPA, namely to think into the future, to anticipate and even promote technological innovations, and to seek out technological developments so as to advance the security of the United States.[53]

DARPA has a long and illustrious legacy in what can be termed recombinant innovation, taking previously unconnected ideas and reassembling them to create new capabilities. An early example was creation of the new field of materials science, in order to develop materials able to withstand the extreme heat of reentry of space capsules into the atmosphere. Or the effort to detect underground nuclear explosions, which required the creation of a global system of monitoring devices and a communication network sending data into one computer network.[54] As with many new areas of scientific study, the spillover effects of new knowledge into unanticipated areas has often proved more important than the original purpose.

Surely the most important and far-reaching advances to come from DARPA are in the area of computing, information technology, and computer networks, in particular, from the ideas of J.C.R. Licklider.[55] DARPA was the organizer of research in several university centers for computer science across the United States and this system was essential for the major advances in computer–human interfaces – such as the computer mouse – that emerged and eventually changed the role of computers in human life.[56] In the 1960s, DARPA was essential in recognizing the potential of a national and even global computer network (what today we call the Internet) and mobilized the funding and knowledge resources in universities and private firms to develop and build a working system in 1969, known as Arpanet. Over the next several years, DARPA worked with universities to develop Internet protocols and deploy a system across the nation for these universities.[57]

During the 1970s, DARPA took steps to promote development of radical advances in chip design with the RISC chip, advances that would lead to new capabilities for personal computers and other applications. And throughout the time from the 1960s to the 1980s, DARPA funded and promoted the development of computer science departments in US universities, thereby creating the knowledge base for development of a much more vigorous software industry.[58] More recently, from 2004–7, DARPA sponsored a race among contestants using driverless cars and awarding a $2 million prize for finishing first over a prescribed course. The goal was to accelerate the development of autonomous vehicles, and the knowledge gained has led Google to deploy self-driving cars.[59]

An essential feature of these processes and successes was the deep linkages between DARPA, universities, and industry through funding and information networks largely created by DARPA. These linkages provided the knowledge and information base for anticipating technology developments and organizing the knowledge teams to implement new technological capabilities. For example, the first truly modern personal computer – the Alto at Xerox PARC – had many of its key software and hardware features supported and developed through DARPA.[60] Contrary to neoliberal ideology, this state unit has been the entrepreneurial agent for the assembly of knowledge resources and the creation, advancement, and dissemination of technologies that have not only improved US security but have added countless trillions of dollars to US and global GDP. The competitive position of the United States in many areas of advanced technology owes much to DARPA.

DARPA's critical role in advancing an array of information and communication technologies along with the development of knowledge-intensive industries should not be surprising.[61] The US government is deeply involved in the knowledge value chain for most advanced technologies, including the biomedical and pharmaceutical industries. The National Institute of Health is a major source of funding for basic research, especially in university medical schools throughout the United States.[62] Of course, this finances not only research but also the education of doctors and researchers. Much of this funding supports risky research with a long and uncertain link to commercialization. The production of knowledge at the level of basic research is mainly the result of a partnership between the US government and the major research universities in the United States. For example, at the Massachusetts Institute of Technology (MIT) in recent years more than $1 billion in research is conducted annually. The federal government supplies about 79 percent of those funds.[63]

This funding, primarily from NIH, NSF, and the Defense Department, does not substitute for but complements the considerable R&D from biomedical-related firms that is even larger. Rather, the knowledge value chain is one in which basic research is conducted at institutions like MIT, while applied research is conducted in for-profit firms. And the profits that ultimately come from this research all redound to these private firms. Profits for US pharmaceutical firms are exceptionally high, measured by profit margin and by return on investment. The knowledge value chain for medical capabilities in the United States and the world includes the US government as an essential partner, not simply as a source of money but as an active participant in knowledge creation, evaluation, and diffusion.[64] The NIH engages in an evaluation of the many applicants for funding and makes choices about which projects are most deserving. And remember, the Food and Drug Administration engages in extensive testing and certification of the efficacy and safety of new drugs.[65] It is not an exaggeration to say the essential input for the biomedical industry – knowledge – and the process for establishing the legitimacy of the products to customers is provided by the US government. But this conclusion is also appropriate for the development of technology across a number of areas.[66]

How are we to understand and explain this vital state role in the development of the most innovative and often most profitable products of the past several decades? Is this just an aberration or are there deeper reasons why governments must be involved? We consider these questions after examining other related cases of state actions in promoting competitiveness.

Israel and Finland Enter Global High-Tech Markets

Can small nations with populations of less than 10 million, and competing in an era of rapid globalization, develop strategies for participating successfully in global markets in the most advanced of products and industries? What kinds of political situations drive nations toward attempting such a daunting task and what kinds of pathways have nations followed in these efforts? What are the sectors for entry into global markets and what strategies lead to success in these markets?

Israel

For Israel, not surprisingly, the somewhat extreme security environment and the importance of military capabilities served as the major force for the development of high-tech capabilities.[67] Israel had an important advantage when the loss of advanced military weaponry from France in 1967 provoked a security crisis that led to the effort to advance an indigenous technology capability. An important base for information technology capabilities already existed in strong universities and a small level of defense-related R&D located in the military. Using a trial and error process and drawing on ideas that emerged from close government–business relationships, the concept emerged of state incentives for the promotion of industry-based R&D in high-technology industries to boost military capabilities and economic growth.

This strategy was premised on the recognition that entrepreneurs in a nation like Israel were very reluctant to assume the risks of investment in developing products for advanced industries through in-house R&D. Standard market signals for investors, financiers, and entrepreneurs do not usually point in this direction, given both the intense global competition and the considerable uncertainty for such investments. At the same time, state and business officials came to believe that with government support the building blocks for creating high-tech industries in Israel could be assembled. With resources focused in two state agencies, competitive grants to supplement business R&D funds were launched in the 1970s. Firms initiated the proposals based on their judgments about market opportunities and the Israeli state provided partial funding that was repaid from royalties. A key ingredient was connections developed by a state agency with the US financial community and with US firms. A primary early strategy was for Israeli firms to develop products that would be designed and made in Israel and sold in the United States by an American partner. The Israeli state agency provided contacts and key knowledge resources for establishing and developing the US connection. Often, this would lead to an initial public offering and listing of the Israeli firm's shares on the US NASDAQ stock exchange.

The Israeli state played an important, even essential, role in the creation and nurturing of high-tech industries in Israel. It was central in supporting the process of knowledge creation, development, and diffusion, in promoting the entrepreneurial and risk-taking ethos, and in sustaining the evolution of the industry in keeping pace with global technological and economic changes. The base of capabilities created by state-firm relations evolved considerably over time. From the 1970s to the present, a globally significant series of Israeli high-tech industries were developed, mainly in information technology, telecommunications, software, and medical technology. The financing for numerous firms was provided by R&D funding and many others grew out of defense-related R&D that was carried into the establishment of private firms. Operating at the global leading edge of technology, Israeli firms became key players, especially in the US technology space. The results for GDP growth are in Table 8.4.

The initial focus on information technology and telecommunications helped spawn a new focus on software, also with government support helping private firms to follow the market, and often by creating the market for new products. The state was the origin of R&D financing, connections to the United States, and frequently of the entrepreneurs themselves. The evolution of Israeli high-tech industries evolved along with the capabilities and strategies of the Israeli state. In the 1980s and 1990s, state agencies promoted new initiatives to create physical and financial opportunities to incubate new technology firms. These were firms with good ideas but with limited business skills. The incubators allowed the firms to form and operate for several years to improve the product and learn business and management skills. A second major state initiative was to develop a venture capital industry in Israel where none previously existed. A state-financed venture capital fund – Yozma – was established to fill a void. Its successes drew out private funding and the knowledge base of managers in Yozma flowed into these private venture capital firms. The Israeli state also was successful in developing R&D consortia that assembled several firms into joint efforts. The result was the blossoming of a complex set of high-technology firms in related industries with global connections and competitive strengths.

Table 8.4 Israel: Real GDP Growth Rate

Country	1999	2000	2002	2003	2004	2005	2006	2007	2008	2009	2010	2011
Israel	2.1	5.9	–1.1	1.3	3.9	5.2	4.8	5.3	4.2	0.2	4.6	4.7

Source: Data from www.indexmundi.com/g/g.aspx?v=66&c=is&l=en; www.indexmundi.com/israel/gdp_real_growth_rate.html

Finland

Finland provides another instructive case in which a very small nation (population 5 million) has been successful in entering global high-tech markets with significant support by the government.[68] The Finns' ability to succeed in the rapidly evolving and turbulent environment of high technology is all the more striking given the traditional basis of the nation's political economy in a system of neo-corporatism, low-tech natural resource industries, and deep economic connections to the Soviet Union. Based on an inclusionary system of stakeholders, with stable and even conservative bargains requiring mutual accommodation and incremental change, such a system seems especially mismatched against a market demanding rapid adaptation. Moreover, long-standing and large trade relations with the Soviets, a country that collapsed as a result of its economically uncompetitive position, would seem a major barrier to operating in any globally competitive industries. Competing in a high-tech world would seem to demand an especially strong commitment to a neoliberal system of labor flexibility, welfare and wage reduction, rapid shifting of financial investment into new products, and upgrading through R&D investment unconnected to existing industries. How did Finland negotiate its way to such an improbable outcome?

Perhaps ironically, the system of political economy that supported a position of natural resource industries was morphed into arrangements that supported leading edge high-technology firms. Neo-corporatist systems used consensus-based decision-making arrangements to guide state direction of the economy. In Finland, this meant government, banking, and industry, with a limited role for labor, engaged in an organized and coordinated system of capitalist competition. The system operated around state-owned enterprises, nationally organized arrangements for accumulating and allocating capital through banks, capital controls, the exclusion of foreign investment, national champion firms focused on natural resource industries such as forestry and paper, slow upgrading into medium-tech products, and with exports concentrated in sales to the neighboring Soviet Union. However, this system of political economy began to break down in the 1970s and 1980s and collapsed entirely with the economic depression that followed the disintegration of the Soviet Union in 1991.

Finland's political and economic leaders realized in the 1970s and early 1980s the existing system could not generate sustainable prosperity and took steps to dramatically shift investment into R&D related to advanced technology. The combination of the global economic crisis of 1973–82, the growing attractiveness of the European Community, and the unattractiveness of the Soviet Union combined to force a radical strategic rethinking. The consensus for large change cut across the collection of stakeholders, with labor acceding because of employment protection and rising benefits to the unemployed. The policies adopted by the government from the 1980s to the 1990s were a mixture of liberalization and state direction for adaptive change. There was some privatization of state-owned firms and increased market-based criteria for those not privatized, a significant relaxation of state control over finance, and an opening to foreign investment. In the 1990s, state subsidies, price cartels, and large budget deficits were reduced to meet European Union (EU) membership criteria and these were combined with further liberalization of finance by increasing the role for equity over debt.

However, Finnish firms requested state help in making the adjustments and realignments needed by the new strategy and this placed a significant limit on liberalization. The most important policy response was to shift capital allocation from promoting industrial expansion to supporting research and development. Significantly, increased public funding for R&D was more than matched by the expansion of private resources as well, largely as a result of the long-standing private acceptance of state leadership. Much of the new policy was coordinated by the same kinds of neo-corporatist associations as previously. Moreover, the state acted to expand the capital available through venture capital funding. The new financial arrangements also involved making support available to all industries and firms rather than targeting large firms and specific industries, as in the past. Through a process of trial and error experimentation and adaptation, Finland was able to make a dramatic and successful transformation in the space of two decades.

The Finnish growth rate has been comparatively high over the twelve years depicted in Table 8.5. However, Finland's success has not been without its difficulties, owing to the extraordinary turbulence in global markets for high technology. The greatest firm in Finland, Nokia, had been the world's largest mobile phone company for more than a decade but has recently slid into second place globally in market share. Nokia came under severe competitive pressure largely from the industry's shift to the smartphone, primarily from the iPhone and Android devices that Nokia was unable to match. Lacking the software capability to develop a smartphone, Nokia saw its revenues plummet and profits eliminated. After teaming up with Microsoft, Nokia has attempted a comeback by concentrating on markets in emerging economies. Notwithstanding

Table 8.5 Finland, Real GDP Growth Rate

Country	1999	2000	2002	2003	2004	2005	2006	2007	2008	2009	2010	2011
Finland	3.5	5.6	1.1	1.9	3	3	5.5	4.5	0.9	−8.1	3.1	2.9

Source: Data from www.indexmundi.com/g/g.aspx?c=fi&v=66; www.indexmundi.com/finland/gdp_real_growth_rate.html

Nokia's difficulties, Finland as a whole remains strong as one of the most competitive and innovative nations in the world by many measures.[69]

Competing through Rule-Making in Regional Trade Agreements/Free Trade Agreements

A primary strategy of the United States for competing in the global economy has been to expand the scale of free trade and open capital markets. However, in recent years the prospects for multilateral trade agreements organized on a global scale through the World Trade Organization (WTO) have declined, thereby blocking forward movement on reducing trade barriers as a mechanism for expanding trade and increasing efficiencies, specialization, and competitiveness. In addition, the pressures for developing systems for managing the increasingly complex forms for trade and investment have increased. The changing structure of global trade, in particular the emergence of regionalized trade in production networks composed of differentiated but complementary forms of specialization distributed across many nations, creates new purposes for regional free trade agreements (FTAs). Most of what we call global production networks involve significant levels of regional production and exchange. Moreover, because production networks are complex and usually require specialized rules, the locus of governance for creating these rules has shifted to regional entities. At the same time, though these agreements have a regional character, the participants may not all be members of the same geographic region.[70] The result has been a significant turn toward regional trade agreements (RTAs) and even bilateral free trade agreements as a substitute for multilateral agreements.

There are numerous examples in recent years of new regional agreements, which generally draw on the experience of the most important regional trade agreement, the European Union. Regional trade agreements are strategies for increasing competitiveness. Beginning in 2013, the United States and the European Union moved toward negotiating a free trade agreement in part as a means for combating the competitive threat from China and more generally from the emerging regional system in Asia. Even though the tariff levels between these economic giants are low, numerous non-tariff barriers exist through areas such as regulatory differences and differences in standards.[71] Eliminating these problems would spur new forms of investment to take advantage of the various complementarities that would emerge from a new trading and production environment. Further, the expansion of markets from such an agreement creates new opportunities for achieving economies of scale and driving down the price at which firms can remain competitive in global markets. Such was the main rationale for the North American Free Trade Agreement (NAFTA), as well as many of the advances toward regional agreements in Asia and Latin America.[72]

Perhaps the most far-reaching preferential trade agreement is the Trans-Pacific Partnership (TPP).[73] The TPP combines a selected set of Western hemisphere and Asian nations in an audacious effort to link developed and developing nations in a system of deep integration. Asian trade represents the most advanced system of integration based on intense specialization by nations in an integrated process of manufacturing.[74] In many ways, the TPP is a response to earlier developments in Asian regionalization and economic integration. For about a decade, the Asian region has begun to develop very limited arrangements for the governance of intraregional integration exclusively by Asian nations. The primary international organization in the area – Association of Southeast Asian Nations (ASEAN) – in conjunction with six other Asian nations, has engaged in repeated efforts to negotiate the terms of governance for regional trade.[75] After the Asian financial crisis of 1997–8, China took a much greater role in developing regional governance for Asian trade. Japan and Korea have also taken an active role in defining regional agreements. Although China has begun to assert a level of leadership in this negotiating forum, the system of existing agreements remains tangled in what some have called a "noodle bowl" set of deals.[76] In 2010, a China–ASEAN FTA was implemented, followed by similar agreements between ASEAN and Japan, Korea, India, Australia, and New Zealand. This set of agreements also served as a springboard for the most important agreement, which has been a commitment to achieving an ASEAN Economic Community by 2015.[77]

The Trans-Pacific Partnership is both more modest and more ambitious.[78] Originating in a 2006 trade agreement among four small Asian nations, TPP negotiations now take place among an unusual mix of twelve nations – United States, Vietnam, Brunei, Singapore, Malaysia, New Zealand, Japan, Australia, Chile, Peru, Canada, and Mexico – operating in considerable secrecy.[79] The context is one of a contest among major Asian powers to define the rules for economic exchange at a deep level of interdependence, with the United States and China being the principal competitors in establishing these rules. The TPP is almost surely designed to serve as a template for a potential expansion of these rules across a much wider group of nations than the present set of negotiators.[80] If successful, the TPP would initially create an agreement that spans across the Asia–Pacific area and then would set the stage for a more comprehensive agreement among a much wider set of nations from this area. A central bargain for successful negotiation could involve trading more access to the US economy for deregulating economies in emerging nations, such as Vietnam. Perhaps the most important consequence of an agreement would be to place the United States squarely within the complex governance rules that now govern trade in the Asia–Pacific area. This must be seen as part of the United States' effort to pivot toward Asia in its global policies.

Creating a more comprehensive system of governance for Asia–Pacific trade is a complicated and daunting task, for the issues involved frequently divide nations from each other and engage conflicting interests within nations. Some of the main topics of negotiation include intellectual property, investor–state relations, and regulations for labor and the environment, along with the large problem of untangling the "noodle bowl" of existing agreements. At the same time, success from a US perspective will come from opening new markets in areas where US firms have a competitive advantage, from creating a more comprehensive set of trade-related rules, and from defining this US-compatible set of rules in the most economically dynamic part of the world. In effect, by defining the rules, the United States is seeking to create a form of structural power. The rules preferred by the United States will tilt national choices toward US conceptions of trade and business and away from Chinese conceptions.[81]

In the longer run, the success of regional trade agreements will depend on the ability to design effective governance for the new set of demands generated by the system of global/regional production networks and related arrangements of investment, specialization, and complex exchange. Further, such a system is subject to significant stress from the rapid changes produced by two related market forces: the continuing efforts by nations to upgrade their capabilities across the value chain and the large turbulence in global markets arising from technological change. The United States' approach to the TPP is primarily related to rules that benefit its competitive advantages and create rules and relationships that boost the structural power of the United States. Whether these goals or those from China are compatible with effective regional governance in Asia remains unclear.

Conclusion: Debating the Role of States in Advancing Competitiveness

There is considerable debate over the merits of an active state involvement in promoting the competitiveness of economic systems. In this concluding section we will review the arguments with an eye toward explaining the substantial and increasing role of the state in an era of supposed neoliberal ascendance. Can the state play an important and even essential role in promoting the competitiveness of a nation? If so, what are the conditions that make for the greatest chance of success?[82]

Why should we expect states to be effective in sustaining and enhancing competitiveness? After all, should not a free market, composed of profit-seeking businesses, be a better judge of where investments should be made? Certainly, markets are powerful institutions for making choices among competing investment options, with businesses making decisions to risk their own money and with significant sanctions (direct losses and even bankruptcy) as the penalty for failure. State actors would seem always to be in an inferior position for making such choices. They operate outside of markets, they may well be influenced by political criteria that negate efficiency, and they are rarely in a position to experience penalties as a result of investment failure. The potential for corruption, lack of information, and the absence of a sanction for failure would seem to provide a convincing case for excluding states from any role in making investment allocation decisions.

But there is also a widespread recognition that markets are poor providers of many of the public goods that markets themselves require for efficiency to happen. The rule of law is a public good for markets and operates to protect business from arbitrary losses. Only governments can supply this. Effective communication and transportation systems are also important public goods that function to expand markets and yet are rarely provided by markets and private firms alone. Airports are an example of public goods that typically are supplied by governments or public–private partnerships. In a knowledge-intensive economy, the development of basic knowledge and of the networks of interaction that diffuse knowledge and support innovation, along with creating the human resources of such an economy, typically require a large government role. Even more important, there may be many situations in which agents in markets, focused on current prices, may be poor judges of investments that have a long time horizon. State-based agents, operating with different criteria for making choices, may have better information than profit-seeking firms operating in markets where the criteria for choice are confined to immediate profits for investors.[83]

Consider the Internet, the basic elements of which were created by DARPA in the 1960s and 1970s. There is no evidence for this time period of any private firms anywhere in the world engaged in R&D or active product development on what became the Internet; indeed, there isn't any evidence that private firms were thinking in these terms at all. Left to private investment choices, it is doubtful the Internet would have been created and certainly not for many years after 1969. The Internet was created because it met other criteria for judgment, which were linked to the mission of DARPA: maintain US technological supremacy and prevent any technological surprises. Development of the Internet required significant knowledge entrepreneurship by DARPA officials, assembling knowledge networks across universities, research institutes, and private consulting firms – a task no private firm could imagine or do. Moreover, the Internet required continuing efforts for many years to organize a research community and develop the large set of integrated protocols and upgrade the hardware for the system. Only after this large, costly, and uncertain public goods investment had been made could the Internet become the wonder we know today and a system that private firms can operate and improve based on profitable opportunities. The Internet is a knowledge public good, consisting of the knowledge that makes up the

Internet system, the capabilities for knowledge exchange the Internet provides, and the knowledge base on which others can build business opportunities.

The theoretical basis for a large state role in knowledge-based industries relates to the weak ability of markets to process the information and the choices related to the provision of the infrastructure for knowledge creation.[84] Universities and other institutions for systematic research into basic science, the systems and incentives for diffusion, and even the knowledge absorptive and processing capacity for firms will be supplied in very small amounts by markets. This does not mean state actors will always have the ability to fill this void. This possibility increases when state actors have close and deep connections to society and to business and knowledge-producing institutions, when state actors possess specialized knowledge themselves, and when they are able to act with some independence of the narrow interests of actors seeking to capture state policy. In this special combination of capabilities, state actors may be in a position to act effectively in promoting targeted innovation and in enhancing competitiveness.[85] We have seen this combination of circumstances in the DARPA, Israel, and Finland cases.

Achieving a higher probability of success for state efforts in targeting specific industries or even firms thus requires an unusual but not impossible set of capabilities.[86] Generally, this means agile and flexible state actions that organize and direct knowledge production and supply demand for products for both proof of concept and potentially to generate economies of scale. Such state actors, to be successful, must be linked effectively into global knowledge networks.[87] Interestingly, perhaps the strongest counterargument against effective state industrial policy is the rapidly diffusing and changing nature of global knowledge systems. Remember, knowledge is the key input for many industries, especially innovating industries. But the combination of increasing complexity, increasing geographic diffusion, and accelerating rates of change for knowledge makes nations by themselves – even the United States – limited as locations for promoting new knowledge-intensive industries.[88] Quite simply, knowledge is becoming globalized and the scale for knowledge development has become globalized as well.

A second form of state competitiveness policies is of a horizontal nature, and involves the creation of knowledge that has multiple applications and significant amount of reuse. This set of policies is sector neutral and designed to bolster capabilities across multiple industries. Examples are actions, such as those in Israel and Finland, that seek to supplement and provide new incentives for R&D at the level of the firm and are focused mainly on product and process development.[89] Such policies may be especially helpful in nations with high levels of existing knowledge capabilities that can be harnessed and leveraged into "fast follower" strategies by firms.

At the same time, relatively few states can support and sustain broad and deep systems for the creation of basic knowledge. Especially agile state actors, such as DARPA, can serve an essential entrepreneurial and catalyzing role in the development of basic knowledge and especially in recombinant innovation. By assembling disparate knowledge resources, developing new incentives for particular research directions, and even acting to orchestrate the creation of new capabilities, some state actors can play an entrepreneurial role in creating knowledge. State actors can possess different and better information and act on that information in ways short-term profit-seeking firms cannot.

But this requires state actors to be able to position themselves deeply within knowledge and business networks and act with significant autonomy. This embeddedness in knowledge, investment, and exchange networks, combined with a different set of goals and criteria for judgment, create the potential for state actors to bring superior information, or at least differentiated information, to a decision about investment. DARPA is an example of this, offering both different and often superior judgment to that available from private firms. These capabilities are especially important in situations such as: large lumpy investments with a temporally distant or highly uncertain payoff and where prices in the present are poorly correlated with prices in the future. Economists assert that in situations of information asymmetry between economic agents, markets break down in the ability to allocate resources efficiently to investments.[90] In situations such as those described, information asymmetry that provides a diversity of perspectives may be important for making investment choices that are superior to those from markets defined by firms alone.[91]

This argument helps explain why, in spite of the so-called free market revolution after 1980, a countervailing force in an increasingly knowledge-intensive economy presses the state to provide sufficient incentives for the creation of knowledge at the frontier. There are few important modern technologies that have been developed without substantial public sector assistance, especially in early stages of their development: just consider commercial aircraft, computers, lasers, biomedicine, biotechnology, and nanotechnology.

The state must become the supplier of knowledge and knowledge infrastructures because the creation of this infrastructure, of advanced knowledge and its distribution, requires a huge society-wide investment in education and research. This very large and very lumpy investment has big payoffs to society but highly uncertain payoffs to individual investors. Once created, the distribution and reuse of knowledge by those who have received the benefits of lumpy investment is collectively very large but individually can be relatively low. At the same time, those who are able to create specialized and innovative knowledge combinations can reap large gains. The production and use of knowledge involve a very large social investment with large payoffs to society as a whole combined with large payoffs to those able to create specialized investments able to tap into low-cost knowledge at the margin and apply it in specialized ways. Only states can supply this knowledge system and infrastructure; in a concomitant fashion, highly specialized firms are able to reap the largest gains from advanced knowledge. This creates a complex partnership of states and firms.

The state in a knowledge-intensive economy is a central player in the value chain of production and as a consumer of knowledge. It is perhaps the key supplier of the central input: knowledge. It is the provider of public education at the basic level of general knowledge capabilities of the population; it is the key supplier at the top of the knowledge chain in universities and research institutes and with funding for research and development in universities (Department of Defense (DoD), NIH, and NSF); and provides a series of subsidies for private universities in the United States. The state is the main partner of firms in the creation and diffusion of knowledge and the development of human capital, thereby supporting and sustaining the processes of innovation that provide the only sustainable competitive advantage for knowledge-intensive firms. Very few firms in the advanced world could operate for long without the very large state role in education of the workforce.

States also assume a central role as broker, assembler, and creator of networked relationships among non-state actors to develop the industrial/knowledge/innovation ecologies that only partially emerge from market relationships. States help create, sustain, and participate in global knowledge networks from which innovation is derived. Large parts of knowledge creation and diffusion, and various forms of exchange, occur outside of markets and instead are based in networks and social relationships. States are key actors in these networks, as a major purchaser, consumer, and repository of knowledge in various departments (Defense, State, EPA, FDA, NSA) and via specialized creators of knowledge efforts such as DARPA. In the role of knowledge purchaser and funder, via NSF/NIH/FDA, the state defines standards and organizes the networks of experts for knowledge validation. This occurs largely outside of markets but in partnerships with firms.

The state is a partner in innovation not only because it provides funding, supports research, and educates human capital; states are themselves repositories of knowledge both at the technical level and at the level of markets and market trends. The state is often a knowledge partner, supplying information to firms. This works especially well when states have a relationship of "embedded autonomy" with firms: deep and close connections but with considerable separation and differentiation of interests. This usually fails when state actors are captured by firms, who are then in a position to subordinate state interests to special industry interests. But in situations of embedded autonomy, states can be effective partners in innovation. The pharmaceutical industry is an example. The state is embedded with information sharing via NIH funding and via FDA with information about safety, and derives some autonomy from both positions.

As we have seen in this chapter, technological developments in recent years have led to enormous turbulence in global markets for firms and nations. As knowledge becomes the most important input in production and becomes more globally dispersed, the pace of competition increases and the role of innovation in competition expands. Notwithstanding the widespread preference in this same period for limiting and reducing the government role in the economy, states have assumed an increasing position in knowledge production, capture, diffusion, and application and especially in building the infrastructure for these processes. No major nation can possibly imagine competing in the global economy without a very substantial role for its government. Firms remain as perhaps the key players in promoting competition but can do so only with states as (sometimes less visible) partners.

Key Concepts (see Glossary)

Competitiveness
  Firm
  Nation
Defense Advanced Research
  Projects Agency (DARPA)
Developmental State
Dispersion of Knowledge
Emerging Economies
General Purpose Technology
Gross Fixed Capital Formation
National Competitiveness System

Research and Development (R&D)
Smile Curve
State Capitalism
Supply Chain (Value Chain, Value
  Added)
Varieties of Capitalism
  Coordinated Market Economies
  Liberal Market Economies
  State-Managed Economies
Zero-Sum Relationship

Discussion Questions

1 What is competitiveness as applied to nations and to firms? How can we measure this concept for nations?

2 What are the main arguments in the debate about whether nations engage in competition with each other?

3 Describe the economic and technological environment within which nations and firms compete. What special role do general purpose technology, knowledge dispersion, global production networks, and the diffusion of economic power to emerging economies play in creating the environment for competition?

4 How does the distribution of gains across the value chain for Apple help to illustrate the large differential gains from the global economy?

5 How and why do nations differ in terms of how much to invest in infrastructure and how the allocation of capital should be made?

6 How do the ideas of a developmental state and state capitalism illustrate different forms and national economic organization and competitiveness?

7 How does DARPA offer a case study of the US government as a partner with innovative firms and universities in technology innovation?

8 Compare the actions of the Israeli and Finnish governments with those of DARPA in enhancing and promoting the development of technology industries.

9 Explain the competitiveness strategy based on establishing the rules for regional trade.

10 Are free markets, operating without state help, likely to be able to create the competitive capabilities for an advanced nation? What are the circumstances in which states can play a key role in promoting competitiveness?

Notes

1 For a discussion of the concept of competitiveness, see World Economic Forum, *The Global Competitiveness Report, 2011–2012*, Geneva, 2012, 4.

2 For a sense of the debate, see Paul Krugman, "Competitiveness: A Dangerous Obsession," *Foreign Affairs* (March–April 1994) 28–48; Gary Pisano and Wally Shih, "Restoring American Competitiveness," *Harvard Business Review* (July–August 2009) 2–13. Scholars of international business and management also use the concept of national competitiveness.

3 World Economic Forum, *The Global Competitiveness Report, 2014–2015*, Geneva, 2015, 4–9.

4 Nations are divided into the three categories for the purpose of weighting based on the level of per capita GDP and the proportion of primary products as a percent of exports. WEF, 2012, 9.

5 For an unsurpassed discussion of the relationship of technology and economic growth, see Joel Mokyr, *The Lever of Riches: Technological Creativity and Economic Progress*, Oxford: Oxford University Press, 1990.

6 Richard Lipsey, Kenneth Karlaw, and Clifford Bekar, *Economic Transformations: General Purpose Technologies and Long Term Growth*, Oxford: Oxford University Press, 2005. Also see, Chris Freeman and Francisco Louca, *As Time Goes On: From the Industrial Revolutions to the Information Revolution*, Oxford: Oxford University Press, 2001; and Timothy Bresnahan and Manuel Trajtenberg, "General Purpose Technologies: 'Engines of Growth'?" *Journal of Econometrics* 65.1 (1995) 83–108.

7 Erik Brynjolfsson and Andrew McAfee, *Race Against the Machine: How the Digital Revolution is Accelerating Innovation, Driving Productivity, and Irreversibly Transforming Employment and the Economy*, Digital Frontier Press, Kindle edition, 2011.

8 Shih-Tse Lo and Dhanoos Sutthiphisal, "Crossover Inventions and Knowledge Diffusion of General Purpose Technologies: Evidence from Electrical Technology," *The Journal of Economic History*, 70.3 (September 2010) 744–64.

9 Lipsey et al., *Economic Transformations*, 131–218.

10 Paul David and Gavin Wright, "General Purpose Technologies and Surges in Productivity: Historical Reflections on the Future of the ICT Revolution," in Paul David and Mark Thomas (eds), *The Economic Future in Historical Perspective*, Oxford: Oxford University Press, 2003, 135–66.

11 As an example, Toyota created the Toyota manufacturing system – sometimes known as lean manufacturing – which consisted of systems for eliminating waste often by managing information, but in a time before widespread computerization. Other firms, borrowing from Toyota, in completely different industries, imitated and even improved this system. For example, a small retail firm in Arkansas – Wal-Mart – decided to adopt lean retailing by investing in new information systems based on barcodes. Later, new software systems were built to permit firms to gain dramatic new management capabilities by substituting information for inventory. Another example is the Internet and the World Wide Web, which had manifold effects on the economy, including the creation of new industries and business models such as paid search.

12 A significant problem in recent years has been the destruction of jobs by technological change, in this case by substituting technology for people. This has resulted in a net loss of jobs from the contemporary process of "creative destruction" and an increase in unemployment along with a decline in the incomes of millions of persons. Even as productivity continues to rise, along with overall national incomes, the distribution of that income favors a well-positioned few. The decade from 2000–10 saw job growth in the United States at roughly zero percent, much lower than in any decade after World War II. In the 1990s, job growth in the United States was nearly 20 percent. Brynjolfsson and McAfee, *Race Against the Machine*, 35.

13 For evidence of this process, see AnnaLee Saxenian, "Brain Circulation and Regional Innovation: the Silicon Valey – Hsinchu – Shanghai Triangle," in Karen Polenske (ed.), *The Economic Geography of Innovation*, Cambridge: Cambridge University Press, 2007, 190–209.

14 Shahid Yusef, Anjum Altaf, and Kaoru Nabeshima (eds), *Global Production Networking and Technological Change in East Asia*, Washington, DC: World Bank, 2004. There is evidence of rethinking the process of offshoring production into global production networks. Tamzin Booth, "Here, There and Everywhere," *The Economist*, January 19, 2013, www.economist.com/news/special-report/21569572-after-decades-sending-work-across-world-companies-are-rethinking-their-offshoring. The scale of this process of offshore outsourcing is large among US firms, rising from about 40 percent to 70 percent of firms in the decade after 2003. *The Economist*, "Herd Instinct," January 19, 2013, www.economist.com/news/special-report/21569575-companies-need-think-more-carefully-about-how-they-offshore-and-outsource-herd-instinct; Dieter Ernst, "Digital Information Systems and Global Flagship Networks: How Mobile is Knowledge in the Global Network Economy," in J.F. Christensen and P. Maskell (eds), *The Industrial Dynamics of the New Digital Economy*, Cheltenham: Edward Elgar, 2003, 151–76.

15 *The Economist*: "Why the Tail Wags the Dog," August 6, 2011, www.economist.com/blogs/dailychart/2011/08/emerging-vs-developed-economies. For a dissenting view on the continuing convergence of rich and developing nations, see Ruchir Sharma, "Broken BRICs: Why the Rest Stopped Rising," *Foreign Affairs*, 91.6 (November/December 2012) 2–7.

16 These profoundly important insights come from Richard Baldwin, "Trade and Industrialisation after Globalisation's Second Unbundling," NBER

Working Paper 17716 (December 2011); Richard Baldwin, "21st Century Regionalism: Filling the Gap Between 21st Century Trade and 20th Century Trade Rules," WTO Working Paper, ESRD 2011–08 (May 2011).

17 Charles Fine, *Clockspeed: Winning Industry Control in an Age of Temporary Advantage*, New York: Basic Books, 1999.

18 Thomas Friedman, "It's PQ and CQ as Much as IQ," *New York Times*, January 30, 2013, A25. ". . . the speed with which every job and industry changes and goes into hypermode. . . . Because of the way every industry – from health care to manufacturing to education – is now being transformed by cheap, fast connected power, the skill required for every decent job is rising as is the necessity of lifelong learning."

19 Steve Pearlstein, "In Tech World: Good to Great To – Gone," *Washington Post*, September 15, 2012, www.washingtonpost.com/business/in-tech-world-good-to-great-to--gone/2012/09/14/a982c512-fabe–11e1–8252–5f89566a35ac_story.html; Erik Brynjolfsson and Michael Schrage, "The New, Faster Face of Innovation," *Wall Street Journal*, August 17, 2009, http://online.wsj.com/articl e/SB10001424052970204830304574130820184260340.html. Interestingly, Amazon has begun to compete against Wal-Mart with potentially dramatic effects.

20 Andrew McAfee and Erik Brynjolfsson, "Investing in the IT that Makes a Difference," Harvard Business Review, 2008, http://hbr.org/2008/07/investing-in-the-it-that-makes-a-competitive-difference/ar/1; Erik Brynjolfsson, Andrew McAfee, Michael Sorell, and Feng Zhu, "Scale Without Mass: Business Process Replication and Industry Dynamics," Harvard Business School Working Paper, 07–016, 2006; "The Volatile U.S. Economy, Industry by Industry," Harvard Business Review, http://hbr.org/web/slideshows/thevolatile-us-economy-industry-by-industry/1-slide; Martin Reeves and Mike Deimler, "Adaptability: The New Competitive Advantage," Harvard Business Review, July 2011, http://hbr.org/2011/07/adaptability-the-new-competitive advantage/ar/1

21 Making a personal computer from the beginnings in 1975–6 involved assembling multiple parts made by different firms. This already fragmented supply chain perhaps facilitated the early globalization of computer production in the 1980s. For a visualization of the Apple supply chain, see www.chinafile.com/who-supplies-apple-it-s-not-just-china-interactive-map

22 *The Economist*, January 21, 2012, 84, www.economist.com/node/21543174; Jason Dedrick and Kenneth Kraemer, "Who Profits from Innovation in Global Value Chains? A Study of iPods and Notebook PCs," *Industrial and Corporate Change*, 19.1 (2009) 81–116.

23 *The Economist*, "Slicing an Apple," August 10, 2011, www.economist.com/blogs/dailychart/2011/08/apple-and-samsungs-symbiotic-relationship; Paul Markillie, "The Third Industrial Revolution," *The Economist*, April 21, 2012, www.economist.com/node/21552901. A similar division of value can be seen in the Nokia smartphone, which is assembled in China and designed in Finland. Jyrki Ali-Yrkko,Petri Rouvinen, Timo Seppälä, and Pekka Ylä-Anttila, "Who Captures Value in Global Supply Chains? Case Nokia N95 Smartphone," *Journal of Industrial Competition and Trade*, 11 (2011) 263–78.

24 Charles Duhigg and Keith Bradsher, "How the U.S. Lost Out on iPhone Work," *New York Times*, January 21, 2012, www.nytimes.com/2012/01/22/business/apple-america-and-a-squeezed-middle-class.html?hp&_r=0

25 Of course, policies and actions that improve the productivity of one nation can also benefit other nations through trade, investment, and knowledge diffusion.

26 For a brief overview of the role of the state in promoting economic growth and competitiveness, see Philippe Aghion and Julia Cage, "Rethinking

Growth and the State," in Otaviano Canuto and Danny Leipziger (eds), *Ascent After Decline*, Washington, DC: IBRD, 2012, 181–200.

27 For a related effort to develop categories of innovation policy, see Bengt-Ake Lundvall and Susana Borras, "Science, Technology, and Innovation Policy," in Jan Fagerberg et al. (eds), *The Oxford Handbook of Innovation*, Oxford: Oxford University Press, 2006, 599–631.

28 Sheldon Garon, "Why the Chinese Save," *Foreign Policy*, January 19, 2012, www.foreignpolicy.com/articles/2012/01/19/why_the_chinese_save; Sheldon Garon, *Why America Spends While the World Saves*, Princeton: Princeton University Press, 2012.

29 Carl Walter and Fraser Howie, *Red Capitalism*, New York: Wiley, 2011; Henry Sanderson and Michael Forsythe, *China's Superbank*, Singapore: Wiley, 2013.

30 Wolfgang Streeck and Kozo Yamamura, *The Origins of Non-Liberal Capitalism: Germany and Japan in Comparison*, Ithaca: Cornell University Press, 2001; Kent Calder, *Strategic Capitalism*, Princeton: Princeton University Press, 1993; Takeo Hoshi and Anil Kashyap, *Corporate Financing and Governance in Japan*, Cambridge, MA: MIT Press, 2001; Pepper Culpepper, "Institutional Change in Contemporary Capitalism: Coordinated Financial Systems Since 1990," *World Politics*, 57 (2005) 173–99.

31 Michael Porter, *The Competitive Advantage of Nations*, New York: Free Press, 1998. For a review of the controversies surrounding this theory, see A.J. Smit, "The Competitive Advantage of Nations: Is Porter's Diamond Framework a New Theory that Explains the International Competitiveness of Countries?" *South African Business Review*, 14.1 (2010) 105–30.

32 Peter Hall and David Soskice (eds), *Varieties of Capitalism: The Institutional Foundations of Comparative Advantage*, Oxford: Oxford University Press, 2001; Suzanne Berger and Ronald Dore (eds), *National Diversity and Global Capitalism*, Ithaca: Cornell University Press, 1996; Herbert Kitschelt and Peter Lange (eds), *Continuity and Change in Contemporary Capitalism*, Cambridge: Cambridge University Press, 1999; Glenn Morgan and Richard Whitley (eds), *Changing Capitalisms?* Oxford: Oxford University Press, 2005.

33 Gregory Jackson and Richard Deeg, "From Comparing Capitalisms to the Politics of Institutional Change," *Review of International Political Economy*, 15.4 (2008) 680–709; Peter Hall and Kathleen Thelen, "Institutional Change in Varieties of Capitalism," *Socio-Economic Review*, 7 (2009) 7–34; Dirk Akkermans, Carolina Castaldi, and Bart Los, "Do Liberal Market Economies Really Innovate More Radically than Coordinated Market Economies? Hall and Soskice Reconsidered," *Research Policy*, 38 (2009) 181–91.

34 Bengt-Ake Lundvall, "National Innovation Systems – Analytical Concept and Development Tool," *Industry and Innovation*, 14.1 (February 2007) 95–119.

35 Chalmers Johnson, *MITI and the Japanese Miracle*, Stanford: Stanford University Press, 1982; Alice Amsden, *Asia's Next Giant*, Oxford: Oxford University Press, 1992; Robert Wade, *Governing the Market*, Princeton: Princeton University Press, 2003.

36 Richard Donor, Bryan Ritchie, and Dan Slater, "Systemic Vulnerability and the Origins of Developmental States," *International Organization*, 59.1 (2005) 327–61.

37 Meagan Greene, *The Origins of the Developmental State in Taiwan*, Cambridge, MA: Harvard University Press, 2008.

38 For a contrary case, in which Asian developmental states were largely unable to make investments that paid off commercially, see Joseph Wong, *Betting on Biotech*, Ithaca: Cornell University Press, 2011.

39 Atul Kohli, *State-Directed Development*, Cambridge: Cambridge University Press, 2004. Yongping Wu, *A Political Explanation of Economic Growth*, Cambridge, MA: Harvard University Press, 2005.

40 Jude Howell, "Reflections on the Chinese State," *Development and Change*, 37.2 (2006) 273–97.

41 Zheng Yongnian, *De Facto Federalism in China*, Singapore: World Scientific, 2007.

42 Richard McGregor, *The Party*, New York: Harper Collins, 2010; David Shambaugh, *China's Communist Party*, Berkeley: University of California Press, 2008.

43 An excellent short description of this process, confirmed by a wealth of additional research by many scholars, is Kenneth Lieberthal, *Managing the China Challenge*, Washington, DC: Brookings, 2011, 16–24, 48–58. Quote is from Christopher McNally, "Sino-Capitalism: China's Reemergence and the International Political Economy," *World Politics*, 64.4 (October 2012) 744. An exceptionally lucid description of state–business relations is in Christopher McNally and Teresa Wright, "Sources of Social Support for China's Current Political Order," *Communist and Post-Communist Studies*, 43 (2010) 189–98. Also see Shu Keng, "Developing into a Developmental State: Explaining the Changing Government–Business Relationships Behind the Kunshan Miracle," in Tse-Kang Leng (ed.), *Dynamics of Local Governance in China During the Reform Era*, Lanham: Rowman and Littlefield, 225–71; Richard Appelbaum, "China's (Not so Hidden) Developmental State," in Fred Block and Matthew Keller (eds), *State of Innovation*, Boulder: Paradigm, 2011, 217–35.

44 Adrian Wooldridge, "The Visible Hand," *The Economist*, January 21, 2012, www.economist.com/node/21542931. For a contrary view about the balance of state and markets in China, see Nicholas Lardy, *Markets Over Mao*, Washington, DC: Peterson Institute, 2014.

45 Sovereign Wealth Fund Institute, www.swfinstitute.org/fund-rankings/. Also see, Ian Bremmer, *The End of the Free Market*, New York: Penguin, 2010.

46 Barry Naughton, "China's Distinctive System: Can it be a Model for Others?" *Journal of Contemporary China* (2010) 437–60.

47 Robert Adkinson and Stephen Ezell, *Innovation Economics*, New Haven: Yale University Press, 2012.

48 The NIH budget was $30.9 billion, www.nih.gov/about/budget.htm; the NSF budget was $7.0 billion, www.nsf.gov/about/congress/112/highlights/cu11_1118.jsp

49 www.whitehouse.gov/sites/default/files/microsites/ostp/fy2013rd_press_release.pdf. For the United States as a nation, R&D spending in 2011 totaled $366 billion. *The Economist*, "Bad Medicine, March 2, 2013, www.economist.com/news/science-and-technology/21572735-cutting-american-health-research-will-harm-world-bad-medicine

50 Gary Pisano and Wally Shih, "Restoring American Competitiveness," *Harvard Business Review* (July–August 2009).

51 *The Economist*, October 1, 2011, www.economist.com/node/21531002

52 The DARPA budget in 2012 was $3.1 billion.

53 Originally named the Special Projects Agency, then beginning life as the Advanced Research Projects Agency (ARPA) and reporting directly to the Secretary of Defense in 1958, DARPA's mission closely resembles the knowledge management mission of today's transnational firms. This raises some interesting points of comparison between firms and government as innovators.

54 Michael Belfiore, *The Department of Mad Scientists*, New York: Harper Collins, 2009, 59–61.
55 M. Mitchel Waldrop, *The Dream Machine*, New York: Penguin, 2002.
56 Belfiore, *The Department of Mad Scientists*, 63–94.
57 www.internetsociety.org/internet/what-internet/history-internet/brief-history-internet
58 Thomas D. Lairson "Charting the Future: Industrial Governance Structures and the Political Economy of High Technology Development," in Iliana Zloch (ed.), *Europe and the World Economy*, Cheltenham: Edward Elgar, 1997, 7–32; David Mowery et al., "Technology Policy and Global Warming: Why New Policy Models are Needed," *Research Policy* 39 (2010) 1016–18.
59 www.darpa.mil/NewsEvents/Releases/2014/03/13.aspx; www.pbs.org/wgbh/nova/darpa/; John Markoff, "Google Cars Drive Themselves, In Traffic," *New York Times*, October 9, 2010, www.nytimes.com/2010/10/10/science/10google.html?pagewanted=all
60 Glenn Fong, "ARPA Does Windows: The Defense Underpinning of the PC Revolution," *Business and Politics*, 3.3 (2001) 213–37; William Bonvillian, "The Connected Science Model for Innovation: The DARPA Role," in Sadao Nagaoka et al. (eds), *21st Century Innovation Systems for Japan and the United States*, Washington, DC: National Academies Press, 2009, 206–37.
61 For an analysis of a DARPA-like strategy applied to energy policy, see William Bonvillian and Richard van Atta, "ARPA-E and DARPA: Applying the DARPA Model to Energy Innovation," *The Journal of Technology Transfer*, 26.5 (October 2011) 469–513. Also see, Erica Fuchs, "Rethinking the Role of the State in Technology Development: DARPA and the Case for Embedded Network Governance," *Research Policy*, 39 (2010) 1133–47. For a comparative analysis of defense-related R&D, see David Mowrey, "Defense-Related R&D as a Model for 'Grand Challenges' Technology Policies," *Research Policy*, 41 (2012) 1701–15; John Markoff, "Making Robots Mimic the Human Hand," *New York Times*, March 29, 2013, www.nytimes.com/2013/03/30/science/making-robots-mimic-the-human-hand.html?hpw
62 Bhaven Sampat, "Mission-Oriented Biomedical Research at the NIH," *Research Policy*, 41 (2012) 1720–41.
63 http://web.mit.edu/fnl/volume/193/canizares.html. One measure in the mid-1990s found that 88 percent of research resources in the life sciences at MIT was federally funded. http://web.mit.edu/newsoffice/1996/biotechmitgov.html
64 Mowery et al., "Technology Policy and Global Warming," 1015–16.
65 Gary Pisano, *Science Business*, Cambridge, MA: Harvard Business School Press, 2006.
66 Fred Block and Matthew Keller (eds), *State of Innovation: The U.S. Government's Role in Technology Development*, Boulder: Paradigm, 2011.
67 This case relies on Dan Breznitz, *Innovation and the State*, New Haven: Yale University Press, 2007, 41–96; Dan Breznitz, "Innovation-Based Industrial Policy in Emerging Economies? The Case of Israel's IT Industry," *Business and Politics*, 8.3 (2006) 1–38; Dan Breznitz, "Industrial Policy as National Policy," *Research Policy*, 36 (2007) 1465–82.
68 Discussion of this case study relies on Darius Ornston, *When Small States Make Big Leaps*, Ithaca: Cornell University Press, 2012, 30–8, 55–91; and Adrian Wooldridge, "The Nordic Countries," *The Economist*, February 2, 2013, www.economist.com/news/special-report/21570840-nordic-countries-are-reinventing-their-model-capitalism-says-adrian
69 Soumitra Doutta, *The Global Innovation Index, 2012*, INSEAD, 2012, xvii, 8, 14.
70 WTO, *World Trade Report, 2011*, 6.

71 Nicholas Kulish and Jackie Calmes, "Obama Bid for Trade Pact With Europe Stirs Hope," *New York Times*, February 14, 2013, www.nytimes.com/2013/02/14/world/europe/obama-bid-for-trade-pact-with-europe-stirs-hope.html

72 Mark Manger, "The Economic Logic of Asian Preferential Trade Agreements: The Role of Intra-Industry Trade," *Journal of East Asian Studies*, 14 (2014) 151–84.

73 The text of the TPP is found at: www.globalresearch.ca/the-full-text-of-the-trans-pacific-partnership-tpp/5486887

74 "Factory Asia" is a term coined to depict this complex system of Asian trade and production. Richard Baldwin, "21st Century Regionalism," 11.

75 The member nations of ASEAN include: Brunei, Burma, Cambodia, Indonesia, Laos, Malaysia, the Philippines, Singapore, Thailand, and Vietnam. Those nations joining with ASEAN in negotiations are referred to as ASEAN + 6, and include China, Japan, Korea, India, Australia, and New Zealand.

76 Richard Baldwin, "Managing the Noodle Bowl: The Fragility of Regionalism in Asia," Asian Development Bank, 2007. As of January 2010, ninety-one free trade agreements relating to ASEAN nations had been concluded and sixty-eight were proposed or under negotiation. Between 2002 and 2011, the annual number of new Asia-related trade agreements increased from two to twenty-three. Hence, the relevance of the "noodle bowl" characterization.

77 www.asean.org/communities/asean-economic-community. The achievement of this goal is very uncertain, given the continuing conflicts among China and its neighbors over control of territories in the oceans off the Chinese coast. China seems willing to sacrifice economic integration for physical control of certain areas. Masahiro Kawai and Ganeshan Wignaraja, "Patterns of Free Trade Areas in Asia," *East–West Center, Policy Studies* 65 (2013).

78 Peter Petri, "Competing Templates for Asia Pacific Economic Integration," in Gilbert Rozman, *Asia at the Tipping Point*, Korea Economic Institute, 2012, 228–45, www.keia.org/publication/asia-tipping-point-korea-rise-china-and-impact-leadership-transitions

79 In March 2013, Japan requested to join the TPP negotiations. Canada and Mexico were added in 2012.

80 Peter Petri, Michael Plummer, and Fan Zhai, "The Trans-Pacific Partnership and Asia-Pacific Integration: A Quantitative Assessment," East–West Center Working Papers, October 24, 2011.

81 Related but distinctive goals motivate the possible US–EU FTA. There, efforts focus on establishing a single market that would create new opportunities for investment and specialization. Howard Schneider, "With Trade Already Flowing, U.S. and European Union Aim for Something Deeper," *Washington Post*, February 13, 2013.

82 The combination of the recent global financial crisis, the economic downturn, and the surging economies in many emerging markets has reopened the discussion of the state role in economic success. Wooldridge, "The Visible Hand"; *The Economist*, "Tinker, Tailor," October 1, 2011, www.economist.com/node/21530958; *The Economist*, "Uncle Sam, Venture Capitalist," March 18, 2013, www.economist.com/blogs/freeexchange/2013/03/innovation; Edward McBride, "America's Competitiveness," *The Economist*, March 16, 2013, www.economist.com/news/special-report/21573229-political-gridlock-may-be-bad-americas-economy-says-edward-mcbride

83 Daron Acemoglu, Philippe Aghion, Leonardo Burszlyn, and David Hemous, "The Environment and Directed Technical Change," *American Economic Review*, 102.1 (February 2012), 131–66; Philippe Aghion and Julia Cage, "Rethinking Growth and the State," in Otaviano Canuto and Danny

Leipziger (eds), *Ascent After Decline*, Washington, DC: World Bank, 2012, 181–200.

84 Philippe Aghion, Paul David, and Dominique Foray, "Science, Technology and Innovation for Economic Growth: Linking Policy Research and Practice in STIG Systems," *Research Policy* (2009) 681–93.

85 Peter Evans, *Embedded Autonomy*, Princeton: Princeton University Press, 1995; Dani Rodrik, "The Return of Industrial Policy, *Project Syndicate*, April 12, 2010, www.project-syndicate.org/commentary/the-return-of-industrial-policy

86 Critics of state efforts in targeted competitiveness policies often point to instances of failure, of which there are many. Usually this comes without defining any standards for judgment and ignores the many successes. This is much like criticizing Ted Williams's hitting in 1941 (when his average was .406) for failing more than 59 percent of the time.

87 Sean O Riain, *The Politics of High-Tech Growth*, Cambridge: Cambridge University Press, 2004.

88 This conclusion is evident in the development of the flat panel industry and can be generalized to others. Thomas Murtha, Stefanie Lenway, and Jeffrey Hart, *Managing New Industry Creation: Global Knowledge Formation and Entrepreneurship in High Technology*, Stanford: Stanford University Press, 2001.

89 Dan Breznitz, "Industrial Policy as a National Policy: Horizontal Technology Policies and Industry-State Co-Evolution in the Growth of the Israeli Software Industry," *Research Policy*, 36 (2007) 1465–82.

90 Joseph Stiglitz, "Information and the Change in the Paradigm in Economics," *American Economic Review*, 92.3 (June 2002) 460–501. Mario Cimoli, Giovanni Dosi, and Joseph Stiglitz (eds), *Industrial Policy and Development*, Oxford: Oxford University Press, 2009.

91 Scott Page, *Diversity and Complexity*, Princeton: Princeton University Press, 2011. An economic case for this assertion is: Dani Rodrik, "Industrial Policy: Don't Ask Why, Ask How," *Middle East Development Journal* (2008) 1–29; and Dani Rodrik, "Normalizing Industrial Policy," Commission on Growth and Development Working Paper No. 3, Washington, DC, 2008.

Further Reading

Timothy Bresnahan and Alfonso Gambardella (eds), *Building High-Tech Clusters*, Cambridge: Cambridge University Press, 2004.
A collection of articles examining the competitiveness implications of high-tech clusters.

Dan Breznitz, *Innovation and the State*, New Haven: Yale University Press, 2007.
A comparative study of the political economy of innovation policies in Israel, Taiwan, and Ireland.

Mario Cimoli, Giovanni Dosi, and Joseph Stiglitz (eds), *Industrial Policy and Development*, Oxford: Oxford University Press, 2009.
A comparative study of industrial policy in developing nations.

Xiaolan Fu and Luc Soete, *The Rise of Technological Power in the South*, New York: Palgrave, 2010.

A series of articles discussing the ability of emerging economies to leverage technology for global competitive advantage.

Sanjaya Lall and Shujiro Urata, *Competitiveness, FDI and Technological Activity in East Asia*, Northampton: Edward Elgar, 2003.
A collection of articles examining the role of technological learning and competitiveness strategies in a variety of Asian states.

James McGregor, *China's Drive for Indigenous Innovation: A Web of Industrial Policies*, US Chamber of Commerce, 2010, www.uschamber.com/sites/default/files/legacy/reports/100728chinareport_0.pdf
Considers the Chinese effort to encourage local firms to engage in innovation.

Sean O Riain, *The Politics of High-Tech Growth*, Cambridge: Cambridge University Press, 2004.
A case study of the developmental network state in Ireland.

Darius Ornston, *When Small States Make Big Leaps: Institutional Innovation and High-Tech Competition in Western Europe*, Ithaca: Cornell University Press, 2012.
A detailed analysis of competitiveness strategies in three small European states.

Karen Polenske (ed.), *The Economic Geography of Innovation*, Cambridge: Cambridge University Press, 2007.
A Western-focused examination of the spatial dimensions of knowledge and innovation.

9 Power, Wealth, and Interdependence in an Era of Advanced Globalization

Globalization is a system of economic, political, social, and cultural relationships that results in a rising level of connections across national boundaries, relative to connections within nations. Much of this book has been devoted to an examination of the nature and development of the processes that create a globalized world. In this chapter we take a somewhat different tack by considering the effects of globalization on the basic concerns of international relations. Scholars of world politics have long focused on the origins and consequences of the power relationships among nations. This has repeatedly led them to consider how economic capabilities and economic ties both create the wealth that contributes to international power and potentially constrains the use of that power to achieve national ends. Especially important is the focus on shifting power relationships, often deriving from different rates of economic growth, and the potential for conflict.

The past thirty years have produced rapid and radical shifts in economic capabilities across the globe, much of it framed within a context of policies, institutions, and actors involving the United States and China. Previous chapters have considered related aspects of these transformations, including the extraordinary increase in economic capabilities in Asia, especially China, and massive global imbalances in saving, investment, and trade between the United States and Asia. There is considerable debate about whether the relative growth of emerging economies can be sustained and whether this marks a truly epochal shift of power. This chapter considers these issues in detail, including the way we measure, analyze, and evaluate the relationship of wealth and power. Put simply, we consider here whether recent global shifts in wealth will continue and, if so, how this can change global systems.

Power and Wealth

Wealth is the basis for power and power is the basis for wealth.[1] This aphorism tells us much about global politics, especially over the past two centuries when wealth in some nations has grown dramatically and rapidly. Large economies provide the basis for acting with great influence in the world but also create large interests across the world. We should remember the titanic and costly struggles fought during the first half of the twentieth century. The scale of the conflicts and the immense destruction and death were made possible by the wealth and technologies available to some nations. The years surrounding World Wars I and II produced very dynamic changes in the relative positions of wealth and power among the main protagonists, as shown in Table 9.1.

If we use gross domestic product (GDP) as an indicator of the wealth position of nations, the eighty years depicted in Table 9.1 show major changes in the positions of most of the nations. Recall the conflict from 1914–18 involved Germany and Austria, Hungary (with less than 1 percent of global GDP in 1913), pitted against Britain, France, Russia, and later the United States; whereas from 1939–45 Germany plus Italy (with about 3 percent of global GDP in 1950) and Japan were in conflict with Britain, France, Russia, and the United States. This period results in a massive increase in the United States' position, a significant rise in the position of Russia (USSR), and declines in the positions of Britain, Germany, and France. In a rapidly growing global economy, the United States increases its proportion of global GDP by more than threefold. The dynamism in the global distribution of wealth was connected to the tragic levels of conflict and war.

Looking at the contemporary world, we can see even more dramatic shifts in the proportions of global GDP in the past thirty years and many have begun to wonder what these changes portend for the future. This chapter examines the relationships of wealth and power in terms of the questions and issues related to the rapid growth of emerging economies, with a special emphasis on China. The rapid gains by emerging economies, particularly China, are the main source of the discussion and debate regarding shifting balances of global power. But achieving such restructuring requires continuing growth relative to developed states and this has been repeatedly called into question. We examine the potential for continuing emerging economy growth, focusing on China, considering and evaluating the main arguments.

Table 9.1 Relative Share of Global GDP, 1900–50 (1990 international Dollars)

	1870	*1913*	*1950*
Great Britain	8.99	8.23	6.52
United States	8.81	18.9	27.3
Germany	6.47	8.67	4.97
Russia (USSR)	7.46	8.49	9.57
France	6.46	5.27	4.12
Japan	2.24	2.63	3.02

Source: Data from Angus Maddison, *The World Economy*, Paris: OECD, 2006, 639.

The discussion of wealth and power often hinges on what counts and how to interpret changes in relative and absolute advantages among states. We will focus on two main elements of this debate, namely how do we measure and evaluate the shifting capabilities of nations and how do we use these indicators to reach conclusions about the implications for global relations and security? Once we have a clear sense of measurement and analysis, a second important issue relates to making predictions about the future growth prospects for emerging economies. Emerging economies have not yet achieved parity and still remain far from dominant in the global economy; achieving either requires continuing growth relative to developed states. Relevant to this is an important hypothesis asserting that many rising nations reach a point where they experience significant declines in growth rates and are unable to achieve advanced positions in the global economy. We consider in some detail the barriers to continuing economic growth in emerging economies by focusing on China and its ability to continue to make the transition from low to high income. A third major topic in this chapter involves making some predictions about the power relationships of the United States and China and developing some alternative scenarios as a basis for developing expectations within a range of likely outcomes. We consider economic and military relationships over a twenty-year time horizon. Finally, we use two major theories connecting wealth and power – power transition theory and theories of economic interdependence – to examine some of the possible outcomes of the shifting power and wealth relationships of China and the United States.

Changes in Economic Relationships through Time

Let's go back to the world of 1980, compare this to the world of today, and analyze the relationships of power and wealth. Consider Table 9.2 and the fourteen nations, which represent both advanced economies and emerging economies, and compare the relative GDP of these nations.

Scholars and analysts frequently use GDP as a proxy measure of potential power, given that a larger economy offers resources that can be converted into various forms of influence. This premise does not solve the problem of measurement: how do you count the size of an economy and, more difficult, how do you determine who is up and who is down? In Tables 9.1 and 9.2, we have used total GDP adjusted for prices changes.[2] An alternative measure, which we provide in Table 9.3, is GDP per capita over time.

The comparison of 1980 and 2012 GDP and per capita GDP levels in Table 9.3 generates several interesting conclusions. Surely the most striking is the stunning increase in the size of the Chinese economy, in 2012 almost twenty-one times larger in real terms than in 1980. At the same time, the Chinese economy in 1980 was extraordinarily small, at

Table 9.2 Relative Economic Capabilities Using Two Measures

Nation	I.		II.	
	1980	*2012*	*1980*	*2010*
Belgium (A)	229	406	199	377
Brazil (E)	513	1,136	594	1,755
Canada (A)	568	1,255	542	1,170
China (E)	216	4,522	1,278	10,122
France (A)	1,283	2,249	1,117	2,022
Germany (A)	1,760	3,069	1,381	2,778
India (E)	203	1,368	752	4,203
Indonesia (E)	80	427	285	975
Japan (A)	2,488	4,711	1,979	3,893
Korea (E)	162	1,078	163	1,312
Mexico (E)	460	997	732	1,407
Turkey (E)	162	628	293	1,007
UK (A)	1,182	2,393	962	2,011
US (A)	5,796	13,518	5,750	13,125

Sources: I. 1980 and 2012: Data from the World Bank, http://data.worldbank.org/indicator/ NY.GDP.MKTP.KD?page=6
II. 1980 and 2010: Data from Penn World Tables, http://cid.econ.ucdavis.edu/data/html

Note: I. 1980 and 2012 GDP in Constant 2005 Terms (billions $US)
II. 1980 and 2010 in Expenditure-side Real GDP at Chained PPP (billions $US)
A = advanced economy; E = emerging economy

Table 9.3 Comparative Per Capita GDP ($US)

Nation	*1980*	*2012*
Belgium (A)	13,730	44,990
Brazil (E)	2,180	11,630
Canada (A)	11,320	50,970
China (E)	220	5,740
France (A)	12,830	41,750
Germany (A)	12,600	44,010
India (E)	270	1,530
Indonesia (E)	510	3,420
Japan (A)	10,670	47,870
Korea (E)	1,810	22,670
Mexico (E)	2,420	9,740
Turkey (E)	1,860	10,830
UK (A)	8,510	38,250
US (A)	12,950	50,120

Source: Data from http://data.worldbank.org/indicator/NY.GNP.PCAP.CD

Note: Figures are World Bank calculations

roughly the same size as tiny Belgium, only slightly larger than Korea and Turkey and half the size of Mexico. Chinese per capita income was an astonishingly low $220. In some ways, China's rate of economic growth is magnified by the low starting point. Advanced economies also grow significantly, with most about double the size in 2012 as in 1980 (see "Comparing Advanced and Emerging Economies, 1980 and 2012" below). Several other emerging economies produce dramatic growth: Korea nearly sevenfold; India, Turkey, and Indonesia rising by about fivefold; and Mexico and Brazil about twice as large. Less clear is whether we should conclude that our sample of emerging economies is catching up to the sample of advanced economies, thereby reducing the power position of the rich world. One major issue associated with answering this question is whether we should make comparisons in absolute or relative terms.

Comparing Advanced and Emerging Economies, 1980 and 2012 (trillions $US)

GDP Ratios, 1980/2012	*Absolute Advantage, 1980/2012*
1980 GDP 13.306/1.796 = 7.41:1	**1980 GDP** 13.306 – 1.796 = $11.510
1980 GDP (PPP)	**1980 GDP (PPP)**
2012 GDP 27.601/10.156 = 2.72:1	**2012 GDP** 27.601 – 10.156 = $17.445
Per Capita Ratios **1980 Average Per Capita** $11,801/1,324 = 8.91:1	**Per Capita Absolute Advantage** **1980 Average Per Capita** $11,801 – $1,324 = $10,477
2012 Per Capita $45,423/$6,127 = 7.4:1	**2012 Per Capita** $45,423 – $6,127 = $39,296

Source: Author's calculations

We get two quite different perspectives on catching up here. On the one hand, we can see the large decline in the ratio of advanced and emerging economy GDPs, from 7.41:1 in 1980 to 2.72:1 in 2012, but the per capita ratio is a much smaller difference from almost 9:1 to 7.4:1. The economies of advanced nations remain significantly larger but by a much smaller proportion. By this reasoning, emerging economies have engaged in significant catch-up, especially if we remember the long two centuries after about 1820 during which these nations fell very far behind. A very different perspective comes from looking at the absolute advantage of rich and poor nations in the right side of "Comparing Advanced and Emerging Economies, 1980 and 2012" above. There we see, in spite of the extraordinary growth by emerging economies, the absolute advantage in GDP size in 1980 has actually gotten larger, growing from $11.5 trillion to $17.48 trillion. If we focus only on China and the United States, a similar finding is reached. The $5.580 trillion gap in 1980 grows to a US advantage of $8.996 trillion in 2012. By this measure, China and other emerging economies have not caught up but have actually fallen farther behind in the last three decades.

There is no standard and accepted way to measure the power relations of nations. One important point to keep in mind is most evidence about our complex world is like this; only rarely do we get a clear and unambiguous finding. Consider a debate about who is the greatest hitter of all time in baseball. There we have an enormous amount of data, most of it very accurate and little debatable (unlike evidence for national wealth and power), but a consensus is hard to reach. What indicator of hitting do we use: batting average, home runs, RBIs, runs per at bat? Or do we use some combination of indicators with what kind of weighting?

Returning to the issue of national power, do we assume that power gradients, such as those found in tables above, are linear? That is, does each movement along a scale measure an equal increment in power? Specifically, does a $200 billion increase from $5.5 trillion to $5.7 trillion in US GDP have the same effect as a $200 billion increase from $200 billion to $400 billion for China? The answer, almost surely, is no and yet we cannot say with precision just how this is true. Consider a related example and the effects on national power. Poor nations experience the effects of growth differently than rich nations. A poor nation, such as Vietnam, has seen its economy grow rapidly from 1993 to the present, as we see in Table 9.4.

In relative terms, the Vietnamese economy is four times larger in 2012 than in 1993. This is a huge relative increase and the result is Vietnamese now have much higher consumption patterns than in the early 1990s.[3] Moreover, not only can consumption rise significantly but spending on infrastructure, education, and national defense also is much higher. But it is less clear whether Vietnam has engaged in any catching up with the United States, where a single year of 1 percent growth (a very bad year)

Table 9.4 Vietnam Economic Growth

	1993	2012
Real GDP (billions $US)	$22.1	$82.7
Per Capita GDP	$170	$1400

Sources: Data from http://data.worldbank.org/indicator/NY.GDP.MKTP.KD?page=6; http://data.worldbank.org/indicator/NY.GNP.PCAP.CD?page=3

Note: GDP figures are adjusted to 2005 dollars. Per capita figures are not so adjusted.

Photo 9.1 A Visual and Ironic Indicator of Economic Growth in Hanoi

Source: Picture taken by Sally Lairson.

Note: A part of the Hua Lo prison is the site for the construction of a large hotel and office building. This prison, often known as the "Hanoi Hilton," was used by the French to imprison Vietnamese political prisoners and as the prison for US POWs during the Vietnam War.

generates more resources in absolute dollars than the nineteen years of growth in Vietnam.

So what do we mean by "catching up" or by "rising?" For our purposes, we can distinguish a rising nation in terms of relative gains – the ability to grow faster than other nations. Catching up only begins when the rising state begins to add more wealth/military than the previously larger state. Or we could find an earlier point when the gains are large enough to affect behavior. This is when the absolute gains are large enough to represent significant gains. Aside from using hard measures, we might consider behavioral changes. For example, we could look for similarities in consumption patterns, in the distribution and availability of advanced communications and transportation (Internet penetration and superhighways), and in market size and scale. In military terms, catching up involves the ability to develop or purchase weapons that can inflict damage on an adversary's homeland and/or the ability to deter an attack on your homeland through the ability to inflict damage on attacking nations. We might also expect to see the rising power more able to gain attention for and accommodation to its positions and preferences as a result of a larger diplomatic presence in international forums.

Can the Rest (Especially China) Keep Rising?

Perhaps the central issue relating to global power and wealth in the twenty-first century is whether emerging economies can continue to achieve rapid economic growth or whether the growth options for these nations have narrowed. This situation will have an enormous impact on how we view shifting power relationships. If the 1965–2016 era, which reversed the income and wealth trends of the previous two centuries, was an aberration, we need have far less concern over a challenge to the rich world by rising emerging economies. Can this new growth continue, especially at a similar pace and scale? More specifically, can the really large emerging economies – such as China and India – sustain growth rates that eventually will bring their economies toward not just relative but absolute catching up?

Much of the questioning of the fate of emerging economies involves understanding and forecasting the nature of profound structural changes in the global economy, a complex and daunting task. This is because structural changes can have opposite effects and reinforcing effects, making prediction very difficult. Sorting out whether a downturn is the start of a long-term trend or just a temporary blip is usually difficult and can generate considerable difference of opinion. Remembering that almost no analysts were able to predict the waves of economic growth that took place in emerging economies after 1965, and only a small and beleaguered minority accurately predicted the 2008–10 financial crisis, why might we think this process of emerging economy catch-up is coming to an end?

One important scholar, Dani Rodrik, points out the economic basis for rapid economic growth, especially for poor nations wanting to advance, has come from industrialization.[4] This was made possible by shifting poor agricultural workers from low-productivity rural jobs into manufacturing, and by selling these products to rich nations. Combining the knowledge and technology of production, very inexpensive workers and high-quality infrastructure yielded a large economic advantage that propelled economic growth. According to Rodrik, this model is becoming much more difficult to follow. This is because manufacturing, even for products of low sophistication, has become much more technology and skill intensive and much less labor intensive. The production of goods no longer requires a large labor force and can no longer serve to move large numbers of the poor out of poverty.

An equally and perhaps more important factor facing emerging economies, according to Rodrik, is the essential importance of achieving the political and institutional capacity to continually restructure the domestic economy so as to catch up with the global knowledge and technology frontier and thereby upgrade human and institutional capabilities.[5] This cannot be done by markets alone, nor by politics alone, but rather by the effective interaction between policies and markets. It is this capacity that sets East Asian nations apart from other emerging economies and which has been responsible for the remarkable continuity of convergence by these nations over five decades. Many other emerging economies have benefited recently from a set of temporary conditions to achieve rapid growth, but have not been successful in developing the ability to push their economic systems toward sustained improvement. Moreover, many advanced nations have rewritten the rules for global competition so as to minimize or even eliminate the ability of emerging economies to engage in these kinds of institutional transformations.

Potentially, the effect of less labor-intensive manufacturing and the political barriers to emerging economies developing institutional improvements makes for a slowdown in the rate of growth for all and significant limits on those nations still far behind the global frontier. The result would be a dramatic decline in the rate of relative catching up by emerging economies and, thereby, less potential for realignment in global power relations.[6] This conclusion draws some support from the downturn in economic growth rates in all of the BRICs.[7] In each of these countries, growth rates declined significantly after 2010. For Brazil, Russia, and India, there is justified concern the governments have not acted effectively to direct resources to the upgrading of firms and institutions so as to sustain high growth rates.

But these conclusions about a permanent and rapid slowing are by no means uniformly shared. One of the strongest counterarguments is to point out the effects of the slowdown in growth in advanced economies, which have recently provided a significant source for the sale of emerging economy products. If these richer nations can resume the average growth of the past, this will help to boost growth in emerging economies. If growth slows in advanced economies over a long time period, emerging economies are still likely to grow faster, thereby closing the gap. Beyond the growth role of advanced economies, the ability of poorer nations to sustain growth is supported by their ability to improve productivity by receiving knowledge and technology from rich nations and applying this to their own economy. Indian workers, for example, produce only 8 percent per person what US workers produce, thereby creating a huge gap to be made up.[8] There remains considerable room for relatively easy growth through the application of readily available knowledge and capital to workers in India.[9] The systems of global knowledge networks and diffusion have not shut down but continue to expand and deepen. Also working in favor of emerging economies is the potential that comes from increasing domestic consumption in China and potentially in India. Rebalancing the Chinese economy toward greater consumption engages the global system of production networks as a source of supply of consumer goods. This system is currently focused on supplying goods to rich nations; the growth of the domestic market in China can boost the economies of many nations, including China. It is not unreasonable to expect both these nations to provide growth poles for themselves and others through rising consumption.

There are other reasons for optimism about continuing emerging economy growth. Perhaps the most important feature of recent emerging economy growth has been the accelerating rate of growth and the widening scope of nations participating in this growth. Over the past fifty years the number of emerging nations with per capita economic growth rates exceeding that of the United States has increased dramatically. From the 1960s to 1990s, 30 percent of emerging economies averaged a 1.5 percent advantage in growth over the United States. But from the late 1990s, the proportion of emerging economies exceeding US growth rates rose to 73 percent and the margin of this advantage to 3.3 percent.[10] This evidence is consistent with the view that important structural changes have taken place in the global economy supporting continuing emerging economy growth.

Because China is a special case and the key player in emerging economies, we turn now to a closer examination of the potential for future growth there.

Is Chinese Growth Sustainable?

China and several other emerging economies have achieved spectacular growth in recent decades. Real per capita income growth in China has averaged nearly 8 percent for over three decades, leading to a dramatic transformation of the physical infrastructure and the real incomes and wealth of the population of the nation. There is little dispute about the reality of economic growth in China; much less consensus exists over interpreting the significance of this growth. Some see this growth as creating the material basis for the elevation of China to the status of a superpower, at least in the near future. Others raise large doubts about the sustainability of this growth while others find the Chinese economy to be much less than it appears, at least in terms of conveying significant global power. Any sign of slower growth in China brings increased skepticism about future growth.[11]

In this section, we will examine three areas of contention over the nature and future of the Chinese economy. First is the view that the Chinese economy, whatever its apparent strengths, contains significant and even fatal flaws that attenuate its capacity for global power. Second, is the prediction that China lacks the capacity for continued development through upgrading its technological capabilities and is doomed to remain trapped at about its present economic level. In a later section we will consider the relationship of China and its capabilities to the rest of the world, focusing on judging how economic and power relationships will affect the potential for war and peace.

In previous chapters, we have examined the globalization of production and exchange through new systems of fragmented value chains distributed across many nations and often focused on an assembly area located in China. This system, for China, has been built by transnational firms through foreign direct investment (FDI) in China and links to global markets. The most obvious result has been the substantial contribution of this system to China's rapid economic growth. Less clear, even controversial, is whether the Chinese economy has developed in such a way that growth is sustainable. This would require that Chinese firms be able to leverage the presence of foreign firms to raise their own capabilities and "move up the value chain" to higher-value products and processes. Possessing this capability would do much to permit continuing growth based on rising wages and productivity.

Students of the Chinese economy reach very different conclusions about the future rates of growth and development and, consequently, make equally different proposals for how to respond to Chinese power. One of the most important comes from Edward Steinfeld, who focuses on control over and the effects of the systems of fragmented production of which China is an important element. Both the manner and the timing of the Chinese entry into the global economy differ from some of its East Asian neighbors. In the 1960s and 1970s, Korea and Taiwan followed the Japanese development model by sharply limiting foreign direct investment, using alternative avenues for obtaining technology and knowledge, and directing capital toward building up several of its domestic firms.[12] Over time, the role of foreign firms in all three nations was relatively small until well after its domestic firms had been built into globally competitive entities.

By contrast, China was ready to bring in foreign capitalist firms, though initially restricted to a small number of locations, almost from the beginning. Benefiting from the relatively wealthy overseas Chinese investors in Hong Kong, Taiwan, and Singapore, China received rising levels of FDI that turned into something of a small flood in the early 1990s and became a near tsunami after World Trade Organization (WTO) accession in 2001. These firms dominated the most economically advanced sectors of the Chinese economy and provided the products associated with much of its exports that also contributed significantly to growth. The Chinese government provided special benefits to entice foreign firms, even to the point of favoring these firms over domestic ones. This led to the odd practice of round-tripping FDI, in which a domestic firm would send funds abroad and reconstitute itself as a foreign firm, move FDI to China, and operate so as to gain the privileges of foreign status. The main question about the overall process is whether the massive presence of foreign firms has expanded, weakened, or left unaffected China's opportunities for future growth.[13]

Steinfeld believes the Chinese have mostly harmed their economic future through such heavy reliance on foreign firms. He argues the emergence of a knowledge-based system of global production creates large differences in the returns to different parts of the value chain. Though the Chinese role in this system is important, the way China has entered the system and the strategies adopted by its firms undermine the ability to gain the greater rewards of the more knowledge-intensive and higher-value-added parts of global production. This failure will place significant restraints on China's capacity to grow and should reduce anxiety over rising Chinese power.[14] Steinfeld asserts that China is distinctly disadvantaged in its ability to upgrade as a result of Western control over the nature and key resources of the system of global production. This structural power of the West means China will not present a serious challenge to the global power balance.

Several features of the Chinese position in global production are distinctive and contribute to a much weaker set of capabilities than are desirable. Though it is certainly true that many very advanced products come from China, the way this works makes Chinese capabilities considerably less than they seem. First, the overwhelming part of high-technology goods exported from China is by firms from advanced economies who have engaged in FDI to create these assembly facilities. The facilities are usually owned and operated by contract manufacturers, such as the Taiwanese firm Foxconn. These products are assembled using high-value components imported into China from other Asian nations, often Taiwan, Korea, and Japan, based on high-value designs and specifications that come from firms in advanced nations, such as Apple, Cisco, or Nokia. By far the greatest returns flow to those advanced firms that create, purchase, brand, and market these products, with secondary returns to component producers, and the least gains to Chinese workers assembling the products.

Chinese firms operating in this environment have frequently settled for focusing at the bottom of the value chain and have thereby consigned themselves to a situation of intense competition for high-volume but very low-margin operations that permit competition only on the basis of price.[15] For some time this has worked well to support growth and rising employment, with millions of Chinese peasants willing to move to cities such as Shenzhen for jobs in assembly factories. But the future looks much less promising for this strategy, as the number of Chinese ready to make this move has declined, labor shortages in Eastern China have increased, and those who have jobs have been able to demand higher wages. Recent years have seen substantial wage increases in Eastern urban areas, with the annual average rise above 20 percent in many areas. One report puts the wage increase from 2004–10 at 150 percent for rural migrant workers.[16]

Perhaps equally or even more important for the Chinese economy has been the exceptional reliance on investment as a basis for economic growth. Even more than its Asian neighbors, China has engaged in a capital mobilizing and investment-based system of promoting growth.

The construction of electric power grids, roads, airports, fast trains and the massive concrete support systems for the tracks, superhighways, factories and the machinery to operate them, schools, apartments, and giant office towers – all this investment has taken place at an unprecedented pace in China.[17] What has been relatively suppressed is consumption and the rise in incomes that would support such spending.[18] Many analysts believe China must shift these proportions significantly in order to sustain an acceptable growth rate. What this means is China needs to institute several related structural transformations that will shift resources from infrastructure investment to household consumption. These changes include altering the structural bias in favor of infrastructure lending – usually directed by local and provincial governments toward state-owned enterprises – and increasing the opportunities for small business and consumer borrowing, increasing the options for investment that is driven by consumer preferences expressed in free markets, and freeing up interest rates related to borrowing and saving to reflect market-derived decisions about investment.[19] China's ability to rebalance its economy will depend on the ability of the political system to engineer these kinds of structural changes in the face of significant political and economic opposition.

A third factor pointing to a slowdown in Chinese growth has to do with resource constraints. The most obvious of these is the size of the labor force. Since the adoption of a one-child policy in the 1970s, China has enjoyed a favorable ratio of workers to dependents. This is rapidly changing as a large cohort of older workers begin to reach retirement age and the workforce as a whole both shrinks and ages. In the coming decades, China will face labor shortages and a growing burden of caring for the elderly.[20]

China's rapid growth and large population have also strained natural resources. Water shortages in north China are forcing planners to make difficult choices among the demands arising from energy, industry, and agriculture.[21] Rising incomes have led to increased meat consumption. As a result, China's grain harvest cannot keep up with demand, resulting in growing dependence upon imports.[22] Air pollution in China is the worst in the world, shaving an estimated 5.5 years off the average lifespan of Northern Chinese.[23]

Sustaining something close to the extraordinary rates of growth that have propelled China into the ranks of great powers will require at least two major economic transformations. First, Chinese firms will need to succeed repeatedly in developing the capabilities for operating at higher levels of the value chain and this will require increasing capabilities for innovation. If successful, these efforts will permit higher wages and allow firms to earn greater profits. Higher wages can only be justified through operating higher-value-added activities. Second, the balance between investment and consumption will need to be altered so that higher-value-added production can take place and Chinese consumers will be able to drive growth with their own purchases. These important changes are well understood by the Chinese government and significant policy efforts have been devoted to strategies for achieving them.[24] What are the chances the needed structural transformations will take place to a degree sufficient to sustain Chinese economic growth?

Reaching judgments about this extremely important issue is made clearer when we establish some distinctions among various types of industrial development and innovation processes, and apply these categories to judgments about China and other emerging economies. For our purposes, there are three broad categories that define important features of improvement in industrial and economic capability that can contribute significantly to continued Chinese growth (see "Types of Upgrading" below). These categories are cumulative, in that capabilities at lower levels are necessary for achieving higher levels, but nations can and do remain stuck at lower levels when they fail to make the kinds of investments and structural changes to continue improvement.[25]

Types of Upgrading

Imitation
Local innovation and upgrading to global standards
Global innovation either at the fast follower or leading edge (first mover) level

---

Each of these levels requires knowledge acquisition and application, but at progressively more sophisticated and complex levels. Imitation involves the ability to effectively borrow (or steal) ideas, techniques, models, and operations of products from other more advanced sources and reengineer and duplicate these capabilities in replicas or variations of products. The "knock-off" products readily available in emerging economies, such as the "Rolex" watch for $4 or the "iPhone" for $20 which work (more or less) for a while, are examples. However much Western firms condemn these products, they do demonstrate a certain level of sophistication in knowledge acquisition and application. A more legitimate example is the Chinese search engine Baidu, which was created as a "knock-off" of Google.[26] Imitation occurs across many areas of an emerging economy and creates a knowledge base that permits upgrading and local innovation.[27] A broader but related capability involves obtaining global knowledge through legitimate means – such as a joint venture – and leveraging that to produce similar products.

Achieving widespread upgrading across the value chain, and even better, significant local innovation in products and processes, has already begun to happen in China. At early stages of industrial development, upgrading and local innovation tend to be combined, as firms are able to improve their value chain position by adding "new to the firm" or local industry capabilities. Sometimes this can represent local innovation by recombining global capabilities with an improvement special to local markets and preferences. An example from China was Haier's addition of a special heavy-duty filter to their washing machine sold in rural China. This permitted customers to wash their vegetables without clogging the washing machine. Such innovation, though it does not enable globally competitive capabilities, does promote firm upgrading that can lead to such capabilities. Private software firms in Hangzhou were found consistently to generate important forms of upgrading to improve such competencies as organizational integration and the transformation of external knowledge.[28] A more important form of upgrading that links local capabilities and global competition occurs in the special ability to produce varying quantities of products, including mass production, with significant options for customization in Chinese factories. This is a globally competitive specialization, focused mainly in the information technology industry, and continued innovation of local capabilities builds China's position in the global value chain.[29]

The ability of Taiwan, Korea, and Singapore to achieve the level of upgrading needed to sustain economic growth, notwithstanding the somewhat easier global environment that is faced by China, bodes well for China's chances.[30] For China has one enormous advantage over these smaller nations: its population provides a massive domestic market, which creates opportunities for producing and selling by Chinese firms, even in competition with foreign firms. Chinese firms in the near term do not need to depend that much on exports, such as smaller Asian tigers have done, to achieve economic growth. Can Chinese firms compete against foreign firms in the China market and engage in upgrading across the value chain?

Perhaps the strongest incentive for Chinese firm upgrading is the intense competition provided by foreign firms operating in China.[31] With some restrictions, the Chinese economy is mostly open to foreign firms, which are able to set up wholly owned operations in China and both produce and sell. These firms create a very competitive environment for domestic Chinese firms, which have very good reasons to work hard to provide value to Chinese consumers. Even in situations where Chinese firms have lost domestic market share to foreign firms, there is considerable evidence of successful efforts to upgrade across the value chain and sustain a viable competitive position. Thus, rather than seeing a set of one-sided gains for foreign firms, Chinese firms have made important gains as well. A complex and highly competitive Chinese auto industry, with foreign firms dominating domestic markets, nonetheless saw the rise of several Chinese firms developing cars just for the Chinese market and achieving important growth in market share at the low end. In the construction equipment industry, which has boomed given immense construction across China, domestic firms hold a dominant market share at the low end of the market. And in the computer numerically controlled machine tool industry, in spite of significant imports, domestic producers dominated the low-end market.

Many of these same domestic firms in each of these three industries have succeeded in leveraging the capabilities in low-end markets into higher-value segments. This is because competition between foreign firms and Chinese firms in Chinese markets can be on a much more level playing field in low-end markets and increasingly in middle-level markets. Not only do Chinese firms have cost advantages over foreign firms, these firms also have matured to the point where they are able to narrow significantly the quality advantages of foreign firms. This has permitted firms in each industry to move successfully into middle market product spaces.[32] Ironically, opportunities for upgrading quality levels by Chinese firms expand as foreign firms, seeking lower costs, increase purchases from local suppliers. This requires efforts to transfer technology and knowledge to these local firms in order to raise their quality. Local Chinese final producers can also reap the gains in quality by buying from these same suppliers and thereby improve their competitive position against foreign firms. Moreover, local original equipment manufacturer (OEM) firms also gain through technology and knowledge transfer directly, as they participate in joint venture relationships with foreign firms and in multiple supply chains. The presence of foreign firms also aids local firms by providing advanced training for Chinese workers who often are hired by local firms or even start up their own firms. Even more important is the growing capacity of Chinese firms to purchase foreign firms and gain access to technology and knowledge.[33]

The most likely form of advanced innovation from China and Chinese firms will not come soon from globally leading edge innovation, but instead from "fast follower" efforts.[34] This is generally the same sort of innovation that comes from many advanced firms and nations around the world and involves a much more advanced form of imitation. An example may help: Samsung, a Korean firm with massive research and development (R&D) capabilities and deeply embedded in global knowledge and innovation networks, responded to Apple's release of the truly innovative iPhone with a "fast follower" smartphone that duplicated many of the features and capabilities of the iPhone and even added some improvements. Achieving this rapid response to a global innovation was itself quite remarkable, based in the massive system of knowledge and production capabilities Samsung owns and manages.[35] A significant number of Chinese and emerging economy firms have the capacity for a "fast follower" strategy or can reasonably aspire to such a role. Chinese examples include the networking firm Huawei, the computer firm Lenovo,[36] the appliance firm Haier, the smartphone firm Xiaomi, and the auto firms Chery and Geely.[37] In one of the most advanced information technology segments, the integrated circuit design industry, only two Chinese firms break into the global top twenty-five firms – a list dominated by the United States and Taiwan – but these Chinese firms rank in the top nine of the fastest growing.[38] For these and other Chinese firms to achieve success in adopting a "fast follower" strategy, they will need to develop substantial internal knowledge, technology, productivity, product development, and marketing capabilities along with a diversified set of connections to global knowledge and trading networks.

Perhaps the most critical element in creating sustained Chinese growth is the ability to access, apply, and leverage knowledge about technologies, products, and processes. This requires a strong domestic knowledge base located in firms, universities, and governments, the ability to apply knowledge to new products and processes, and significant connections to global knowledge networks. There are multiple pathways for access – many legitimate, many not, many in-between – whereas application and leveraging depends on incentives, opportunities, and capabilities.[39] Not surprisingly, given the remaining large distance between the Chinese knowledge base and the global frontier, the Chinese government is deeply involved in organizing efforts to obtain knowledge from abroad. These governmental activities include both military and commercial areas and involve large institutes in China designed to receive, organize, and diffuse foreign-obtained knowledge.[40] Another option for knowledge acquisition by China comes from using its vast holdings of foreign exchange to purchase foreign firms and obtain knowledge by buying and owning it. Some recent prominent examples include an effort by Chinese machine tool companies to upgrade capabilities by purchasing small and medium-sized German machine tool firms and the purchase of the Swedish auto firm Volvo by the Chinese firm Geely. These efforts can also provide access into global knowledge networks.[41]

Achieving innovation at more advanced and even globally leading edge levels requires a diverse set of capabilities. One of the most important is a high level of effectiveness from firms, universities, and governments along with deep connections with each other and from each of these institutions into global knowledge networks. Some Chinese innovation regions succeed better than others in these tasks.[42] At an even broader level, a nation seeking to become a global technology and innovation leader needs to achieve a level of breadth, depth, and diffusion of knowledge. China has a limited set of firms, universities, and other institutions where this has been achieved. This means R&D spending, which has risen rapidly, remains too diffuse rather than diffused, and operates more to support a process of learning rather than actually advancing basic and applied research.[43] Nonetheless, China has made enormous strides in achieving this level of innovative capability and has positioned itself for a likely move to global parity within a relatively few years. The accomplishments of China can be seen in:

- high education levels (97 percent literacy);
- numbers of well-trained science and technology personnel;[44]
- rising R&D spending;
- global firms' R&D centers in China;
- students studying abroad;
- patents – which can be interpreted as a closing or a widening gap;
- substantial resources directed toward targeted industries and technologies.

China has achieved much in the past three decades, not only in its astounding growth rates, but equally in the repeated structural transformations in the economy to adapt to new stages in the growth process and to changes in the global economy. There are simply too many Chinese firms that have been very successful in the competitive environment of China and the global economy, China is too deeply connected to global knowledge networks, and the current and potential size of the Chinese market is simply too big to accept the pessimistic view of China's economic future.[45]

Predicting Chinese Growth

The most likely Chinese scenario for the next several decades is for growth to continue, but at a slower pace, perhaps in the 5–7 percent range.[46] For the United States, the most likely scenario is to continue to average 2.5 percent growth over the next twenty years. The following chart (Table 9.5) creates a range of outcomes in GDP size for China and the United States based on these averages.

At an average of 7 percent real growth, the Chinese economy will double in size every ten years. This means in 2034 the Chinese economy will be four times larger than in 2014. Using purchasing power parity (PPP) calculations for analysis, the Chinese economy is approximately $10 trillion in 2014 and would thus be $40 trillion in twenty years. If the United States experiences average real growth of 2.5 percent over the

Table 9.5 Alternative Scenarios for China and US GDP in 2034

Country/Growth Rate	2034 GDP
United States @ 2.5%	$26.2 trillion
China @ 7%	$40.0 trillion
China @ 6%	$32.0 trillion
China @ 5%	$26.5 trillion

same twenty years, the economy will total about $26 trillion, substantially smaller than the Chinese economy growing at 7 percent.[47] But 7 percent growth continuing in China for another twenty years is unlikely. More realistic would be a 5–6 percent rate sustained for this period. But, even at this growth rate China will at least equal or surpass the size of the US economy. How will changes like this affect the stability not only of the global economy but global politics as well?

Alternative Perspectives on Chinese Growth

We have just concluded that the most likely outcome of the shifting economic relationship between China and the United States over the next twenty years is for China to achieve a rough parity and perhaps surpass the United States in economic size. Such an outcome suggests the possibility of a major transformation in global relations. At the same time, we have made clear the wide range of possible outcomes that also have a significant probability. We now consider how someone might disagree with this conclusion. The first dissenting perspective sees a long period of continuing US dominance; the second perspective anticipates the emergence of China's dominance over the global system.

One scholar in particular has been widely viewed as dissenting from the view that China will be the most powerful nation in the world in relatively short order. Michael Beckley argues instead that China may be rising but is not catching up.[48] Beckley is an especially strong advocate of the view that measures of absolute advantage are more important than measures of relative advantage. By this standard, China remains farther behind the United States today than twenty-five years ago. Moreover, US power rests on its innovation capabilities and its ability to design a global system that disproportionately benefits the United States. Much of this US advantage rests on the advanced and unmatched capacity for innovation in basic science, applying science to products and production, and the management of knowledge-based industries. Like Steinfeld, Beckley sees China's technological position as relatively weak, overwhelmingly dependent on foreign firms, and receding from the United States' position. In sum, Beckley believes we are wrong to anticipate an end to the unipolar world of American dominance.[49]

Contrasting sharply with both Beckley and this chapter, two scholars have been outspoken in predicting a coming era of Chinese dominance. Subramanian and Jacques, in separate books,[50] chart a future of Chinese dominance and "rule" significantly at variance with the conclusions of this chapter. Each focuses on economic power as the origin of national power. Subramanian places a special emphasis on financial power, with the debtor–creditor relationship between the United States and China having a defining importance. China will be able to translate its significant economic power – based in GDP, trade, and finance – into the achievement of the RMB as the key currency in the coming years. The author's measures of relative economic capabilities already show China at near parity with the United States in 2010 and projections indicate an index of Chinese economic advantage of as much as 80 percent by 2030. Indeed, these predictions suggest China's economic power will roughly equal that of the United States and the European Union (EU) combined in 2030. At the same time, Subramanian expects China will remain deeply linked to the global economy and will not seek to overthrow the system.[51]

As we see, making predictions is very hard, especially when it is about the future.[52] Reputable scholars come to widely varying conclusions about the future of China's economic position. Some see the Chinese economy as much weaker than it appears and facing significant decline in growth rates. Others see China as much stronger than we realize and likely to continue its rapid rise. We have argued that China has achieved much in the past thirty years, and though it remains well behind global techno-logical frontier and per capita income levels, it retains great capacity to sustain significant economic growth into the next several decades. In about twenty years, China will have achieved rough parity with the United States in many measures but will remain behind in per capita income, techno-logical capabilities, and military strength. We now turn to a second facet of this analysis, one with equally large room for disagreement: how will the new world of power and wealth affect the potential for global coop-eration and conflict?

Power, Wealth, Conflict, and Peace in the Twenty-First Century

The relationship between the United States and China will have an outsized impact on global relations in the twenty-first century and, conse-quently, this topic has drawn commentary and predictions from many scholars, pundits, and political commentators. There is no lack of posi-tions about what will happen, and the real challenge is to sort through the array of ideas and understand the reasons for the differences. Not surprisingly, differences in conclusions are often related to difference in theories and perspectives. Some of the best of these studies work to use a perspective to identify a single element that will influence overall rela-tions and then spin out a scenario based on that element. Some focus on power, some on the process of power changes, yet others on financial relations. Two main groups of conclusions arise from this: those who expect an increasingly conflicted world and those who look toward a relatively peaceful system of interactions. We will review the perspectives and the analysis they provide for the political economy of power and wealth in the twenty-first century. The greatest value from such an exer-cise is to identify those main causal forces that are likely to affect outcomes and the causal processes by which this may happen.

The examination of United States–China relations has been dominated by three schools of thought, each of which offers important insights but none of which is adequate to assess the range of potential outcomes. The first school is neorealism, which defines the relationship in terms of power, based on decline and rise. Power in this conception is almost always linear and its effects are defined by the capacity for political influence and the potential for military conflict. The second school is neoliberalism, which examines the effects of economic interdependence and liberal international institutions. These are thought to be supportive of a peaceful relationship among nations. The third sees relations affected by the ideas of elites and the political systems of the nations.[53]

However, these schools may be overly narrow for trying to understand such a complex and dynamic relationship. These ideas need to be supplemented by perspectives that are able to see more complex processes that permit several possible outcomes with some sense of the probability of each happening. The analytical approach adopted in this section is distinct in two ways: first, we consider a range of possible outcomes in the United States–China power relationship; second, we consider multiple causal elements and the interaction of these elements as forces affecting United States–China relations.[54] Projecting the economic and military power capabilities will be based on varying sets of assumptions, each with a different probability of being realized. This permits a range of outcomes with different probabilities; from these we attempt to focus on a subset with the greatest likelihood of happening. But readers will be able to make their own judgments about the realism of the choices. In addition, we work to combine different theoretical perspectives in ways that permit a more complex and nuanced analysis of the processes that can lead to war or peace.

United States and China Power Scenarios

In this section we examine in more detail the elements of national power and the relation to wealth, recognizing the many dimensions of this relationship. National power is a relational concept – the interactions among nations – but is equally a complex combination of capabilities by any particular nation – many complementary elements must work together to create national power.[55] We focus now on the level of current military spending and make a range of predictions for the next twenty years. Data is found in Tables 9.6 and 9.7.

Tables 9.6 and 9.7 demonstrate that, at present, the United States has overwhelming dominance in military spending. The United States in 2015 represents 36 percent of global military spending, which roughly equals the military spending of the next ten nations combined.[56] At the same time, we can see that China has a rapidly growing level of military spending as a proportion of US military spending.[57] One prediction is

Table 9.6 United States and China, Comparative Military Spending 1990–2013 (constant 2011 billions $US)

	1990	1995	2000	2005	2008	2010	2012	2013
US	527.1	411.7	394.2	580.0	649.0	720.4	668.8	618.7
China	19.8	23.1	37.0	71.5	106.8	136.5	157.6	171.4
China as % of US	3.75	5.61	9.38	12.33	16.45	18.94	23.56	27.70

Source: Data from www.sipri.org/research/armaments/milex/milex_database

Table 9.7 Global Military Spending, 2015
World Share of the Fifteen Nations with the Highest Level of Military Spending

Nation	% World Share
United States	36.0
China	13.0
Saudi Arabia	5.2
Russia	4.0
United Kingdom	3.3
India	3.1
France	3.0
Japan	2.4
Germany	2.4
South Korea	2.2
Brazil	1.5
Italy	1.4
Australia	1.4
UAE	1.4
Israel	1.0

- These fifteen nations account for 81 percent of world military spending
- The United States and China together account for nearly one-half of all military spending

Source: adapted from data provided by SIPRI at http://books.sipri.org/files/FS/SIPRIFS1604.pdf

that China will equal US military spending beginning in the early 2030s and then surpass the United States.[58]

How are we to judge this recent process of change? Remembering that we can examine this in terms of relative advantage or absolute advantage, the Chinese are making relative advances and recently perhaps now even absolute advances. In 1990, China had 3.75 percent of US military spending, about the same as South Korea and India. In 2013, China had 27.7 percent of US military spending, which is almost as large as the next three nations – Russia, Saudi Arabia, and France – combined. In relative terms, this is a major improvement. In absolute terms, China has made less progress. In 1990, the United States held an absolute advantage in spending of $527.2 billion; in 2013, the absolute difference in military spending had declined somewhat, to $447.3 billion. When military spending is calculated as a percent of GDP, we see that for both China and the United States spending has declined. US spending as a percent of GDP has declined from 5.3 percent in 1990 to 4.4 percent in 2012; for China, military spending has declined from 2.5 percent of GDP in 1990 to 2.0 percent in 2012.[59]

How do we interpret this and other data about the wealth and power relationship of China and the United States? The range of discussion and conclusion is very wide. Some analysts foresee a rapid transition from a dominant United States to a dominant China. Others expect the dominance of the United States to last for a considerable period of time. And a third group finds the wealth relationship more complex. The term "dominance" would seem to have a clear meaning, but that is not necessarily so. It should mean the ability to prevail consistently in having the preferences of one state define outcomes in international affairs, even as no other state is able to achieve its preferences except as these correspond to the dominant state. Is it reasonable to expect continued dominance by the United States, the ascendance of China to dominance, or the emergence of a more bipolar world with both the United States and China contending to achieve their preferences on a range of issues?

If we focus just on projections of relative/absolute GDP, share of global GDP, and military spending, what kind of material power analysis emerges?[60] There is considerable value in examining different assumptions as the basis for making projections. What are the consequences of making alternative assumptions?

The calculations in Tables 9.8[61] and 9.9[62] show the substantial variance that can result from making seemingly small changes in assumptions. But the conclusion from this data, where we have the highest confidence, is the unlikely outcome of either US or Chinese dominance. If we accept the combination of the most favorable United States scenario with the most unfavorable China scenario, the result is a replication of

Table 9.8 Projecting US and Chinese Power

	2013	2033
Real GDP PPP (2013 $)		
US	$16 trillion	$26.2 trillion
China	$10 trillion	$32.0 trillion
% World GDP		
US	22.8%	18.7%
China	14.2%	22.8%
Military Spending		
US	$618.7 billion	$1.15 trillion
China	$171.4 billion	$1.12 trillion

Table 9.9 Projecting US and Chinese Power, Alternative Scenario

	2013	2033
Real GDP PPP (2013 $)		
US (1.5%–3.5%)	$16 trillion	$21.5–$31.8 trillion
China (3%–5%)	$10 trillion	$18.1–$25.5 trillion
% World GDP		
US	22.8%	15.3%–22.7%
China	14.2%	12.9%–18.2%
Military Spending		
US (3.5% GDP)	$618 billion	$.946–$1.4 trillion
China	$157.6 billion	$.633–$.893 trillion

GDP and military spending and proportion of global GDP similar to the present. To the extent the United States is dominant today, we can expect that to continue into the future. But this scenario combination is exceedingly unlikely and would require dramatic and long-term shifts from present trends. Nonetheless, this outcome is not impossible. The most pessimistic growth rates for China – 3 percent – are much higher than growth rates for Japan from 1990–2012 – about 1 percent. The assumed high range growth rate for the United States – 3.5 percent – is probably the least likely, but not inconceivable. What makes this scenario most improbable is the *combination* of two low-probability events: high US growth *and* low Chinese growth.

The combination of the most favorable growth rates: for China – 7 percent – and least favorable for the United States – 1.5 percent – creates a scenario that is only slightly more likely. Here the result is wide Chinese advantages in GDP, global proportion of GDP, and military spending. This scenario comes close to simply projecting recent trends across the next two decades. Though this is not impossible, there are good reasons not to expect this to happen. Most important, rapid Chinese growth will be difficult to achieve without at least significant US growth. This makes the *combination* of high Chinese growth *and* exceptionally low US growth a low-probability outcome. But even here, can we realistically impute Chinese dominance to a situation where the United States is spending nearly $1 trillion on defense?

The most likely outcome is a world in which China's GDP is larger than that of the United States by about 25 percent, with a per capita income less than one-half that of the United States, and with military spending roughly equal to the United States. China will likely have closed part of the technology gap with the United States, but a significant difference in economic and military capability favoring the United States will likely persist. China will certainly have risen, but it will not be dominant. A much more probable outcome is a rough equality of capability, with each nation enjoying advantages in some areas and also dealing with important areas of disadvantage as well. Moreover, several other nations will possess significant global economic power, including Germany, Japan, Britain, and India, and perhaps Brazil and Russia. Economic capabilities will likely be even more widely distributed across many states, which will possess a variety of specializations that feed into global production systems and global innovation systems. With no nation possessing more than one-quarter of global GDP, the world of 2033 will be multipolar in terms of the distribution of power resources. If we use this conclusion as a baseline for analysis, what are the consequences for global power relations, conflict, and peace?

Power, Wealth, and Conflict

The wealth of nations and the power relations among them are closely related and in constant flux. Growth rates through time vary considerably and power capabilities typically mirror these changes. Somewhat more unusual are persistent variations among the largest nations that lead to significant shifts in the economic, military, and political capabilities affecting global systems. In the past two centuries, we have witnessed several such transformations. Between about 1800 and 1850, Great Britain emerged as the nation with the greatest economic and military power and stood as a hegemonic force in global affairs. Between 1870 and 1945, three nations – Germany, the United States, and Japan – grew rapidly and achieved positions of great global power. Horrific wars were part of this global shift, and from this the United States emerged as hegemonic. Though the Soviet Union seemed for a time to challenge the United States, by the mid-1980s the United States stood alone as the dominant state. Over the past twenty years, the growth of China has transformed this nation from economic and military insignificance into a new potential challenger to the United States.

China is an exceptional case of a rising state; the only really comparable example is the United States from about 1870–1950. The combination of rapidly rising wealth, large geographic size, and large population is very unusual. A similar situation is the rising Soviet Union from 1935–75. But in some important respects China is unique. Its population, at about 17 percent of world population, is much greater than for the United States or Soviet Union. The rate of growth in its economy also exceeds that of any large state in history, propelling China from desperate poverty to moderate wealth in three decades. In one other sense is China unique. Neither the United States nor Soviet Union was deeply connected to the global economy during the period of rapid growth; China has rapidly deepened its connection to the global economy and in some respects is as globally integrated as any other nation. Finally, China has reached a point where it has begun to close the absolute gap in its economy with the United

States. At 7 percent growth, China adds $700 billion to its productive wealth each year; at 2 percent growth, the United States adds $320 billion in productive wealth each year.

Scholars have devoted considerable attention to this process of rise and fall, developing theories and examining evidence designed to understand the political implications of economic change.

> Of the various international relations theories, power transition theory is probably the most widely used by scholars seeking to better understand the likely dynamics and consequences of the rise of China in the contemporary global systems.[63]

The theory of power transitions focuses on the shift from one hegemon in relative decline to another hegemon in relative expansion and the effects of this transition on the potential for war and peace. The theory makes somewhat specific predictions concerning the circumstances in which the process of transition is likely to lead to war or intensified conflict.[64]

The essential proposition of power transition theory is that the process of a rising power overtaking a declining hegemon creates considerable potential for conflict and war, especially if the rising power is very dissatisfied with the nature of the global system created by the incumbent hegemon.[65] In these circumstances, conflict and even war are seen to arise in several ways. The rising power, with expectations for gains from creating a new global system based on its preferences, acts to hasten this through war against the hegemonic state in decline. By contrast, another path to war comes from the declining hegemon acting to initiate preventive war while it still retains an advantage. This outcome is tempered and even eliminated should the rising state and declining hegemon share common values and similar preferences for the nature of international order.

It is not difficult to find cases that correspond to the situations described by power transition theory. The aforementioned cases of rising powers in Germany, Japan, and the United States present trajectories that seem to correspond to the basic facts of power transition theory. The rise of the United States to economic preeminence between 1880 and 1940 did not result in a war between the United States and Great Britain, presumably because these nations held very consistent preferences for the nature of global political economy. By contrast, the rise of Germany from 1870–1940 and of Japan from 1900–40 did result in global war provoked in large part by these nations. Germany initiated war against Britain and its allies twice between 1914 and 1939 in a reach for global dominance and as a way to overturn the British–American global order. Japan initiated war against the United States in 1941 hoping to achieve regional dominance in Asia and thereby create a Japanese economic zone to match that of the United States.[66] Importantly, neither Germany nor Japan at the point of initiating war had achieved parity with their adversaries, especially the coalition of states allied with their adversaries. Rather, both Germany and Japan saw war and conquest as the *means* to achieving parity or even superiority against those adversaries.

Power transition theory provides an important framework and set of propositions for thinking about exceptionally powerful rising and falling states. At the same time, there is considerable ambiguity about the circumstances that lead to war during the process of power transition.[67] At what point does a rising state initiate war: to hasten the shift in power as it approaches parity with the hegemon or after it has already achieved dominance? How do we know a priori whether a rising state is satisfied or dissatisfied? Do characteristics of global weapons systems affect the calculations of costs and benefits of war? For example, is it reasonable for power transition theorists (and neorealists) to discount the role of nuclear weapons in affecting the calculations relating to war? Can we imagine a set of circumstances where Chinese and US leaders would opt for a nuclear war as a rational act?

Perhaps most important, power transition theory makes assumptions about the incentives for war that are too simple, ignoring too much the role of economic interdependence in generating reasons for avoiding war and discounting the role of nuclear weapons. And finally, the theory fails to consider how relationships within one region, such as among China, the United States, and other Asian states, can influence outcomes in the broader global system. A resolution of potential hostilities in East and Southeast Asia, or the breakdown into war, can affect significantly the global relationship of China and the United States.

Too much of the thinking about this process comes from simple calculations of power relationships defined too narrowly, and with incentives defined by judgments of gains from military conflict. Far too little of the analysis examines the calculations based on the multiple and complex dimensions of global systems, from complex conceptions of power relationships and from the gains and losses from the many interactions other than military conflict.[68] These arrangements generate an array of very important incentives affecting national calculations. To its credit, power transition theory does acknowledge the degree to which a rising power is satisfied with the system, but gives little guidance as to where this comes from or how to integrate this into calculations based on traditional power relations. Dividing states into satisfied and dissatisfied is too simple and offers little guidance as to how we judge China in the present and over the next several decades. We have indications of satisfaction–dissatisfaction as being the result of the level of congruence of political economies of the various states, a version of the democratic peace theory.

So the really important question is whether China could become so dissatisfied as to engage in war or the risk of war to change that system. Is the power relationship with the United States the only calculation that will affect this judgment? Could China design a military strategy that would permit it to defeat the United States and all its allies, and then redesign a global system in China's own image? Are the power relationships among the various states such that chances for success for this kind of global strategy can be high? Perhaps most important, does the vast global structure of institutions and economic interdependence affect the decisions of states to initiate war in order to resolve conflicts?

Expectations of a Conflict-Prone World

Closely related to the analysis of power transition theory are the ideas of traditional realist and neorealist scholars, who generally find the coming era of power shifts to be ominously one of rising conflict. Two important thinkers providing such an analysis are Aaron Friedberg and John Mearsheimer. Friedberg sees the United States and China locked in an "increasingly intense struggle for power and influence" driven by the confluence of a power shift from a democratic dominant state to an authoritarian rising state.[69] A rising state, like China, will reject and resist the existing international order created by the dominant hegemon, like the United States. Further, as China's power grows relative to that of the United States, its leaders will expansively define China's interests to include a much larger influence over Asia and over access to vital resources around the world. These efforts will likely meet resistance from the established power, and nations have historically settled such conflicts with force. Adding to the conflict and inhibiting the creation of trust that might ameliorate the differences is the liberal democratic political order of the United States and the authoritarian political order of China. US leaders fear the aggressive potential of an authoritarian state and Chinese leaders fear the aggressive US efforts to contain and remove their regime. Friedberg believes that the best chance for reducing conflict between China and the United States is a regime change to a democratic China.

John Mearsheimer seconds Friedberg's worries with the view that power shifts favoring China and unfavorable to the United States will create a significant potential for rising conflict, predicting that "China cannot rise peacefully."[70] This is because the nature of international politics – with no international government or police to maintain peace – leads nations in a rising–falling relationship to distrust each other, work to build offsetting military force, see even the defensive actions of each other as adversarial and threatening, and develop goals consonant with their respective power positions. The critical factor will be a Chinese effort to achieve regional dominance, which requires the United States as the current dominant power in Asia to give way. That, according to Mearsheimer, cannot happen peacefully. Discounting the importance of political differences and of economic interdependence, Mearsheimer forecasts a bleak future, especially as the Chinese military begins to achieve parity with the United States.

An especially strong and important counter to the pessimism of these realist scholars comes from other realists who focus on the revolution in military relationships brought on by nuclear weapons. Robert Jervis has stated the conclusions of many when he asserts that the combination of society-killing destruction from nuclear weapons and the inability to defend against their use makes war among heavily armed nuclear states very difficult to imagine.[71] The high level of conflict between the United States and the Soviet Union during the Cold War did not lead to actual war between these nations. This can be attributed in part to the restraining effect of nuclear weapons. Both the United States and China possess nuclear weapons and each nation is able to inflict horrific damage on the other. The United States possesses by far the larger and more sophisticated system of nuclear weapons and delivery systems. Nonetheless, China's nuclear capabilities are more than sufficient to provide an effective deterrent against nuclear attack, even by the United States.[72] Such capabilities provide a major barrier to war, because even in a conventional conflict the risk of escalation to nuclear war is significant and operates to prevent one nuclear nation from much more than minimal risk taking.

Global Interdependence, Power, and Conflict

An examination of global economic systems can provide a more complete understanding of the broader array of incentives affecting the way national leaders assess their international environments and the calculations relating to strategy and war. Nearly four decades ago, in the early days of the current wave of globalization, scholars began to reformulate many of these concerns in terms of the relationship of power and rising global interdependence.[73] At that time, the ties among nations were overwhelmingly concentrated in already wealthy nations. What we think of today as emerging economies, in nations like Korea, Taiwan, and especially China and India, were just a small feature of the reality of interdependence at that time. Can the nature of global economy, especially the complexity and depth of interdependence among nations, affect the outcome of the rise of China?

Scholars have long and often examined the impact of economic exchange on the propensity for international conflict, but have not agreed on just what about economic exchange affects the chances for war or how this happens. Open markets, high levels of exchange, foreign investment, contact and communication, and achieving the gains from trade all in some fashion contribute to interdependence and create a set of incentives to those engaged in these activities to prefer peace over war. Some of the assertions claim that economic interdependence influences mainly those actors directly engaged in economic exchange, who then must influence national decision-makers regarding conflict and war. This strongly suggests that some form of democracy is a necessary condition for interdependence to constrain conflict. But some propose that interdependence affects national choices and policymakers more directly by changing the strategic incentives relating to choices about war and peace. Many scholars see the need to include the effects of the system of global institutions and shared assumptions held by global political and economic elites, both of which can serve to reinforce or undermine the effects of economic interdependence. Finally, understanding the impact of interdependence on conflict is not likely to hold under all circumstances and time periods. Spelling out when, where, and why this happens is vital to judging the role of interdependence on conflict in the twenty-first century in a situation of shifting power relationships.[74]

For our discussion, we will focus on interdependence as a type of complex global system, with a number of interacting elements that change through time. Trade has an important impact on interdependence, not just from the volume of trade but also from the structural connections associated with product development, production, and distribution on a global scale. But, interdependence is more – much more – than trade. It also includes financial flows and holding of foreign currency, ownership, and investment patterns, and knowledge, innovation, and technology capabilities and flows. Interdependence also includes the norms and institutions created to facilitate and enhance global political and economic interactions. The working assumptions about global relations – often shared by leaders and elites across many nations – deeply affect and frame issues and options.[75] And finally, interdependence includes the feedback relationships among the various elements of interdependence – the system effects that reinforce arrangements through increasing returns, or that can reduce or nullify connections through decreasing returns. This means we must consider whether the elements of interdependence are reinforcing each other or whether these elements neutralize each other.

Thus, interdependence is best understood as a complex system with multiple components involved in dynamic relationships that generate differentiated incentives for states over time. What are the characteristics of global interdependence that are likely to have the largest impact on national decisions about conflict and war? We should expect complex interdependence to generate strong and consistent incentives against military conflict and in favor of cooperation when this entire combination of systemic characteristics is present:

- Economic relationships among nations are defined by multiple layers of differentiated but reinforcing forms of interaction, including trade, investment, knowledge flows, and strongly complementary and globalized systems of specialization and innovation.

- Institutions and norms relating to the global economy are strongly and consistently biased toward cooperation to achieve mutual gains; norms and institutions relating to global security are consistent with and reinforce cooperative gains and discourage efforts to achieve unilateral relative gains.
- Feedback relationships between economic exchange and institutions/norms are positive.

This argument identifies a large number of variables that could potentially compose a system of interdependence. However, we can hypothesize that certain values for these variables tend to correlate and cohere as a result of various forms of feedback and thereby produce a typology of systems of global interdependence. For purposes of example, we can define variation in global systems of interdependence that generate three types corresponding to the historical systems of 1814, 1914, and 2014 (see "Global Systems of Interdependence" below).[76] How are these systems of interdependence different and how do they influence war and international conflict?[77] A summary of these historical systems is provided in the text box below.

Global Systems of Interdependence: 1814, 1914, 2014

1814

The system of 1814–20 was based on new thinking about the nature of international relations and the value of defining regular procedures and forums for resolving international conflicts through the norms of political concert, equilibrium, and mutual restraint on the use of military power to achieve gains. Perhaps most important for this era was the emergence of systemic thinking in relation to international security, which provided a normative and political base for interdependence.[1]

In contrast to the new thinking in political relations, economic interdependence in 1814 was based on trade embedded in mercantilist and protectionist behaviors and norms. This meant the effects of economic interdependence were small but did not reinforce the emerging thinking regarding the need for managing the security relations of Europe. Though interdependence was shallow and had limited effects, these norms and behaviors provided negative feedback in relation to the much stronger security regime norms. Overall, interdependence in 1814 was mixed though successful in limiting the use of military force among the great powers for at least the next forty and perhaps one hundred years (see Table 9.10).

1914

The global economy in 1914 had achieved very high levels of basic interdependence, with large volumes of trade and investment among independent states. At the same time, the global economy was equally defined by the relationships of imperialism and power politics. The result was systems of economic interdependence were embedded in somewhat contradictory relationships of security and power relations. Trade was generally based on production within one nation followed by the export of a finished product to other nations. Investment was dominated by portfolio investment, which meant the funds involved could be quickly withdrawn, and loans, which created a relationship of dependency. Exchange and investment were also embedded in norms defined by the nationalistic struggle for power and advantage, with rising protectionism after 1880 offset by falling costs of transportation. The spectrum of elite opinion in all major powers operated within the bounds of intense nationalism in security and economy and did not venture into the massive intellectual and structural changes needed for international economic and political integration.[2]

As a result, the considerable economic interdependence in Europe in 1914,[3] rather than operating to dampen the potential for war, actually reinforced norms of conflict because of weak institutions and equally weak cooperative norms. Interdependence between France and Germany was substantial but contributed much to German insecurity and to German designs on obtaining control over French markets and industry. In 1914, interdependence was but part of a system of policies, resources, and relationships bound by the nation-centered system of production, the extension of the nation through imperialism, and the role of trade in relation to achieving international power. Global economic institutions were limited, beyond the gold standard, with rules for exchange constructed as much by traders as by states.[4] The potentially pacifying incentives from interdependence conflicted dramatically with those of imperialism, nationalism, and international security and, as such, frequently were incorporated into the incentives of these conflict-oriented systems. Largely undeveloped were the domestic and international political foundations that would permit stronger relationships of interdependence and thereby create incentives for peace. Thus, nationalistic and highly competitive assumptions about trade reinforced similar views about security.

2014

The global system of 2014 presents a substantially distinct, even qualitatively different, system of interdependence. Not only are economic relationships bound together into complex, deep, and widely distributed systems of interdependence, but equally important, systems of global institutions relating both to economy and security are framed around a strong recognition of the mutual gains from cooperation. For those nations most closely connected to the existing global order, these systems create powerful and even compelling incentives to attenuate the use or threats to use military force to achieve the aims of states.

Global exchange has become much deeper and more complex as a result of the massive increase in the geographic scale of production and the global diffusion of the capacity to produce for global markets. This was achieved through global knowledge networks, the fragmentation and diffusion of production into complementary specializations, the creation of these systems by transnational firms through related networks of FDI, strategic alliances, and global innovation processes. Firms were also engaged in partnerships with nations seeking investment, with nations providing the soft and hard infrastructure needed to operate and upgrade production. The system that emerges is defined by high-density, tightly coupled, and complementary exchange diffused across much of the planet.

Equally important is the supportive system of norms and institutions relating both to security and economic exchange that provide the rules and the political and governance base for globalization. Unprecedented in human history, this system creates the stability necessary for a global system of exchange to operate. The norms that undergird these arrangements consist of systemic thinking: recognition of security and economic interdependence, the gains to be had from cooperation for mutual gains, the mutual losses from failure to cooperate, and the absolute need for political management of these relationships. The core institutions of NATO, WTO, IMF, World Bank, and the myriad layers of associated and complementary institutions and non-governmental organizations both create and reinforce these norms.

1 T.C.W. Blanning, "Paul W. Schroeder's Concert of Europe," *International History Review*, 16.4 (1994) 701–14; Paul Schroeder, *The Transformation of European Politics, 1763–1848*, Oxford: Oxford University Press, 1994; G. John Ikenberry, *After Victory*, Princeton: Princeton University Press, 2001; Jennifer Mitzen, *Power in Concert*, Chicago: University of Chicago Press, 2013.

2 Paul Schroeder, "Economic Integration and the European International System in the Era of World War I," *American Historical Review*, 98.4 (October 1993) 1130–7.

3 Carl Strikwerda, "The Troubled Origins of European Economic Integration: International Iron and Steel and Labor Migration in the Era of World War I," *American Historical Review*, 98.4 (October 1993) 1106–29.

4 Christof Dejung and Niels Petersson (eds), *The Foundations of Worldwide Economic Integration: Power, Institutions and Global Markets, 1850–1930*, Cambridge: Cambridge University Press, 2013.

Table 9.10 Global Systems of Interdependence 1814, 1914, 2014

Economic Exchange	Institutions/Norms	Feedback
	1814	
Shallow and simple interdependence	Informal institutions Strong security norms	Low and Negative
	1914	
Extensive and shallow interdependence	Strong expectations for economic and military conflict	Positive
	2014	
Complex, deep, distributed interdependence	Strong and mutually reinforcing for cooperation	Strong and Positive

This discussion identifies three different types of global interdependence based on the complexity and depth of economic interdependence, the nature of international institutions and norms, and whether these factors have a reinforcing or negative relationship. How can this be used to evaluate the effects of interdependence on contemporary China?

Analyzing Global Interdependence and the Rise of China

There is no compelling evidence that would permit a definitive test of a hypothesis relating interdependence and war, especially given the dynamic and complex nature of such systems.[78] Rather, we can at best assemble evidence that tends to support or refute expectations we can link to such a hypothesis and draw only tentative conclusions. The evidence needs to identify key features of the global system and the ways the system affects the incentives for states relating to conflict and war. We will review evidence in two related situations, each involving the behavior of states in relation to this system. The first considers how "outsider" states to the emerging global system have interacted with this system: to what extent have "outsider" states been ready to join the global capitalist economy and to what extent have these states worked to resist this system? The behavior of these states helps us to judge the impact of the global system on the propensity for cooperation, conflict, and war. We are especially interested in nations that are already hostile to this system. Do these nations resist, even to the point of using force to destroy this system, or do they choose to join it? If a system of economic interdependence did not promote cooperation and the avoidance of war, we would expect very few, if any, hostile states to join it and commit their security and prosperity to such an order. Instead we would expect, given such hostility, at least significant preparation for war and high levels of conflict from such nations directed toward leading nations and significant efforts to remain apart from such a system. A system so attractive from an economic and security standpoint that it attracts "outsider" and "hostile" states must have a very strong capacity for promoting mutual gains and managing the potential for conflict.

The period from 1970–2014 is instructive on this question. Here, many illiberal states[79] chose to join the liberal international order – an order of economic, political, and security liberalism – and persisted in integrating ever deeper into the system over time. At the same time, a significant but declining number of nations remained outside this order, either by choice or by exclusion.

China, which in the 1950–72 period was intensely hostile to the system of global capitalism and was ready to mobilize many nations to resist if not fight this system, chose to join the liberal order in the 1970s and dramatically reorient its global strategy and domestic system of political economy in order to do so. This involved a calculation of the security implications of, as well as the economic restructuring required from, such a decision. Joining a system of global interdependence based on capitalism, at a time when China was quite weak economically and militarily, strongly suggests that Chinese leaders – from Mao to Deng – did not fear this order.[80] The many other states like China, which also joined the system, must have concluded joining would not increase but rather would decrease their security problems and would provide significant economic gains.[81]

The second form of evidence relating to interdependence and war relates to how closely illiberal states align themselves to the global liberal order: shallow involvement is consistent with incentives that do not attenuate the potential for war and conflict; deep integration is consistent with high expectations of a reduction in the chances for war and conflict. Here the evidence again suggests acknowledgment and acceptance of the security gains from close alignment. This is because joining this system in most instances has involved accepting both economic and security norms: basic systems of economic exchange, and more complex rules for resolving trade conflicts, for dealing with economic competition, and for managing global financial instability, went together with the norms of managing global security, which were also part of the bargain.

The post-1970 system was open to new members and clearly began providing large gains to those that joined. In the 1960s and 1970s, those states joining the European Economic Community (EEC)/EU and poor states such as Korea, Thailand, Singapore, Taiwan, and Malaysia integrating into the system achieved much faster economic growth, with manageable consequences for the domestic political economy and an improved security position. The system of economic exchange, global institutions, and norms did not threaten or reduce security; rather it enhanced security through systems of stability and through economic growth.[82] Notwithstanding the fact that the system was and is dominated by economically and politically liberal nations – with strong preferences for markets, democracy, and private firms – nations with quite antithetical values not only joined the system but were ready to make large changes in their values and institutions in order to facilitate participation. Further, those nations failing to integrate found themselves caught outside the economic and technological gains that contributed to dynamic economic restructuring. The most spectacular of these nations was the Soviet Union, which found itself in a catastrophic spiral of decline.[83]

The long-standing Soviet effort to compete militarily with the United States, and with the global liberal system while remaining outside of that system, could not be sustained. This strategy failed in economic terms to generate growth, but even more so failed to generate the dynamic structural and rapid technological changes found in the liberal system. Perhaps most telling, rather than attempting a military response to its decline the Soviet Union first attempted to join the global economy and engage in security cooperation with the United States and, when that failed to stem the tide of decline, simply imploded, with its former members now free to join the liberal system. The Soviets had little choice but to acquiesce in the loss of control over Eastern Europe and the reunification of Germany.[84] Even more revealing for the connection between interdependence and conflict, the collapse of the Soviet Union and the Tiananmen crisis in China could have led the Chinese to reverse direction and retreat from the global capitalist order. Instead, by 1992 Deng Xiaoping was successfully pressing to integrate China even more into this system.[85] The deep connections between wealth and power are demonstrated very clearly by the fate of the Soviet Union. At the same time, the impact of the global capitalist order on decisions relating to integration or conflict with this system is demonstrated by the choices of virtually all of the nations in the global communist order in the 1978–95 period.[86]

Moreover, the global system was itself in the process of morphing into new and more complex forms after 1970.[87] The rising tide of market-based global economic exchange and the revolutionary changes in the technologies of communication and transportation were being extended and transformed by the expansion of new members. Especially important were those poor nations that began to integrate hundreds of millions of new, inexpensive workers into the global capitalist economy. As we have seen in previous chapters, dramatically new forms of production emerged around the fragmentation of the value chain, with new forms of specialization, extraordinary increases in global FDI, and new forms of knowledge, technology, and innovation networks. Much of this new system was defined and directed by new actors, often non-state actors operating in intimate partnerships with states.[88] The result was a new form of global economy, able to produce higher-quality products at much lower prices, create new products through rapid and cumulating innovation, and raise and lower production levels with extraordinary flexibility. Governance of the system came through strong norms and institutions promoting cooperation and through multiple rules and norms governing interaction. It was a new system for creating economic value and wealth; virtually no states were in a position to gain benefits from it through military attack but only by joining and adapting to it. This is a world dramatically different from the global interdependence of 1914 or 1814.[89]

This global system of interdependence deepened and became more complex, in the sense that feedback loops were reinforcing, thereby extending existing systems of exchange. The rising gains from the system were coupled to an increase in the density of connections as new participants encouraged more complex forms of exchange, which led to greater integration and even more new members. Existing international institutional corollaries of this system not only survived these changes but also adapted to and reinforced the processes of global exchange. The International Monetary Fund (IMF) found itself as the central player in managing the inevitable instabilities of a system defined by rapid and radical change, which seemed to manifest in repeated financial crises.[90] By acting to contain the destructive effects of these crises, the IMF not only preserved the system but also reinforced the process of transformation and the value of such institutions for the system. Likewise the WTO, which managed the complex and difficult integration of China into the global system on terms that reinforced but did not destabilize the system, operated to contribute to the rising tide of complex and deep interdependence. These arrangements have no corollary in past systems of global interdependence. And the development of the system in these terms supports the hypothesis that contemporary interdependence is both qualitatively different from interdependence in the past and facilitates the integration of a rising power into the system.[91]

Nations that might not initially have fully understood the effects of joining the global capitalist system would, over time, have little doubt about the consequences. The incentives for joining generally cumulated. Once nations have joined the system, this has rarely been followed by withdrawal. Even in instances where nations have suffered considerable pain – such as in the Asian financial crisis of 1997–8 – no nation so affected chose to withdraw from the system.[92] Participation in the global liberal order has not produced levels of domestic economic or political pain that would lead nations to even imagine withdrawal.[93] The global order rests on very firm domestic and international political foundations and represents a powerful pull on nations.

What does all this mean for forecasting the position of China in global affairs for the next two decades? China is surely the best example of an illiberal nation that has benefited dramatically from joining the global liberal system. And of all the illiberal states taking this step, China began in the 1970s with very little connection to the global capitalist system and has become by far the most deeply integrated into this system. Global firms play a very large role in the Chinese economy, as a vital source of investment, technology, knowledge, and competition for Chinese firms, and providing access to global markets. Global production networks – spread across much of Asia and the world – create the avenues for a constant flow of components to China that end as Chinese exports to the rest of the world. China has a large, growing, and unbreakable set of links to global knowledge networks.

How does participation in the global economy and the global security order generate incentives that affect China's foreign policy choices? Earlier in this chapter we have considered the question of China's ability to sustain its remarkable economic growth, mainly through continuous upgrading of firms' ability to improve the quality and capabilities of products. For this to happen, we have described the essential role of connections to global knowledge networks, global production networks, and global markets, and the role of domestic competition from foreign firms. Already evident and expected to accelerate is a new form of Chinese connection to the global economy: outward foreign direct investment. One estimate forecasts $1 trillion in Chinese outward FDI by 2020, creating a gigantic and continuing system of new interests in global relations.[94] Access to global markets, knowledge, and production networks and massive external investments makes the preservation of deep interdependence with the global economy a vital interest of China, at least for the foreseeable future. The ability to upgrade across the value chain, and even more so achieving innovation in the contemporary global economy, cannot take place through a strategy of knowledge and technology autarchy. No nation, even the most advanced, can possibly hope to succeed in keeping pace with global technology and knowledge advances while cutting itself off from the global knowledge system.[95] The Chinese government clearly understands this reality, with its encouragement of Chinese efforts to expand access to knowledge through actions such as the purchase of German machine tool firms by Chinese firms. Any effort to alter significantly the global rules and norms relating to innovation, trade, and investment would carry a major risk of damage to the capabilities of this system and thereby to China. Any significant use of military force by China would contain considerable risk of a rupture of the Chinese connections to the global system. Even an effort to alter the global order based on Chinese preferences would carry large risks of disruption and threaten China's future economic prosperity.[96]

Seen in these terms, the global system of deep interdependence generates not only powerful incentives to join and remain but equally important incentives to preserve it, including avoiding the risks of war that could unravel the system. The way we think about power is affected by the existence of a system capable of having these effects. In 1914, the system of interdependence produced considerable incentives for nations to prepare for and use war as a primary instrument for achieving national ends. We have usually understood this to define power itself. But the global system has evolved into a different kind of system since then and our understanding of the nature of power must evolve as well. Structural power is much more important today than the power to hurt and coerce. What we call structural power involves the ability to create the system of exchange, innovation, knowledge, finance, institutions, and norms. And structural power, which results from the nature of the existing global system, resides overwhelmingly with the United States.

The United States is able, as a result of its long period of hegemony, to define rules, control access to vital resources, define the military calculations and choices of potential adversaries, and generally shape outcomes that extend far beyond its apparent military and economic position. Structural power is embedded in systems of deep and complex interdependence and derives from asymmetries in the ability to define rules and control resources others need for success. Situations that appear to be positions of US weakness – such as the massive holdings of dollar-denominated assets by the Chinese government – are actually positions of US strength. The Chinese cannot credibly threaten to sell these assets, and by holding this money China provides US benefits in lower interest rates and permits US purchases of imports on a credit card that doesn't have to be paid off. At the same time, holding these assets allows the Chinese to preserve an exchange rate for the RMB that favors Chinese exports. This form of structural power derives from the position of the US dollar as the global key currency combined with the power created by the size and global importance of the US market.[97] But most important, this and other forms of structural power derive from the system of complex and deep interdependence represented by this relationship between China and the United States. This is a system in which both gain, which neither wants to unravel, and which requires cooperative management to maintain.

The effects of deep and complex interdependence on military conflict do not mean that other forms of conflict and certainly competition will not continue and thereby affect global political relations. One somewhat unexpected result may be to change the role of power in interstate relations, mainly by shifting power equations away from the capacity to hurt toward the capacity to define the standards, norms, and rules for the global system. Following the example of structural power, we can already see efforts by the Chinese to enhance their capacity for structural power. This comes from repositioning the RMB and the Chinese financial system for the RMB to play a role as a key currency, at least regionally and in areas with large amounts of trade with China, such as parts of Africa.[98] In addition, efforts to rebalance the Chinese economy through expanding domestic consumption will certainly create a giant consumer market that already serves as a magnet for sales, global investment, and product design.[99] Both efforts will require time and discipline by the Chinese government, traits they have already demonstrated. The nature of a world composed of dueling systems of structural power is somewhat murky from today's vantage point. Competition and even significant conflict over efforts to define rules for global exchange, investment, intellectual property, and the role for states in economies will persist and even expand. But creating structural power tends to reinforce the existing system, not undermine it. Thus, the use of war and the threat of war will likely be attenuated by the overriding reality of deep and complex interdependence and the gains to be had from cooperation.[100]

Conclusion: Power, Wealth, and Conflict

The power transition from the United States to China will most likely result in a raw advantage in economic size and military spending for China, but will leave China substantially constrained by the global system of deep interdependence, institutional arrangements, norms, and governance. Theories based on the analysis of power transitions, economic interdependence, and elite ideas all point to the same basic conclusion. As long as this global system remains adaptable to Chinese preferences and able to sustain global prosperity, these constraints will hold. Should either break down, that is, should the global system fail to provide the incentives for cooperation, the Chinese will at some point have the capacity to break this system but perhaps not the capacity to make a new one. In such an environment, military struggle could return as a predominant form of interaction.

We should recognize that for the highest probability outcome to materialize – that is, for China to remain committed to preservation of the main parameters of the current global system and avoid major military confrontations with the United States – many of the basic patterns from the past several centuries in global politics will need to be different. The case for conflict made by realists and power transition theories is strong, and identifies many pathways leading toward war between rising and declining powers. We have identified three main reasons why the patterns of the past are unlikely to repeat themselves in the contemporary system. First, China is quite unlikely to achieve the level of wealth and power advantages in the next two decades that could lead to decisions for war with the United States. The United States will retain significant advantages in per capita income and innovation and a qualitative military advantage. Second, nuclear weapons provide a very important deterrent against choices for war and risk-taking involving war between great powers. Third, the global system generates large gains for those who remain in the system and potentially larger risks and costs for those who operate outside the system. It is difficult to design scenarios leading China either to withdraw from or act to transform the contemporary system, one or both of which is a prerequisite for war.

Key Concepts (see Glossary)

Deep Interdependence	Move Up the Value Chain
Fast Follower	Nuclear Revolution
Illiberal States	Power Transition Theory
Imitation	Relative Gains
Local Innovation	

Discussion Questions

1 Describe and evaluate the data for shifts in the relative positions of nations in size of GDP.

2 Discuss and evaluate the debate over whether rapid growth in emerging economies is likely to slow.

3 Analyze the varying positions about the ability of China to sustain economic growth.

4 What is the probable range of possible outcomes over the next two decades in the economic balance of China and the United States?

5 Analyze the methodology of developing scenarios and attaching probabilities to these scenarios as a basis for predicting future outcomes.

6 When we combine military and economic capabilities, does the prediction of a rough balance between China and the United States seem valid?

7 What are the central ideas, conclusions, and most important limitations for power transition theory in estimating the potential for war or peace between the United States and China?

8 What combination of the elements of interdependence needs to be present to have a tempering effect on the potential for war? Compare the systems of interdependence in 1814, 1914, and 2014 in terms of these relationships:

- Depth, density, and complexity of interdependence generate massive gains to participating states.
- Reinforcing elements and incentives relating to interdependence promote cooperation to create and preserve the global system.
- Global security and economic institutions formalize and reinforce the gains and informal/formal norms among elites deriving from economic interdependence and undermine gains from military action.

9 How persuasive is the evidence that the nature of contemporary interdependence is such that it will constrain the potential for war between the United States and China?

Notes

1 For excellent overviews of these relationships, see Ronald Finlay and Kevin O'Rourke, *Power and Plenty*, Princeton: Princeton University Press, 2007; Lance Davis and Robert Huttenback, *Mammon and the Pursuit of Empire*, Cambridge: Cambridge University Press, 1988. The Chinese term is *fuquiang*. Orville Schell and John Delury, *Wealth and Power*, New York: Random House, 2013.

2 This is accomplished by adjusting the figures for each year to prices in 2005.

3 For example, in 1993 there were virtually no passenger cars on Hanoi streets, essentially only bicycles and motorbikes. You could stand for several minutes on an important street in midday and see no cars. In 2014, the same streets are choked with cars.

4 Dani Rodrik, "The Future of Economic Convergence," NBER Working Paper No. 17400, September 2011; Dani Rodrik, "The Past, Present and Future of Economic Growth," Global Citizen Foundation, Working Paper 1, June 2013.

5 The difficulty in achieving this outcome can be seen when we try to model the processes associated with innovation. See Christiano Antionelli, "The Economic Complexity of Technological Change: Knowledge Interaction and Path Dependence," in Antionelli (ed.), *Handbook on the Economic Complexity of Technological Change*, Cheltenham: Edward Elgar, 2011, 3–59.

6 Ruchir Sharma, "Broken BRICs: Why the Rest Stopped Rising," *Foreign Affairs*, 91.6 (November/December 2012) 2–7; Nelson Antoine, "Emerging Markets, Hitting a Wall," *New York Times*, June 22, 2013; *The Economist*, "When Giants Slow Down," June 27, 2013; Nathaniel Popper, "Old Economies Rise as Growing Markets Begin to Falter," *New York Times*, August 14, 2013.

7 Brazil, Russia, India, and China.

8 *The Economist*, "Is the Fastest Period of Emerging Economy Growth Behind Us?" August 20, 2013, www.economist.com/debate/days/view/1001

9 Of course, this will require large and effective efforts by the Indian government to develop educational and other institutions that can provide workers able to utilize this knowledge.

10 Arvind Subramanian and Martin Kessler, "The Hyperglobalization of Trade and Its Future," Peterson Institute Working Paper, 13–6 (July 2013).

11 Alexandra Stevenson, "China's Economy Expands at Slowest Rate in Quarter-Century," *New York Times*, January 20, 2015, www.nytimes.com/2015/01/20/business/international/china-gdp-growth-rate-slowest-since–1990.html?ref=business

12 Atul Kohli, *State-Directed Development*, Cambridge: Cambridge University Press, 25–123; Alice Amsden, *Asia's Next Giant*, Oxford: Oxford University Press, 1989; Robert Wade, *Governing the Market*, Princeton: Princeton University Press, 2004; Yongping Wu, *A Political Explanation of Economic Growth*, Cambridge, MA: Harvard University Press, 2005.

13 For a thorough discussion of FDI in China, see Yuqing Xing, "Facts About and Impacts of FDI on China and the World Economy," *China: An International Journal*, 8.2 (September 2010) 309–27.

14 Edward Steinfeld, *Playing Our Game*, Oxford: Oxford University Press, 2010, 70–119.

15 Pankaj Ghemawat and Thomas Hout, "Tomorrow's Global Giants: Not the Usual Suspects," *Harvard Business Review*, November 2008, 80–8.

16 Shaohua Zhan and Lingli Huang, "Rural Roots of Current Labor Migrant Shortage in China," *Studies in Comparative International Development*, 48

(2013) 84–7. The coming decline in the size of the workforce in China adds to the wage pressure. Mitali Das and Papa N'Diaye, "The End of Cheap Labor," *Finance and Development*, June 2013, 34–7.

17 David Barboza, "In China, Projects to Make Great Wall Feel Small," *New York Times*, January 12, 2015, www.nytimes.com/2015/01/13/business/international/in-china-projects-to-make-great-wall-feel-small-.html?action=click&pgtype=Homepage&version—oth-Visible&module=inside-nyt-region&region=inside-nyt-region&WT.nav=inside-nyt-region&_r=0§ory-continues–1

18 The share of investment in China's GDP hovers near 50 percent, well above that in the high investing nations of Asia and more than double that of many Western nations. Consumption spending is consistently below 40 percent of GDP, dramatically below levels of most nations, and even more dramatically lower than the consumer-driven economy of the United States.

19 Simon Cox, "Pedaling Prosperity," *The Economist*, May 26, 2012, www.economist.com/node/21555762; Nicholas Lardy, *Sustaining China's Economic Growth After the Financial Crisis*, Washington, DC: Brookings, 2012.

20 Yanzhong Huang, "Population Aging in China: A Mixed Blessing," Asia Unbound (Council on Foreign Relations), November 4, 2013.

21 Elisabeth Economy, "China's Growing Water Crisis," *World Politics Review*, August 9, 2011.

22 Damien Ma and William Adams, "Comment: Why Feeding China Could Leave the Rest of the World Hungry," *Foreign Policy* (October 2, 2013).

23 Louise Watt, "Air Pollution Cuts Northern China Lifespans," *Associated Press*, July 8, 2013. Delhi seems to be competing for the world's worst air pollution with Beijing. Gardiner Harris, "Delhi Wakes Up to an Air Problem It Cannot Ignore," *New York Times*, February 14, 2015.

24 Details on these efforts can be found in The World Bank, *China 2030*, Washington, DC: International Bank for Reconstruction and Development, 2012; Yasheng Huang, "China's Great Rebalancing: Promise and Peril," *McKinsey Quarterly*, June 2013; Ian Johnson, "The Great Uprooting: Moving 250 Million into Cities," *New York Times*, June 15, 2013, www.nytimes.com/2013/06/16/world/asia/chinas-great-uprooting-moving–250-million-into-cities.html?hp&_r=0

25 Barry Naughton, *The Chinese Economy*, Cambridge, MA: MIT Press, 2007, 349–74. Linsu Kim, *Imitation to Innovation*, Cambridge, MA: Harvard Business School Press, 1997.

26 Of course, Google was a "knock-off" of Yahoo. And the initial versions of Microsoft's Windows in the 1980s were a knock-off of the look and feel of Apple's operating system, which itself was a knock-off of the operating system from Xerox PARC's Alto. Westerners tend to forget how much imitation without payment occurs here.

27 Kal Raustiala and Christopher Sprigman, "Fake It Till You Make It," *Foreign Affairs* (July/August 2013) 25–30.

28 Mark Greeven and Zhao Xiaodong, "Developing Innovative Competencies in an Emerging Business System: New Private Enterprises in Hangzhou's Software Industry," ERIM Report ERS–2009, 2009, http://hdl.handle.net/1765/16599

29 Dan Breznitz and Michael Morphree, *Run of the Red Queen: Government, Innovation, Globalization and Economic Growth in China*, New Haven: Yale University Press, 2011. G.E. Anderson, *Designated Drivers*, Singapore: John Wiley, 2012; Dieter Ernst and Barry Naughton, "China's Emerging Industrial Economy," in Christopher McNally, *China's Emergent Political Economy*, London: Routledge, 2008, 40–59. For discussion of the limitations

of the Chinese model for the auto industry, see Crystal Chang, "Center-Local Politics and the Limits of China's Production Model," in Dan Breznitz and John Zysman, *The Third Globalization*, Oxford: Oxford University Press, 2013, 82–98.

30 John Mathews, *Dragon Multinationals*, Oxford: Oxford University Press, 2002.

31 Loren Brandt and Eric Thun, "The Fight for the Middle: Upgrading, Competition, and Industrial Development in China," *World Development*, 38.11 (2010) 1555–74.

32 In addition to Brandt and Thun, "The Fight for the Middle," see Loren Brandt and Johannes Van Biesebroeck, "Capability Building in China's Auto Supply Chains," University of Toronto, www.rotman.utoronto.ca/offshoring/ Ch4.pdf; Kazuyuki Motohashi and Yuan Yuan, "Productivity Impact of Technological Spillover from Multinationals to Local Firms," *Research Policy*, 39 (2010) 790–8; Edward Tse et al., "China's Mid-Market Innovators," *Strategy+Business*, 67 (Summer 2012) 32–6.

33 See a series of articles in *East Asia Forum*, 4.2 (April–June 2012); Paul Geitner, "China, Amid Uncertainty at Home and in Europe, Looks to Germany, *New York Times*, April 22, 2012, www.nytimes.com/2012/04/23/ business/ global/china-invests-in-germany-amid-uncertainty.html?_r=2&ref=world&

34 John Mathews, Mei-Chih Hu, and Ching-Yan Wu, "Fast-Follower Industrial Dynamics: The Case of Taiwan's Emergent Solar Photovoltaic Industry," *Industry and Innovation*, 18.2 (2011) 177–202.

35 *The Economist*, "Samsung: The Next Big Bet," October 1, 2011, www. economist.com/node/21530976. Part of Samsung's advantage in developing a rival smartphone comes from its partnership role with Apple in producing the iPhone.

36 Wei Xie and Steven White, "Sequential Learning in a Chinese Spin-off: The Case of Lenovo Group Limited," *R&D Management*, 34.4 (2004) 407–22.

37 Qing Mu and Keun Lee, "Knowledge Diffusion, Market Segmentation and Technological Catch-up: The Case of the Telecommunication Industry in China," *Research Policy*, 34 (2005) 759–83; Geert Duysters, Jojo Jacob, Charmainne Lemmens, and Yu Jintian, "Internationalization and Technological Catching up of Emerging Multinationals: A Comparative Case Study of China's Haier Group," *Industrial and Corporate Change*, 18.2 (2009) 325–49.

38 Dieter Ernst and Barry Naughton, "Global Technology Sourcing in China's Integrated Circuit Design Industry," East–West Center Working Papers, No. 131 (August 2012) 17–18.

39 Dieter Ernst, "Can Chinese IT Firms Develop Innovative Capabilities Within Global Knowledge Networks?" in Henry Rowen et al. (eds), *Greater China's Quest for Innovation*, Stanford: Shorenstein Center, 2008, 197–216; Dieter Ernst, *A New Geography of Knowledge in the Electronics Industry?* Honolulu: East–West Center, 2009.

40 Edward Wong and Didi Tatlow, "China Seen in Push to Gain Technology Insights," *New York Times*, June 5, 2013, www.nytimes.com/2013/06/06/ world/asia/wide-china-push-is-seen-to-obtain-industry-secrets. html?ref=edwardwong; William Hannas, James Mulvernon, and Anna Puglisi, *Chinese Industrial Espionage: Technology Acquisition and Military Modernisation*, Abingdon: Routledge, 2013.

41 Colum Murphy and John Stoll, "Geely's Li Doubles Down on Volvo," *Wall Street Journal* (June 5, 2013), http://online.wsj.com/article/SB10001424 12788732406330457852653294475858.html; Yipeng Liu and Michael

Woywood, "Chinese M&A in Germany," in Ilan Alon, Marc Fetscherin, and Phillipe Guglar (eds), *Chinese International Investments*, London: Palgrave, 2012, 212–33; Thilo Hanemann, "Building a Global Portfolio: What China Owns Abroad," http://rhg.com/notes/building-a-global-portfolio-what-china-owns-abroad

42 Tse-Kang Leng and Jenn-Hwan Wang, "Local States, Institutional Changes and Innovation Systems: Beijing and Shanghai Compared," *Journal of Contemporary China*, 22.80 (2013) 219–36.

43 Martin Schaaper, "Measuring China's Innovation System," OECD STI Working Paper 2009/1, www.oecd-ilibrary.org/science-and-technology/oecd-science-technology-and-industry-working-papers_18151965. For an analysis that evaluates China from the standard of a leading edge knowledge economy, see Vincent Shie, Craig Meer, and Nian-Feng Shin, "Locating China in the 21st Century Knowledge-Based Economy," *Journal of Contemporary China*, 21 (2012) 113–30.

44 Denis Fred Simon and Cong Cao, *China's Emerging Technological Edge*, Cambridge: Cambridge University Press, 2009. Notwithstanding the massive number of graduates, in many cases there is good reason to question the quality of their training. Also see, Li-Kai Chen, Mona Mourshed, and Andrew Grant, "The $250 Billion Dollar Question: Can China Close the Skills Gap?" McKinsey, 2013, www.mckinsey.com/industries/social-sector/our-insights/the–250-billion-question-can-china-close-the-skills-gap

45 Nicholas Lardy, *Sustaining China's Economic Growth*, Washington, DC: Petersen Institute, 2012; Mary Teagarden and Dong Hong Cai, "Developmental Lessons from China's Global Companies," *Organizational Dynamics*, 38.1 (2009) 73–81.

46 *The Economist*, "When Giants Slow Down," July 27, 2013, www.economist.com/news/briefing/21582257-most-dramatic-and-disruptive-period-emerging-market-growth-world-has-ever-seen. The rates of increase projected are net of price increases. This makes the figures priced in 2013 dollars.

47 This figure is in 2013 dollars. Assuming no additional population growth in China, per capita income in 2034 with 7 percent average growth would be about $30,000, closer to but still considerably below the US per capita income in 2034 of about $75,000. At 6 percent growth, per capita income would be $24,000 and at 5 percent the figure is near $20,000.

48 Michael Beckley, "China's Century? Why America's Edge Will Endure," *International Security*, 36.3 (Winter 2011/12) 41–78.

49 For an effective critical commentary on Beckley's thesis and his response, see Joshua Itzkowitz Shifrinson and Michael Beckley, "Debating China's Rise and U.S. Decline," *International Security*, 37.3 (Winter 2012/13) 172–81.

50 Arvind Subramanian, *Eclipse: Living in the Shadow of China's Economic Dominance*, Washington, DC: Peterson Institute, 2011; Martin Jacques, *When China Rules the World: The End of the Western World and the Birth of a New Global Order*, New York: Penguin, 2012. Also valuable is *The Economist*, "Global Economic Dominance," September 9, 2011, www.economist.com/node/21528591

51 Jacques presents a less optimistic prediction for China, expecting its proportion of global GDP to surpass that of the United States by 25 percent in 2050. Nonetheless, he expects China to be able to leverage this advantage into overwhelming global power. This is somewhat improbable, given his own calculations.

52 With apologies to that insightful philosopher, Yogi Berra. For an academic analysis of this problem, see Philip Tetlock, "Theory-Driven Reasoning about

Plausible Pasts and Probable Futures in World Politics," *American Journal of Political Science*, 43.2 (April 1999) 335–66.

53   An excellent review of the variations from each school for analyzing US–China relations is Aaron Friedberg, "The Future of U.S.–China Relations: Is Conflict Inevitable?" *International Security*, 30.2 (Fall 2005) 7–45. Also see, Peter Katzenstein, *The Culture of National Security*, New York: Columbia University Press, 1996.

54   Put another way, we opt for "analytical eclecticism" over "paradigmatic clashes." Peter Katszenstein and Nobuo Okawara, "Japan, Asian-Pacific Security and the Case for Analytical Eclecticism," *International Security*, 26.3 (2001) 153–85. Bruce Gilley, "Beyond the Four Percent Solution: Explaining the Consequences of China's Rise," *Journal of Contemporary China*, 20.72 (November 2011) 795–811.

55   For a discussion of the many dimensions that "rising" might take, see Sheena Chestnut and Alastair Iain Johnston, "Is China Rising?" in Eva Paus, Penelope Prime, and John Western (eds), *Global Giant*, New York: Palgrave, 2009, 239–42.

56   And, most of those ten nations are US allies or are closely related to the United States. It would be very difficult for any adversary of the United States to assemble a coalition of nations that could come close to matching just US military capabilities, much less the United States and potential allies.

57   For some nations, such as China, measures of defense spending can vary widely. For an alternate measure that places Chinese defense spending at a considerably lower level, see http://armscontrolcenter.org/issues/securityspending/articles/2012_topline_global_defense_spending/

58   *The Economist*, April 7, 2012, www.economist.com/node/21552193

59   www.sipri.org/research/armaments/milex/milex_database. Notably, both the United States and China have seen a decline in the percent of GDP devoted to military spending in recent years.

60   For an alternative effort to project economic power into the future, using data that incorporates finance and trade, see Subramanian, *Eclipse*. Another scenario-based analysis comes from the National Intelligence Council, "Global Trends 2025: A Transformed World," NIC, 003, 2008, www.aicpa.org/research/cpahorizons2025/globalforces/downloadabledocuments/global-trends.pdf

61   If we calculate real global GDP rising at 3.5 percent, global GDP will increase from about $70 trillion today to about $140 trillion dollars in 2033. For military spending, we assume US military spending remains at 4.4 percent of GDP and China's military spending rises to 3.5 percent of GDP. Each is a very conservative assumption: there will be considerable pressure in the United States to cut military spending and in China considerable pressure to raise military spending.

62   The Chinese National Bureau of Statistics measured the size of China's GDP at PPP in 2014 at $10.6 trillion. This is the basis for our estimate of a $10 trillion economy in 2013, www.stats.gov.cn/enGliSH/. There is considerable variance in these estimates. Both the IMF and the World Bank estimate China's 2013 GDP PPP at above $16 trillion. The CIA estimates this figure at $13 trillion.

63   Jack Levy, "Power Transition Theory and the Rise of China," in Robert Ross and Zhu Feng (eds), *China's Ascent*, Ithaca: Cornell University Press, 2008, 18.

64   Ronald Tammen (ed.), *Power Transitions: Strategies for the 21st Century*, New York: Seven Bridges, 2000; A.F.K. Organski, *World Politics*, New York: Knopf, 1958; Robert Gilpin, *War and Change in World Politics*, New York: Cambridge University Press, 1981; Ronald Tammen and Jacek Kugler,

"Power Transition and China–US Conflicts," *Chinese Journal of International Politics*, 1 (2006) 35–55; Paul Kennedy, *The Rise and Fall of the Great Powers*, New York: Vintage, 1987; Jonathan DiCicco and Jack Levy, "Power Shifts and Problem Shifts: The Evolution of the Power Transition Research Program," *Journal of Conflict Resolution*, 43.6 (December 1999) 675–704; Steve Chan, *China, The U.S. and the Power-Transition Theory: A Critique*, New York: Routledge, 2008.

65 The expectation of conflict is seconded by neorealist theories, though without the qualification regarding the satisfaction of the rising power. Aaron Friedberg, "The Future of U.S.–China Relations: Is Conflict Inevitable?" *International Security*, 30.2 (Fall 2005) 7–45.

66 Michael Barnhart, *Japan Prepares for Total War*, Ithaca: Cornell University Press, 1987.

67 Keir Lieber, "The New History of World War I and What It Means for International Relations Theory," *International Security*, 32.2 (Fall 2007) 155–91.

68 The effects of the security dilemma on national choices – in which efforts to engage in a purely defensive military expansion threaten other nations and lead to counterveiling efforts by opponents and an escalation to war – are not integrated into power transition theory. Robert Jervis, "Cooperation Under the Security Dilemma," *World Politics*, 30.2 (January 1978) 167–214. Charles Glasser, "The Security Dilemma Revisited," *World Politics*, 50.1 (October 1997) 171–201.

69 Aaron Friedberg, *A Contest for Supremacy: China, America and the Struggle for Mastery in Asia*, New York: Norton, 2011; Aaron Friedberg, "Hegemony With Chinese Characteristics," *The National Interest* (July/August 2011) 18–27.

70 John Mearsheimer, "The Gathering Storm: China's Challenge to U.S. Power in Asia," *The Chinese Journal of International Politics*, 3 (2010) 382.

71 Robert Jervis, *The Meaning of the Nuclear Revolution*, Ithaca: Cornell University Press, 1989.

72 Elbridge Colby and Abraham Denmark, *Nuclear Weapons and U.S.–China Relations*, CSIS, 2013, http://csis.org/files/publication/130307_Colby_USChinaNuclear_Web.pdf

73 Robert Keohane and Joseph Nye, *Power and Interdependence*, Boston, MA: Little Brown, 1977.

74 A review of these ideas is Edward Mansfield and Brian Pollins, "Interdependence and Conflict: An Introduction," in Mansfield and Pollins (eds), *Economic Interdependence and International Conflict*, Ann Arbor: University of Michigan Press, 2003, 10–37. Further, there are other scholars, mostly realists, who assert that economic relationships bear little influence on the choices that result in war, which are related instead to the distribution of power in the international system.

75 Paul Schroeder, "Economic Integration and the European International System in the Era of World War I," *American Historical Review*, 98.4 (October 1993) 1130–7, provides a discussion of the intersection of elite assumptions in pre-World War I Europe about international competition as a zero sum game linking both military and economic struggles.

76 The first date, 1813, is not precisely accurate, as the system we will discuss did not come into place until about 1818. But, for purposes of symmetry with the other dates, 1914 and 2014, we choose 1814.

77 A detailed discussion and debate about the changes in global systems from the eighteenth to the twenty-first centuries is: Peter Kruger and Paul Schroeder, *The Transformation of European Politics, 1763–1848: Episode or Model in Modern History?* Munster: LIT, 2002.

78 Except for the outbreak of systemic war among the most powerful states. Such evidence would certainly cast large doubt on the conflict-reducing effects of interdependence.

79 Fareed Zakaria, "The Rise of Illiberal Democracy," *Foreign Affairs*, 76.6 (November/December 1997) 22–43.

80 For an analysis of the adjustments made by China resulting from joining the system of global capitalist interdependence, see Andrew Nathan and Andrew Scobell, *China's Search for Security*, New York: Columbia University Press, 2012, especially chapter 10.

81 Quddus Snyder, "Integrating Rising Powers: Liberal Systemic Theory and the Mechanism of Competition," *Review of International Studies*, 39 (2013) 209–31.

82 Stephan Haggard and Beth Simmons, "Theories of International Regimes," *International Organization*, 41.3 (Summer 1987) 491–517.

83 Stephen Brooks and William Wohlforth, "Power, Globalization and the End of the Cold War," *International Security*, 25.3 (Winter 2000) 5–53. There is a large and important literature relating changes in ideas by Soviet and other leaders as a key source of the end of the Cold War. However, the analysis of economic constraints and ideas is not necessarily a competing hypothesis. Richard Ned Lebow and Thomas Risse-Kappen (eds), *International Relations Theory and the End of the Cold War*, New York: Columbia University Press, 1995.

84 Stephen Brooks and William Wohlforth, "Economic Constraints and the Turn Towards Superpower Cooperation in the 1980s," in Olav Njolstad (ed.), *The Last Decade of the Cold War*, New York: Cass, 2004, 69–117; Stephen Brooks and William Wohlforth, "Economic Constraints and the End of the Cold War," in William Wohlforth (ed.), *Cold War Endgame*, University Park: Penn State University Press, 2003, 273–309.

85 Ezra Vogel, *Deng Xiaoping and the Transformation of China*, Cambridge, MA: Harvard University Press, 2011, 664–90.

86 Especially significant were the decisions to integrate by communist Vietnam between 1992 and 1995.

87 The new system of interdependence calls for new forms of understanding. Previously, interdependence has been conceptualized as a bilateral relationship. This is too simple for thinking about interdependence today. We need a more complex set of ideas: interdependence must be understood in multilateral terms, as a relationship between individual states and a global system, and as a system of relationships among a multitude of states and non-state actors. For a conception based on bilateral thinking, see John Kroll, "The Complexity of Interdependence," *International Studies Quarterly*, 37.3 (September 1993) 321–47.

88 Stephen Brooks, *Producing Security*, Princeton: Princeton University Press, 2005. Thomas D. Lairson, "Deep Interdependence and the Political Economy of Power Relations in Asia," paper presented at the June 2013 Asian Studies on the Pacific Coast Conference, Monterey.

89 Erik Gartzke, "The Capitalist Peace," *American Journal of Political Science*, 51.1 (January 2007) 166–91. The major outsider states were North Korea and Cuba; the major non-state actor ready to attack the system was Al Qaeda and affiliates.

90 See Chapter 7 for discussion of global financial crises in the 1980s, 1990s, and 2000s. Also see, Mark Copelovitch, *The International Monetary Fund in the Global Economy*, Cambridge: Cambridge University Press, 2010.

91 G. John Ikenberry, "The Rise of China: Power, Institutions and Western Order," in Robert Ross and Zhu Feng (eds), *China's Ascent*, Ithaca: Cornell University Press, 2008, 89–114. A similar analysis can be made for the

World Bank. Ngaire Woods, *The Globalizers: The IMF, the World Bank, and Their Borrowers*, Ithaca: Cornell University Press, 2006.

92 Malaysia did choose to reinstitute capital controls during the financial crisis but remained otherwise deeply integrated in the global economy.

93 Even Greece, which has recently suffered a massive economic depression from its relationship to the euro, has not moved to withdraw from this system, much less withdraw from the global economy. The outcome of the Brexit vote remains to be seen, but if continued does portend conflicting evidence on this point.

94 Daniel Rosen and Thilo Hanemann, *An American Open Door? Maximizing the Benefits of Chinese Foreign Direct Investment*, Washington, DC: Asia Society, 2011, http://asiasociety.org/policy/center-us-china-relations/american-open-door

95 This was clearly true for the Soviets two decades ago and is even more true today.

96 One group of scholars, focusing only on US–China dimensions of economic interdependence, describes a situation of "mutual assured economic destruction" that prevails from any significant military engagement between these nations. James Dobbins, David Gompert, David Shlapak, and Andrew Scobell, "Conflict With China," RAND, Occasional Paper, 2011.

97 Michael Mastanduno, "System Maker and Privilege Taker: U.S. Power and the International Political Economy," 61.1 (January 2009) 121–54. Carla Norrlof, *America's Global Advantage*, Cambridge: Cambridge University Press, 2010.

98 Eswar Prasad and Lei Ye, *The Renminbi's Role in the Global Monetary System*, Washington, DC: Brookings, 2012; Economist Intelligence Unit, "China: Towards a Redback World," September 24, 2013, www.eiu.com/industry/article/1550992339/china-towards-a-redback-world/2013–09–24; Arvind Subramanian and Martin Kessler, "The Renminbi Bloc is Here: Asia Down, Rest of the World to Go?" Petersen Institute for International Economics, Working Paper 12–19, October 2012.

99 See the discussion of Chinese rebalancing in Chapter 7.

100 In China's case, a vital issue for consideration is the relationship between external conflict, including efforts to overturn the existing international system, and regime survival. Can the Chinese Communist Party maintain its level of domestic control in an external environment defined by great instability? This question may have a sobering effect on Chinese decision making. M. Taylor Fravel, "Regime Insecurity and International Cooperation: Explaining China's Compromises in Territorial Disputes," *International Security*, 30.2 (Fall 2005) 46–83.

Further Reading

Stephen Brooks, *Producing Security*, Princeton: Princeton University Press, 2005.
An exceptionally insightful analysis of the complex relationships of global production and international security.

Elbridge Colby and Abraham Denmark, *Nuclear Weapons and U.S.–China Relations*, Washington, DC: CSIS, 2013, http://csis.org/files/publication/130307_Colby_USChinaNuclear_Web.pdf
A useful examination of the nuclear relationship of the United States and China.

Aaron Friedberg, *A Contest for Supremacy: China, America and the Struggle for Mastery in Asia*, New York: Norton, 2011.
One of the primary forecasts of a likely military conflict between China and the United States.

Robert Jervis, *The Meaning of the Nuclear Revolution*, Ithaca: Cornell University Press, 1989.
The best analysis of the impact of nuclear weapons on global politics.

Peter Kruger and Paul Schroeder (eds), *The Transformation of European Politics, 1763–1848: Episode or Model in Modern History?* Munster: LIT, 2002.
Examination of systemic change and the potential for war.

Nicholas Lardy, *Sustaining China's Economic Growth After the Financial Crisis*, Washington, DC: Brookings, 2012.
A lucid and compelling analysis of the Chinese economy.

Andrew Nathan and Andrew Scobell, *China's Search for Security*, New York: Columbia University Press, 2012.
An important study of the making and content of Chinese foreign and security policy.

Barry Naughton, *The Chinese Economy*, Cambridge, MA: MIT Press, 2007.
Though a little dated, the best single source on the Chinese economy.

Edward Steinfeld, *Playing Our Game*, Oxford: Oxford University Press, 2010.
A detailed analysis of China's position in the global economy.

Arvind Subramanian, *Eclipse: Living in the Shadow of China's Economic Dominance*, Washington, DC: Peterson Institute, 2011.
Provides a detailed analysis of Chinese current and future economic power.

Part III
Sustainability

10 Population, Hunger, Food, and Health

Between 1798 and 1826, British mathematician Thomas Malthus published six editions of *An Essay on the Principle of Population.*[1] In this influential tract, Malthus inveighed against the possibility of perpetual human progress. He argued that human populations would always expand to consume all available resources. Indeed, times of prosperity tended to encourage an excess of births over deaths. But since the amount of arable land remained fixed and improvements to agricultural productivity were assumed to be gradual and limited, population growth would quickly exhaust available resources and produce growing immiseration as food supplies were divided among a growing number of mouths. Equilibrium would be restored as famine and disease raised the death rate to match births. For Malthus, the possibilities for lifting the mass of peoples above an economic state of bare subsistence were dim.

Considered against the long span of human history, Malthus's thesis has much to commend it. For most societies prior to the past two centuries, economic growth was so slow as to be imperceptible within the lifetimes of most inhabitants. Populations were in fact subject to fluctuations around a low-level equilibrium and few people enjoyed a standard of living much beyond mere subsistence. Periods of rapid population growth were regularly followed by painful corrections as societies breached the carrying capacity of the natural environment.

At just the point that Malthus so eloquently expounded upon this dismal record, however, the relationship between population, food, and health entered a period of radical departure from any prior human experience. Over the past two centuries, the world's population has grown more than seven times, the quantity and quality of per capita food consumption has greatly improved, and advances in human health have allowed even common people to survive into old age. These unprecedented advances have arisen from two sources: rapid growth in scientific understanding of nature and the globalization of this knowledge through improvements in transportation, communication, and models of social organization. As a result, the human ability to manipulate the environment so as to extend nature's carrying capacity has disproven Malthus's dire predictions.

Yet precisely because this dramatic growth in human populations and resource consumption is so recent and unique in human history, it would be folly to abandon the idea that natural limits to further economic and population do exist. Historically, when human societies have overshot the carrying capacity of local eco-systems, there remained other resource-abundant locations to which humans could migrate. Such options are narrowing in contemporary times. The environmental strains placed upon the planet are global in scope and extend to forests, fisheries, coral reefs, and fresh water supplies around the world.

In this chapter and the next, we explore two questions: What factors account for the ability of humans to expand in both population size and quality of life over the past two centuries? Are there limits to our ability to extend these recent gains into the future? In this chapter, we examine the relationships among population growth, food and hunger, and human health. In the next chapter, we explore issues related to energy, climate change, and sustainable development. In each chapter, we place these issues within the context of globalization, including the ways in which tightening links of interdependence both facilitate and impede solutions to pressing human and environmental problems.

Population

It took over a million years for the world's human population to pass the 1 billion mark. Yet the passage from 6 billion to 7 billion in population was accomplished in little more than a decade. Much of this increase is concentrated in poor societies that must struggle to provide the schooling, jobs, and social services that are necessary to offer a decent standard of living for rapidly growing numbers of claimants. Excessive population growth holds back economic development, contributes to social and political frictions, strains scarce resources, and triggers sometimes-destabilizing cross-border immigration flows. In a myriad of ways, population pressures are likely to play the dominant role in the political, social, and economic lives of many societies across the globe in the twenty-first century. These include not only continued growth in the absolute number of people, which is not expected to peak until the end of the century, but also in the shifting profile and geographic distribution of populations (see Table 10.1).

A variety of data sheds light on population trends. The global rate of annual population growth peaked in 1963 at 2.2 percent and has since fallen to 1.2 percent in 2011. Globally, the average number of children born per woman has dropped by half since 1950.[2] Nevertheless, the absolute number of people added to the world's population continued to climb through the 1970s and 1980s, reaching a peak of almost 90 million per

Table 10.1 World Population Milestones

World Population Reached:	
Level	Year
1 billion	1804
2 billion	1927 (123 years later)
3 billion	1960 (33 years later)
4 billion	1974 (14 years later)
5 billion	1987 (13 years later)
6 billion	1999 (12 years later)
7 billion	2011 (12 years later)
Projections:	
8 billion	2024 (13 years later)
9 billion	2042 (18 years later)
10 billion	2082 (40 years later)

Source: Data from United Nations Population Division of the Department of Economic and Social Affairs, 2010 Revision of the World Population Prospects, May 3, 2011. Future projections reflect medium population variant.

year in the early 1990s. This figure has since declined to about 78 million additional people per year.[3] In 2011, the world's population passed the 7 billion mark.[4] United Nations' (UN) projections suggest that population levels will grow to around 10 billion people by the end of the century, although the actual figure could be higher or lower, depending upon the speed of progress in lowering birth rates.[5]

Because birth rates in much of the developed world are already at or even below replacement levels, 98 percent of additional population growth in the years ahead will occur in the developing world.[6] Already, 90 percent of those between the ages of 10 and 24 live in the developing world, creating enormous pressures on governments there to generate a sufficient number of new jobs and in some cases threatening political stability.[7] Africa's population is projected to triple during this century – while there existed three Europeans for every African in 1950, the ratio will shift to 5:1 in favor of Africans by 2100.[8] Although the South's share of total world population stood at 68 percent in 1950, this proportion is expected to rise to 84 percent by 2025.[9] Much of this growth will take place in cities. In 2008, the number of urban dwellers surpassed the number living in rural areas for the first time. Cities in Africa and Asia are projected to double in size by 2030. Already, China is home to 160 cities with populations exceeding 1 million, compared with only nine of that size in the United States. By 2020, the number of urban slum-dwellers is expected to reach 1.4 billion, double the number of 1990[10] (see Table 10.2).

The Demographic Transition

Why have Southern populations expanded at such a rapid rate? Population experts believe that the developing world is passing through

Table 10.2 Developing World Population and Growth Rates, by Region

	Total Population in Millions, 2011	Average Annual Growth Rate (%)
East Asia	1,581	0.5
Southeast Asia	602	1.3
Latin America and Caribbean	596	1.2
Middle East	238	1.9
South Central Asia	1,795	1.6
Sub-Saharan Africa	883	2.6

Source: Data from Population Reference Bureau, 2011 World Populations Data Sheet, 2011, www.prb.org/pdf11/2011population-data-sheet_eng.pdf, 6–9.

the same sort of demographic transition that led to growing population levels in Europe and North America from the late eighteenth through the early twentieth centuries. According to this theory, rapid population growth is essentially a byproduct of the early stages of economic development. Prior to industrialization and economic development, population levels are generally stable. High birth rates are matched by high death rates. After development produces rising incomes and increased wealth, however, death rates begin to fall dramatically. Better nutrition and sanitation, combined with less physical toil and improved access to increasingly sophisticated medical care, lead to reduced infant mortality rates and rising life expectancy. Globally, the number of infant deaths has fallen by more than half since 1960.[11] Because birth rates are initially unaffected, a declining rate of death produces an imbalance that results in a population explosion.

As incomes continue to rise, birth rates begin to decline as well (for reasons explained later) and may eventually catch up with still-falling death rates. After birth rates and death rates are equalized at low levels, population stability again appears, only now on a much higher plateau. The sequence posited by the demographic transition theory is thus: (1) high death rate/high birth rate, (2) falling death rate/high birth rate, (3) falling death rate/falling birth rate, and (4) low death rate/low birth rate.[12]

Due to a phenomenon known as population momentum, however, population growth will persist for a lengthy period even after couples begin to limit family size to the long-run replacement level of roughly two children each. Following a rapid burst of population growth, younger generations will account for a disproportionately large share of the overall population as compared with older generations. As these younger people move through their childbearing years, they will produce children at a faster rate than the comparatively small number of elderly people reach the end of their lives. Thus for birth rates to fall far enough to match death rates at low levels, two things must happen: family size must decline, and the age distribution must even out as the first generations produced by the population boom move past their childbearing years.[13]

As population growth slows and moves toward stability, one consequence is that the average age rises. North America, Europe, and Japan have already experienced this phenomenon, as fewer children are born and larger numbers of people live longer lives. Globally, the estimated median age was 25 in 1995. As population growth slows, the median age worldwide is expected to approach 40 by 2050. The proportion of the global population composed of persons 65 years of age or older is expected to rise from 6.5 percent today to almost 20 percent in 2050. Global life expectancy is expected to rise from 68 at present to 81 by the end of the century.[14] Aging populations pose different sorts of problems. The need for education and other services for children declines, while the medical costs of caring for a growing elderly population rises.[15]

The demographic transition theory fits Europe's experience well. It also appears to explain trends in the developing world, although the South's population explosion has been far more intense than Europe's earlier boom. Due to the spread of antibiotics and other medical advances originating in the North, Southern death rates fell at a far steeper rate during the initial stages of development. Birth rates also fell more slowly in the South, thus extending the transitional period of high growth. Nevertheless, fertility rates have fallen across most developing regions since the 1960s. A major exception is Africa, where fertility rates remain stubbornly high.[16] Overall, 42 percent of the world's people live in countries where average fertility rates have fallen beneath the replacement level of 2.1 children per woman.[17]

The spread of modern contraceptives is helping to bring down birth rates in many places. In 1960, an estimated 10 percent of married women in Third World countries used some method of fertility control. Today this figure has risen to 62 percent.[18] Nevertheless, an estimated 215 million women in the developing world currently lack access to modern contraception, resulting in 80 million unplanned pregnancies each year.[19] Contraception use rates are particularly low in Africa, ranging between 9 percent and 47 percent depending upon the country (and 20 percent for all of sub-Saharan Africa). Unfortunately, international funding for family planning programs in developing countries has fallen over the past two decades.[20]

Contraceptives help to avoid only unplanned births. Yet the majority of children born in Southern countries are conceived by choice. World Bank economist Lant Pritchett notes that "desired levels of fertility account for 90 percent of differences across countries in total fertility rates."[21] In some cases, the desire for large families is influenced by culture or religion. By and large, however, the incentives that most powerfully affect preferences about family size are economic. It is here, in the household economy of the family, that we can discover clues as to how best to go about restraining population growth.

Research has shown that the three most important factors affecting family size choices are income, education, and rural or urban status. Counterintuitively, poorer, less-educated rural families are likely to prefer larger numbers of children than are high-income, better-educated urban families. The reasons for this finding have to do with the economic costs and benefits of having additional children for families in differing circumstances.[22]

Poor, rural couples have two strong incentives to prefer a large family. In developing countries, agriculture is typically very labor intensive. On small farms, children provide a cheap source of added labor from a relatively early age. Their contributions can help to expand production and thereby augment family income. The costs of an additional child are relatively small for such households; chiefly, the expenses are associated with food and clothing. At low-income levels, moreover, it may be impossible for parents to save money for their old age, and few such families have access to the type of social security benefits that are available to elderly people in the North. For parents, then, a large number of offspring increases the chances that enough children will survive to adulthood and prosper sufficiently to take care of their parents after the latter are unable to provide for themselves.

As incomes rise, however, the incentives for rural families to prefer more children begin to diminish. A wealthier farmer may now have the means to hire skilled adult labor to help with the farm or to acquire labor-saving machinery. This lessens the family's degree of dependence upon the children's contribution. Better-off rural families are also more capable of setting aside savings for the parents' later years.

As households move from the countryside to the city, the incentives shaping choices about family size change still further. In urban areas, compulsory education laws are better enforced, and educational opportunities are more readily available. Thus children are more likely to be in school for longer periods rather than contributing to the family income through work. In any case, paid employment for children is scarce in urban areas, particularly where child labor laws are strict. The costs associated with each additional child, on the other hand, tend to rise in urban settings. Housing is more expensive. Moreover, urban parents are more likely to work at a distance from the home, increasing the costs of supervising a large number of children.

Education, particularly that of women, also plays a role in reducing family size. Better-educated parents are more likely to use modern contraceptives. Education is also associated with delayed marriage, reducing the opportunities for adding more children during a woman's childbearing years. As women gain more education and skills, they become more likely to engage in work outside the home, making a large family less attractive. Better-educated women also possess greater power within the marriage and are more likely to challenge traditional gender roles and expectations.

Indeed, the social status and education of women have been found to constitute the most powerful predictor of fertility rates. In societies where women have made progress against legal and social discrimination and where educational and economic opportunities are open to them, fertility rates are dramatically lower than in societies that offer women little social or economic power. A World Bank study highlights the importance of women's education in curbing population growth. In parts of the developing world where women are excluded from secondary education, the average fertility rate is seven. Where at least 40 percent of women go on to the secondary level, the average number of children born drops to three. Similarly, illiterate women in Brazil bear an average of 6.5 children during their lifetimes while women who have completed secondary education have an average of 2.5 children.[23]

The task of improving women's lives will be a huge one. A disproportionate number of the world's poor are women. Twice as many women as men are illiterate. Many societies and cultures devalue women and continue to deny them access to education, the right to own property, or the freedom to engage in political life.[24]

The foregoing analysis suggests that population pressures are greatest among the rural poor. Bottom-up development strategies that seek to improve the income and status of the poor majority will also be the most effective at bringing down birth rates. Inequitable, top-down strategies that concentrate benefits at the top of the income scale will, on the other hand, fail to alter the incentives that give rise to exploding populations.[25]

At the 1994 UN-sponsored International Conference on Population and Development held in Cairo, 180 nations endorsed a twenty-year Program of Action on population control. In addition to increased spending on traditional population control measures, such as family planning outreach and the distribution of contraceptives, the conference focused on efforts to improve the socioeconomic and educational status of poor women. Aside from their intrinsic value, such measures promise to bring down birth rates more quickly.[26]

Population and Economic Development

As more countries pass through the demographic transition, the possibilities for economic growth shift over time. In the early stages, when birth rates remain high, the working age population must support a large number of young dependents. Under these conditions, rising population serves as a drag on economic growth. Yet once birth rates plunge and the larger previous cohort reaches young adulthood, the society enters a demographic sweet spot often associated with rapid development. The working-age population rises as a proportion of the total. With working adults supporting relatively few children or elderly, living standards and savings rates both rise. Whether a country can take advantage of such favorable demographic circumstances depends upon its ability to generate jobs for the growing number of new job seekers and channel savings toward productive uses. The International Labor Organization estimates that the global economy will need to generate 400 million jobs over the next decade to ensure against rising unemployment and many more if the current levels of 200 million unemployed are to be reduced.[27]

Finally, once the "baby boom" generation reaches retirement age, the ratio of workers to dependents falls. Retirees draw down savings, taxes rise in order to provide support for non-working seniors, and the working-age population declines in relative and often absolute terms.

Consider countries positioned at different stages in the process of demographic transition. Still at an early stage, Nigeria remains burdened by a high birth rate and a large number of dependent youth relative to the working-age population. As a result, over 50 percent of the population lives in poverty while annual per capita GDP (purchasing power parity (PPP)) growth has averaged a modest 4–5 percent in recent years. Nigeria's prospects will remain dim until birth rates fall further and the ratio of workers to dependents rises (see Table 10.3).

India, by contrast, has recently entered the demographic sweet spot. India's working-age population will grow by 136 million people over the next decade even as the proportion of young dependents declines.[28] India has already begun to reap the rewards of this demographic profile. Economic growth has averaged better than 7 percent per year over the past decade.

China is approaching the downward slope of the demographic transition. Beginning in the 1970s, China's one child policy led to sharply declining birth rates. Over time, therefore, the relative size of China's

Table 10.3 Comparing Countries at Different Stages in Demographic Transition, 2011

	Birth Rate (annual % growth)	% of Population under 15 years	% of Population Ages 15 to 64	Median Age (years)
Nigeria	1.93%	40.9%	55.9%	19
India	1.34%	29.7%	64.9%	26
China	0.49%	17.6%	73.6%	35
South Korea	0.23%	15.7%	72.9%	38
Japan	−0.28	13.1%	64%	45

Source: Data from CIA World Factbook, www.cia.gov/library/publications/the-world-factbook/

working-age population has rapidly grown. Considered alongside the movement of a large proportion of Chinese women into the workforce and the migration of hundreds of millions of people from low-productivity rural employment to high-productivity manufacturing and construction jobs in urban areas, it is little surprise that the world's most populous country has become the world's factory. As China's pre–1970s baby boomers enter retirement, however, the nation's dependency ratio will quickly begin to rise. The proportion of China's population aged 60 or older will rise from 12.5 percent in 2010 to 20 percent in 2020 while over the same decade the number of people between 20 and 25 years of age will fall by 50 percent.[29] While in 1980 China's median age was 22.1, the median will rise to 46.3 by 2050.[30] As a result of these trends, China's grossly underfunded pension system will require massive infusions of new cash and its economic growth rate seems certain to fall.

Finally, a group of relatively wealthy countries has entered a period of rapid aging and declining population. At 20 percent, Japan's proportion of senior citizens is already the highest in the world and will continue rising to 30 percent in 2030.[31] By 2050, Japan's median age will be 56. Fertility rates in Hong Kong, Taiwan, and South Korea are well below replacement levels and among the lowest in the world.[32] By 2060, an astonishing 40 percent of Taiwan's population will be aged 65 or older.[33] Along with an older age profile, these societies, along with much of Europe, face a future of shrinking populations. In 2050, developed countries will have twice as many people aged 60 or older as under 15. The exception among rich countries is the United States, where birth rates slightly exceed replacement levels, while the continued flow of relatively large numbers of young immigrants (one-quarter of Americans under the age of 18 are immigrants or the children of immigrants[34]) ensure continued population growth and a more gently rising age profile. With an expected median age of 40 in 2050, America will be a much younger society than its rich country peers.[35] By the end of this century, the US population is expected to rise to 478 million from the current level of 311 million.[36]

International Migration

The United Nations estimates that 214 million people currently reside outside of the country where they were born.[37] This total represents an historical high and follows a 37 percent increase in global migration over the past two decades.[38] Yet the number of migrants today still represents only 3 percent of the world's population and does not match, in relative terms, the levels of international mobility experienced during the first era of globalization of the late nineteenth and early twentieth centuries.[39]

While immigration within the developing world is significant – at 40 percent of the total – virtually all of the recent growth in migration has involved movements of people from relatively poor to relatively rich countries. In general, international migrants have claimed a growing share of developed country populations and a declining share of developing country populations. In absolute terms, the United States is home to the largest number of foreign-born residents at 35 million. As a share of total population, however, the US level of 12.5 percent foreign born ranks well down the list.[40]

The various motivations that prompt people to leave their country of origin can be divided into two categories: push factors and pull factors. In some cases, people are pushed to emigrate by fears of violence, civil war, and political persecution in their home country. Individuals fleeing such circumstances may be recognized by recipient states and/or international agencies as political refugees. This status ensures certain legal protections, including that against forcible repatriation. As political violence and repression have lessened in many parts of the developing world over the past two decades, the number of such refugees has declined – 21 million refugees were repatriated between 1990 and 2005 and refugee populations in the developing world shrank by roughly one-third during this period.[41] However, the number of people internally displaced as they flee violence within their own country has risen in recent years.[42]

Push factors also include natural and manmade disasters, including drought, flooding, disease, or famine. Such conditions particularly give rise to cross-border movements of people when the home country government is unable or unwilling to respond to the crisis with measures that effectively address the survival needs of its people.

International migration is also a product of pull factors: perceiving a lack of opportunity at home, people leave in search of a better, more secure, and more prosperous life elsewhere. As a result, migrants tend to prefer destinations that offer some promise of economic opportunity. The attraction is understandable. Just by crossing a border, a migrant who succeeds in landing a job can often experience a threefold to fifteenfold increase in income even for doing the same kind of work as in his or her country of origin. Beyond perceived economic opportunity, however, other factors also influence migration flows, including language, geographical proximity, family ties, levels of cultural tolerance in the recipient country, and the degree of openness in the recipient country's immigration laws and regulations. The factors most likely to attract migrants are highly concentrated in a small number of locations: twenty-eight recipient countries account for 75 percent of all migrants worldwide.[43]

Migrants often send money back to family members in their country of birth. These remittances have grown to become a major economic force in the world economy. Official remittances reached $440 billion in 2010 (this does not include illegal or irregular flows that bypass banks and legal money transfer firms), with $325 billion of this total destined for developing countries. The latter figure was triple the size of all official development assistance during the same year. Two dozen countries depend upon remittances for more than 10 percent of national income and the figure reaches over 20 percent for nine of the countries on this list.[44]

Remittances to family members can raise household incomes and alleviate poverty. Yet much of the money goes toward immediate consumption rather than the kinds of investments that might produce long-term economic development for the society as a whole. To encourage the latter, many governments have established special programs designed to steer remittances into priority development projects by offering matching funds and the prospect of attractive investment returns.

Remittances are just one way in which today's migrants are more closely connected to their country of origin than in earlier periods. The declining costs of transportation and the spread of cheap and easily accessible communication technologies, such as the Internet and cell phones, allow today's migrants to retain strong ties of family, culture, and community with their birth country. Such connections facilitate economic exchanges that go beyond simple remittances. A doubling in the number of immigrants from a particular country produces a 9 percent increase in trade between that country and the recipient country.[45] Immigrant ties also hasten the movement of ideas and technology across borders. Some immigrant communities play important roles in the political arenas in the countries of both their birth and their current residence, even influencing the character of diplomatic relations between the respective governments. Reverse immigration is also significant. Having accumulated some degree of wealth and education abroad, returnees bring these assets with them to their country of origin. Half of all immigrants return home within five years.[46]

From the standpoint of global economic efficiency, reduced barriers to the international movement of labor have the same overall positive impact as reductions in barriers to trade in goods, services, and finance. Yet in contrast with trade or finance, there exist no formal multilateral rules or institutions at the global level to govern or ease migration flows across borders. As economist Dani Rodrik has observed, the economic gains to be had from liberalizing labor flows dwarf those that can be expected from any further reductions in already low tariff barriers.[47] Freer transnational labor movement would also speed the convergence of wages across the divide between developed and developing countries. The absence of global institutions aimed at achieving such ends is a reflection of the political sensitivity of population movements in many countries.

Food and Hunger

In November 1996, diplomats from countries around the globe gathered in Rome for a World Food Summit. The Rome Declaration issued by the assembled delegates pledged action toward the goal of cutting in half the number of people suffering from chronic hunger and malnutrition by the year 2015.[48] This pledge was echoed in the UN Millennium Declaration issued at the close of the Millennium Summit of 2000. Among the eight principal development goals outlined in that document, goal number one focused on the reduction of poverty and hunger, pledging to reduce by half between 1990 and 2015 the number of people suffering from hunger.

These promises have not been kept. On the one hand, the proportion of the developing world population that suffered from chronic hunger and malnutrition fell by more than one-third from the 1970s through the 1990s, despite large increases in population. Across the Third World as a whole, the daily caloric intake per capita rose by 21 percent between 1965 and 1990. Yet some of these gains have been reversed over the past decade. The number of hungry people in the world rose from 815 million in 1990 to more than 1 billion in 2009, before falling back to 925 million in 2010.[49] An estimated 18,000 children die each day due to hunger and malnutrition.[50]

Ensuring an adequate diet requires attention not just to caloric intake, but also to the supply of key micronutrients necessary to good health. In developing countries, zinc, iron, iodine, and vitamin A are chronically undersupplied. The lack of vitamin A causes blindness and even death.

Shortages of zinc result in brain dysfunction and account for 400,000 deaths per year. One-half of women of childbearing age in the poorest countries consume too little iron, leading to anemia and weakened immune systems.[51]

The proximate cause of growing hunger in recent years has been rising food prices. Poor harvests combined with global financial jitters in 2007 and 2008 prompted a sharp spike in grain prices. Markets were further shaken when Russia and Argentina banned wheat exports and Vietnam halted rice exports for a time.[52] While prices moderated in 2009, another upward spike began in June 2010, forcing an estimated 44 million people below the poverty line. In 2011, the Food and Agriculture Organization's global food price index reached a record high twelve-month average.[53] One result was political turmoil as violent protests spread to more than forty countries.

This disappointing record in fighting hunger is not due to an inadequate quantity of food in the world, but rather to its inequitable distribution. Like other commodities, food is mainly allocated through the market. Using what income they have at their disposal, consumers bid for the food that is available. Those able to pay the market price receive the food they need, and sometimes more. Indeed, the number of people in the world who are overweight roughly equals the number of those who are undernourished.[54] Those lacking either the means to grow their own food or the money needed to purchase it in sufficient quantities simply go hungry. For the world's poorest, food purchases take up to 50–70 percent of household income.[55] Many households lack sufficient income to compete for the food they need even in the best of times. When prices rise, many more find themselves unable to divert enough income from other needs in order to avoid hunger. In short, the principal cause of hunger is poverty. Although nutritional programs run by governments or international agencies provide some relief, these efforts reach only a fraction of the chronically malnourished.

Food Aid

Indeed, developed countries have not followed through on commitments to promote developing country agriculture and get food to the hungry. The agricultural sector's share of official development assistance fell from 20 percent in 1979 to 5 percent in 2011.[56] In real dollars, aid spending for agriculture fell by 58 percent between 1980 and 2005. The budget of the UN World Food Program, for instance, declined from $5 billion in 2008 to $3.7 billion in 2010 during a period of grain shortages and rising hunger.[57] Overall, the quantity of food delivered through all assistance programs has declined from 17 million metric tons in 1993 to only 5.5 metric tons in 2010, despite the increase in the absolute numbers of malnourished people over this time span. While rich country governments pledged in 2008 to spend $22 billion over the coming years on agricultural investment in the developing world, only one-half of the total represented new money and relatively little of the pledged amount has been dispersed. Of the $3.5 billion pledged by the United States, for instance, only $1.9 billion was subsequently approved by the Congress.[58]

Food aid, in any case, is itself a controversial response to hunger. Consider, for instance, the United States Food for Peace program, which is the largest source of food aid. US law requires that food aid be grown and processed in the United States and shipped on US-flagged vessels. The US Government Accounting Office estimates that a 10 percent reduction in the one-third of US food aid costs which go toward shipping would allow for the feeding of an additional 850,000 people. When other costs are factored in, only one-third of the Food for Peace budget actually goes toward purchasing food. As such costs rose between 2002 and 2007, the amount of food delivered to the hungry fell by half.[59]

In response to these problems, recent presidents have proposed that a growing portion of the US food aid budget be devoted to purchasing food from markets close to the area of need, which would reduce transportation costs, support agricultural markets in developing countries, and reduce delays in the delivery of food during periods of shortage. However, an Iron Triangle of agribusiness interests, shipping firms, and non-profit groups that depend upon the funding raised when food aid is sold abroad in developing countries has sidelined such reforms in

Congress.[60] Critics of reform argue that local food would not be available in sufficient quantities during times of urgent need and that large purchases in regional markets would drive up prices. They also contend that political support for food aid will disappear if not supplied from US sources.[61] The latter argument, however, only highlights the most important purpose of food aid – to satisfy farming interests in rich countries by providing an outlet for agricultural surpluses. Another objective of food aid is to reward politically friendly countries. Owen Cylke, former acting director of the US Food for Peace program, has commented: "it's used as a slush fund of the State Department to meet political requirements around the world."[62]

The influx of cheap, subsidized, Northern food into poor Third World countries can encourage dependence and vulnerability. Insecure governments prefer to keep food prices low so as to appease politically active urban populations. However, this practice denies rural farmers adequate revenue, thus discouraging agricultural investment and production as well as perpetuating rural poverty. The result is that cities swell with rural immigrants, while the country becomes vulnerable should food aid levels fall due to poor harvests and dwindling surpluses in the North.[63] Food aid is therefore often resisted by rural residents who make up the majority of the population in many developing countries. In 1990, Indonesian officials appealed to the US ambassador to stop the shipments of 700,000 tons of US grain after local farmers protested that they would be forced out of business due to the influx of aid.[64]

The most defensible form of food aid is emergency assistance designed to compensate for shortfalls during times of drought and famine. Under these circumstances, outside food can save hundreds of thousands of lives. The need for such assistance has grown, rather than lessened, over time, particularly in the case of many African countries that have experienced repeated food shortages over the last three decades. At the beginning of the 1990s, only one-third of all food aid shipments provided by the World Food Program were devoted to emergency assistance. The remaining two-thirds were designed to serve longer-term development objectives. In 2009, however, over 80 percent of the World Food Program budget was devoted to emergency needs.[65]

Yet while emergency food aid has played a necessary role in alleviating much hunger and misery, such programs have been plagued by problems. Famine is rarely the result of natural factors alone. It is often exacerbated by government policies that discourage food production, the failure to set aside adequate food reserves during good years, slowness on the part of the governments and outside donors in reacting to signs of impending shortages, and the dislocations caused by war or political instability. These essentially political sources of hunger not only serve to heighten the probability of famine, but also hinder efforts to assist the hungry after outside help is needed. Conflicts between the local government and international relief agencies are common. Government authorities are often slow to acknowledge the prospect of famine for fear of shouldering the political blame for the country's desperate condition. Moreover, the distribution of food and medical supplies is fraught with political implications in severely divided societies. This often gives rise to intense bargaining between local governments and outside donors over the control of distribution activities.

In the summer of 2011, the worst famine in sixty years stalked the peoples of Somalia and other parts of the Horn of Africa. The United Nations estimated in July that 3.7 million people – half of the country's population – were at risk of severe hunger or starvation. Somalia has lacked a functioning government since the early 1990s, when the country became overwhelmed by civil war and economic collapse. As international agencies mobilized to provide assistance in the summer and fall of 2011, their operations were hampered by a militia called al-Shabab that blocked aid groups out of fear that assistance would strengthen rival groups.[66] Similar circumstances prompted US and UN intervention in 1992–3 when Somalis confronted famine conditions. While that earlier intervention succeeded in savings hundreds of thousands of lives, US and UN troops came under attack by local armed gangs, leading to the deaths of eighteen US marines in Mogadishu (an episode captured by a book titled *Black Hawk Down* and a subsequent film of the same title). In the wake of that event, President Bill Clinton wound down US military involvement in Somalia.

In 2011, al-Shabab blocked the departure of tens of thousands of Somalis who sought to flee to neighboring Kenya and Ethiopia. The group also banned immunizations against measles and cholera in areas under its control. Much of the country remained a zone of lawlessness despite the efforts of 9,000 African Union troops to prop up a fledgling government in Mogadishu. Dozens of aid workers have been killed in recent years, forcing aid agencies to rely upon local workers rather than more experienced foreign staff.

Even in areas where food deliveries have been possible, efforts to alleviate the Somali famine have been plagued by allegations of theft and corruption.[67] Moreover, donors have provided only 62 percent of the $1 billion that the World Food Program estimated was needed in order to address urgent needs.[68] These complexities are hardly unique to the case of Somalia. Failed governance, political violence, corruption, inefficient distribution systems, and inadequate provisions of aid are common features of emergency assistance under conditions of famine or severe food shortages.

Emergency aid often arrives too late or fails to reach those in greatest need. The European Community pledged food assistance in 1984 when much of sub-Saharan Africa faced famine conditions. Yet, actual food deliveries did not begin until 400 days later. The slow response of the international community as well as that of local governments prompted many African farmers to abandon their land and migrate to enormous famine camps. Many who survived failed to return to their farms in time to sow new crops after the rains returned.[69]

After aid began arriving in 1985, the huge quantities of food overwhelmed port, storage, and transportation facilities. Only 75 percent of the food delivered to Ethiopia was distributed, while the figure for the Sudan was 64 percent. Moreover, food aid failed to end when the famine finally lifted. Aid continued to pour into Kenya after returning rains allowed a record harvest in 1985. The overabundance of food flooded markets, depressed prices, and lowered rural incomes.[70] Two decades later, similar problems arose when Niger experienced serious food shortages in 2005. By the time international food aid arrived, famers had harvested a bumper crop of millet. This combination sent food prices tumbling, which undermined farm incomes. A more ironic case of misdirected food aid occurred in the wake of the 1976 earthquake in Guatemala. Large quantities of food were delivered despite the fact that agricultural production remained unaffected by the quake and no food shortages existed.[71]

One bright spot in the story of nutritional aid is Plumpy'nut – an inexpensive, tasty peanut-based paste that can be locally produced and which can restore a malnourished child to health within one to two months. When Doctors Without Borders distributed Plumpy'nut to 60,000 severely malnourished children in Niger, 90 percent made a complete recovery. Early childhood nutrition – from birth to age 2 – is especially important in the development of brain and immune system functions. In Guatemala, boys who participated in early childhood nutrition programs earned wages as men 46 percent higher than those who did not. Still, Plumpy'nut and similar nutritional aids only reach 10–15 percent of those in need.[72]

Food Production

The Green Revolution, launched in the 1960s, harnessed modern science to the challenge of feeding a hungry world. Through cross-breeding techniques, scientists developed new varieties of wheat, rice, and other food crops that offered higher yields, better resistance to pests and disease, increased tolerance to environmental stresses, and quicker crop rotation. As a result, world cereal production increased 2.5 times between 1970 and 2007. Bountiful harvests helped to reduce the incidence of hunger in many parts of the world. India, a country repeatedly plagued by famine over the centuries, became self-sufficient in food. The global food supply today equals an ample 2,700 calories daily for each person on the planet.

As discussed, poverty and inequality, rather than genuine scarcity, account for much of the hunger in today's world. Yet the future could bring genuine shortages and skyrocketing prices if food production fails to keep pace with population growth and changing consumption patterns. Recent trends are troubling. After rising at a relatively steady pace of 3 percent per year throughout much of the post-World War II period, grain harvests have expanded at the anemic rate of only 1 percent per year since 1984. With the world's population growing at a faster clip, this means that global per capita grain production has been falling for more than two decades. Moreover, global warming is expected to reduce wheat yields by 2 percent per decade and corn yields by 1 percent per decade compared with a future without warming.[73] This trend is especially worrisome because grain is a staple of diets around the world and accounts for the majority of the food consumed by humans.

A declining number of countries are self-sufficient in food. Two-thirds of countries are net importers of food. Production of the major grain crops is heavily concentrated. Five countries account for 70 percent of the world's rice production, three countries produce 80 percent of all soybeans, and five countries harvest 70 percent of the world's corn.[74]

Many observers once believed that the world's oceans could serve as a growing source of food and protein. The total global fish catch quintupled from 1950 to 1990. However, the tonnage of wild fish caught each year peaked in 2000 and has declined since. On a global per capita basis, wild fish production has declined since the late 1960s. The UN Food and Agriculture Organization estimates that 85 percent of the world's fish stocks are being exploited above sustainable levels.[75] Fish consumption has been sustained through the rapid growth in aquaculture. More than one-half of the fish consumed by humans now comes from fish farms. Aquaculture itself, however, places strains on natural eco-systems. Carnivorous fish must be fed several times their weight in feeder fish. In general, the ability of the world's lakes, rivers, and oceans to keep up with expected increases in the demand for food appears limited.[76]

Using median population projections, food production must increase 70 percent by the year 2050 in order to maintain present levels of per capita consumption. If the goal is to improve diets enough to eliminate malnutrition, then food production will need to more than double. To meet these goals, grain yields will need to rise at a minimum of 1.5 percent per year. Only corn exceeds that rate at present. As *The Economist* magazine notes: "farmers will have to grow more wheat and maize in the next 40 years than was grown in the previous 500."[77]

Predictions as to whether this challenge can be met vary enormously. The former director-general of the International Food Policy Research Institute, Per Pinstrup-Anderson, has declared that "Our estimates show that the world is perfectly capable of feeding 12 billion people 100 years from now."[78] To the contrary, population experts Paul Ehrlich and Anne Ehrlich argue in their book *The Population Explosion* that "Human numbers are on a collision course with massive famines. . . . If humanity fails to act, nature will end the population explosion for us—in very unpleasant ways—well before 10 billion is reached."[79]

That knowledgeable observers could reach such opposed conclusions provides some clue as to the complexity of the issues involved in charting the future relationships among food, hunger, and population. Many factors – political, economic, biological, and demographic – must be taken into account. The following discussion highlights some of the principal issues that are central to an analysis of world hunger in the coming decades.

One certainty is that much more food will be required in the future than is presently produced. Even if population control efforts are relatively successful, the number of consumers will continue to grow and, as living standards rise, they will seek enhanced diets. Most of additional demand for food will come in the developing world. From where will the food to meet this demand come?

One way to increase food production is to expand the total land under cultivation. Growth in agricultural land was rapid between 1850 and 1950. The expansion of new farmland slowed considerably after World War II, however, and has actually reversed in the developed world and some Southern countries over the past decade. Between 1972 and 1989, the total land area harvested increased by only 3.6 percent, and the amount of arable land per capita has been declining for decades. Since the early 1960s, the vast majority of increased food production has come as a result of higher yields, with the expansion of land under cultivation playing only a minor role in raising output.[80]

Nor is there much prospect that the growing food demands of coming decades can be met by opening new fields to production. Little arable land remains unexploited in Asia. There exists greater potential for expanding agriculture in Africa and Latin America, but the best land is already under production. Much of the arable land that remains is only marginally suited to support agriculture and is incapable of sustaining high yields. Indeed, the environmental costs of clearing new farmland are considerable because new land is typically obtained by burning or clear-cutting forests; 70–80 percent of deforestation worldwide is a result of agricultural expansion.[81]

Against this, however, must be set the farmland lost to urbanization and the harmful effects of modern agricultural practices. Nearly 1 percent of all irrigated land is lost each year due to salinization or waterlogging, both attributable to poor drainage. If this rate of loss continues, nearly 50 percent of all presently irrigated land will be lost by 2050. Land is also lost to chemical pollution, a result of the overuse of fertilizers and pesticides. The greatest threat, however, comes from soil erosion. Topsoil is currently being lost at a rate many times faster than it is being replaced. If current trends persist, the world will be robbed of 30 percent of its global soil inventory by 2050.[82]

Over the past decade, a great deal of land once devoted to growing food crops for human consumption has been diverted to the production of crops used in the production of biofuels. Forty percent of the US corn harvest is used to produce ethanol to fuel automobiles. The energy gains from this diversion are minimal since ethanol production consumes one unit of energy for every 1.5 units produced. Many countries have set ambitious goals for increased biofuel production. Were these to be met, 10 percent of global cereals production would have to be diverted from food production or vast amounts of forest cleared for farming.[83]

If the net gain in agricultural land is likely to be small in coming decades, then the main burden for increasing food supplies must be placed on techniques designed to raise the productivity of existing land. This was the aim of the Green Revolution of the 1960s. Since then, scientific research into ways to enhance Third World food production has been conducted under the auspices of an informal international regime. International cooperation in this field began with the founding of the International Rice Research Institute (IRRI) in the Philippines in 1961. The IRRI developed new rice strains that dramatically raised yields throughout Asia. The Centro Internacional de Major-amiento de Maiz y Trige (CIMMYT), located in Mexico, soon duplicated this success by devising new wheat varieties that served to stimulate the Green Revolution in India, Pakistan, and elsewhere.

In many ways, the work of implementing the Green Revolution is still unfinished. Only 3 percent of the corn seeds planted in Ghana are hybrids, while only 10 percent of farmers on the African continent plant new and higher yielding varieties of sorghum and cassava.[84] Bringing high-yield seeds into more common use throughout the Third World could lead to substantial gains in food output. Unfortunately, this goal is not easily met. Green Revolution grain varieties achieve their high yields by virtue of their responsiveness to liberal quantities of fertilizer and water. Irrigation is particularly important. Although only 20 percent of the world's grain-producing lands are irrigated, these fields produce 40 percent of all the grain harvested each year.[85]

But irrigation is expensive. The most bountiful and affordable sites for irrigated agriculture have already been exploited. Future expansion of irrigated land will require large investments. As previously mentioned, existing irrigated lands are threatened by salinization and waterlogging. In some cases, the dams and reservoirs upon which many irrigation systems depend are becoming clogged with silt. In other instances, underground water tables are being depleted much faster than they are being replenished. This is true of the aquifer that lies beneath India's bountiful Punjab wheatfields, which is falling by 1 meter per year. Africa, which lacks the plentiful river systems of Asia, has considerable untapped underground water reserves. But the investment needed to access this water has been slow to emerge.[86] Globally, the rate at which new irrigated land is brought into production has been falling since the 1960s. By 2020, the per capita amount of irrigated land is expected to fall 17–28 percent below the 1978 peak. Considering all uses, humans already consume more water than can be sustainably extracted.[87]

Fertilizers can boost yields substantially, especially if used in conjunction with modern seed varieties. Lacking either self-generated capital or access to credit, many owners of small farms in the developing world simply cannot, however, afford the expense of purchasing commercial fertilizers for their fields. In many places where fertilizer use is already heavy, farmers have begun to experience declining marginal returns. Additional quantities of fertilizer produce increasingly smaller enhancements to yield[88] (see Figure 10.1).

Africa is one part of the developing world that has been almost entirely bypassed by the Green Revolution and other modern farming advances. Africa does not enjoy the extensive river systems that allow widespread irrigation in Asia. An underdeveloped transportation system makes it difficult to get crops to market. Credit and storage facilities are also in short supply.[89] Only 5 percent of Africa's farmers plant high-yield varieties of seed. The fertilizer use rate in Africa is only 3 percent that of the United States. Due to the devastating effects upon livestock of diseases spread by the tsetse fly, relatively few African farms rely upon animal power and only a tiny minority have access to modern farm machinery. Cereal yields in Africa are less than one-quarter of those achieved in the United States, one-third of those in the Far East, and less than one-half of those of Latin America.[90] While cereal yields tripled in Asia between

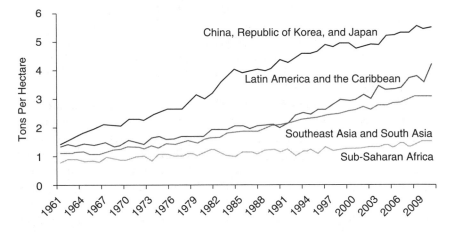

Figure 10.1 Crop Yields by Region.

Source: Adapted from World Bank, *World Development Report, 2013*, World Bank, 2012. Data from FAOSTAT-Agriculture (database), Food and Agriculture Organization, Rome.

Note: Figures are weighted averages of yields for wheat, rice, and coarse crops.

1965 and 2005, yields in Africa over the same period rose by only 30 percent and failed to keep pace with population growth.[91]

When provided with adequate resources, African farmers are capable of substantially improved performance. Norman Borlaug, one of the fathers of Asia's Green Revolution, helped to transplant Green Revolution techniques to 150,000 African farms between 1986 and 1992. These farms realized average increases in yield of 3.5 times previous levels.[92] A doubling of fertilizer use could produce a corresponding increase in yield. A combination of factors, including general economic stagnation, repeated drought, and, in many countries, civil violence, robs African agriculture of the investments needed to realize these sorts of results on a broad-scale basis.

Since 2008, African food production has outpaced population growth for the first time in decades.[93] But Africa's ability to sustain this positive trend is in doubt. Population pressures have reduced the amount of land used to pasture livestock. As a result, the amount of manure available to fertilize fields is falling. For similar reasons, fallow periods, which are essential to replenish land with organic matter, have dropped from fifteen years in the 1970s to two years today. Commercial fertilizers can help compensate for these deficiencies. But whenever rising energy prices push up the costs of fertilizer, a diminishing number of farmers can afford to purchase needed supplies. Finally, climate change has resulted in erratic rainfall patterns, which makes it difficult for farmers to judge the best time to plant. Some observers fear that these factors raise the prospect of exhausted soils and declining productivity.[94]

Even where the Green Revolution has been pursued most vigorously, however, its effects have not been entirely positive. In many places, large farmers who could afford the investments required to reap the benefits from the new varieties of seed gained power and economic status relative to small farmers who lacked sufficient resources to undertake such investments. In the Punjab region of India, this led to an increasing concentration of land ownership, with nearly a quarter of all small farms disappearing between 1970 and 1980.[95]

The Green Revolution has also had negative environmental impacts that limit its sustainability, including increased soil erosion, the depletion of water tables, and chemical pollution. Moreover, because farmers in some regions have abandoned the plethora of traditional varieties of wheat or corn in favor of a small handful of new high-yielding varieties, a disturbing loss of genetic diversity is occurring.[96] Native crops that may have useful characteristics, such as resistance to certain diseases, are threatened with extinction before scientists can even ascertain and exploit their beneficial qualities. The genetic uniformity of modern grain production also increases the risk that new diseases might wipe out entire crops or that pests will become increasingly resistant and invulnerable to modern pesticides. Traditional farming practices guarded against these risks by planting a variety of grains, each with different vulnerabilities. This diversity reduces the chances that one disease will damage the entire crop.[97]

Some observers argue that the "industrial" model of agriculture represented by the Green Revolution is the wrong path. Capital- and water-intensive methods to produce grain are unsustainable, according to critics, and are accompanied by the diversion of food to raise livestock and fuel automobiles. Instead, developing countries should invest in more diversified, low-input, small-holding agriculture that promotes greater self-sufficiency and gets food to those most in need.[98]

Despite these cautionary notes, scientific advances will undoubtedly play a role in boosting future food production. The Consultative Group on International Agricultural Research (CGIAR), founded in 1972, has meshed the efforts of a growing number of agricultural research organizations. CGIAR today encompasses eighteen research centers and draws funding from forty public and private sources, including Northern and Southern governments, development banks, private foundations, and international agencies. Although CGIAR's initial emphasis was on enhancing productivity through higher yields, it has since broadened its research into sustainable agriculture, including environmental concerns and resource management.[99] New rice varieties created by CGIAR affiliate International Rice Research Institute could raise total rice production by as much as one-quarter after they are planted on a widespread basis. Many such breakthroughs must be realized, however, if food production is to keep pace with growing populations.

Yet funding for agricultural research and improvement has declined in recent years. The amount of Official Development Assistance (ODA) targeted toward agriculture dropped by 57 percent between 1988 and 1996. On average, developing country governments devote only 7.4 percent of state budgets to agricultural development.[100] The rate of investment in developing country agriculture must rise by at least 50 percent if production is to keep up with growing demand.[101]

Genetic modification offers one potential tool for tackling future food scarcity. Genetic marking, for instance, can greatly speed and simplify traditional cross-breeding methods in the development of a given species of plant or animal. With knowledge of a particular plant genome, for instance, scientists can ascertain beforehand whether organisms have the specific gene that is desired for cross-breeding. This technology is relatively uncontroversial and may allow for swifter, though still incremental, gains in yield and pest resistance.[102]

Far more controversial are genetic engineering techniques that involve the transfer of genes from one species to another. The promise of such advances is alluring, although still largely unrealized to date. Most stunning has been the development of so-called "golden rice." Scientists have succeeded in producing a yellow-hued strain of rice that is rich in vitamin

A through trans-genetic modification. This new rice could bring tremendous health benefits in the many parts of the developing world where vitamin A deficiency is a major problem. An estimated 124 million children worldwide suffer from a lack of sufficient dietary vitamin A. Two million children die of vitamin A deficiency each year while another 500,000 go blind from the same lack.

Although its release has been delayed by patent disputes, cooperation involving the Rockefeller Institute, several agricultural research organizations, and large biotechnology companies calls for the establishment of non-profit holding companies that would distribute "golden rice" seeds free to poor farmers in the developing world. The vitamin-rich rice would be cross-bred with local varieties and the seeds saved for planting in future years. Such is the popular distrust of genetically modified organisms, however, that activists destroyed a field where golden rice was planted in the Philippines in 2013.[103]

There exist other promising applications for these techniques. Some scientists, for instance, believe that genetic engineering could save an estimated 1–3 percent of the world's crops that are presently lost to pests and disease.[104] The cropland planted with genetically engineered plants grew from 5 million acres in 1996 to 250 million acres in 2006.[105]

Yet genetic engineering of modified foodstuffs has also encountered stiff opposition from some quarters. Environmentalists warn that the introduction of genetically modified organisms (GMOs) into natural ecosystems could produce unexpected and harmful effects, such as the development of fast-spreading and pesticide-resistant "superweeds" or chemical-resistant pests. Others express concerns about the consumption of genetically modified foods on human health. Scientific research into such risks has been scant thus far and one authoritative review of existing studies concludes that it is not yet possible to draw firm conclusions about the safety of genetically modified foods.[106] It remains unclear whether GMOs can deliver the increased yields that have been promised. One survey of relevant research found that GMO varieties had produced no yield gains in wheat or soybeans and only marginal gains from GMO corn.[107]

To date, little progress has been made toward developing widely accepted national or international standards and regulations with regard to genetically modified foods. Without such oversight, consumer confidence in the safety of such foodstuffs may stand in doubt. In 1999, negotiations on international rules regarding trade in genetically modified organisms based upon the Biosafety Protocol of the 1992 Convention on Biological Diversity ended in disagreement and failure. Later in the same year, efforts to establish a "Working Party on Biotechnology" under the auspices of the World Trade Organization (WTO) also came to naught.

In general, the United States prefers open trade in genetically modified organisms and minimal regulation. Most European countries, on the other hand, are highly skeptical about genetic engineering and the European Union (EU) has imposed what amounts to a near-ban on the importation of genetically modified food and seeds. The European Union's stance on this issue has slowed the spread of genetically engineered strains to developing countries, since the latter fear that the food grown from such seeds would be ineligible for export to European markets. Coming years promise to bring continued political strife over how to balance the promise and the risks of genetic engineering.[108]

There exist other measures that can help make more food available in the future. At least 30 percent of food production is not consumed due to waste. Better management should be able to save much of the 6 percent of all grain that is presently lost through poor storage and distribution practices. A project funded by the African Development Bank aims to reduce food waste by 20 percent over a seven-year period. In the United States, one-quarter of all food is lost at the retail, consumer, and food service levels.[109]

The world's farms could feed far more people if a large proportion of the grain presently fed to livestock was instead consumed directly by humans. Livestock, such as cattle and sheep, now graze roughly one-half of the earth's total land area. One-quarter of the world's cropland is devoted to the production of grain and other feeds for livestock. These animals consume 38 percent of the grain produced worldwide.[110]

Although the grain fed to livestock is converted to meat, which is eventually consumed by humans, the process is quite inefficient. It takes 7 kilograms of grain, for instance, to produce 1 kilogram of beef. Up to the point of slaughter, a 240-pound hog raised in the United States consumes 600 pounds of corn and 100 pounds of soybean meal. The meat thereby produced could supply one person with a diet of 2,200 calories per day for forty-nine days. The same corn and soybean, if consumed directly, could sustain one person at the same rate of caloric intake for 500 days. A decline in meat consumption would free up much grain for direct human consumption and help the world's agricultural system to accommodate the demands of a growing global population. Unfortunately, proportional meat consumption is more likely to rise than to fall in the coming years. Experience suggests that as Southern incomes rise, people who had previously been able to afford only a vegetarian diet will begin to consume larger quantities of meat. In the United States, a 10 percent rise in income is associated with a 1.1 percent rise in meat consumption. But in China, a 10 percent rise in income results in an 11.5 percent rise in meat consumption.[111] In response to rising demand, world meat output doubled between 1980 and 2007. Overall, the demand for meat in developing countries is expected to double between 1995 and 2020.[112]

Much will depend upon policy reform as well. If Southern agriculture is to modernize quickly enough to provide for rapidly growing populations, then the development priorities of many Third World governments must change. Three sets of policy biases common to many governments work against producers of basic staple food crops: an industrial bias, an urban bias, and a cash crop bias. Policymakers often equate development with industrialization. As a result, scarce capital is marshaled toward the manufacturing sector, while agriculture suffers from a paucity of investment. Indeed, some governments deliberately manipulate food prices downward so as to please politically potent urban constituencies. The results of this urban bias are to depress rural incomes and to undermine both the ability and the incentive for farmers to modernize and expand production. Even within the agricultural sector, crucial inputs such as credit, infrastructure, and the best land are targeted principally at cash crops, such as coffee, tea, cocoa, or sugar, which can be exported to the North in return for scarce foreign exchange.

Brazil's experience in recent years offers a bright spot in the otherwise worrisome trends in global food production. Since 1996, the Brazilian Agricultural Research Corporation (Embrapa), established in 1973, has introduced a series of innovations that have transformed Brazil's cerrado into a major food-producing region. The addition of lime lowered the acidity of the soil. New high-yielding grasses allowed increased cattle farming. Improved soybean strains adapted to mature in shorter cycles led to increased yields and the ability to harvest two crops per year on the same land. Brazil pioneered no-till agriculture, which allows leftover crop residue to replenish the soil while limiting soil erosion. Embrapa also introduced schemes for integrating forests, agriculture, and live-stock. As a result of these policy innovations, the total value of Brazil's agricultural output more than tripled between 1996 and 2006. Soybean production quadrupled and Brazil has become the largest exporter of beef, sugar cane, and ethanol. All of this was accomplished even while agricultural subsidies in Brazil remain less than one-quarter in relative terms than those in the United States and Europe. There is hope that some of these techniques can be transferred to parts of Africa.[113]

Climate change represents a wild card in all projections about future food production. On the one hand, rising levels of carbon dioxide may, in theory, stimulate accelerated plant growth. Yet even this slim basis for optimism has recently been called into question.[114] Overall, a warming earth will almost certainly have harmful effects on agriculture. Wheat is particularly vulnerable to heat stress. A 2 degree Celsius rise in average temperature is thus expected to reduce wheat yields by 20 percent.[115] Climate will impact agriculture by producing more extremes of drought and flooding. Africa, in particular, is likely to experience more frequent episodes of drought. One estimate suggests that crop yields from rain-fed fields in Africa may decline by 50 percent if efforts to slow global warming are not successful.[116]

It remains unclear whether the world can achieve sufficient increases in food production to avoid any dramatic lowering of present consumption levels, much less to improve the diets of the millions of malnourished. Four factors appear critical to achieving a positive outcome: (1) continued progress must be made in reducing the rate of population growth, (2) ongoing scientific research must continue to devise increasingly reliable and higher-yielding staple crop varieties, (3) increased economic investment must be directed to agricultural modernization, particularly in the Third World, and (4) greater efforts must be made to bring about the more equitable distribution of food supplies. Much will depend upon the priorities of political leaders in both the North and South. What does seem apparent, however, is that the margin of error is slim when it comes to organizing the world's agricultural resources over the coming decades.

Global Public Health

The past century has witnessed astonishing improvements in human health. Global average life expectancy rose from 31 years in 1900 to 69 years in 2010. Infant mortality has declined by 75 percent over the past 120 years. Moreover, the greatest gains in recent decades have come in the least developed countries. In 1950, life spans in the poorest countries were only one-half of those in the richest countries. By the end of the century, the ratio was two-thirds. Despite almost no growth in per capita income and a tripling of population, Africa has experienced a ten-year rise in life expectancy since 1960, while childhood (under 5 years of age) mortality has fallen from 27 percent to 15 percent[117] (see Figure 10.2).

The stunning progress in improving health outcomes in even the poorest countries is primarily due to three factors: the globalization of health technologies and knowledge, the growing availability of cheap public health interventions, and an increasingly robust global health infrastructure that encompasses the World Health Organization (WHO), national public health agencies, major foundations, non-governmental organizations (NGOs), and private firms and health providers.

Advances in knowledge about health and the development of new medicines and technologies are responsible for major improvements in health. The germ theory of disease led to more effective public health measures related to sanitation and the containment of contagions. Antibiotics have reduced the length and costs of bacterial diseases. Vaccines against many common communicable diseases have saved millions of lives. Once acquired, medical knowledge disseminates widely and quickly from the point of origin, especially where public health authorities carry out aggressive health education campaigns.

Many effective health interventions are surprisingly inexpensive. An insecticide-treated bed net that serves to reduce the odds of contracting malaria costs only $5 and remains effective for several years. Oral rehydration therapy to offset the dangerous effects of dysentery requires a combination of clean water, sugar, and salt. Treatment to prevent

Sub-Saharan Africa — 180 (1990), 129 (2008)
Southern Asia — 122 (1990), 69 (2008)
Oceania — 76 (1990), 59 (2008)
CIS, Asia — 78 (1990), 37 (2008)
South-Eastern Asia — 73 (1990), 36 (2008)
Western Asia — 66 (1990), 31 (2008)
Northern Africa — 80 (1990), 26 (2008)
Latin America & the Caribbean — 52 (1990), 23 (2008)
Eastern Asia — 45 (1990), 19 (2008)
Commonwealth of Independent States, Europe — 26 (1990), 13 (2008)
Transition Countries of South-Eastern Europe — 31 (1990), 11 (2008)
Developed Regions — 12 (1990), 6 (2008)
Developing Regions — 99 (1990), 66 (2008)

1990
2008

0   50   100   150   200

Figure 10.2 Under-5 Mortality Rate Per 1,000 Live Births, 1990 and 2008.

Source: Adapted from "The Millennium Development Goals Report," United Nations, 2010, www.un.org/millenniumgoals/pdf/MDG%20Report%202010%20En%20r15%20 -low%20res%2020100615%20-.pdf#page=28&gt

elephantiasis costs 3 cents per year. Iodized salt can fight iodine deficiency, which is a cause of mental retardation. Vitamin A boosters for children cost 2 cents each. Medicine for intestinal worms comes in at the same price. The human and economic returns from cheap health interventions are considerable. Deworming reduces school absenteeism by 25 percent, while a child who avoids chronic hookworm will enjoy a 50 percent higher income as an adult. The campaign against measles has achieved a global vaccination rate of 85 percent, saving the lives of 9 million children as infections fell by 75 percent over the first decade of the twenty-first century. [118]

Indeed, where effective and committed coalitions develop among national governments, international donors, and civil society, astonishing progress can be achieved in even very poor countries. One study found that of sixty-nine indicators of quality of life, only three were strongly correlated with income.[119] This suggests that countries do not have to wait until they become rich in order to provide a better and healthier life for their citizens. For example, programs aimed at empowering women over the past decade have brought dramatic declines in birth rates, teen pregnancies, and infant mortality in Bangladesh. In Rwanda, the implementation of an efficient, cost-effective universal health insurance program has resulted, over the course of a single decade, in a rise in life expectancy from 48 to 58 years, a drop in under–5 child mortality by half, and a two-thirds decline in deaths from malaria.[120]

While cheap public health interventions have brought major progress, major challenges remain. Three billion people lack access to sanitation services. One billion people have no access to clean drinking water despite an international campaign that has halved that figure in recent years. Diseases from contaminated water kill 5–10 million people per year. Intestinal worms take 180,000 lives per year. Two billion people suffer from iodine deficiency. At any given time, roughly half of people in the developing world suffer from one of the following: diarrhea, cholera, typhoid, trachoma, and parasitic worms. Two million people die each year from exposure to indoor air pollution caused by household cooking fires.[121]

A recent study found 1.24 million deaths attributable to malaria in 2010, double the estimate previously arrived at by the WHO.[122] While other studies suggest that the death rate from malaria has declined by almost one-half since 2000, the fact that malaria may remain a far deadlier killer than previously appreciated is alarming.[123] It also serves as a reminder of the difficulties of gathering reliable data on health conditions in the world's poorest countries.

If inexpensive solutions are available for many of these health problems, why do so many still lack access to them? Much of the answer has to do with the lack of public health infrastructure in many countries. Especially where poor transportation systems limit access to remote rural populations, health delivery systems struggle to reach those in need. Public health systems are also constrained by a lack of financial resources, whether due to skewed political priorities or economic penury. Indeed, all of the governments of sub-Saharan Africa combined spend only $30 billion per year on health – about as much as Poland.[124] In some countries, internal conflict and violence inflict suffering, disrupt health services, and force people to flee their homes and communities.

While health is considered a public as well as private good in much of the world, national and global health systems are also enmeshed in commercial networks that commodify health resources. For instance, pharmaceutical companies focus their research and development investments on drugs most likely to generate healthy profits rather than drugs that would have the greatest health benefits for the greatest number of people. A promising vaccine that was found to be effective in protecting monkeys from the Ebola virus went untested in humans for over a decade due to lack of interest among drug-makers.[125] Thus, few private dollars are devoted to research into cures for tropical diseases. Moreover, patent rights grant a monopoly market position to their owners. This encourages investment in new drugs but also drives up drug prices until the patent expires and cheaper generic versions become available.

The Agreement on Trade Related Aspects of Intellectual Property (TRIPs), negotiated as part of the World Trade Organization in 1994, required member states to meet international standards in providing legal protection for patent and copyright claims. As a result, patented drugs that could be manufactured and sold by developing country firms at a fraction of the price charged by the big, Western drug companies are simply unaffordable for the vast majority of the world's population. In the case of HIV/AIDS drugs, TRIPs rules were reinterpreted to allow compulsory licensing so that generic versions could be produced and sold at low prices, saving many lives. Despite the opposition of the United States, developing countries are now seeking the right to produce or import generic versions of drugs for non-communicable diseases such as cancer, heart disease, and diabetes, all of which are rising problems in the developing world.[126] Indian drug firms claim that they can produce cancer drugs for one-third of the price charged by the global pharmaceutical companies. In a direct challenge to existing interpretations of TRIPs, Indian authorities recently authorized a local manufacturer to produce a cancer drug patented by Bayer under compulsory licensing. Although this was the first case of its kind, it is unlikely to be the last.[127]

Pandemic Diseases

The global public health agenda includes campaigns to contain or eliminate the spread of pandemic diseases. This section focuses on three such cases: influenza, polio, and HIV/AIDS.

Influenza

Influenza is the most deadly and unpredictable threat among communicable diseases. A global outbreak of the Spanish flu in 1918 killed an estimated 50–100 million people worldwide. In the United States, a normal flu season results in 200,000 hospitalizations and 38,000 deaths, despite annual vaccination campaigns.[128]

There are many different strains of the influenza virus. New versions are developing at a rapid rate, many jumping from animals to humans. Avian flu was first detected in Southern China in 1997. Human victims typically acquire the bug from contact with infected chickens. The mortality rate from Avian flu is particularly frightful. So far, however, Avian flu has not been found to spread through human-to-human contact, although such a possibility remains a future threat.

In 2009, a new version of the flu that jumped from pigs to humans – labeled H1N1 – was identified. Unlike most influenza strains, this one posed a greater threat to young people than the elderly. Emergency efforts to produce and distribute 90 million vaccine doses in the United States helped to avert the direst scenario that year.[129]

Some experts believe that a major influenza outbreak on the scale of 1918 (or greater, given the much larger world population) is unavoidable. New strains of the flu virus, along with other infectious diseases, are migrating from animals to humans at an increasing rate as humans penetrate previously virgin forests and expand livestock herds. Moreover, denser urban populations and the increased mobility offered through global transportation networks allow diseases to spread more quickly.[130]

Although influenza can be combated with vaccines, it takes time to develop effective vaccines in response to new strains. Moreover, vaccines are never 100 percent effective. The manufacture of vaccines is slow and complex and the number of commercial firms engaged in vaccine production has dwindled, as profits are modest and producers face legal risks since vaccines can sometimes pose health risks themselves. Even if public and private efforts produced a quick and effective vaccine in response to a new and virulent strain of influenza, the beneficiaries would likely be limited to residents of wealthy countries, leaving the vast majority of poorer people in the developing world exposed.

Facing a major pandemic, health authorities may be tempted to close down schools, public meetings, and transportation links in an effort to contain the spread of disease. In 2003, the World Health Organization responded to reported cases of Severe Acute Respiratory Syndrome (SARS) in Toronto, Canada by issuing an advisory against non-essential travel to that city. However, the effectiveness of such measures is uncertain and the economic consequences can be substantial – the decline of tourism alone cost Toronto hundreds of millions of dollars in lost revenue.[131]

In 2001, the World Health Organization adopted the Pandemic Influenza Preparedness Framework, stressing knowledge, preparedness, responsiveness, and access to drugs. The World Health Assembly passed the International Health Regulations Framework in 2007 to promote better coordination among national public health authorities in response to transnational health emergencies.[132] Despite such steps to enhance global capacity and coordination, the risks of a major outbreak of influenza or other infectious diseases are considerable while the ability of health authorities to respond in an effective manner is uncertain.

Polio Eradication

Both the promise and the challenge of global public health can be witnessed in global efforts to eradicate polio. In 1981, 65,000 new polio cases were reported worldwide. Thanks to a massive international vaccination campaign, this figure had fallen to only 223 in 2012. An estimated 5 million children were spared paralysis due to the dissemination of the polio vaccine. The ultimate goal of this global effort – sponsored by the WHO, UNICEF, the Rotary and Gates Foundations, and other groups – is to eradicate polio completely, thus duplicating an earlier successful campaign that achieved the goal of eliminating naturally occurring smallpox in 1979.[133]

Reaching final victory over polio has proven more difficult, costly, and time-consuming than originally expected. Costs run to roughly $1 billion each year. Unlike smallpox, polio symptoms emerge slowly, thus making it difficult to organize rapid and timely responses to new outbreaks. Also, a course of three vaccine doses is required. Moreover, the standard oral version of the polio vaccine itself carries a small risk of passing along the disease. Thus, even after a region has succeeded in ridding itself of the polio virus, health workers must continue to administer an inactivated version of the vaccine for five to ten years in order to ensure against renewed outbreaks.[134]

There has also been resistance to vaccination among Muslim communities in some countries driven by a combination of fear, ignorance, and political calculation. The American Central Intelligence Agency employed a Pakistani doctor who had been a major leader in the polio vaccination campaign to gather intelligence as part of the United States' effort to locate and kill Osama bin Laden. Citing this mingling of humanitarianism with covert operations, the Taliban in June 2012 banned the delivery of polio vaccines to areas of North Waziristan under their control. This delayed scheduled vaccinations for 161,000 children in the country with the highest rate of polio infections in the world.[135] After years of steady progress, the number of new polio cases rose in 2013.[136]

The polio campaign, despite its evident successes, has drawn criticism for diverting scarce health resources from other perhaps more immediate priorities. Defenders argue that the future benefits should the campaign succeed in eradicating polio are incalculable. Moreover, any slackening of effort could once again lead to spread of the virus.

HIV/AIDS

In 2001, the UN General Assembly held a Special Session on HIV/AIDS which declared that "the global HIV/AIDS epidemic is a global emergency and one of the most fundamental challenges to human life and dignity, as well as to the enjoyment of human rights." Thus was launched what has become the world's largest coordinated global health campaign to date. AIDS has now become the fourth biggest cause of death in the world. An estimated 33 million people presently suffer from this terrible disease and each year brings an additional 2.5 million cases of infection. Especially harmful from a social and economic perspective is the fact that one-half of those infected are between the ages of 15 and 24. AIDS has already claimed nearly 25 million lives and accounts for 1.8 additional deaths each year.[137] Ninety-five percent of AIDS sufferers are located in the developing world. Hardest hit is sub-Saharan Africa, which alone accounts for 70 percent of all AIDS cases worldwide. AIDS has produced 12 million orphans in Africa.[138]

The attention given to HIV/AIDS provided the political will needed to create the Global Fund to Fight AIDS, Tuberculosis, and Malaria, which was founded as a public–private partnership in 2001. The Global Fund draws together resources from governments, international organizations, non-governmental organizations, private donors, and corporations for the purpose of preventing, treating, and alleviating the suffering associated with three major diseases. The Global Fund has an annual budget of over $22 billion, which supports 1,000 programs in 150 countries. The Global Fund claims to have saved over 7.7 million lives through programs that provide treatment for 3.3 million AIDS patients and 8.6 million tuberculosis victims. The Global Fund also makes available 230 million insecticide-treated bed nets to populations in malarial zones.[139]

These and other responses to the HIV/AIDS pandemic offer hope. Most promising are education and prevention programs. In Africa, 80 percent of HIV infections are spread through heterosexual contact. The rapid growth in condom use in many African countries has slowed the spread of the disease. Babies born to HIV-positive mothers are at risk of being born with the disease. The odds of infection decline by half, however, if the mother receives anti-retroviral drugs prior to childbirth. The proportion of expectant mothers receiving such therapy in the developing world has risen from 10 percent in 2004 to 50 percent in 2009. The use of infant formula can reduce chances of babies catching HIV from the mother as a result of breastfeeding, although the use of infant formula itself carries health risks if mixed with dirty water. The number of infants contracting HIV during birth or through breastfeeding fell from 500,000 in 2001 to 370,000 in 2009. Circumcised males are 60 percent less likely to become infected with HIV. One million males worldwide have undergone circumcision since 2007, with 75 percent of these operations paid for by the US Agency for International Development (AID). As a result of these preventive measures, the rate of new HIV infections has fallen by half in a group of 25 low- and middle-income countries, most located in Africa.[140]

The lives of individuals infected with HIV can be extended through drug treatment. Until recent years, however, the so-called "AIDS cocktail" was too expensive for widespread use in the developing world. In 2004, the yearly cost of drug treatment in Africa was over $1,000 per patient, a figure far beyond the financial means of the vast majority of African AIDS sufferers. A combination of pressures from AIDS activists, African governments, and media coverage compelled large Northern drug companies to drastically cut their prices on AIDS drugs sold in Africa and other developing countries to cost or below. Also, Indian and Chinese firms now produce generic versions of some AIDS drugs for both domestic use and export under compulsory patent licensing arrangements. As a result, the cost of drug treatment for AIDS patients has fallen to 20 cents per day, a level that allows national and international health agencies to vastly extend the numbers of patients treated. Indeed, 6 million AIDS victims in the developing world now receive regular drug treatment, up from only 2,000 patients in 2001.[141] This led to a 19 percent decline in deaths among the HIV positive population between 2004 and 2009. Another 10 million AIDS victims, however, still lack access to drug therapy.

One-half of those receiving AIDS treatment are supported by the Global Fund, while most of the remainder are covered by an American program called the President's Emergency Plan for AIDS Relief (PEPFAR). The financial strain of providing lifetime treatment for a growing number of AIDS patients came into sharp relief in 2010 when donors failed to pledge enough money to finance what the Global Fund considered an "austerity level" budget.[142] In 2012, the Global Fund's financial circumstances became so dire that it was forced to declare a two-year hiatus in considering new grants. As government support waned, the Bill and Melinda Gates Foundation stepped up with a $750 million donation, though this still left the Global Fund far short of its funding goals.[143]

There have been other setbacks in the fight against HIV/AIDS. In southern and eastern Africa, many women rely upon a hormone shot given every three months for contraceptive purposes. The advantages of this form of contraceptive is that the shots are safe, long lasting, and do not require a visit to a doctor. Recent research, however, has revealed that this contraceptive treatment doubles the risk of HIV infection among women. The risk of infection also doubles for the male sexual partners of already HIV-positive women who receive the shot.[144]

The massive international response to HIV/AIDS has drawn the same kinds of criticisms as those leveled against the polio eradication effort. Critics argue that global health dollars tend to focus on particular diseases in isolation rather than taking an holistic approach to improved health. More cost-effective interventions, such as providing neonatal care or insuring access to safe drinking water, would prevent more suffering and death. In addition, the high-profile campaigns mounted by international agencies and non-governmental organizations often bypass local health authorities and thus do little to strengthen the capacity of health systems over the long term.

Indeed, international agencies and NGOs often lure health practitioners away from local public health bureaucracies that cannot afford to offer salaries competitive with those available from outside employers. In fact, the short-term infusion of expatriate health workers into poor countries is more than offset by the loss of trained health providers who migrate to rich countries. One-fourth of doctors in the United States, the United Kingdom, Canada, and Australia were born elsewhere and between 40 percent and 75 percent of the latter originate from poor countries.[145] The proportions are even more lopsided for nurses. In 1994, the US Congress passed a law that allows foreign medical students to remain in the United States on J-1 visas if they practice in communities that have too few doctors. This is a response to the problem that not enough doctors and nurses are being trained within the United States itself. Indeed, one study predicts a shortage of 200,000 doctors in the United States a decade from now. Meanwhile, however, such shortage of trained medical personnel is far more acute in the developing countries from which medical personnel are being recruited. Zambia, for instance, has only one doctor for every 23,000 people compared with one for 416 in the United States.[146]

The international community has become somewhat more sensitive to these complaints. In 2005, donor countries signed on to the Paris Declaration on Aid Effectiveness, which attempts to improve coordination among donors and between donors and recipients. In 2010, WHO member states adopted the Global Code of Practice on the International Recruitment of Health Personnel in an effort to slow the exodus of health practitioners from poor to rich countries.[147] In recognition of this medical brain drain, some international donors are providing funds to raise the salaries of doctors and nurses in poor countries.[148]

Conclusion: Managing the Population Challenge

Contrary to Malthus, the past two centuries have witnessed the coincidence of rapid population growth and quickly improving human welfare. Despite huge and growing income gaps between the haves and the have-nots, gains in health and welfare have extended to even the world's poorest societies. The keys to these achievements have been expanding scientific knowledge, the spread and application of this knowledge on a global basis and the development of cheap health interventions that extend and improve the quality of human life.

At the same time, enormous challenges remain. One out of seven humans suffers from malnourishment and millions of premature deaths each year are attributable to preventable or treatable diseases. The environmental and resource strains produced by the combination of rising population and growing consumption levels present challenges that might yet redeem Malthus's pessimism. The key question is whether economic and human development can be rendered environmentally sustainable. Energy and climate change, the focal points of the next chapter, lie at the center of this puzzle.

Key Concepts (see Glossary)

Carrying Capacity

Demographic Transition

Global Fund

Green Revolution

Pandemic Diseases

Public Health

Remittances

Sustainable Development

Tragedy of the Commons

Discussion Questions

1 Are Malthus's ideas about population and resources of contemporary relevance?

2 What are the main factors that determine the pace of population growth?

3 Are rapidly rising populations a spur or a drag upon economic growth?

4 Given vast income differentials between rich and poor countries, why has immigration from developing to developed economies been so restrained?

5 Which is the more effective response to global hunger – increasing the supply of food or distributing the existing supply of food more equitably?

6 Does food aid help or hurt recipient countries?

7 What are the biggest challenges to increasing global food supplies? What are the most promising solutions?

8 How has globalization figured into the improvements in life expectancy and health in even the poorest countries?

Notes

1 Thomas Malthus, *An Essay on the Principle of Population*, New York: Penguin Books, 1985.

2 United Nations, Department of Economic and Social Affairs, Population Division, Population Estimates and Projections Section (http://esa.un.org/unpd/wpp/unpp/p2k0data.asp), 2011.
3 US Census Bureau, World POPClock Projection, January 5, 2012 (www.census.gov/population/popclockworld.html).
4 Justin Gillis and Celia W. Dugger, "U.N. Forecasts 10.1 Billion People by Century's End," *New York Times*, May 3, 2011; Natalie Wolchover, "5 Ways the World Will Change Radically This Century," *Life's Little Mysteries*, October 19, 2011, www.livescience.com/16625-world-century.html
5 A recent study predicts that populations will fail to stabilize during this century and could reach more than 12 billion. Patrick Gerland, Adrian E. Raftery, Hana Ševčíková, Nan Li, Danan Gu, Thomas Spoorenberg, Leontine Alkema, Bailey K. Fosdick, Jennifer Chunn, Nevana Lalic, Guiomar Bay, Thomas Buettner, Gerhard K. Heilig, and John Wilmoth, "World Population Stabilization Unlikely this Century," *Science*, vol. 346, no. 6206 (October 10, 2014) 234–7.
6 Erla Zwingle, "Women and Population," *National Geographic* (October 1998) 38.
7 Somini Sengupta, "United Nations Forecasts Persistently High Unemployment for the Young," *New York Times*, May 21, 2014; Gwynn Guilford, "The Lost Generation of Young Men is Threatening Global Stability," *Quartz* (March 11, 2014).
8 Gillis and Dugger, "U.N. Forecasts."
9 Lester Brown, Nicholas Lenssen, and Hal Kane, *Vital Signs, 1995: The Trends That Are Shaping Our Future*, New York: W.W. Norton & Company (Worldwatch Institute), 1995, 94–5.
10 Matthew Quirk, "Bright Lights, Big Cities," *The Atlantic Monthly* (December 2007).
11 Malcolm Potts and Martha Campbell, "The Myth of 9 Billion," *Foreign Policy* (May 9, 2011).
12 Charles Kegley, Jr. and Eugene R. Wittkopf, *World Politics: Trend and Transformation*, New York: St. Martin's Press, 5th ed., 1995, 305.
13 For a discussion of population momentum, see Kegley and Wittkopf, *World Politics*, 299–300.
14 United Nations Population Division of the Department of Economic and Social Affairs, "2010 Revision of the World Population Prospects," May 3, 2011.
15 On the aging of the world's population, see Nicholas Eberstadt, "World Population Implosion?" in Timothy C. Lim (ed.), *Stand! Contending Ideas and Opinions: Global Issues*, Bellevue: Coursewise Publishing, 1999.
16 "Fertility Declines Have Stalled in Many Countries in Sub-Saharan Africa," *International Family Planning Perspectives*, vol. 34, no. 3 (September 2008).
17 United Nations Population Division of the Department of Economic and Social Affairs, "2010 Revision of the World Population Prospects," May 3, 2011.
18 William Schmidt, "U.N. Population Report Urges Family-Size Choice for Women," *New York Times*, August 18, 1994; "Population: Battle of the Bulge," *The Economist*, September 3, 1994, 24. Andreea A. Creanga, Duff Gillespie, Sabrina Karklins, and Amy O. Tsui, "Low Use of Contraception among Poor Women in Africa: An Equity Issue," *Bulletin of the World Health Organization*, 89 (2011) 258–66.
19 Potts and Campbell, "The Myth of 9 Billion."
20 Potts and Campbell, "The Myth of 9 Billion"; Gillis and Dugger, "U.N. Forecasts"; and "African Demography: Fertility Treatment," *The Economist*, March 8, 2014.

21 "Population: Battle of the Bulge," 25.

22 The following discussion is based upon William W. Murdoch, *The Poverty of Nations: The Political Economy of Hunger and Population*, Baltimore: Johns Hopkins University Press, 1980, 15–58.

23 Barbara Crossette, "16% World Illiteracy to Grow, Study Says," *New York Times*, December 9, 1998.

24 "The World's Women, 2010: Trends and Statistics," United Nations Department of Economic and Social Affairs, 2010, http://unstats.un.org/unsd/demographic/products/Worldswomen/WW_full report_color.pdf

25 See Murdoch, *The Poverty of Nations*, 59–83.

26 Schmidt, "U.N. Population Report."

27 "Global Employment Trades, 2014," International Labor Organization, 2014, www.ilo.org/wcmsp5/groups/public/---dgreports/---dcomm/---publ/documents/publication/wcms_233953.pdf

28 "A Bumpier but Freer Road," *The Economist*, September 30, 2010.

29 "Getting On: The Consequences of an Ageing Population," *The Economist*, June 23, 2011.

30 United Nations Department of Economic and Social Affairs, *World Population Prospects: The 2012 Revision*, 2012.

31 "Japan. Ikonoclast. Debating Issues in Japanese Politics? What a Droll Idea," *The Economist*, May 18, 2006.

32 "An Exercise in Fertility," *The Economist*, September 16, 2010.

33 "An Exercise in Fertility."

34 Jason DeParle, "Global Migration: A World Ever More on the Move," *New York Times*, June 25, 2010.

35 United Nations Department of Economic and Social Affairs, *World Population Prospects: The 2012 Revision*, 2012.

36 Mereya Navarro, "Breaking a Long Silence on Population Control," *New York Times*, October 31, 2011; Ted C. Fishman, "As Populations Age, a Chance for Younger Nations," *New York Times*, October 14, 2010.

37 Only those who have lived abroad for at least a year are classified as migrants by the UN.

38 DeParle, "Global Migration."

39 Pankaj Ghemawat, *World 3.0: Global Prosperity and How to Achieve It*, Boston, MA: Harvard Business Review Press, 2011, 27, 174.

40 Eric Weiner, "Debunking Global Migration Myths," *NPR News*, June 6, 2007.

41 *International Migration Report 2006: A Global Assessment*, United Nations Department of Social and Economic Affairs, Population Division, 2009.

42 Nick Cumming-Bruce, "Number of People Displaced by Violence Highest in 20 Years, Agency Says," *New York Times*, May 14, 2014.

43 *International Migration Report 2006: A Global Assessment*.

44 Migration Policy Institute Data Hub, www.migrationinformation.org/datahub/remittances.cfm, accessed January 28, 2012.

45 Ghemawat, *World 3.0*, 82.

46 Ghemawat, *World 3.0*, 179.

47 Dani Rodrik, *The Globalization Paradox: Democracy and the Future of the World Economy*, New York: W.W. Norton & Company, 2011. Also see, Tyler Cowen, "A Strategy for Rich Countries: Absorb More Immigrants," *New York Times*, November 8, 2014.

48 Rome Declaration on Food Security, www.fao.org/docrep/003/w3613e/w3613e00.htm

49 Justin Gillis, "A Warming Planet Struggles to Feed Itself," *New York Times*, June 4, 2011.

50 Edith M. Lederer, "18,000 Kids Die Daily of Hunger, Malnutrition, U.N. Food Chief Says," *Des Moines Register*, February 18, 2007.
51 "Agriculture and Nutrition: Hidden Hunger," *The Economist*, March 24, 2011.
52 "Food: The Hidden Driver of Global Politics," National Public Radio, May 18, 2011.
53 "FAO Food Price Index Ends Year with Sharp Decline," *Food and Agricultural Organization* (January 12, 2012).
54 Charles Kenny, *Getting Better: Why Global Development is Succeeding – and How We Can Improve the World Even More*, New York: Basic Books, 2011.
55 Lester R. Brown, "The New Geopolitics of Food," *Foreign Policy*, May/June 2011.
56 "Investment" How to Feed the World 2050: High-Level Expert Forum, Rome, October 1, 2009.
57 Uwe Buse, "The Challenge of Deciding Who to Feed," *Spiegel Online*, January 7, 2011.
58 Gillis, "A Warming Planet."
59 Celia W. Dugger, "Bush Administration Gains Support for New Approach on Foreign Aid," *New York Times*, April 22, 2007.
60 Dugger, "Bush Administration Gains Support"; Dugger, "Oversight Report Says U.S. Food Aid Practices Are Wasteful," *New York Times International*, April 14, 2007. Ron Nixon, "Proposal for Changes in Food Aid Sets Off Infighting in Congress," *New York Times*, May 2, 2013.
61 Celia W. Dugger, "Kenyan Farmers' Fate Caught Up in U.S. Aid Rules," *New York Times*, July 31, 2007.
62 William Schmidt, "U.N. Population Report Urges Family-Size Choice for Women," *New York Times*, August 18, 1994.
63 Lloyd Timberlake, "The Politics of Food Aid," in Edward Goldsmith and Nicholas Hildyard (eds), *The Earth Report*, London: Mitchell Beazley, 1988, 29.
64 Martha Ann Overland, "Lawmakers Seek to Remove Politics from Foreign Aid," *Des Moines Register*, July 22, 1990.
65 *World Food Program Annual Report 2010*, http://givewell.org/files/DisasterRelief/WFP/WFP. Annual report 2010.pdf
66 Jeffrey Gettleman, "Famine Hits Somalia in a World Less Likely to Intervene," *New York Times*, September 15, 2011; Jeffrey Gettleman, "Somalis Waste Away as Insurgents Block Escape from Famine," *New York Times*, August 1, 2011; Jeffrey Gettleman, "Food Crisis in Somalia Is a Famine, U.N. Says," *New York Times*, July 20, 2011; Gettleman, "Contractors Are Accused in Large-Scale Theft of Food Aid in Somalia," *New York Times*, August 16, 2011; "Somali Famine 'Will Kill Tens of Thousands,'" *BBC News*, January 15, 2012.
67 Gettleman, "Contractors Are Accused in Large-Scale Theft."
68 Joanna M. Foster, "Report Sees Tight Global Cereal Markets," *New York Times*, October 10, 2011.
69 Timberlake, "The Politics of Food Aid," 24.
70 Timberlake, "The Politics of Food Aid," 23–4.
71 Timberlake, "The Politics of Food Aid," 24. For a critique of emergency and disaster assistance programs in Africa, see Alex de Waal, *Famine Crimes: Politics & the Disaster Relief Industry in Africa*, Indianapolis: Indiana University Press, 2009.
72 Andrew Rice, "The Peanut Solution," *New York Times*, September 2, 2010.
73 Eduardo Porter, "Old Forecast of Famine May Yet Come True," *New York Times*, April 1, 2014.

74 Pascal Lamy, "Feeding the World: The 9-Billion People Question," World Trade Organization, February 8, 2012.

75 Nina Chestney, "World Lacks Enough Food, Fuel as Population Soars: U.N." *Reuters*, January 30, 2012.

76 "Half of Fish Consumed Globally is Now Raised on Farms, Study Says," *Science Daily*, September 7, 2009; "Eco-Economy Indicators: Fish Catch," Earth Policy Institute, June 22, 2005, www.earth-policy.org/indicators/C55

77 "A Special Report on Feeding the World: Doing More with Less," *The Economist*, February 24, 2011; "A Special Report on Feeding the World: How Much is Enough?" *The Economist*, February 24, 2011.

78 "Will the World Starve?" *The Economist*, June 10, 1995.

79 Quoted in John Bongaarts, "Can the Growing Human Population Feed Itself?" *Scientific American* (March 1994).

80 Bongaarts, "Can the Growing Human Population Feed Itself?"; Margaret R. Biswas, "Agriculture and Environment: A Review, 1972–1992," *Ambio* (May 1994) 192–3; Donald L. Plucknett, "International Agricultural Research for the Next Century," *BioScience* (July/August 1993) 433.

81 Bongaarts, "Can the Growing Human Population Feed Itself?"; Henry W. Kendall and David Pimentel, "Constraints on the Expansion of the Global Food Supply," *Ambio*, vol. 23, no. 3 (May 1994) 199.

82 Kendall and Pimentel, "Constraints on the Expansion of the Global Food Supply," 200; Per Pinstrup-Anderson, Rajul Pandya-Lorch, and Mark W. Rosegrant, "The World Food Situation: Recent Developments, Emerging Issues and Long-Term Prospects," Food Policy Report of the International Food Policy Research Institute, Washington, DC, 1997.

83 "A Special Report on Feeding the World: Plagued by Politics," *The Economist*, February 24, 2011.

84 "A Special Report on Feeding the World: Doing More with Less," *The Economist*, February 24, 2011.

85 Laura Tangley, "Beyond the Green Revolution," *BioScience* (March 1987); MacKenzie, "Will Tomorrow's Children Starve?"; "A Special Report on Feeding the World: No Easy Fix," *The Economist*, February 24, 2011.

86 Alan MacDonald, "Africa's Hidden Water Wealth," *New York Times*, June 17, 2012.

87 MacKenzie, "Will Tomorrow's Children Starve?"; Bongaarts, "Can the Growing Human Population Feed Itself?"; Kendall and Pimentel, "Constraints on the Expansion of the Global Food Supply"; Sandra Postel, "Redesigning Irrigated Agriculture," in Worldwatch Institute, *State of the World 2000*, New York: W.W. Norton & Company, 2000, 40–1; "A Special Report on Feeding the World."

88 MacKenzie, "Will Tomorrow's Children Starve?"

89 Celia W. Dugger, "In Africa, Prosperity from Seeds Falls Short," *New York Times*, October 10, 2007.

90 Richard Critchfield, "Bring the Green Revolution to Africa," *New York Times*, September 14, 1992; Tangley, "Beyond the Green Revolution"; Kendall and Pimentel, "Constraints on the Expansion of the Global Food Supply"; Biswas, "Agriculture and Environment: A Review, 1972–1992"; Bongaarts, "Can the Growing Human Population Feed Itself?"; USAID Policy Paper, "Food Aid and Food Security," February 1995.

91 Jeffrey Sachs, "Challenges of Sustainable Development under Globalization," *International Journal of Development Issues*, vol. 4, no. 2 (December 2005) 1–20.

92 Critchfield, "Bring the Green Revolution to Africa."

93 "A Special Report on Feeding the World: Doing More with Less."

94 Roland Bunch, "Africa's Soil Fertility Crisis and the Coming Famine," the Worldwatch Institute, *State of the World 2011: Innovations that Nourish the Planet*, New York: W.W. Norton & Company, 2011, 60–1.
95 Vandana Shiva, "The Green Revolution in the Punjab," *The Ecologist* (March/April 1991).
96 "A Special Report on Feeding the World: No Easy Fix."
97 Shiva, "The Green Revolution in the Punjab"; Kendall and Pimentel, "Constraints on the Expansion of the Global Food Supply"; Bongaarts, "Can the Growing Human Population Feed Itself?"
98 Mark Bittman, "How to Feed the World," *New York Times*, October 14, 2013.
99 Plucknett, "International Agricultural Research for the Next Century"; Nienke M. Beintema and Gert-Jan Stads, "Measuring Agricultural Research Investments: A Revised Global Picture," *Agricultural Science & Technology Indicators*, Background Note (October 2008).
100 MacKenzie, "Will Tomorrow's Children Starve?"; Robert Paarlberg, "The Global Food Fight," *Foreign Affairs* (May/June 2000) 35.
101 How to Feed the World 2050: High-Level Expert Forum, Rome, October 1, 2009, www.fao.org/fileadmin/templates/wsfs/docs/expert_paper/How_to_Feed_the_World_in_2050.pdf.
102 Andrew Pollack, "Gene Research Finds New Use in Agriculture," *New York Times*, March 7, 2001.
103 Jon Christensen, "Golden Rice in a Grenade-Proof Greenhouse," *New York Times*, November 21, 2000; "Golden Rice Commercial Production Starts in '13," *Manila Standard Today* (February 11, 2012); Amy Harmon, "Golden Rice: Lifesaver?" *New York Times*, August 24, 2013.
104 George Anthan, "Many Countries Produce Biotech Food to Meet Shortages," *Des Moines Register* (December 15, 2000); Anne Simon Moffat, "Developing Nations Adapt Biotech for Own Needs," *Science* (July 1994).
105 Norman Borlaug, "Science Technology Can Help Advance the Green Revolution," *Des Moines Register* (July 25, 2007).
106 Carol Kaesuk Yoon, "Modified-Crop Studies are Called Inconclusive," *New York Times*, December 14, 2000.
107 Doug Gurian-Sherman, *Failure to Yield: Evaluating the Performance of Genetically Engineered Crops*, Union of Concerned Scientists, April 2009.
108 Kristin Dawkins, "The International Food Fight: From Seattle to Montreal," *Multinational Monitor*, January/February, 2000; Paarlberg, "The Global Food Fight"; Kristin Dawkins, "Unsafe In Any Seed: US Obstructionism Defeats Adoption of an International Biotechnology Safety Agreement," *Multinational Monitor*, vol. 20, no. 3 (March 1999).
109 "A Special Report on Feeding the World: Waste Not, Want Not," *The Economist*, February 24, 2011.
110 "A Special Report on Feeding the World: Waste Not, Want Not."
111 Kevin Rafferty, "Global Food Policies a Recipe for Disaster," *South China Morning Post*, January 25, 2011.
112 Kendall and Pimentel, "Constraints on the Expansion of the Global Food Supply"; Vaclav Smil, *Feeding the World: A Challenge for the Twenty-First Century*, Cambridge, MA: MIT Press, 2000, 209; Debora MacKenzie, "Will Tomorrow's Children Starve?"; Bongaarts, "Can the Growing Human Population Feed Itself?"; T. R. Reid, "Feeding the Planet," *National Geographic*, October 1998, vol. 195, no. 4, 58–74; C. Ford Runge and Benjamin Senauer, "A Removable Feast," *Foreign Affairs* (May/June 2000) 40.

113 "The Miracle of the Cerrado," *The Economist*, August 26, 2010.

114 Gillis, "A Warming Planet."

115 "A Special Report on Feeding the World: No Easy Fix."

116 Elizabeth Dickson, "The Future of Food," *Foreign Policy* (May/June 2011).

117 Kenny, *Getting Better*, 75–9.

118 Nicholas D. Kristof, "Attack of the Worms," *New York Times*, July 2, 2007; Dugger, "A Joint Attack on Many Perils of Africa's Young," *New York Times*, December 23, 2006; "Measles Deaths Said to Drop," *New York Times*, April 25, 2012.

119 Kenny, *Getting Better*, 106.

120 Bettina Wassener, "Success in a Land Known for Disasters," *New York Times*, April 9, 2012; Tina Rosenberg, "In Rwanda, Health Care Coverage that Eludes the U.S." *New York Times*, July 3, 2012.

121 Elisabeth Malkin, "At World Forum, Support Erodes for Private Management of Water," *New York Times*, March 20, 2006; Kristof, "Attack of the Worms"; Dugger, "Toilets Underused to Fight Disease, U.N. Study Finds," *New York Times International*, November 10, 2006; Annie Lawrey, "Dire Poverty Falls Despite Global Slump, Report Finds," *New York Times*, March 6, 2012; Vivek Dehejia, "The Cookstove Conundrum," *New York Times*, April 23, 2012.

122 "New Estimate of Malaria Deaths: Concern and Opportunity," *The Lancet*, vol. 379, issue 9814 (February 4, 2012) 385.

123 "Fragile Gains Against Malaria," *New York Times*, December 13, 2014.

124 Sabrina Tavernise, "Chronic Diseases are Killing More in Poorer Countries," *New York Times*, December 4, 2014.

125 Denise Grady, "Without Lucrative Market, Potential Ebola Vaccine Was Shelved for Years," *New York Times*, October 23, 2014.

126 Tavernise, "Chronic Diseases Are Killing More in Poorer Countries."

127 Gardiner Harris, "China and India Making Inroads in Biotech Drugs," *New York Times*, September 18, 2011; Vikas Bajaj and Andrew Pollack, "India Orders Bayer to License a Patented Drug," *New York Times*, March 12, 2012; "Battling Borderless Bugs," *The Economist*, January 7, 2012. Gardiner Harris, "India's Efforts to Aid Poor Worry Drug Makers, *New York Times*, December 29, 2013.

128 Michael T. Osterholm, "Preparing for the Next Pandemic," *Foreign Affairs* (July/August 2005); Laurie Garrett, "The Next Pandemic?" *Foreign Affairs* (July/August 2005).

129 Steve Sternberg, "1 Year Later: Pandemic is Over, but H1N1 Flu Remains Active," *USA Today* (April 21, 2010).

130 Rachel Nuwer, "From the Jungle to J.F.K., Viruses Cross Borders in Monkey Meat," *New York Times*, January 13, 2012; "Hot Spots," *The Economist*, February 10, 2011.

131 "The Economic Impact of SARS," *CBC News*, July 8, 2003, www.cbc.ca/news2/background/sars/economicimpact.html

132 Ilona Kickbusch, "Advancing the Global Health Agenda," *UN Chronicle*, December 2011.

133 Charles Kenny, "The Eradication Calculation," *Foreign Policy*, January 17, 2012.

134 Kenny, "The Eradication Calculation."

135 Declan Walsh, "Taliban Block Vaccinations in Pakistan," *New York Times*, June 18, 2011.

136 "Eradicating Polio Everywhere," *New York Times*, January 14, 2014. Dan Bilefsky and Rick Gladstone, "Polio Spreading at Alarming Rates, World Health Organization Declares," *New York Times*, May 5, 2014.

137 Katherine Seelye, "Gore to Preside at Security Council Session on AIDS Crisis," *New York Times*, January 10, 2000; "Aid for AIDs," *The Economist*, April 29, 2000; Claire Nullis, "AIDS Massacres African Teenagers," *Des Moines Register* (June 28, 2000).

138 "A Turning Point for AIDs?" *The Economist*, July 15, 2000; "Orphans of the Virus," *The Economist*, August 14, 1999; Seelye, "Gore to Preside at Security Council Session"; "Aid for AIDs."

139 The Global Fund: www.theglobalfund.org/en/about/secretariat/

140 Ezekiel J. Emanuel, "Foreign Aid is Not a Rathole," *New York Times*, November 30, 2011; Donald G. McNeil, Jr., "New HIV Cases Falling in Some Poor Nations, but Treatment Still Lags," *New York Times*, November 20, 2012.

141 Harry Dunphy, "US to Offer African AIDS Funds," *Associate Press*, July 19, 2000; Ellen Knickmeyer, "Africa Skirts HIV Drug Patents," *Des Moines Register*, March 20, 2001; Melody Peterson and Donald G. McNeil, Jr., "Maker Yielding Patent in Africa for AIDS Drug," *New York Times*, March 15, 2001.

142 Donald G. McNeil, Jr., "Global Fight Against AIDS Falters as Pledges Fail to Reach Goal of $13 Billion," *New York Times*, October 5, 2010.

143 Donald G. McNeil, Jr., "Bill Gates Donates $750 Million to Shore Up Disease-Fighting Fund," *New York Times*, January 26, 2012. Paul Farmer, "Why the Global Fund Matters," *New York Times*, February 1, 2012.

144 Pam Belluck, "Contraceptive Used in Africa May Double Risk of H.I.V.," *New York Times*, October 3, 2011.

145 "Physician, Heal Thy Country," *The Atlantic Monthly* (January/February 2006).

146 Matt McAllester, "America is Stealing the World's Doctors," *New York Times*, March 7, 2012.

147 Ilona Kickbusch, "Advancing the Global Health Agenda," *UN Chronicle* (December 2011).

148 Kickbusch, "Advancing the Global Health Agenda"; McAllester, "America is Stealing the World's Doctors."

Further Reading

Angus Deaton, *The Great Escape: Health, Wealth and the Origins of Inequality*, Princeton: Princeton University Press, 2013.

Examines the emergence of global inequalities in health and development over the past two centuries and prospects for enhancing well-being in those areas left behind.

Debra DeLaet and David DeLaet, *Global Health in the 21st Century: The Globalization of Disease and Wellness*, St. Paul, MN: Paradigm Publishers, 2011.

A readable overview of basic concepts and evidence relating to the politics and sociology of public health around the world.

Paul R. Ehrlich and Anne H. Ehrlich, *The Population Explosion*, New York: Simon & Schuster, 1990.

A pessimistic and alarming perspective on runaway population growth and its consequences.

Paul Farmer, *Pathologies of Power: Health, Human Rights and the New War on the Poor*, Berkeley: University of California Press, 2004.
A radical critique of the power structures that give rise to inequitable access to health care and well-being.

Laurie Garrett, *Betrayal of Trust: The Collapse of Global Public Health*, New York: Hyperion, 2001.
A science journalist surveys the landscape of global public health at both the national and international levels, arguing that increased attention and funding for public health are often misdirected.

Vandana Shiva, *The Violence of the Green Revolution: Third World Agriculture, Ecology and Politics*, London: Zed Books, 1991.
A radical critique of the Green Revolution.

Vaclav Smil, *Feeding the World: A Challenge for the Twenty-First Century*, Cambridge, MA: MIT Press, 2000.
A thorough and scientific look at the world's capacity to feed growing populations. Reaches cautiously optimistic conclusions.

The Worldwatch Institute, *State of the World 2014: Governing for Sustainability*, New York: W.W. Norton & Company, 2014.
Statistic-laden and up-to-date collection of essays on various environmental trends and topics. The theme varies from year to year.

11 Sustainability and the Environment

The entire edifice of economic globalization rests upon a fragile natural eco-system. The demands that humans place upon their natural environment have risen to unprecedented and destructive levels in recent decades. Global population will continue to grow through this century, while rising incomes fuel increased consumption. These trends raise questions about whether nature can accommodate ever-increasing resource demands for food, water, energy, minerals, and timber. Already, scientists warn that our massive appetite for fossil fuels may have altered the earth's atmosphere and set in motion an irreversible pattern of global warming, with dire consequences for future generations.

Biologists use the notion of carrying capacity to measure the limits of nature's ability to sustain increasing numbers of a given species. When nature's carrying capacity is breached, resource scarcity serves to correct excess population levels in a most brutal manner. Humans differ from other species, of course, in that they possess the ability to manipulate their natural environment and thus to extend its carrying capacity in various ways. Still, this biological metaphor aptly serves to raise the question of limits. How many people can the earth support? Where do the limits to rising consumption lie? What are the consequences should we overshoot the earth's carrying capacity?

These questions can be explored by reference to two key concepts: sustainable development and the global commons. Both have become the central focus of international environmental diplomacy over recent decades. These transnational efforts to forge environmental cooperation have engaged not only states, but also private corporations, scientific communities, and civil society. Recasting notions of economic development to consider the problem of sustainability and developing mechanisms to guard against overexploitation of the oceans and atmosphere that humans and other species share in common are central to the ongoing challenges of globalization.

Our discussion of sustainability will examine and compare three large-scale global gatherings that have served as milestones in the evolution of environmental diplomacy. We then turn to the global commons and the threats to the earth's atmosphere posed by ozone depletion and global warming. We will ask why the collective response to the thinning of the ozone layer has been more successful than international efforts to address global warming. We also explore the available alternatives for limiting the warming of the earth and the consequences of failure.

Global Summits for Sustainable Development

Sustainable development can be defined as the ability of present generations of humans to provide for their own needs without so harming the natural environment as to endanger the ability of future generations to do the same.[1] There are growing indications that the current mode of global economic accumulation falls short of this standard. Indeed, a recent United Nations report bluntly states: "The current global development model is unsustainable."[2] The warning signs are many. Consider, for instance, the following examples of human-produced environmental damage and resource scarcity:

- Of the 50,000 plants that have been found to hold medicinal value for humans, over one-third are at risk of extinction.[3] The same is true for one-third of all amphibians and one-half of all primates.[4]
- 85 percent of the world's fish stocks are overexploited or depleted.[5]
- 5.2 million hectares of forest – an area close to the size of Ireland – are lost each year.[6]
- The world's wetlands have shrunken by one-half since 1900.[7]
- Without major conservation efforts, coral reefs, which sustain one-quarter of marine fish species, will shrink by half within thirty years.[8]
- India is expected to exhaust 60 percent of the nation's aquifers by 2030.[9] Similarly, the water table beneath China's northern wheat-growing region is falling by one meter per year and could be exhausted by 2030.[10]

While growing populations contribute to these strains on eco-systems, resource consumption in high-income countries plays a more significant role. On average, per capita resource consumption rates in the developed world are thirty-two times those in the developing countries.[11]

These alarming trends have forced policymakers to move environmental issues higher on national and international policy agendas. While many environmental problems are local or national in scope, recent decades have brought increasing awareness that international efforts to share information, disseminate best practices, support research, and marshal collective resources are needed. This is especially true with respect to the world's oceans and atmosphere, which together make up the global commons upon which all nations rely.

International cooperation emerges through a process of environmental diplomacy. At present, over two hundred international environmental agreements have come into force.[12] While international environmental cooperation is continuous and ongoing, three major global summits – held in 1972, 1992, and 2012 – have played key roles in providing direction to the process. This section reviews the aspirations, process, and progress of these key episodes in global environmental diplomacy.

The concept of sustainable development first achieved widespread recognition at the United Nations (UN) Conference on the Human Environment held in Stockholm, Sweden in 1972. This was the most ambitious exercise in multilateral environmental diplomacy to date. Representatives from 114 governments and 400 intergovernmental or non-governmental organizations met from June 3rd through 14th to discuss national and international responses to a variety of environmental challenges. The conference produced agreement on twenty-six environmental principals and an Action Plan containing 109 recommendations. The conference also gave rise to the United Nations Environmental Program, which supports research, coordinates environmental activities by UN bodies, advises developing countries on environmental policies, and provides funding for projects designed to meet environmental threats.

Together with the first Earth Day, held on April 22, 1970, the Stockholm conference is often credited with helping to launch the modern environmental movement. The Action Plan provided a template for environmental protection legislation in many countries around the world. The conference also strengthened transnational ties among non-governmental organizations engaged in research, education, and advocacy surrounding environmental issues.

While the Stockholm conference placed a spotlight on the need to conserve resources and confront environmental degradation, developing countries were also keen on ensuring that environmental cooperation did not endanger their rights to pursue economic growth or impinge upon their sovereignty and cultural autonomy. The Statement of Principles emphasized that national and international measures designed to protect the environment should "enhance and not adversely affect the present or future development potential of developing countries." The Statement also acknowledged that states retain the "sovereign right to exploit their own resources." Furthermore, international environmental rules and regulations should respect the "systems of values prevailing in each country" and refrain from imposing "standards which are valid for the most advanced countries but which may be inappropriate and of unwarranted social cost for the developing countries."[13] These tensions between environmental sustainability on the one hand and the priorities given to economic growth and state sovereignty on the other would continue to bedevil future negotiations.

The Stockholm conference served as a model for the United Nations Conference on Environment and Development (UNCED), held June 3–14, 1992, in Rio de Janeiro, Brazil.[14] Popularly known as the Earth Summit, this meeting brought together representatives from over 150 nations, including 118 heads of state, to focus on the connections between threats to the global environment and economic development. The UN General Assembly resolution authorizing UNCED established that its purpose was to "elaborate strategies and measures to halt and reverse the effects of environmental degradation in the context of increased national and international efforts to promote sustainable and environmentally sound development in all countries."[15]

Rio was also the site of a parallel meeting of 1,400 non-governmental organizations called the Global Forum. Private environmental and citizens groups from around the world shared ideas, built ongoing networks, and lobbied government representatives on behalf of a more environmentally sustainable future. As compared with Stockholm, the larger scale of the non-governmental organization (NGO) forum at the Rio Summit provided a measure of the rapid growth in the broader environmental movement over the intervening two decades and the intensifying transnational networks that allowed for coordinated action across countries.

The Rio conference produced five major documents:

- The Rio Declaration established twenty-seven basic principles of sustainable development.
- The Convention on Biodiversity sought to address three major goals: (1) to commit governments to the preservation of endangered plant and animal species and habitats, (2) to encourage the sustainable use of biological resources, and (3) to establish the right of Southern nations to compensation from Northern commercial exploitation of products based upon Southern gene stocks.
- The Climate Convention addressed the problem of global warming, brought on by the emission of greenhouse gases, such as carbon dioxide. One hundred and fifty-three nations committed themselves to curbing the emission of such gases to 1990 levels by the year 2000.
- The Forest Principles document specified seventeen nonbinding principles of sustainable forest management.
- Agenda 21, an 800-page document, provided a work plan or agenda for action covering all major areas of sustainable development.

The most important new international institution to emerge from the Earth Summit was the Sustainable Development Commission. This organization was given responsibility for integrating the planning and activities of all UN bodies responsible for projects related to both environmental protection and economic development. The Commission was also given the job of monitoring and reporting on progress toward fulfillment of the aims and programs spelled out in Agenda 21. National governments were invited to provide annual reports to the Commission on the state of environmental and development goals within their countries. The Commission periodically holds high-level conferences on topics related to its mandate and bargains with governments and international organizations on issues of mutual concern.

In many ways, the Earth Summit was a success. Never before had so many of the world's people and governments focused such concentrated attention on the major environmental challenges of modern life. With eight thousand journalists in attendance, media coverage was extensive. Broad agreement was reached on the critical importance of coupling environmental and economic issues and on many of the principles and strategies necessary to move in the direction of sustainability. The national reports prepared by most governments for submission at the summit enhanced the information base regarding environmental conditions in many parts of the globe. The creation of new institutions, such as the Sustainable Development Commission, ensured continued international attention and regularized consultation regarding environmental problems. The Climate Convention launched international efforts to combat global warming and set the stage for the more far-reaching Kyoto Protocol, which was agreed to in 1997 (to be discussed in greater depth later in this chapter). The Global Forum helped to strengthen cooperation among hundreds of nongovernmental environmental organizations from all parts of the world and illustrated the potential political clout of citizen-based groups.

Nevertheless, the Earth Summit fell short of its ambitious mandate in other ways. Disagreements plagued the deliberations surrounding many important issues. Due to differing interests and perspectives, final drafts of the forestry and climate change agreements were considerably watered down. Northern and Southern countries clashed over the assignment of responsibility for various environmental problems.

The most significant conflict emerged over how to finance the expensive programs elaborated in Agenda 21. UNCED's secretariat estimated that comprehensive implementation of the provisions of Agenda 21 in the South would cost $600 billion per year. The suggested share of this amount to be provided by Northern countries was $125 billion, with the remainder to be allocated by developing countries themselves. In fact, the Rio conference produced Northern pledges of increased aid for environmental programs in the South amounting to only an estimated $6 to $7 billion. Between 1991 and 1998, the Global Environment Facility, created to combat global warming, ozone depletion, and other environmental threats, skimped by with a budget of less than $2 billion per year.[16] At best, Agenda 21 outlined a set of goals and strategies that could be realized only slowly through an incremental process.

The third in this trio of environmental summits was the United Nations Conference on Sustainable Development, which met in Rio de Janeiro in

June 2012. The meeting drew 50,000 participants, including 10,000 officials and 100 heads of state or government from 190 countries, 40,000 NGO representatives, and 1,500 corporate leaders.

Rio+20, as it was dubbed, lacked either the novelty of the 1972 meeting in Stockholm or the ambition of the 1992 gathering. Expectations that international diplomacy could mobilize the resources or political will to halt or reverse the most worrying environmental trends had taken a beating over the four decades since the first major conference. There have been successes, of course, during this period. Conference host Brazil, for example, could point to a 70 percent reduction in the rate of deforestation in the Amazon and the passage of laws that placed 50 percent of forest land under protection from logging, farming, and mining. On a global scale, however, overall resource consumption doubled and carbon dioxide emissions rose by 40 percent during the two decades between the first and the second Rio meetings.[17]

Unlike the Earth Summit, Rio+20 produced no major international agreements. A European Union (EU) proposal for an accord to protect the high seas was defeated by resistance from the United States, Venezuela, Russia, Canada, and Japan. So were proposals to phase out subsidies for fossil fuels, to require that large corporations prepare environmental reports on their operations and to strengthen the UN Environmental Program.[18] The text of the conference report, a 283-page document titled "The Future We Want," was finalized by lower-level officials before top government ministers even arrived at the meeting. As a result, controversial text was simply deleted and no high-level negotiations took place.[19]

The most ambitious agreement was to develop a set of UN-backed Sustainable Development Goals (SDGs) to replace the Millennium Development Goals due to expire in 2015. While the Millennium Development Goals focused on poverty, hunger, and health, the Sustainable Development Goals will shift attention to environmental and resource issues. Once set, the SDGs will serve to orient and focus the work of aid agencies, research institutions, national governments, NGOs, and private-sector partners. Yet, the process established for reaching consensus on a new set of Sustainable Development Goals is hopelessly complex, leaving in doubt whether the established timetable can be kept.[20]

Evaluations of Rio+20 by participants and observers were often harsh. United Kingdom (UK) Deputy Prime Minister labeled the result "insipid," while Care International declared the meeting a "charade." Greenpeace denounced what it described as "a failure of epic proportions" and the World Wildlife Fund lamented the "colossal failure of leadership and vision."[21]

The timing of the conference, coming amidst continuing financial instability and government budget-cutting in the developed world, worked against the possibility of expensive new commitments. Moreover, divisions between developed and developing nations and between oil-exporting and oil-importing countries also made agreement difficult in the context of a UN process that prioritized unanimity. The deeper reality is that most environmental problems are local or national in scope and the challenges vary quite dramatically from one country to the next. Under these circumstances, united action at the global level is difficult to organize.

The glimmers of hope that emerged from Rio+20 reflected this point. Much of the action took place not in negotiating sessions among diplomats haggling over the wording of the conference report, but instead in the informal interactions among participants representing many varied interests and entities. While no binding multilateral agreements were achieved, for instance, individual governments and corporations announced 200 new voluntary pledges of action. The Maldives, for example, committed to creating the world's largest marine reserve by 2017. Microsoft announced a plan to ensure that its corporate operations were carbon-neutral by the end of 2013. Big city mayors from around the world met to share models for reducing greenhouse emissions. A group of international development banks unveiled a $175 billion initiative to provide financing for the expansion of mass transit systems and bike lanes.[22]

Assessing the Utility of Global Environmental Summits

How should we assess the practice of organizing global summits as a means for reconciling the imperatives of environmental sustainability with the continued need for economic development? In an anarchic international system composed of competing nation-states, it is perhaps remarkable that international efforts to tackle such a complex array of problems on a global scale take place at all. The three global summits held thus far have undoubtedly educated publics around the world and raised the political salience of environmental challenges. The concept of sustainability and many of the principals associated with it have assumed a central place in thinking about economic development. New international institutions have been created and financial resources marshaled. Intergovernmental and civil society networks have been strengthened.

Nevertheless, as the scale and scope of global environmental summitry has expanded, the concrete achievements have shrunken. In part, this may be because previous meetings have already laid in place the basic principles and modalities of international environmental cooperation and the emphasis has shifted to the more prosaic task of implementation. A more critical perspective, however, points to the limitations of this sort of environmental diplomacy.

Most obviously, the complexity of a negotiation process that involves close to 200 states with the world's media and thousands of NGOs in the background limits what can be accomplished. Also, the quest for universal, binding multilateral agreements has proven less fruitful than expected. Efforts to corral the support of a handful of recalcitrant states often result in the dilution of final agreements. Cases of diplomatic failure breed cynicism about the merits of multilateralism. Most importantly, an overly legalistic approach to environmental cooperation neglects the fact that international law is ultimately no stronger than the political will of national leaders and the level of domestic political support they enjoy for such commitments. At this stage in the evolution of international environmental diplomacy, a better approach might involve smaller groups of interested and consequential states tasked with more focused agendas and seeking less formal and less legalistic forms of cooperation.

Another lesson is that environmental issues are perhaps too varied, too complex, and too interwoven with broader social, political, and economic spheres to leave to diplomats or even environmental ministers. The search for solutions ultimately involves shifting networks of finance ministers, bureaucrats, activists, politicians, scientists, journalists, and corporate leaders that function on a continuing basis, not only once every two decades.

Atmospheric Pollution and the Tragedy of the Commons

The world's atmosphere constitutes a classic "commons." Any resource which is freely available for common use by everyone and which is not easily partitioned by the allocation of exclusive ownership rights can be considered a commons. The earth's atmosphere meets these criteria. All nations, groups, and individuals have access to the atmosphere, whether to inhale its air or to emit pollutants. Atmospheric circulation patterns do not respect national borders and ensure that pollutants released in one country often travel to other parts of the globe.

The so-called "tragedy of the commons" refers to the fact that resources held in common are easily and often overexploited.[23] Individual users enjoy all of the benefits of exploiting common resources but are able to push the costs of doing so onto the community as a whole. The classic example is a village commons, where villagers can freely graze individually owned sheep. Each villager has an incentive to increase the size of his or her herd since more sheep means more wool and a greater income. When all follow this logic, however, the number of sheep feeding on the commons area quickly exceeds the carrying capacity of the land. The pasture gives out, sheep die for want of food, and the villagers all suffer.[24]

This problem could be avoided in one of several ways. The commons could be divided into private property, with each villager taking a well-defined parcel. In this way, the costs of overgrazing would be borne entirely by the individual herder and could not be passed along to the community. This would enhance the incentive for each herder to exercise restraint in managing herd size. Another solution would be to combine all sheep under community ownership, eliminating private herds. Rather than each individual making separate decisions about the size of his or her herd, the community as a whole would balance costs and benefits in making a single decision that maximized the return to the village as a whole.

Neither of these solutions is available in managing the earth's atmosphere. As mentioned, wind currents make it impossible to confine pollutants to the air space of the emitting country. So partition is not an option. Global ownership of the atmosphere under a single decision-making authority is conceivable, but most unlikely given the division of the world into more than two hundred sovereign nations.

A third solution is external regulation. Individuals continue to exploit the commons for their own gain, but under regulations imposed by some common authority. In the domestic sphere, this is the solution often adopted to protect local commons, such as streams and lakes. National or local governments impose limits on the activities of businesses and individuals.

At the global level, of course, there exists no world government that could impose binding regulations on states in relation to exploitation of the earth's atmosphere. Yet regulation remains an option if nations accept mutually agreed-upon rules and limitations on a voluntary basis. This is the approach that has been adopted in attempts to deal with the two most important threats to the world's atmosphere: ozone depletion and global warming. In both cases, global negotiations have aimed at agreement on a set of rules to which individual governments would voluntarily consent and comply.

The obstacles to the success of this approach to protecting the atmospheric commons are numerous. Agreement must be gained from all or most of those countries responsible for polluting the atmosphere. Yet states differ widely in power, economic interests, culture, political systems, and ability to adjust to new conditions. Nations have incentives to push the most difficult costs of adjustment onto others. The prospect that some countries will cheat or renege on agreements both makes such agreements more difficult to achieve and threatens their effectiveness once in force. These problems do not render environmental cooperation impossible, but they do raise questions about our ability to cope as a species with complex threats to the health of the global commons. The following sections examine and compare efforts to carve out voluntary global agreements dealing with the issues of ozone depletion and global warming.

Ozone Depletion

Over the past several decades, scientists have monitored the gradual thinning of the earth's ozone layer over certain portions of the planet. Early findings focused on Antarctica. Subsequently, extensive thinning has been detected in the Arctic region as well. Ozone "holes" over these areas have continued to expand and thinning has been detected in the populated areas of northern Europe, Canada, and the northern United States. The ozone hole over the Antarctic extends over an area larger than the size of the United States, Canada, and Mexico and reached its largest range ever in September 2000.[25]

The concerns raised by these measurements stem from the fact that the ozone layer in the upper atmosphere serves to protect plant and animal life on earth from the harm potentially done by the sun's intense ultraviolet rays. Scientists estimate that a 1 percent loss in stratospheric ozone leads to a 2 percent increase in the incidence of skin cancer among exposed humans and a 1 percent increase in eye cataracts.[26] Ozone loss endangers marine life through its harmful impact on sea plankton. Some types of terrestrial plant life are also threatened.

Ozone thinning was first linked to the release of chloroflourocarbons (CFCs) into the atmosphere in the 1970s. Among other applications, CFCs are used as industrial solvents and as coolants for refrigeration. In the 1970s, the United States was the first nation to take steps to limit CFC emissions by banning their use in aerosols. Over the subsequent years, scientists have identified other types of chemical emissions that deplete ozone, including halons, methyl bromide, and hydrochlorofluorocarbons (HCFCs).

The first steps toward multilateral regulation of CFCs began in the 1980s and culminated in the Montreal Protocol on Substances that Deplete the Ozone Layer, signed by representatives from industrial countries in 1987. The Montreal Protocol called for a 50 percent reduction in CFC production by the year 2000. As further scientific evidence revealed an accelerated loss of ozone in subsequent years, more far-reaching limitations were agreed to in the follow-up accords of 1992 and 1996. The latter agreement mandated a total phase-out of CFC production in Northern countries by 2000 and in the developing world by 2010. The Montreal Protocol has nearly eliminated emissions of 100 types of chemicals and production of ozone-depleting chemicals has dropped to less than one-tenth of 1990 levels.[27]

Other classes of chemicals, including HCFCs and hydroflourocarbons (HFCs), were originally considered acceptable substitutes for CFCs in many industrial uses. Subsequently, it was determined that these substances also contribute to ozone depletion, although they are less potent and less long-lasting compared with CFCs. HCFCs have also been found to worsen the global warming problem – as warming agents, they are thousands of times more powerful than carbon dioxide. Atmospheric concentrations of HCFC–22 – widely used in air-conditioning units – have doubled in the past two decades. Under current agreements, HCFCs will be phased out by 2020 in developed countries. Developing countries were required to begin reductions in 2010, leading to a total phase-out by 2040. Nevertheless, while the United States has banned HCFC–22 in new air-conditioners, it remains in use in 140 million older air-conditioners and US import controls have been circumvented through smuggling from Mexico and China. HFCs have also been widely used as an ozone-friendly substitute for CFCs. Like HCFCs, however, HFCs are potent contributors to global warming. One hundred and eight countries have called for new regulations under the Montreal Protocol to phase out HFCs more quickly, and the United States and China reached agreement in 2013 to move in this direction.[28]

The initial moves to regulate CFC production were opposed by the chemical industry. Public pressure, along with the possibility of developing and marketing substitutes, eventually reduced the level of industry opposition. Southern countries were excluded from the Montreal Protocol at first. In 1996, developing countries agreed to phase out CFC production, albeit with a ten-year grace period. At present, 197 countries have ratified the agreement. Developed countries provide financial support for transition projects in developing countries through the Multilateral Fund for the Implementation of the Montreal Protocol.

The series of accords dealing with ozone depletion represents the most far-reaching and successful example of international environmental cooperation to date. Indeed, since many ozone-depleting chemicals also contribute to global warming, it is estimated that the Montreal Protocol has made a far greater contribution to slowing global warming than the Kyoto Protocol itself.[29] Nevertheless, the underlying problem of ozone depletion itself has not been fully solved. The deadlines for phasing out some classes of ozone-depleting chemicals still lay years into the future. Moreover, CFCs remain active in the atmosphere for up to 100 years. The Antarctic ozone hole has begun to stabilize, reaching its second smallest extent of the past two decades in 2012.[30] By mid-century, scientists expect that the ozone layer will recover to pre-1980 levels outside of the polar regions as the previous buildup of ozone-destroying chemicals in the atmosphere subsides and new emissions continue to decline. Full recovery at the poles will take additional decades.[31] Thus, ozone depletion will remain a concern for decades yet to come.

Global Warming and the Kyoto Protocol

Global warming is the most serious environmental threat yet faced by humankind. The problem stems from the growing concentration of so-called greenhouse gases in the earth's atmosphere. While greenhouse gases make up a natural part of the atmosphere and are indeed necessary to life on earth, human activities have released such chemicals into the atmosphere in ever-growing amounts over the past century and a half, where some of them remain for many decades. Carbon dioxide accounts for over one-half of such emissions, with methane, CFCs, and other greenhouse gases making up the remainder. Levels of carbon dioxide, which is a byproduct of the burning of fossil fuels and the combustion or decomposition of plant life, such as forests, have risen 40 percent since the mid-nineteenth century. Methane is released during the cultivation of rice and the raising of livestock.[32]

As they build up in the atmosphere, these gases serve to trap solar radiation as it is transformed into heat by reflecting off the earth's surface. Greenhouse gases prevent this heat from escaping into space, much as a greenhouse captures the sun's rays to retain warmth within even on a cold winter day. As the concentration of such gases in the earth's atmosphere has grown fourfold since 1950, the earth's average temperature has begun to climb. The earth's surface temperature has warmed by 0.8 degrees Celsius since the beginning of the Industrial Revolution. May 2012 marked the 327th month that the average global temperature exceeded the global average for the twentieth century; 2014 was the hottest year in recorded history and the ten warmest years globally have all come since 1997.[33]

The consequences of global warming are already apparent. Sea ice coverage in the Arctic has shrunk by one-third, reaching a record low in the summer of 2012, as temperatures in that region are rising twice as fast as for the globe as a whole. The thickness of Arctic ice has fallen by one-half since 1979 to the lowest level of the past 8,000 years. Ocean acidity, another side-effect of warming, has increased by one-third, threatening the health of coral reefs and the abundant diversity of life that they support. Atmospheric humidity over the oceans has risen by 5 percent, leading to more frequent and more violent storms, such as Hurricane Sandy, which devastated the Northeastern United States in October 2012. The effects of such coastal storms have been amplified by the 8-inch rise in global sea levels that has occurred since 1880.[34]

The science underlying these findings has been collected in a series of reports prepared by the Intergovernmental Panel on Climate Change. The most recent report, issued in 2014, offered a series of dire predictions.[35] Scientists warn of rising sea levels as the polar ice caps recede, threatening to flood many islands and heavily populated coastal areas.[36] Scientists have recently concluded that the collapse of the West Antarctic ice sheet has already begun and is most likely unstoppable. As this monumental event slowly unfolds over the next century and more, ocean levels will eventually rise by an estimated 10 feet, wiping out major coastal cities.[37] Weather patterns will become more extreme, with more frequent episodes of hurricanes, severe hot spells, heavy rainfall, and flooding in some areas and drought in others.[38] A warmer climate will allow tropical diseases such as malaria and dengue fever to spread to previously temperate zones. Eco-systems will be disrupted. Entire forests may die off as native tree species are suddenly exposed to climate conditions to which they are poorly adapted. While food production may flourish in some areas, many existing agricultural regions will suffer and the adjustment costs will be great. Overall, the United Nations Environmental Program has estimated that without decisive steps to reduce the rate of global warming, the consequences of a warmer earth could produce global costs of $300 billion annually by the year 2050.[39] A report prepared by a group of retired US military officers in 2014 warned that global warming could bring heightened threats to international security in the form of destabilizing refugee flows, resource conflicts, and political instability.[40]

While these threats have prompted extensive international dialogue over what to do about global warming, the results so far have been disappointing. The Rio Earth Summit produced the UN Framework Convention on Climate Change, which came into force in March 1994 and has been ratified by 181 nations. The Framework Convention called for voluntary reductions in greenhouse gas emissions and committed the signatories to meet periodically to review progress and consider additional steps toward combating global warming. Such a meeting was held in Kyoto, Japan in 1997. One hundred and ninety countries eventually signed and ratified the resulting Kyoto Protocol, which called for developed countries to reduce their collective greenhouse gas emissions to 5.2 percent below 1990 levels by the year 2010.[41]

To facilitate progress toward this goal, the agreement also established the Climate Development Mechanism that allowed developed countries to meet a part of their obligations by purchasing tradeable credits tied to emission reduction projects in the developing world. A similar emissions trading system was adopted by the European Union in 2003.

Developing world countries successfully resisted binding commitments under Kyoto on the grounds that Northern countries were largely responsible for the buildup of greenhouse gases to date, accounting for 73 percent of global carbon dioxide emissions. Developing countries argued that those most responsible for creating the problem should bear the greater burden toward its solution. The United States, in particular, objected to the failure of developing countries to set targets for reducing their emissions, pointing out that rapidly growing energy production in the developing world meant that overall greenhouse gas emissions among this group of countries would surpass the collective total of the industrialized world by 2010. The Kyoto Protocol's failure to require greenhouse gas reductions by developing countries has been cited by many congressional opponents for the United States' failure to ratify the agreement.[42]

The conflict between North and South is rooted in differing conceptions of fairness in allocating the burdens of addressing climate change as well as the zero sum nature of the problem. Scientists have calculated a "carbon budget" – the maximum amount of carbon that can be emitted into the atmosphere before rising temperatures breach a minimally acceptable threshold. That limit is thought to be around 1 trillion tons. More than half of this amount has already been spewed into the atmosphere since the beginning of the Industrial Revolution. This upper bound on carbon emissions would be breached by 2040 at current levels of emissions. From the standpoint of international negotiations, the key question is how to divvy up among countries the rights to emit the remaining allowable carbon emissions. Should the rich countries that have higher per capita emissions claim a bigger slice of the carbon pie? Or should developing countries, whose emissions are growing more quickly due to fast economic growth, be allotted a growing piece of the pie?[43]

In recognition of the Kyoto Protocol's limitations, signatory countries convened another meeting at the Hague in the Fall of 2000 in an effort to hammer out more detailed mechanisms for ensuring progress toward the goals set out in the earlier accord. These negotiations, however, collapsed in disagreement and failure in late November 2000. While some governments and environmental groups held out for a compromise between polarized positions, in the end no common ground could be found. Dr. Michael Grub of Britain's Imperial College observed that, "When something like this is killed, it is killed by an alliance of those who want too much with those who don't want anything." Business interests, led by large oil companies and represented at the meeting by over three hundred lobbyists, argued that the emission reduction goals being considered were too stringent. Some environmental groups, on the other hand, believed that the compromise proposals under discussion were too weak. According to Bill Hare of Greenpeace International, "We are better off with no deal than a bad deal."[44]

Subsequent to the failure of the Bonn meeting, newly elected US President George Bush declared in March 2001 that his administration was no longer committed to the Kyoto Protocol, despite the fact that the United States had already signed (but not ratified) the accord under President Clinton. Bush stated: "I will not accept a plan that will harm our economy and hurt American workers."[45]

Even without US participation and despite unsatisfactory progress at the Bonn meeting, 164 nations signed the final agreement. The conclusion of negotiations on the Kyoto agreement represented a significant accomplishment. Under the treaty, countries that are party to the agreement committed to reduce their overall greenhouse gas emissions to 5 percent below 1990 levels by the year 2012.[46]

As the 2012 expiration date for the Kyoto Protocol grew closer, negotiators met in Copenhagen, Denmark in December 2009 in hopes of negotiating a successor accord. Instead, Copenhagen represented a low point in the difficult effort to achieve international cooperation around global warming. The negotiations were plagued by a host of conflicts and handicaps, including the failure of the US Congress to pass proposed climate change legislation prior to the meeting, disputes between rich and poor countries over financing for climate change mitigation and adaptation in the developing world, and the unwillingness of China and India to accept binding emissions targets.

Joining the conference in its last days, US President Barack Obama succeeded in obtaining a non-binding political agreement among five major players: the United States, China, India, South Africa, and Brazil. The agreement called for these and other countries to set national goals for emissions reduction, subject to international monitoring, pledged future funding from wealthy countries to assist developing countries, and set a goal of limiting the rise in average global temperatures to 2 degrees Celsius above pre-industrial levels by 2050. The agreement did not set out a process or timetable for achieving a binding international treaty.[47] Obama announced the agreement to the press before delegates from most of the 193 countries represented at the meeting were notified of its existence. Subsequently, the assembly as a whole agreed only to "take note" of the five-party agreement. Incremental progress continued through a series of annual meetings Cancun, Mexico (2010), Doha, Qatar (2011), Durban, South Africa (2012), and Lima, Peru (2014).[48]

Developments in 2014 shed a ray of hope. The United States has long been considered a laggard for its failure to take substantial steps toward lowering greenhouse gas emissions. In 2010, the Congress rejected the Obama Administration's proposal for a carbon trading system designed to cap emissions.[49] But in June 2014, the Obama Administration bypassed Congress by issuing new regulations that require a 30 percent cut from 2005 levels in carbon emissions from coal-fired power plants by 2030. With this significant step under his belt, Obama then negotiated an agreement with China committing the United States to cut greenhouse gas emissions in the United States by 26 percent from 2005 levels by 2025. For its part, China agreed to ensure that its emissions peak by 2030, at the latest, and to increase the share of non-fossil fuels in its energy mix to 20 percent over the next fifteen years.

In some respects, these commitments were less than they seemed. For both countries, the goals did little more than reinforce targets already achievable under current plans. While China stated a target year for peaking emissions, it did not say how high those emissions would reach. Moreover, both countries will come under pressure to do far more in the coming years as the dire consequences of global warming unfold.[50] Nevertheless, this was the first time that China had made a public commitment to place a limit on carbon emissions and the US pledge was seen as more credible than previous targets by virtue of the earlier steps to rein in coal.

Another important development during this time period was the emergence of a global movement to place pressure on governments to act. In September 2014, prior to a UN meeting on climate change, a crowd of 400,000 took part in the People's Climate March in New York City while solidarity events were organized in cities around the world. In another sign that climate change had gained popular salience, the organization

Fossil Free announced on December 2, 2015 that 500 institutions – universities, religious bodies, unions, municipalities, etc. – had pledged to divest from investment holdings in fossil fuel companies.[51]

Joint action by the top two greenhouse gas emitters along with growing grassroots pressure paved the way for progress at the global level. Negotiations held in Paris in December 2015 produced voluntary commitments to reduce or limit greenhouse emissions by every country in the world. This was the first time that developing countries as a bloc had agreed to take such a step. Unlike the Kyoto Protocol, which took the form of a treaty that committed countries to legally binding targets, the Paris Accord is built around voluntary national plans for reducing greenhouse gas emissions by amounts that the countries themselves specify.[52]

While there is no guarantee that the resulting plans will significantly restrain emissions or that plans will be implemented once adopted, the Lima Accord depends upon peer pressure from other nations, or "naming and shaming," to ensure good faith efforts by individual countries. This approach averts the seemingly impossible task of reaching agreement on a set of globally binding targets and ensures broad participation among both developed and developing countries. For the United States, in particular, the Paris Accord provides a way for the executive branch to set targets without the need for Senate ratification – which would be unlikely – of a formal treaty.[53]

The Paris agreement included:[54]

- A commitment to hold the global temperature rise to no more than 2 degrees Celsius, while also pledging to work toward the even more ambitious goal of a 1.5 degree Celsius cap. The latter represented a concession to developing countries, which argued that even a 2 degree Celsius rise in temperature rise would pose unacceptable costs.
- A strengthened commitment to preserve and restore the world's major forests, which absorb and retain atmospheric carbon.
- A commitment by developed countries to fund mitigation and adaptation efforts in developing countries. The preamble, which is not legally binding, mentions a figure of $100 billion per year, though this number is omitted from the main body of the agreement.
- A commitment to build a transparent system for holding countries accountable for keeping the national pledges to control greenhouse gases.
- A plan to reconvene a meeting of the conferees every five years, with individual countries expected to update their national plans in the direction of more ambitious goals.

The Paris agreement represents the most ambitious multilateral international response to climate change to date. However, it is estimated that the national pledges, if met, would together bring the world only halfway toward meeting the greenhouse gas reductions necessary to ensure an average temperature increase of no more than 2 degrees Celsius. Moreover, the commitments do not extend beyond 2030. As a result, global efforts will need to ratchet up over time, eventually leading to the phasing out of fossil fuel energy altogether.[55] That is a tall order given the repeated failure of countries to meet previous commitments to seriously combat global warming over the past quarter-century.

Comparison of the Ozone and Climate Change Negotiations

International negotiation has yet to provide full or lasting solutions for either of the major problems of atmospheric pollution reviewed here. Clearly, however, progress has been swifter and more significant in dealing with ozone depletion than in the case of global warming. Why the difference? What lessons can we learn from comparing these two cases?

Several points of comparison deserve attention. First, negotiations are more likely to succeed the smaller the number of key parties involved in seeking agreement. In the case of the Montreal Protocol, a relatively small number of industrial countries accounted for 85 percent of global production of CFCs and other ozone-depleting chemicals. Since developing countries contributed so little to the problem, they were granted a generous grace period before they would be expected to eliminate CFC production. In the case of global warming, much of past greenhouse gas emissions can be attributed to a small number of industrial countries. Yet today and in the future, the majority of such emissions come from developing countries, especially China. The broader scope of responsibility for greenhouse gas emissions, as compared with the ozone case, led to disagreement over who should be included under the rules of an emerging global regime, thus greatly complicating negotiations.[56]

Second, scientists offered a clearer and more urgent message in the ozone case. The scientific evidence linking ozone depletion to CFC emissions was overwhelming and the consequences of inaction were clearly spelled out. Moreover, the ozone hole could be easily monitored and graphically displayed to the public. As ozone thinning began to appear over populated areas in the middle latitudes, the dangers could no longer be ignored. It took longer for a scientific consensus to emerge over the reality of global warming, due, in part, to the difficulties of distinguishing human-induced temperature changes from natural fluctuations. Only in its fourth report of 2007 did the Intergovernmental Panel on Climate Change (IPCC) finally issue an unqualified endorsement of the view that global warming was a product of human activity. Even today, uncertainty continues to exist over key questions, such as the pace and ultimate extent of warming, the eventual environmental consequences, and the best ways to either minimize or cope with these consequences. The normal gaps and uncertainties in scientific knowledge have been exploited by skeptics and self-interested actors to create and amplify unwarranted levels of public disbelief about the realities of global warming.[57]

Third, the economic and social costs and disruptions associated with proposed solutions were clearly far more manageable in the case of ozone depletion than in the global warming case. Coping with the problem of ozone depletion meant eliminating a relatively small class of chemical emissions for which substitutes could be developed at a reasonable cost. Fewer than forty companies were involved in producing CFCs and just two firms accounted for one-half of the market.[58] The chemical industry giants responsible for most CFC production could afford to eventually accept regulation because revenues from CFC sales accounted for only a small proportion of their total income. Moreover, the same companies could hope to profit from developing substitutes. In the case of global warming, a large share of the problem could be traced to the carbon dioxide emissions that are an inevitable product of burning fossil fuels and difficult to replace.

Given the world's overwhelming reliance upon oil, coal, and natural gas for current energy needs, the adjustment costs of lowering green-house gas emissions are potentially huge. This fact alone explains much of the reluctance to tackle the problem of global warming with more potent measures. In addition, the economic interests opposed to limits on carbon dioxide were much broader and more politically mobilized in the case of climate change. In 1989, the National Association of Manufacturers joined with a group of US oil and automobile firms to form the Global Climate Coalition. The Coalition lobbied Congress against domestic and international regulation, conducted a public campaign against the Kyoto Protocol, and funded climate skeptics who produced studies casting doubt upon the idea that global warming was a product of human activity.[59]

Prospects for the Earth's Climate

To date, international negotiations have failed to fully address the challenge of global warming. Indeed, movement to date has mostly been in the opposite direction. During the 1990s, carbon dioxide emissions grew by 1 percent per year. Due to rapid growth in China and India, the rate increased to 3 percent per year in the first decade of the twenty-first century prior to the global recession of 2008–9, when emissions temporarily fell. As the world economy recovered in 2010, however, carbon dioxide emissions rose by 5.9 percent – the largest one-year jump ever recorded. More hopefully, emissions from energy production fell slightly in 2015, the first such decline during a period of economic growth.[60] This was mostly attributable to slowing economic growth and reduced coal consumption in China. Overall, heat-trapping greenhouse gas emissions have risen 29 percent since 1990.[61] The great majority of this growth is accounted for by the developing countries, which are now responsible for 57 percent of total emissions.[62] Even were greenhouse gas emissions to magically end, the gases already added to the atmosphere ensure an additional half degree of warming.

In order to meet the Copenhagen target of ensuring that the earth's average temperature would not rise more than 2 degrees Celsius above pre-industrial levels, annual carbon dioxide emissions would have to fall from the current annual level of 47 billion tons to less than 20 billion tons by 2050. Former IPCC head Bob Watson has called this scenario "a wishful dream."[63]

The International Energy Agency estimates that if all existing national emissions reduction commitments were fully realized, the global climate would warm by 3.5 degrees Celsius during this century. While a 2 degree Celsius rise in average temperature would pose unprecedented challenges of adaptation, a 3.5 degree Celsius increase would be the stuff of apocalyptic science fiction. The melting of the permafrost that circles the upper levels of the Northern Hemisphere would release enormous quantities of methane, which is itself a potent greenhouse gas.[64] The shrinkage of the polar ice caps would replace highly reflective ice coverage with darker land and sea surfaces, thus heightening the warming effect. At the extreme, these positive feedback effects could unleash a runaway warming process.

A 3.5 degree Celsius increase in average temperatures would mean that by 2090 the probability of a summer warmer than any on record would reach 90 percent in many places.[65] Low-lying islands and coastal cities would vanish beneath rising oceans. The world's plant and animal species would disappear at a rate to rival the five Great Extinctions of earth's history. In countless ways, human life would be radically altered and diminished.

Can such a future be avoided? The fundamental problem lies in our reliance upon fossil fuels. Before the past two centuries, economic and social development, as well as the size of the human population, was sharply limited by the paucity of available energy, which depended heavily upon the muscle power of humans and domesticated animals. The technological advances that have brought about the discovery and exploitation of fossil fuels for the purposes of transportation and manufacturing unleashed both spectacular human progress and a set of environmental consequences that could undermine these gains over a time period that represents a mere blip in human existence.

The world's energy economy is marked by an underlying market failure. The prices of fossil fuels fail to reflect the negative externalities associated with their use. As an example, one study estimated that the costs to the United States from the air pollution produced by coal-fired power plants exceeded the total value of the energy produced by those plants. Matters are not helped by the fact that energy from fossil fuels has been heavily subsidized by governments over many decades – currently at a rate of more than $75 billion per year[66] (see Figure 11.1).

When the actual life-cycle costs of a good are not represented in the price of that good, then it will be overconsumed relative to its true economic value. In the case of fossil fuels, low prices have encouraged waste and inefficiency while discouraging and delaying the development of cleaner and more sustainable alternative forms of energy.

Governments can correct the failure of markets to incorporate negative externalities into price levels by imposing a tax. Tax levels on oil, coal, and natural gas vary greatly across countries, but nowhere capture the full costs of fossil fuel consumption. In the United States, the average tax on a gallon of gasoline is less than 50 cents – a tenth of the average level in Europe. A progressive rise in taxes on carbon emissions would represent one of the simpler and more effective steps that could be taken to begin the shift toward a post-fossil fuel future.

Unfortunately, however, the political costs of raising energy taxes – even were the proceeds to be returned by reducing other taxes – are imposing in many countries given the resistance of energy producers, energy-intensive industries, and consumers. The political challenge is deepened by the lack of public understanding of the realities and risks of climate change. While in 2006 79 percent of Americans acknowledged that the climate is warming, this figure fell to 50 percent in 2011.

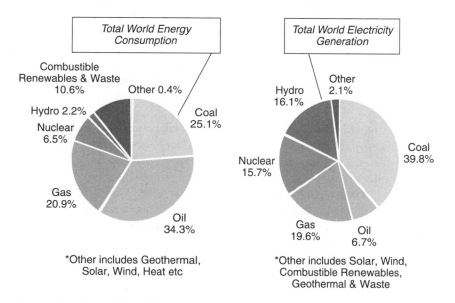

Figure 11.1 Total World Energy Consumption and Electricity Generation.

Source: Adapted from Alternative Energy Renewables, Global Greenhouse Warming, www.global-greenhouse-warming.com/alternative-energy.html

Moreover, only 40 percent of Americans surveyed expressed a willingness to pay more for clean energy if it were necessary in order to mitigate climate change.[67]

While carbon dioxide is the most worrisome greenhouse gas due to the enormous quantities released through fossil fuel combustion and because it can persist in the atmosphere for decades, 40 percent of greenhouse gas emissions consist of short-lived chemicals that remain in the atmosphere for anywhere from days to a few years. The three most important of these are HFCs, methane, and black carbon. As previously mentioned, HFCs are already being phased out under the Montreal Protocol. Methane emissions can be reduced by fixing leaky pipes, draining rice fields of water more often, and capturing methane that is released from landfills. Black carbon is a byproduct of diesel engines and the millions of inefficient brick kilns and cookstoves common in the developing world. When it settles in polar regions, black carbon contributes to warming by reducing the reflectivity of surface ice.[68]

In February 2012, the United States, Canada, Sweden, Ghana, Mexico, and Bangladesh announced an initiative to reduce emissions of short-lived greenhouse gases, working through the UN Environmental Program. Separately, a UN-backed public–private partnership called the Global Alliance for Clean Cookstoves hopes to distribute 100 million clean-burning (and safer – indoor air pollution from dirty cookstoves takes 2 million lives per year) cookstoves by 2020.[69] If successful, efforts to reduce short-lived greenhouse gas emissions could buy time to address the far more difficult problem of fossil fuel emissions.

Conservation – both of energy and of the forests that absorb carbon dioxide – offers another route to slow global warming. Energy intensity is a measure of the amount of energy needed to produce a unit of GDP. Due to both efficiency gains and the shrinking share of production accounted for by energy-intensive industries, global energy intensity declined by 20 percent between 1981 and 2010, though most of the improvement took place during the 1980s and 1990s. With appropriate price and government incentives, future efficiency gains could be substantial. Higher fuel efficiency standards imposed by the US Congress, for instance, will save 4.3 million barrels of oil per year by 2025, while an additional 2.5 million barrels in savings could be achieved were electric vehicles to achieve a 20 percent share of the US automobile fleet by 2050. China managed to reduce energy intensity by 15 percent between 2005 and 2010. Considerable efficiency gains are possible through newer building designs and even in retrofitting older buildings. After the Empire State Building received an energy makeover, for instance, energy costs fell by 40 percent.[70]

Forest conservation must also be a part of any solution to global warming. Forests absorb carbon dioxide when healthy and release it back into the atmosphere when burned to make way for agriculture or urban development. Forest destruction accounts for roughly 20 percent of carbon emissions. From 2000–12, the earth experienced a net loss of 1.5 square kilometers of forest cover due to logging, fire, disease, and storms – an area equivalent to six Californias.[71] The UN Reducing Emissions from Deforestation and Forest Degradation Program was created in 2008 to provide funding for forest preservation in developing countries, although the program has been plagued by allegations of fraud and waste.[72]

These measures – reducing emissions of short-lived greenhouse gases, improving energy efficiency, and conserving forests – can delay the process of global warming, but cannot halt it. Only radically reduced reliance upon fossil fuels can stop the inexorable rise in carbon dioxide concentrations in the atmosphere. The challenge of doing so is staggering. At present, the world relies upon fossil fuel for 80 percent of energy consumption. While oil, coal, and natural gas are finite resources, technological advances in exploration and recovery ensure ample supplies for many decades to come. Indeed, proven fossil fuel reserves exceed by five times the amount that can safely be consumed without pushing the climate beyond the 2 degree warming target set at Copenhagen.[73]

Some way must be found to accelerate the development of alternative energy sources or to render fossil fuels more climate-friendly. The chief renewable sources of energy are hydro-electric, solar, and wind. Because the best sites for hydro-electric dams have already been exploited, growth from this source is expected to be modest. Solar and wind power are each growing rapidly, as prices have fallen dramatically in recent years. Wind energy production rose by two-thirds from 1998 to 2008 and solar power increased by a factor of fifteen over the same period. Yet the absolute increase in coal-produced power over this decade was 5.8 times the increase from wind and 823 times the increase from solar. In 2010, a single coal mine in Kentucky produced enough coal to provide three-quarters as much energy as all of the solar panels in the United States combined. Solar and wind are also intermittent – available only when the sun is shining or the wind is blowing – which presents challenges in maintaining stability across the electrical grid, although new methods for energy storage show promise. All types of renewable energy together accounted for only 3 percent of installed electrical capacity globally in 2012, though these sources represented 50 percent of new capacity added from 2007–9.[74]

Although nuclear power makes a significant contribution to present electrical capacity, its share is shrinking as a result of daunting investment costs, a tough regulatory climate, nuclear proliferation concerns, the lack of solutions to the problem of nuclear waste, and public worries over safety. The Fukushima nuclear disaster prompted Japan to shut down all but two of its fifty-four nuclear plants and some other countries, including Germany, to launch efforts to scale back future dependence upon nuclear power.[75]

Over the long term, alternatives to fossil fuels do exist and will come to play a growing role as a result of technological improvements, declining costs, and government support. Yet it seems unavoidable that fossil fuels will continue to dominate energy supplies well into the present century. Some therefore argue that any solution must seek ways to render such fuels less destructive to the earth's atmosphere.

Coal lies at the center of such discussions. Coal is, in many places, the lowest-cost source of electricity. It is also, by far, the dirtiest. Even as new technology has improved the efficiency of the most advanced coal power plants, they still emit far more carbon dioxide per unit of energy than natural gas, the most common alternative. While the United States and Europe have imposed strict limits on the construction of new coal facilities, existing plants continue, in the case of the United States, to account for one-half of electrical production. Globally, however, 1,200 new coal plants are planned for the coming decades, two-thirds of them in China and India.[76] Despite massive investments in energy efficiency, solar, wind, and nuclear power, China still depends upon coal for 70 percent of its still rapidly growing electricity needs.[77] In short, the problem of global warming is in large part defined by reliance upon coal.

Efforts are currently underway to develop economical systems to capture and store beneath the earth much of the carbon dioxide emitted by coal power plants. If successful, carbon capture and storage would serve to reconcile our dependence upon coal with progress toward slowing global warming. The practicality of this solution is, however, much debated. The technology is expensive and uncertain. New coal plants equipped with carbon capture and storage systems cost twice the investment of conventional plants. Refitting older coal plants with the technology would be even more uneconomical. The incentives for utilities to bear such added costs or to recover such investments from rate-payers do not currently exist. Moreover, there are uncertainties about whether leakage of buried carbon dioxide can be avoided and what to do were such leakage to take place. The International Energy Agency has called for the construction of 100 carbon and capture coal plants by 2020 and 3,400 by 2050. As of 2012, however, there existed only eight such plants, none operated on a commercial basis.[78]

The IPCC estimates that effective mitigation measures would have only a marginally negative impact on global economic growth. However, the incentives necessary to produce a rapid shift toward a low-carbon future are not yet in place and the longer the world waits before undertaking the needed investments, the higher the cost of limiting warming to a manageable level becomes.[79]

To summarize, the issue of global warming has a number of characteristics that render it especially problematic from a political and an economic point of view:

1   Commons: As a global commons, the atmosphere cannot be partitioned among the world's 200 independent states. It is thus vulnerable to exploitation, and collective efforts to induce restraint are hampered by free-rider problems and the competitive nature of international politics.

2   Market failure: The market price of fossil fuels is set in a manner that fails to reflect the full social and environmental costs of production and consumption. As a result, oil, coal, and natural gas are overconsumed and renewable sources of energy face greater obstacles.

3   Timescale: The negative consequences of global warming will emerge gradually over time, with the worst effects decades in the future. Effective mitigation measures, however, require large, immediate, upfront investments. This misalignment of effort and reward is particularly problematic for politicians whose political horizon is the next election two or four years hence.

4   Scope: Meeting the challenge of global warming requires revolutionary changes in the entire global energy complex – the world economy's most foundational industry and one that is heavily controlled by politically powerful actors who have invested deeply in the continued centrality of fossil fuels.

Conclusion: Sustainable Globalization?

Both rising incomes and rising populations have been based upon constantly improving technologies for exploiting the earth's natural resources. Perhaps more than any other factor, the consumption of fossil fuels has powered a period of human progress and development unprecedented in history. Yet a scant two centuries into the fossil fuel era, the same technologies and consumption patterns that have provided increased material comfort to many also threaten to render the planet a far less hospitable place for humans and many other forms of life in the future.

To avoid the worst consequences, wrenching changes will be required. Yet the very nature of the global commons diffuses responsibility and renders collective action difficult. The fragmented and competitive structure of the world's political and economic systems has the same effect. These obstacles have not prevented governments and other actors from working across national boundaries to forge shared understandings of problems and taking cooperative actions to address them. Yet the processes of environmental diplomacy have moved too slowly and without sufficient political commitment to redirect economic development and globalization along sustainable paths. The fate of globalization itself will depend upon greater future progress in meeting the challenge of reconciling growth with the limits imposed by nature.

Key Concepts (see Glossary)

Earth Summit

Global Commons

Global Warming

Greenhouse Gases

Kyoto Protocol

Market Failure

Millennium Development Goals
   (MDGs)

Montreal Protocol

Ozone Depletion

Renewable Energy

Rio Earth Summit

Sustainable Development

Tragedy of the Commons

Discussion Questions

1   Does the earth have a fixed "carrying capacity"?

2   Are the notions of "development" and "sustainability" in conflict with one another?

3   Is the history of environmental diplomacy one of success or disappointment?

4   With respect to the health of the world's air and oceans, what is the best approach to avoiding the "tragedy of the commons"?

5   Why have global negotiations to deal with ozone depletion been relatively more productive than those focusing on global warming?

6   Can technological fixes alone successfully address global warming? Or will major lifestyle changes be required?

7   What ethical criteria should be applied in allocating the costs of mitigating and adapting to climate change among rich and poor countries?

Notes

1   This definition is adapted from one offered by the Bruntland Commission in World Commission on Environment and Development (WCED), *Our Common Future*, New York: Oxford University Press, 1987, 8.

2   Nina Chestney, "World Lacks Enough Food, Fuel as Population Soars: U.N." *Reuters*, January 30, 2012.

3   Gary C. Bryner, *Protecting the Global Environment*, New York: Paradigm Publishers, 2011, 18.

4   Jim Robbins, "Global Trade Spreads a Fatal Amphibian Disease," *New York Times*, November 24, 2011; Kelsey Russell and Lisa Mastny, "State of the World: A Year in Review," in *State of the World 2011: Innovations that Nourish the Planet*, Worldwatch Institute, New York: W.W. Norton & Company, 2011, xxiv–xxix.

5   Chestney, "World Lacks Enough Food."

6   Chestney, "World Lacks Enough Food."

7   Bryner, *Protecting the Global Environment*, 19.

8   Bryner, *Protecting the Global Environment*, 21–2.

9   Bryner, *Protecting the Global Environment*, 21.

10   Jonathan Watts, "China Told to Reduce Food Production or Face 'Dire' Water Levels," *The Guardian*, June 28, 2011.

11 Bryner, *Protecting the Global Environment*, 34.
12 Bryner, *Protecting the Global Environment*, 47.
13 "Declaration of the United Nations Conference on the Human Environment," United Nations Environmental Program, www.unep.org/Documents. Multilingual/Default.asp?DocumentID=97&ArticleID=1503&l=en
14 Much of the information given next on UNCED has been culled from Edward Parson, Peter Haas, and Marc Levy, "A Summary of the Major Documents Signed at the Earth Summit and the Global Forum," *Environment*, October 1992; Peter Haas, Marc Levy, and Edward Parson, "The Earth Summit: How Should We Judge UNCED's Success?" *Environment*, October 1992; and Jerald Schnoor, "The Rio Earth Summit: What Does It Mean?" *Environment, Science and Technology*, vol. 27, no. 1 (1993).
15 Haas, Levy, and Parson, "The Earth Summit," 8.
16 World Bank, *World Development Report, 1999/2000*, New York: Oxford University Press, 2000, 94.
17 Fred Pearce, "Beyond Rio, Green Economics Can Give Us Hope," *The Guardian*, June 28, 2012.
18 Phasing out all fossil fuel subsidies would reduce carbon dioxide emissions by an estimated 13 percent. Tim Worstall, "Eliminating Energy Subsidies Could Reduce Emissions by 13 Percent," *Forbes*, April 27, 2013.
19 Fred Pearce, "Beyond Rio, Green Economics Can Give Us Hope," *The Guardian*, June 28, 2012; Nina Chestney, "Rio Summit: Environmentalists Slam Agreements as Too Weak," *The Christian Science Monitor*, June 20, 2012.
20 Stephen Hale, "Sustainable Development Goals: UN Must Take Simple, Sensible Approach," *The Guardian*, July 3, 2012. An interim report can be found at www.post2015hlp.org/wp-content/uploads/2013/05/UN-Report.pdf
21 Richard Black, "Rio Summit: Little Progress, 20 Years On," *BBC*, June 12, 2012; Fred Pearce, "Beyond Rio"; Simon Romero and John M. Broder, "Progress on Sidelines as Rio Conference Ends," *New York Times*, June 23, 2012.
22 Black, "Rio Summit"; Nina Chestney, "Rio Summit."
23 The term itself was coined by Garrett Hardin in "The Tragedy of the Commons," *Science* (December 1968).
24 For a more optimistic view on the ability of users to cooperate for the purpose of sustainability, see Elinor Ostrom, "A General Framework for Analyzing Sustainability of Social–Ecological Systems," *Science*, vol. 235 (July 24, 2009).
25 National Atmospheric and Oceanic Administration, US Department of Commerce, "Antarctic Hole Second Smallest in 20 Years," October 24, 2012, www.noaanews.noaa.gov/stories2012/20121024_antarcticozonehole.html
26 Jessica Vellette Revere, "Ozone Depletion and Global Warming," *Foreign Policy in Focus* (October 12, 2005).
27 Mario Molina and Durwood Zaelke, "A Climate Success Story to Build On," *New York Times*, September 25, 2012, and Roger Coate, "Ignoring the Earth Comes with Consequences," *The InterDependent*, vol. 4, no. 2 (Summer 2006).
28 Molina and Zaelke, "A Climate Success Story to Build On"; Elisabeth Rosenthal and Andrew W. Lehren, "As Coolant is Phased Out, Smugglers Reap Large Profits," *New York Times*, September 7, 2012; Rosenthal and Lehren, "Effort to Curb Dangerous Coolant Falters, Sometimes at Home," *New York Times*, September 22, 2012; and Rosenthal and Lehren, "Relief in

Every Window, but Global Worry Too," *New York Times*, June 20, 2012; "United States and China Agree to Work Together on Phase Down of HFCs," Office of the Press Secretary, The White House, June 8, 2013.

29 Molina and Zaelke, "A Climate Success Story to Build On."
30 National Atmospheric and Oceanic Administration, US Department of Commerce, "Antarctic Hole Second Smallest in 20 Years."
31 "New Report Highlights Two-way Link between Ozone Layer and Climate Change," *UNEP News Center*, November 16, 2010, www.unep.org/Documents.Multilingual/Default.asp?DocumentID=647&ArticleID=6751&l=en&t=long
32 Charles Kegley, Jr., and Eugene R. Wittkopf, *World Politics: Trend and Transformation*, New York: St. Martin's Press, 5th ed., 1995, 380; "This Year was the 2nd Hottest, Confirming a Trend, U.N. Says," *New York Times*, December 19, 2001; Justin Gillis, "Carbon Emissions Show Biggest Jump Ever Recorded," *New York Times*, December 4, 2011.
33 Justin Gillis, "2014 Was the Warmest Year Ever Recorded on Earth," *New York Times*, January 16, 2015.
34 Associated Press, "World Temps Maintain the Heat of Global Warming," *New York Times*, November 29, 2011; Justin Gillis, "Rising Sea Levels Seen as Threat to Coastal U.S.," *New York Times*, March 13, 2012; "Beating a Retreat," *The Economist*, September 24, 2011; Nick Cumming-Bruce, "Agency Says 2012 Ranks Among Hottest Years," *New York Times*, November 28, 2012; Bill McKibben, "Global Warming's Terrifying New Math," *Rolling Stone*, July 19, 2012.
35 Justin Gillis, "U.N. Climate Panel Warns Speedier Action is Needed to Avert Disaster," *New York Times*, April 13, 2014.
36 Justin Gillis, "How High Could the Tide Go?" *New York Times*, January 21, 2013.
37 Justin Gillis and Kenneth Chang, "Scientists Warn of Rising Oceans as Antarctic Ice Melts," *New York Times*, May 12, 2014.
38 Sarah Lyall, "Heat, Flood or Icy Cold, Extreme Weather Rages Worldwide," *New York Times*, January 10, 2013; Justin Gillis, "Climate Change Study Finds U.S. is Already Widely Affected," *New York Times*, May 6, 2014.
39 Kegley and Wittkopf, *World Politics*, 382.
40 CNA Military Advisory Board, "National Security and the Accelerating Risks of Climate Change," CNA Analysis and Solutions, March 2014, www.cna.org/cna_files/pdf/MAB_5-8-14.pdf
41 Daniel Sarewitz and Roger Pielke, Jr., "Breaking the Global-Warming Gridlock," *The Atlantic Monthly* (July 2000) 58, 62; "Emission Impossible?" *Foreign Policy* (November/December 2000) 31.
42 Kegley and Wittfopf, *World Politics*, 383; Sarewitz and Pielke, "Breaking the Global-Warming Gridlock," 62.
43 Justin Gillis, "Climate Panel Says Upper Limit on Emissions is Nearing," *New York Times*, September 27, 2013; Justin Gillis, "How to Slice a Global Carbon Pie?" *New York Times*, October 7, 2013.
44 Andrew C. Revkin, "Odd Culprits in Collapse of Climate Talks," *New York Times*, November 28, 2000; "Corporate Campaign to Corrupt the Kyoto Protocol Continues After COP-6," *Corporate Europe Observer*, issue 8 (2000).
45 Cat Lazaroff, "UN Secretary General Denounces U.S. Global Warming Stance," *Environment News Service*, May 21, 2001.
46 "This Year was the 2nd Hottest, Confirming a Trend, U.N. Says."
47 See text of the agreement at http://unfccc.int/resource/docs/2009/cop15/eng/l07.pdf

48 Melissa Low, "How Was Doha Different and What's Next?" Eco-Business. com, January 10, 2013; Syed Mujtaba Hussain, "Doha Climate Change Conference Another Lost Opportunity to Enhance Ambition," *The Nation*, December 31, 2012; Janet Redman, "What Next for the Green Climate Fund After Doha Dud?" *Responding to Climate Change (RTCC)*, January 14, 2013; Tom Bawden, "Fiddling While Rome Burns – the £3trn Cost of Climate Delay," *The Independent*, January 13, 2013.

49 Stephen Power, "Senate Halts Effort to Cap CO2 Emissions," *Wall St. Journal*, July 23, 2010.

50 Editorial Board, "A Major Breakthrough on Climate Change," *New York Times*, November 12, 2014.

51 Nick Visser, "Hundreds of Thousands Turn Out for People's Climate March in New York City," *The Huffington Post*, September 21, 2014; Melanie Mattauch, "In the Space of Just 10 Weeks . . .," *Fossil Free* (December 2, 2015), http://gofossilfree.org/in-the-space-of-just–10-weeks/

52 Coral Davenport, "A Climate Accord Based upon Global Peer Pressure," *New York Times*, December 14, 2014.

53 Michael Greenstone, "Surprisingly, a Voluntary Climate Treaty Could Actually Work," *New York Times*, February 13, 2015.

54 Coral Davenport, Justin Gillis, Sewell Chan, and Melissa Eddy, "Inside the Paris Climate Deal," *New York Times*, December 12, 2015.

55 Hannah Fairfield and Josh Williams, "The Climate Change Pledges Are In. Will They Fix Anything?" *New York Times*, November 23, 2015.

56 Kevin Jianjun Yu, "Only a New Bloc Can Save the Climate," *Carnegie Endowment for International Peace* (December 26, 2012).

57 See, for example, Stephen Coll's discussion of the Exxon Corporation's efforts to influence the debate over climate change. Stephen Coll, *Private Empire: ExxonMobil and American Power*, New York: Penguin Press, 2012, 67–92.

58 Daniel Yergin, *The Quest: Energy, Security and the Remaking of the Modern World*, New York: Penguin Books, rev. ed., 2012.

59 Robert Falkner, "Business Conflict and U.S. International Environmental Policy: Ozone, Climate and Biodiversity," in Paul G. Harris (ed.), *The Environment, International Relations, and US Foreign Policy*, Washington, DC: Georgetown University Press, 2001, 168.

60 Joby Warrick, "Surprisingly Good News for the Earth's Climate: Greenhouse Gas Pollution Dropped this Year," *Washington Post*, December 7, 2015.

61 Associated Press, "Climate Deal Doesn't Make Things Worse – or Better," *New York Times*, December 11, 2011.

62 Gillis, "Carbon Emissions Show Biggest Jump Ever Recorded."

63 Nicholas Stern, "Climate Changer," *South China Morning Post*, October 30, 2011; "Adapting to Climate Change: Facing the Consequences," *The Economist*, November 25, 2010.

64 Existing permafrost holds twice as much carbon as the earth's atmosphere. As the permafrost melts, the released carbon will eventually come to equal one-third of the annual emissions from human activities. Justin Gillis, "As Permafrost Thaws, Scientists Study the Risks," *New York Times*, December 16, 2011; Matt McGrath, "Arctic Methane 'Time Bomb' Could Have Huge Economic Costs," *BBC*, July 24, 2013.

65 "Adapting to Climate Change: Facing the Consequences," *The Economist*, November 25, 2010.

66 James Kanter, "Cost of Subsidizing Fossil Fuels is High, but Cutting Them is Tough," *New York Times*, October 23, 2011.

67 Vivek Dehejia, "The Developing World, Leading on Climate Change?" *New York Times*, November 9, 2011.

68 Elisabeth Rosenthal, "Burning Fuel Particles Do More Damage to Climate Than Thought, Study Says," *New York Times*, January 15, 2013; David G. Victor, Charles F. Kennel, and Veerabhadran Ramanathan, "The Climate Threat That We Can Beat," *Foreign Affairs* (May/June 2012).

69 Victor, Kennel, and Ramanathan, "The Climate Threat That We Can Beat"; John M. Broder, "U.S. Pushes to Cut Emissions of Some Pollutants That Hasten Climate Change," *New York Times*, February 15, 2012; Dehejia, "The Cookstove Conundrum."

70 Sheldon Yoder, "Energy Intensity of Global Economy Rises, Reversing Longtime Trend," Worldwatch Institute, January 18, 2013, www.world-watch.org/energy-intensity-energy-efficiency-gross-world-product-emerging-economies-infrastructure-development; Clifford Krauss, "Can We Do Without the Mideast?" *New York Times*, March 30, 2011; Justin Gillis, "Tax Plan to Turn Old Building 'Green' Finds Favor," *New York Times*, September 19, 2011.

71 "Brazil Says Amazon Deforestation Rose 28% in a Year," *BBC*, November 15, 2013; Ritchie King, "The World Has Lost Almost Six Californias Worth of Forest Since, 2000," *Quartz*, November 15, 2013.

72 Audrey Belford, "Indonesia's Billion-Dollar Forest Deal is At Risk," *New York Times*, November 28, 2010.

73 McKibben, "Global Warming's Terrifying New Math."

74 James Fallows, "Dirty Coal, Clean Future," *The Atlantic*, December 2010.

75 Mark Scott, "Out of Africa (and Elsewhere): More Fossil Fuels," *New York Times*, April 10, 2012.

76 Andrew C. Revkin, "Coal Boom Unabated in Asia," *New York Times*, November 12, 2012.

77 Fallows, "Dirty Coal, Clean Future."

78 James Kanter, "Obstacles to Capturing Carbon Gas," *New York Times*, July 31, 2011; Stanley Reed, "Energy Solution Faces Economic Obstacles," *New York Times*, November 28, 2012; Matthew L. Wald, "Study Finds Setbacks in Carbon Capture Projects," *New York Times*, October 10, 2013.

79 Damian Carrington, "IPCC Climate Change Report: Averting Catastrophe is Eminently Affordable," *The Guardian*, April 13, 2014.

Further Reading

Erik Assadourian and Michael Renner, *State of the World 2012: Moving Toward a Sustainable Prosperity*, Washington, DC: Worldwatch Institute, 2012.
Annual edition of Worldwatch Institute series that provides up-to-date data and perspective on sustainable development.

Richard Elliot Benedick, *Ozone Diplomacy: New Directions in Safeguarding the Planet*, Cambridge, MA: Harvard University Press, 2nd ed., 1998.
An account of the negotiations that led to the Montreal Protocol.

Stephen Coll, *Private Empire: ExxonMobil and American Power*, New York: Penguin Press, 2012.
An examination of the political and economic power of the world's largest private oil company.

Naomi Klein, *This Changes Everything: Capitalism vs. the Climate*, New York: Simon & Schuster, 2014.

Klein argues that combating climate change requires a broad-based restructuring and democratization of political and economic power.

Amory Lovins, *Reinventing Fire: Bold Solutions for the New Energy Era*, Burlington, VT: Chelsea Green Publishing, 2011.
Lovins, head of the Rocky Mountain Institute, offers a hopeful and detailed look at emerging energy technologies and solutions that point toward a post-fossil fuel future.

Bill McKibben, *Earth: Making a Life on a Tough New Planet*, New York: St. Martin's Griffin, 2011.
A lead environmentalist examines how humans have altered the global ecology.

R.K. Pachauri and A. Reisinger (eds), *Climate Change 2007: Synthesis Report*, Geneva: Intergovernmental Panel on Climate Change, 2007.
A summary of the three working group reports issued by the IPCC in 2007. Provides an overview of scientific findings related to climate change.

Daniel Yergin, *The Quest: Energy, Security and the Remaking of the Modern World*, London: Penguin Books, rev. ed., 2012.
An examination of the role that oil has played in the world economy during the post-Cold War era, with attention to climate change and the development of alternative energy sources.

12 Conclusion
The International Political Economy of Globalization

The focus of our book has been on understanding the development of the global economy through the lens of international political economy, an analysis rooted in the ways political and economic processes are intertwined. We have worked to help you understand what has happened, the various reasons for these developments, and the consequences. In the concluding chapter, we hope to do three things. First, provide a basic overview of some of the main issues discussed and how the study of international political economy provides unique and valuable insights. Second is to think about how the global economy might develop in the near future, perhaps over the next twenty years. Third, we reflect on some of the important controversies brewing in international political economy.

Globalization in the past forty years has altered the basic character of many economic relationships, by moving us from an international economy to a global economy. The system has changed from one largely defined by nations and their economic interactions to one defined much more by transnational economic interactions. This new global economic environment has become one in which the scale, density, distribution, organization of production, and complexity of economic relationships have made for a different kind of system from what we have had before. In the process, markets for goods, services, and money have become more deeply integrated; the process of production has been distributed across a much wider geographic space and incorporated into nations now richer for this; knowledge, technology, and ideas have been linked together in webs and networks of global scope; new forms of political cooperation among nations have emerged and a vast array of partnerships among nations and firms for development and enhanced competitiveness have been formed; and the level of volatility and even turbulence in the global economy has intensified.

The global connections of markets can be seen easily from the connections in price movements in stock markets around the world over the past eight years, as shown in Figure 12.1. The chart shows how price movements from three very different kinds of markets not only follow each other across broad trends but also through many short and small cycles.

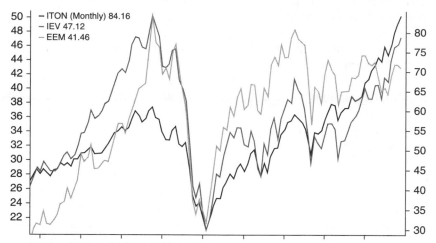

Figure 12.1 Price Movements of Exchange Traded Funds for the United States, EU, and Emerging Markets Stock Markets, 2005–13.

Source: Adapted from Street Authority, "Expect 2014 to be Hugely Profitable for this Beaten Down Sector," http://finance.yahoo.com/news/expect–2014-hugely-profitable-beaten–160000253.html, courtesy of StockCharts.com.

Your study of international political economy now permits not only the ability to understand and analyze such a chart as in Figure 12.1, but also to reflect on how we should study this and other features of the global economy. We turn first to a discussion about the special value added of international political economy.

The Value of International Political Economy

The developments in the global economy over the past forty years have been momentous. For the first time in human history, a truly global economy has emerged from the rapid growth of economic transactions, global firms, and institutions. The changes in the global distribution of wealth across nations and firms in this period rival those of the 150 years after 1820. Clearly, this system of global economic relationships has immense consequences for the lives of most people on the planet, affecting prosperity and poverty, war and peace, and environmental degradation and sustainability.

The expansion of global markets has produced significant effects for the relative and absolute prosperity of literally billions of people. In many nations, a relatively small number of persons especially well positioned to take advantage of expanding markets, have seen their incomes and wealth grow much, much faster than others. This is not particularly surprising, as free markets always accentuate economic advantages and disadvantages.

Somewhat more unexpected is that one of the most important of the groups affected by globalization is concentrated in the poorest nations. This is a remarkably large number of persons who have seen their lives and those of their children changed from wretched poverty to at least ones of minimal income and a little wealth. This is the most surprising effect of globalization: not that the rich have gotten much richer, but that hundreds of millions of the poorest have benefited. These have primarily been persons living in poor nations, who have been best positioned to take advantage of new global markets. A combination of factors, mostly linked to globalization, has led to substantial improvements in global health. In China, which has achieved some of the greatest economic growth, perhaps 500 million persons have been moved above the line of absolute poverty. Of course, many Chinese have achieved much larger economic rewards and, notwithstanding the improvements by the poorest, economic inequality in China has also increased dramatically. This does not mean that all nations with good growth records have been so fortunate. India, though trailing China in rates of GDP growth, achieved quite fast growth between 1991 and 2010. And yet, this has benefited the poorest in India much less.[1]

One result we have described is how India remains a nation where far too many people are afflicted by malnutrition and hunger. We have considered the effects of poverty in poor (and rich) nations, including population growth, malnutrition, disease, and war – scourges that have always afflicted humans. Rising incomes, especially for those who are poorest, can have the effect of reducing the incidence of these terrible problems and remain the best hope for improving the human lot as a whole. At the same time, market relations that bring economic growth typically also work against the weakest of the world in terms of income distribution and the allocation of basic necessities such as food, shelter, and medicine. Efforts to overcome these problems, organized outside of free markets, typically cut against the interests of those who are most powerfully positioned in these markets. One example we have considered is the difficulty in the United States in implementing a food aid policy that provides food to the hungry instead of profits to rich famers and shippers. As we have seen, improving the health of the poorest is also undermined by many of the same rules that facilitate global trade. Though globalization has led to improvements in the incomes, health, and wealth of many people in poor nations, the impact of markets and the interests of the powerful differentially benefit the strong and this process cannot be counted on to improve the lot of much of humankind.

We should also remember the epic expansion of global markets has been accompanied by, and sustained by, equally important changes in technology. The digital revolution, with personal computers, software, mobile devices, the Internet, and computer chips in thousands of products, has created new forms of economic value and also altered the distribution of gains. Much of these transformations come from new forms of productivity that some nations and firms are able to master and some are not. Over the past forty years, 40 percent of gains in global productivity has come from the falling prices of semiconductor chips and the related innovations in information and communication technologies.[2] At the same time that technology has generated enormous gains in human welfare, these gains have been largely distributed to those best positioned to take advantage of these changes.

Surely one of the most important of these distributional transformations is the increasing proportion of national income for holders of capital and a decreasing proportion for those whose economic resource is their labor.[3] This means workers in advanced and emerging economies see their incomes fall relative to those who are owners of capital. One obvious effect of this process is increasing levels of inequality within nations. The reason is a complex interaction between global markets and technology. Bringing hundreds of millions of very low-paid workers into the global workforce – much of this made possible by technological advances – is part of the story. But the productivity of workers in all nations has continued to rise and historically these improvements have provided the economic basis for rising incomes. However, rather than workers as a whole, technology and the capital investment associated with technology seem to have been the main engines of rising productivity. This has been responsible for the largest part of the shift in relative income between workers and capital.[4]

Perhaps the most important idea from this book relates to how we try to understand these huge changes. We believe this can best be done through the concepts and theories of international political economy, broadly construed. Big events like globalization are never just about economic efficiency and markets, nor just about governments and power. Rather, globalization is about how markets and power interact and thereby require new kinds of ideas to capture this reality.

How is this true? Consider the origins of globalization. Make no mistake, globalization could not have happened without the active efforts and support of powerful interests, in and outside of government. (It is naive to assert that globalization is just the result of expanding free markets.) Perhaps the most important power relationship is the close partnership of the governments of the most advanced nations and the greatest of global firms, especially financial firms. In addition, the case for globalization has been consistently made by global media, policy, and academic elites, many of whom themselves have personal interests in the success of this venture. As we have seen, the political leaders of the US government after World War II pressed hard for a global policy of open markets and democratization. By the 1960s, governments in Western Europe were largely in favor of such a policy and by the 1970s had been pushed by global banking interests into accepting much larger economic freedom across national borders for finance. The late 1970s and early 1980s were a crucial period for the shift to a much more consistent and aggressive posture of open and free markets, led by the United States and Great Britain. The past thirty-five years have produced the globalization we have discussed in detail in this book, which involves the massive changes in global development and economic redistribution.

Consider again one of the large issues and questions that now dominate the global economic agenda and the value of international political economy in understanding how and why these events happen: the origin and consequences of the Global Financial Crisis. Particularly important is a United States–China relationship involving government debt and the effects of the bond-buying strategy by wealthy nations to bolster their economies. International political economy offers a focus on the power calculations, strategies, and preferences of the most powerful states as a basis for understanding outcomes. The crisis itself also makes clear the limits imposed by markets on the ability to achieve preferences held by other groups.

One of the most significant features of the globalization process, especially after 2001, was the rapid development of China and the sale of its products to the United States, resulting in a large current account deficit by the United States. Much of this process took place through the actions of global firms, engaged in FDI and knowledge transfers, and often in partnership with various levels of the Chinese central and local governments engaged in infrastructure development to support global production. Left alone, free markets would have produced adjustments in prices to deal with the large imbalances resulting from the US current account deficit. Specifically, the deficit would have led to a significant rise in the exchange rate of the RMB and decline in the exchange rate of the US dollar. However, these market-based adjustments were unacceptable to both the US and Chinese governments. Such changes would have reduced the value of producing in China: a value captured by many US corporations and consumers who benefited from this system and a value greatly boosting economic growth in China. So, instead of allowing markets to adjust, the Chinese government controlled the RMB exchange rate and accumulated US dollars. And, in order to obtain some return on its newfound dollar assets, the Chinese purchased US government bonds. This made it much easier for the Bush Administration to keep interest rates low and sustain the large budget deficits resulting from the large tax cuts that mostly benefited the wealthiest Americans.

The Global Financial Crisis disrupted this cozy arrangement, mainly by pushing the Chinese to begin rebalancing away from export-driven growth and to reduce their willingness to hold US government debt. The US government moved to support its collapsing economy with much larger budget deficits and desperately needed to keep interest rates low. This led to the innovation by the Federal Reserve known as Quantitative

Easing, which was then emulated by Europe and Japan. The various programs of bond buying by the Federal Reserve and other central banks, known as QE 1–3, led to a massive accumulation of assets by the Fed, to the tune of $4 trillion, the flip side of a massive increase in global liquidity.[5] In turn, the actions associated with Quantitative Easing spilled out into the rest of the world, flooding the United States and much of the world with globally useable dollars. This contributed to inflationary pressures in China, along with considerable stimulus to the economy of India and the rupee's exchange rate.[6] The Fed's decision to scale back or taper Quantitative Easing, in late 2013, prompted not only a stock market selloff in the United States, and rising interest rates, but also a sinking Indian stock market and falling exchange rates. Emerging markets more generally were sent into a swoon by the Fed's new policies. The damage done to emerging economies came back to produce significant declines in US and European markets because of a new threat of global economic slowing.

International political economy helps us focus on the failures of markets, which after all are composed of human beings who often make bad judgments. It is difficult to deny that major market players individually and collectively made a continuing stream of bad investment choices, often the result of a herd instinct rather than careful and dispassionate analysis. An important source of these failures resulted from the investment climate created by government policies, in particular an almost religious belief in the benefits of free markets. At the same time, the global expansion of free markets was a cornerstone of a broader strategy to advance the power of the United States.

This strategy developed through a partnership relationship of global financial institutions and the US government, in which deregulation was seen as a means to advance the position and profits of US firms. And the US government was able to expand its influence through global financial markets and firms were able to increase their profits through larger markets. The considerable risks of larger and freer financial markets were ignored or explained away, perhaps because of the enormous profits and power to be won. This form of analysis – always a core feature of international political economy – helps reinforce the conclusion that global economic systems are in part the result of strategic calculations and actions by the largest nations; that is, the shape of such systems is a result of the preferences of the major powers. As such, it is impossible to understand the market-based system of globalization without an appreciation of the strategic actions and gains that led the United States to promote such a system and the importance of understanding how structural power both is the basis of such actions and is enhanced by these same actions.

Beyond the search for gains is the essential role of governments in stabilizing and managing markets, especially evident in systemic financial crises. Immense resources have been devoted to compensate for some of the losses of the recent crisis and to prop up national economies and the global economy, and these resources come from governments. The near unanimity of this state intervention, combined with the dynamic adjustments made by governments to support and sustain national and firm competitiveness, makes calls for free markets sound somewhat whimsical and atavistic. The study of international political economy helps us understand the many profound relationships of politics and markets and the impossibility of achieving effective analysis of events without such a perspective.

Economic Growth and Change in the Next Twenty Years?

Prediction is not something social scientists undertake lightly. The deep complexities in the global economy mean that interaction effects can and will produce consequences that cannot be anticipated. Nonetheless, we believe the study of international political economy permits us to define some of the parameters within which change in the coming years is likely to occur. Perhaps the easiest to predict, and most important feature of the contemporary global economy, is the unremitting demands on most nations to restructure their economies to keep pace with rapid and far-reaching technological, political, organizational, and economic changes. The nature of these changes varies considerably from nation to nation, as do the abilities to direct these changes. Much of the character of the global economy of the next twenty years will be shaped by the patterns of success and failure in economic restructuring. We will also consider the fate of globalization during this period, which will hinge not only on the ability of constituent nations and firms to make the needed adjustments but also on the ability of nations to provide the political support systems that make globalization possible.

The context for the current phase of restructuring is the Global Financial Crisis and the widespread economic dislocation that lies in its wake. The problems for many advanced nations include the huge overhang of public and private debt that created the crisis, along with the huge additions to government debt that derive from the budget deficits created by the near depression. Not only does the debt serve as a drag on growth, but conflict over new spending cripples the capacity for making the kinds of public investment in infrastructure, innovative research, and human resources such as education that are essential for creating dynamic growth opportunities. The global imbalances of trade and debt, the damage to private credit markets from the bursting of debt bubbles, and the rising inequalities of wealth and income also represent important barriers to economic restructuring and resumed growth. Perhaps the largest problems are political, with paralysis resulting from deep ideological divisions over economic policy and a wide variety of other issues. These political problems are enhanced by the legacy of the old growth model, rooted in a financial industry looking to preserve its privileged position.

New policies and significant restructuring are needed to reinvigorate the economies of many advanced nations, where growth rates after the financial crisis have been anemic. At the beginning of 2014, only a small number of advanced nations have what appears to be a promising near future. One is the United States, where growth is starting to accelerate based on an energy boom in natural gas and solar power, a potential reemergence of manufacturing as labor costs rise in China and fall (with worker's wages) in the United States, several technologies, such as 3D printing, robotics, smart chips for new products, genetic-based medicine, and nanotechnology, hold promise for new investment, and immigration continues to produce young entrepreneurial talent. At the same time, none of these trends holds much promise for generating a broad-based economic growth that benefits most of the population. Instead, these new areas generally continue a long-run secular trend in which gains from growth flow overwhelmingly to those already wealthy and who possess significant knowledge resources. Only a massive reinvestment strategy, financed and directed by the US government, can alter this trend and create growth that also builds a broad base of political support.

Some other advanced nations, such as Japan, Australia, and Germany, hold promise for resuming or continuing economic growth, and several small nations (Nordic nations, Israel, Korea, and Singapore) are well positioned to engage in restructuring that can yield sustained growth. But many advanced nations – especially in Europe – offer much more pessimistic signs and remain bogged down in the consequences of the financial crisis. Among advanced nations, where can we expect significant restructuring to take place? Interestingly, the answer can come from the operation of markets and from the actions of governments. Much of the advances for the United States come from entrepreneurs responding to market signals that have been shaped by government policies. We can easily see this process in the energy industry, while virtually all advanced technologies have significant origins in government-sponsored research, and immigration levels are directly linked to national policy. National political leadership can provide both a strategic vision and a set of integrated policies, but successful actions like this seem restricted to a limited set of small and somewhat homogenous states. Most large, democratic nations today have a limited capacity for state-led restructuring. This may be due to the contradictory politics required by the simultaneous need to preserve wealth and make significant changes that involve transforming economic relationships. To the extent the United States follows a coherent national economic strategy, it will likely be defined by actions that do the least harm to existing powerful interests and coherence may result from the capacity of powerful interests to act collectively outside the political system.

There are two major near- and long-term issues that affect this expectation of modest growth: radical technological breakthroughs and climate change.[7] The potential for some transcendent technological breakthrough – such as a new kind of material, or energy source, or computer implant – able to drive large increases in investment that would generate new gains to society, is a realistic possibility. We have several previous examples, such as railroads, internal combustion, electricity, and computers, that have defined the forms of investment which generate extraordinary benefits to society and lead to substantial and sustained economic growth. Though these economic processes are typically very disruptive, usually eliminating and/or transforming many forms of previous economic value, the net gains are very large. At the same time, recent trends in technology may continue to exacerbate the current deficit in middle-class jobs for persons with only moderate skills. Historically, technology has typically destroyed jobs but also created even more, usually with higher wages. Recently and perhaps into the future, the number of new jobs will be small and technological changes will on balance reduce the number of jobs.[8] This development does not bode well for economic growth that benefits most people in a nation.

Much more predictable, but still operating within a significant range of uncertainty, is the potential for dramatically negative consequences from rapid climate change resulting from human use of carbon-based energy. In late 2013 and again in late 2015, large parts of China were dramatically affected by large particulate air pollution, leading to shutting down many of the normal economic functions of several major cities. These negative consequences are directly connected to the operation of the Chinese economy. China uses quite dirty coal to generate 70 percent of its electricity and, although coal is plentiful in China, the nation imports about 30 percent of its requirements from Australia, and these transactions account for 16 percent of Australia's exports. The economic gains from coal make any rapid alteration in the use of coal very difficult. China (and India) represent the extreme end of the continuum of dirty air, but the effects of pollution on the entire planet are likely to be significant and even extremely bad for almost everyone. This is a crisis where there is no place to hide, even for the very rich.[9] At the same time, we can be sure that the costs of climate change will be disproportionately borne by the poorest of the earth.

Looming on the horizon are economic disruptions from climate change that will be impossible to avoid. The difficulties in China, while inconvenient and even potentially deadly, pale in comparison to the possible effects of rapid climate change. These forms of climate change have happened in the past and the climatic system on the Earth is such that tipping points can and already have been reached, mainly as a consequence of rising levels of gases released from burning fossil fuels. The extinction of multiple species from rising temperatures, some of which play a crucial role in ecological systems, has been happening for several years. Perhaps the most likely events relate to extreme weather changes that render previously productive areas, such as land for cultivation and estuaries for fishing, much less productive or even not productive at all. Once such tipping points have been reached, they can even begin to cumulate to generate new forms of effects we cannot now anticipate. The range of uncertainty about the potential for such events is large, but the consequences are so immense for the global economy that conservative and prudent humans need to take steps to reduce the chances.

Unfortunately, there is limited evidence of such willingness, and the probability of catastrophic events rises with inaction. Even the decisions in Paris to develop global plans for limiting global warming may be too little, too late.[10] Humans are not likely to make major adjustments in the absence of brutally obvious evidence, that is, after the fact. Thus, any economic prediction for the coming years must include the possibility of significant economic disruption from drastic weather and ecological events. In political terms, these issues often play out in a conflict between those with a significant economic interest in fossil fuels and those who call for rapid and radical restructuring to shift the kinds and amount of energy we consume. Allied with the former are those consumers – most of us in rich nations – who are able to heat and cool homes, cook food, and travel using fossil fuels at a relatively low cost. We enjoy these benefits today even as we defer the costs onto generations (maybe even ourselves) in the near future. Quickly joining this coalition are the rising numbers of consumers in emerging market economies who have a similar set of interests in fossil fuels. The bond between producers and consumers is strong and powerful, creating a major barrier to change. Few governments are willing to endure the political and economic pain to reap a seemingly distant and diffuse benefit.[11]

Closely related to climate change, but with a more regional and longer-term perspective, is the overall carrying capacity of the earth. The destructive power of humans on our planet, through the processes of globalization, is immense and growing. The truly sad part is with the commitment of a relatively small amount of resources – perhaps 2 percent of global GDP – much of the negative impact could be dramatically ameliorated. This amounts to a lot of money, but the rich world alone could afford this, and yet we humans are so shortsighted and so selfish that we typically cannot act to save even ourselves until it is too late. Our record of collective commitment to solving these problems is poor and not improving. To be sure, we are asking humans to do something with no precedent in human history. And we are asking those – rich and poor – whose daily well-being is linked to these same destructive actions to make changes and sacrifices. For all the reasons we have considered in this book, solving global problems faces huge obstacles: collective action, differential gains and losses, differential capacity to bear the costs, local and regional issues, competing nations and the absence of global government, generalized but low levels of citizen concern, the tragedy of the commons, free riders, denial, short-term incentives, and simplistic thinking.[12] The outcome of the efforts to achieve sustainable development through international diplomacy can be summarized as "more talk and less action." Most families in rich nations purchase insurance on lives and property. Perhaps if we could think of the saving of the planet in relation to an insurance policy, which prudent and conservative people buy all the time, we could improve the chances for action.

The Fate of Globalization

Another of the most important features of international political economy and this book is the emphasis on taking a long historical perspective for understanding the global economy. You have learned about the changes in the form of the global economy as a consequence of the revolution in manufacturing, steam technology, and communications in the nineteenth century. And you can now appreciate how globalization has expanded and contracted and itself taken different forms over the past two centuries. So, asking whether globalization can continue cannot be a surprising question.

Globalization happens because powerful nations and firms promote it to reap the gains from this process. The gains from globalization for these nations and firms in recent decades have certainly been large, suggesting that it will continue. We have argued that China and other emerging economies, somewhat surprisingly, have been among the largest winners, creating new and powerful interests in perpetuating and expanding a global economy. We have also seen how the recent form of globalization has been quite different from that in the nineteenth century. Then, one of the main forces in globalization was imperialism – which involved the forced taking of territories and incorporating these areas into the economy of the imperialist nation, usually on somewhat exploitative terms. The globalization of the last four decades has been organized quite differently. Poor nations have welcomed the firms of rich nations because they brought investment, access to foreign markets, and, more importantly, knowledge, which could be leveraged into rapid growth. A close partnership of national governments and global firms emerged. Also facilitating globalization was the fragmentation of the value chain and the distribution of the process of production to many nations, thereby lowering the barriers to entry to participation in the global economy.

The first great wave of globalization in the nineteenth century was brought to a halt about a century ago as a result of World War I. During the twenty years after war began in 1914, nations acted to shield themselves from the global economy and the result was a retreat from globalization. What followed was an even more devastating conflict brought on by aggressive and expansionist capitalist states. Today, there is some reason to expect the broad set of interests supporting globalization will resist the potential for war as a way of resolving conflict in order to prevent the same outcome as in the past. The more likely force undermining globalization at present is the inability of national leaders to act to control the negative externalities of globalization: global warming, rising income inequality, resource depletion, population growth, and the disruptive effects on people's lives.

The other great force affecting globalization is technology. In the period from the 1970s to the early twenty-first century, technological change largely favored poor nations with a combination of large labor pools and decent to improving infrastructure. New forms of communication and management led to a massive shift of low-skilled jobs to these kinds of nations and rapid growth. To an increasing extent, this has begun to change with the rise of smart machines able to make products with much lower labor input. Visit a steel mill in Shanghai, an auto factory in Georgetown, Kentucky, a motorbike factory in Hanoi, or a noodle factory in Tianjin and you will be surprised at the small number of workers.[13] As the labor value in products declines and as wages in emerging economies such as China increase, it has become profitable to return some manufacturing to the United States. But this shift now comes without the large number of low-skilled jobs. Rather, there is a small number of very high-skilled jobs for those persons who can manage and program these very sophisticated machines doing the actual production. In this case, technology rebalances the economic equation between China and the United States but exacerbates the distributional effects between owners of capital and knowledge and those who offer only their muscle power.[14] How this new trend in technology will affect the global economy remains unclear, but its impact on class relations is likely to be negative and perhaps will erode further support for globalization.

The processes of economic globalization have important but sometimes indirect and unexpected political consequences, some of which pose a significant threat to globalization. One of the most interesting is the increasing importance in many advanced nations of identity politics, in which national or local cultures are threatened as a result of advancing globalization, often in the form of immigration or through the mixing of cultures from trade and tourism. Right-wing populism in the United States with the Tea Party, and in Europe with the Danish People's Party, the Law and Justice Party in Poland, or the French National Front has been politically effective in mobilizing those who feel threatened by the encroachment of different peoples and cultures. Often these feelings are mixed together with economic fears associated with global economic competition or potential changes in welfare benefits.[15] The Brexit vote in Britain and the presidential candidacies of Donald Trump and Bernie Sanders also provide a striking challenge to globalizing elites and to the broad direction of global policy since 1945. The specter of a reversal of trade, immigration, security alliance, and global integration efforts is not likely to be easily altered without some form of significant policy accommodation to those groups harmed by globalization. The unraveling of the global economic and security system would almost surely lead to greater conflict and declining global growth. Neoliberal elites promoting globalization have long been blind to dealing with the negative effects; to continue in this fashion poses a threat to everyone.

Populist forms of anti-globalization may rise and fall with economic distress and growth. But this time may be different. The continuation of a protracted era of low growth, with continuing redistribution of income and wealth, has the potential for the development of a major backlash against globalization, especially if also combined with the negative effects of global climate change.[16] What can we expect for globalization? The best estimate is the interests of powerful nations and firms will adjust to the challenges to globalization and will continue to support the preservation of a relatively open global economy, and technology will continue to create cost advantages from operating across borders. At the same time, technology is also likely to produce difficult to manage restructuring of domestic and global economies. And the near certainty of large negative consequences from climate change will add to the stress on the global system of the political economy. Once the gains from globalization begin to decline, the constraints of interdependence on nations may also wither and the potential for rising international conflict may return.

What of International Political Economy?

This book has provided a detailed tour of globalization through the lens of international political economy. Now you may want to step back and develop some additional perspective on this process by considering one of the main controversies within international political economy. This concerns how such studies should and should not proceed. We will consider some of these issues by examining the disputes over theory and methodology in international political economy. This involves a focus on the strengths and weaknesses, as we see them, of some of the main approaches to international political economy. You may want to give some thought to how and whether the topics of this book could be studied differently and more effectively using different theories and methods of analysis. The study of international political economy is made very exciting by an appreciation of the intellectual disputes that mark both the richness of inquiry and the importance of the issues under debate.

Much is often made of Robert Gilpin's now decades-old division of international political economy into intellectual camps of liberalism, realism (mercantilism), and radicalism. But the actual practice of international political economy today is much more differentiated and complex, as is the behavior of firms and nations.[17] In this book, we have acknowledged these categories but have not felt ourselves bound by them. For example, we have repeatedly described how there are no purely liberal nations. All advanced nations permit and encourage free markets for many products and services. At the same time, these same nations engage in repeated and significant market interventions to transfer income and wealth, manage the terms for market exchange, participate in efforts to create economic resources such as innovation and education, create rules that affect international trade, protect citizens from environmental damage, and support one group over another. It is also true that nations differ significantly in the degree to which and the way in which these actions are taken. At best, liberalism, realism, and radicalism are ideal types – intellectual constructs designed to highlight certain features of policy or action – that can be used as a baseline for discussion.

Though scholars may be a little more consistent in their thinking, there are very few pure liberals who would either deny or dispute the points just made. Instead, most scholarly work in international political economy begins with a theoretical perspective that is far more nuanced than the three categories would suggest with the ideas of free markets, state interests, or class struggle. At various points in this book, we have woven together all three ideas into the same analysis. Very few scholars would succumb to either worshiping free markets or condemning them completely. This is not to say that ideological conflict among various interests does not often descend into such behavior. Though the academic world is often influenced by the ideological world of clashing interests, it cannot and should not be reduced to the level of mere ideology.

This is because you cannot understand more than a small part of what happens in the world of nations, firms, and economies from the lens of only one of these ideal types. Ideologues may try to spin all events to conform to their preferred worldview, but scholars have a higher calling, namely an obligation to work toward as accurate and complete an understanding as is possible. Indeed, it was this very point – the striking limitations for understanding what was happening in the 1970s – that led to the development of international political economy in the first place. And the importance of this effort is even greater today.

How can we understand the Global Financial Crisis if we only consider state interests or free markets or class relations? We would need to leave out the allocative power and success of financial markets, the structural power of finance, the political and economic importance of economic stabilization, the dramatic asymmetries of power and privilege that are starkly revealed from these events, and the deep connections between governments and markets. The value of international political economy comes from the eclecticism in bringing these and other perspectives to bear on such events and not from the clash of paradigms that some might prefer. Should we follow the lead with any one of the three perspectives, we would be equally deficient in trying to understand the nature of Chinese capitalism, the development of preferential trade agreements, efforts to cooperate in developing global environmental policies, or almost any other important global issue. This is not to say that many advocates of policy, bound to a particular set of interests, typically spin their arguments to conform to the narrow thinking of an ideology. The value of international political economy is that it incorporates, integrates, and moves beyond such shallow understanding.

Open Economy Politics as a "Dominant" International Political Economy Perspective

Nevertheless, a case can be made for adopting a somewhat more narrow and less complex perspective for analysis. Yet, even this effort advances far beyond the tripartite Gilpin schema. Several leading scholars in international political economy have declared one emergent perspective to be the "dominant approach" and the "single, unifying paradigm" for international political economy: the Open Economy Politics (OEP) perspective.[18] This perspective operates to define somewhat narrowly the questions to be asked and the kinds of answers that can be given by scholars of international political economy. By narrowing the scope of international political economy and the mode of analysis, "scientific accumulation" is thought to be enhanced. This comes from having a community of scholars focused on the same questions and developing answers based on the same methodology. Though a commendable goal, it is not clear whether international political economy or most social sciences have reached a point where such narrowing is possible or valuable.

Two primary questions are asked by the OEP perspective: (1) "how, when, and why do countries choose to open themselves to transborder flows of goods and services, capital, and people?" and (2) "how does integration (or not) into the international economy affect the interests of individuals, sectors, factors of production, or countries and, in turn, national policies?" These are questions certainly worthy of considerable inquiry, but may not be sufficient to define the entirety of international political economy, nor even the principal direction of research. Equally important is the theoretical perspective OEP brings to bear on these questions. OEP adopts the approach of neoclassical economics and trade theory to develop answers to these questions. This means assuming, most importantly, the primacy of the interests of various groups in driving outcomes and the sources of these interests in economic relationships. Thus, the political interests of firms, sectors, factors of production, and even nations are derived from the economic interests of these actors as they are positioned in relationship to the global economy.

The effort to explain the choices related to economic opening is linked to the ways such policies affect various firms, sectors, or factors; that is, do these entities gain or lose from such policies? OEP works to predict interests from assumptions about the production profile of different groups and thereby how these groups will benefit or lose from opening policies. Firms can be distinguished in terms of how their products compete (or not) in the global economy, and factors in terms of their relative scarcity or abundance in relation to the global economy. The competing interests of winners and losers are filtered through political institutions, and assumptions about this process are used to predict whether a policy will be adopted. The main points of contention in OEP relate to determining the appropriate groups which share common interests associated with economic opening: firms, sectors, or factors of production.

Getting to policy by deducing the interests of different groups within the economy requires some sense of the political process associated with political institutions that aggregate interests and structure bargaining. Institutions provide information about power relationships among different economic groups, often through the processes by which policy is made. Will this be through votes, bribes, or ideology; will there be large or small constituencies and many or few veto points; and do institutions provide compensation to groups and firms that lose from policy choices? OEP has also considered how the distribution of gains from globalization and opening can affect political struggles over the locus of political decisions and the shape of domestic institutions. Though OEP has identified many factors affecting how conflicting interests are translated into policy, this has not led to substantial precision in predicting actual policy outcomes.

In addition to domestic institutions, international institutions and bargaining among states also affect policy choices and outcomes, and OEP has extended its thinking here as well. Scholars consider the manner and extent to which international institutions facilitate cooperation among bargaining nations and provide a context for structuring the bargaining conflict over the distribution of gains and losses among nations. But international institutions may also act to affect domestic interests within nations. The impact of WTO membership for China's calculation of the gains from international opening could be significant.

OEP has also considered a set of interesting issues involving strategic behavior relating to economic opening. These include efforts by one nation through economic opening to affect the distribution of gains and therefore the configuration of political interests in another nation. In the 1840s, the British decision to repeal the Corn Laws and open their economy included expectations that sectional agricultural interests in the United States would become motivated to align and reciprocate by voting to reduce tariffs as well. Similar effects can be seen in agricultural protectionism and in decisions relating to the opening to capital flows in the contemporary world. In addition, economies of scale in various industries – in which costs per unit of production fall significantly as output rises – can lead to distortions in the distributions of gains and therefore interests. More important, strategic efforts by the state to promote an industry with large economies of scale can lead to a created comparative advantage and to the ability to dominate globally through lower costs. A contemporary example of this comes from Chinese government subsidies to solar power panel producers and a subsequent drop in costs per unit as a means to capture global market share.[19]

OEP provides an important arena for research and has advanced our understanding of the international political economy of globalization and opening. Many scholars, from a variety of perspectives, have contributed to research framed around the approach of OEP. The dynamics associated with significant economic change, as from expanding global markets and the opening of national economies to trade and investment, is an exceptionally important part of the study of international political economy. And yet, evaluating OEP as the core and predominant approach of international political economy, as its proponents have claimed, creates a very high standard.

How well do we understand these dynamics with a theory rooted in the narrowly defined interests of economic actors? First, there are many cases in which much can be learned from the examination of the political relationships among the winners and losers from economic liberalization.[20] At the same time, there is much that is lost from this perspective. As with almost all theories based in neoclassical economics, there is little to be said about state interests and calculations, and yet states are clearly key players in these processes.[21] Equally important, international political economy must consider the impact of global systems, as systems, because these relationships very frequently confound the efforts of individual interests and even states to achieve their purposes.[22] The bargaining relationship among states can even play a key role in the definition of state interests, apart from the interests of domestic groups.[23] A third significant limitation of OEP is its near exclusive emphasis on democratic societies, where domestic interests can be (somewhat) realistically assumed to have a major impact on policy. OEP assumptions have much less applicability to non-democratic and authoritarian societies, such as China. The analysis of the domestic sources of free trade policies in non-democratic societies can require important variations on the OEP theoretical agenda.[24] Leaving out states, as states, and international systems, as systems, and focusing only on democratic societies can be justified by OEP scholars only if these forces have limited effects on outcomes and the theoretical perspective of OEP gives us a large (or even complete) part of an understanding of outcomes. There are good reasons to doubt this. Indeed, as we have discussed, some of the trends in OEP research already acknowledge the limitations of the existing approach, by branching into examination of how the domestic interests of a nation and its choices are linked to the choices of other nations and the effects of global institutions. That is, these interests and choices can be defined by their global production profile but must be seen as part of a larger political and economic system.

How differently have we in this book explained globalization and its outcomes? Earlier in this chapter, we provided a summary of the origins of globalization, which had important parallels with OEP. Like OEP, we also find the analysis framed by the political struggle among winners and losers from globalization to be instructive. And we find an analysis of the political dynamics and relationships among these interests to provide important insights.

But there are also important points of departure from OEP that fill in much of the valuable details left out by a reliance on this perspective. One is that interests relating to economic liberalization are constructed in a political process and not simply a result of inferred economic gains and losses.[25] We have emphasized the historical process creating a partnership relationship of advanced states and large transnational corporations (TNCs), especially global banks, a partnership somewhat organized by state actors but also defined by the structural power of finance in a capitalist society.[26] The ability of large global banks to escape regulation and provide financial support to states tipped the scales of policy in the 1960s and 1970s to one much more favorable to these interests. At the same time, in the 1980s the US and British governments were able to recast international strategy so as to reap new gains from the structural power of expanding global markets. The choices by many nations in the 1980s and 1990s to expand opening to the global economy, including the series of choices by the Chinese state, were heavily influenced by this same structural power related to access to US markets, global TNCs, and the technology and knowledge they possessed.

Equally important were the political dynamics related to the considerable pressure applied by the US government to encourage policies of opening.[27] Moreover, globalization is not confined just to decisions by states to open their economies but equally important requires active management by states, especially during times of economic crisis. The relationships of cooperation and conflict among states during the recent Global Financial Crisis involved managing events so as to preserve and often exploit various forms of structural power. A very important example is the effort to stimulate the US economy through Quantitative Easing by the US Federal Reserve, with the effects of artificially boosting and distorting the financial systems in emerging economies; and the actions to develop new forms of financial leverage by China in order to protect itself from the actions of the United States.[28]

The perspectives of this book, drawn from international political economy, offer a broader conception of politics and power, in particular a much broader sense of the political arrangements available to the powerful, an explanation more sensitive to the contingencies of events, less determined by simple generalizations about power and institutions,[29] and acknowledging the broader systemic effects that affect and distort choices and preferences by states, firms, and sectors. Our criticism of OEP is more about its narrow, somewhat mechanical and idealized sense of political economy, especially the relationship of state interests to domestic socioeconomic interests, but also its neoclassical conception of markets.[30] The neoliberal understanding of political economy is based on an idealization of democracy: pressure group lobbying. However, the pattern of relationship of the most powerful economic interests to states – perhaps especially the United States – is often one of partnership, in which the economic interests of firms are accommodated to the interests of state actors through a global economic strategy.[31] States are also key agents of market-shaping policies. Domestic economic systems have often been constructed through concerted state action, especially in emerging economies.[32] Global markets are frequently constructed by the largest of states and firms and can be manipulated by these actors; but these same actions often have pernicious consequences for all involved and must then be rebuilt and restructured through the actions of states, sometimes in partnerships with firms.[33] At the same time, the recent financial crisis shows the limits of control even very powerful states can exert over global markets.[34]

In short, there is much to be said for resisting an exclusive or a predominant perspective offered by OEP and thereby incorporating a range of competing ideas, often through a much more eclectic analysis. International political economy has much to say about the global economy and its development and pluralism in practice, and in theory, will keep this new field alive and well.

Key Concepts (see Glossary)

Open Economy Politics (OEP)

Discussion Questions

1   What are some of the key features of the new global economy? How are these different from the past?

2   How can we describe the broad features of income changes resulting from globalization? How does international political economy provide explanations for these patterns, especially through a consideration of power and markets?

3   How does international political economy offer an important perspective for understanding the origins and consequences of the Global Financial Crisis?

4   What conclusions can we reach about the significance of the strategic interests of the most powerful states in shaping the global economy?

5   Explain how "the unremitting demands on most nations to restructure their economies to keep pace with rapid and far-reaching technological, political, organizational and economic changes" can affect the policies and actions of nations.

6   How does international political economy offer insights into the potential for various nations to achieve economic growth in the coming decades?

7   How does international political economy offer a perspective on the political capacity to respond effectively to climate change?

8   How does analysis of the economic interests of powerful states give us a basis for predicting the continuation of globalization?

9   How do you react to the discussion of OEP and the issues raised about how to study international political economy?

Notes

1   Pankaj Mishra, "Which India Matters?" *New York Review of Books*, November 21, 2013, 51–3.

2   Harald Bauer et al., "Moore's Law: Repeal or Renew?" *Insights and Publications*, McKinsey & Company (December 2013), www.mckinsey.com/Insights/
High_Tech_Telecoms_Internet/Moores_law_Repeal_or_renewal?cid=other-eml-alt-mip-mck-oth–1312

3   *The Economist*, "A Shrinking Slice," November 2, 2013, www.economist.com/news/
leaders/21588860-labours-share-national-income-has-fallen-right-remedy-help-workers-not-punish

4   *The Economist*, "Labour Pains," November 2, 2013, www.economist.com/news/
finance-and-economics/21588900-all-around-world-labour-losing-out-capital-labour-pains

5   Federal Reserve Bank of the US, www.federalreserve.gov/releases/h41/Current/

6   Shyam Saran, "Quantitative Easing: Impact on Emerging and Developing Economies," *Inter Press Service*, June 5, 2013, www.ipsnews.net/2013/06/quantitative-easing-impact-on-emerging-and-developing-economies/

7   National Academy of Sciences, "Abrupt Impacts of Climate Change: Anticipating Surprises," December 2013, www.nap.edu/catalog.php?record_id=18373. Justin Gillis, "U.N. Says Lag in Confronting Climate Woes Will Be Costly," *New York Times*, January 16, 2014, www.nytimes.com/2014/01/17/science/earth/un-says-lag-in-confronting-climate-woes-will-be-costly.
html?hp&_r=0. For the debate about the existence of tipping points in global climate, see Barry W. Brook et al., "Does the Terrestrial Biosphere Have Planetary Tipping Points?" *Trends in Ecology & Evolution*, 2013.

8   *The Economist*, "The Future of Jobs: The Onrushing Wave," January 18, 2014, www.economist.com/news/briefing/21594264-previous-technological-innovation-has-always-delivered-more-long-run-employment-not-less;   Erik Brynjolfsson and Andrew McAfee, *The Second Machine Age*, New York: Norton, 2014.

9   Our research and this book give little credence to the self-serving palliatives of the fossil fuel industries and to those who look to these groups for

guidance on climate science. Within the scientific community, there is no debate on the role of humans in affecting climate. Rather, discussion now is focused on the magnitude and speed of the consequences.

10 A more optimistic view is found at *The Economist*, "Deal Done," December 12, 2015, www.economist.com/news/international/21683990-paris-agreement-climate-change-talks?zid=301&ah=e8eb01e57f7c9b43a3c864613973b57f

11 Michael Klare, "Three Signs of Retreat in the Global War on Climate Change," *The Huffington Post*, February 15, 2014, www.huffingtonpost.com/michael-t-klare/signs-of-retreat-on-climate-change_b_4780835.html

12 Deborah Yashar, "Globalization and Collective Action," *Comparative Politics*, 34.3 (April 2002) 355–75.

13 Stephanie Clifford, "U.S. Textile Plants Return, with Floors Largely Empty of People," *New York Times*, September 19, 2013, www.nytimes.com/2013/09/20/business/us-textile-factories-return.html?pagewanted=all&_r=0

14 Brynjolfsson and McAfee, *The Second Machine Age. The Economist*, "Closing the Gap: America's Labour Market Has Suffered Permanent Harm," February 15, 2014, www.economist.com/news/finance-and-economics/21596529-americas-labour-market-has-suffered-permanent-harm-closing-gap

15 Yotam Margalit. "Lost in Globalization: International Economic Integration and the Sources of Popular Discontent," *International Studies Quarterly*, 56 (2012) 484–500; Andrew Higgins, "Right Wing's Surge in Europe Has the Establishment Rattled," *New York Times*, November 8, 2013, www.nytimes.com/2013/11/09/world/europe/right-wings-surge-in-europe-has-the-establishment-rattled.html?pagewanted=1&hp. Also see, Nate Cohn, "Right-Wing Populism is Prevailing in Left-Wing Strongholds Around the World," *New York Times*, June 27, 2016.

16 Neil Irwin, "We're In a Low-Growth World. How Did We Get Here?" *New York Times*, August 6, 2016.

17 Matthew Watson, "Theoretical Traditions in Global Political Economy," in John Ravenhill (ed.), *Global Political Economy*, Oxford: Oxford University Press, 2nd ed., 2008, 27–66.

18 The overview of OEP relies on David Lake's discussion in two similar articles. David Lake, "International Political Economy: A Maturing Interdiscipline," in Barry R. Weingast and Donald Wittman (eds), *The Oxford Handbook of Political Economy*, New York: Oxford University Press, 2008, 757–77; and David Lake, "Open Economy Politics: A Critical Review," *Review of International Organizations*, 4 (2009) 219–44.

19 Usha Haley and George Haley, *Subsidies to Chinese Industry: State Capitalism, Business Strategy and Trade Policy*, Oxford: Oxford University Press, 2013.

20 Mireya Solis, "Can FTAs Deliver Market Liberalization in Japan? A Study on Domestic Political Determinants," *Review of International Political Economy*, 17.2 (May 2010) 209–37.

21 Vivien Schmidt, "Putting the Political Back Into Political Economy by Bringing the State Back In Yet Again," *World Politics*, 61.3 (July 2009) 516–46. At best, OEP treats states as institutions that may passively affect outcomes through rules that affect domestic interests. The possibility of state interests formed apart from some aggregation of social interests is not part of the analysis. For an example of state interests affecting opening decisions, see Thomas Richter, "When Do Autocracies Start to Liberalize Foreign Trade?" *Review of International Political Economy*, 20.4 (2013) 760–87.

22 Thomas Oatley, "The Reductionist Gamble: Open Economy Politics in the Global Economy," *International Organization*, 65 (Spring 2011) 311–41. Robert Jervis, *System Effects: Complexity in Political and Social Life*,

Princeton: Princeton University Press, 1997. As an obvious example, consider the importance of transnational policy networks. David Bach and Abraham Newman, "Transgovernmental Networks and Domestic Policy Convergence: Evidence from Insider Trading Regulation," *International Organization*, 64.3 (Summer 2010) 505–28.

23 John Ravenhill, "The New East Asian Regionalism: A Political Domino Effect," *Review of International Political Economy*, 17.2 (May 2010) 178–208.

24 Yang Jiang, "China's Pursuit of Free Trade Agreements: Is China Exceptional?" *Review of International Political Economy*, 17.2 (May 2010) 238–61.

25 Cornelia Woll, *Firm Interests*, Ithaca: Cornell University Press, 2008.

26 Carole Biau, "Whose Globalization is it Anyway?" *Review of International Political Economy*, 16.2 (May 2009) 350–70.

27 Oatley, "The Reductionist Gamble," focuses on systemic forces that affect choices and outcomes unnoticed by the OEP approach. The discussion of contagion effects – in which characteristics of the system affect the probability of speculative attacks on a currency – is especially important.

28 Leonardo Martinez-Diaz, *Globalizing in Hard Times*, Ithaca: Cornell University Press, 2009.

29 Juliet Johnson et al., "The Future of International Political Economy," *Review of International Political Economy*, 20.5 (2013) 1009–23.

30 Kathleen McNamara, "Of Intellectual Monocultures and the Study of IPE," *Review of International Political Economy*, 16.1 (February 2009) 72–84.

31 The recent global financial crisis is a clear example, but there are many others. David Tyfield, "Enabling TRIPs: The Pharma-Biotech-University Patent Coalition," *Review of International Political Economy*, 15.4 (October 2008) 533–66.

32 Ben Ross Schneider, "A Comparative Political Economy of Diversified Business Groups: or How States Organize Big Business," *Review of International Political Economy*, 16.2 (May 2009) 178–201.

33 Hubert Buch-Hansen and Angela Wigger, "Revisiting 50 Years of Market-Making: The Neoliberal Transformation of European Competition Policy," *Review of International Political Economy*, 17.1 (February 2010) 20–44.

34 Scholars have noted how the narrowness of OEP is reflected in the muteness regarding the origins of the global financial crisis. Peter Katzenstein and Stephen Nelson, "Reading the Right Signals and Reading the Signals Right: IPE and the Financial Crisis of 2008," *Review of International Political Economy*, 20.5 (2013) 1101–31.

Further Reading

Juliet Johnson, *Priests of Prosperity: How Central Bankers Transformed the Postcommunist World*, Ithaca: Cornell University Press, 2016.
Considers how central bank actors were able to redefine norms and rules for other central bank actors in postcommunist regimes.

Barry Naughton and Kellee Tsai (eds), *State Capitalism, Institutional Adaptation, and the Chinese Miracle*, Cambridge: Cambridge University Press, 2015.
A collection of readings providing perspective on the ability of states to define a wide array of economic choices.

Deepak Nayar, *Catch Up: Developing Countries in the World Economy*, Oxford: Oxford University Press, 2013.
Offers an exceptional analysis and explanation for the shifts in the global distribution of income and wealth since 1820.

John Ravenhill (ed.), *Global Political Economy*, Oxford: Oxford University Press, 2nd ed., 2008.
An exceptional and diverse collection of essays considering the state of scholarship in international political economy.

Glossary

Absolute Advantage   The ability of one nation to produce a particular good more efficiently than another nation. See also Comparative Advantage.

Absolute Gains   A relationship in which both parties to an exchange can improve their position relative to their initial starting points. International cooperation is easier to organize when all parties can realize absolute gains. See also relative gains.

ASEAN Free Trade Agreement (AFTA)   An agreement among ASEAN nations that involves common tariffs among the members but nationally set tariffs for external trade.

Association of Southeast Asian Nations (ASEAN)   An organization of ten nations in Southeast Asia involving cooperation on political and economic issues.

Asymmetrical Interdependence   A form of mutual dependence between two parties in which one partner is more dependent upon the relationship than the other. The less dependent party holds potential leverage over the more dependent party.

Autarchy   An economic policy designed to promote an extreme version of economic self-sufficiency. This leads to closing off domestic markets from external trade as well as severely restricting exports. Such a policy frequently is designed to defend the nation against political and ideological imports that accompany trade along with organization of the economy for war.

Balance of Payments   An accounting system designed to measure all transactions a nation has with the rest of the world over some period of time. See also Current Account; Capital Account.

Border Effects   The dampening effect of political borders on the intensity of economic exchange.

Bretton Woods System   A set of new institutions and regimes for global economic management created by a meeting of major governments at Bretton Woods, New Hampshire. These included a system of fixed exchange rates, the International Monetary Fund (IMF), and the World Bank, and set the stage for the International Trade Organization.

Budget Deficit/Surplus   These are outcomes of fiscal policy. A *deficit* in the government accounts occurs when spending exceeds tax revenues, a *surplus* occurs when revenues exceed spending.

Capital Account   An item in the balance of payments that measures the investment of resources abroad and in the home country by foreigners. See also Direct Foreign Investment; Portfolio Investment.

Capital Accumulation   The process in a capitalist society by which investment capital is created and located in the hands of those able to make choices about how to allocate these resources.

Capital Controls   A system of regulations and controls enacted by a government restricting or even prohibiting moving capital (money) into or out of a nation.

Capitalism   A system of economic organization in which capital is systematically accumulated and allocated to economically rational and efficient investments.

Capital Liberalization   The process of removing and/or reducing capital controls.

Carrying Capacity   Refers to the maximum sustainable rate of resource extraction for a given geographical area. When the carrying capacity of a given area is exceeded, the long-term ability of the land to sustain future generations is compromised.

Central Bank   All advanced nations have a government-owned bank with the responsibility for managing the money supply and acting as the lender of last resort to banks.

Class   Groups of individuals who share the same relationship to the means of production, such as workers and owners.

Collateralized Debt Obligations (CDOs)   A derivative backed by other assets, which generate a regular stream of income. An important example is a CDO backed by a bundle of home mortgages.

Collective Goods   Benefits that meet two strict requirements: consumption by any one person or nation does not reduce the supply of the good, and no one can be excluded from consumption. An important issue in the theory of hegemony is the nature and extent to which hegemons provide collective goods to the international system.

Collective Interests   Interests shared by the largest number of people in a society. Such interests may or may not be consistent with the interests of each individual.

Command Economy   A system of political economy in most communist states in which decisions about what to produce and about prices for goods are made by central political authorities.

Commercial Services   A component of measuring global trade involving various kinds of services, which are non-tangible but valuable products that support merchandise trade and provide value for transactions. Examples include transportation, communication and telecommunications, and insurance, financial, and computer services.

Common Agricultural Policy (CAP) An important form of protectionism and income support for farmers in the European Community. Arranged in the 1950s and 1960s, CAP provides for funds to maintain high prices for farm products and for tariffs to protect these prices from external competition. See also European Community.

Commonwealth of Independent States (CIS) The successor political organization to the Soviet Union, organized late in 1991. The character, composition, and durability of this organization remain unclear.

Comparative Advantage A situation affecting global trade in which one nation has relative advantages in the production of a particular good or service.

Competitiveness
Firm – the ability to achieve profitability through its efforts in global markets in relation to other firms.
Nation – the ability to achieve economic growth and a rising standard of living when substantially exposed to the global economy through trade and capital flows.

Complex Interdependence A theoretical model of international relations that contrasts with traditional models of realism. Complex interdependence posits a world where economic issues are not less important than security issues, where linkages among nations reduce government control over foreign affairs, and where military power is essentially unimportant.

Cooperation A situation in which two or more nations bargain over modifying their behavior and/or preferences in order to receive some reciprocal act from each other. The aim of these complementary concessions is coordination of their actions in order to gain some benefit they cannot have alone.

Corn Laws A set of tariff laws on agricultural imports in Great Britain during the nineteenth century. Repeal of these laws ushered in a British policy of free trade.

Credit Default Swaps (CDSs) A financial arrangement that functions somewhat like an insurance policy, in which one party (the seller) agrees to compensate a creditor (the buyer) in the event of a default on a loan this creditor has made.

Creditor Nation This is a measurement of a nation's net foreign position which indicates that it holds more assets abroad than foreigners hold of its assets. See also Debtor Nation.

Currency Appreciation/Depreciation Terms that refer to a currency rising in value (in terms of its exchange rate) or falling in value.

Currency Convertibility A policy choice for each government that permits the currency to be traded in global financial markets. See also Exchange Rates.

Current Account This is a summary item in the balance of payments that measures the net of exports and imports of merchandise and services, investment income and payments, and government transactions.

Deficit – a situation in which items such as imports and other negative items in the current account exceed positive items such as exports.

Surplus – a situation in which items such as exports and other positive items in the current account exceed negative items such as imports.

Dawes Plan A proposal made in 1924 by a private US citizen, Charles Dawes, calling for a reduction in reparation payments made by Germany to Britain and France and loans by US banks to Germany.

Debtor Nation This is a measurement of a nation's net foreign position that indicates that it holds fewer assets abroad than foreigners hold of its assets. See also Creditor Nation.

Deep Interdependence Denotes a global system of exceptionally strong connections among states and firms. This comes from the multiple, cross-cutting, and reinforcing forms of economic and political relationships among states and firms. Trade and investment networks, knowledge and information networks, negotiated rules, regimes, institutions and governance, and people exchange create tightly coupled, complementary, and thick networks and relationships that affect the interests and preferences of states and firms.

Defense Advanced Research Projects Agency (DARPA) A unit of the US Defense Department formed in the wake of Sputnik and charged with advancing the technological prowess of the United States.

Demographic Transition A theory which posits that rapid population growth begins when a country enters the initial stages of economic development, but later slows as incomes reach moderate levels and the economy matures.

Dependency A theory of development designed to explain the gap between living standards in the North and the South. Beginning with colonialism, Southern development has been constrained by the Third World's dependent or peripheral role in the international economy. North–South economic ties are marked by Northern exploitation of the South. Genuine, self-sustained economic development will require changes in the relationship of Southern countries to the international economic order.

Derivative A security, the value of which depends on the value of another security or asset.

Developmental State A particular kind of governmental strategy for achieving rapid economic growth based on significant engagement with the global economy and continuing efforts to upgrade the competitive capabilities of the nation and at least some of its firms. Typically, this involves a strong governmental commitment to achieving rapid economic growth, typically in order to enhance the security position of the nation.

Dirty Float   A system of floating exchange rates in which governments occasionally intervene to prevent unwanted swings in the price of their currency. See also Exchange Rate Systems.

Discount Rate   An anchor interest rate set by the Federal Reserve, which is the rate charged to member banks that borrow from a regional branch of the Fed. See also Central Bank.

Dispersion of Knowledge   The diffusion of advanced economic and technological knowledge across the world, primarily as a result of globalization.

Earth Summit   A milestone international environmental meeting held in 1992.

Economic and Monetary Union (EMU)   A term that refers to the elimination of all barriers to trade in the European Community by the end of 1992 and the development of a single currency later in the decade.

Economic Growth   An expansion of the production of goods and services in a nation.

Efficiency   An economic outcome of markets able to allocate resources to the most productive uses. Such a system should effectively link consumer demand and supply and produce products at the lowest cost.

Elasticity   A technique for being more precise in stating the relationship between a change in price and resulting changes in demand or supply. When percentage changes in the quantity of demand or supply are greater than percentage changes in price, we speak of an elastic demand (or supply) of a product. When percent changes in demand are less than percent changes in price, this is a case of inelastic demand. For purists, this can be seen in the slope of the demand (or supply) curve.

Embedded Liberalism   A system of domestic and international political economy developed after World War II, lasting about three decades. Arrangements emphasizing free markets were tempered by broad acceptance of limits on the ability of the world economy to influence developments in the domestic economy. Free trade was accepted only as a goal and widespread limits on capital flows permitted nations to formulate independent domestic economic policies.

Emerging Economies   A group of relatively poor nations able to achieve rapid and sustained economic growth during the latest era of globalization, after about 1980.

Eurocurrency (Eurodollar)   A development in the 1950s and 1960s in which dollars were deposited in European banks and came to be bought, sold, and borrowed. In the 1970s and 1980s, this expanded to include other currencies.

European Central Bank (ECB)   The central bank of the European Union.

European Currency Unit (ECU)   A weighted average of currencies in the Exchange Rate Mechanism of the European Community used as a benchmark to fix exchange rates among these nations.

European (Economic) Community (EC, EEC)   Officially begun in 1958, the European Economic Community established a set of stages for the elimination of tariffs and other barriers to trade. Originally composed of six nations, by 1986 the EEC expanded to twelve members and in 1991 agreed to add six additional members. In 1986, the nations of the EEC committed themselves to a single market by 1992 and to the political arrangements needed to achieve this result. After this decision, the EEC became known as the European Community. See also Common Agricultural Policy; European Currency Unit; Economic and Monetary Union; European Monetary System; Exchange Rate Mechanism.

European Monetary System (EMS)   A monetary arrangement created after the breakdown of the Bretton Woods system and designed to maintain a fixed exchange rate system among some of the countries in the European Community. See also European Currency Unit; Exchange Rate Mechanism.

European Union (EU)   The most important and far-reaching form of international political and economic integration. It is composed of twenty-eight nations, with 500 million people, and with various forms of common political decision-making processes along with systems for economic integration through a single market and a single currency (for some but not all nations), the euro.

Eurozone   The set of nations in the EU that have adopted the euro as their currency.

Exchange Rate Mechanism (ERM)   The specific means by which a system of fixed exchange rates is maintained in the European Monetary System. Exchange rates are tied to the European Currency Unit (with small room for fluctuation). Governments act to peg interest rates to those in Germany and intervene in foreign exchange markets to maintain the fixed value of their currency. See also European Currency Unit; European Monetary System.

Exchange Rate Systems   These systems are created by global markets for foreign exchange, which are composed of many traders, those purchasing foreign exchange for purposes of trade in goods and services, but mostly large institutions engaged in speculation. The variety of exchange rate systems include:

Fixed – governments intervene in foreign exchange markets to prevent little change in the value of their currency.

Floating – markets are mostly free, with supply and demand determining exchange rates.

Dirty Float – a system of floating exchange rates in which governments occasionally intervene to prevent unwanted swings in the price of their currency.

Export-Led Industrialization (ELI) Pursued most successfully by a group of East Asian newly industrializing countries, a strategy of Export-Led Industrialization focuses on the production of manufactured goods for export to Northern markets.

Factor of Production The primary inputs to the production of goods and services, typically land, physical labor, capital, and human capital.

Fast Follower A competitiveness strategy by firms and nations requiring the ability to rapidly emulate the products and processes of the most advanced firms.

Federal Reserve Bank The central bank of the United States.

Fed Funds Rate A key interest rate managed by the Federal Reserve, which is the rate member banks charge when lending to each other.

Financialization An increasing role for financial firms in the domestic economy of the United States and in the global economy. Some features include: the expansion of credit as a percent of the overall economy; the deregulation of finance; an increase in the number and size of financial firms; and the relative weight of these firms in generating profits and political power. The globalization of finance, with financial firms extending their operations to a global scale, was associated with the shifting of political power toward the largest financial firms in New York and London and was sustained through the use of US political power to press nations to liberalize their financial systems and to open them to global financial firms.

Fiscal Policy The taxing and spending policy of a government.

Foreign Direct Investment (FDI) An investment in a nation by foreigners in which real assets are purchased. These include real estate or plant and equipment assets and involve some effort to manage. See also Portfolio Investment.

Foreign Exchange Reserves Holdings of convertible and widely traded foreign currencies by a nation's central bank.

Fragmentation of the Value Chain Breaking up various elements of the value chain and offshore outsourcing them to an independent firm.

Free Trade A policy adopted by a nation that places few, if any, restrictions on the process of importing goods and services into a nation. Free trade is often contrasted with a policy of protectionism.

Free Trade Agreement A system of economic cooperation among nations in which tariffs, quotas, and other barriers to free trade are removed. Typically, this arrangement does not extend to establishing a common external tariff or to the development of elaborate institutions for cooperation.

General Agreement on Tariffs and Trade (GATT) A system of treaties among more than a hundred nations establishing rules for the conduct of international trade. Most rules relate to tariffs and quotas, though some arrangements have been made regarding other non-tariff barriers. The rules are the result of a series of negotiating sessions that began in the 1940s. See also Free Trade; Non-tariff Barrier.

General Purpose Technology　A set or system of related technologies that provide significant improvements in products and processes, usually through simultaneously lowering the costs and significantly enlarging the capabilities of products and processes.

Geoeconomics　An explanation for variation in development trajectories that emphasizes the effects of geography, climate, and other natural factors.

Gini Coefficient　A measure of inequality that ranges from 0 (perfect equality) to 1 (perfect inequality).

Global and Regional Production Networks (GRPNs)　A new system of production involving a partnership of TNCs, governments, and local firms to reorganize the scale and geography of production based on the capabilities of information technology. This requires creating local infrastructure and labor resources to attract FDI and a globalized management system operated by TNCs. This process is organized around national specialization in different elements of a fragmented value chain.

Global Commons　Resources that are shared in common among states, such as the seas and the atmosphere.

Global Economy　The system of economic exchange for the entire world.

Global Fund　International agency established to fight HIV/AIDS, Tuberculosis, and Malaria.

Globalization　The process of deepening and tightening of interdependence among actors in the world economy after 1973. Much higher levels of international financial transactions and increasing international production are key features.

Global Network Flagship Firm　The central firm in a global production network (GPN) because it organizes the relationships among suppliers, usually controls the brand and design of products, and reaps the largest profits from the network.

Global Production　A measure of the total production of goods and services by firms, whether inside or outside of the home country. This includes production for domestic consumption, production for export from any nation, and production for domestic consumption abroad.

Global Warming　The product of the build-up of heat-trapping gases in the atmosphere, global warming poses multiple threats to the environmental health of the planet and to the social, economic, and political stability of human populations.

Gold Standard　Generally, a system of domestic and international monetary relations during the nineteenth and early twentieth centuries.

Member nations defined their monetary unit in terms of a fixed amount of gold. The ratio of gold in the currencies of different countries thereby provided an exchange rate among these currencies.

Greenfield Investment   A form of FDI in which the foreign investing firm creates an entirely new business to operate in another nation.

Greenhouse Gases   Gases that serve to trap heat as they accumulate within the earth's atmosphere.

Green Revolution   The Green Revolution was launched with the introduction of high-yield strains of wheat, along with changed agricultural practices, in India, Pakistan, and Bangladesh in the 1960s. The Green Revolution helped to end the cycles of famine that had previously afflicted these countries.

Gross Domestic Product (GDP)   A common measure of the size of a nation's economy, this is the sum of all the goods and services produced in a nation over a period of time, usually one year.

Gross Fixed Capital Formation   An important measure of national investment in infrastructure related to production and includes expenditures on improvements for land, plant, equipment and machinery, roads, bridges, schools, hospitals, offices, and residential housing.

Group of 20 (G–20)   The Group of 20, formed in 1999, brings together finance ministers and central bankers from twenty major economies. Since 2011, the G–20 has held annual summit meetings of heads of state.

Hegemony   An international system in which one dominant state takes on the role of organizing and managing the world economic system. This means supplying capital, defining the rules for international trade, promoting political and military security, and having its money operate as a key currency.

Human Development Index (HDI)   A statistical tool for measuring and comparing national development and human welfare. Developed by the United Nations Development Program, the Human Development Index is a composite of four individual measures of human welfare: life expectancy, adult literacy, mean years of schooling, and per capita income, adjusted for the local cost of living. Scores on this composite index vary between 0 (the lowest measure of human development) and 1 (the highest measure of human development).

Illiberal States   A government that rejects at least some of the standards of a liberal society, substituting somewhat authoritarian rule and some of the trappings of democracy.

Imitation   A competitiveness strategy of firms and states involving copying the products, processes, and business models of leading firms and nations.

Imperialism   Expansion of political control by one country over another society.

Import Substitution Industrialization (ISI)   An inward-directed strategy of industrialization focused on the production of manufactured goods intended for sale in the domestic market. Typically, an ISI strategy provides trade protection or other forms of state assistance to import-substituting firms and industries.

Inflation   A measure of the prices of goods and services in which prices on average rise over some period of time.

Institution-Led Globalization   A form of globalization in which governance is characterized by a thick web of international rules and institutions.

Interdependence   A situation in world affairs in which the linkages among nations make their fate on certain issues mutually dependent. See also Asymmetrical, Complex, and Deep Interdependence.

Interest Groups   Typically, this is an organization designed to promote the economic, political, and ideological interests of a group of persons.

Interest Rates   The cost of borrowing money.

International Cooperation   A process whereby two or more nations align their actions and policies, often by compromising with each other.

International Institutions   Formal organizations that extend across national boundaries for the purpose of creating and promoting special and particular rules for how nations, firms, and other actors interact.

International Monetary Fund (IMF)   An international financial institution funded and governed by member states. Provides financing to countries experiencing balance-of-payments shortfalls. Has played a key role in the Third World debt crisis by conditioning financial assistance upon debtor country policy reforms.

Key Currency   A currency widely accepted as payment in global transactions and frequently used as a store of value. This conveys considerable structural power on the nation that issues a key currency.

Keynesianism   An economic policy common in capitalist societies after World War II and named in honor of the British economist, John Maynard Keynes. The purpose was to reduce the severity of economic recessions through government spending, which often included deficits in fiscal accounts.

Knowledge-Intensive Production   The production of a good or service in the predominant value lies in knowledge in the product/service and/or in the process by which it is made or created.

Kyoto Protocol   An international treaty completed in 1997 that committed signatories to reductions in greenhouse gas emissions.

Lender of Last Resort   Typically a central bank that lends to banks during an extreme financial crisis when credit markets have collapsed. The loans are designed to reduce fears of an economic collapse and stabilize the economy.

Leverage The use of borrowed money to make part of an investment, thereby magnifying the returns on the amount of the investment.

Liberalism A policy toward the world economy emphasizing the benefits of free markets and free trade. These views originated with Adam Smith and David Ricardo about two hundred years ago and today infuse the policies of many governments, international businesses, and international economic organizations.

Liberalization A policy that leads to greater market freedom for firms through lower tariffs, reduced capital controls, or fewer restrictions and regulations.

Liquidity A term referring to the level of cash held by a nation or firm. This also refers to the ability to convert an asset to cash quickly.

Local Innovation The ability to develop innovative products and processes in comparison to the capabilities of local markets.

Macroeconomic Policy A governmental policy directed toward affecting the national economy as a whole. Examples include tax policy, spending policy, and monetary policy.

Market Failure A condition in which markets fail to produce optimum private and/or social returns due to various factors that depart from perfect competition. Examples include monopoly, negative externalities, high barriers to entry, and increasing returns to scale.

Market-Led Globalization A perspective on globalization that advocates maximum freedom for the exchange of goods, capital, information, and people across borders with minimal regulation at either the national or global levels.

Markets A system of buyers, sellers, prices, a medium of exchange (money), and information relating to goods and/or services.

Market Segmentation A situation in which the prices for similar goods are significantly different in different areas or markets.

Marshall Plan A proposal by US Secretary of State George Marshall in 1947 calling for massive aid to Europe. The purpose was to secure a US position of strength in Europe and reduce Soviet strength

Marxism A critical approach to the study of capitalist societies based upon the ideas of Karl Marx. Marxism assumes fundamental conflicts of interest among social classes within capitalist societies.

Mercantilism A strategy adopted by most nations before the nineteenth century in which war and trade were designed to benefit the national treasury and punish adversaries in international relations.

Merchandise Trade Typically the trade of goods through exports and imports.

Merger and Acquisition (M&A) A form of FDI, in which a firm purchases part or complete ownership of a firm abroad.

Millennium Development Goals (MDGs) Launched in 2002 by the United Nations and member governments, the MDGs set a series of poverty reduction targets to be met by 2015 through the coordinated efforts of aid providers, development agencies, and national governments.

Modernization   A theory of development designed to explain the gap between living standards in the North and South. The North's economic prosperity is attributed to its successful transition from traditional to modern forms of social, political, and economic life. The economic backwardness of Southern countries is traced to the persistence of traditional social values and institutions. Southern development is thus dependent upon modernizing domestic reforms.

Monetary Policy   Decisions normally made by a nation's central bank concerning interest rates, the growth of the money supply, and exchange rates. See also Discount Rate; Open Market Operations.

Money Supply   The total of all money (currency and demand deposits) in a nation at a point in time.

Montreal Protocol   An international treaty committing signatories to reduce emissions of substances that deplete the global ozone layer. Completed in 1987.

Moral Hazard   The fear that, as a result of a central bank supporting commercial banks and shielding them from bankruptcy, banks will develop even more reckless behavior in the future.

Most Favored Nation (MFN)   A rule relating to trade policy adopted by nations. The rule requires that the terms of an agreement reached by a nation be available to all nations with whom it has an MFN agreement.

Move Up the Value Chain   The ability of a firm and/or nation to improve its position in the production of goods and services by developing productive capabilities in higher-valued products and processes.

National Competitiveness System   The scientific, business, and risk-taking environment of a nation and the impact on the capacity of a nation and its firms to compete in the global economy.

Neoliberalism   An approach to international trade and development that stresses the key role of free markets in economic growth. See also Washington Consensus.

Non-Tariff Barriers (NTBs)   Trade policies other than tariffs used to reduce or even block the import of certain goods and services. Various kinds of rules, procedures, regulations, and actions can have this effect.

Nuclear Revolution   The transformation of the thinking and behavior of nuclear-armed states with regard to the nature and desirability of war and of taking actions that could lead to war.

Offshore Outsourcing   The process of outsourcing some part of the value chain to a firm located in another country.

Oligopoly   A market dominated by a few large sellers.

Open Economy Politics (OEP)   A singular approach to international political economy based in neoclassical economics, advocating the analysis of the processes of global integration from the standpoint of the economic interests of private actors.

Open-Market Operations   An action of a nation's central bank involving the sale or purchase of government securities in the market. The purpose is to drain funds from the economy – by selling securities, the central bank ends up with more money – or pumping funds into the economy – buying securities results in the central bank exchanging securities for money. This is a key instrument for managing the overall level of the money supply. See also Central Bank; Monetary Policy.

Organization of Petroleum Exporting Countries (OPEC)   Formed in 1960, OPEC is a cooperative arrangement among many of the world's major oil exporting countries. Its purpose is to facilitate common agreement among member states on matters relating to oil policy, such as production levels and pricing.

Ozone Depletion   The ozone layer in the earth's atmosphere protects plants and animals from excessive exposure to ultraviolet radiation from the sun's rays. The release of various chemicals into the atmosphere – especially chlorofluorocarbons used as refrigerants – depletes ozone levels, thus posing health and environmental threats. The Montreal Protocol and its follow-on agreements set timelines toward the eventual phasing out of the production and use of ozone-depleting substances.

Pandemic Diseases   Communicable diseases that spread rapidly across populations.

Per Capita   A measurement of economic value per person. GDP is often measured in per capita terms. This is done by dividing the population size into GDP, giving a measure of GDP per person.

Political Coalitions   Formal and informal alliances among various groups in a society for the purpose of achieving political power and influence.

Post-Communism   A descriptive term used to refer to nations that have dropped some or all of their Communist political and economic policies. In Europe and the former Soviet Union, this has meant an end to communist political control and an end to command economies. In Asia, this has meant significant economic liberalization directed by communist governments.

Poverty Trap   The idea that the lack of ability to fulfill basic needs hampers the ability of the poor to improve their condition.

Power Relationships   Efforts to measure and analyze the military, economic, and political power capabilities of nations and evaluate how these capabilities compare to each other.

Power Transition Theory   An important theory about the effects of a declining hegemon interacting with a rising challenger state.

Preferential Trade Agreements (PTAs)   A trade agreement the terms of which are limited to those who have signed it.

Prime Rate   The interest rate charged by banks to their best customers, usually large and well-run businesses.

Privatization   A system for transferring control over government-owned enterprises to private hands. The focus of this effort is in post-Communist states of the Commonwealth of Independent States and Eastern Europe. Some successful transfers of government corporations to private hands took place in Great Britain during the 1980s.

Product Cycle   A term defining a set of stages in the development, production, and sale of a product in which the stages are associated with the comparative advantage of different countries. The creation and development of a product usually take place in advanced industrial countries with large scientific complexes, but once the method of production has matured, manufacture can take place where costs are lowest.

Productivity   Broadly, this is the quantity of output of a good or service measured by the amount of input. For example, the amount of a good one worker can produce in a period of time is a measure of productivity.

Protection(ism)   An economic policy in which restrictions and barriers, in the form of tariffs and/or rules, procedures, and laws, are placed on importing goods and services. See also Free Trade.

Public Health   Interventions aimed at improving the health of populations.

Purchasing Power Parity (PPP)   An adjustment in measurement for different price levels in different nations, the purpose of which is to equalize price levels. Thus, when price levels in one nation are higher than another, adjusting for PPP increases the value of goods and services in the lower price nation so as to reflect the globally higher value of this nation's economic output.

Quantitative Easing   A special policy of the central banks of several nations following the 2008 Global Financial Crisis. This involved large purchases by the central bank of various types of securities held by banks. The purchases are made using new created money.

Realism   An approach to international relations and international political economy that stresses the competitive and conflictual nature of the international state system. Conflict and war arise from international anarchy and the insecurity that such a condition produces for individual states.

Real Terms   An adjustment to economic measures for inflation. When measured in real terms, the economic value of some quantity has been reduced by an amount equal to inflation in the prices of goods and services.

Regime   A relationship among nations in which there is a convergence of beliefs, expectations, norms, and procedures for making decisions relating to a particular problem or issue in international affairs. A regime is important to the extent that it affects the actions and choices of nations associated with the regime.

Regional Comprehensive Economic Partnership Agreement (RCEP) An ASEAN-based negotiation, but with six other Asian nations, to create a regional PTA.

Regionalism The growing intensification of economic interdependence within a geographic region as compared with economic ties across regions.

Relative Gains A relationship in which the parties are primarily concerned about how exchange affects their relative power or standing vis-à-vis one another. Where relative gains are a priority for states, international cooperation is more difficult to achieve. See also Absolute Gains.

Remittances Money that immigrants send from the host country to family in the home country.

Renewable Energy Energy drawn from sustainable sources.

Research and Development (R&D) Expenditures by a nation's firms, universities, and research institutes on basic and applied efforts to develop scientific knowledge and to develop new and enhanced products and processes.

Resource Cartels Efforts by resource exporting countries to push up international prices by restricting supply.

Reverse Engineering A process for learning and often for duplicating the capabilities of a product. The device is disassembled and reconstructed to understand how it works.

Rio Earth Summit Formally called the United Nations Conference on Environment and Development (UNCED), the Rio Earth Summit brought together representatives from 150 nations in June 1992 with the purpose of elaborating "strategies and measures to halt and reverse the effects of environmental degradation in the context of increased national and international efforts to promote sustainable and environmentally sound development in all countries."

Smile Curve A figure depicting how the returns to different parts of the value chain have changed from globalization. Returns to low-skilled workers have declined and returns to high-skilled workers and capital have increased.

Smoot–Hawley Tariff A tariff proposal enacted in 1930 by US protectionists during the Great Depression and signed by President Hoover. This led other capitalist states to adopt similar tariffs and contributed to a crushing decline in world trade and worsening depression in the United States and elsewhere.

Socialism An economic system in which private ownership and control of economic activity are significantly restrained with arrangements designed to direct much more of the gains from the economy to workers and the poor. Much higher levels of resources are devoted to income maintenance programs, access to health care, and retirement benefits in a socialist economy. These costs are usually paid for with high tax levels on the wealthy. In addition, many of the most important industries are owned by the government and operated for the public welfare instead of for private gain.

Sovereignty A characteristic of states, by which states assert control over territory and make the rules that define how people interact within that area. States also possess the military forces needed to enforce those rules and the combination of territory and military makes it difficult for actors other than states to challenge this power.

Sovereign Wealth Fund (SWF) This is an investment fund owned by a government and used to make purchases of financial and other assets for strategic and economic purposes.

Special Economic Zone (SEZ) An area of a nation designated for special treatment and rules relating to the promotion of economic growth. Rules might include the ability to import certain goods without tariffs and special resources may be devoted to reliable energy, water, roads, and communication. This is designed to attract investment by domestic and foreign firms.

Specialization A situation in which a nation or a firm focuses its production on products or services in which it has some kind of competitive advantage.

State A centralized system of power that organizes a society and provides order within and protection from without. Typically, this system of power is based on various forms of organized support from groups within the society. States claim to monopolize the use of legitimate force within a society and also develop considerable physical power to defend the society from external threats and attacks.

State Capitalism A system of political economy in which the state strategically influences market relations for purposes of national and even global economic and political gain.

State-Led Globalization A perspective on globalization that emphasizes the need for strong national-level regulation so as to manage the risks of globalization and prevent mobile capital from undermining organized labor and weakening social and environmental safety nets.

State-Owned Enterprises (SOEs) A firm owned in whole or part by a local or national government.

Statism A theoretical perspective on economic development that emphasizes the importance of strong state intervention to stimulate growth and create productive areas of comparative advantage.

Strategic Alliance An arrangement between two or more firms that creates some continuing cooperative relationship. This could involve production, marketing, and/or research and development, such that the sharing and transfer of information, products, and/or production take place.

Strategic Trade   An international trade policy in which various forms of governmental aid are directed at a specific industry or industries so as to boost their competitive advantages in global markets. The industries selected for targeting typically have substantial positive consequences for the economy or have a cost or market structure that promotes a small number of producers.

Structural Adjustment   In contrast with traditional project loans, which finance particular development investments or activities, the World Bank began shifting part of its lending to structural-adjustment financing in the 1980s. Typically, this newer type of financing provides balance-of-payment support to countries which have committed themselves to bank-sponsored policy reforms.

Structural Power   The possession of resources – such as a large market or the ability to provide public goods such as security or credit – that are so important other actors must make choices based on the effects of these resources.

Supply Chain (Value Chain, Value Added)   The organization of activities that lead to the production of a product and/or service. A value chain links the various activities of a supply chain to the price or cost of each activity, thereby placing judgments about the relative contribution to the process of production. This is often referred to as the value added of an activity.

Sustainable Development   The term "sustainable development" was first brought into common use by the World Commission on Environment and Development, also called the Brundtland Commission, in 1987. Brundtland defined sustainable development as that which "meets the needs of the present generation without compromising the needs of future generations."

Systemic Crisis   A financial crisis so severe and far reaching as to threaten the stability of the entire economic system and threaten the incomes and wealth of the entire population.

Trade Surplus/Deficit   A situation in a nation's balance of payments when exports exceed imports (surplus) or when imports exceed exports (deficit).

Tragedy of the Commons   Associated with the work of Garrett Hardin, this term refers to the idea that resources held in common are likely to be overexploited without adequate regulation. The concept helps to explain why it has been difficult to prevent unsustainable exploitation of the global commons – the oceans and the atmosphere.

Transatlantic Trade and Investment Partnership (TTIP)   A proposed free trade agreement between the United States and the European Union. Negotiations over the agreement began in July 2013.

Transfer Pricing   An accounting practice by which multinational corporations adjust prices on intrafirm trade in order to shift profits from subsidiaries located in high-tax countries to those residing in low-tax countries or to escape restrictions of the repatriation of profits imposed by host-country governments.

Transnational Corporations (TNCs)   Firms engaged in substantial FDI abroad and producing and selling in global markets.

Trans-Pacific Partnership (TPP)   A proposed preferential trade agreement among certain Asian and Western Hemisphere nations that would develop common rules to enhance trade.

Triad of Global Production   A term describing the geographic pattern of global trade, which is concentrated in three regions: North America, Europe, and Asia.

Varieties of Capitalism

Coordinated market economies – nations in which important economic decisions, such as the allocation of capital, involve a partnership of the government and private banks. Germany and Norway are examples.

Liberal market economies – nations with a relatively high emphasis on free markets as the basis for economic policies and action. Great Britain and the United States are examples.

State-managed economies – nations in which the government takes a leading role in directing resources toward investment and national economic strategy. China and Singapore are examples.

Washington Consensus   This term was coined in 1989 by economist John Williamson to describe what he saw as an emerging consensus among Latin American countries on the need for pro-market policies and a shrunken role for states in managing economic development. See also Neoliberalism.

World Bank   This term actually refers to a group of related international financial institutions, including the International Bank for Reconstruction and Development (IBRD), the International Development Agency (IDA), and the International Finance Corporation (IFC). Funded largely by capital infusions from Northern governments, these agencies provide financing for Third World development projects or programs.

World Systems Theory   A theoretical model for understanding the expansion and structure of capitalism on a global scale. Proposed by Immanuel Wallerstein, world systems theory views the economic development of any particular country as embedded within and determined by its place within the overall international economic order. The global economy is divided into core, semi-periphery, and periphery, with the development of the core countries coming largely at the expense of the semi-peripheral and peripheral countries.

World Trade Organization (WTO)   A global trade organization created to oversee the implementation of agreements emerging out of the Uruguay Round of international trade negotiations.

Zaibatsu/Keiretsu   Two related forms of industrial organization in Japan in which family-centered holding companies act to organize and integrate many different firms. Often, large banks operate to supply capital, and in other cases complex systems of manufacturers and suppliers are the main forms of organization. *Zaibatsu* refers to such enterprise systems prior to 1945; *keiretsu* refers to such systems after 1945.

Zero-Sum Relationship   A form of interaction between two agents, in which the gains for either agent come at the expense of the other.

Index

Note: page numbers in *italic* refer to Figures; those in **bold** refer to Tables.